Jean-Claude **Corbeil**
Ariane **Archambault**

VISUAL
FRENCH
DICTIONARY

ACKNOWLEDGEMENTS FROM QA INTERNATIONAL

Our deepest gratitude to the individuals, institutions, companies and businesses that have provided us with the latest technical documentation for use in preparing the *Visual French Dictionary*.

Arcand, Denis (réalisateur); Association Internationale de Signalisation Maritime; Association canadienne des paiements (Charlie Clarke); Association des banquiers canadiens (Lise Provost); Automobiles Citroën; Automobiles Peugeot; Banque du Canada (Lyse Brousseau); Banque Royale du Canada (Raymond Chouinard, Francine Morel, Carole Trottier); Barrett Xplore inc.; Bazarin, Christine;Bibliothèque du Parlement canadien (Service de renseignements); Bibliothèque nationale du Québec (Jean-François Palomino); Bluechip Kennels (Olga Gagne); Bombardier Aéronautique; Bridgestone-Firestone; Brother (Canada); Canadien National; Casavant Frères ltée; C.O.J.O. ATHENES 2004 (Bureau des Médias Internationaux); Centre Eaton de Montréal; Centre national du Costume (Recherche et de Diffusion); Cetacean Society International (William R. Rossiter); Chagnon, Daniel (architecte D.E.S. – M.E.Q.); Cohen et Rubin Architectes (Maggy Cohen); Commission Scolaire de Montréal (École St-Henri); Compagnie de la Baie d'Hudson (Nunzia Iavarone, Ron Oyama); Corporation d'hébergement du Québec (Céline Drolet); École nationale de théâtre du Canada (Bibliothèque); Élevage Le Grand Saphir (Stéphane Ayotte); Énergie atomique du Canada ltée; Eurocopter; Famous Players; Fédération bancaire française (Védi Hékiman); Fontaine, PierreHenry (biologiste); Future Shop; Garaga; Groupe Jean Coutu; Hôpital du Sacré-Cœur de Montréal; Hôtel Inter-Continental; Hydro-Québec; I.P.I.Q. (Serge Bouchard); IGA Barcelo; International Entomological Society (Dr. Michael Geisthardt); Irisbus; Jérôme, Danielle (O.D.); La Poste (Colette Gouts); Le Groupe Canam Manac inc.; Lévesque, Georges (urgentologue); Lévesque, Robert (chef machiniste); Manutan; Marriot Spring Hill suites; MATRA S.A.; Métro inc.; ministère canadien de la Défense nationale (Affaires publiques); ministère de la Défense, République Française; ministère de la Justice du Québec (Service de la gestion immobilière – Carol Sirois); ministère de l'Éducation du Québec (Direction de l'équipement scolaire-Daniel Chagnon); Muse Productions (Annick Barbery); National Aeronautics and Space Administration; National Oceanic and Atmospheric Administration; Nikon Canada inc.; Normand, Denis (consultant en télécommunications); Office de la langue française du Québec (Chantal Robinson); Paul Demers & Fils inc.; Phillips (France); Pratt & Whitney Canada inc.; Prévost Car inc.; Radio Shack Canada ltée; Réno-Dépôt inc.; Robitaille, Jean-François (Département de biologie, Université Laurentienne); Rocking T Ranch and Poultry Farm (Pete and Justine Theer); RONA inc.; Sears Canada inc.; Secrétariat d'État du Canada : Bureau de la traduction ; Service correctionnel du Canada; Société d'Entomologie Africaine (Alain Drumont); Société des musées québécois (Michel Perron); Société Radio-Canada; Sony du Canada ltée; Sûreté du Québec; Théâtre du Nouveau Monde; Transports Canada (Julie Poirier); Urgences-Santé (Éric Berry); Ville de Longueuil (Direction de la Police); Ville de Montréal (Service de la prévention des incendies); Vimont Lexus Toyota; Volvo Bus Corporation; Yamaha Motor Canada Ltd.

The Visual French Dictionary is created and produced by
QA International, a division of
Les Éditions Québec Amérique inc.
329, rue de la Commune Ouest, 3ᵉ étage
Montréal (Québec) H2Y 2E1 Canada
T 514.499.3000 F 514.499.3010

British Library Cataloguing In Publication Data
Data available
Library of Congress Cataloging In Publication Data
Data available

Printed and bound in Slovakia.
www.qa-international.com

Staff – QA International

EDITORIAL STAFF

Publisher: Jacques Fortin

Authors: Jean-Claude Corbeil et Ariane Archambault

Editorial Director: François Fortin

Editor-in-Chief: Serge D'Amico

Graphic Design: Anne Tremblay

PRODUCTION

Mac Thien Nguyen Hoang

Guylaine Houle

TERMINOLOGICAL RESEARCH

Jean Beaumont

Catherine Briand

Nathalie Guillo

ILLUSTRATION

Art Direction: Jocelyn Gardner

Jean-Yves Ahern

Rielle Lévesque

Alain Lemire

Mélanie Boivin

Yan Bohler

Claude Thivierge

Pascal Bilodeau

Michel Rouleau

Anouk Noël

Carl Pelletier

LAYOUT

Pascal Goyette

Janou-Ève LeGuerrier

Véronique Boisvert

Josée Gagnon

Karine Raymond

Geneviève Théroux Béliveau

DOCUMENTATION

Gilles Vézina

Kathleen Wynd

Stéphane Batigne

Sylvain Robichaud

Jessie Daigle

DATA MANAGEMENT

Programmer : Daniel Beaulieu

Nathalie Fréchette

REVISION

Marie-Nicole Cimon

PREPRESS

Sophie Pellerin

Tony O'Riley

Staff – Oxford University Press

EDITORIAL STAFF

Natalie Pomier

Catherine Soanes

CONTRIBUTIONS

QA International wishes to thank the following for their contribution to the *Visual French Dictionary* :

Jean-Louis Martin, Marc Lalumière, Jacques Perrault, Stéphane Roy, Alice Comtois, Michel Blais, Christiane Beauregard, Mamadou Togola, Annie Maurice, Charles Campeau, Mivil Deschênes, Jonathan Jacques, Martin Lortie, Raymond Martin, Frédérick Simard, Yan Tremblay, Mathieu Blouin, Sébastien Dallaire, Hoang Khanh Le, Martin Desrosiers, Nicolas Oroc, François Escalmel, Danièle Lemay, Pierre Savoie, Benoit Bourdeau, Marie-Andrée Lemieux, Caroline Soucy, Yves Chabot, Anne-Marie Ouellette, Anne-Marie Villeneuve, Anne-Marie Brault, Nancy Lepage, Daniel Provost, François Vézina.

Introduction to the
Visual French Dictionary

The *Visual French Dictionary* is the result of a collaboration between QA International and Oxford University Press. With over 3,600 illustrations combined with thousands of specialist and general terms, the *Visual French Dictionary* provides a rich source of knowledge that is both clear and attractive to use.

EDITORIAL POLICY

The *Visual French Dictionary* takes an inventory of the physical environment of a person who is part of today's technological age and who knows and uses a large number of specialized terms in a wide variety of fields.

Designed for the general public, it responds to the needs of anyone seeking the precise, correct terms for a wide range of personal or professional reasons: finding an unknown term, checking the meaning of a word, advertising, additional teaching material, etc.

The target user has guided the choice of contents for the *Visual French Dictionary*, which aims to bring together in one volume the technical terms required to express in French or in English the contemporary world, in the specialized fields that shape our daily experience.

STRUCTURE OF THE VISUAL FRENCH DICTIONARY

This book has three sections: the preliminary pages, including the list of themes and table of contents; the body of the text, i.e. the detailed treatment of each theme; the index.

Information is presented moving from the most abstract to the most concrete: theme, sub-theme, title, subtitle, illustration, terminology.

The content of the *Visual French Dictionary* is divided into 17 THEMES, from Astronomy to Sports. More complex themes are divided into SUB-THEMES. For example, the theme Earth is divided into Geography, Geology, Meteorology and Environment.

The TITLE has a variety of functions: to name the illustration of a unique object, of which the principal parts are identified (for example, glacier, window); to bring together under one designation illustrations that belong to the same conceptual sphere, but that represent a variety of elements, each with its own designations and terminology (e.g. configuration of the continents, household appliances).

At times, the chief members of a class of objects are brought together under the same SUB-TITLE, each with its own name but without a detailed terminological analysis. (e.g. under space probe, examples of space probes).

The ILLUSTRATION shows realistically and precisely an object, a process or a phenomenon, and the most significant details from which they are constructed. It serves as a visual definition for each of the terms presented.

TERMINOLOGY

Each word in the *Visual French Dictionary* has been carefully selected following examination of high-quality documentation, at the required level of specialization.

There may be cases where different terms are used to name the same item. In such instances, the word most frequently used by the most highly regarded authors has been chosen.

The *Visual French Dictionary* contains 13,750 index entries, or more than 23,700 English words with their French equivalent.

The INDEXES list all words in the dictionary in alphabetical order.

METHODS OF CONSULTATION

One may gain access to the contents of the *Visual French Dictionary* in a variety of ways:

- from the list of THEMES on the back of the book and at the end of the preliminary pages;

- with the French or English INDEX the user can consult the *Visual French Dictionary* from a word, so as to see what it corresponds to, or to verify accuracy by examining the illustration that depicts it;

- the most original aspect of the *Visual French Dictionary* is the fact that the illustrations enable the user to find a word even if he or she only has a vague idea of what it is. The dictionary is unique in this feature, as consultation of any other dictionary requires the user first to know the word.

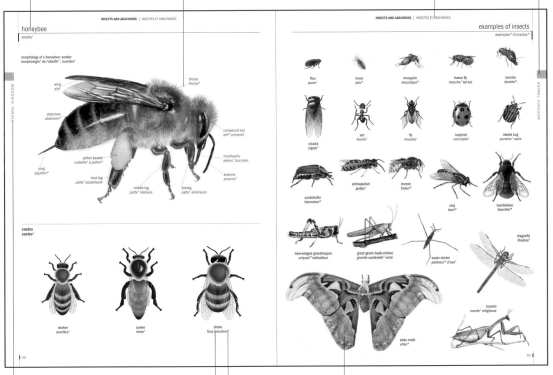

Contents

List of chapters

ASTRONOMY

solar system

système^M solaire

outer planets
planètes^F externes

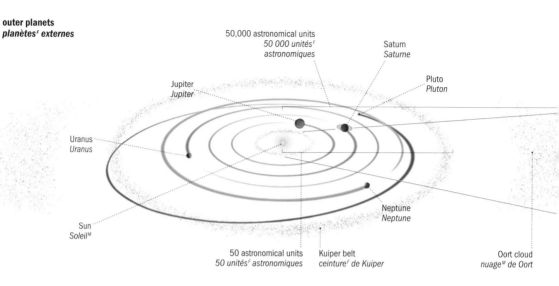

50,000 astronomical units
50 000 unités^F astronomiques

Saturn
Saturne

Pluto
Pluton

Jupiter
Jupiter

Uranus
Uranus

Neptune
Neptune

Sun
Soleil^M

50 astronomical units
50 unités^F astronomiques

Kuiper belt
ceinture^F de Kuiper

Oort cloud
nuage^M de Oort

planets and moons

planètes^F et satellites^M

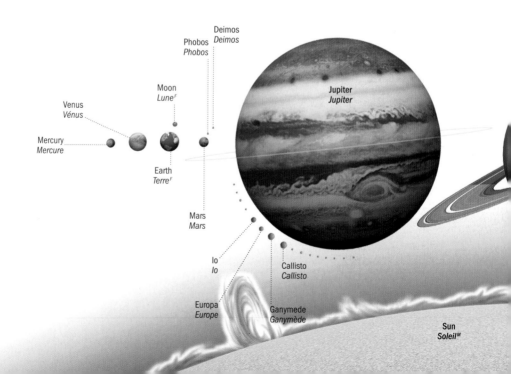

Deimos
Deimos

Phobos
Phobos

Moon
Lune^F

Venus
Vénus

Mercury
Mercure

Jupiter
Jupiter

Earth
Terre^F

Mars
Mars

Io
Io

Callisto
Callisto

Europa
Europe

Ganymede
Ganymède

Sun
Soleil^M

solar system

inner planets
*planètes*F *internes*

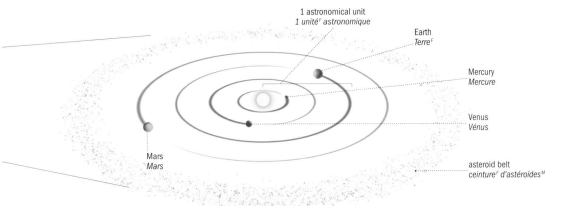

1 astronomical unit
*1 unité*F *astronomique*

Earth
*Terre*F

Mercury
Mercure

Venus
Vénus

Mars
Mars

asteroid belt
*ceinture*F *d'astéroïdes*M

planets and moons

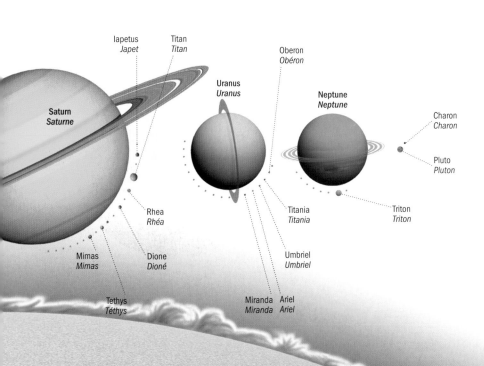

Iapetus
Japet

Titan
Titan

Oberon
Obéron

Uranus
Uranus

Neptune
Neptune

Saturn
Saturne

Charon
Charon

Pluto
Pluton

Rhea
Rhéa

Titania
Titania

Triton
Triton

Mimas
Mimas

Dione
Dioné

Umbriel
Umbriel

Tethys
Téthys

Miranda   Ariel
Miranda *Ariel*

Sun

Soleil[M]

ASTRONOMY

structure of the Sun
structure[F] du Soleil[M]

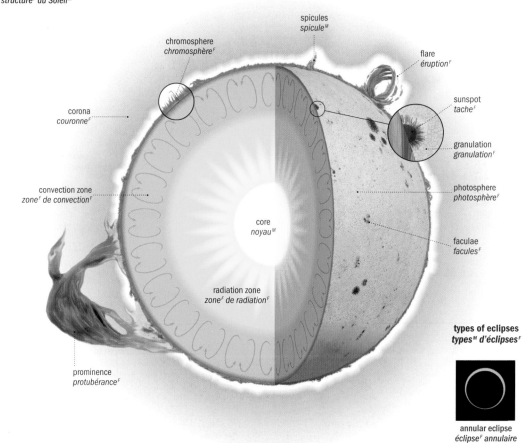

chromosphere
chromosphère[F]

spicules
spicule[M]

flare
éruption[F]

corona
couronne[F]

sunspot
tache[F]

granulation
granulation[F]

convection zone
zone[F] de convection[F]

core
noyau[M]

photosphere
photosphère[F]

faculae
facules[F]

radiation zone
zone[F] de radiation[F]

prominence
protubérance[F]

types of eclipses
types[M] d'éclipses[F]

annular eclipse
éclipse[F] annulaire

solar eclipse
éclipse[F] de Soleil[M]

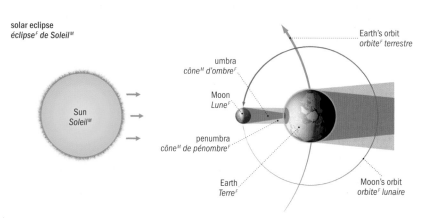

Earth's orbit
orbite[F] terrestre

umbra
cône[M] d'ombre[F]

Moon
Lune[F]

Sun
Soleil[M]

penumbra
cône[M] de pénombre[F]

Earth
Terre[F]

Moon's orbit
orbite[F] lunaire

partial eclipse
éclipse[F] partielle

total eclipse
éclipse[F] totale

Moon
Lune[F]

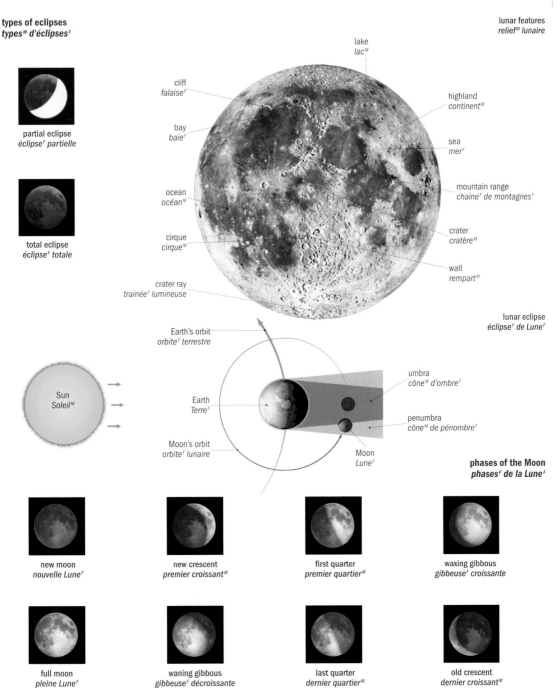

types of eclipses
types[M] d'éclipses[F]

partial eclipse
éclipse[F] partielle

total eclipse
éclipse[F] totale

lunar features
relief[M] lunaire

lake
lac[M]

cliff
falaise[F]

highland
continent[M]

bay
baie[F]

sea
mer[F]

ocean
océan[M]

mountain range
chaine[F] de montagnes[F]

cirque
cirque[M]

crater
cratère[M]

crater ray
trainée[F] lumineuse

wall
rempart[M]

lunar eclipse
éclipse[F] de Lune[F]

Earth's orbit
orbite[F] terrestre

umbra
cône[M] d'ombre[F]

Sun
Soleil[M]

Earth
Terre[F]

penumbra
cône[M] de pénombre[F]

Moon's orbit
orbite[F] lunaire

Moon
Lune[F]

phases of the Moon
phases[F] de la Lune[F]

new moon
nouvelle Lune[F]

new crescent
premier croissant[M]

first quarter
premier quartier[M]

waxing gibbous
gibbeuse[F] croissante

full moon
pleine Lune[F]

waning gibbous
gibbeuse[F] décroissante

last quarter
dernier quartier[M]

old crescent
dernier croissant[M]

ASTRONOMY

galaxy

galaxie[F]

Milky Way
Voie[F] lactée

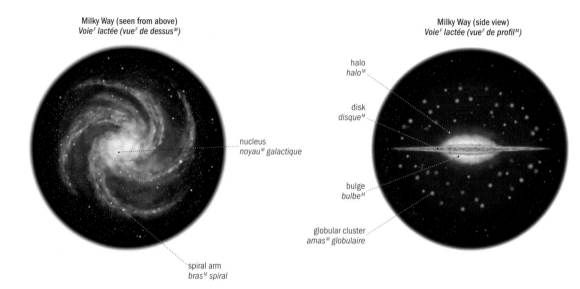

Milky Way (seen from above)
Voie[F] lactée (vue[F] de dessus[M])

Milky Way (side view)
Voie[F] lactée (vue[F] de profil[M])

nucleus
noyau[M] galactique

spiral arm
bras[M] spiral

halo
halo[M]

disk
disque[M]

bulge
bulbe[M]

globular cluster
amas[M] globulaire

comet

comète[F]

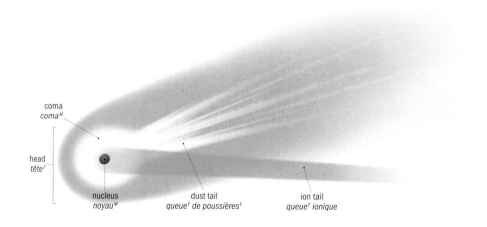

coma
coma[M]

head
tête[F]

nucleus
noyau[M]

dust tail
queue[F] de poussières[F]

ion tail
queue[F] ionique

Hubble space telescope

télescope*M* spatial Hubble

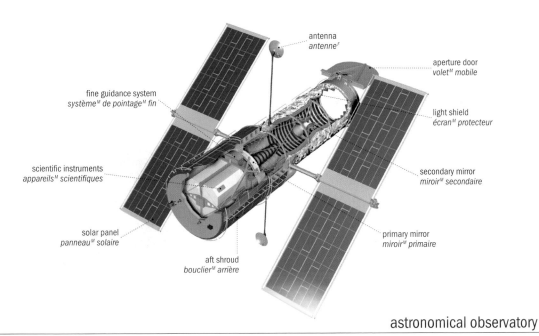

antenna
antenne*F*

aperture door
volet*M* mobile

fine guidance system
système*M* de pointage*M* fin

light shield
écran*M* protecteur

scientific instruments
appareils*M* scientifiques

secondary mirror
miroir*M* secondaire

solar panel
panneau*M* solaire

primary mirror
miroir*M* primaire

aft shroud
bouclier*M* arrière

astronomical observatory

observatoire*M* astronomique

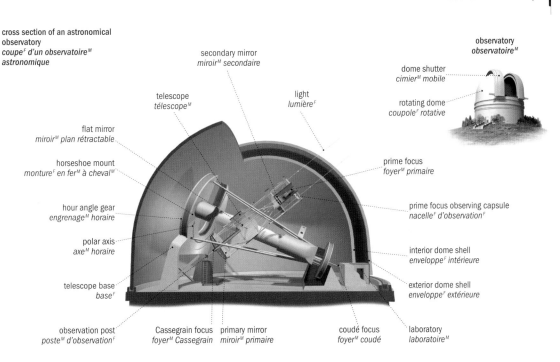

cross section of an astronomical
observatory
coupe*F* d'un observatoire*M*
astronomique

secondary mirror
miroir*M* secondaire

observatory
observatoire*M*

light
lumière*F*

dome shutter
cimier*M* mobile

telescope
télescope*M*

rotating dome
coupole*F* rotative

flat mirror
miroir*M* plan rétractable

prime focus
foyer*M* primaire

horseshoe mount
monture*F* en fer*M* à cheval*M*

prime focus observing capsule
nacelle*F* d'observation*F*

hour angle gear
engrenage*M* horaire

polar axis
axe*M* horaire

interior dome shell
enveloppe*F* intérieure

telescope base
base*F*

exterior dome shell
enveloppe*F* extérieure

observation post
poste*M* d'observation*F*

Cassegrain focus
foyer*M* Cassegrain

primary mirror
miroir*M* primaire

coudé focus
foyer*M* coudé

laboratory
laboratoire*M*

refracting telescope

lunette^F astronomique

finderscope
chercheur^M

cradle
bride^F de fixation^F

main tube
tube^M

lens hood
pare-soleil^M

eyepiece
oculaire^M

eyepiece holder
tube^M porte-oculaire^M

star diagonal
oculaire^M coudé

declination setting scale
cercle^M de déclinaison^F

focusing knob
bouton^M de mise^F au point^M

azimuth clamp
vis^F de blocage^M (azimut^M)

altitude clamp
vis^F de blocage^M (latitude^F)

azimuth fine adjustment
réglage^M micrométrique (azimut^M)

altitude fine adjustment
réglage^M micrométrique (latitude^F)

right ascension setting scale
cercle^M d'ascension^F droite

fork
fourche^F

counterweight
contrepoids^M

tripod accessories shelf
plateau^M pour accessoires^M

tripod
trépied^M

cross section of a refracting telescope
coupe^F d'une lunette^F astronomique

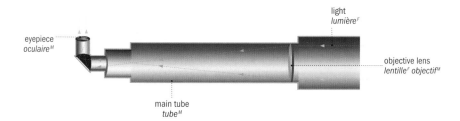

light
lumière^F

eyepiece
oculaire^M

objective lens
lentille^F objectif^M

main tube
tube^M

reflecting telescope

télescope^M

finderscope
chercheur^M

eyepiece
oculaire^M

cradle
bride^F de fixation^F

support
support^M de fixation^F

main tube
tube^M

focusing knob
bouton^M de mise^F au point^M

declination setting scale
cercle^M de déclinaison^F

right ascension setting scale
cercle^M d'ascension^F droite

azimuth clamp
vis^F de blocage^M (azimut^M)

azimuth fine adjustment
réglage^M micrométrique (azimut^M)

altitude clamp
vis^F de blocage^M (latitude^F)

altitude fine adjustment
réglage^M micrométrique
(latitude^F)

cross section of a reflecting telescope
coupe^F d'un télescope^M

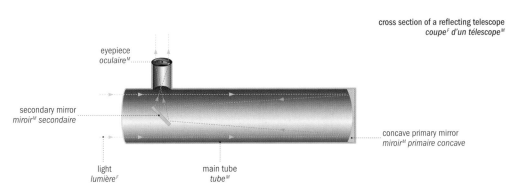

eyepiece
oculaire^M

secondary mirror
miroir^M secondaire

concave primary mirror
miroir^M primaire concave

light
lumière^F

main tube
tube^M

spacesuit

scaphandre^M spatial

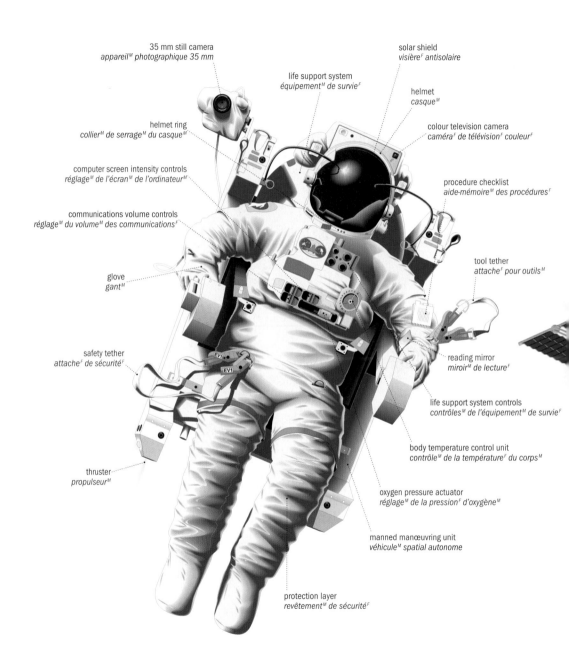

35 mm still camera
appareil^M photographique 35 mm

solar shield
visière^F antisolaire

life support system
équipement^M de survie^F

helmet
casque^M

helmet ring
collier^M de serrage^M du casque^M

colour television camera
caméra^F de télévision^F couleur^F

computer screen intensity controls
réglage^M de l'écran^M de l'ordinateur^M

procedure checklist
aide-mémoire^M des procédures^F

communications volume controls
réglage^M du volume^M des communications^F

tool tether
attache^F pour outils^M

glove
gant^M

reading mirror
miroir^M de lecture^F

safety tether
attache^F de sécurité^F

life support system controls
contrôles^M de l'équipement^M de survie^F

body temperature control unit
contrôle^M de la température^F du corps^M

thruster
propulseur^M

oxygen pressure actuator
réglage^M de la pression^F d'oxygène^M

manned manœuvring unit
véhicule^M spatial autonome

protection layer
revêtement^M de sécurité^F

international space station

station^F spatiale internationale

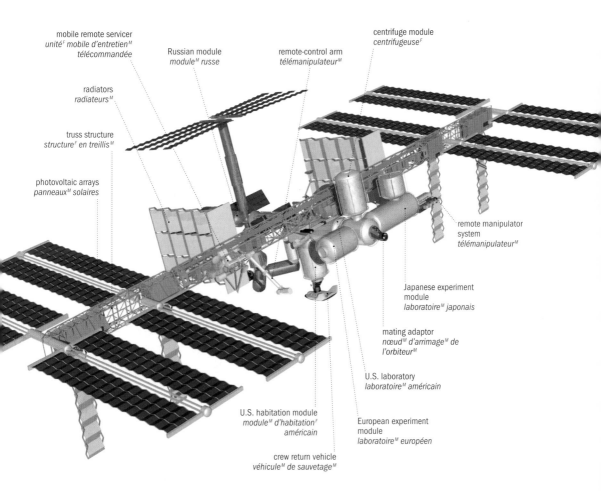

mobile remote servicer
*unité^F mobile d'entretien^M
télécommandée*

Russian module
module^M russe

remote-control arm
télémanipulateur^M

centrifuge module
centrifugeuse^F

radiators
radiateurs^M

truss structure
structure^F en treillis^M

photovoltaic arrays
panneaux^M solaires

remote manipulator
system
télémanipulateur^M

Japanese experiment
module
laboratoire^M japonais

mating adaptor
*nœud^M d'arrimage^M de
l'orbiteur^M*

U.S. laboratory
laboratoire^M américain

U.S. habitation module
*module^M d'habitation^F
américain*

European experiment
module
laboratoire^M européen

crew return vehicle
véhicule^M de sauvetage^M

ASTRONOMY

space shuttle

navette^F spatiale

space shuttle at takeoff
navette^F spatiale au décollage^M

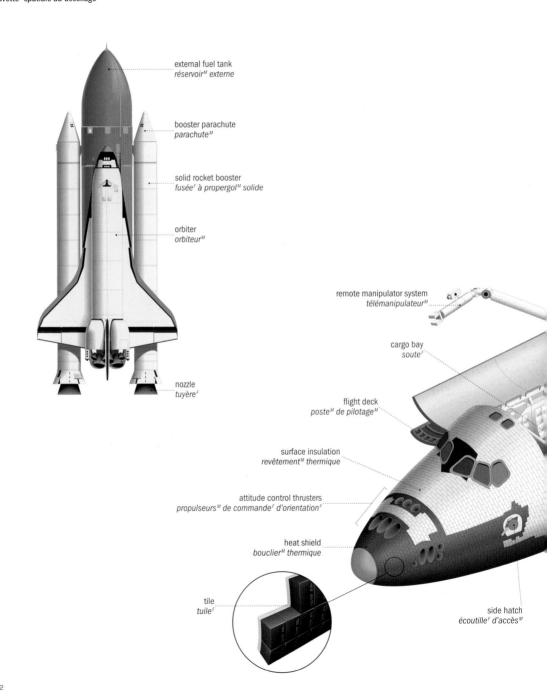

external fuel tank
réservoir^M externe

booster parachute
parachute^M

solid rocket booster
fusée^F à propergol^M solide

orbiter
orbiteur^M

nozzle
tuyère^F

remote manipulator system
télémanipulateur^M

cargo bay
soute^F

flight deck
poste^M de pilotage^M

surface insulation
revêtement^M thermique

attitude control thrusters
propulseurs^M de commande^F d'orientation^F

heat shield
bouclier^M thermique

tile
tuile^F

side hatch
écoutille^F d'accès^M

orbiter
orbiteur^M

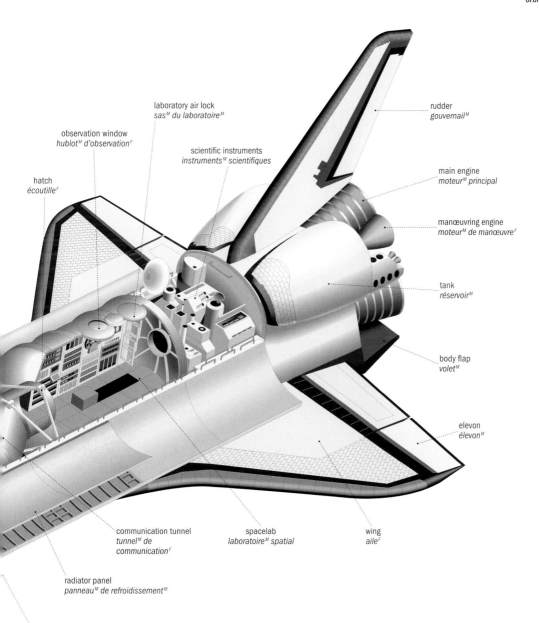

laboratory air lock
sas^M *du laboratoire*^M

observation window
hublot^M *d'observation*^F

scientific instruments
instruments^M *scientifiques*

hatch
écoutille^F

rudder
gouvernail^M

main engine
moteur^M *principal*

manœuvring engine
moteur^M *de manœuvre*^F

tank
réservoir^M

body flap
volet^M

elevon
élevon^M

communication tunnel
tunnel^M *de communication*^F

spacelab
laboratoire^M *spatial*

wing
aile^F

radiator panel
panneau^M *de refroidissement*^M

cargo bay door
porte^F *de la soute*^F

configuration of the continents

configuration^F des continents^M

planisphere
planisphère^M

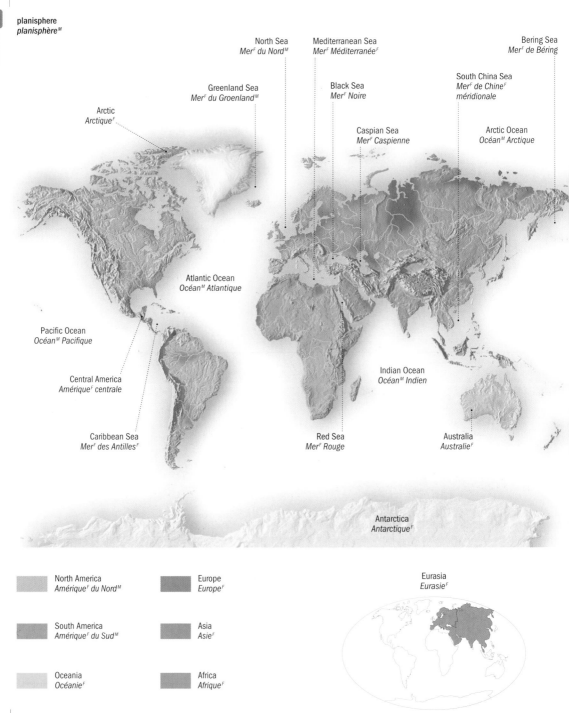

North Sea
Mer^F du Nord^M

Mediterranean Sea
Mer^F Méditerranée^F

Bering Sea
Mer^F de Béring

Greenland Sea
Mer^F du Groenland^M

Black Sea
Mer^F Noire

South China Sea
*Mer^F de Chine^F
méridionale*

Arctic
Arctique^F

Caspian Sea
Mer^F Caspienne

Arctic Ocean
Océan^M Arctique

Atlantic Ocean
Océan^M Atlantique

Pacific Ocean
Océan^M Pacifique

Central America
Amérique^F centrale

Indian Ocean
Océan^M Indien

Caribbean Sea
Mer^F des Antilles^F

Red Sea
Mer^F Rouge

Australia
Australie^F

Antarctica
Antarctique^F

North America
Amérique^F du Nord^M

Europe
Europe^F

Eurasia
Eurasie^F

South America
Amérique^F du Sud^M

Asia
Asie^F

Oceania
Océanie^F

Africa
Afrique^F

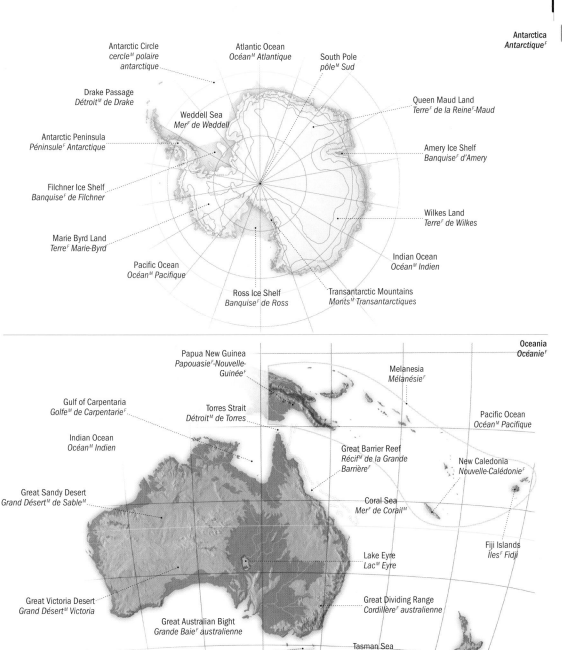

Antarctica
Antarctique[F]

EARTH

Antarctic Circle
cercle[M] *polaire*
antarctique

Atlantic Ocean
Océan[M] *Atlantique*

South Pole
pôle[M] *Sud*

Drake Passage
Détroit[M] *de Drake*

Queen Maud Land
Terre[F] *de la Reine*[F]*-Maud*

Weddell Sea
Mer[F] *de Weddell*

Antarctic Peninsula
Péninsule[F] *Antarctique*

Amery Ice Shelf
Banquise[F] *d'Amery*

Filchner Ice Shelf
Banquise[F] *de Filchner*

Wilkes Land
Terre[F] *de Wilkes*

Marie Byrd Land
Terre[F] *Marie-Byrd*

Indian Ocean
Océan[M] *Indien*

Pacific Ocean
Océan[M] *Pacifique*

Ross Ice Shelf
Banquise[F] *de Ross*

Transantarctic Mountains
Monts[M] *Transantarctiques*

Oceania
Océanie[F]

Papua New Guinea
Papouasie[F]*-Nouvelle-*
Guinée[F]

Melanesia
Mélanésie[F]

Gulf of Carpentaria
Golfe[M] *de Carpentarie*[F]

Torres Strait
Détroit[M] *de Torres*

Pacific Ocean
Océan[M] *Pacifique*

Indian Ocean
Océan[M] *Indien*

Great Barrier Reef
Récif[M] *de la Grande*
Barrière[F]

New Caledonia
Nouvelle-Calédonie[F]

Great Sandy Desert
Grand Désert[M] *de Sable*[M]

Coral Sea
Mer[F] *de Corail*[M]

Fiji Islands
Îles[F] *Fidji*

Great Victoria Desert
Grand Désert[M] *Victoria*

Lake Eyre
Lac[M] *Eyre*

Great Dividing Range
Cordillère[F] *australienne*

Great Australian Bight
Grande Baie[F] *australienne*

Bass Strait
Détroit[M] *de Bass*

Tasman Sea
Mer[F] *de Tasman*

Tasmania
Tasmanie[F]

New Zealand
Nouvelle-Zélande[F]

Cook Strait
Détroit[M] *de Cook*

configuration of the continents

EARTH

North America
Amérique^F du Nord^M

Beaufort Sea
Mer^F de Beaufort

Mackenzie River
Mackenzie^M

Hudson Bay
Baie^F d'Hudson

Baffin Island
Terre^F de Baffin

Bering Strait
Détroit^M de Béring

Greenland
Groenland^M

Great Lakes
Grands Lacs^M

Gulf of Alaska
Golfe^M d'Alaska

Newfoundland Island
Île^F de Terre-Neuve

Aleutian Islands
Îles^F Aléoutiennes

Rocky Mountains
Montagnes^F Rocheuses

Saint Lawrence River
Saint-Laurent^M

Grand Canyon
Grand Canyon^M

Appalachian Mountains
Appalaches^F

Mississippi River
Mississippi^M

Gulf of California
Golfe^M de Californie^F

Gulf of Mexico
Golfe^M du Mexique^M

West Indies
Antilles^F

Yucatan Peninsula
Péninsule^F du Yucatan^M

Caribbean Sea
Mer^F des Antilles^F

Central America
Amérique^F centrale

Isthmus of Panama
Isthme^M de Panama^M

South America
Amérique^F du Sud^M

Orinoco River
Orénoque^M

Amazon River
Amazone^F

Gulf of Panama
Golfe^M de Panama^M

equator
équateur^M

Andes Cordillera
Cordillère^F des Andes^F

Lake Titicaca
Lac^M Titicaca

Atacama Desert
Désert^M d'Atacama

Paraná River
Paraná^M

Patagonia
Patagonie^F

Falkland Islands
Îles^F Falkland

Tierra del Fuego
Terre^F de Feu^M

Cape Horn
Cap^M Horn

Drake Passage
Détroit^M de Drake

configuration of the continents

EARTH

Europe
Europe^F

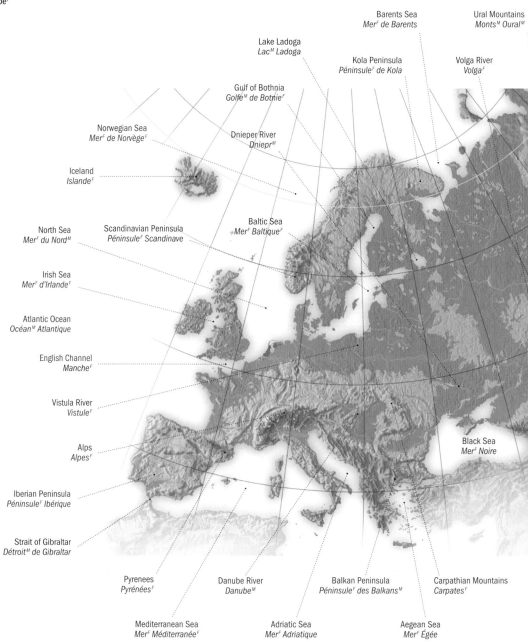

Barents Sea
Mer^F de Barents

Ural Mountains
Monts^M Oural^M

Lake Ladoga
Lac^M Ladoga

Kola Peninsula
Péninsule^F de Kola

Volga River
Volga^F

Gulf of Bothnia
Golfé^M de Botnie^F

Norwegian Sea
Mer^F de Norvège^F

Dnieper River
Dniepr^M

Iceland
Islande^F

Baltic Sea
Mer^F Baltique^F

North Sea
Mer^F du Nord^M

Scandinavian Peninsula
Péninsule^F Scandinave

Irish Sea
Mer^F d'Irlande^F

Atlantic Ocean
Océan^M Atlantique

English Channel
Manche^F

Vistula River
Vistule^F

Black Sea
Mer^F Noire

Alps
Alpes^F

Iberian Peninsula
Péninsule^F Ibérique

Strait of Gibraltar
Détroit^M de Gibraltar

Pyrenees
Pyrénées^F

Danube River
Danube^M

Balkan Peninsula
Péninsule^F des Balkans^M

Carpathian Mountains
Carpates^F

Mediterranean Sea
Mer^F Méditerranée^F

Adriatic Sea
Mer^F Adriatique

Aegean Sea
Mer^F Égée

Asia
Asie[F]

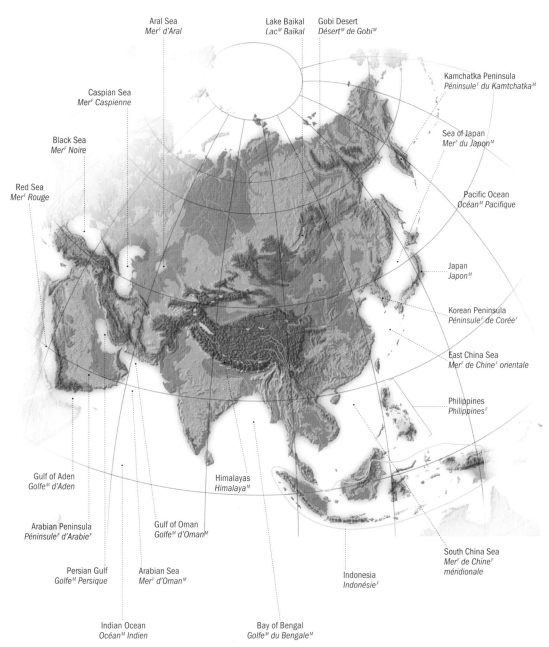

Aral Sea
Mer[F] *d'Aral*

Lake Baikal
Lac[M] *Baïkal*

Gobi Desert
Désert[M] *de Gobi*[M]

Kamchatka Peninsula
Péninsule[F] *du Kamtchatka*[M]

Caspian Sea
Mer[F] *Caspienne*

Sea of Japan
Mer[F] *du Japon*[M]

Black Sea
Mer[F] *Noire*

Pacific Ocean
Øcéan[M] *Pacifique*

Red Sea
Mer[F] *Rouge*

Japan
Japon[M]

Korean Peninsula
Péninsule[F] *de Corée*[F]

East China Sea
Mer[F] *de Chine*[F] *orientale*

Philippines
Philippines[F]

Gulf of Aden
Golfe[M] *d'Aden*

Himalayas
Himalaya[M]

Arabian Peninsula
Péninsule[F] *d'Arabie*[F]

Gulf of Oman
Golfe[M] *d'Oman*[M]

South China Sea
Mer[F] *de Chine*[F]
méridionale

Persian Gulf
Golfe[M] *Persique*

Arabian Sea
Mer[F] *d'Oman*[M]

Indonesia
Indonésie[F]

Indian Ocean
Océan[M] *Indien*

Bay of Bengal
Golfe[M] *du Bengale*[M]

configuration of the continents

Africa
Afrique[F]

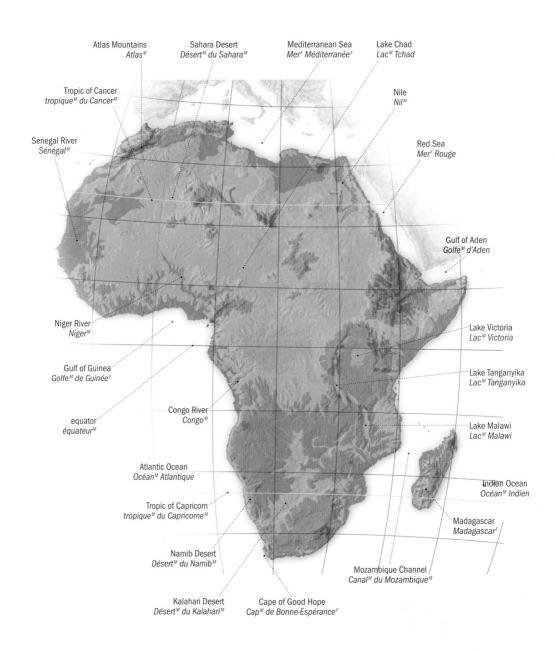

Atlas Mountains
Atlas[M]

Sahara Desert
Désert[M] *du Sahara*[M]

Mediterranean Sea
Mer[F] *Méditerranée*[F]

Lake Chad
Lac[M] *Tchad*

Tropic of Cancer
tropique[M] *du Cancer*[M]

Nile
Nil[M]

Senegal River
Sénégal[M]

Red Sea
Mer[F] *Rouge*

Gulf of Aden
Golfe[M] *d'Aden*

Niger River
Niger[M]

Lake Victoria
Lac[M] *Victoria*

Gulf of Guinea
Golfe[M] *de Guinée*[F]

Lake Tanganyika
Lac[M] *Tanganyika*

equator
équateur[M]

Congo River
Congo[M]

Lake Malawi
Lac[M] *Malawi*

Atlantic Ocean
Océan[M] *Atlantique*

Indian Ocean
Océan[M] *Indien*

Tropic of Capricorn
tropique[M] *du Capricorne*[M]

Madagascar
Madagascar[F]

Namib Desert
Désert[M] *du Namib*[M]

Mozambique Channel
Canal[M] *du Mozambique*[M]

Kalahari Desert
Désert[M] *du Kalahari*[M]

Cape of Good Hope
Cap[M] *de Bonne-Espérance*[F]

cartography
cartographie^F

Earth coordinate system
coordonnées^F *terrestres*

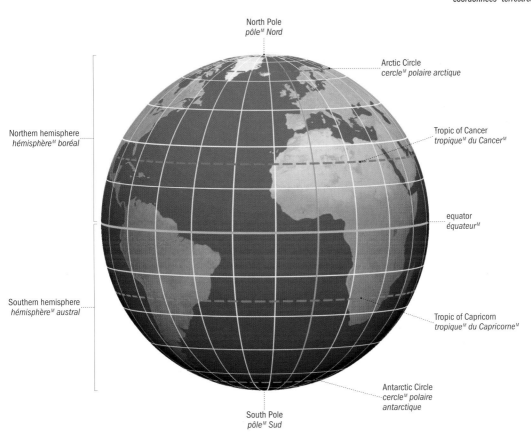

North Pole
pôle^M *Nord*

Arctic Circle
cercle^M *polaire arctique*

Northern hemisphere
hémisphère^M *boréal*

Tropic of Cancer
tropique^M *du Cancer*^M

equator
équateur^M

Southern hemisphere
hémisphère^M *austral*

Tropic of Capricorn
tropique^M *du Capricorne*^M

Antarctic Circle
cercle^M *polaire*
antarctique

South Pole
pôle^M *Sud*

hemispheres
hémisphères^M

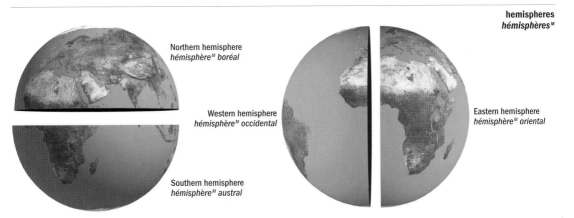

Northern hemisphere
hémisphère^M *boréal*

Western hemisphere
hémisphère^M *occidental*

Eastern hemisphere
hémisphère^M *oriental*

Southern hemisphere
hémisphère^M *austral*

cartography

grid system
divisions^F cartographiques

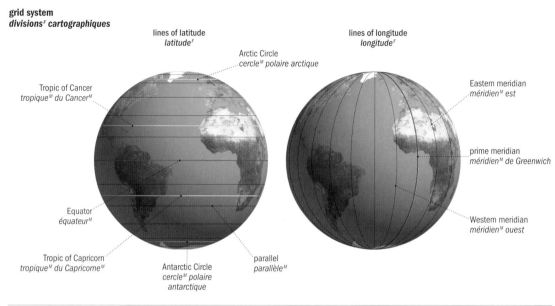

lines of latitude
latitude^F

lines of longitude
longitude^F

Arctic Circle
cercle^M polaire arctique

Tropic of Cancer
tropique^M du Cancer^M

Eastern meridian
méridien^M est

prime meridian
méridien^M de Greenwich

Equator
équateur^M

Western meridian
méridien^M ouest

Tropic of Capricorn
tropique^M du Capricorne^M

Antarctic Circle
*cercle^M polaire
antarctique*

parallel
parallèle^M

map projections
projections^F cartographiques

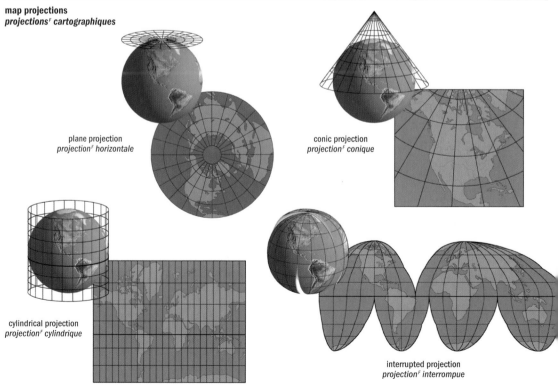

plane projection
projection^F horizontale

conic projection
projection^F conique

cylindrical projection
projection^F cylindrique

interrupted projection
projection^F interrompue

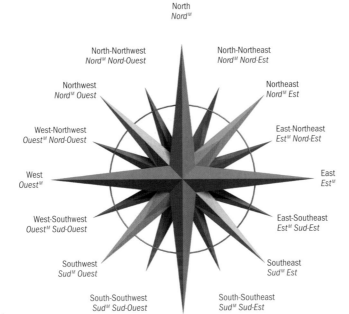

North
Nord[M]

North-Northwest
Nord[M] *Nord-Ouest*

North-Northeast
Nord[M] *Nord-Est*

Northwest
Nord[M] *Ouest*

Northeast
Nord[M] *Est*

West-Northwest
Ouest[M] *Nord-Ouest*

East-Northeast
Est[M] *Nord-Est*

West
Ouest[M]

East
Est[M]

West-Southwest
Ouest[M] *Sud-Ouest*

East-Southeast
Est[M] *Sud-Est*

Southwest
Sud[M] *Ouest*

Southeast
Sud[M] *Est*

South-Southwest
Sud[M] *Sud-Ouest*

South-Southeast
Sud[M] *Sud-Est*

South
Sud[M]

political map
carte[F] *politique*

province
province[F]

internal boundary
division[F] *territoriale*

city
grande ville[F]

frontier
frontière[F]

capital
capitale[F]

state
état[M]

country
pays[M]

CANADA

UNITED STATES

MEXICO

Edmonton

Calgary

Vancouver

Seattle

Winnipeg

Montréal

Ottawa

Toronto

Detroit

New York

Washington

Chicago

San Francisco

Denver

Los Angeles

San Diego

Atlanta

Dallas

Houston

Miami

Monterrey

Guadalajara

Ciudad de México

cartography

EARTH

physical map
carte^F physique

sea
mer^F

bay
baie^F

strait
détroit^M

mountain range
chaîne^F de montagnes^F

island
île^F

ocean
océan^M

prairie
prairie^F

massif
massif^M montagneux

estuary
estuaire^M

river
rivière^F

lake
lac^M

plateau
plateau^M

archipelago
archipel^M

gulf
golfe^M

peninsula
péninsule^F

cape
cap^M

plain
plaine^F

river
fleuve^M

isthmus
isthme^M

urban map
plan^M urbain

railway
chemin^M de fer^M

railway station
gare^F

bridge
pont^M

park
parc^M

suburbs
banlieue^F

cemetery
cimetière^M

river
fleuve^M

monument
monument^M

woods
bois^M

ring road
boulevard^M périphérique

roundabout
rond-point^M

motorway
autoroute^F

district
arrondissement^M

street
rue^F

avenue
avenue^F

public building
édifice^M public

boulevard
boulevard^M

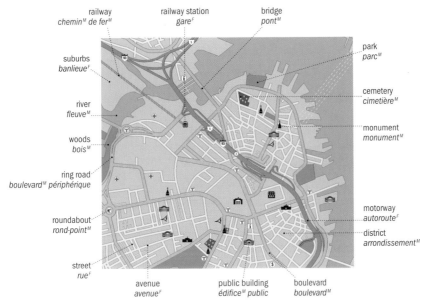

road map
carte^F routière

motorway number
numéro^M d'autoroute^F

road
route^F

motorway
autoroute^F

road number
numéro^M de route^F

rest area
aire^F de repos^M

airport
aéroport^M

service area
aire^F de service^M

national park
parc^M national

ring motorway
autoroute^F de ceinture^F

scenic route
parcours^M pittoresque

secondary road
route^F secondaire

point of interest
curiosité^F

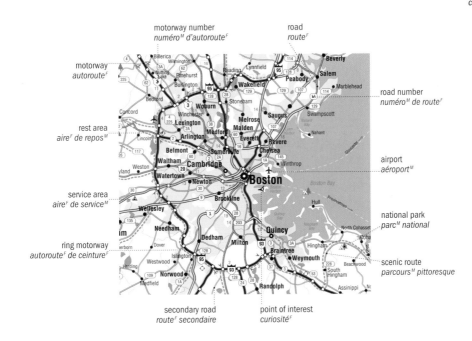

section of the Earth's crust

coupe^F de la croûte^F terrestre

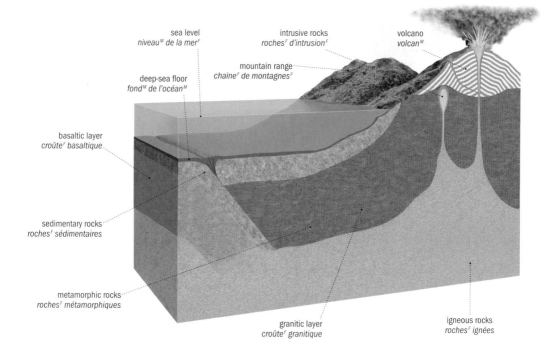

sea level
niveau^M de la mer^F

intrusive rocks
roches^F d'intrusion^F

volcano
volcan^M

mountain range
chaîne^F de montagnes^F

deep-sea floor
fond^M de l'océan^M

basaltic layer
croûte^F basaltique

sedimentary rocks
roches^F sédimentaires

metamorphic rocks
roches^F métamorphiques

granitic layer
croûte^F granitique

igneous rocks
roches^F ignées

structure of the Earth

structure^F de la Terre^F

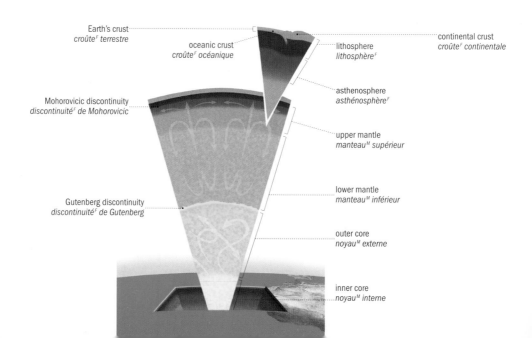

Earth's crust
croûte^F terrestre

oceanic crust
croûte^F océanique

continental crust
croûte^F continentale

lithosphere
lithosphère^F

asthenosphere
asthénosphère^F

Mohorovicic discontinuity
discontinuité^F de Mohorovicic

upper mantle
manteau^M supérieur

lower mantle
manteau^M inférieur

Gutenberg discontinuity
discontinuité^F de Gutenberg

outer core
noyau^M externe

inner core
noyau^M interne

tectonic plates
plaques^F tectoniques

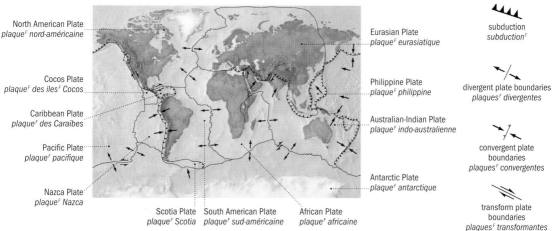

North American Plate
plaque^F nord-américaine

Cocos Plate
plaque^F des îles^F Cocos

Caribbean Plate
plaque^F des Caraïbes

Pacific Plate
plaque^F pacifique

Nazca Plate
plaque^F Nazca

Scotia Plate
plaque^F Scotia

South American Plate
plaque^F sud-américaine

African Plate
plaque^F africaine

Eurasian Plate
plaque^F eurasiatique

Philippine Plate
plaque^F philippine

Australian-Indian Plate
plaque^F indo-australienne

Antarctic Plate
plaque^F antarctique

subduction
subduction^F

divergent plate boundaries
plaques^F divergentes

convergent plate
boundaries
plaques^F convergentes

transform plate
boundaries
plaques^F transformantes

earthquake
séisme^M

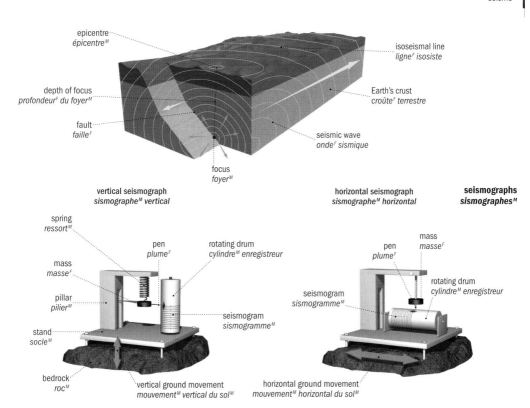

epicentre
épicentre^M

isoseismal line
ligne^F isosiste

depth of focus
profondeur^F du foyer^M

Earth's crust
croûte^F terrestre

fault
faille^F

seismic wave
onde^F sismique

focus
foyer^M

vertical seismograph
sismographe^M vertical

horizontal seismograph
sismographe^M horizontal

**seismographs
sismographes^M**

spring
ressort^M

pen
plume^F

rotating drum
cylindre^M enregistreur

mass
masse^F

pillar
pilier^M

stand
socle^M

seismogram
sismogramme^M

bedrock
roc^M

vertical ground movement
mouvement^M vertical du sol^M

pen
plume^F

mass
masse^F

rotating drum
cylindre^M enregistreur

seismogram
sismogramme^M

horizontal ground movement
mouvement^M horizontal du sol^M

volcano

volcan^M

volcano during eruption
volcan^M en éruption^F

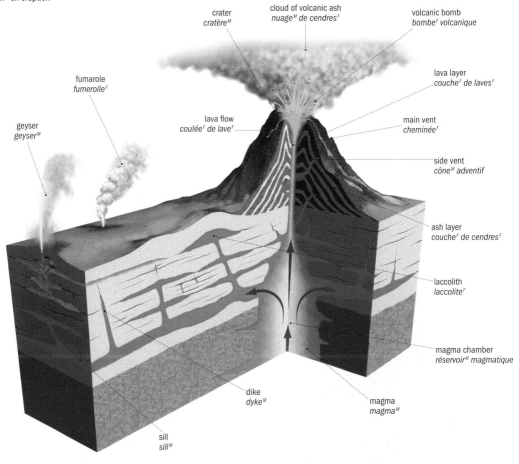

crater
cratère^M

cloud of volcanic ash
nuage^M de cendres^F

volcanic bomb
bombe^F volcanique

fumarole
fumerolle^F

lava layer
couche^F de laves^F

geyser
geyser^M

lava flow
coulée^F de lave^F

main vent
cheminée^F

side vent
cône^M adventif

ash layer
couche^F de cendres^F

laccolith
laccolite^F

magma chamber
réservoir^M magmatique

dike
dyke^M

magma
magma^M

sill
sill^M

examples of volcanoes
exemples^M de volcans^M

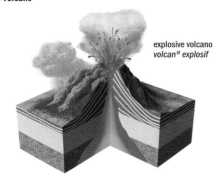

explosive volcano
volcan^M explosif

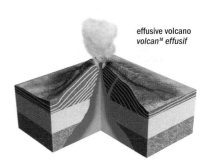

effusive volcano
volcan^M effusif

mountain
montagne[F]

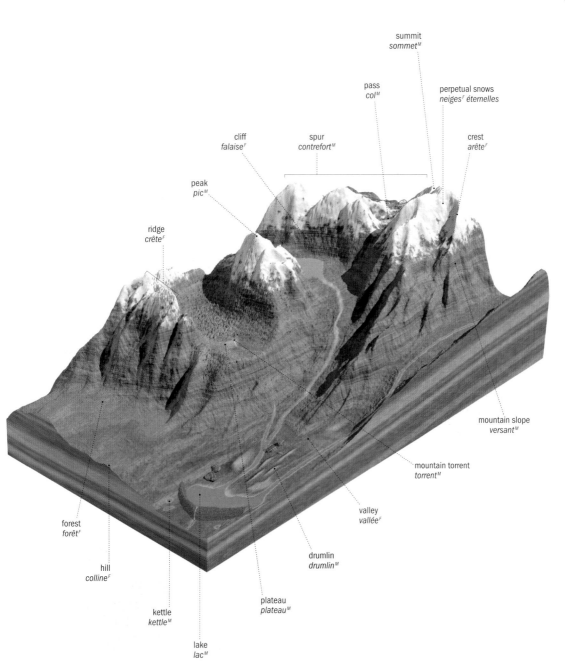

summit
sommet[M]

pass
col[M]

perpetual snows
neiges[F] *éternelles*

cliff
falaise[F]

spur
contrefort[M]

crest
arête[F]

peak
pic[M]

ridge
crête[F]

mountain slope
versant[M]

mountain torrent
torrent[M]

valley
vallée[F]

forest
forêt[F]

drumlin
drumlin[M]

hill
colline[F]

plateau
plateau[M]

kettle
kettle[M]

lake
lac[M]

glacier

glacier^M

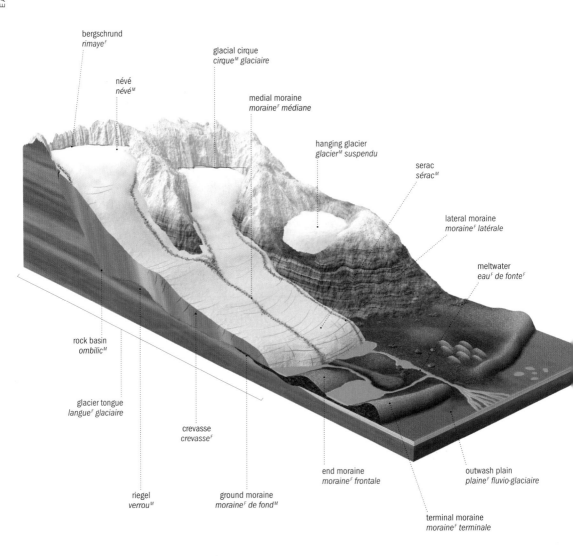

bergschrund
rimaye^F

glacial cirque
cirque^M *glaciaire*

névé
névé^M

medial moraine
moraine^F *médiane*

hanging glacier
glacier^M *suspendu*

serac
sérac^M

lateral moraine
moraine^F *latérale*

meltwater
eau^F *de fonte*^F

rock basin
ombilic^M

glacier tongue
langue^F *glaciaire*

crevasse
crevasse^F

end moraine
moraine^F *frontale*

outwash plain
plaine^F *fluvio-glaciaire*

riegel
verrou^M

ground moraine
moraine^F *de fond*^M

terminal moraine
moraine^F *terminale*

cave

grotte[F]

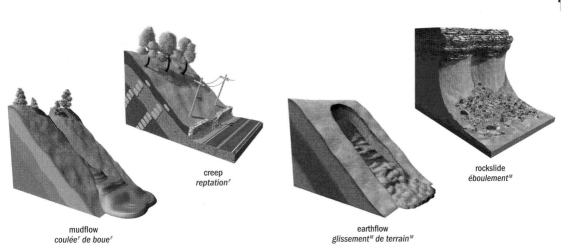

pothole
aven[M]

grike
lapiaz[M]

stalactite
stalactite[F]

dolina
doline[F]

gorge
gorge[F]

waterfall
chute[F]

swallow hole
gouffre[M]

gour
gour[M]

water table
nappe[F] phréatique

column
colonne[F]

subterranean stream
rivière[F] souterraine

stalagmite
stalagmite[F]

dry gallery
galerie[F] sèche

resurgence
résurgence[F]

landslides

mouvements[M] de terrain[M]

creep
reptation[F]

rockslide
éboulement[M]

mudflow
coulée[F] de boue[F]

earthflow
glissement[M] de terrain[M]

EARTH

watercourse

cours^M d'eau^F

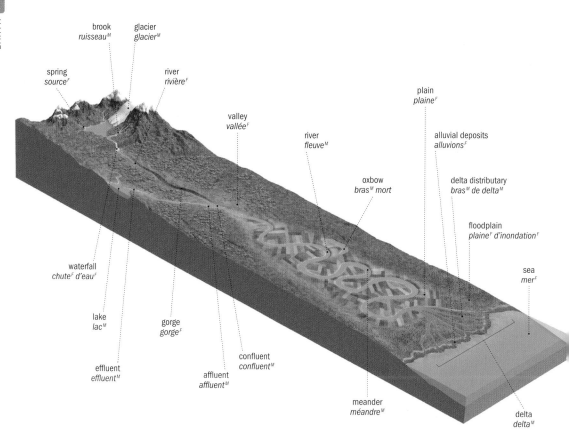

brook
ruisseau^M

glacier
glacier^M

spring
source^F

river
rivière^F

valley
vallée^F

plain
plaine^F

river
fleuve^M

alluvial deposits
alluvions^F

oxbow
bras^M mort

delta distributary
bras^M de delta^M

floodplain
plaine^F d'inondation^F

waterfall
chute^F d'eau^F

sea
mer^F

lake
lac^M

gorge
gorge^F

confluent
confluent^M

effluent
effluent^M

affluent
affluent^M

meander
méandre^M

delta
delta^M

lakes

lacs^M

glacial lake
lac^M d'origine^F glaciaire

volcanic lake
lac^M d'origine^F volcanique

tectonic lake
lac^M d'origine^F tectonique

oxbow lake
lac^M en croissant^M

oasis
oasis^F

artificial lake
lac^M artificiel

wave

vague^F

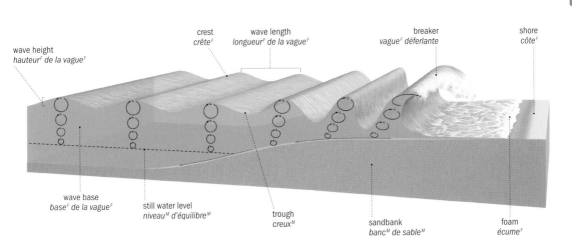

wave height
hauteur^F de la vague^F

crest
crête^F

wave length
longueur^F de la vague^F

breaker
vague^F déferlante

shore
côte^F

wave base
base^F de la vague^F

still water level
niveau^M d'équilibre^M

trough
creux^M

sandbank
banc^M de sable^M

foam
écume^F

ocean floor

fond^M de l'océan^M

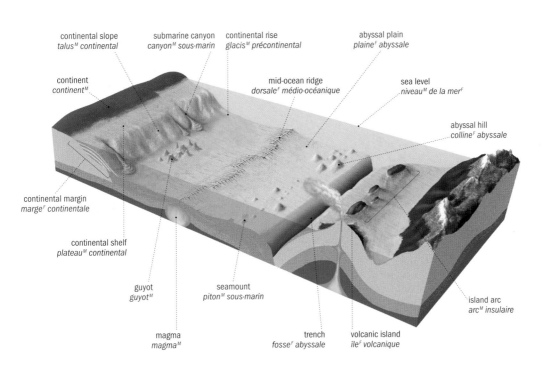

continental slope
talus^M continental

submarine canyon
canyon^M sous-marin

continental rise
glacis^M précontinental

abyssal plain
plaine^F abyssale

continent
continent^M

mid-ocean ridge
dorsale^F médio-océanique

sea level
niveau^M de la mer^F

abyssal hill
colline^F abyssale

continental margin
marge^F continentale

continental shelf
plateau^M continental

guyot
guyot^M

seamount
piton^M sous-marin

magma
magma^M

trench
fosse^F abyssale

volcanic island
île^F volcanique

island arc
arc^M insulaire

ocean trenches and ridges

fosses^F et dorsales^F océaniques

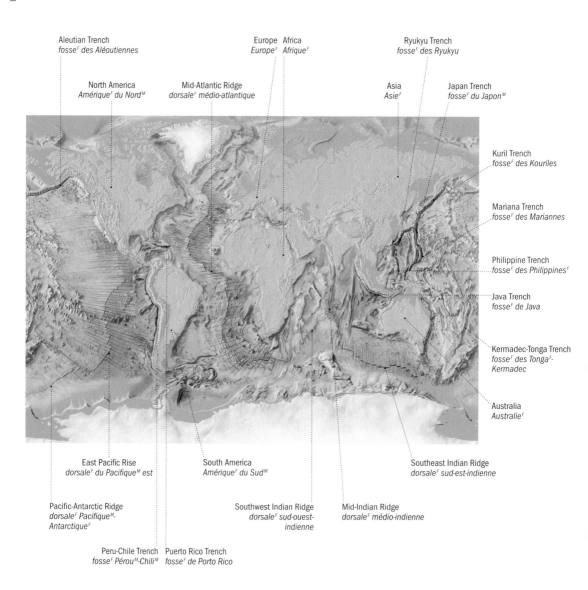

Aleutian Trench
fosse^F des Aléoutiennes

Europe Africa
Europe^F Afrique^F

Ryukyu Trench
fosse^F des Ryukyu

North America
Amérique^F du Nord^M

Mid-Atlantic Ridge
dorsale^F médio-atlantique

Asia
Asie^F

Japan Trench
fosse^F du Japon^M

Kuril Trench
fosse^F des Kouriles

Mariana Trench
fosse^F des Mariannes

Philippine Trench
fosse^F des Philippines^F

Java Trench
fosse^F de Java

Kermadec-Tonga Trench
*fosse^F des Tonga^F-
Kermadec*

Australia
Australie^F

East Pacific Rise
dorsale^F du Pacifique^M est

South America
Amérique^F du Sud^M

Southeast Indian Ridge
dorsale^F sud-est-indienne

Pacific-Antarctic Ridge
*dorsale^F Pacifique^M-
Antarctique^F*

Southwest Indian Ridge
*dorsale^F sud-ouest-
indienne*

Mid-Indian Ridge
dorsale^F médio-indienne

Peru-Chile Trench
fosse^F Pérou^M-Chili^M

Puerto Rico Trench
fosse^F de Porto Rico

common coastal features
configuration^F du littoral^M

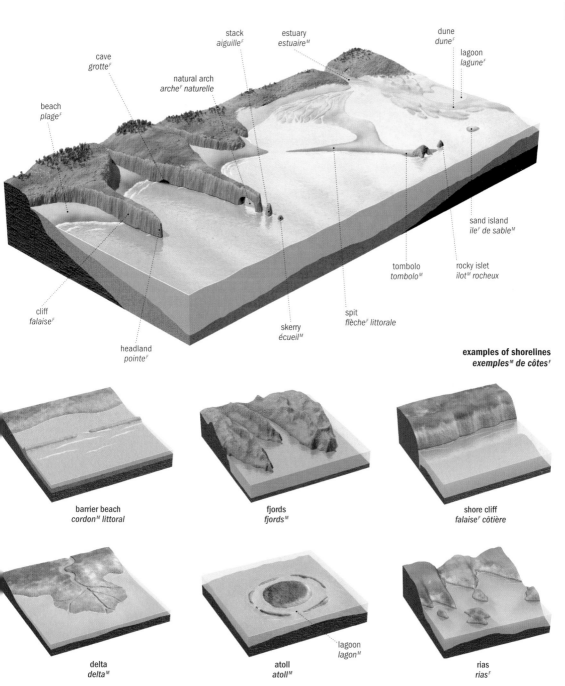

stack
aiguille^F

estuary
estuaire^M

dune
dune^F

lagoon
lagune^F

cave
grotte^F

natural arch
arche^F naturelle

beach
plage^F

sand island
ile^F de sable^M

tombolo
tombolo^M

rocky islet
ilot^M rocheux

cliff
falaise^F

spit
flèche^F littorale

skerry
écueil^M

headland
pointe^F

examples of shorelines
exemples^M de côtes^F

barrier beach
cordon^M littoral

fjords
fjords^M

shore cliff
falaise^F côtière

delta
delta^M

atoll
atoll^M

lagoon
lagon^M

rias
rias^F

desert

désert^M

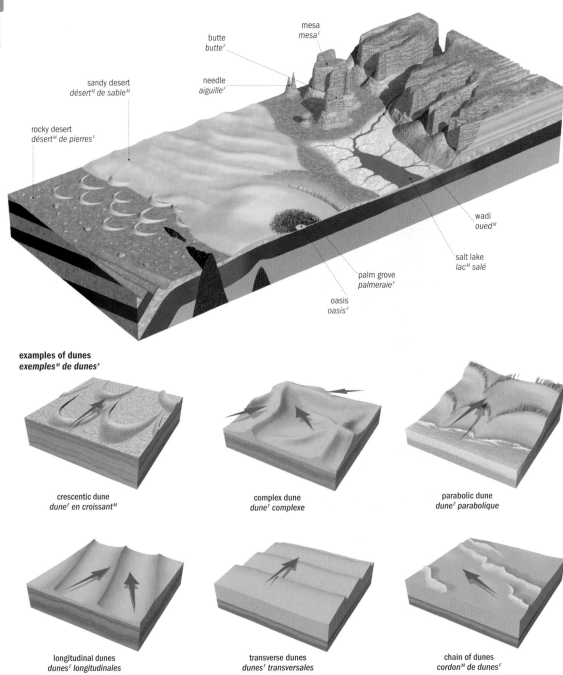

mesa
mesa^F

butte
butte^F

needle
aiguille^F

sandy desert
désert^M de sable^M

rocky desert
désert^M de pierres^F

wadi
oued^M

salt lake
lac^M salé

palm grove
palmeraie^F

oasis
oasis^F

examples of dunes
exemples^M de dunes^F

crescentic dune
dune^F en croissant^M

complex dune
dune^F complexe

parabolic dune
dune^F parabolique

longitudinal dunes
dunes^F longitudinales

transverse dunes
dunes^F transversales

chain of dunes
cordon^M de dunes^F

profile of the Earth's atmosphere

coupe^F de l'atmosphère^F terrestre

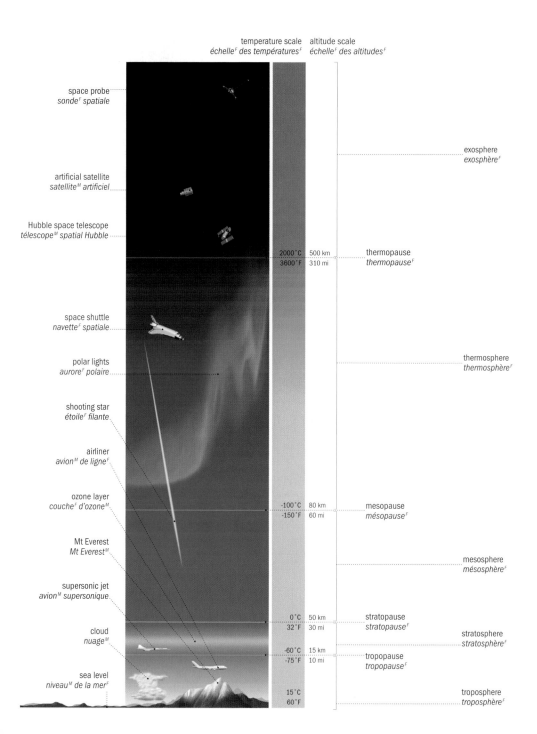

temperature scale
échelle^F des températures^F

altitude scale
échelle^F des altitudes^F

space probe
sonde^F spatiale

exosphere
exosphère^F

artificial satellite
satellite^M artificiel

Hubble space telescope
télescope^M spatial Hubble

2000°C   500 km   thermopause
3600°F   310 mi   thermopause^F

space shuttle
navette^F spatiale

polar lights
aurore^F polaire

thermosphere
thermosphère^F

shooting star
étoile^F filante

airliner
avion^M de ligne^F

ozone layer
couche^F d'ozone^M

-100°C   80 km   mesopause
-150°F   60 mi   mésopause^F

Mt Everest
Mt Everest^M

mesosphere
mésosphère^F

supersonic jet
avion^M supersonique

0°C   50 km   stratopause
32°F   30 mi   stratopause^F

cloud
nuage^M

stratosphere
stratosphère^F

-60°C   15 km   tropopause
-75°F   10 mi   tropopause^F

sea level
niveau^M de la mer^F

15°C
60°F

troposphere
troposphère^F

seasons of the year

cycle^M des saisons^F

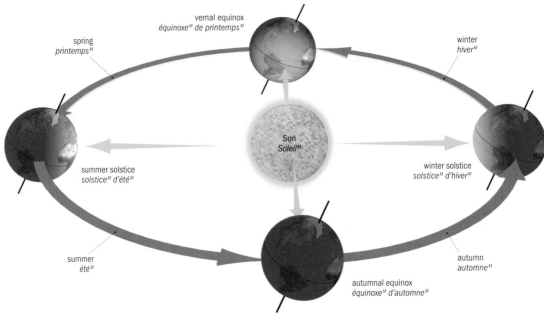

vernal equinox
équinoxe^M de printemps^M

spring
printemps^M

winter
hiver^M

Sun
Soleil^M

summer solstice
solstice^M d'été^M

winter solstice
solstice^M d'hiver^M

summer
été^M

autumn
automne^M

autumnal equinox
équinoxe^M d'automne^M

meteorological forecast

prévisions^F météorologiques

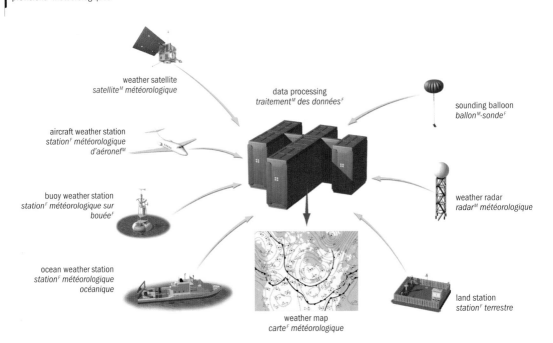

weather satellite
satellite^M météorologique

data processing
traitement^M des données^F

sounding balloon
ballon^M-sonde^F

aircraft weather station
station^F météorologique
d'aéronef^M

buoy weather station
station^F météorologique sur
bouée^F

weather radar
radar^M météorologique

ocean weather station
station^F météorologique
océanique

land station
station^F terrestre

weather map
carte^F météorologique

weather map
carte^F météorologique

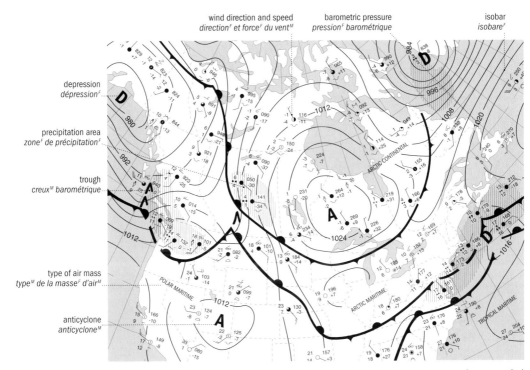

wind direction and speed
direction^F et force^F du vent^M

barometric pressure
pression^F barométrique

isobar
isobare^F

depression
dépression^F

precipitation area
zone^F de précipitation^F

trough
creux^M barométrique

type of air mass
type^M de la masse^F d'air^M

anticyclone
anticyclone^M

station model
disposition^F des informations^F d'une station^F

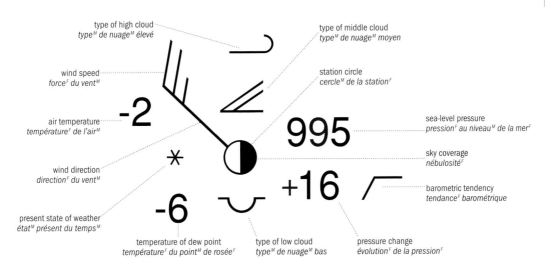

type of high cloud
type^M de nuage^M élevé

type of middle cloud
type^M de nuage^M moyen

wind speed
force^F du vent^M

station circle
cercle^M de la station^F

air temperature
température^F de l'air^M

sea-level pressure
pression^F au niveau^M de la mer^F

wind direction
direction^F du vent^M

sky coverage
nébulosité^F

barometric tendency
tendance^F barométrique

present state of weather
état^M présent du temps^M

temperature of dew point
température^F du point^M de rosée^F

type of low cloud
type^M de nuage^M bas

pressure change
évolution^F de la pression^F

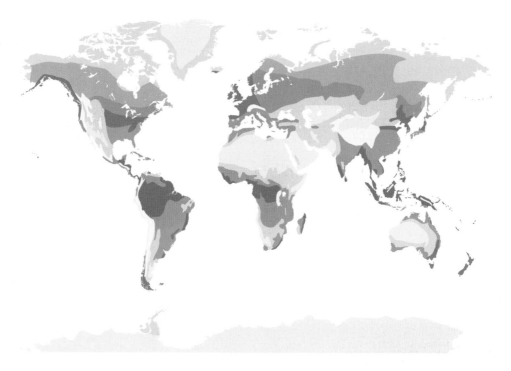

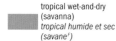

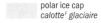

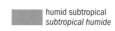

climates of the world

climats*M* du monde*M*

EARTH

tropical climates
*climats*ᴹ *tropicaux*

  tropical rain forest
  tropical humide

  tropical wet-and-dry
  (savanna)
  *tropical humide et sec
  (savane*ᶠ*)*

dry climates
*climats*ᴹ *arides*

  steppe
  *steppe*ᶠ

  desert
  *désert*ᴹ

cold temperate climates
*climats*ᴹ *tempérés froids*

  humid continental - hot
  summer
  *continental humide, à été*ᴹ
  chaud

  humid continental - warm
  summer
  *continental humide, à été*ᴹ
  frais

  subarctic
  subarctique

warm temperate climates
*climats*ᴹ *tempérés chauds*

  humid subtropical
  subtropical humide

  Mediterranean subtropical
  méditerranéen

  marine
  océanique

polar climates
*climats*ᴹ *polaires*

  polar tundra
  *toundra*ᶠ

  polar ice cap
  *calotte*ᶠ *glaciaire*

highland climates
*climats*ᴹ *de montagne*ᶠ

  highland
  *climats*ᴹ *de montagne*ᶠ

precipitations

précipitations^F

winter precipitations
précipitations^F
hivernales

warm air
air^M chaud

cold air
air^M froid

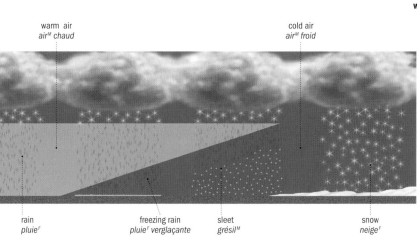

rain
pluie^F

freezing rain
pluie^F verglaçante

sleet
grésil^M

snow
neige^F

stormy sky
ciel^M d'orage^M

cloud
nuage^M

lightning
éclair^M

rainbow
arc-en-ciel^M

rain
pluie^F

dew
rosée^F

mist
brume^F

fog
brouillard^M

rime
givre^M

glazed frost
verglas^M

41

clouds

nuages^M

EARTH

high clouds
nuages^M de haute altitude^F

middle clouds
nuages^M de moyenne
altitude^F

low clouds
nuages^M de basse
altitude^F

cirrostratus
cirro-stratus^M

cirrocumulus
cirro-cumulus^M

cirrus
cirrus^M

altostratus
alto-stratus^M

altocumulus
alto-cumulus^M

stratocumulus
strato-cumulus^M

nimbostratus
nimbo-stratus^M

cumulus
cumulus^M

stratus
stratus^M

clouds with vertical development
nuages^M à développement^M vertical

cumulonimbus
cumulo-nimbus^M

tornado and waterspout

tornade^F et trombe^F marine

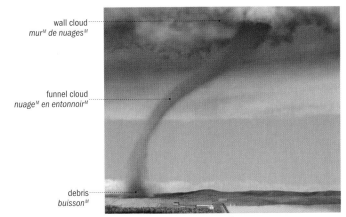

wall cloud
mur^M de nuages^M

funnel cloud
nuage^M en entonnoir^M

debris
buisson^M

waterspout
trombe^F marine

tornado
tornade^F

tropical cyclone

cyclone^M tropical

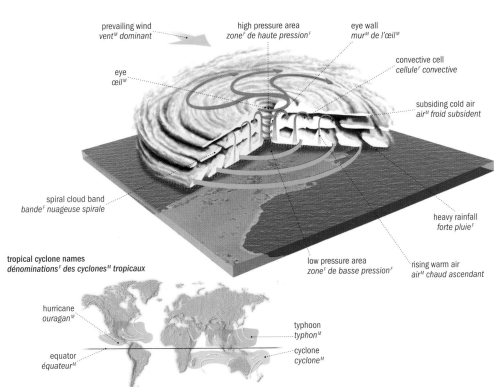

prevailing wind
vent^M dominant

high pressure area
zone^F de haute pression^F

eye wall
mur^M de l'œil^M

eye
œil^M

convective cell
cellule^F convective

subsiding cold air
air^M froid subsident

spiral cloud band
bande^F nuageuse spirale

heavy rainfall
forte pluie^F

tropical cyclone names
dénominations^F des cyclones^M tropicaux

low pressure area
zone^F de basse pression^F

rising warm air
air^M chaud ascendant

hurricane
ouragan^M

typhoon
typhon^M

equator
équateur^M

cyclone
cyclone^M

vegetation and biosphere

végétation^F et biosphère^F

vegetation regions
distribution^F de la végétation^F

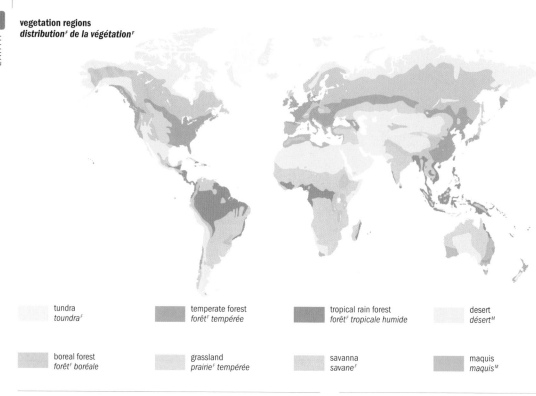

tundra *toundra^F*	temperate forest *forêt^F tempérée*	tropical rain forest *forêt^F tropicale humide*	desert *désert^M*
boreal forest *forêt^F boréale*	grassland *prairie^F tempérée*	savanna *savane^F*	maquis *maquis^M*

elevation zones and vegetation
paysage^M végétal selon l'altitude^F

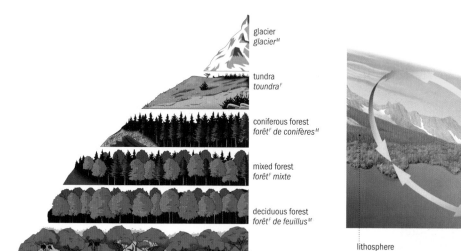

glacier
glacier^M

tundra
toundra^F

coniferous forest
forêt^F de conifères^M

mixed forest
forêt^F mixte

deciduous forest
forêt^F de feuillus^M

tropical forest
forêt^F tropicale

structure of the biosphere
structure^F de la biosphère^F

atmosphere
atmosphère^F

lithosphere
lithosphère^F

hydrosphere
hydrosphère^F

food chain

chaîne^F alimentaire

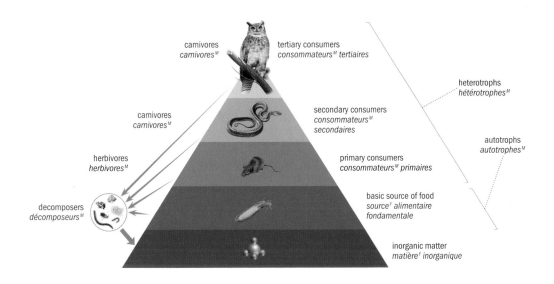

carnivores
carnivores^M

tertiary consumers
consommateurs^M *tertiaires*

heterotrophs
hétérotrophes^M

carnivores
carnivores^M

secondary consumers
consommateurs^M
secondaires

herbivores
herbivores^M

primary consumers
consommateurs^M *primaires*

autotrophs
autotrophes^M

decomposers
décomposeurs^M

basic source of food
source^F *alimentaire*
fondamentale

inorganic matter
matière^F *inorganique*

hydrologic cycle

cycle^M de l'eau^F

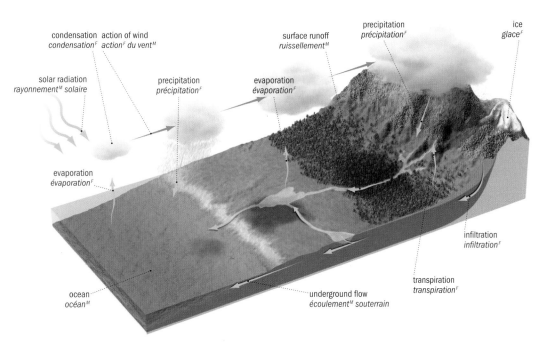

condensation
condensation^F

action of wind
action^F *du vent*^M

surface runoff
ruissellement^M

precipitation
précipitation^F

ice
glace^F

solar radiation
rayonnement^M *solaire*

precipitation
précipitation^F

evaporation
évaporation^F

evaporation
évaporation^F

infiltration
infiltration^F

ocean
océan^M

underground flow
écoulement^M *souterrain*

transpiration
transpiration^F

greenhouse effect

effet^M de serre^F

natural greenhouse effect
effet^M de serre^F naturel

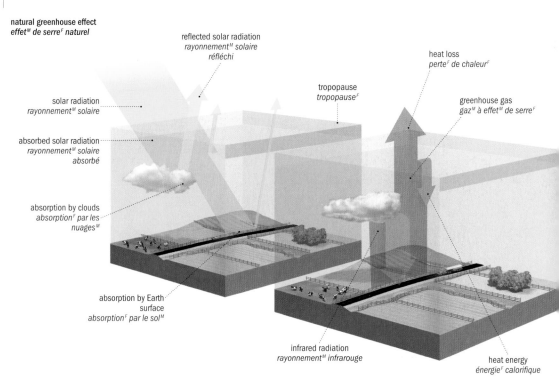

reflected solar radiation
*rayonnement^M solaire
réfléchi*

heat loss
perte^F de chaleur^F

tropopause
tropopause^F

greenhouse gas
gaz^M à effet^M de serre^F

solar radiation
rayonnement^M solaire

absorbed solar radiation
*rayonnement^M solaire
absorbé*

absorption by clouds
*absorption^F par les
nuages^M*

absorption by Earth
surface
absorption^F par le sol^M

infrared radiation
rayonnement^M infrarouge

heat energy
énergie^F calorifique

enhanced greenhouse effect
*augmentation^F de l'effet^M
de serre^F*

greenhouse gas
concentration
*concentration^F des gaz^M à
effet^M de serre^F*

fossil fuel
combustible^M fossile

global warming
réchauffement^M de la planè

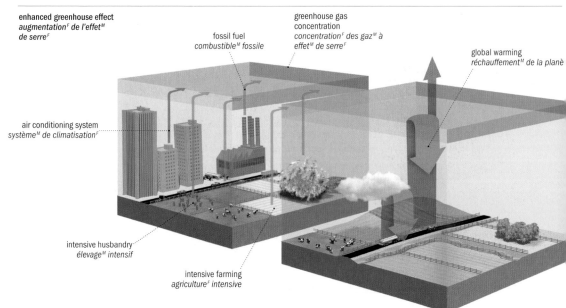

air conditioning system
système^M de climatisation^F

intensive husbandry
élevage^M intensif

intensive farming
agriculture^F intensive

air pollution
pollution^F de l'air^M

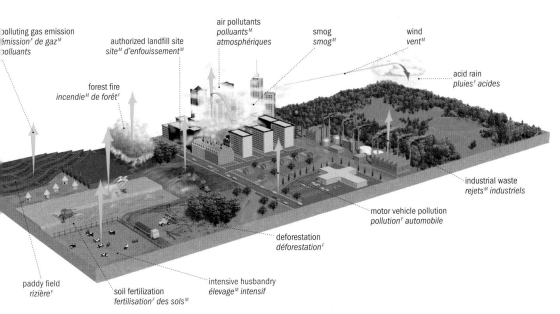

polluting gas emission
émission^F de gaz^M
polluants

authorized landfill site
site^M d'enfouissement^M

air pollutants
polluants^M
atmosphériques

smog
smog^M

wind
vent^M

acid rain
pluies^F acides

forest fire
incendie^M de forêt^F

industrial waste
rejets^M industriels

motor vehicle pollution
pollution^F automobile

deforestation
déforestation^F

paddy field
rizière^F

soil fertilization
fertilisation^F des sols^M

intensive husbandry
élevage^M intensif

land pollution
pollution^F du sol^M

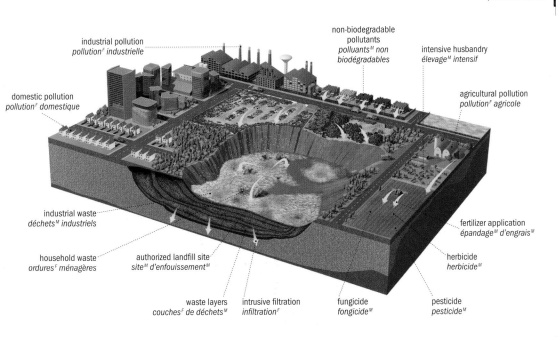

industrial pollution
pollution^F industrielle

non-biodegradable
pollutants
polluants^M non
biodégradables

intensive husbandry
élevage^M intensif

domestic pollution
pollution^F domestique

agricultural pollution
pollution^F agricole

industrial waste
déchets^M industriels

fertilizer application
épandage^M d'engrais^M

household waste
ordures^F ménagères

authorized landfill site
site^M d'enfouissement^M

herbicide
herbicide^M

waste layers
couches^F de déchets^M

intrusive filtration
infiltration^F

fungicide
fongicide^M

pesticide
pesticide^M

water pollution

pollution*F* de l'eau*F*

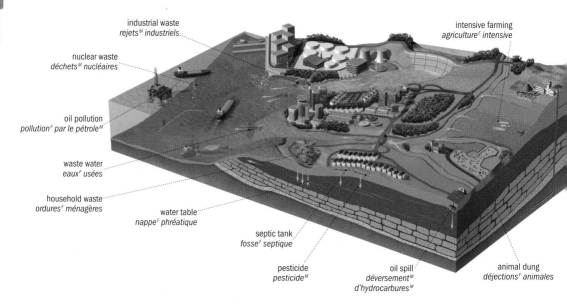

industrial waste
*rejets*M *industriels*

nuclear waste
*déchets*M *nucléaires*

intensive farming
*agriculture*F *intensive*

oil pollution
*pollution*F *par le pétrole*M

waste water
*eaux*F *usées*

household waste
*ordures*F *ménagères*

water table
*nappe*F *phréatique*

septic tank
*fosse*F *septique*

pesticide
*pesticide*M

oil spill
*déversement*M
*d'hydrocarbures*M

animal dung
*déjections*F *animales*

acid rain

pluies*F* acides

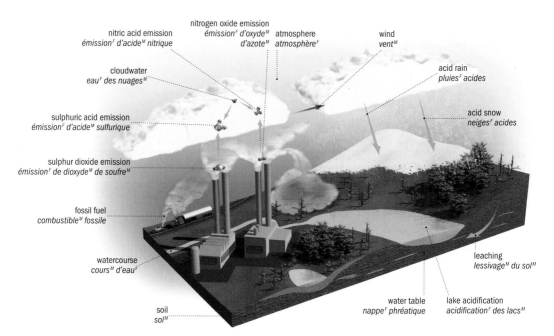

nitrogen oxide emission
*émission*F *d'oxyde*M
*d'azote*M

nitric acid emission
*émission*F *d'acide*M *nitrique*

atmosphere
*atmosphère*F

wind
*vent*M

cloudwater
*eau*F *des nuages*M

acid rain
*pluies*F *acides*

sulphuric acid emission
*émission*F *d'acide*M *sulfurique*

acid snow
*neiges*F *acides*

sulphur dioxide emission
*émission*F *de dioxyde*M *de soufre*M

fossil fuel
*combustible*M *fossile*

watercourse
*cours*M *d'eau*F

leaching
*lessivage*M *du sol*M

soil
*sol*M

water table
*nappe*F *phréatique*

lake acidification
*acidification*F *des lacs*M

selective sorting of waste

tri^M sélectif des déchets^M

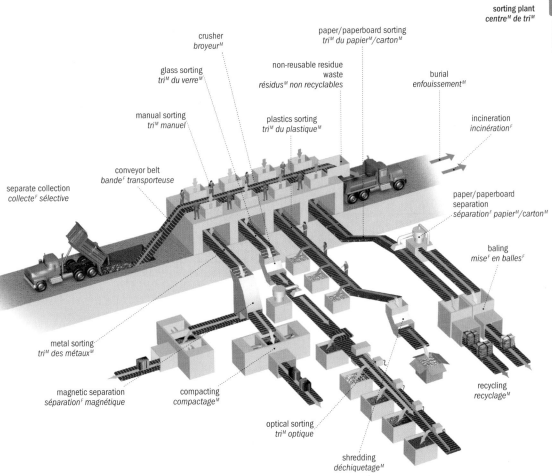

sorting plant
centre^M de tri^M

crusher
broyeur^M

paper/paperboard sorting
tri^M du papier^M/carton^M

glass sorting
tri^M du verre^M

non-reusable residue
waste
résidus^M non recyclables

burial
enfouissement^M

manual sorting
tri^M manuel

plastics sorting
tri^M du plastique^M

incineration
incinération^F

conveyor belt
bande^F transporteuse

separate collection
collecte^F sélective

paper/paperboard
separation
séparation^F papier^M/carton^M

baling
mise^F en balles^F

metal sorting
tri^M des métaux^M

magnetic separation
séparation^F magnétique

compacting
compactage^M

recycling
recyclage^M

optical sorting
tri^M optique

shredding
déchiquetage^M

---

recycling containers
conteneurs^M de collecte^F
sélective

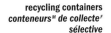

paper recycling container
conteneur^M à papier^M

aluminum recycling container
conteneur^M à boîtes^F
métalliques

glass collection unit
colonne^F de collecte^F du
verre^M

recycling bin
bac^M de recyclage^M

glass recycling container
conteneur^M à verre^M

paper collection unit
colonne^F de collecte^F du
papier^M

plant cell

cellule^F végétale

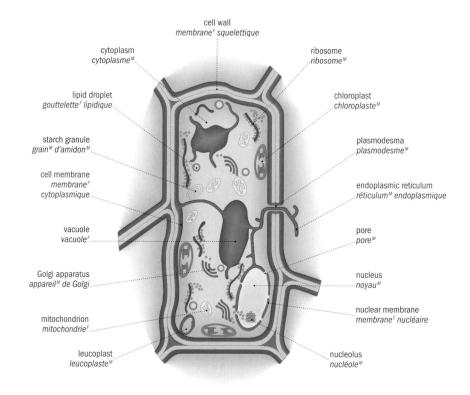

cell wall
membrane^F squelettique

cytoplasm
cytoplasme^M

ribosome
ribosome^M

lipid droplet
gouttelette^F lipidique

chloroplast
chloroplaste^M

starch granule
grain^M d'amidon^M

plasmodesma
plasmodesme^M

cell membrane
membrane^F
cytoplasmique

endoplasmic reticulum
réticulum^M endoplasmique

vacuole
vacuole^F

pore
pore^M

Golgi apparatus
appareil^M de Golgi

nucleus
noyau^M

mitochondrion
mitochondrie^F

nuclear membrane
membrane^F nucléaire

leucoplast
leucoplaste^M

nucleolus
nucléole^M

lichen

lichen^M

structure of a lichen
structure^F d'un lichen^M

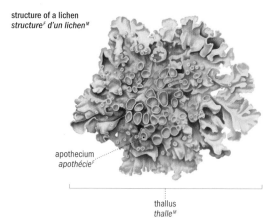

apothecium
apothécie^F

thallus
thalle^M

examples of lichens
exemples^M de lichens^M

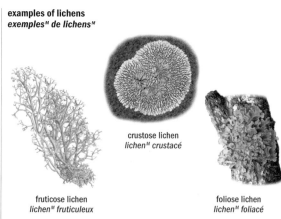

crustose lichen
lichen^M crustacé

fruticose lichen
lichen^M fruticuleux

foliose lichen
lichen^M foliacé

structure of a moss
structure[F] d'une mousse[F]

examples of mosses
exemples[M] de mousses[F]

capsule
capsule[F]

stalk
pédicelle[M]

leaf
feuille[F]

stem
tige[F]

rhizoid
rhizoïde[M]

prickly sphagnum
sphaigne[F] squarreuse

common hair cap moss
polytric[M] commun

structure of an alga
structure[F] d'une algue[F]

examples of algae
exemples[M] d'algues[F]

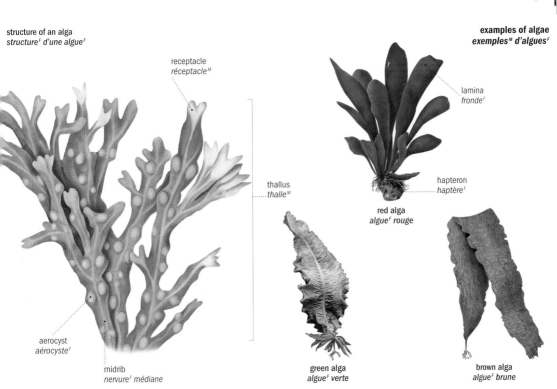

receptacle
réceptacle[M]

lamina
fronde[F]

thallus
thalle[M]

hapteron
haptère[F]

red alga
algue[F] rouge

aerocyst
aérocyste[F]

midrib
nervure[F] médiane

green alga
algue[F] verte

brown alga
algue[F] brune

mushroom

champignon^M

PLANT KINGDOM

structure of a mushroom
structure^F d'un champignon^M

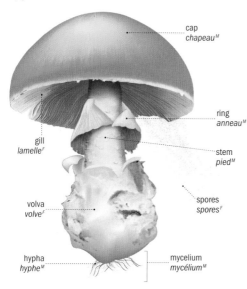

cap
chapeau^M

ring
anneau^M

gill
lamelle^F

stem
pied^M

volva
volve^F

spores
spores^F

hypha
hyphe^M

mycelium
mycélium^M

**deadly poisonous
mushroom
*champignon^M mortel***

destroying angel
amanite^F vireuse

**poisonous mushroom
*champignon^M
vénéneux***

fly agaric
fausse oronge^F

fern

fougère^F

structure of a fern
structure^F d'une fougère^F

examples of ferns
exemples^M de fougères^F

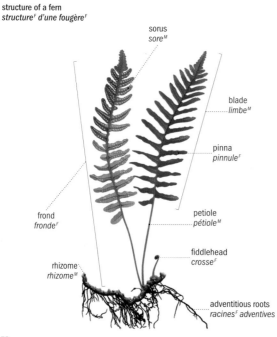

sorus
sore^M

blade
limbe^M

pinna
pinnule^F

frond
fronde^F

petiole
pétiole^M

fiddlehead
crosse^F

rhizome
rhizome^M

adventitious roots
racines^F adventives

tree fern
fougère^F arborescente

trunk
tronc^M

common polypody
polypode^M commun

bird's nest fern
fougère^F nid^M d'oiseau^M

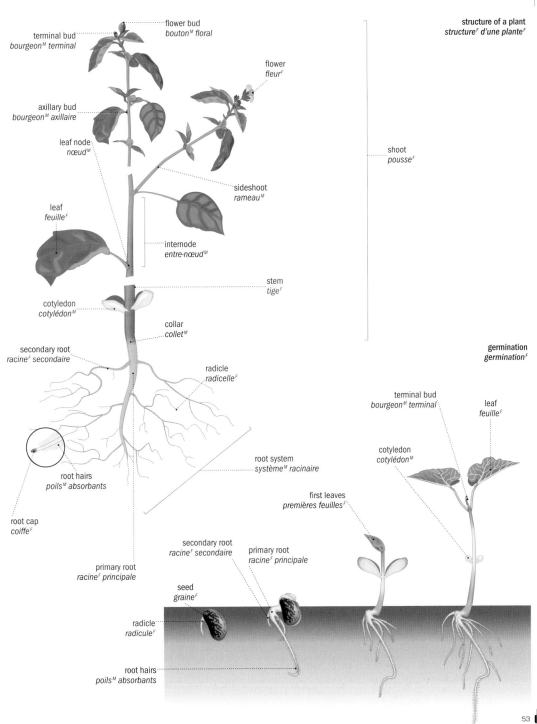

structure of a plant
structure[F] *d'une plante*[F]

terminal bud
bourgeon[M] *terminal*

flower bud
bouton[M] *floral*

flower
fleur[F]

axillary bud
bourgeon[M] *axillaire*

leaf node
nœud[M]

sideshoot
rameau[M]

leaf
feuille[F]

internode
entre-nœud[M]

shoot
pousse[F]

stem
tige[F]

cotyledon
cotylédon[M]

collar
collet[M]

secondary root
racine[F] *secondaire*

radicle
radicelle[F]

root system
système[M] *racinaire*

root hairs
poils[M] *absorbants*

root cap
coiffe[F]

primary root
racine[F] *principale*

secondary root
racine[F] *secondaire*

primary root
racine[F] *principale*

seed
graine[F]

radicle
radicule[F]

root hairs
poils[M] *absorbants*

germination
germination[F]

terminal bud
bourgeon[M] *terminal*

leaf
feuille[F]

cotyledon
cotylédon[M]

first leaves
premières feuilles[F]

53

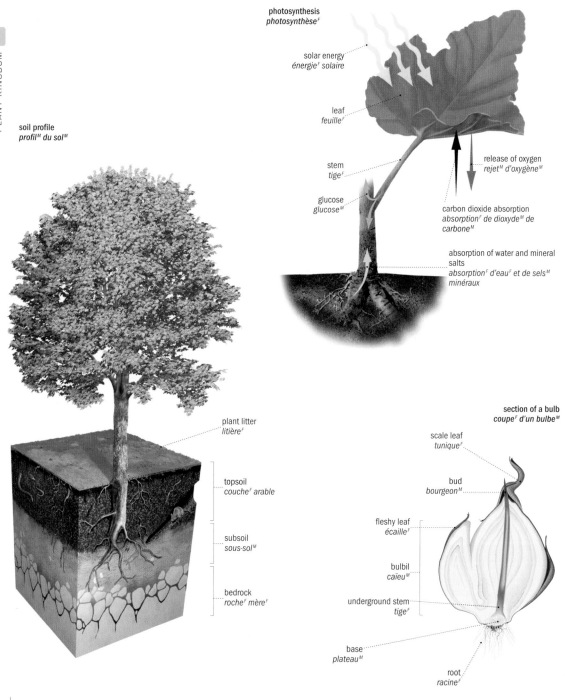

photosynthesis
photosynthèse^F

solar energy
énergie^F *solaire*

leaf
feuille^F

stem
tige^F

glucose
glucose^M

release of oxygen
rejet^M *d'oxygène*^M

carbon dioxide absorption
absorption^F *de dioxyde*^M *de carbone*^M

absorption of water and mineral salts
absorption^F *d'eau*^F *et de sels*^M *minéraux*

soil profile
profil^M *du sol*^M

plant litter
litière^F

topsoil
couche^F *arable*

subsoil
sous-sol^M

bedrock
roche^F *mère*^F

section of a bulb
coupe^F *d'un bulbe*^M

scale leaf
tunique^F

bud
bourgeon^M

fleshy leaf
écaille^F

bulbil
caïeu^M

underground stem
tige^F

base
plateau^M

root
racine^F

simple leaves
feuilles^F simples

cordate
cordée

reniform
réniforme

orbiculate
arrondie

spatulate
spatulée

linear
linéaire

hastate
hastée

ovate
ovoïde

lanceolate
lancéolée

peltate
peltée

structure of a leaf
structure^F d'une feuille^F

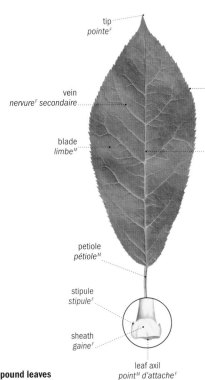

tip
pointe^F

vein
nervure^F secondaire

blade
limbe^M

margin
bord^M

midrib
nervure^F principale

petiole
pétiole^M

stipule
stipule^F

sheath
gaine^F

leaf axil
point^M d'attache^F

compound leaves
feuilles^F composées

trifoliate
trifoliée

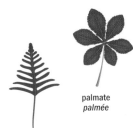

pinnatifid
pennée

palmate
palmée

paripinnate
paripennée

odd pinnate
imparipennée

leaf margins
bord^M d'une feuille^F

serrate
denté

doubly toothed
doublement denté

crenate
crénelé

ciliate
cilié

entire
entier

lobate
lobé

flower

*fleur*F

structure of a flower
*structure*F *d'une fleur*F

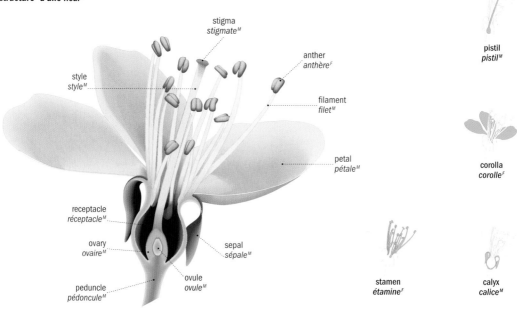

stigma
*stigmate*M

anther
*anthère*F

style
*style*M

filament
*filet*M

petal
*pétale*M

receptacle
*réceptacle*M

ovary
*ovaire*M

sepal
*sépale*M

peduncle
*pédoncule*M

ovule
*ovule*M

pistil
*pistil*M

corolla
*corolle*F

stamen
*étamine*F

calyx
*calice*M

examples of flowers
*exemples*M *de fleurs*F

orchid
*orchidée*F

daffodil
*jonquille*F

poppy
*coquelicot*M

tulip
*tulipe*F

lily of the valley
*muguet*M

carnation
*œillet*M

rose
*rose*F

begonia
*bégonia*M

lily
*lis*M

violet
*violette*F

crocus
*crocus*M

sunflower
*tournesol*M

types of inflorescence
modes^M d'inflorescence^F

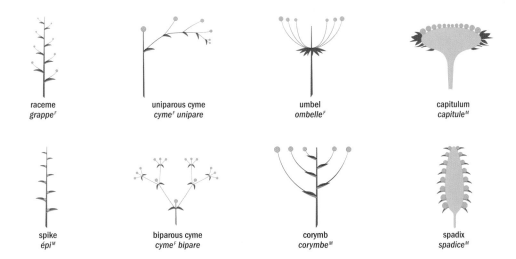

raceme
grappe^F

uniparous cyme
cyme^F unipare

umbel
ombelle^F

capitulum
capitule^M

spike
épi^M

biparous cyme
cyme^F bipare

corymb
corymbe^M

spadix
spadice^M

fruits
fruits^M

fleshy stone fruit
fruit^M charnu à noyau^M

technical terms
termes^M techniques

section of a peach
coupe^F d'une pêche^F

usual terms
termes^M familiers

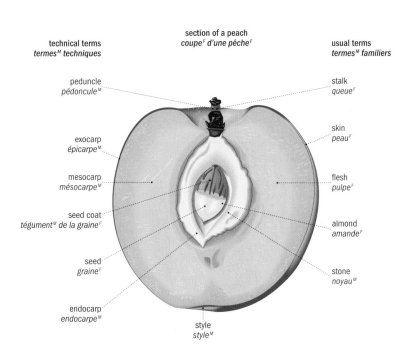

peduncle
pédoncule^M

stalk
queue^F

exocarp
épicarpe^M

skin
peau^F

mesocarp
mésocarpe^M

flesh
pulpe^F

seed coat
tégument^M de la graine^F

almond
amande^F

seed
graine^F

stone
noyau^M

endocarp
endocarpe^M

style
style^M

fleshy pome fruit
fruit^M charnu à pépins^M

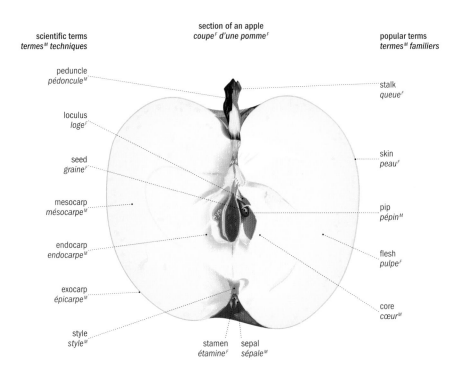

section of an apple
coupe^F d'une pomme^F

scientific terms
termes^M techniques

popular terms
termes^M familiers

peduncle
pédoncule^M

stalk
queue^F

loculus
loge^F

seed
graine^F

skin
peau^F

mesocarp
mésocarpe^M

pip
pépin^M

endocarp
endocarpe^M

flesh
pulpe^F

exocarp
épicarpe^M

core
cœur^M

style
style^M

stamen
étamine^F

sepal
sépale^M

fleshy fruit: citrus fruit
fruit^M charnu : agrume^M

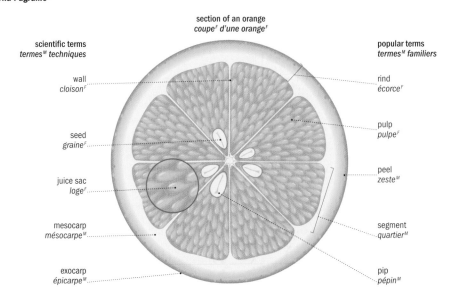

section of an orange
coupe^F d'une orange^F

scientific terms
termes^M techniques

popular terms
termes^M familiers

wall
cloison^F

rind
écorce^F

seed
graine^F

pulp
pulpe^F

juice sac
loge^F

peel
zeste^M

mesocarp
mésocarpe^M

segment
quartier^M

exocarp
épicarpe^M

pip
pépin^M

fleshy fruit: berry fruit
fruitᴹ charnu : baieᶠ

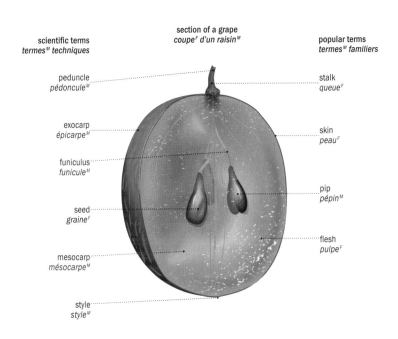

section of a grape
coupeᶠ d'un raisinᴹ

scientific terms
termesᴹ techniques

popular terms
termesᴹ familiers

peduncle
pédonculeᴹ

stalk
queueᶠ

exocarp
épicarpeᴹ

skin
peauᶠ

funiculus
funiculeᴹ

pip
pépinᴹ

seed
graineᶠ

flesh
pulpeᶠ

mesocarp
mésocarpeᴹ

style
styleᴹ

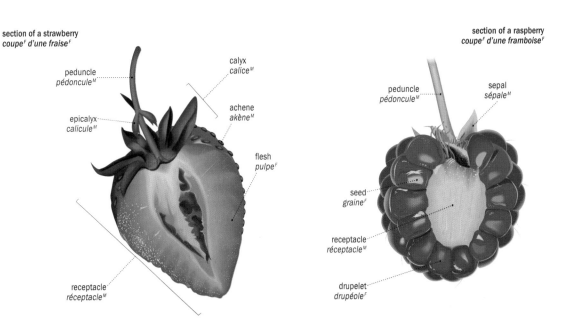

section of a strawberry
coupeᶠ d'une fraiseᶠ

section of a raspberry
coupeᶠ d'une framboiseᶠ

peduncle
pédonculeᴹ

calyx
caliceᴹ

peduncle
pédonculeᴹ

sepal
sépaleᴹ

epicalyx
caliculeᴹ

achene
akèneᴹ

flesh
pulpeᶠ

seed
graineᶠ

receptacle
réceptacleᴹ

receptacle
réceptacleᴹ

drupelet
drupéoleᶠ

dry fruits
fruits^M secs

fruits^M *secs*

husk
brou^M

section of a follicle: star anise
coupe^F *d'un follicule*^M *: anis*^M *étoilé*

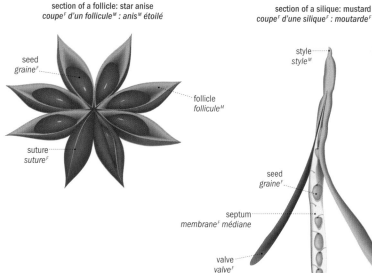

seed
graine^F

follicle
follicule^M

suture
suture^F

section of a silique: mustard
coupe^F *d'une silique*^F *: moutarde*^F

style
style^M

seed
graine^F

septum
membrane^F *médiane*

valve
valve^F

section of a hazelnut
coupe^F *d'une noisette*^F

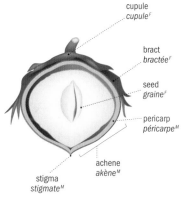

cupule
cupule^F

bract
bractée^F

seed
graine^F

pericarp
péricarpe^M

achene
akène^M

stigma
stigmate^M

section of a legume: pea
coupe^F *d'une gousse*^F *: pois*^M

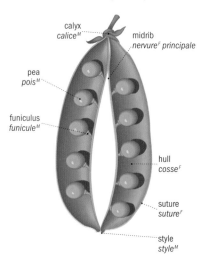

calyx
calice^M

midrib
nervure^F *principale*

pea
pois^M

funiculus
funicule^M

hull
cosse^F

suture
suture^F

style
style^M

section of a capsule: poppy
coupe^F *d'une capsule*^F *: pavot*^M

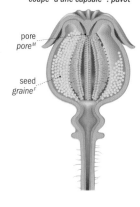

pore
pore^M

seed
graine^F

section of a walnut
coupe^F *d'une noix*^F

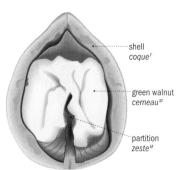

shell
coque^F

green walnut
cerneau^M

partition
zeste^M

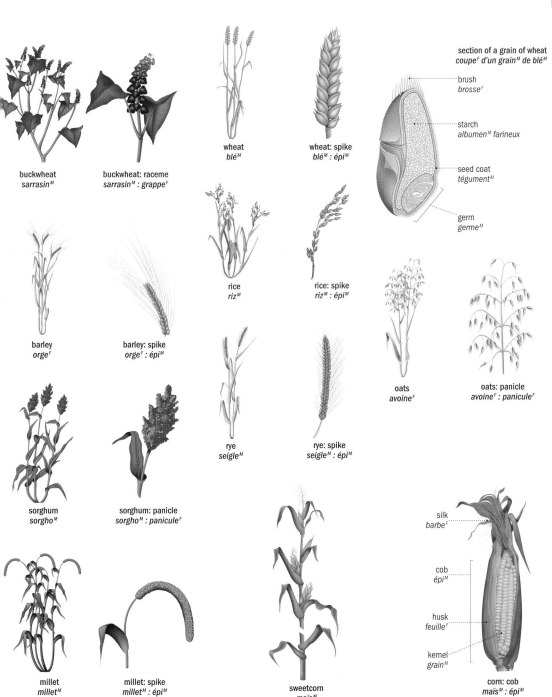

PLANT KINGDOM

buckwheat
sarrasin^M

buckwheat: raceme
sarrasin^M : *grappe*^F

wheat
blé^M

wheat: spike
blé^M : *épi*^M

section of a grain of wheat
coupe^F *d'un grain*^M *de blé*^M

brush
brosse^F

starch
albumen^M *farineux*

seed coat
tégument^M

germ
germe^M

barley
orge^F

barley: spike
orge^F : *épi*^M

rice
riz^M

rice: spike
riz^M : *épi*^M

oats
avoine^F

oats: panicle
avoine^F : *panicule*^F

sorghum
sorgho^M

sorghum: panicle
sorgho^M : *panicule*^F

rye
seigle^M

rye: spike
seigle^M : *épi*^M

silk
barbe^F

cob
épi^M

husk
feuille^F

kernel
grain^M

millet
millet^M

millet: spike
millet^M : *épi*^M

sweetcorn
maïs^M

corn: cob
maïs^M : *épi*^M

grape

vigne^F

bunch of grapes
grappe^F *de raisins*^M

vine stock
cep^M *de vigne*^F

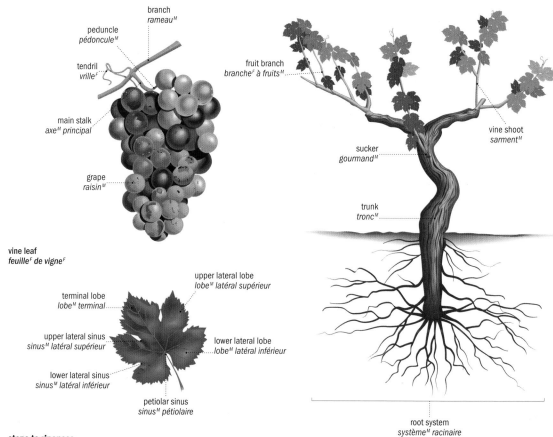

branch
rameau^M

peduncle
pédoncule^M

tendril
vrille^F

fruit branch
branche^F *à fruits*^M

vine shoot
sarment^M

main stalk
axe^M *principal*

sucker
gourmand^M

grape
raisin^M

trunk
tronc^M

vine leaf
feuille^F *de vigne*^F

upper lateral lobe
lobe^M *latéral supérieur*

terminal lobe
lobe^M *terminal*

upper lateral sinus
sinus^M *latéral supérieur*

lower lateral lobe
lobe^M *latéral inférieur*

lower lateral sinus
sinus^M *latéral inférieur*

petiolar sinus
sinus^M *pétiolaire*

root system
système^M *racinaire*

steps to ripeness
étapes^F *de maturation*^F

flowering
floraison^F

fruiting
nouaison^F

ripening
véraison^F

ripeness
maturité^F

structure of a tree
structure^F *d'un arbre*^M

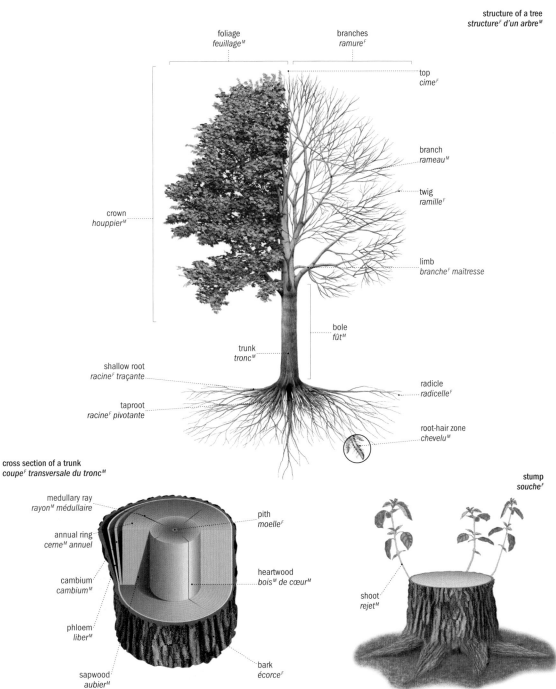

foliage
feuillage^M

branches
ramure^F

top
cime^F

branch
rameau^M

twig
ramille^F

crown
houppier^M

limb
branche^F *maîtresse*

bole
fût^M

trunk
tronc^M

shallow root
racine^F *traçante*

taproot
racine^F *pivotante*

radicle
radicelle^F

root-hair zone
chevelu^M

cross section of a trunk
coupe^F *transversale du tronc*^M

stump
souche^F

medullary ray
rayon^M *médullaire*

pith
moelle^F

annual ring
cerne^M *annuel*

cambium
cambium^M

heartwood
bois^M *de cœur*^M

phloem
liber^M

shoot
rejet^M

sapwood
aubier^M

bark
écorce^F

examples of broadleaved trees
exemples^M d'arbres^M feuillus

oak
chêne^M

birch
bouleau^M

weeping willow
saule^M pleureur

poplar
peuplier^M

palm tree
palmier^M

maple
érable^M

beech
hêtre^M

walnut
noyer^M

branch
rameau^M

male cone
cône^M *mâle*

female cone
cône^M *femelle*

cone
cône^M

pine seed
pignon^M

examples of leaves
***exemples*^M *de feuilles*^F**

fir needles
aiguilles^F *de sapin*^M

pine needles
aiguilles^F *de pin*^M

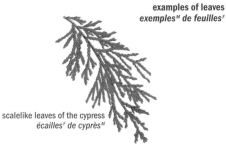

scalelike leaves of the cypress
écailles^F *de cyprès*^M

examples of conifers
***exemples*^M *de conifères*^M**

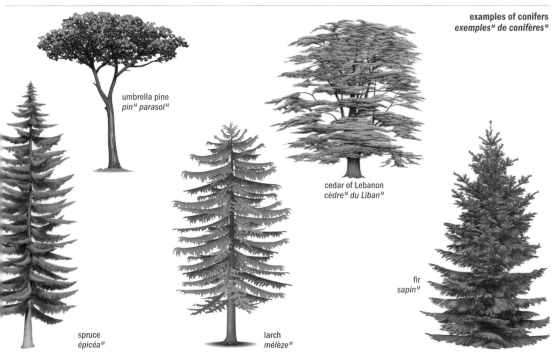

umbrella pine
pin^M *parasol*^M

cedar of Lebanon
cèdre^M *du Liban*^M

fir
sapin^M

spruce
épicéa^M

larch
mélèze^M

animal cell

cellule^F animale

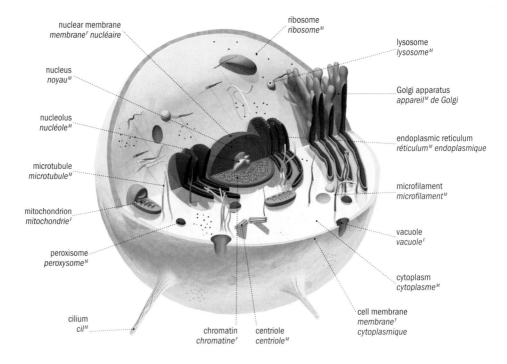

nuclear membrane
membrane^F nucléaire

nucleus
noyau^M

nucleolus
nucléole^M

microtubule
microtubule^M

mitochondrion
mitochondrie^F

peroxisome
peroxysome^M

cilium
cil^M

ribosome
ribosome^M

lysosome
lysosome^M

Golgi apparatus
appareil^M de Golgi

endoplasmic reticulum
réticulum^M endoplasmique

microfilament
microfilament^M

vacuole
vacuole^F

cytoplasm
cytoplasme^M

cell membrane
membrane^F
cytoplasmique

chromatin
chromatine^F

centriole
centriole^M

unicellulars

unicellulaires^M

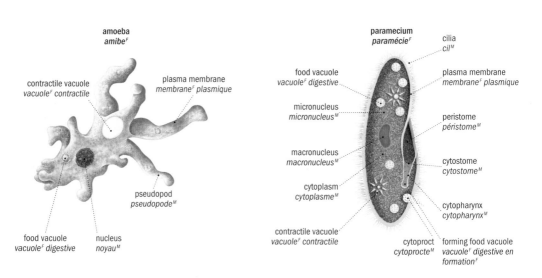

amoeba
amibe^F

contractile vacuole
vacuole^F contractile

plasma membrane
membrane^F plasmique

food vacuole
vacuole^F digestive

nucleus
noyau^M

pseudopod
pseudopode^M

paramecium
paramécie^F

cilia
cil^M

food vacuole
vacuole^F digestive

plasma membrane
membrane^F plasmique

micronucleus
micronucleus^M

peristome
péristome^M

macronucleus
macronucleus^M

cytostome
cytostome^M

cytoplasm
cytoplasme^M

cytopharynx
cytopharynx^M

contractile vacuole
vacuole^F contractile

cytoproct
cytoprocte^M

forming food vacuole
vacuole^F digestive en
formation^F

butterfly
papillon^M

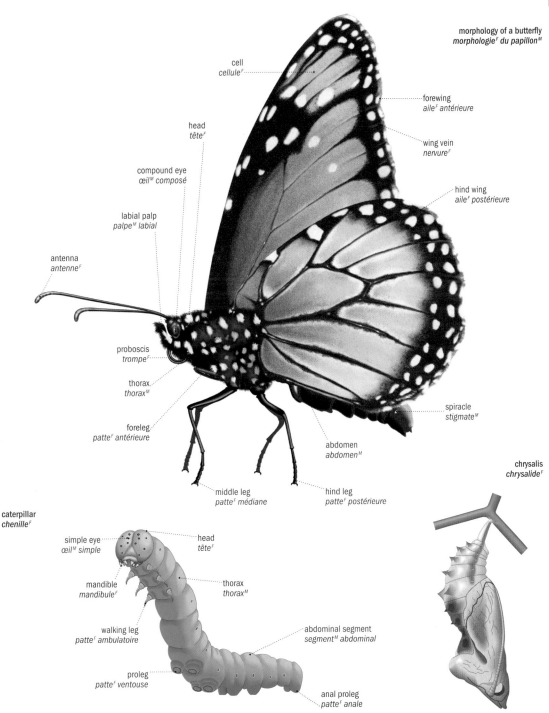

morphology of a butterfly
morphologie^F *du papillon*^M

cell
cellule^F

forewing
aile^F *antérieure*

head
tête^F

wing vein
nervure^F

compound eye
œil^M *composé*

hind wing
aile^F *postérieure*

labial palp
palpe^M *labial*

antenna
antenne^F

proboscis
trompe^F

thorax
thorax^M

spiracle
stigmate^M

foreleg
patte^F *antérieure*

abdomen
abdomen^M

middle leg
patte^F *médiane*

hind leg
patte^F *postérieure*

chrysalis
chrysalide^F

caterpillar
chenille^F

simple eye
œil^M *simple*

head
tête^F

mandible
mandibule^F

thorax
thorax^M

walking leg
patte^F *ambulatoire*

abdominal segment
segment^M *abdominal*

proleg
patte^F *ventouse*

anal proleg
patte^F *anale*

honeybee

abeille^F

morphology of a honeybee: worker
morphologie^F de l'abeille^F : ouvrière^F

wing
aile^F

thorax
thorax^M

abdomen
abdomen^M

compound eye
œil^M composé

sting
aiguillon^M

pollen basket
corbeille^F à pollen^M

mouthparts
pièces^F buccales

antenna
antenne^F

hind leg
patte^F postérieure

middle leg
patte^F médiane

foreleg
patte^F antérieure

castes
castes^F

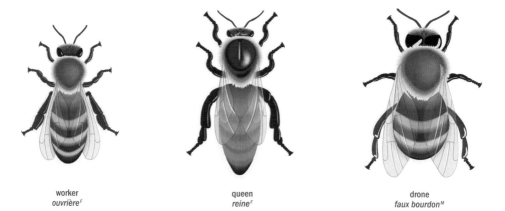

worker
ouvrière^F

queen
reine^F

drone
faux bourdon^M

examples of insects
exemples^M d'insectes^M

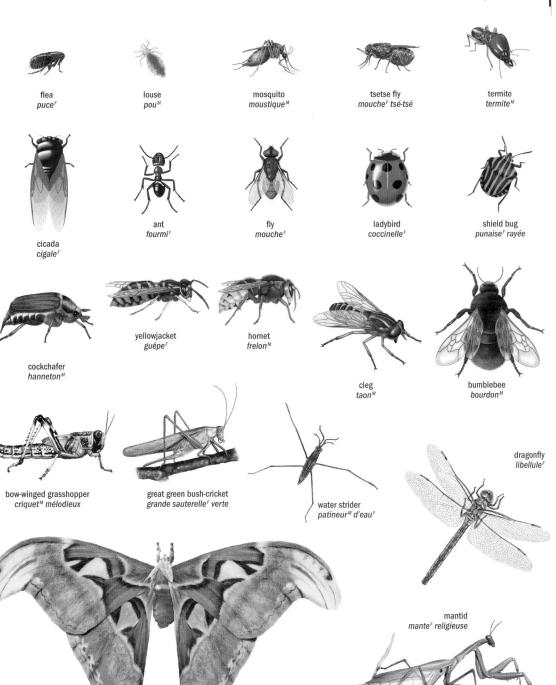

flea
puce^F

louse
pou^M

mosquito
moustique^M

tsetse fly
mouche^F tsé-tsé

termite
termite^M

cicada
cigale^F

ant
fourmi^F

fly
mouche^F

ladybird
coccinelle^F

shield bug
punaise^F rayée

cockchafer
hanneton^M

yellowjacket
guêpe^F

hornet
frelon^M

cleg
taon^M

bumblebee
bourdon^M

bow-winged grasshopper
criquet^M mélodieux

great green bush-cricket
grande sauterelle^F verte

water strider
patineur^M d'eau^F

dragonfly
libellule^F

mantid
mante^F religieuse

atlas moth
atlas^M

spider

araignée^F

ANIMAL KINGDOM

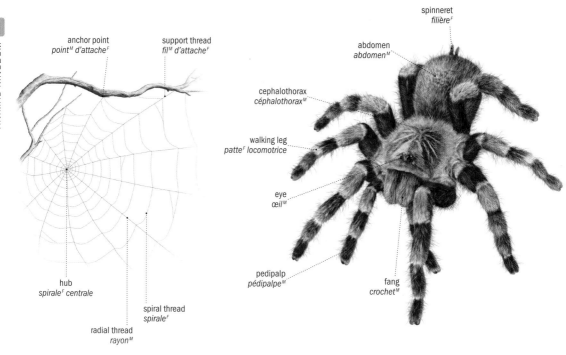

spider web
toile^F d'araignée^F

morphology of a spider
morphologie^F de l'araignée^F

anchor point
point^M d'attache^F

support thread
fil^M d'attache^F

spinneret
filière^F

abdomen
abdomen^M

cephalothorax
céphalothorax^M

walking leg
patte^F locomotrice

eye
œil^M

hub
spirale^F centrale

spiral thread
spirale^F

radial thread
rayon^M

pedipalp
pédipalpe^M

fang
crochet^M

examples of arachnids

exemples^M d'arachnides^M

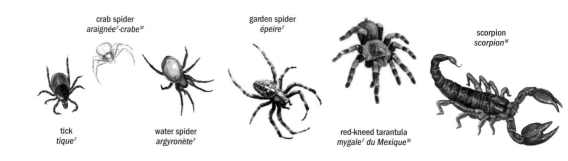

crab spider
araignée^F-crabe^M

garden spider
épeire^F

scorpion
scorpion^M

tick
tique^F

water spider
argyronète^F

red-kneed tarantula
mygale^F du Mexique^M

lobster

homard^M

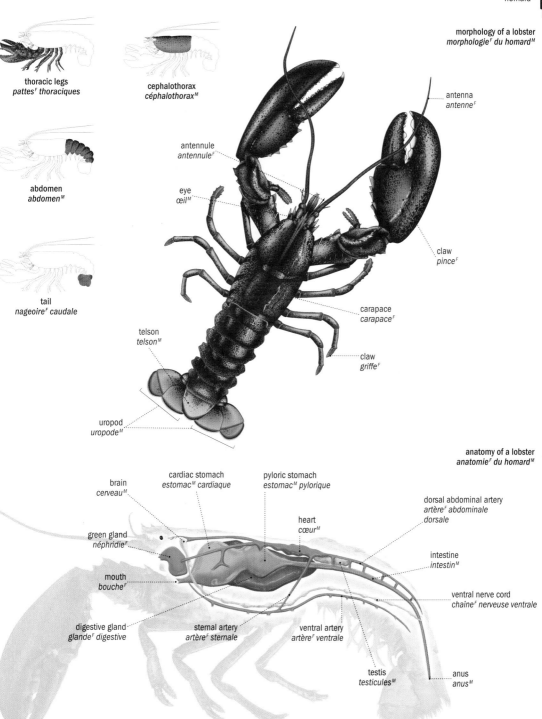

thoracic legs
pattes^F thoraciques

cephalothorax
céphalothorax^M

abdomen
abdomen^M

tail
nageoire^F caudale

morphology of a lobster
morphologie^F du homard^M

antenna
antenne^F

antennule
antennule^F

eye
œil^M

claw
pince^F

carapace
carapace^F

claw
griffe^F

telson
telson^M

uropod
uropode^M

anatomy of a lobster
anatomie^F du homard^M

brain
cerveau^M

cardiac stomach
estomac^M cardiaque

pyloric stomach
estomac^M pylorique

dorsal abdominal artery
artère^F abdominale dorsale

heart
cœur^M

green gland
néphridie^F

intestine
intestin^M

mouth
bouche^F

ventral nerve cord
chaîne^F nerveuse ventrale

digestive gland
glande^F digestive

sternal artery
artère^F sternale

ventral artery
artère^F ventrale

testis
testicules^M

anus
anus^M

ANIMAL KINGDOM

71

snail

escargot^M

morphology of a snail
morphologie^F de l'escargot^M

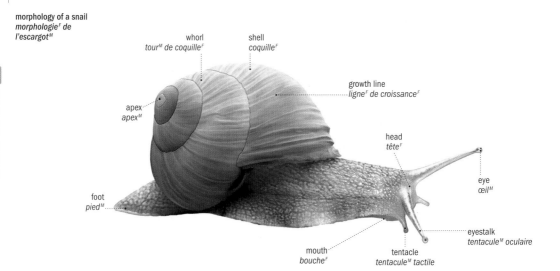

whorl
tour^M de coquille^F

shell
coquille^F

growth line
ligne^F de croissance^F

apex
apex^M

head
tête^F

eye
œil^M

foot
pied^M

eyestalk
tentacule^M oculaire

mouth
bouche^F

tentacle
tentacule^M tactile

octopus

pieuvre^F

morphology of an octopus
morphologie^F de la pieuvre^F

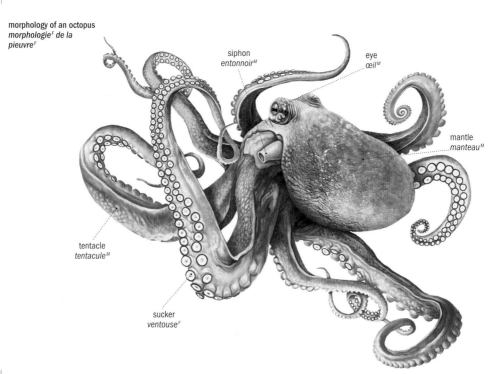

siphon
entonnoir^M

eye
œil^M

mantle
manteau^M

tentacle
tentacule^M

sucker
ventouse^F

univalve shell
coquille^F univalve

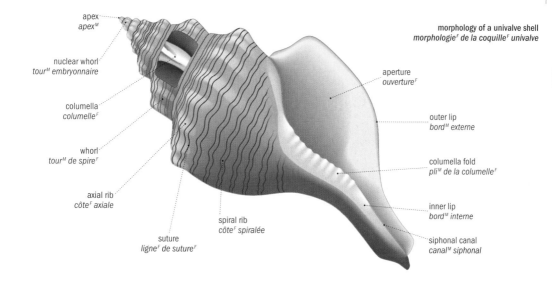

morphology of a univalve shell
morphologie^F de la coquille^F univalve

apex
apex^M

nuclear whorl
tour^M embryonnaire

columella
columelle^F

whorl
tour^M de spire^F

axial rib
côte^F axiale

suture
ligne^F de suture^F

spiral rib
côte^F spiralée

aperture
ouverture^F

outer lip
bord^M externe

columella fold
pli^M de la columelle^F

inner lip
bord^M interne

siphonal canal
canal^M siphonal

bivalve shell
coquille^F bivalve

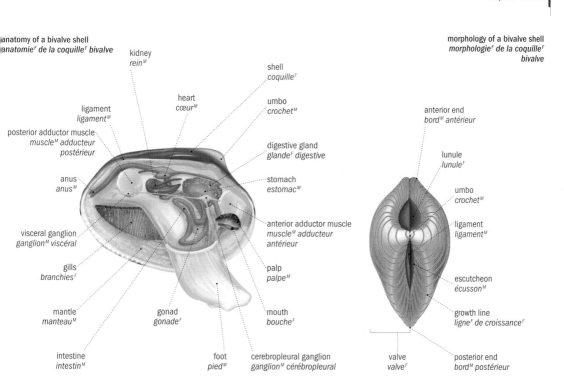

anatomy of a bivalve shell
anatomie^F de la coquille^F bivalve

morphology of a bivalve shell
morphologie^F de la coquille^F bivalve

kidney
rein^M

heart
cœur^M

ligament
ligament^M

posterior adductor muscle
muscle^M adducteur postérieur

anus
anus^M

visceral ganglion
ganglion^M viscéral

gills
branchies^F

mantle
manteau^M

intestine
intestin^M

foot
pied^M

gonad
gonade^F

cerebropleural ganglion
ganglion^M cérébropleural

shell
coquille^F

umbo
crochet^M

digestive gland
glande^F digestive

stomach
estomac^M

anterior adductor muscle
muscle^M adducteur antérieur

palp
palpe^M

mouth
bouche^F

anterior end
bord^M antérieur

lunule
lunule^F

umbo
crochet^M

ligament
ligament^M

escutcheon
écusson^M

growth line
ligne^F de croissance^F

valve
valve^F

posterior end
bord^M postérieur

cartilaginous fish

poisson^M cartilagineux

morphology of a shark
morphologie^F du requin^M

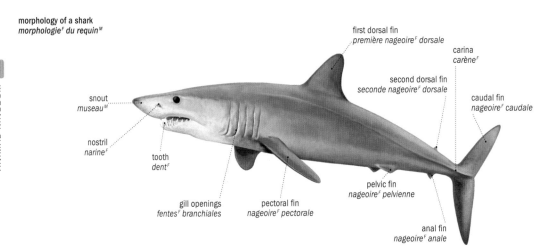

first dorsal fin
première nageoire^F dorsale

carina
carène^F

second dorsal fin
seconde nageoire^F dorsale

caudal fin
nageoire^F caudale

snout
museau^M

nostril
narine^F

tooth
dent^F

gill openings
fentes^F branchiales

pectoral fin
nageoire^F pectorale

pelvic fin
nageoire^F pelvienne

anal fin
nageoire^F anale

bony fish

poisson^M osseux

morphology of a perch
morphologie^F de la perche^F

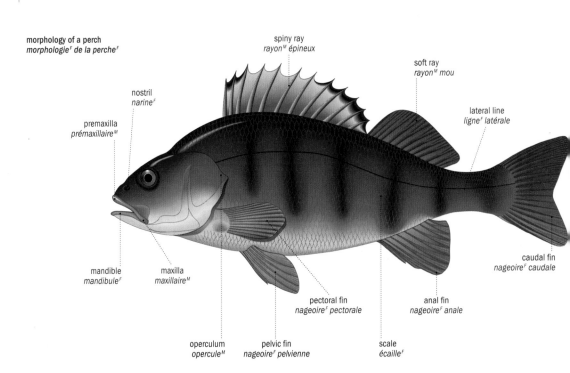

spiny ray
rayon^M épineux

soft ray
rayon^M mou

lateral line
ligne^F latérale

nostril
narine^F

premaxilla
prémaxillaire^M

mandible
mandibule^F

maxilla
maxillaire^M

caudal fin
nageoire^F caudale

pectoral fin
nageoire^F pectorale

anal fin
nageoire^F anale

operculum
opercule^M

pelvic fin
nageoire^F pelvienne

scale
écaille^F

ANIMAL KINGDOM

frog
grenouille^F

morphology of a frog
morphologie^F de la grenouille^F

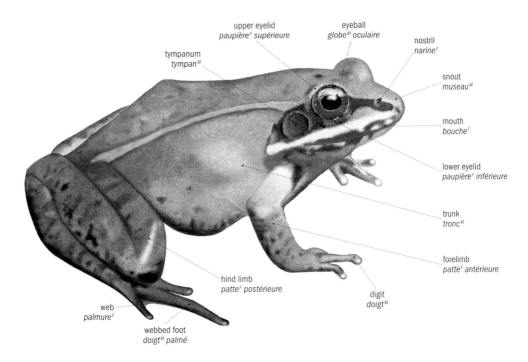

upper eyelid
paupière^F supérieure

eyeball
globe^M oculaire

nostril
narine^F

tympanum
tympan^M

snout
museau^M

mouth
bouche^F

lower eyelid
paupière^F inférieure

trunk
tronc^M

forelimb
patte^F antérieure

hind limb
patte^F postérieure

digit
doigt^M

web
palmure^F

webbed foot
doigt^M palmé

examples of amphibians
exemples^M d'amphibiens^M

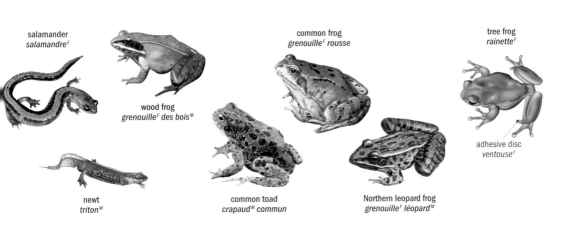

salamander
salamandre^F

wood frog
grenouille^F des bois^M

common frog
grenouille^F rousse

tree frog
rainette^F

adhesive disc
ventouse^F

newt
triton^M

common toad
crapaud^M commun

Northern leopard frog
grenouille^F léopard^M

snake

serpent^M

morphology of a venomous snake: head
morphologie^F du serpent^M venimeux : tête^F

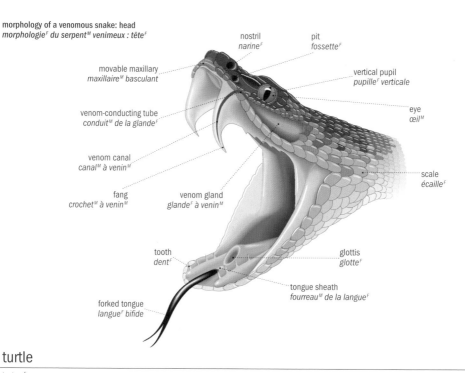

nostril
narine^F

pit
fossette^F

movable maxillary
maxillaire^M basculant

vertical pupil
pupille^F verticale

venom-conducting tube
conduit^M de la glande^F

eye
œil^M

venom canal
canal^M à venin^M

scale
écaille^F

fang
crochet^M à venin^M

venom gland
glande^F à venin^M

tooth
dent^F

glottis
glotte^F

tongue sheath
fourreau^M de la langue^F

forked tongue
langue^F bifide

turtle

tortue^F

morphology of a turtle
morphologie^F de la tortue^F

vertebral shield
plaque^F vertébrale

costal shield
plaque^F costale

carapace
dossière^F

eyelid
paupière^F

pygal shield
plaque^F supra-caudale

eye
œil^M

tail
queue^F

horny beak
bec^M corné

leg
patte^F

neck
cou^M

scale
écaille^F

claw
griffe^F

plastron
plastron^M

marginal shield
plaque^F marginale

ANIMAL KINGDOM

examples of reptiles
exemples^M de reptiles^M

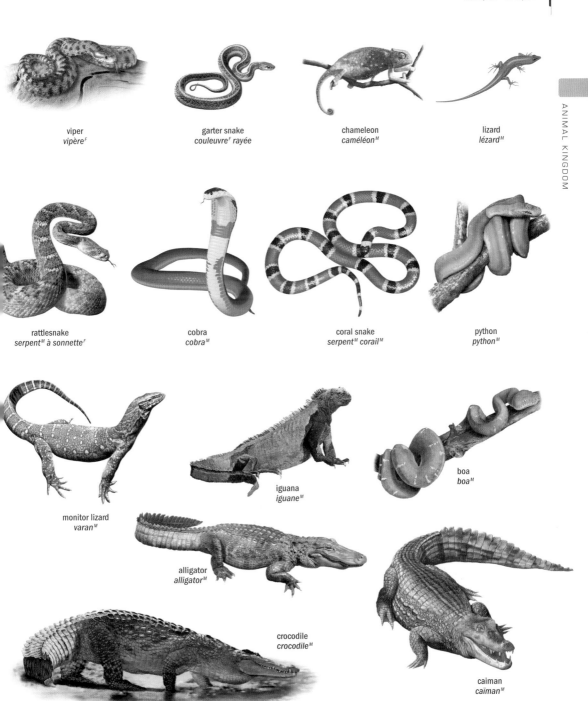

viper
vipère^F

garter snake
couleuvre^F *rayée*

chameleon
caméléon^M

lizard
lézard^M

rattlesnake
serpent^M *à sonnette*^F

cobra
cobra^M

coral snake
serpent^M *corail*^M

python
python^M

iguana
iguane^M

boa
boa^M

monitor lizard
varan^M

alligator
alligator^M

crocodile
crocodile^M

caiman
caiman^M

bird

oiseau^M

morphology of a bird
morphologie^F de l'oiseau^M

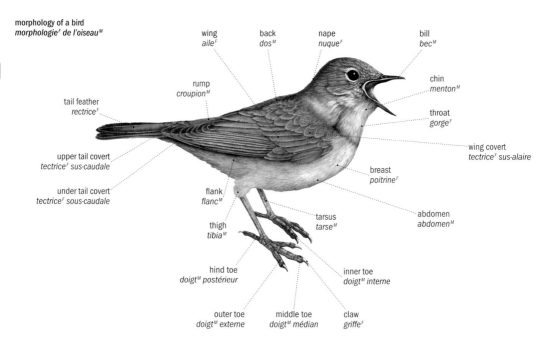

wing
aile^F

back
dos^M

nape
nuque^F

bill
bec^M

chin
menton^M

rump
croupion^M

throat
gorge^F

tail feather
rectrice^F

wing covert
tectrice^F sus-alaire

upper tail covert
tectrice^F sus-caudale

breast
poitrine^F

under tail covert
tectrice^F sous-caudale

flank
flanc^M

abdomen
abdomen^M

tarsus
tarse^M

thigh
tibia^M

hind toe
doigt^M postérieur

inner toe
doigt^M interne

outer toe
doigt^M externe

middle toe
doigt^M médian

claw
griffe^F

head
tête^F

forehead
front^M

crown
calotte^F

nostril
narine^F

eyebrow stripe
raie^F sourcilière

upper mandible
maxillaire^M supérieur

auriculars
région^F auriculaire

lower mandible
mandibule^F

malar region
région^F malaire

lore
lorum^M

eye ring
anneau^M oculaire

wing
aile^F

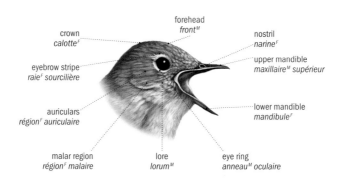

primary covert
tectrice^F primaire

alula
alule^F

middle covert
moyenne sus-alaire^F

primaries
rémige^F primaire

lesser covert
petite sus-alaire^F

middle primary covert
moyenne tectrice^F primaire

scapular
scapulaire^F

greater covert
grande sus-alaire^F

secondaries
rémige^F secondaire

tertial
rémige^F tertiaire

bird

ANIMAL KINGDOM

egg
œuf^M

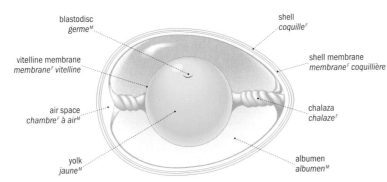

blastodisc
germe^M

shell
coquille^F

vitelline membrane
membrane^F *vitelline*

shell membrane
membrane^F *coquillière*

air space
chambre^F *à air*^M

chalaza
chalaze^F

yolk
jaune^M

albumen
albumen^M

examples of bills
exemples^M *de becs*^M

aquatic bird
oiseau^M *aquatique*

granivorous bird
oiseau^M *granivore*

bird of prey
oiseau^M *de proie*^F

insectivorous bird
oiseau^M *insectivore*

wading bird
oiseau^M *échassier*

examples of feet
exemples^M *de pattes*^F

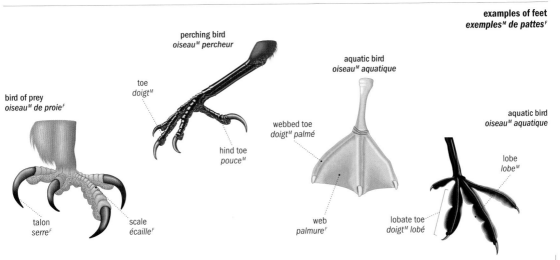

perching bird
oiseau^M *percheur*

aquatic bird
oiseau^M *aquatique*

toe
doigt^M

bird of prey
oiseau^M *de proie*^F

aquatic bird
oiseau^M *aquatique*

hind toe
pouce^M

webbed toe
doigt^M *palmé*

lobe
lobe^M

talon
serre^F

scale
écaille^F

web
palmure^F

lobate toe
doigt^M *lobé*

examples of birds

exemples^M d'oiseaux^M

hummingbird
colibri^M

European robin
rouge-gorge^M

finch
pinson^M

kingfisher
martin-pêcheur^M

nightingale
rossignol^M

sparrow
moineau^M

swallow
hirondelle^F

starling
étourneau^M

jay
geai^M

cardinal
cardinal^M

swift
martinet^M

partridge
perdrix^F

condor
condor^M

raven
corbeau^M

toucan
toucan^M

vulture
vautour^M

macaw
ara^M

woodpecker
pic^M

penguin
manchot^M

albatross
albatros^M

heron
héron^M

pelican
pélican^M

stork
cigogne^F

examples of birds

pheasant
faisan^M

great horned owl
grand duc^M *d'Amérique*^F

falcon
faucon^M

quail
caille^F

eagle
aigle^M

hen
poule^F

duck
canard^M

pigeon
pigeon^M

turkey
dindon^M

guinea fowl
pintade^F

goose
oie^F

rooster
coq^M

ostrich
autruche^F

peacock
paon^M

flamingo
flamant^M

rodent

rongeur^M

morphology of a rat
morphologie^F du rat^M

pinna
pavillon^M

vibrissa
vibrisse^F

nose
nez^M

digit
doigt^M

claw
griffe^F

fur
pelage^M

tail
queue^F

examples of rodents

exemples^M de mammifères^M rongeurs^M

field mouse
mulot^M

chipmunk
tamia^M

jerboa
gerboise^F

hamster
hamster^M

squirrel
écureuil^M

rat
rat^M

guinea pig
cobaye^M

porcupine
porc-épic^M

groundhog
marmotte^F

beaver
castor^M

examples of lagomorphs

exemples^M de mammifères^M lagomorphes^M

pika
pika^M

rabbit
lapin^M

hare
lièvre^M

horse
cheval^M

morphology of a horse
morphologie^F *du cheval*^M

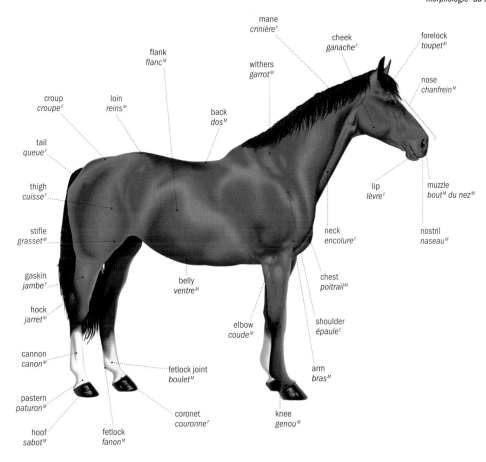

mane
crinière^F

cheek
ganache^F

forelock
toupet^M

flank
flanc^M

withers
garrot^M

nose
chanfrein^M

croup
croupe^F

loin
reins^M

back
dos^M

tail
queue^F

thigh
cuisse^F

lip
lèvre^F

muzzle
bout^M *du nez*^M

stifle
grasset^M

neck
encolure^F

nostril
naseau^M

gaskin
jambe^F

belly
ventre^M

chest
poitrail^M

hock
jarret^M

elbow
coude^M

shoulder
épaule^F

cannon
canon^M

fetlock joint
boulet^M

arm
bras^M

pastern
paturon^M

coronet
couronne^F

knee
genou^M

hoof
sabot^M

fetlock
fanon^M

gaits
allures^F

walk
pas^M

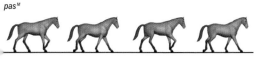

amble
amble^M

trot
trot^M

gallop
galop^M

examples of ungulate mammals

exemples^M de mammifères^M ongulés

ANIMAL KINGDOM

peccary
pécari^M

wild boar
sanglier^M

pig
porc^M

goat
chèvre^F

antelope
antilope^F

sheep
mouton^M

calf
veau^M

white-tailed deer
cerf^M de Virginie

mouflon
mouflon^M

reindeer
renne^M

Canadian elk
cerf^M du Canada

okapi
okapi^M

ass
âne^M

mule
mulet^M

cow
vache^F

zebra
zèbre^M

llama
lama^M

bison
bison^M

buffalo
buffle^M

ANIMAL KINGDOM

ox
bœuf^M

yak
yack^M

horse
cheval^M

elk
élan^M

camel
chameau^M

dromedary
dromadaire^M

rhinoceros
rhinocéros^M

hippopotamus
hippopotame^M

giraffe
girafe^F

elephant
éléphant^M

dog

chien^M

morphology of a dog
morphologie^F du chien^M

stop
stop^M

muzzle
museau^M

cheek
joue^F

withers
garrot^M

back
dos^M

flews
babines^F

thigh
cuisse^F

shoulder
épaule^F

elbow
coude^M

hock
jarret^M

tail
queue^F

forearm
avant-bras^M

knee
genou^M

wrist
poignet^M

toe
orteil^M

dog breeds

races^F de chiens^M

bulldog
bouledogue^M

collie
colley^M

dalmatian
dalmatien^M

poodle
caniche^M

schnauzer
schnauzer^M

Saint Bernard
saint-bernard^M

Great Dane
danois^M

German shepherd
berger^M allemand

cat
chat^M

ANIMAL KINGDOM

cat's head
tête^F

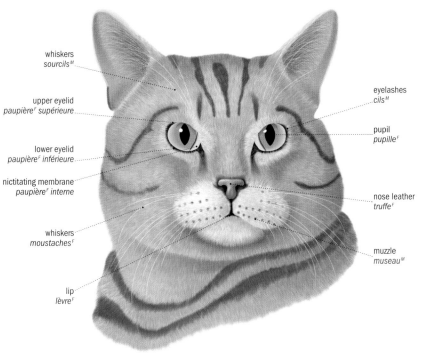

whiskers
sourcils^M

upper eyelid
paupière^F supérieure

lower eyelid
paupière^F inférieure

nictitating membrane
paupière^F interne

whiskers
moustaches^F

lip
lèvre^F

eyelashes
cils^M

pupil
pupille^F

nose leather
truffe^F

muzzle
museau^M

cat breeds
races^F de chats^M

Siamese
siamois^M

Abyssinian
abyssin^M

Persian
persan^M

Maine Coon
Maine coon^M

Manx
chat^M de l'île^F de Man

examples of carnivorous mammals

exemples^M de mammifères^M carnivores

ANIMAL KINGDOM

weasel
belette^F

mink
vison^M

stone marten
fouine^F

marten
martre^F

fox
renard^M

raccoon
raton^M *laveur*

fennec
fennec^M

river otter
loutre^F *de rivière*^F

mongoose
mangouste^F

badger
blaireau^M

skunk
moufette^F

hyena
hyène^F

lynx
lynx^M

wolf
loup^M

cougar
puma^M

ANIMAL KINGDOM

cheetah
guépard^M

leopard
léopard^M

lion
lion^M

jaguar
jaguar^M

tiger
tigre^M

polar bear
ours^M *polaire*

black bear
ours^M *noir*

ANIMAL KINGDOM

dolphin

dauphin[M]

morphology of a dolphin
morphologie[F] du dauphin[M]

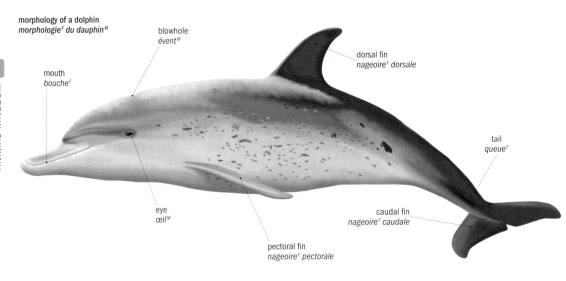

blowhole
évent[M]

dorsal fin
nageoire[F] dorsale

mouth
bouche[F]

tail
queue[F]

eye
œil[M]

caudal fin
nageoire[F] caudale

pectoral fin
nageoire[F] pectorale

examples of marine mammals

exemples[M] de mammifères[M] marins

killer whale
orque[F]

seal
phoque[M]

rorqual
rorqual[M]

whale
baleine[F]

sperm whale
cachalot[M]

sea lion
otarie[F]

gorilla
gorille^M

morphology of a gorilla
morphologie^F du gorille^M

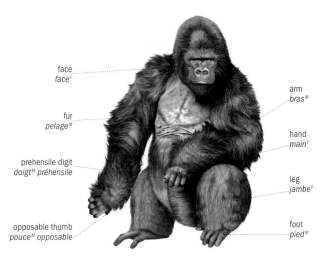

face
face^F

arm
bras^M

fur
pelage^M

hand
main^F

prehensile digit
doigt^M *préhensile*

leg
jambe^F

opposable thumb
pouce^M *opposable*

foot
pied^M

examples of primates
exemples^M *de mammifères*^M *primates*

tamarin
tamarin^M

baboon
babouin^M

macaque
macaque^M

marmoset
ouistiti^M

orangutan
orang-outan^M

chimpanzee
chimpanzé^M

lemur
lémurien^M

gibbon
gibbon^M

man

homme^M

anterior view
face^F antérieure

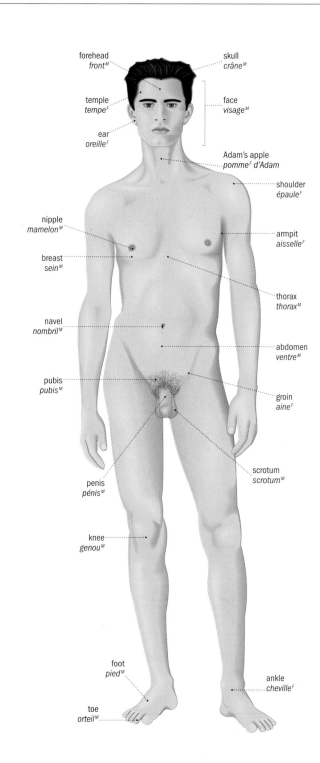

forehead
front^M

skull
crâne^M

temple
tempe^F

face
visage^M

ear
oreille^F

Adam's apple
pomme^F d'Adam

shoulder
épaule^F

nipple
mamelon^M

armpit
aisselle^F

breast
sein^M

thorax
thorax^M

navel
nombril^M

abdomen
ventre^M

pubis
pubis^M

groin
aine^F

scrotum
scrotum^M

penis
pénis^M

knee
genou^M

foot
pied^M

ankle
cheville^F

toe
orteil^M

man

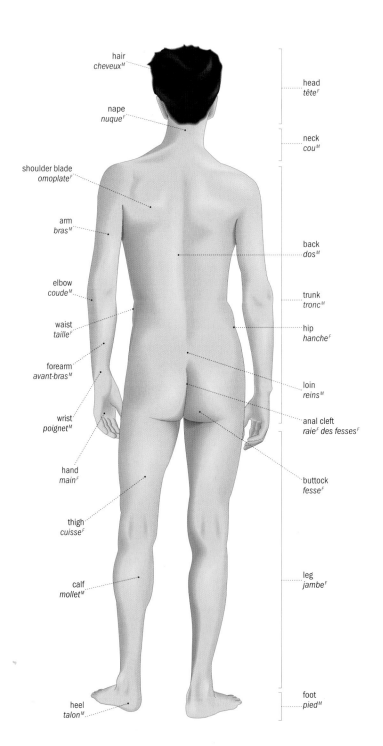

posterior view
*face*F *postérieure*

hair
*cheveux*M

head
*tête*F

nape
*nuque*F

neck
*cou*M

shoulder blade
*omoplate*F

arm
*bras*M

back
*dos*M

elbow
*coude*M

trunk
*tronc*M

waist
*taille*F

hip
*hanche*F

forearm
*avant-bras*M

loin
*reins*M

wrist
*poignet*M

anal cleft
*raie*F *des fesses*F

hand
*main*F

buttock
*fesse*F

thigh
*cuisse*F

calf
*mollet*M

leg
*jambe*F

foot
*pied*M

heel
*talon*M

woman

femme^F

anterior view
face^F antérieure

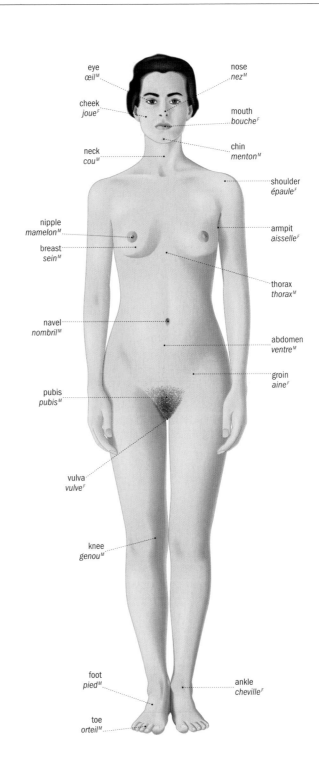

eye
œil^M

nose
nez^M

cheek
joue^F

mouth
bouche^F

neck
cou^M

chin
menton^M

shoulder
épaule^F

nipple
mamelon^M

armpit
aisselle^F

breast
sein^M

thorax
thorax^M

navel
nombril^M

abdomen
ventre^M

groin
aine^F

pubis
pubis^M

vulva
vulve^F

knee
genou^M

foot
pied^M

ankle
cheville^F

toe
orteil^M

HUMAN BEING

posterior view
face^F postérieure

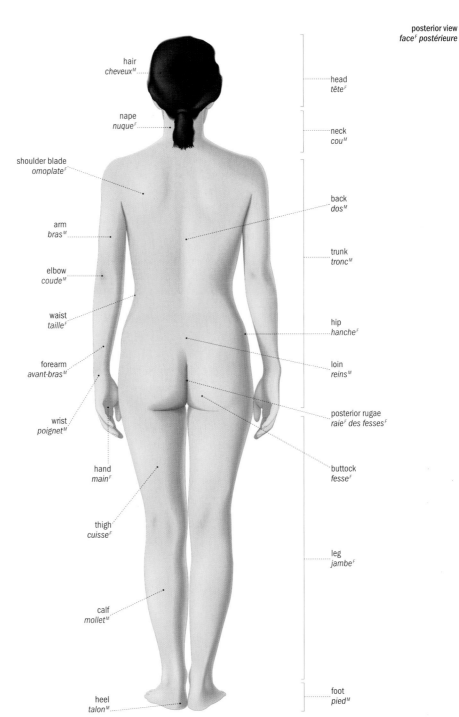

hair
cheveux^M

nape
nuque^F

shoulder blade
omoplate^F

arm
bras^M

elbow
coude^M

waist
taille^F

forearm
avant-bras^M

wrist
poignet^M

hand
main^F

thigh
cuisse^F

calf
mollet^M

heel
talon^M

head
tête^F

neck
cou^M

back
dos^M

trunk
tronc^M

hip
hanche^F

loin
reins^M

posterior rugae
raie^F des fesses^F

buttock
fesse^F

leg
jambe^F

foot
pied^M

muscles

muscles^M

anterior view
face^F antérieure

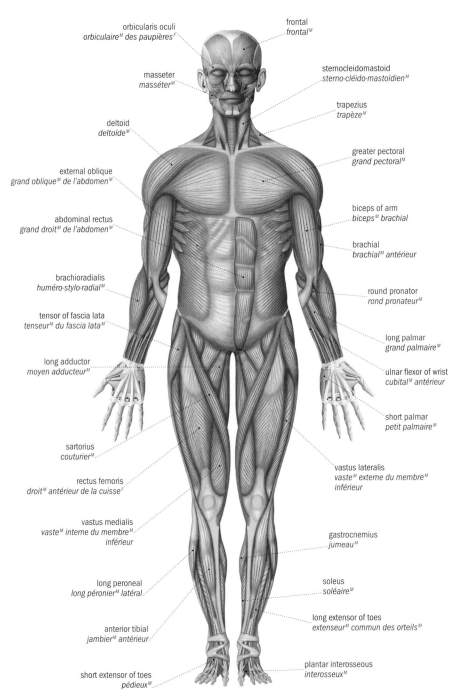

orbicularis oculi
orbiculaire^M des paupières^F

frontal
frontal^M

masseter
masséter^M

sternocleidomastoid
sterno-cléido-mastoïdien^M

deltoid
deltoïde^M

trapezius
trapèze^M

external oblique
grand oblique^M de l'abdomen^M

greater pectoral
grand pectoral^M

abdominal rectus
grand droit^M de l'abdomen^M

biceps of arm
biceps^M brachial

brachial
brachial^M antérieur

brachioradialis
huméro-stylo-radial^M

round pronator
rond pronateur^M

tensor of fascia lata
tenseur^M du fascia lata^M

long palmar
grand palmaire^M

long adductor
moyen adducteur^M

ulnar flexor of wrist
cubital^M antérieur

short palmar
petit palmaire^M

sartorius
couturier^M

vastus lateralis
*vaste^M externe du membre^M
inférieur*

rectus femoris
droit^M antérieur de la cuisse^F

vastus medialis
*vaste^M interne du membre^M
inférieur*

gastrocnemius
jumeau^M

long peroneal
long péronier^M latéral

soleus
soléaire^M

long extensor of toes
extenseur^M commun des orteils^M

anterior tibial
jambier^M antérieur

short extensor of toes
pédieux^M

plantar interosseous
interosseux^M

muscles

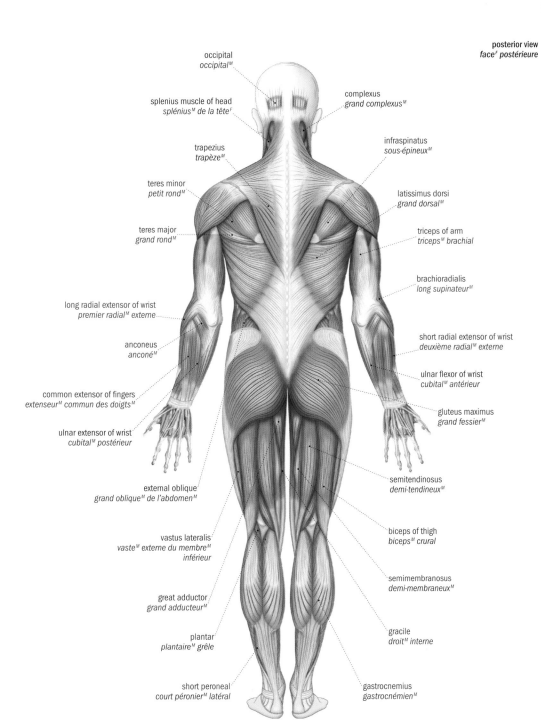

posterior view
face^F postérieure

occipital
occipital^M

complexus
grand complexus^M

splenius muscle of head
splénius^M de la tête^F

infraspinatus
sous-épineux^M

trapezius
trapèze^M

teres minor
petit rond^M

latissimus dorsi
grand dorsal^M

teres major
grand rond^M

triceps of arm
triceps^M brachial

brachioradialis
long supinateur^M

long radial extensor of wrist
premier radial^M externe

short radial extensor of wrist
deuxième radial^M externe

anconeus
anconé^M

ulnar flexor of wrist
cubital^M antérieur

common extensor of fingers
extenseur^M commun des doigts^M

gluteus maximus
grand fessier^M

ulnar extensor of wrist
cubital^M postérieur

semitendinosus
demi-tendineux^M

external oblique
grand oblique^M de l'abdomen^M

biceps of thigh
biceps^M crural

vastus lateralis
*vaste^M externe du membre^M
inférieur*

semimembranosus
demi-membraneux^M

great adductor
grand adducteur^M

gracile
droit^M interne

plantar
plantaire^M grêle

short peroneal
court péronier^M latéral

gastrocnemius
gastrocnémien^M

skeleton

squelette^M

anterior view
vue^F antérieure

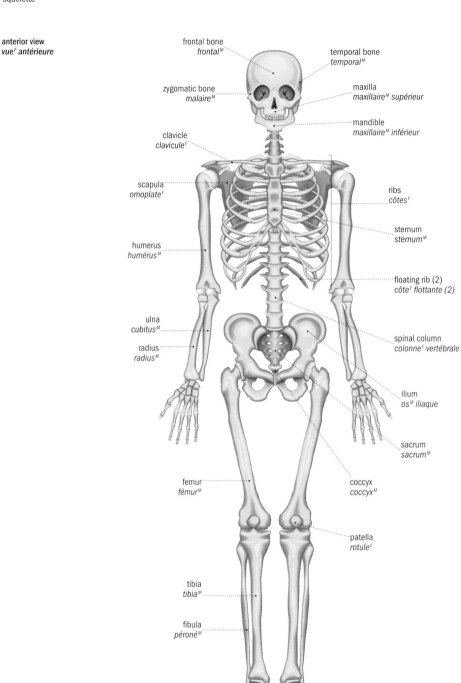

frontal bone
frontal^M

temporal bone
temporal^M

zygomatic bone
malaire^M

maxilla
maxillaire^M supérieur

mandible
maxillaire^M inférieur

clavicle
clavicule^F

scapula
omoplate^F

ribs
côtes^F

sternum
sternum^M

humerus
humérus^M

floating rib (2)
côte^F flottante (2)

ulna
cubitus^M

spinal column
colonne^F vertébrale

radius
radius^M

ilium
os^M iliaque

sacrum
sacrum^M

femur
fémur^M

coccyx
coccyx^M

patella
rotule^F

tibia
tibia^M

fibula
péroné^M

posterior view
vue^F postérieure

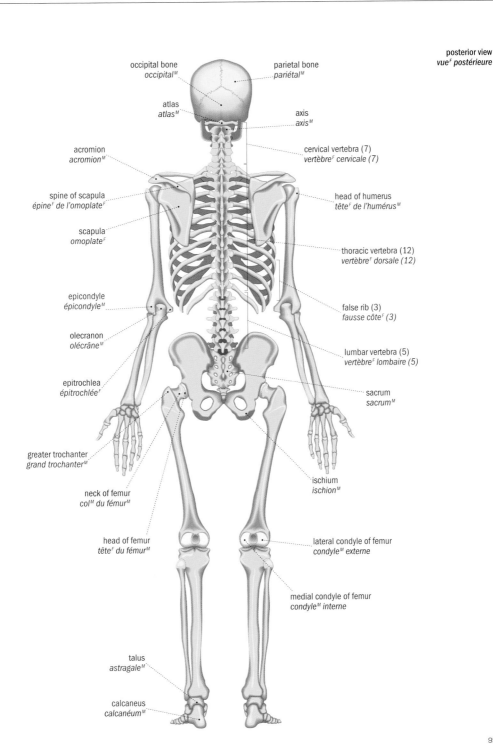

occipital bone
occipital^M

parietal bone
pariétal^M

atlas
atlas^M

axis
axis^M

acromion
acromion^M

cervical vertebra (7)
vertèbre^F cervicale (7)

spine of scapula
épine^F de l'omoplate^F

head of humerus
tête^F de l'humérus^M

scapula
omoplate^F

thoracic vertebra (12)
vertèbre^F dorsale (12)

epicondyle
épicondyle^M

false rib (3)
fausse côte^F (3)

olecranon
olécrâne^M

lumbar vertebra (5)
vertèbre^F lombaire (5)

epitrochlea
épitrochlée^F

sacrum
sacrum^M

greater trochanter
grand trochanter^M

ischium
ischion^M

neck of femur
col^M du fémur^M

head of femur
tête^F du fémur^M

lateral condyle of femur
condyle^M externe

medial condyle of femur
condyle^M interne

talus
astragale^M

calcaneus
calcanéum^M

skeleton

HUMAN BEING

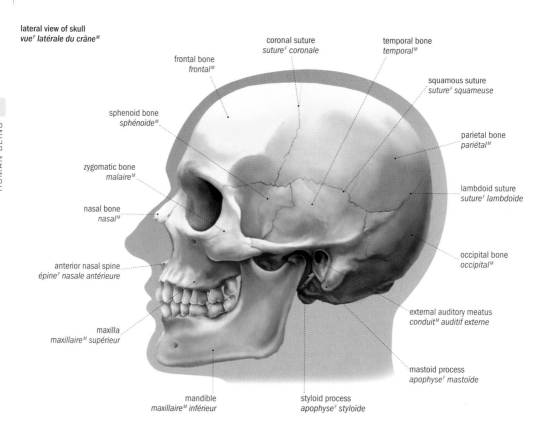

lateral view of skull
vue^F latérale du crâne^M

coronal suture
suture^F coronale

temporal bone
temporal^M

frontal bone
frontal^M

squamous suture
suture^F squameuse

sphenoid bone
sphénoïde^M

parietal bone
pariétal^M

zygomatic bone
malaire^M

lambdoid suture
suture^F lambdoïde

nasal bone
nasal^M

anterior nasal spine
épine^F nasale antérieure

occipital bone
occipital^M

external auditory meatus
conduit^M auditif externe

maxilla
maxillaire^M supérieur

mastoid process
apophyse^F mastoïde

mandible
maxillaire^M inférieur

styloid process
apophyse^F styloïde

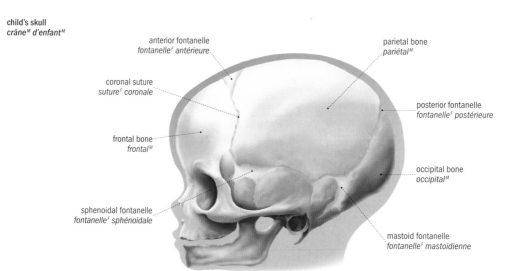

child's skull
crâne^M d'enfant^M

anterior fontanelle
fontanelle^F antérieure

parietal bone
pariétal^M

coronal suture
suture^F coronale

posterior fontanelle
fontanelle^F postérieure

frontal bone
frontal^M

occipital bone
occipital^M

sphenoidal fontanelle
fontanelle^F sphénoïdale

mastoid fontanelle
fontanelle^F mastoïdienne

teeth

human denture
denture^F humaine

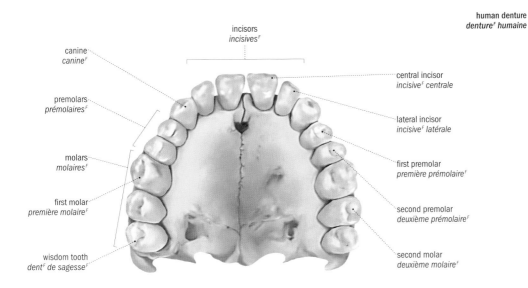

incisors
incisives^F

canine
canine^F

premolars
prémolaires^F

molars
molaires^F

first molar
première molaire^F

wisdom tooth
dent^F de sagesse^F

central incisor
incisive^F centrale

lateral incisor
incisive^F latérale

first premolar
première prémolaire^F

second premolar
deuxième prémolaire^F

second molar
deuxième molaire^F

cross section of a molar
coupe^F d'une molaire^F

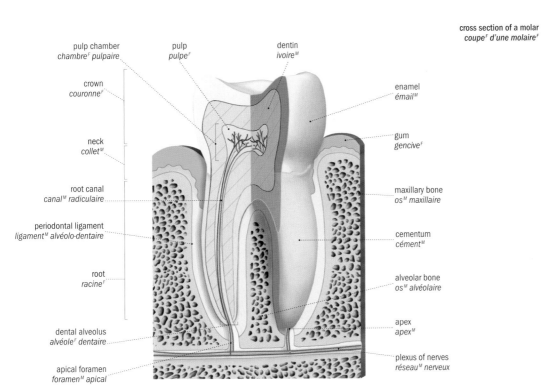

pulp chamber
chambre^F pulpaire

crown
couronne^F

neck
collet^M

root canal
canal^M radiculaire

periodontal ligament
ligament^M alvéolo-dentaire

root
racine^F

dental alveolus
alvéole^F dentaire

apical foramen
foramen^M apical

pulp
pulpe^F

dentin
ivoire^M

enamel
émail^M

gum
gencive^F

maxillary bone
os^M maxillaire

cementum
cément^M

alveolar bone
os^M alvéolaire

apex
apex^M

plexus of nerves
réseau^M nerveux

blood circulation

circulation[F] sanguine

principal veins and arteries
principales veines[F] et artères[F]

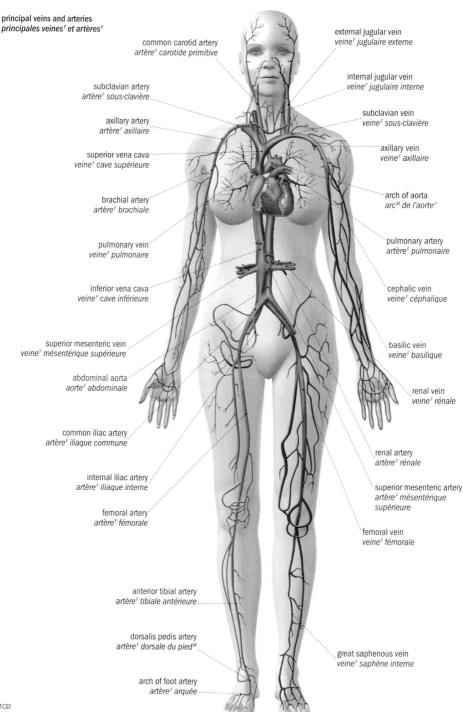

external jugular vein
veine[F] jugulaire externe

common carotid artery
artère[F] carotide primitive

internal jugular vein
veine[F] jugulaire interne

subclavian artery
artère[F] sous-clavière

subclavian vein
veine[F] sous-clavière

axillary artery
artère[F] axillaire

axillary vein
veine[F] axillaire

superior vena cava
veine[F] cave supérieure

arch of aorta
arc[M] de l'aorte[F]

brachial artery
artère[F] brachiale

pulmonary vein
veine[F] pulmonaire

pulmonary artery
artère[F] pulmonaire

inferior vena cava
veine[F] cave inférieure

cephalic vein
veine[F] céphalique

superior mesenteric vein
veine[F] mésentérique supérieure

basilic vein
veine[F] basilique

abdominal aorta
aorte[F] abdominale

renal vein
veine[F] rénale

common iliac artery
artère[F] iliaque commune

renal artery
artère[F] rénale

internal iliac artery
artère[F] iliaque interne

superior mesenteric artery
artère[F] mésentérique
supérieure

femoral artery
artère[F] fémorale

femoral vein
veine[F] fémorale

anterior tibial artery
artère[F] tibiale antérieure

dorsalis pedis artery
artère[F] dorsale du pied[M]

great saphenous vein
veine[F] saphène interne

arch of foot artery
artère[F] arquée

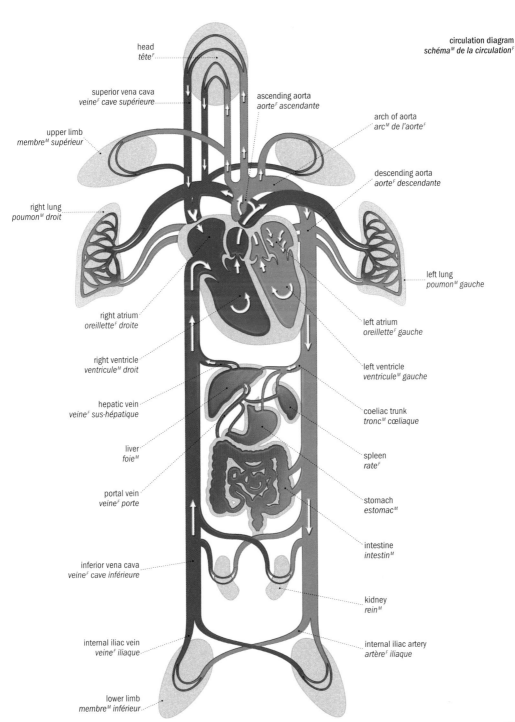

circulation diagram
schéma^M de la circulation^F

head
tête^F

superior vena cava
veine^F cave supérieure

ascending aorta
aorte^F ascendante

arch of aorta
arc^M de l'aorte^F

upper limb
membre^M supérieur

descending aorta
aorte^F descendante

right lung
poumon^M droit

left lung
poumon^M gauche

right atrium
oreillette^F droite

left atrium
oreillette^F gauche

right ventricle
ventricule^M droit

left ventricle
ventricule^M gauche

hepatic vein
veine^F sus-hépatique

coeliac trunk
tronc^M cœliaque

liver
foie^M

spleen
rate^F

portal vein
veine^F porte

stomach
estomac^M

intestine
intestin^M

inferior vena cava
veine^F cave inférieure

kidney
rein^M

internal iliac vein
veine^F iliaque

internal iliac artery
artère^F iliaque

lower limb
membre^M inférieur

blood circulation

composition of the blood
composition^F du sang^M

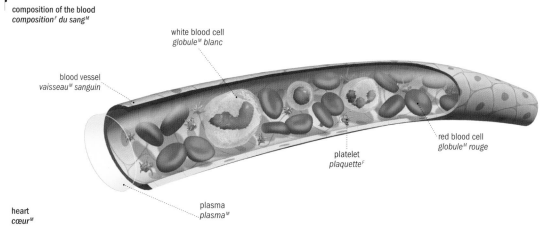

white blood cell
globule^M blanc

blood vessel
vaisseau^M sanguin

red blood cell
globule^M rouge

platelet
plaquette^F

plasma
plasma^M

heart
cœur^M

oxygenated blood
sang^M oxygéné

deoxygenated blood
sang^M désoxygéné

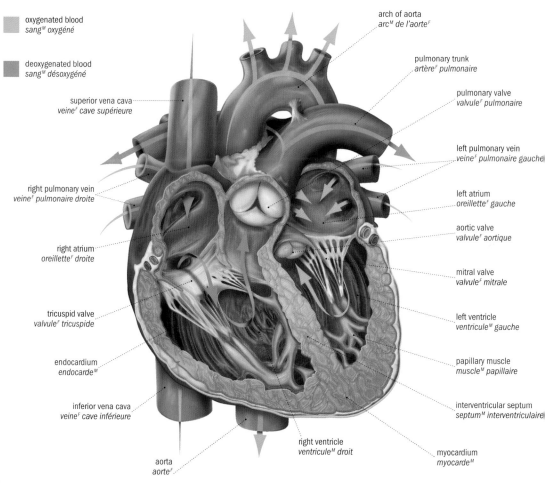

arch of aorta
arc^M de l'aorte^F

pulmonary trunk
artère^F pulmonaire

pulmonary valve
valvule^F pulmonaire

superior vena cava
veine^F cave supérieure

left pulmonary vein
veine^F pulmonaire gauche

left atrium
oreillette^F gauche

right pulmonary vein
veine^F pulmonaire droite

aortic valve
valvule^F aortique

right atrium
oreillette^F droite

mitral valve
valvule^F mitrale

tricuspid valve
valvule^F tricuspide

left ventricle
ventricule^M gauche

papillary muscle
muscle^M papillaire

endocardium
endocarde^M

interventricular septum
septum^M interventriculaire

inferior vena cava
veine^F cave inférieure

right ventricle
ventricule^M droit

myocardium
myocarde^M

aorta
aorte^F

respiratory system

appareil^M respiratoire

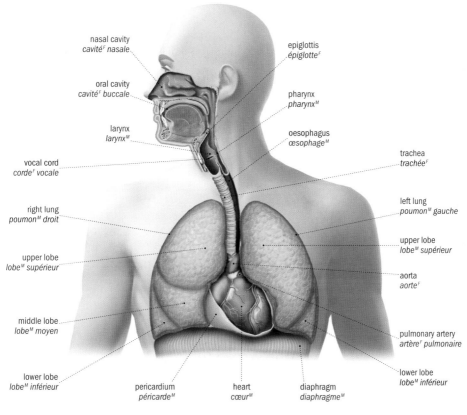

nasal cavity
cavité^F nasale

oral cavity
cavité^F buccale

larynx
larynx^M

vocal cord
corde^F vocale

right lung
poumon^M droit

upper lobe
lobe^M supérieur

middle lobe
lobe^M moyen

lower lobe
lobe^M inférieur

pericardium
péricarde^M

heart
cœur^M

diaphragm
diaphragme^M

epiglottis
épiglotte^F

pharynx
pharynx^M

oesophagus
œsophage^M

trachea
trachée^F

left lung
poumon^M gauche

upper lobe
lobe^M supérieur

aorta
aorte^F

pulmonary artery
artère^F pulmonaire

lower lobe
lobe^M inférieur

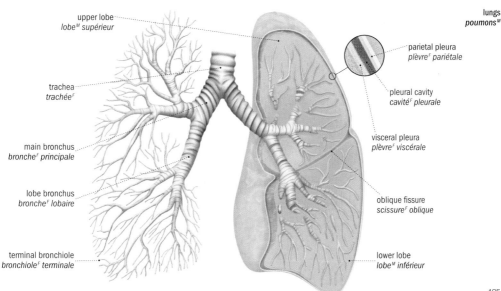

upper lobe
lobe^M supérieur

trachea
trachée^F

main bronchus
bronche^F principale

lobe bronchus
bronche^F lobaire

terminal bronchiole
bronchiole^F terminale

lungs
poumons^M

parietal pleura
plèvre^F pariétale

pleural cavity
cavité^F pleurale

visceral pleura
plèvre^F viscérale

oblique fissure
scissure^F oblique

lower lobe
lobe^M inférieur

digestive system

appareil^M digestif

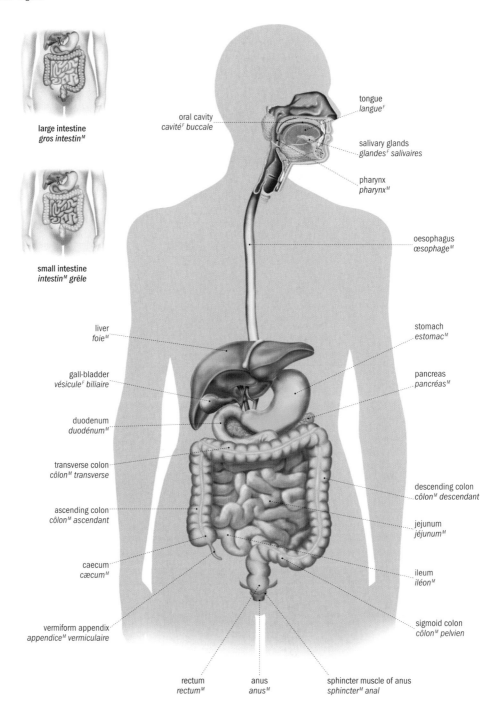

large intestine
gros intestin^M

small intestine
intestin^M grêle

oral cavity
cavité^F buccale

tongue
langue^F

salivary glands
glandes^F salivaires

pharynx
pharynx^M

oesophagus
œsophage^M

liver
foie^M

stomach
estomac^M

gall-bladder
vésicule^F biliaire

pancreas
pancréas^M

duodenum
duodénum^M

transverse colon
côlon^M transverse

descending colon
côlon^M descendant

ascending colon
côlon^M ascendant

jejunum
jéjunum^M

caecum
cæcum^M

ileum
iléon^M

vermiform appendix
appendice^M vermiculaire

sigmoid colon
côlon^M pelvien

rectum
rectum^M

anus
anus^M

sphincter muscle of anus
sphincter^M anal

urinary system
appareil^M urinaire

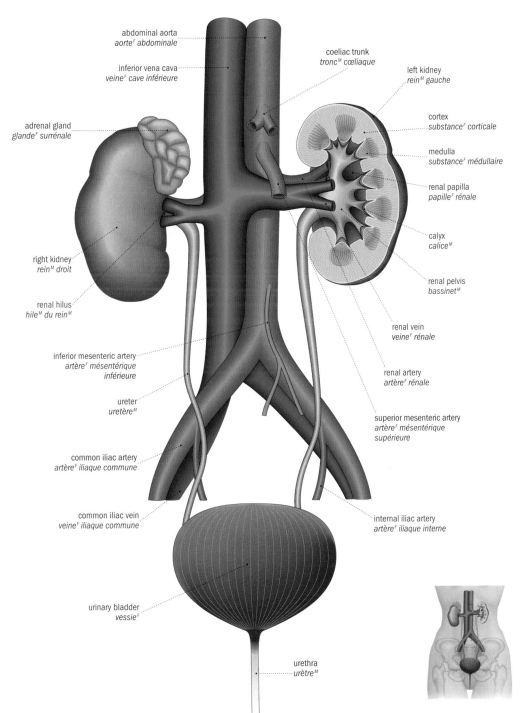

abdominal aorta
aorte^F abdominale

inferior vena cava
veine^F cave inférieure

coeliac trunk
tronc^M cœliaque

left kidney
rein^M gauche

cortex
substance^F corticale

adrenal gland
glande^F surrénale

medulla
substance^F médullaire

renal papilla
papille^F rénale

calyx
calice^M

right kidney
rein^M droit

renal pelvis
bassinet^M

renal hilus
hile^M du rein^M

renal vein
veine^F rénale

inferior mesenteric artery
*artère^F mésentérique
inférieure*

ureter
uretère^M

renal artery
artère^F rénale

common iliac artery
artère^F iliaque commune

superior mesenteric artery
*artère^F mésentérique
supérieure*

common iliac vein
veine^F iliaque commune

internal iliac artery
artère^F iliaque interne

urinary bladder
vessie^F

urethra
urètre^M

HUMAN BEING

nervous system

système^M nerveux

peripheral nervous system
système^M nerveux
périphérique

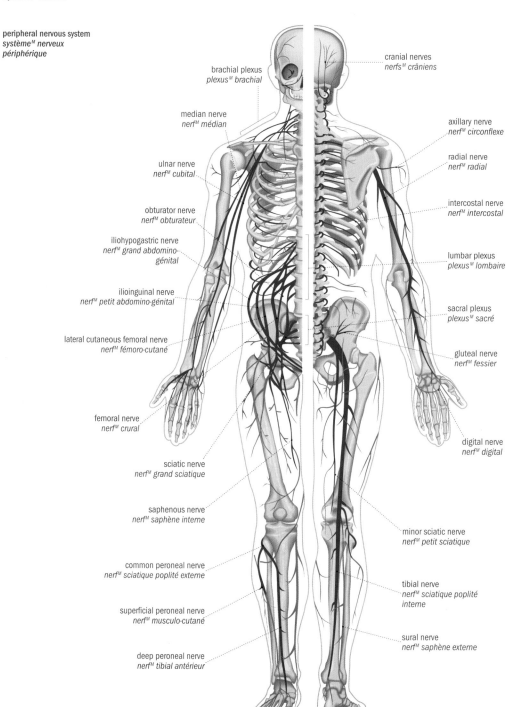

brachial plexus
plexus^M brachial

cranial nerves
nerfs^M crâniens

median nerve
nerf^M médian

axillary nerve
nerf^M circonflexe

ulnar nerve
nerf^M cubital

radial nerve
nerf^M radial

intercostal nerve
nerf^M intercostal

obturator nerve
nerf^M obturateur

iliohypogastric nerve
nerf^M grand abdomino-
génital

lumbar plexus
plexus^M lombaire

ilioinguinal nerve
nerf^M petit abdomino-génital

sacral plexus
plexus^M sacré

lateral cutaneous femoral nerve
nerf^M fémoro-cutané

gluteal nerve
nerf^M fessier

femoral nerve
nerf^M crural

digital nerve
nerf^M digital

sciatic nerve
nerf^M grand sciatique

saphenous nerve
nerf^M saphène interne

minor sciatic nerve
nerf^M petit sciatique

common peroneal nerve
nerf^M sciatique poplité externe

tibial nerve
nerf^M sciatique poplité
interne

superficial peroneal nerve
nerf^M musculo-cutané

sural nerve
nerf^M saphène externe

deep peroneal nerve
nerf^M tibial antérieur

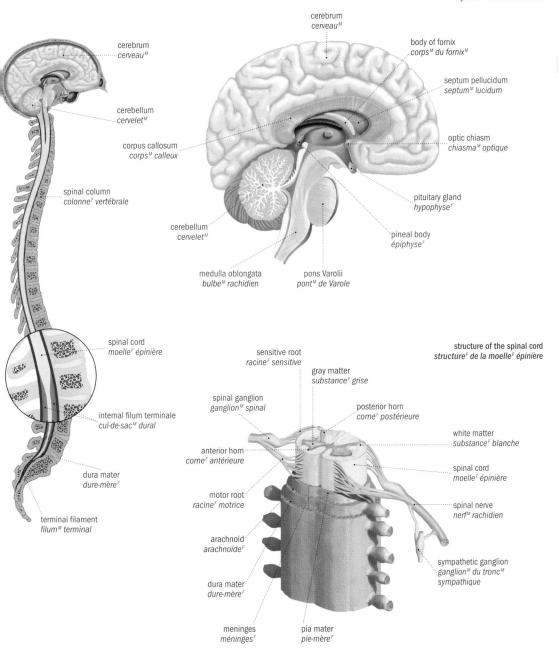

central nervous system
système^M *nerveux central*

cerebrum
cerveau^M

cerebrum
cerveau^M

body of fornix
corps^M *du fornix*^M

septum pellucidum
septum^M *lucidum*

cerebellum
cervelet^M

optic chiasm
chiasma^M *optique*

corpus callosum
corps^M *calleux*

spinal column
colonne^F *vertébrale*

pituitary gland
hypophyse^F

cerebellum
cervelet^M

pineal body
épiphyse^F

medulla oblongata
bulbe^M *rachidien*

pons Varolii
pont^M *de Varole*

spinal cord
moelle^F *épinière*

structure of the spinal cord
structure^F *de la moelle*^F *épinière*

sensitive root
racine^F *sensitive*

gray matter
substance^F *grise*

spinal ganglion
ganglion^M *spinal*

posterior horn
corne^F *postérieure*

internal filum terminale
cul-de-sac^M *dural*

white matter
substance^F *blanche*

anterior horn
corne^F *antérieure*

spinal cord
moelle^F *épinière*

dura mater
dure-mère^F

motor root
racine^F *motrice*

spinal nerve
nerf^M *rachidien*

terminal filament
filum^M *terminal*

arachnoid
arachnoïde^F

sympathetic ganglion
ganglion^M *du tronc*^M
sympathique

dura mater
dure-mère^F

meninges
méninges^F

pia mater
pie-mère^F

chain of neurons
chaine^F de neurones^M

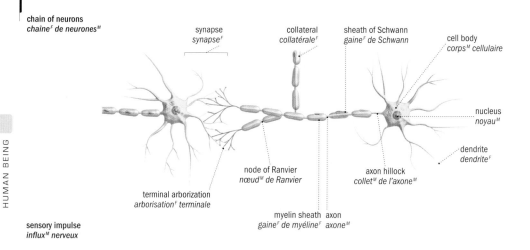

synapse
synapse^F

collateral
collatérale^F

sheath of Schwann
gaine^F de Schwann

cell body
corps^M cellulaire

nucleus
noyau^M

dendrite
dendrite^F

axon hillock
collet^M de l'axone^M

node of Ranvier
nœud^M de Ranvier

terminal arborization
arborisation^F terminale

myelin sheath axon
gaine^F de myéline^F axone^M

sensory impulse
influx^M nerveux

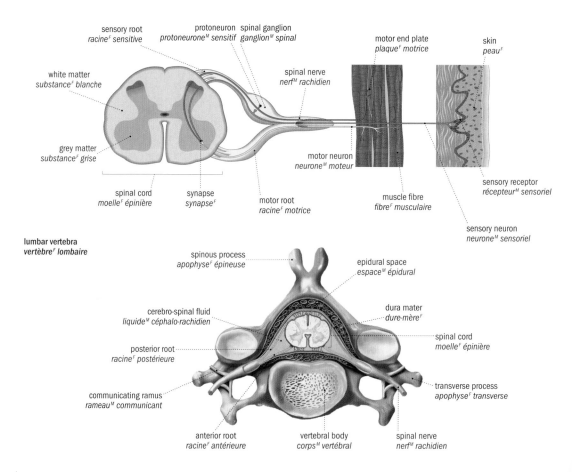

sensory root
racine^F sensitive

protoneuron spinal ganglion
protoneurone^M sensitif ganglion^M spinal

motor end plate
plaque^F motrice

skin
peau^F

white matter
substance^F blanche

spinal nerve
nerf^M rachidien

grey matter
substance^F grise

motor neuron
neurone^M moteur

spinal cord
moelle^F épinière

synapse
synapse^F

motor root
racine^F motrice

muscle fibre
fibre^F musculaire

sensory receptor
récepteur^M sensoriel

sensory neuron
neurone^M sensoriel

lumbar vertebra
vertèbre^F lombaire

spinous process
apophyse^F épineuse

epidural space
espace^M épidural

cerebro-spinal fluid
liquide^M céphalo-rachidien

dura mater
dure-mère^F

posterior root
racine^F postérieure

spinal cord
moelle^F épinière

communicating ramus
rameau^M communicant

transverse process
apophyse^F transverse

anterior root
racine^F antérieure

vertebral body
corps^M vertébral

spinal nerve
nerf^M rachidien

male genital organs
organes^M génitaux masculins

sagittal section
coupe^F sagittale

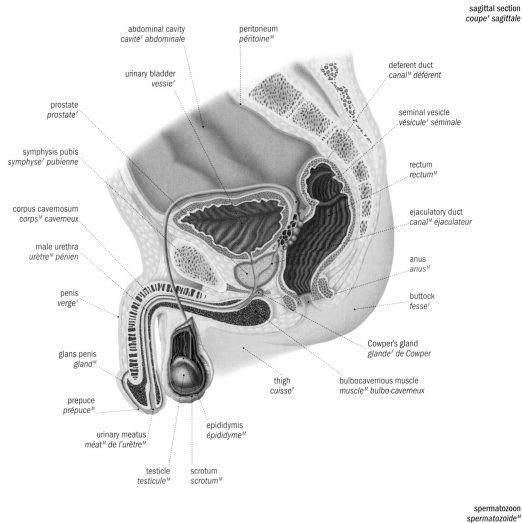

abdominal cavity
cavité^F abdominale

peritoneum
péritoine^M

urinary bladder
vessie^F

deferent duct
canal^M déférent

seminal vesicle
vésicule^F séminale

prostate
prostate^F

rectum
rectum^M

symphysis pubis
symphyse^F pubienne

corpus cavernosum
corps^M caverneux

ejaculatory duct
canal^M éjaculateur

male urethra
urètre^M pénien

anus
anus^M

penis
verge^F

buttock
fesse^F

glans penis
gland^M

Cowper's gland
glande^F de Cowper

prepuce
prépuce^M

thigh
cuisse^F

bulbocavernous muscle
muscle^M bulbo-caverneux

urinary meatus
méat^M de l'urètre^M

epididymis
épididyme^M

testicle
testicule^M

scrotum
scrotum^M

spermatozoon
spermatozoïde^M

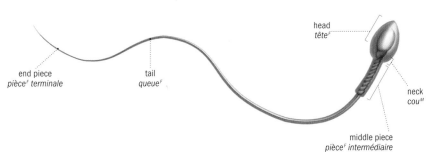

head
tête^F

end piece
pièce^F terminale

tail
queue^F

neck
cou^M

middle piece
pièce^F intermédiaire

female genital organs

organes^M génitaux féminins

sagittal section
coupe^F sagittale

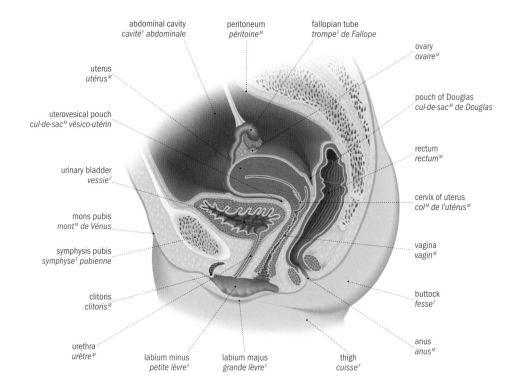

abdominal cavity
cavité^F abdominale

peritoneum
péritoine^M

fallopian tube
trompe^F de Fallope

ovary
ovaire^M

uterus
utérus^M

pouch of Douglas
cul-de-sac^M de Douglas

uterovesical pouch
cul-de-sac^M vésico-utérin

rectum
rectum^M

urinary bladder
vessie^F

cervix of uterus
col^M de l'utérus^M

mons pubis
mont^M de Vénus

symphysis pubis
symphyse^F pubienne

vagina
vagin^M

clitoris
clitoris^M

buttock
fesse^F

urethra
urètre^M

labium minus
petite lèvre^F

labium majus
grande lèvre^F

thigh
cuisse^F

anus
anus^M

egg
ovule^M

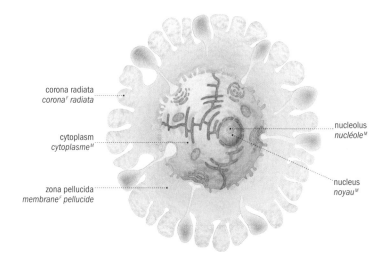

corona radiata
corona^F radiata

nucleolus
nucléole^M

cytoplasm
cytoplasme^M

nucleus
noyau^M

zona pellucida
membrane^F pellucide

posterior view
vue^F postérieure

ampulla of fallopian tube
ampoule^F de la trompe^F utérine

isthmus of fallopian tube
isthme^M de la trompe^F utérine

infundibulum of fallopian tube
pavillon^M de la trompe^F utérine

ovary
ovaire^M

uterus
utérus^M

broad ligament of uterus
ligament^M large de l'utérus^M

labium minus
petite lèvre^F

vagina
vagin^M

labium majus
grande lèvre^F

fallopian tubes
trompes^F de Fallope

vulva
vulve^F

breast

sein^M

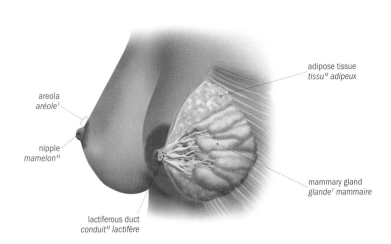

adipose tissue
tissu^M adipeux

areola
aréole^F

nipple
mamelon^M

mammary gland
glande^F mammaire

lactiferous duct
conduit^M lactifère

touch

toucher^M

skin
peau^F

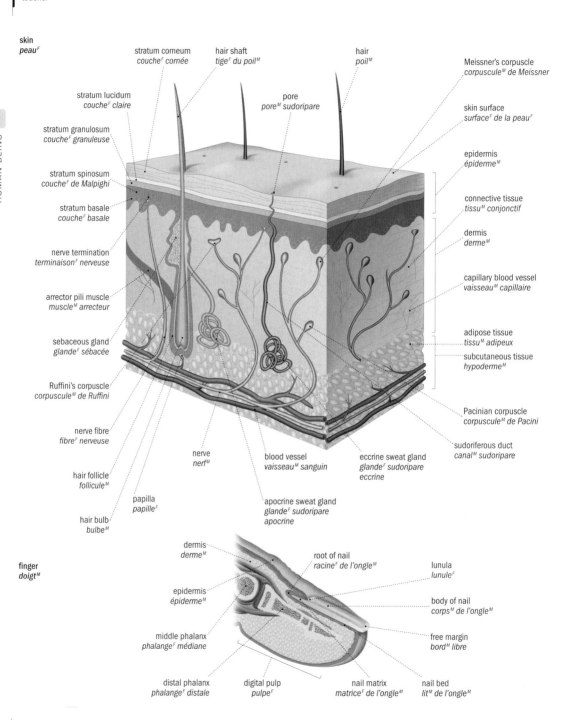

stratum corneum
couche^F cornée

hair shaft
tige^F du poil^M

hair
poil^M

pore
pore^M sudoripare

stratum lucidum
couche^F claire

stratum granulosum
couche^F granuleuse

stratum spinosum
couche^F de Malpighi

stratum basale
couche^F basale

nerve termination
terminaison^F nerveuse

arrector pili muscle
muscle^M arrecteur

sebaceous gland
glande^F sébacée

Ruffini's corpuscle
corpuscule^M de Ruffini

nerve fibre
fibre^F nerveuse

hair follicle
follicule^M

nerve
nerf^M

papilla
papille^F

hair bulb
bulbe^M

blood vessel
vaisseau^M sanguin

apocrine sweat gland
glande^F sudoripare
apocrine

eccrine sweat gland
glande^F sudoripare
eccrine

Meissner's corpuscle
corpuscule^M de Meissner

skin surface
surface^F de la peau^F

epidermis
épiderme^M

connective tissue
tissu^M conjonctif

dermis
derme^M

capillary blood vessel
vaisseau^M capillaire

adipose tissue
tissu^M adipeux

subcutaneous tissue
hypoderme^M

Pacinian corpuscle
corpuscule^M de Pacini

sudoriferous duct
canal^M sudoripare

finger
doigt^M

dermis
derme^M

epidermis
épiderme^M

middle phalanx
phalange^F médiane

distal phalanx
phalange^F distale

digital pulp
pulpe^F

root of nail
racine^F de l'ongle^M

nail matrix
matrice^F de l'ongle^M

lunula
lunule^F

body of nail
corps^M de l'ongle^M

free margin
bord^M libre

nail bed
lit^M de l'ongle^M

touch

hand
*main*F

palm
*paume*F

back
*dos*M

middle finger
*majeur*M

third finger
*annulaire*M

index finger
*index*M

little finger
*auriculaire*M

thumb
*pouce*M

fingernail
*ongle*M

lunula
*lunule*F

wrist
*poignet*M

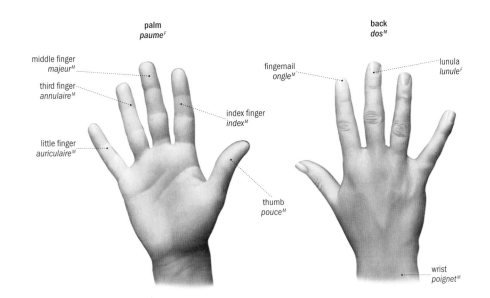

HUMAN BEING

hearing
*ouïe*F

auricle
*pavillon*M

helix
*hélix*M

antihelix
*anthélix*M

triangular fossa
*fossette*F *de l'anthélix*M

concha
*conque*F

crus of helix
*racine*F *de l'hélix*M

intertragic notch
*échancrure*F *de la conque*F

anterior notch
*sillon*M *antérieur*

antitragus
*antitragus*M

tragus
*tragus*M

tail of helix
*queue*F *de l'hélix*M

acoustic meatus
*orifice*M *du conduit*M
auditif

lobule
*lobule*M

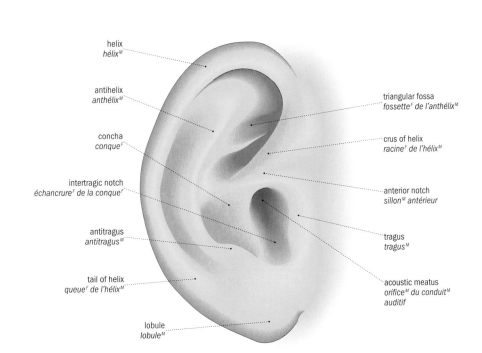

hearing

structure of the ear
structure^F de l'oreille^F

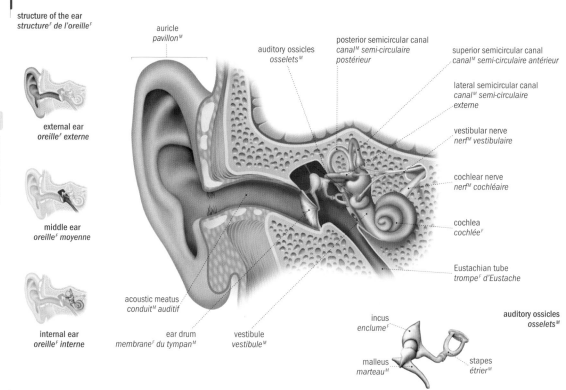

external ear
oreille^F externe

middle ear
oreille^F moyenne

internal ear
oreille^F interne

auricle
pavillon^M

auditory ossicles
osselets^M

posterior semicircular canal
canal^M semi-circulaire postérieur

superior semicircular canal
canal^M semi-circulaire antérieur

lateral semicircular canal
canal^M semi-circulaire externe

vestibular nerve
nerf^M vestibulaire

cochlear nerve
nerf^M cochléaire

cochlea
cochlée^F

Eustachian tube
trompe^F d'Eustache

acoustic meatus
conduit^M auditif

ear drum
membrane^F du tympan^M

vestibule
vestibule^M

incus
enclume^F

auditory ossicles
osselets^M

malleus
marteau^M

stapes
étrier^M

smell and taste

odorat^M et goût^M

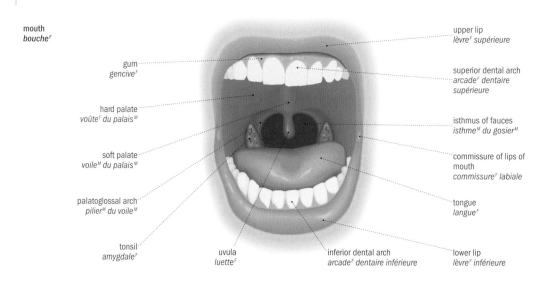

mouth
bouche^F

gum
gencive^F

hard palate
voûte^F du palais^M

soft palate
voile^M du palais^M

palatoglossal arch
pilier^M du voile^M

tonsil
amygdale^F

uvula
luette^F

inferior dental arch
arcade^F dentaire inférieure

upper lip
lèvre^F supérieure

superior dental arch
arcade^F dentaire supérieure

isthmus of fauces
isthme^M du gosier^M

commissure of lips of mouth
commissure^F labiale

tongue
langue^F

lower lip
lèvre^F inférieure

HUMAN BEING

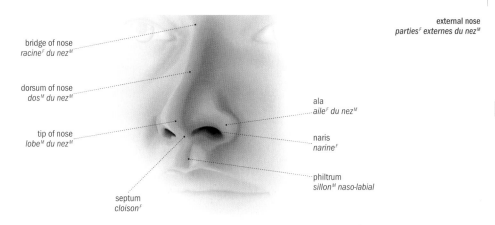

external nose
parties^F externes du nez^M

bridge of nose
racine^F du nez^M

dorsum of nose
dos^M du nez^M

ala
aile^F du nez^M

tip of nose
lobe^M du nez^M

naris
narine^F

philtrum
sillon^M naso-labial

septum
cloison^F

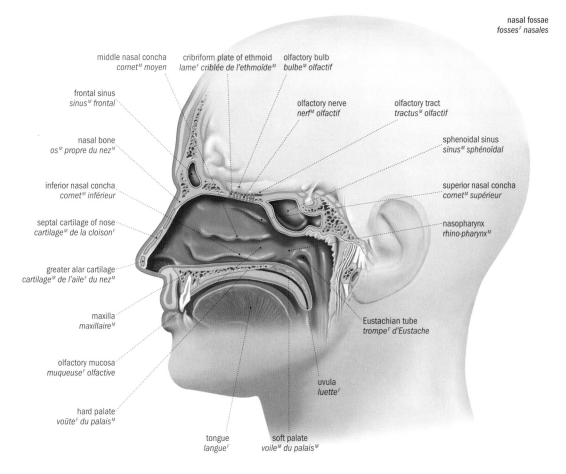

nasal fossae
fosses^F nasales

middle nasal concha
cornet^M moyen

cribriform plate of ethmoid
lame^F criblée de l'ethmoïde^M

olfactory bulb
bulbe^M olfactif

frontal sinus
sinus^M frontal

olfactory nerve
nerf^M olfactif

olfactory tract
tractus^M olfactif

nasal bone
os^M propre du nez^M

sphenoidal sinus
sinus^M sphénoïdal

inferior nasal concha
cornet^M inférieur

superior nasal concha
cornet^M supérieur

septal cartilage of nose
cartilage^M de la cloison^F

nasopharynx
rhino-pharynx^M

greater alar cartilage
cartilage^M de l'aile^F du nez^M

maxilla
maxillaire^M

Eustachian tube
trompe^F d'Eustache

olfactory mucosa
muqueuse^F olfactive

uvula
luette^F

hard palate
voûte^F du palais^M

tongue
langue^F

soft palate
voile^M du palais^M

smell and taste

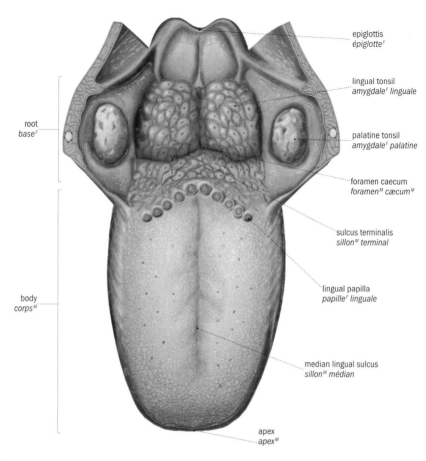

dorsum of tongue
dos^M de la langue^F

root
base^F

body
corps^M

epiglottis
épiglotte^F

lingual tonsil
amygdale^F linguale

palatine tonsil
amygdale^F palatine

foramen caecum
foramen^M cæcum^M

sulcus terminalis
sillon^M terminal

lingual papilla
papille^F linguale

median lingual sulcus
sillon^M médian

apex
apex^M

taste receptors
récepteurs^M du goût^M

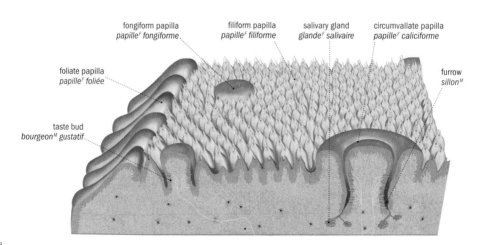

fongiform papilla
papille^F fongiforme

filiform papilla
papille^F filiforme

salivary gland
glande^F salivaire

circumvallate papilla
papille^F caliciforme

foliate papilla
papille^F foliée

furrow
sillon^M

taste bud
bourgeon^M gustatif

sight
vue^F

eye
œil^M

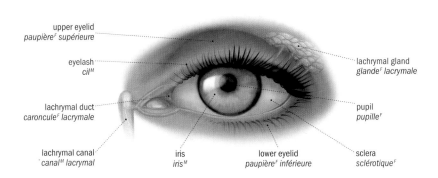

upper eyelid
paupière^F supérieure

eyelash
cil^M

lachrymal duct
caroncule^F lacrymale

lachrymal canal
canal^M lacrymal

lachrymal gland
glande^F lacrymale

pupil
pupille^F

iris
iris^M

lower eyelid
paupière^F inférieure

sclera
sclérotique^F

eyeball
globe^M oculaire

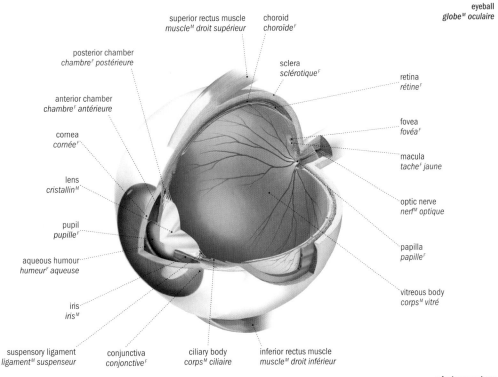

superior rectus muscle
muscle^M droit supérieur

choroid
choroïde^F

posterior chamber
chambre^F postérieure

sclera
sclérotique^F

anterior chamber
chambre^F antérieure

retina
rétine^F

cornea
cornée^F

fovea
fovéa^F

macula
tache^F jaune

lens
cristallin^M

optic nerve
nerf^M optique

pupil
pupille^F

papilla
papille^F

aqueous humour
humeur^F aqueuse

vitreous body
corps^M vitré

iris
iris^M

suspensory ligament
ligament^M suspenseur

conjunctiva
conjonctive^F

ciliary body
corps^M ciliaire

inferior rectus muscle
muscle^M droit inférieur

photoreceptors
photorécepteurs^M

cone
cône^M

rod
bâtonnet^M

supermarket

supermarché^M

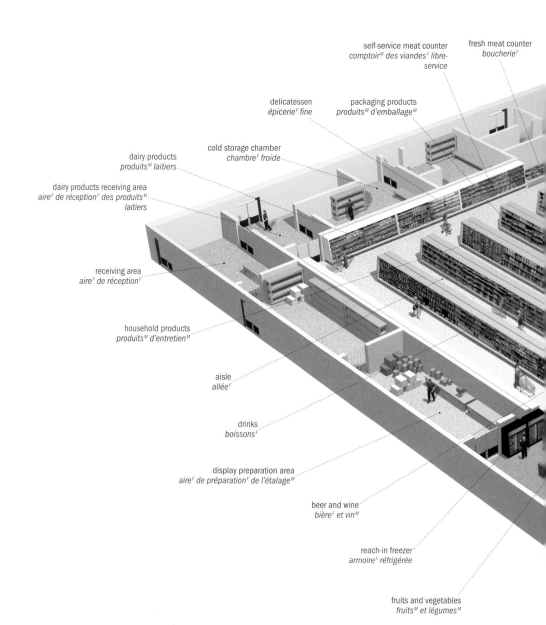

self-service meat counter
comptoir^M des viandes^F libre-
service

fresh meat counter
boucherie^F

delicatessen
épicerie^F fine

packaging products
produits^M d'emballage^M

cold storage chamber
chambre^F froide

dairy products
produits^M laitiers

dairy products receiving area
aire^F de réception^F des produits^M
laitiers

receiving area
aire^F de réception^F

household products
produits^M d'entretien^M

aisle
allée^F

drinks
boissons^F

display preparation area
aire^F de préparation^F de l'étalage^M

beer and wine
bière^F et vin^M

reach-in freezer
armoire^F réfrigérée

fruits and vegetables
fruits^M et légumes^M

FOOD AND KITCHEN

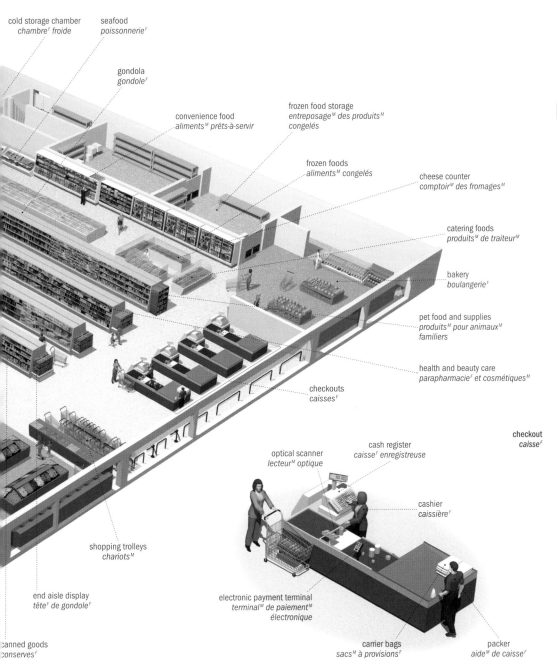

cold storage chamber
chambre^F froide

seafood
poissonnerie^F

gondola
gondole^F

convenience food
aliments^M prêts-à-servir

frozen food storage
entreposage^M des produits^M
congelés

frozen foods
aliments^M congelés

cheese counter
comptoir^M des fromages^M

catering foods
produits^M de traiteur^M

bakery
boulangerie^F

pet food and supplies
produits^M pour animaux^M
familiers

health and beauty care
parapharmacie^F et cosmétiques^M

checkouts
caisses^F

checkout
caisse^F

optical scanner
lecteur^M optique

cash register
caisse^F enregistreuse

cashier
caissière^F

shopping trolleys
chariots^M

end aisle display
tête^F de gondole^F

electronic payment terminal
terminal^M de paiement^M
électronique

canned goods
conserves^F

carrier bags
sacs^M à provisions^F

packer
aide^M de caisse^F

farmstead

ferme^F

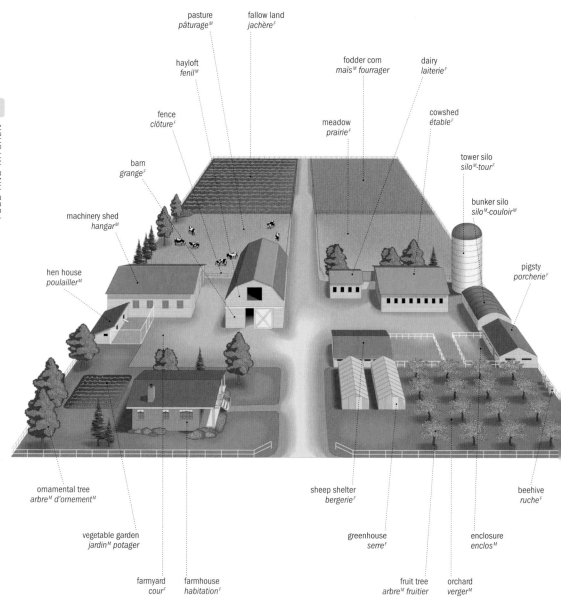

pasture
pâturage^M

fallow land
jachère^F

fodder corn
maïs^M fourrager

dairy
laiterie^F

hayloft
fenil^M

meadow
prairie^F

cowshed
étable^F

fence
clôture^F

barn
grange^F

tower silo
silo^M-tour^F

bunker silo
silo^M-couloir^M

machinery shed
hangar^M

hen house
poulailler^M

pigsty
porcherie^F

ornamental tree
arbre^M d'ornement^M

sheep shelter
bergerie^F

beehive
ruche^F

vegetable garden
jardin^M potager

greenhouse
serre^F

enclosure
enclos^M

farmyard
cour^F

farmhouse
habitation^F

fruit tree
arbre^M fruitier

orchard
verger^M

mushrooms

truffle
truffe^F

wood ear
oreille-de-Judas^F

royal agaric
oronge^F vraie

delicious lactarius
lactaire^M délicieux

enoki mushroom
collybie^F à pied^M velouté

oyster mushroom
pleurote^M en forme^F d'huitre^F

cultivated mushroom
champignon^M de couche^F

green russula
russule^F verdoyante

morel
morille^F

edible boletus
cèpe^M

shiitake
shiitake^M

chanterelle
chanterelle^F commune

seaweed

arame
aramé^M

wakame
wakamé^M

kombu
kombu^M

spirulina
spiruline^F

Irish moss
mousse^F d'Irlande^F

hijiki
hijiki^M

sea lettuce
laitue^F de mer^F

agar-agar
agar-agar^M

nori
nori^M

dulse
rhodyménie^M palmé

vegetables

légumes^M

bulb vegetables
légumes^M bulbes^M

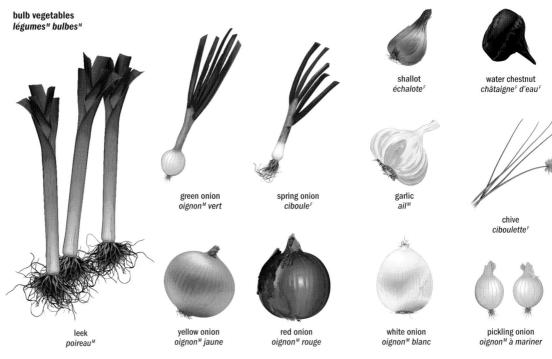

shallot
échalote^F

water chestnut
châtaigne^F d'eau^F

green onion
oignon^M vert

spring onion
ciboule^F

garlic
ail^M

chive
ciboulette^F

leek
poireau^M

yellow onion
oignon^M jaune

red onion
oignon^M rouge

white onion
oignon^M blanc

pickling onion
oignon^M à mariner

tuber vegetables
légumes^M tubercules^M

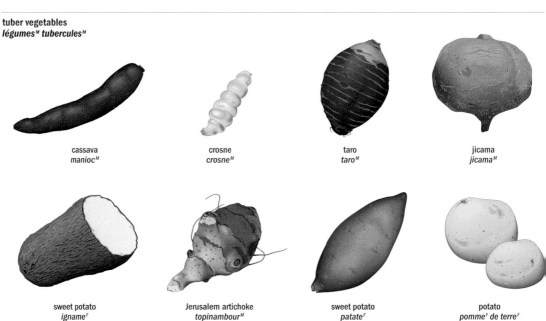

cassava
manioc^M

crosne
crosne^M

taro
taro^M

jicama
jicama^M

sweet potato
igname^F

Jerusalem artichoke
topinambour^M

sweet potato
patate^F

potato
pomme^F de terre^F

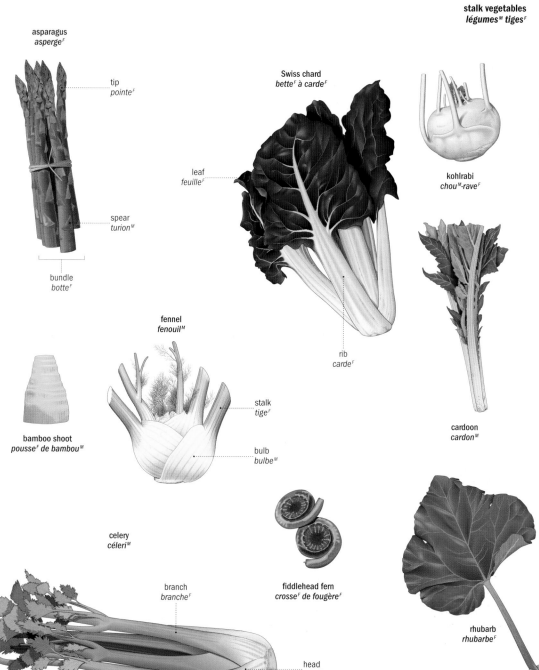

stalk vegetables
légumes^M tiges^F

asparagus
asperge^F

tip
pointe^F

spear
turion^M

bundle
botte^F

Swiss chard
bette^F à carde^F

leaf
feuille^F

rib
carde^F

kohlrabi
chou^M-rave^F

fennel
fenouil^M

stalk
tige^F

bulb
bulbe^M

bamboo shoot
pousse^F de bambou^M

cardoon
cardon^M

celery
céleri^M

branch
branche^F

fiddlehead fern
crosse^F de fougère^F

head
pied^M

rhubarb
rhubarbe^F

vegetables

leaf vegetables
légumes^M feuilles^F

leaf lettuce
laitue^F frisée

cos lettuce
romaine^F

celtuce
laitue^F asperge^F

sea kale
chou^M marin

collards
chou^M cavalier^M

escarole
scarole^F

butterhead lettuce
laitue^F pommée

iceberg lettuce
laitue^F iceberg^M

radicchio
chicorée^F de Trévise

ornamental kale
chou^M laitue^F

curly kale
chou^M frisé

vine leaf
feuille^F de vigne^F

Brussels sprouts
choux^M de Bruxelles

red cabbage
chou^M pommé rouge

white cabbage
chou^M pommé blanc

savoy cabbage
chou^M de Milan

green cabbage
chou^M pommé vert

pe-tsai
pe-tsaï^M

pak-choi
pak-choï^M

purslane
pourpier^M

nettle
ortie^F

watercress
cresson^M de fontaine^F

dandelion
pissenlit^M

corn salad
mâche^F

rocket
roquette^F

spinach
épinard^M

garden cress
cresson^M alénois

garden sorrel
oseille^F

curly endive
chicorée^F frisée

chicory
endive^F

inflorescent vegetables
légumes^M fleurs^F

cauliflower
chou^M-fleur^F

broccoli
brocoli^M

Gai-lohn
Gai lon^M

broccoli raab
brocoli^M italien

artichoke
artichaut^M

fruit vegetables
légumes^M *fruits*^M

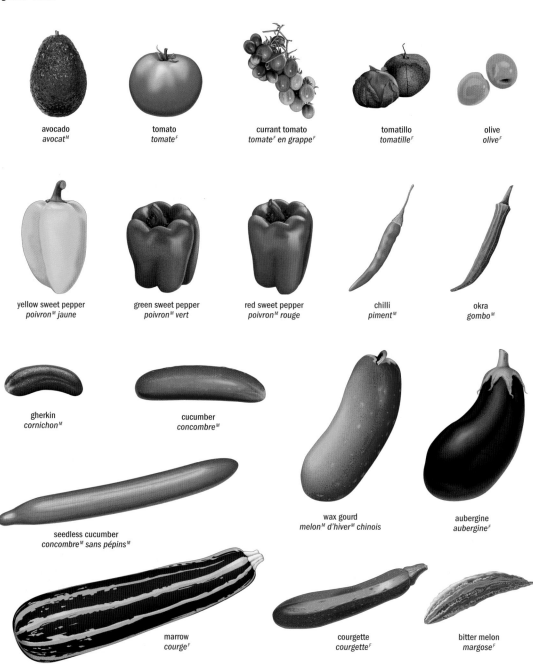

avocado
avocat^M

tomato
tomate^F

currant tomato
tomate^F *en grappe*^F

tomatillo
tomatille^F

olive
olive^F

yellow sweet pepper
poivron^M *jaune*

green sweet pepper
poivron^M *vert*

red sweet pepper
poivron^M *rouge*

chilli
piment^M

okra
gombo^M

gherkin
cornichon^M

cucumber
concombre^M

seedless cucumber
concombre^M *sans pépins*^M

wax gourd
melon^M *d'hiver*^M *chinois*

aubergine
aubergine^F

marrow
courge^F

courgette
courgette^F

bitter melon
margose^F

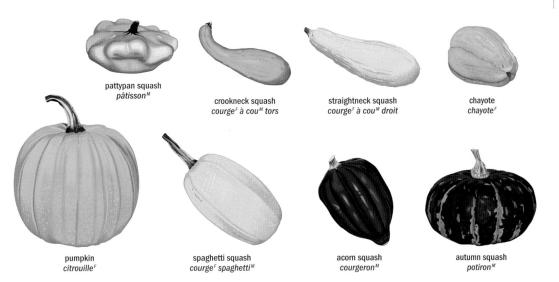

pattypan squash
pâtisson^M

crookneck squash
courge^F à cou^M tors

straightneck squash
courge^F à cou^M droit

chayote
chayote^F

pumpkin
citrouille^F

spaghetti squash
courge^F spaghetti^M

acorn squash
courgeron^M

autumn squash
potiron^M

root vegetables
légumes^M racines^F

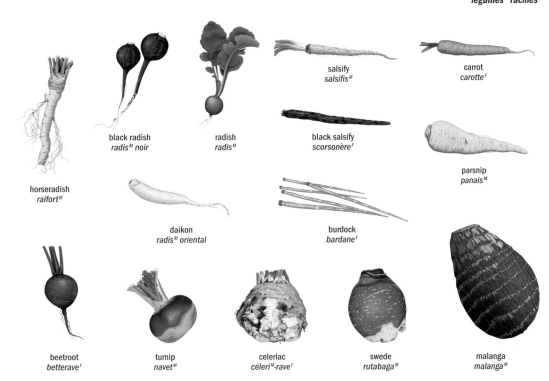

salsify
salsifis^M

carrot
carotte^F

black radish
radis^M noir

radish
radis^M

black salsify
scorsonère^F

parsnip
panais^M

horseradish
raifort^M

daikon
radis^M oriental

burdock
bardane^F

beetroot
betterave^F

turnip
navet^M

celeriac
céleri^M-rave^F

swede
rutabaga^M

malanga
malanga^M

legumes

légumineuses^F

lupine
lupin^M

lentils
lentilles^F

peanut
cacahuète^F

broad beans
fèves^F

alfalfa
luzerne^F

peas
pois^M

dolichos beans
doliques^M

chick peas
pois^M *chiches*

split peas
pois^M *cassés*

black-eyed pea
dolique^M *à œil*^M *noir*

lablab bean
dolique^M *d'Égypte*^F

green peas
petits pois^M

mangetout
pois^M *mange-tout*^M

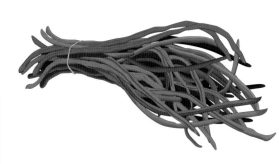

yard-long bean
dolique^M *asperge*^F

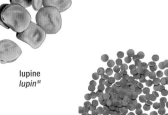

beans
haricots^M

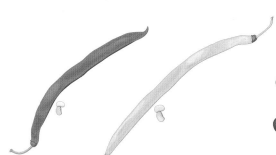

green bean
haricot^M *vert*

wax bean
haricot^M *jaune*

roman bean
haricot^M *romain*

adzuki bean
haricot^M *adzuki*

scarlet runner bean
haricot^M *d'Espagne*^F

mung bean
haricot^M *mungo*

Lima bean
haricot^M *de Lima*

pinto bean
haricot^M *pinto*

red kidney bean
haricot^M *rouge*

black gram
haricot^M *mungo à grain*^M
noir

black bean
haricot^M *noir*

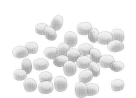

soybeans
graine^F *de soja*^M

soybean sprouts
germes^M *de soja*^M

flageolet
flageolet^M

fruits

fruits^M

berries
baies^F

redcurrant
groseille^F à grappes^F

blackcurrant
cassis^M

gooseberry
groseille^F à maquereau^M

grape
raisin^M

blueberry
myrtille^F d'Amérique^F

bilberry
myrtille^F

red whortleberry
airelle^F

alkekengi
alkékenge^M

cranberry
canneberge^F

raspberry
framboise^F

blackberry
mûre^F

strawberry
fraise^F

stone fruits
fruits^M à noyau^M

apricot
abricot^M

plum
prune^F

peach
pêche^F

nectarine
nectarine^F

cherry
cerise^F

date
datte^F

dry fruits
fruits^M secs

macadamia nut
noix^F de macadamia^M

ginkgo nut
noix^F de ginkgo^M

pistachio nut
pistache^F

pine nut
pignon^M

cola nut
noix^F de cola^M

pecan nut
noix^F de pécan^M

cashew
noix^F de cajou^M

almond
amande^F

hazelnut
noisette^F

walnut
noix^F

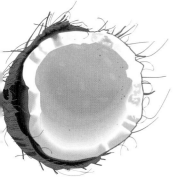

coconut
noix^F de coco^M

chestnut
marron^M

beechnut
faine^F

Brazil nut
noix^F du Brésil^M

pome fruits
fruits^M à pépins^M

pear
poire^F

quince
coing^M

apple
pomme^F

medlar
nèfle^F du Japon^M

fruits

citrus fruits
agrumes[M]

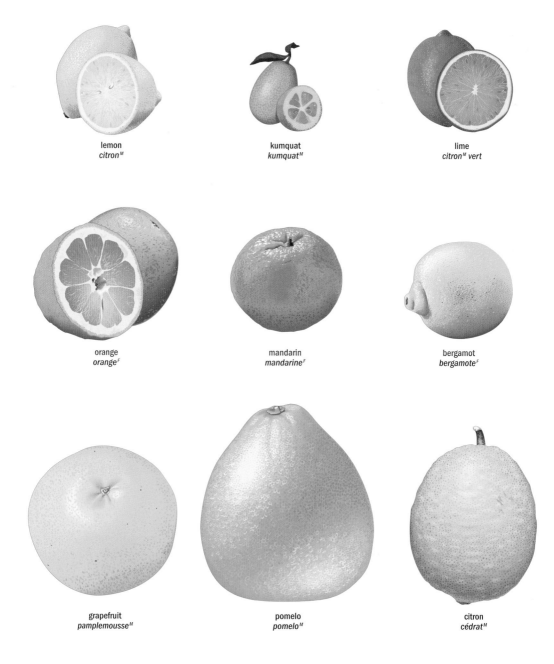

lemon
citron[M]

kumquat
kumquat[M]

lime
citron[M] *vert*

orange
orange[F]

mandarin
mandarine[F]

bergamot
bergamote[F]

grapefruit
pamplemousse[M]

pomelo
pomelo[M]

citron
cédrat[M]

melons
melons^M

cantaloupe
cantaloup^M

casaba melon
melon^M *Casaba*

honeydew melon
melon^M *miel*^M

muskmelon
melon^M *brodé*

canary melon
melon^M *d'Espagne*^F

watermelon
pastèque^F

Ogen melon
melon^M *d'Ogen*

fruits

tropical fruits
fruits^M tropicaux

plantain
banane^F plantain^M

banana
banane^F

longan
longane^M

tamarillo
tamarillo^M

passion fruit
fruit^M de la Passion^F

horned melon
melon^M à cornes^F

mangosteen
mangoustan^M

kiwi
kiwi^M

pomegranate
grenade^F

cherimoya
chérimole^F

jackfruit
jaque^M

pineapple
ananas^M

jaboticaba
jaboticaba^M

litchi; lychee
litchi^M

fig
figue^F

jujube
jujube^M

sapodilla
sapotille^F

guava
goyave^F

rambutan
ramboutan^M

Japanese persimmon
kaki^M

prickly pear
figue^F *de Barbarie*

carambola
carambole^F

Asian pear
pomme^F-*poire*^F

mango
mangue^F

durian
durian^M

papaya
papaye^F

pepino
pepino^M

feijoa
feijoa^M

spices

épices^F

juniper berry
baie^F de genièvre^M

clove
clou^M de girofle^M

allspice
piment^M de la Jamaïque^F

white mustard
moutarde^F blanche

black mustard
moutarde^F noire

black pepper
poivre^M noir

white pepper
poivre^M blanc

pink pepper
poivre^M rose

green pepper
poivre^M vert

nutmeg
noix^F de muscade^F

caraway
carvi^M

cardamom
cardamome^F

cinnamon
cannelle^F

saffron
safran^M

cumin
cumin^M

curry
curry^M

turmeric
curcuma^M

fenugreek
fenugrec^M

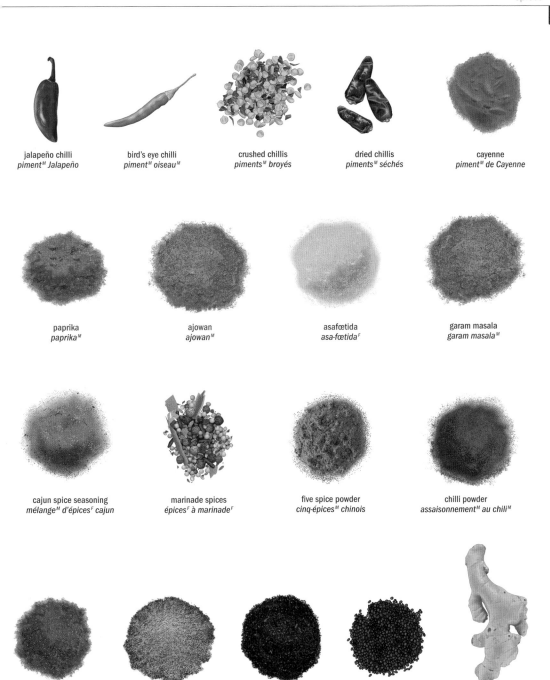

jalapeño chilli
piment^M Jalapeño

bird's eye chilli
piment^M oiseau^M

crushed chillis
piments^M broyés

dried chillis
piments^M séchés

cayenne
piment^M de Cayenne

paprika
paprika^M

ajowan
ajowan^M

asafœtida
asa-fœtida^F

garam masala
garam masala^M

cajun spice seasoning
mélange^M d'épices^F cajun

marinade spices
épices^F à marinade^F

five spice powder
cinq-épices^M chinois

chilli powder
assaisonnement^M au chili^M

ground pepper
poivre^M moulu

ras el hanout
ras-el-hanout^M

sumac
sumac^M

poppy seeds
graines^F de pavot^M

ginger
gingembre^M

condiments

condiments^M

Tabasco™ sauce
sauce^F Tabasco®

Worcestershire sauce
sauce^F Worcestershire

tamarind paste
pâte^F de tamarin^M

vanilla extract
extrait^M de vanille^F

tomato paste
concentré^M de tomate^F

tomato coulis
coulis^M de tomate^F

hummus
hoummos^M

tahini
tahini^M

hoisin sauce
sauce^F hoisin

soy sauce
sauce^F soja^M

powdered mustard
moutarde^F en poudre^F

wholegrain mustard
moutarde^F à l'ancienne^F

Dijon mustard
moutarde^F de Dijon

German mustard
moutarde^F allemande

English mustard
moutarde^F anglaise

American mustard
moutarde^F américaine

FOOD AND KITCHEN

plum sauce
sauce^F aux prunes^F

mango chutney
chutney^M à la mangue^F

harissa
harissa^F

sambal oelek
sambal oelek^M

ketchup
ketchup^M

wasabi
wasabi^M

table salt
sel^M fin

coarse salt
gros sel^M

sea salt
sel^M marin

balsamic vinegar
vinaigre^M balsamique

rice vinegar
vinaigre^M de riz^M

cider vinegar
vinaigre^M de cidre^M

malt vinegar
vinaigre^M de malt^M

wine vinegar
vinaigre^M de vin^M

herbs

fines herbes^F

dill
aneth^M

anise
anis^M

bay
laurier^M

oregano
origan^M

tarragon
estragon^M

basil
basilic^M

sage
sauge^F

thyme
thym^M

mint
menthe^F

parsley
persil^M

chervil
cerfeuil^M

coriander
coriandre^F

rosemary
romarin^M

hyssop
hysope^F

borage
bourrache^F

lovage
livèche^F

savory
sarriette^F

lemon balm
mélisse^F

cereals
céréales^F

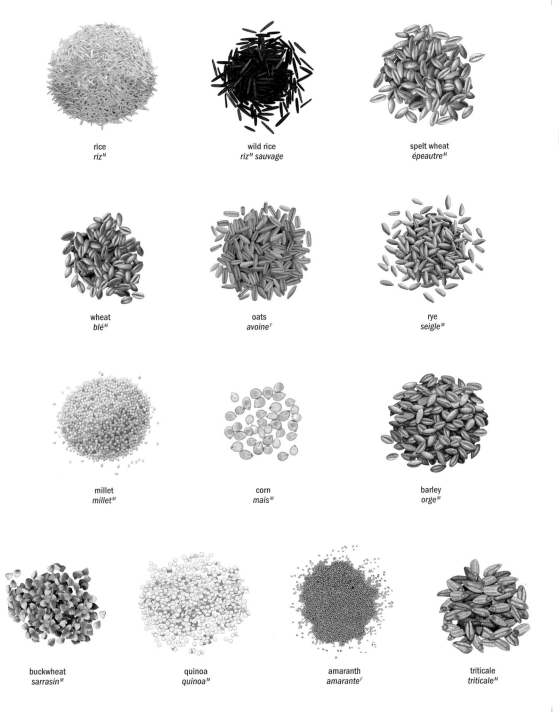

rice
riz^M

wild rice
riz^M sauvage

spelt wheat
épeautre^M

wheat
blé^M

oats
avoine^F

rye
seigle^M

millet
millet^M

corn
maïs^M

barley
orge^M

buckwheat
sarrasin^M

quinoa
quinoa^M

amaranth
amarante^F

triticale
triticale^M

FOOD AND KITCHEN

cereal products

produits^M céréaliers

produits^M céréaliers

flour and semolina
farine^F et semoule^F

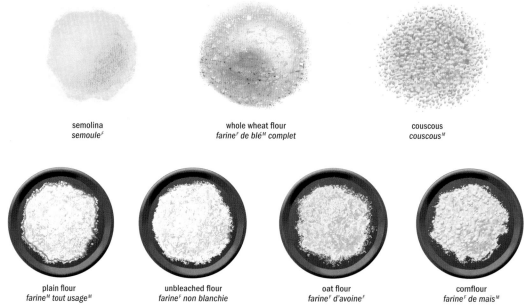

semolina
semoule^F

whole wheat flour
farine^F de blé^M complet

couscous
couscous^M

plain flour
farine^M tout usage^M

unbleached flour
farine^F non blanchie

oat flour
farine^F d'avoine^F

cornflour
farine^F de maïs^M

bread
pain^M

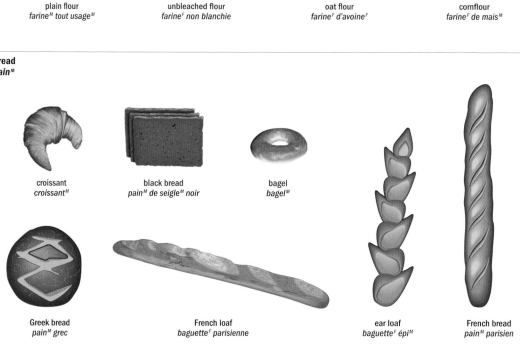

croissant
croissant^M

black bread
pain^M de seigle^M noir

bagel
bagel^M

Greek bread
pain^M grec

French loaf
baguette^F parisienne

ear loaf
baguette^F épi^M

French bread
pain^M parisien

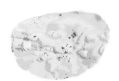

Indian chapati bread
pain^M chapati indien

tortilla
tortilla^F

pitta bread
pain^M pita

Indian naan bread
pain^M naan indien

rye crispbread
cracker^M de seigle^M

filo dough
pâte^F phyllo^F

unleavened bread
pain^M azyme

Danish rye bread
pain^M de seigle^M danois

white bread
pain^M blanc

multigrain bread
pain^M multicéréales

Scandinavian crispbread
cracker^M scandinave

Jewish challah
pain^M tchallah juif

American corn bread
pain^M de maïs^M américain

German rye bread
pain^M de seigle^M allemand

Russian black bread
pain^M noir russe

farmhouse loaf
pain^M de campagne^F

wholemeal bread
pain^M complet

Irish soda bread
pain^M irlandais

cottage loaf
pain^M de mie^F

cereal products

FOOD AND KITCHEN

pasta
pâtes^F alimentaires

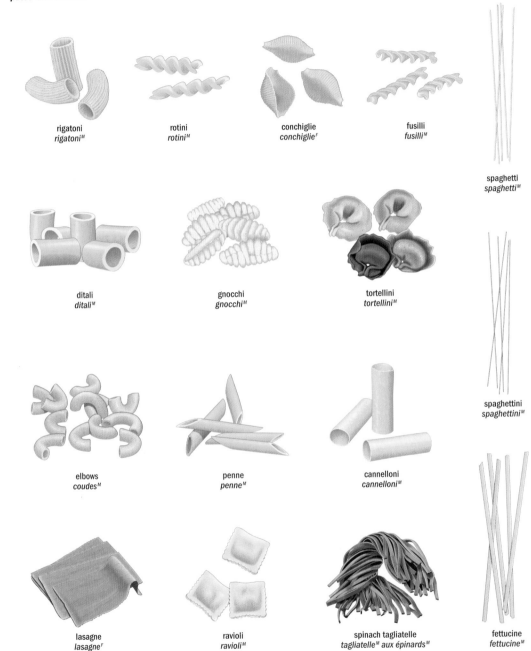

rigatoni
rigatoni^M

rotini
rotini^M

conchiglie
conchiglie^F

fusilli
fusilli^M

spaghetti
spaghetti^M

ditali
ditali^M

gnocchi
gnocchi^M

tortellini
tortellini^M

spaghettini
spaghettini^M

elbows
coudes^M

penne
penne^M

cannelloni
cannelloni^M

lasagne
lasagne^F

ravioli
ravioli^M

spinach tagliatelle
tagliatelle^M aux épinards^M

fettucine
fettucine^M

Asian noodles
nouilles^F asiatiques

soba noodles
nouilles^F soba

somen noodles
nouilles^F somen

udon noodles
nouilles^F udon

rice papers
galettes^F de riz^M

rice noodles
nouilles^F de riz^M

bean thread cellophane noodles
nouilles^F de haricots^M mungo

egg noodles
nouilles^F aux œufs^M

rice vermicelli
vermicelles^M de riz^M

won ton skins
pâtes^F won-ton

rice
riz^M

white rice
riz^M blanc

brown rice
riz^M complet

parboiled rice
riz^M étuvé

basmati rice
riz^M basmati

FOOD AND KITCHEN

coffee and infusions

café^M et infusions^F

FOOD AND KITCHEN

coffee
café^M

green coffee beans
grains^M de café^M verts

roasted coffee beans
grains^M de café^M torréfiés

herbal teas
tisanes^F

linden
tilleul^M

chamomile
camomille^F

verbena
verveine^F

tea
thé^M

green tea
thé^M vert

black tea
thé^M noir

oolong tea
thé^M oolong

tea bag
thé^M en sachet^M

chocolate

chocolat^M

dark chocolate
chocolat^M noir

milk chocolate
chocolat^M au lait^M

cocoa
cacao^M

white chocolate
chocolat^M blanc

sugar

granulated sugar
sucre^M granulé

powdered sugar
sucre^M glace^F

brown sugar
cassonade^F

rock candy
sucre^M candi

molasses
mélasse^F

corn syrup
sirop^M de maïs^M

maple syrup
sirop^M d'érable^M

honey
miel^M

FOOD AND KITCHEN

fats and oils
huiles^F et matières^F grasses

corn oil
huile^F de maïs^M

olive oil
huile^F d'olive^F

sunflower-seed oil
huile^F de tournesol^M

peanut oil
huile^F d'arachide^F

sesame oil
huile^F de sésame^M

shortening
saindoux^M

lard
lard^M

margarine
margarine^F

149

dairy products

produits*M* laitiers

yogurt
*yaourt*M

ghee
*ghee*M

butter
*beurre*M

cream
*crème*F

whipping cream
*crème*F *épaisse*

sour cream
*crème*F *aigre*

milk
*lait*M

homogenized milk
*lait*M *homogénéisé*

goat's milk
*lait*M *de chèvre*F

evaporated milk
*lait*M *concentré*

buttermilk
*babeurre*M

powdered milk
*lait*M *en poudre*F

fresh cheeses
*fromages*M *frais*

cottage cheese
*cottage*M

mozzarella
*mozzarella*F

goat's-milk cheeses
*fromages*M *de chèvre*F

Chèvre cheese
*chèvre*M *frais*

ricotta
*ricotta*F

cream cheese
*fromage*M *à tartiner*

Crottin de Chavignol
*crottin*M *de Chavignol*

pressed cheeses
fromages M *à pâte* F *pressée*

Jarlsberg
jarlsberg M

Emmenthal
emmenthal M

Raclette
raclette F

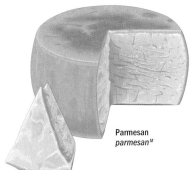

Parmesan
parmesan M

Gruyère
gruyère M

Romano
romano M

blue-veined cheeses
fromages M *à pâte* F *persillée*

Roquefort
roquefort M

Stilton
stilton M

Gorgonzola
gorgonzola M

Danish Blue
bleu M *danois*

soft cheeses
fromages M *à pâte* F *molle*

Pont-l'Évêque
pont-l'évêque M

Coulommiers
coulommiers M

Munster
munster M

Camembert
camembert M

Brie
brie M

meat
viande^F

cuts of beef
découpes^F de bœuf^M

steak
bifteck^M

beef cubes
cubes^M de bœuf^M

minced beef
bœuf^M haché

shank
jarret^M

tenderloin roast
filet^M de bœuf^M

rib roast
rôti^M de côtes^F

back ribs
côtes^F levées de dos^M

cuts of veal
découpes^F de veau^M

veal cubes
cubes^M de veau^M

minced veal
veau^M haché

shank
jarret^M

roast
rôti^M

steak
bifteck^M

chop
côte^F

FOOD AND KITCHEN

cuts of lamb
découpes^F d'agneau^M

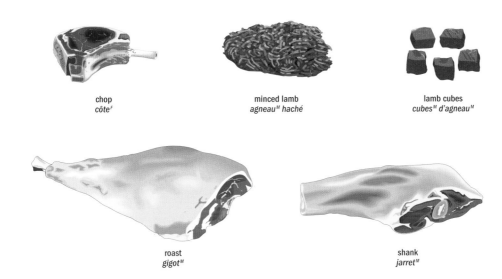

chop
côte^F

minced lamb
agneau^M haché

lamb cubes
cubes^M d'agneau^M

roast
gigot^M

shank
jarret^M

cuts of pork
découpes^F de porc^M

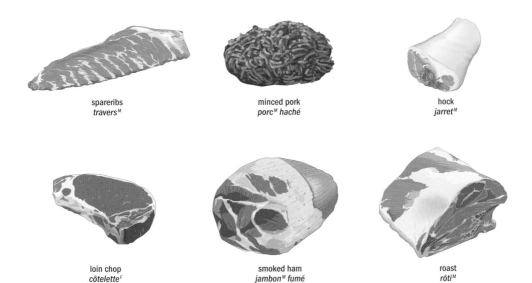

spareribs
travers^M

minced pork
porc^M haché

hock
jarret^M

loin chop
côtelette^F

smoked ham
jambon^M fumé

roast
rôti^M

FOOD AND KITCHEN

offal
abats^M

sweetbreads
ris^M

heart
cœur^M

liver
foie^M

marrow
moelle^F

tongue
langue^F

kidney
rognons^M

brains
cervelle^F

tripe
tripes^F

game
gibier^M

quail
caille^F

pigeon
pigeon^M

hare
lièvre^M

guinea fowl
pintade^F

pheasant
faisan^M

rabbit
lapin^M

poultry

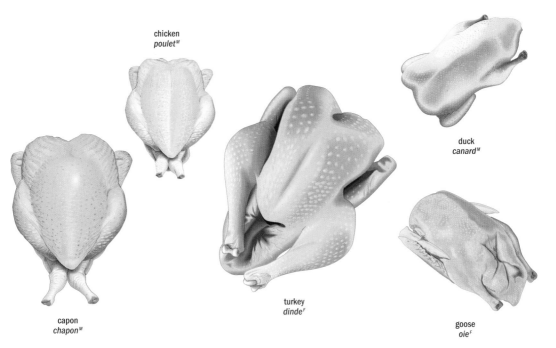

chicken
poulet^M

duck
canard^M

capon
chapon^M

turkey
dinde^F

goose
oie^F

eggs

quail egg
œuf^M *de caille*^F

pheasant egg
œuf^M *de faisane*^F

goose egg
œuf^M *d'oie*^F

ostrich egg
œuf^M *d'autruche*^F

duck egg
œuf^M *de cane*^F

hen egg
œuf^M *de poule*^F

delicatessen

charcuterie^F

rillettes
rillettes^F

foie gras
foie^M *gras*

prosciutto
prosciutto^M

kielbasa sausage
saucisson^M *kielbasa*

mortadella
mortadelle^F

black pudding
boudin^M

chorizo
chorizo^M

pepperoni
pepperoni^M

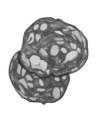

Genoa salami
salami^M *de Gênes*

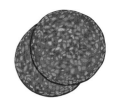

German salami
salami^M *allemand*

Toulouse sausage
saucisse^F *de Toulouse*

merguez sausage
merguez^F

andouillette
andouillette^F

chipolata sausage
chipolata^F

frankfurter
saucisse^F *de Francfort*

pancetta
pancetta^F

cooked ham
jambon^M *cuit*

American bacon
bacon^M *américain*

Canadian bacon
bacon^M *canadien*

FOOD AND KITCHEN

molluscs

molluscs^M

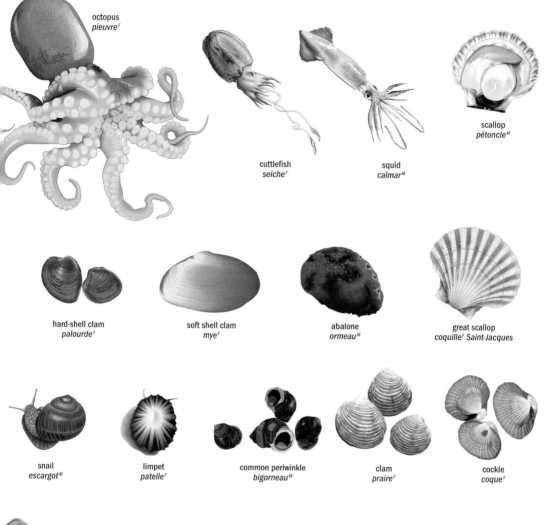

octopus
pieuvre^F

cuttlefish
seiche^F

squid
calmar^M

scallop
pétoncle^M

hard-shell clam
palourde^F

soft shell clam
mye^F

abalone
ormeau^M

great scallop
coquille^F Saint-Jacques

snail
escargot^M

limpet
patelle^F

common periwinkle
bigorneau^M

clam
praire^F

cockle
coque^F

razor clam
couteau^M

oyster
huître^F plate

oyster
huître^F creuse du
Pacifique^M

blue mussel
moule^F

whelk
buccin^M

157

crustaceans

crustacés^M

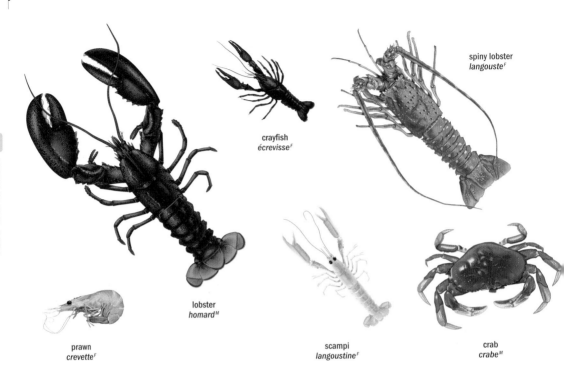

crayfish
écrevisse^F

spiny lobster
langouste^F

lobster
homard^M

prawn
crevette^F

scampi
langoustine^F

crab
crabe^M

cartilaginous fishes

poissons^M cartilagineux

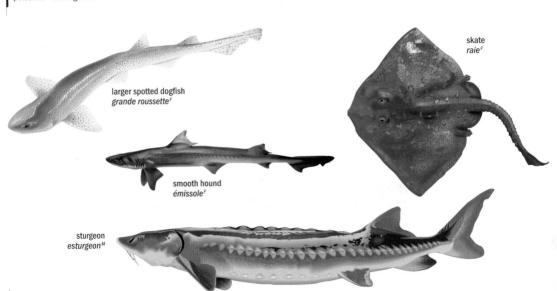

larger spotted dogfish
grande roussette^F

skate
raie^F

smooth hound
émissole^F

sturgeon
esturgeon^M

bony fishes

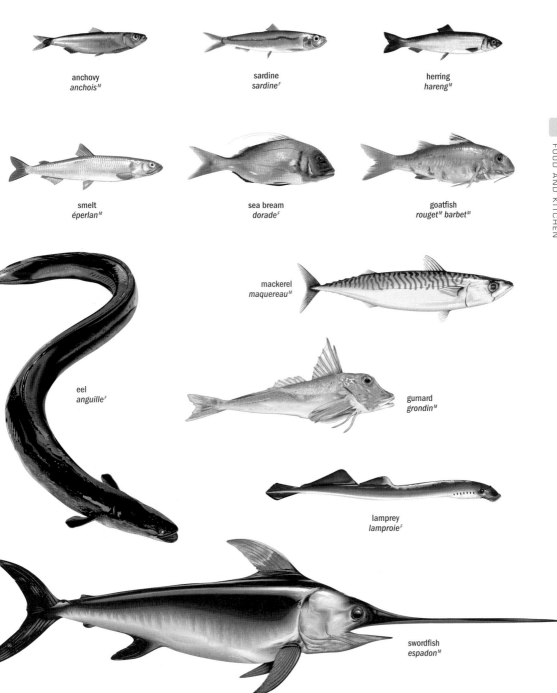

anchovy
anchois^M

sardine
sardine^F

herring
hareng^M

smelt
éperlan^M

sea bream
dorade^F

goatfish
rouget^M *barbet*^M

mackerel
maquereau^M

eel
anguille^F

gurnard
grondin^M

lamprey
lamproie^F

swordfish
espadon^M

bony fishes

bass
perche[F] *truitée*

mullet
mulet[M]

carp
carpe[F]

perch
perche[F]

shad
alose[F]

pike
brochet[M]

pike perch
sandre[M]

bluefish
tassergal[M]

sea bass
bar[M] *commun*

monkfish
baudroie[F]

tuna
thon[M]

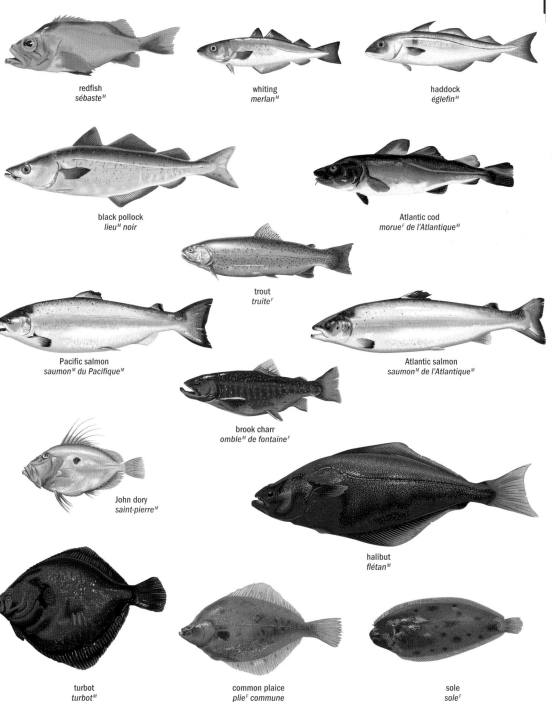

redfish
sébaste^M

whiting
merlan^M

haddock
églefin^M

black pollock
lieu^M *noir*

Atlantic cod
morue^F *de l'Atlantique*^M

trout
truite^F

Pacific salmon
saumon^M *du Pacifique*^M

Atlantic salmon
saumon^M *de l'Atlantique*^M

brook charr
omble^M *de fontaine*^F

John dory
saint-pierre^M

halibut
flétan^M

turbot
turbot^M

common plaice
plie^F *commune*

sole
sole^F

packaging

emballage^M

pouch
sachet^M

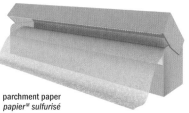

parchment paper
papier^M *sulfurisé*

aluminium foil
papier^M *aluminium*^M

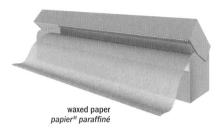

waxed paper
papier^M *paraffiné*

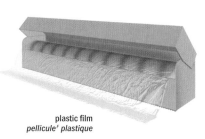

plastic film
pellicule^F *plastique*

freezer bag
sac^M *de congélation*^F

egg carton
boite^F *à œufs*^M

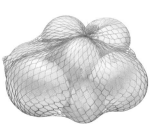

mesh bag
sac^M*-filet*^M

canisters
boites^F *alimentaires*

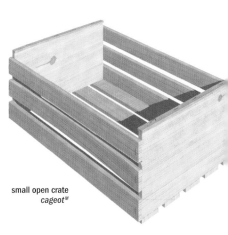

food tray
barquette^F

small crate
caissette^F

small open crate
cageot^M

FOOD AND KITCHEN

FOOD AND KITCHEN

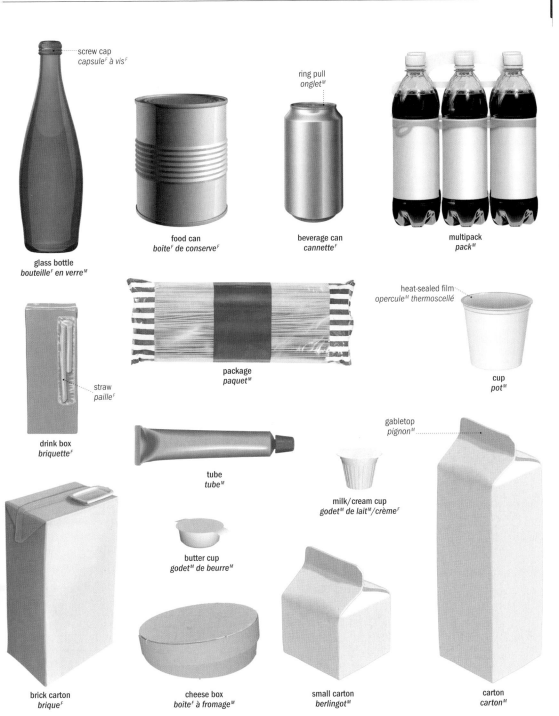

screw cap
capsule^F *à vis*^F

glass bottle
bouteille^F *en verre*^M

food can
boîte^F *de conserve*^F

ring pull
onglet^M

beverage can
cannette^F

multipack
pack^M

package
paquet^M

heat-sealed film
opercule^M *thermoscellé*

cup
pot^M

straw
paille^F

drink box
briquette^F

tube
tube^M

gabletop
pignon^M

milk/cream cup
godet^M *de lait*^M/*crème*^F

butter cup
godet^M *de beurre*^M

brick carton
brique^F

cheese box
boîte^F *à fromage*^M

small carton
berlingot^M

carton
carton^M

kitchen

cuisine^F

FOOD AND KITCHEN

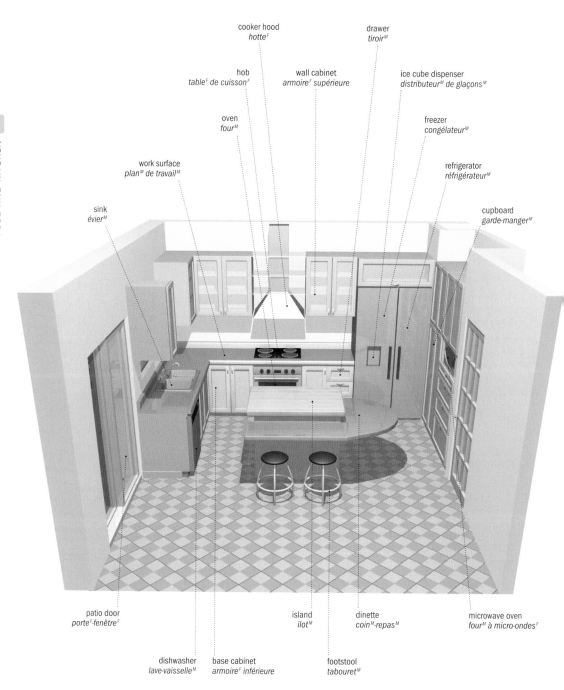

cooker hood
hotte^F

drawer
tiroir^M

hob
table^F *de cuisson*^F

wall cabinet
armoire^F *supérieure*

ice cube dispenser
distributeur^M *de glaçons*^M

oven
four^M

freezer
congélateur^M

work surface
plan^M *de travail*^M

refrigerator
réfrigérateur^M

sink
évier^M

cupboard
garde-manger^M

patio door
porte^F*-fenêtre*^F

island
îlot^M

dinette
coin^M*-repas*^M

microwave oven
four^M *à micro-ondes*^F

dishwasher
lave-vaisselle^M

base cabinet
armoire^F *inférieure*

footstool
tabouret^M

glassware

liqueur glass
verre^M à liqueur^F

port glass
verre^M à porto^M

champagne glass
coupe^F à mousseux^M

brandy glass
verre^M à cognac^M

hock glass
verre^M à vin^M d'Alsace^F

burgundy glass
verre^M à bourgogne^M

bordeaux glass
verre^M à bordeaux^M

white wine glass
verre^M à vin^M blanc

water goblet
verre^M à eau^F

cocktail glass
verre^M à cocktail^M

tall tumbler
verre^M à gin^M

whisky tumbler
verre^M à whisky^M

beer glass
chope^F à bière^F

champagne flute
flûte^F à champagne^M

carafe
carafon^M

decanter
carafe^F

FOOD AND KITCHEN

crockery

vaisselle^F

demitasse
tasse^F à café^M

tea cup
tasse^F à thé^M

coffee mug
chope^F à café^M

cream jug
crémier^M

sugar bowl
sucrier^M

saltcellar
salière^F

pepperpot
poivrière^F

gravy boat
saucière^F

butter dish
beurrier^M

ramekin
ramequin^M

soup bowl
bol^M

rim soup bowl
assiette^F creuse

dinner plate
assiette^F plate

salad plate
assiette^F à salade^F

side plate
assiette^F à dessert^M

teapot
théière^F

serving dish
plat^M ovale

vegetable dish
légumier^M

fish dish
plat^M à poisson^M

hors d'oeuvre dish
ravier^M

water jug
pichet^M

salad bowl
saladier^M

salad dish
bol^M à salade^F

soup tureen
soupière^F

FOOD AND KITCHEN

cutlery
couverts^M

knife
couteau^M

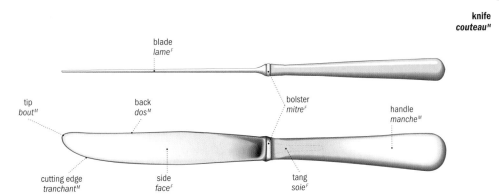

blade
lame^F

bolster
mitre^F

handle
manche^M

tip
bout^M

back
dos^M

cutting edge
tranchant^M

side
face^F

tang
soie^F

fork
fourchette^F

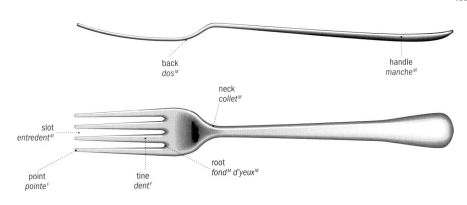

back
dos^M

handle
manche^M

neck
collet^M

slot
entredent^M

point
pointe^F

tine
dent^F

root
fond^M *d'yeux*^M

spoon
cuiller^F

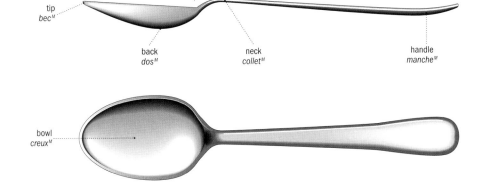

bowl
cuilleron^M

tip
bec^M

back
dos^M

neck
collet^M

handle
manche^M

bowl
creux^M

FOOD AND KITCHEN

cutlery

examples of forks
exemples^M de fourchettes^F

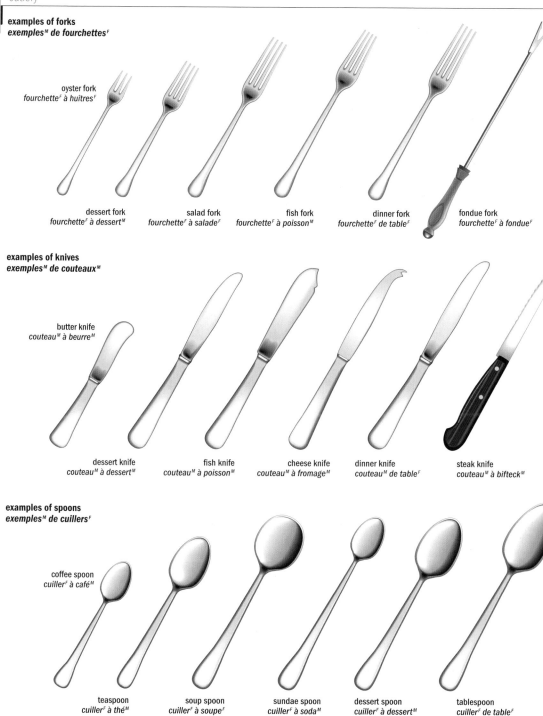

oyster fork
fourchette^F à huîtres^F

dessert fork
fourchette^F à dessert^M

salad fork
fourchette^F à salade^F

fish fork
fourchette^F à poisson^M

dinner fork
fourchette^F de table^F

fondue fork
fourchette^F à fondue^F

examples of knives
exemples^M de couteaux^M

butter knife
couteau^M à beurre^M

dessert knife
couteau^M à dessert^M

fish knife
couteau^M à poisson^M

cheese knife
couteau^M à fromage^M

dinner knife
couteau^M de table^F

steak knife
couteau^M à bifteck^M

examples of spoons
exemples^M de cuillers^F

coffee spoon
cuiller^F à café^M

teaspoon
cuiller^F à thé^M

soup spoon
cuiller^F à soupe^F

sundae spoon
cuiller^F à soda^M

dessert spoon
cuiller^F à dessert^M

tablespoon
cuiller^F de table^F

FOOD AND KITCHEN

kitchen utensils
ustensiles^M de cuisine^F

kitchen knife
couteau^M de cuisine^F

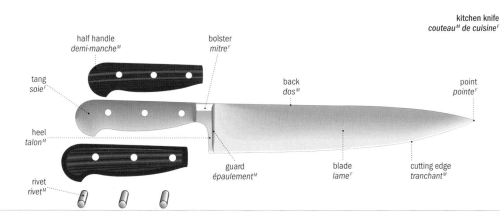

half handle
demi-manche^M

bolster
mitre^F

tang
soie^F

back
dos^M

point
pointe^F

heel
talon^M

guard
épaulement^M

blade
lame^F

cutting edge
tranchant^M

rivet
rivet^M

examples of kitchen knives
exemples^M de couteaux^M de cuisine^F

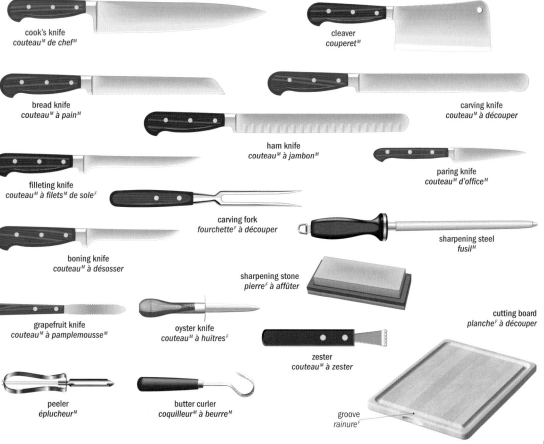

cook's knife
couteau^M de chef^M

cleaver
couperet^M

bread knife
couteau^M à pain^M

carving knife
couteau^M à découper

ham knife
couteau^M à jambon^M

paring knife
couteau^M d'office^M

filleting knife
couteau^M à filets^M de sole^F

carving fork
fourchette^F à découper

sharpening steel
fusil^M

boning knife
couteau^M à désosser

sharpening stone
pierre^F à affûter

cutting board
planche^F à découper

grapefruit knife
couteau^M à pamplemousse^M

oyster knife
couteau^M à huîtres^F

zester
couteau^M à zester

peeler
éplucheur^M

butter curler
coquilleur^M à beurre^M

groove
rainure^F

kitchen utensils

for opening
pour ouvrir

tin opener
ouvre-boîtes^M

bottle opener
décapsuleur^M

wine waiter corkscrew
tire-bouchon^M de sommelier^M

lever corkscrew
tire-bouchon^M à levier^M

for grinding and grating
pour broyer et râper

nutcracker
casse-noix^M

mortar
mortier^M

pestle
pilon^M

mincer
hachoir^M

garlic press
presse-ail^M

lemon squeezer
presse-agrumes^M

nutmeg grater
râpe^F à muscade^F

rotary cheese grater
râpe^F à fromage^M cylindrique

pusher
poussoir^M

grater
râpe^F

crank
manivelle^F

drum
tambour^M

handle
poignée^F

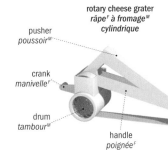

pasta maker
machine^F à faire les pâtes^F

food mill
moulin^M à légumes^M

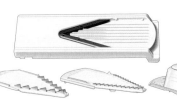

mandoline
mandoline^F

FOOD AND KITCHEN

for measuring
pour mesurer

measuring spoons
cuillers^F doseuses

measuring cups
mesures^F

sugar thermometer
thermomètre^M à sucre^M

instant-read thermometer
thermomètre^M à mesure^F instantanée

measuring jug
tasse^F à mesurer

meat thermometer
thermomètre^M à viande^F

oven thermometer
thermomètre^M de four^M

measuring beaker
verre^M à mesurer

kitchen timer
minuteur^M

egg timer
sablier^M

kitchen scale
balance^F de cuisine^F

---

for straining and draining
pour passer et égoutter

mesh strainer
passoire^F fine

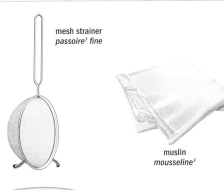

muslin
mousseline^F

chinois
chinois^M

funnel
entonnoir^M

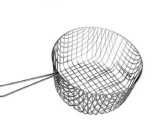

colander
passoire^F

frying basket
panier^M à friture^F

sieve
tamis^M

salad spinner
essoreuse^F à salade^F

kitchen utensils

baking utensils
pour la pâtisserie^F

icing syringe
piston^M *à décorer*

pastry cutting wheel
roulette^F *de pâtissier*^M

pastry brush
pinceau^M *à pâtisserie*^F

egg beater
batteur^M *à œufs*^M

whisk
fouet^M

pastry bag and nozzles
poche^F *à douilles*^F

sifter
tamis^M *à farine*^F

biscuit cutters
emporte-pièces^M

dredger
saupoudreuse^F

pastry blender
mélangeur^M *à pâtisserie*^F

mixing bowls
bols^M *à mélanger*

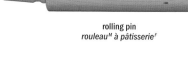

rolling pin
rouleau^M *à pâtisserie*^F

baking sheet
plaque^F *à pâtisserie*^F

bun tin
moule^M *à muffins*^M

soufflé dish
moule^M *à soufflé*^M

charlotte mould
moule^M *à charlotte*^F

removable-bottomed tin
moule^M *à fond*^M *amovible*

pie tin
moule^M *à tarte*^F

quiche tin
moule^M *à quiche*^F

cake tin
moule^M *à gâteau*^M

set of utensils
jeu^M d'ustensiles^M

skimmer
écumoire^F

draining spoon
cuiller^F à égoutter

spatula
spatule^F

slice
pelle^F

ladle
louche^F

potato masher
pilon^M

miscellaneous utensils
ustensiles^M divers

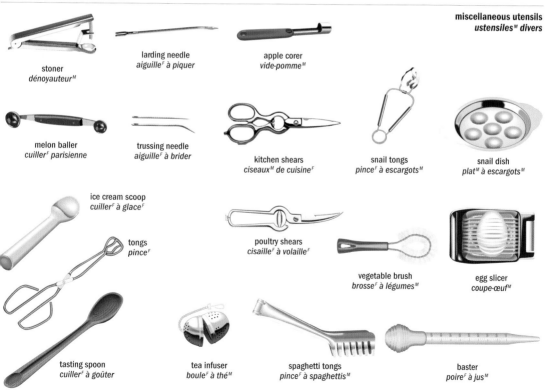

stoner
dénoyauteur^M

larding needle
aiguille^F à piquer

apple corer
vide-pomme^M

melon baller
cuiller^F parisienne

trussing needle
aiguille^F à brider

kitchen shears
ciseaux^M de cuisine^F

snail tongs
pince^F à escargots^M

snail dish
plat^M à escargots^M

ice cream scoop
cuiller^F à glace^F

tongs
pince^F

poultry shears
cisaille^F à volaille^F

vegetable brush
brosse^F à légumes^M

egg slicer
coupe-œuf^M

tasting spoon
cuiller^F à goûter

tea infuser
boule^F à thé^M

spaghetti tongs
pince^F à spaghettis^M

baster
poire^F à jus^M

FOOD AND KITCHEN

cooking utensils

batterie^F de cuisine^F

wok set
wok^M

lid
couvercle^M

rack
grille^F

wok
wok^M

burner ring
collier^M

tajine
tajine^M

fondue set
service^M à fondue^F

fondue pot
caquelon^M

stand
support^M

burner
réchaud^M

fish kettle
poissonnière^F

strainer
grille^F

lid
couvercle^M

dripping pan
lèchefrite^F

terrine
terrine^F

roasting pans
plats^M à rôtir

pressure cooker
autocuiseur^M

pressure regulator
régulateur^M de pression^F

safety valve
soupape^F

Dutch oven
faitout^M

stock pot
marmite^F

couscous kettle
couscoussier^M

frying pan
poêle^F *à frire*

steamer
cuit-vapeur^M

egg poacher
pocheuse^F

sauté pan
sauteuse^F

small saucepan
poêlon^M

diable
diable^M

pancake pan
poêle^F *à crêpes*^F

steamer basket
panier^M *cuit-vapeur*^M

double boiler
bain-marie^M

saucepan
casserole^F

175

domestic appliances

appareils^M électroménagers

for mixing and blending
pour mélanger et battre

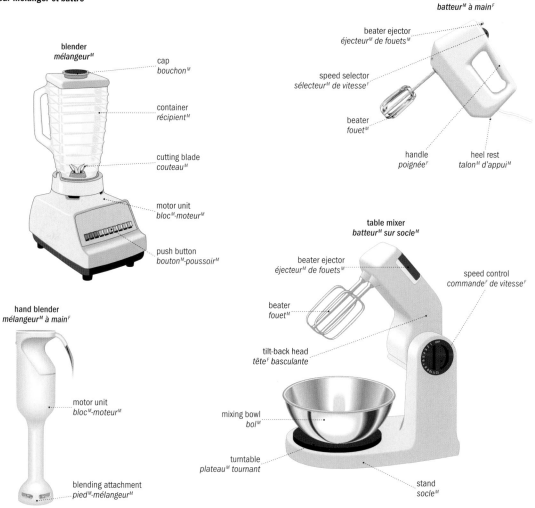

blender
mélangeur^M

cap
bouchon^M

container
récipient^M

cutting blade
couteau^M

motor unit
bloc^M-moteur^M

push button
bouton^M-poussoir^M

hand mixer
batteur^M à main^F

beater ejector
éjecteur^M de fouets^M

speed selector
sélecteur^M de vitesse^F

beater
fouet^M

handle
poignée^F

heel rest
talon^M d'appui^M

table mixer
batteur^M sur socle^M

beater ejector
éjecteur^M de fouets^M

speed control
commande^F de vitesse^F

beater
fouet^M

tilt-back head
tête^F basculante

mixing bowl
bol^M

turntable
plateau^M tournant

stand
socle^M

hand blender
mélangeur^M à main^F

motor unit
bloc^M-moteur^M

blending attachment
pied^M-mélangeur^M

beaters
fouets^M

four-blade beater
fouet^M quatre pales^F

spiral beater
fouet^M en spirale^F

wire beater
fouet^M à fil^M

dough hook
crochet^M pétrisseur

FOOD AND KITCHEN

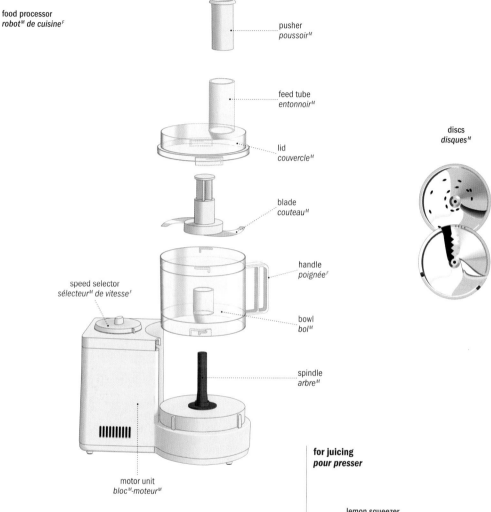

food processor
*robot*ᴹ *de cuisine*ᶠ

pusher
*poussoir*ᴹ

feed tube
*entonnoir*ᴹ

lid
*couvercle*ᴹ

blade
*couteau*ᴹ

speed selector
*sélecteur*ᴹ *de vitesse*ᶠ

handle
*poignée*ᶠ

bowl
*bol*ᴹ

spindle
*arbre*ᴹ

motor unit
*bloc*ᴹ*-moteur*ᴹ

for cutting
pour couper

discs
*disques*ᴹ

for juicing
pour presser

electric knife
*couteau*ᴹ *électrique*

power cord
*cordon*ᴹ *d'alimentation*ᶠ

blade
*lame*ᶠ

on-off switch
*interrupteur*ᴹ

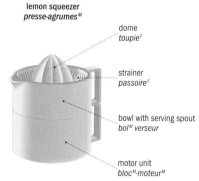

lemon squeezer
*presse-agrumes*ᴹ

dome
*toupie*ᶠ

strainer
*passoire*ᶠ

bowl with serving spout
*bol*ᴹ *verseur*

motor unit
*bloc*ᴹ*-moteur*ᴹ

domestic appliances

for cooking
pour cuire

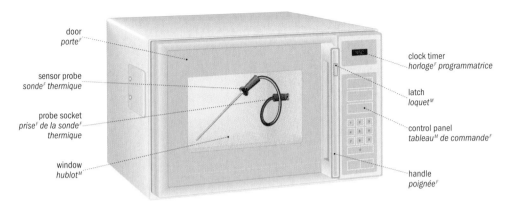

microwave oven
four^M à micro-ondes^F

door
porte^F

sensor probe
sonde^F thermique

probe socket
prise^F de la sonde^F
thermique

window
hublot^M

clock timer
horloge^F programmatrice

latch
loquet^M

control panel
tableau^M de commande^F

handle
poignée^F

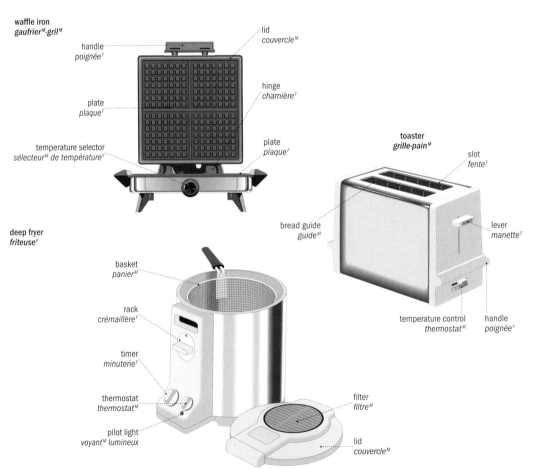

waffle iron
gaufrier^M-gril^M

handle
poignée^F

plate
plaque^F

temperature selector
sélecteur^M de température^F

lid
couvercle^M

hinge
charnière^F

plate
plaque^F

toaster
grille-pain^M

slot
fente^F

bread guide
guide^M

lever
manette^F

temperature control
thermostat^M

handle
poignée^F

deep fryer
friteuse^F

basket
panier^M

rack
crémaillère^F

timer
minuterie^F

thermostat
thermostat^M

pilot light
voyant^M lumineux

filter
filtre^M

lid
couvercle^M

domestic appliances

raclette with grill
raclette^F-gril^M

electric steamer
cuit-vapeur^M électrique

dish
poêlon^M

cooking plate
surface^F de cuisson^F

base
socle^M

cooking dishes
bols^M de cuisson^F

water level indicator
*indicateur^M de niveau^M
d'eau^F*

signal lamp
voyant^M lumineux

timer
minuterie^F

indoor electric grill
gril^M barbecue^M

insulated handle
poignée^F isolante

dripping pan
bac^M ramasse-jus^M

cooking surface
surface^F de cuisson^F

adjustable thermostat
thermostat^M réglable

bread maker
robot^M boulanger^M

lid
couvercle^M

control panel
tableau^M de commande^F

window
hublot^M

loaf pan
moule^M à pain^M

griddle
gril^M électrique

cooking surface
surface^F de cuisson^F

handle
poignée^F

detachable control
commande^F amovible

grease well
collecteur^M de graisse^F

miscellaneous domestic appliances

appareils^M électroménagers divers

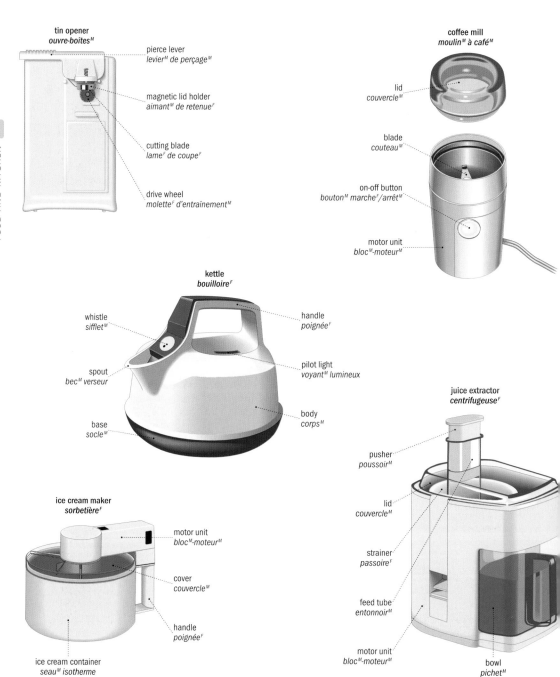

tin opener
ouvre-boîtes^M

pierce lever
levier^M de perçage^M

magnetic lid holder
aimant^M de retenue^F

cutting blade
lame^F de coupe^F

drive wheel
molette^F d'entraînement^M

coffee mill
moulin^M à café^M

lid
couvercle^M

blade
couteau^M

on-off button
bouton^M marche^F/arrêt^M

motor unit
bloc^M-moteur^M

kettle
bouilloire^F

whistle
sifflet^M

handle
poignée^F

spout
bec^M verseur

pilot light
voyant^M lumineux

base
socle^M

body
corps^M

juice extractor
centrifugeuse^F

pusher
poussoir^M

ice cream maker
sorbetière^F

lid
couvercle^M

motor unit
bloc^M-moteur^M

strainer
passoire^F

cover
couvercle^M

feed tube
entonnoir^M

handle
poignée^F

ice cream container
seau^M isotherme

motor unit
bloc^M-moteur^M

bowl
pichet^M

coffee makers
cafetières[F]

FOOD AND KITCHEN

automatic filter coffee maker
cafetière[F] filtre[M]

reservoir
réservoir[M]

water level
niveau[M] d'eau[F]

pilot light
voyant[M] lumineux

on-off switch
interrupteur[M]

lid
couvercle[M]

filter
panier[M]

jug
verseuse[F]

warming plate
plaque[F] chauffante

Neapolitan coffee maker
cafetière[F] napolitaine

espresso machine
machine[F] à espresso[M]

on-off switch
interrupteur[M]

tamper
presse-café[M]

drip tray
cuvette[F] ramasse-gouttes[M]

steam nozzle
buse[F] vapeur[F]

steam control knob
manette[F] vapeur[F]

filter holder
porte-filtre[M]

water tank
réservoir[M] d'eau[F]

vacuum coffee maker
cafetière[F] à infusion[F]

upper bowl
tulipe[F]

stem
tige[F]

lower bowl
ballon[M]

cafetière with plunger
cafetière[F] à piston[M]

espresso coffee maker
cafetière[F] espresso[M]

percolator
percolateur[M]

spout
bec[M] verseur

pilot light
voyant[M] lumineux

exterior of a house

extérieur^M d'une maison^F

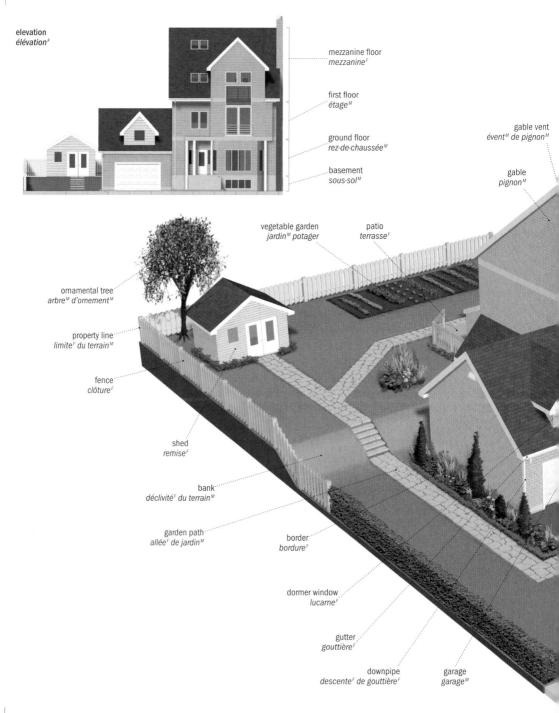

elevation
élévation^F

mezzanine floor
mezzanine^F

first floor
étage^M

ground floor
rez-de-chaussée^M

basement
sous-sol^M

gable vent
évent^M de pignon^M

gable
pignon^M

vegetable garden
jardin^M potager

patio
terrasse^F

ornamental tree
arbre^M d'ornement^M

property line
limite^F du terrain^M

fence
clôture^F

shed
remise^F

bank
déclivité^F du terrain^M

garden path
allée^F de jardin^M

border
bordure^F

dormer window
lucarne^F

gutter
gouttière^F

downpipe
descente^F de gouttière^F

garage
garage^M

HOUSE

ight
erneau^M

lightning conductor
paratonnerre^M

chimney pot
mitron^M

chimney
cheminée^F

roof
toit^M

cornice
corniche^F

stone steps
perron^M

basement window
fenêtre^F *de sous-sol*^M

hedge
haie^F

lawn
pelouse^F

bed
massif^M

pavement
trottoir^M

porch
porche^M

driveway
entrée^F *de garage*^M

site plan
plan^M *du terrain*^M

pool
piscine^F

above ground swimming pool
piscine^F hors sol^M

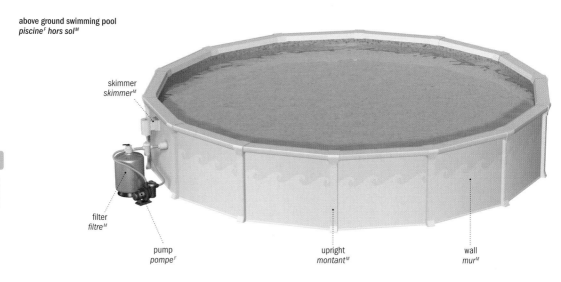

skimmer
skimmer^M

filter
filtre^M

pump
pompe^F

upright
montant^M

wall
mur^M

sunken swimming pool
piscine^F enterrée

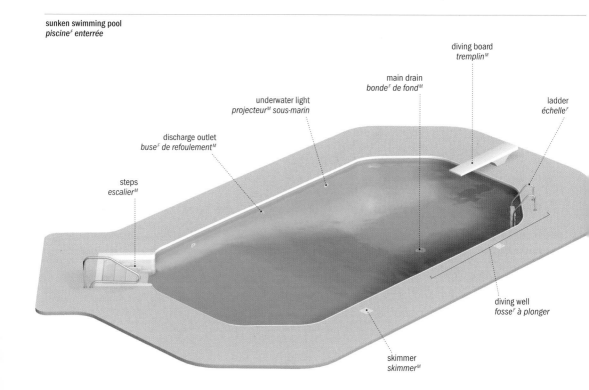

diving board
tremplin^M

main drain
bonde^F de fond^M

underwater light
projecteur^M sous-marin

ladder
échelle^F

discharge outlet
buse^F de refoulement^M

steps
escalier^M

diving well
fosse^F à plonger

skimmer
skimmer^M

exterior door
porte^F extérieure

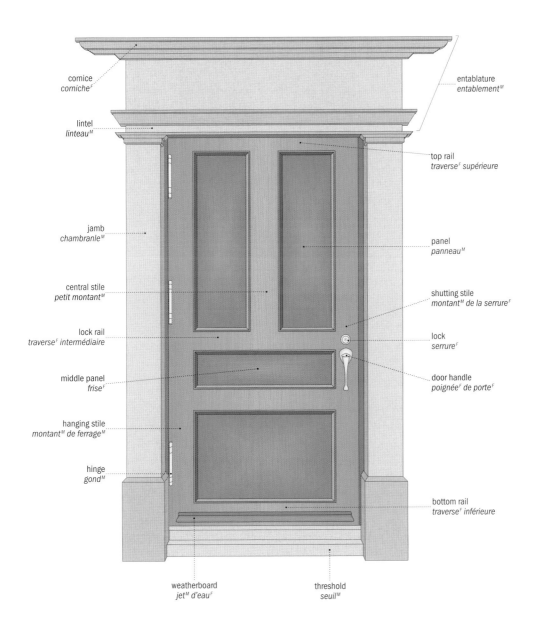

cornice
corniche^F

entablature
entablement^M

lintel
linteau^M

top rail
traverse^F supérieure

jamb
chambranle^M

panel
panneau^M

central stile
petit montant^M

shutting stile
montant^M de la serrure^F

lock rail
traverse^F intermédiaire

lock
serrure^F

middle panel
frise^F

door handle
poignée^F de porte^F

hanging stile
montant^M de ferrage^M

hinge
gond^M

bottom rail
traverse^F inférieure

weatherboard
jet^M d'eau^F

threshold
seuil^M

lock

serrure^F

general view
vue^F d'ensemble^M

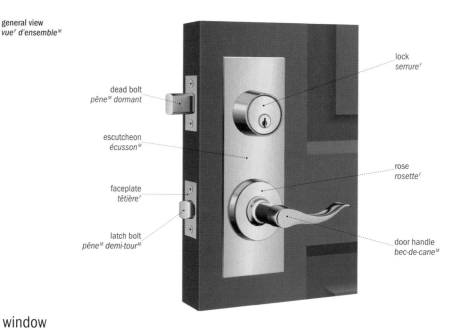

lock
serrure^F

dead bolt
pêne^M dormant

escutcheon
écusson^M

rose
rosette^F

faceplate
têtière^F

latch bolt
pêne^M demi-tour^M

door handle
bec-de-cane^M

window

fenêtre^F

structure
structure^F

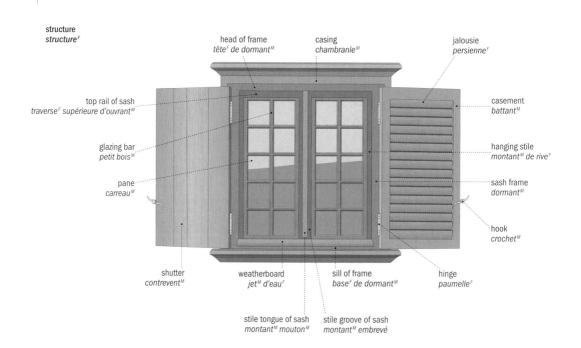

head of frame
tête^F de dormant^M

casing
chambranle^M

jalousie
persienne^F

top rail of sash
traverse^F supérieure d'ouvrant^M

casement
battant^M

glazing bar
petit bois^M

hanging stile
montant^M de rive^F

pane
carreau^M

sash frame
dormant^M

hook
crochet^M

shutter
contrevent^M

weatherboard
jet^M d'eau^F

sill of frame
base^F de dormant^M

hinge
paumelle^F

stile tongue of sash
montant^M mouton^M

stile groove of sash
montant^M embrevé

timber frame

charpente^F

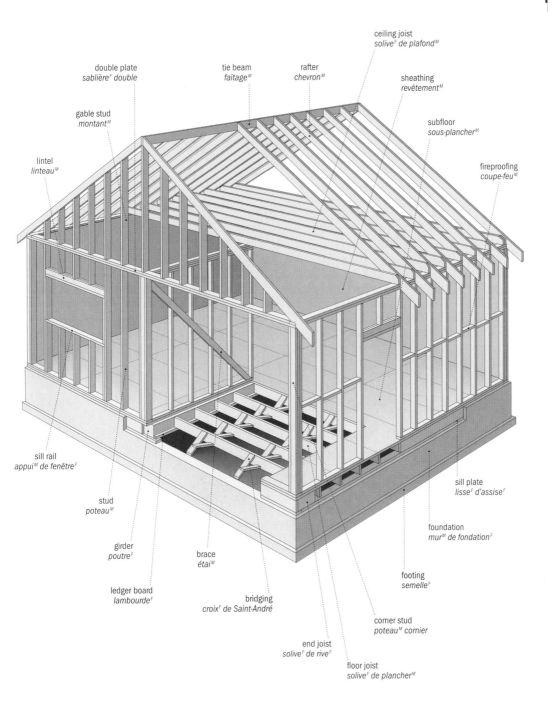

ceiling joist
solive^F *de plafond*^M

double plate
sablière^F *double*

tie beam
faîtage^M

rafter
chevron^M

sheathing
revêtement^M

gable stud
montant^M

subfloor
sous-plancher^M

lintel
linteau^M

fireproofing
coupe-feu^M

sill rail
appui^M *de fenêtre*^F

sill plate
lisse^F *d'assise*^F

stud
poteau^M

foundation
mur^M *de fondation*^F

girder
poutre^F

brace
étai^M

footing
semelle^F

ledger board
lambourde^F

bridging
croix^F *de Saint-André*

corner stud
poteau^M *cornier*

end joist
solive^F *de rive*^F

floor joist
solive^F *de plancher*^M

main rooms

principales pièces^F d'une maison^F

HOUSE

ground floor
rez-de-chaussée^M

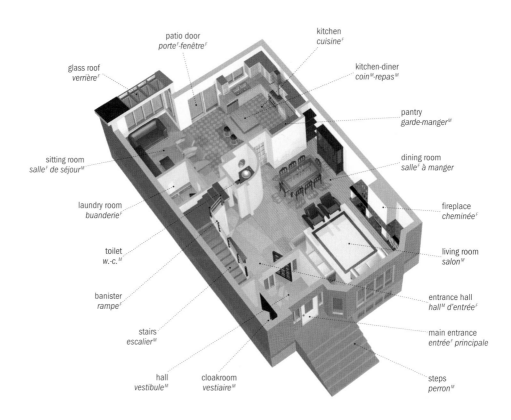

patio door
porte^F-fenêtre^F

kitchen
cuisine^F

glass roof
verrière^F

kitchen-diner
coin^M-repas^M

pantry
garde-manger^M

sitting room
salle^F de séjour^M

dining room
salle^F à manger

laundry room
buanderie^F

fireplace
cheminée^F

toilet
w.-c.^M

living room
salon^M

banister
rampe^F

entrance hall
hall^M d'entrée^F

stairs
escalier^M

main entrance
entrée^F principale

hall
vestibule^M

cloakroom
vestiaire^M

steps
perron^M

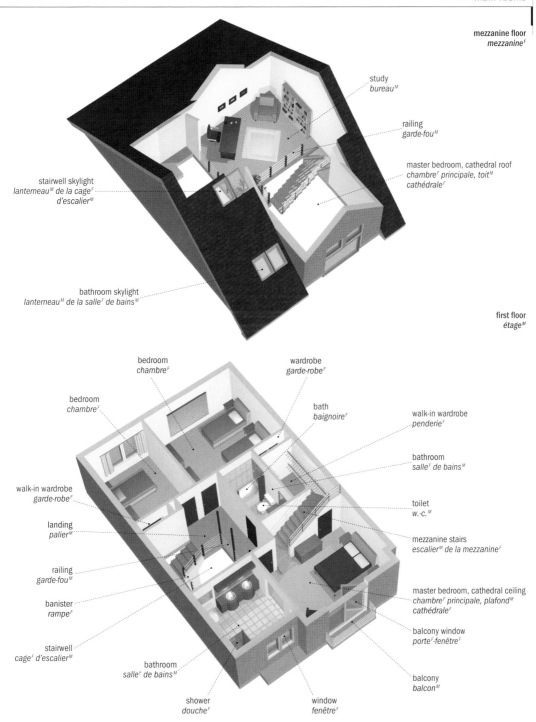

mezzanine floor
mezzanine^F

study
bureau^M

railing
garde-fou^M

master bedroom, cathedral roof
chambre^F *principale, toit*^M
cathédrale^F

stairwell skylight
lanterneau^M *de la cage*^F
d'escalier^M

bathroom skylight
lanterneau^M *de la salle*^F *de bains*^M

first floor
étage^M

bedroom
chambre^F

wardrobe
garde-robe^F

bath
baignoire^F

walk-in wardrobe
penderie^F

bedroom
chambre^F

bathroom
salle^F *de bains*^M

walk-in wardrobe
garde-robe^F

toilet
w.-c.^M

landing
palier^M

mezzanine stairs
escalier^M *de la mezzanine*^F

railing
garde-fou^M

master bedroom, cathedral ceiling
chambre^F *principale, plafond*^M
cathédrale^F

banister
rampe^F

balcony window
porte^F*-fenêtre*^F

stairwell
cage^F *d'escalier*^M

bathroom
salle^F *de bains*^M

shower
douche^F

window
fenêtre^F

balcony
balcon^M

HOUSE

wood flooring

parquet^M

wood flooring on cement screed
parquet^M sur chape^F de ciment^M

wood flooring on wooden base
parquet^M sur ossature^F de bois^M

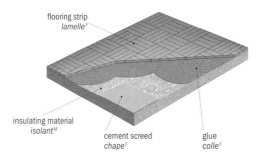

flooring strip
lamelle^F

insulating material
isolant^M

cement screed
chape^F

glue
colle^F

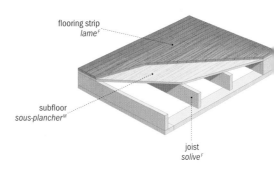

flooring strip
lame^F

subfloor
sous-plancher^M

joist
solive^F

wood flooring types
arrangements^M des parquets^M

woodstrip flooring
parquet^M à coupe^F perdue

brick-bond woodstrip flooring
parquet^M à coupe^F de pierre^F

herringbone parquet
parquet^M à bâtons^M rompus

herringbone pattern
parquet^M en chevrons^M

inlaid parquet
parquet^M mosaïque^F

basket weave pattern
parquet^M en vannerie^F

Arenberg parquet
parquet^M d'Arenberg

Chantilly parquet
parquet^M Chantilly

Versailles parquet
parquet^M Versailles

textile floor coverings

revêtements^M de sol^M textiles

rug
tapis^M

pile carpet
moquette^F

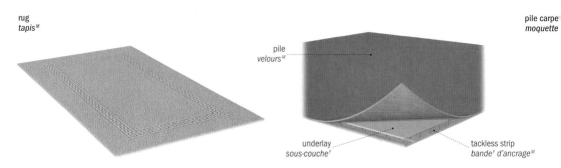

pile
velours^M

underlay
sous-couche^F

tackless strip
bande^F d'ancrage^M

HOUSE

stairs
escalier^M

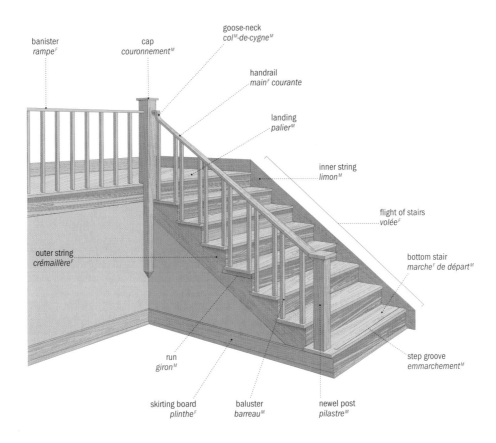

banister
rampe^F

cap
couronnement^M

goose-neck
col^M-*de-cygne*^M

handrail
main^F *courante*

landing
palier^M

inner string
limon^M

flight of stairs
volée^F

outer string
crémaillère^F

bottom stair
marche^F *de départ*^M

run
giron^M

step groove
emmarchement^M

skirting board
plinthe^F

baluster
barreau^M

newel post
pilastre^M

HOUSE

step
marche^F

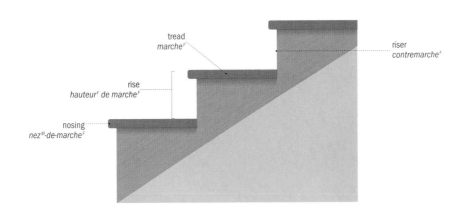

tread
marche^F

riser
contremarche^F

rise
hauteur^F *de marche*^F

nosing
nez^M-*de-marche*^F

wood firing

chauffage^M au bois^M

HOUSE

fireplace
cheminée^F à foyer^M ouvert

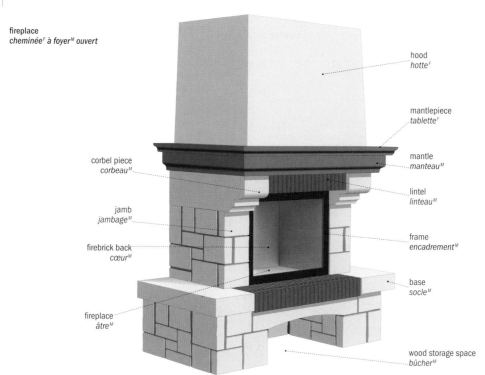

hood
hotte^F

mantlepiece
tablette^F

mantle
manteau^M

lintel
linteau^M

frame
encadrement^M

base
socle^M

wood storage space
bûcher^M

corbel piece
corbeau^M

jamb
jambage^M

firebrick back
cœur^M

fireplace
âtre^M

slow-burning stove
*poêle^M à combustion^F
lente*

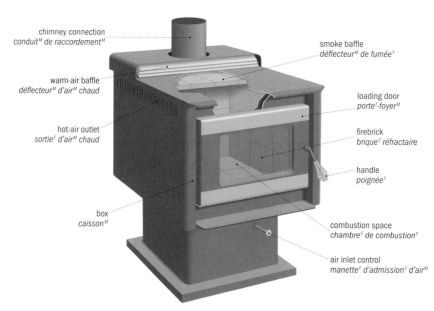

chimney connection
conduit^M de raccordement^M

warm-air baffle
déflecteur^M d'air^M chaud

hot-air outlet
sortie^F d'air^M chaud

box
caisson^M

smoke baffle
déflecteur^M de fumée^F

loading door
porte^F-foyer^M

firebrick
brique^F réfractaire

handle
poignée^F

combustion space
chambre^F de combustion^F

air inlet control
manette^F d'admission^F d'air^M

chimney
cheminée^F

fire irons
accessoires^M *de foyer*^M

rain cap
mitre^F

roof
toit^M

storm collar
collet^M

flashing
solin^M

ceiling
plafond^M

ceiling collar
collier^M *coupe-feu*^M

pipe section
section^F *de conduit*^M

ceiling collar
collier^M *coupe-feu*^M

floor
plancher^M

capped tee
té^M *de base*^F

poker
tisonnier^M

broom
balai^M

tongs
pince^F

shovel
pelle^F

andirons
chenets^M

log carrier
porte-bûches^M

fireplace screen
pare-feu^M

plumbing system

circuit^M de plomberie^F

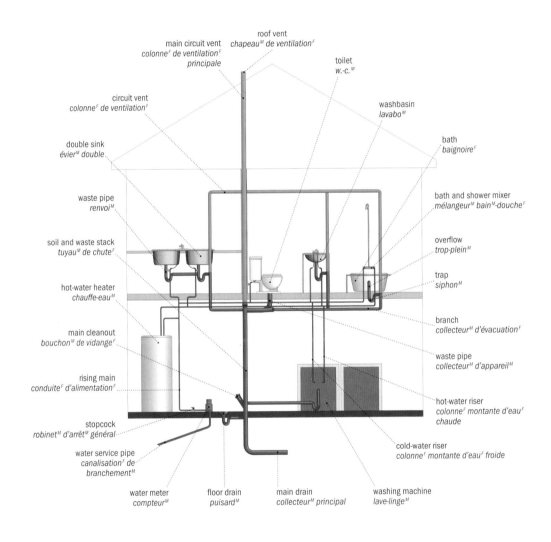

roof vent
chapeau^M de ventilation^F

main circuit vent
colonne^F de ventilation^F
principale

toilet
w.-c.^M

circuit vent
colonne^F de ventilation^F

washbasin
lavabo^M

double sink
évier^M double

bath
baignoire^F

waste pipe
renvoi^M

bath and shower mixer
mélangeur^M bain^M-douche^F

soil and waste stack
tuyau^M de chute^F

overflow
trop-plein^M

hot-water heater
chauffe-eau^M

trap
siphon^M

main cleanout
bouchon^M de vidange^F

branch
collecteur^M d'évacuation^F

waste pipe
collecteur^M d'appareil^M

rising main
conduite^F d'alimentation^F

hot-water riser
colonne^F montante d'eau^F
chaude

stopcock
robinet^M d'arrêt^M général

water service pipe
canalisation^F de
branchement^M

cold-water riser
colonne^F montante d'eau^F froide

water meter
compteur^M

floor drain
puisard^M

main drain
collecteur^M principal

washing machine
lave-linge^M

ventilating circuit
circuit^M de ventilation^F

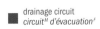

drainage circuit
circuit^M d'évacuation^F

cold-water circuit
circuit^M d'eau^F froide

hot-water circuit
circuit^M d'eau^F chaude

bathroom

salle^F de bains^M

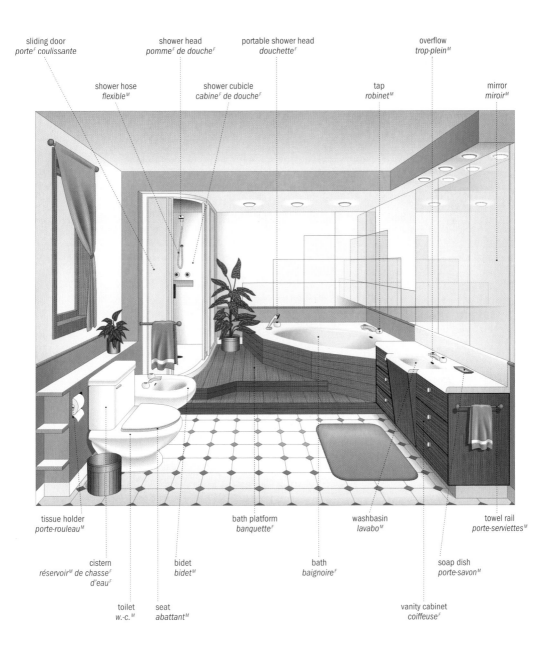

sliding door
porte^F coulissante

shower head
pomme^F de douche^F

portable shower head
douchette^F

overflow
trop-plein^M

shower hose
flexible^M

shower cubicle
cabine^F de douche^F

tap
robinet^M

mirror
miroir^M

tissue holder
porte-rouleau^M

bath platform
banquette^F

washbasin
lavabo^M

towel rail
porte-serviettes^M

cistern
réservoir^M de chasse^F
d'eau^F

bidet
bidet^M

bath
baignoire^F

soap dish
porte-savon^M

toilet
w.-c.^M

seat
abattant^M

vanity cabinet
coiffeuse^F

toilet

w.-c.^M

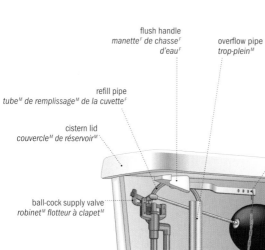
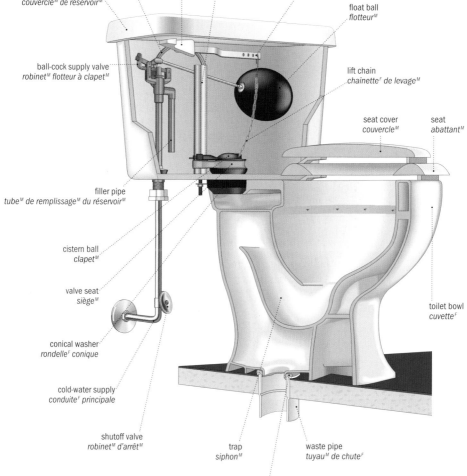

flush handle
*manette^F de chasse^F
d'eau^F*

overflow pipe
trop-plein^M

refill pipe
tube^M de remplissage^M de la cuvette^F

trip lever
levier^M de déclenchement^M

cistern lid
couvercle^M de réservoir^M

float ball
flotteur^M

ball-cock supply valve
robinet^M flotteur à clapet^M

lift chain
chaînette^F de levage^M

seat cover
couvercle^M

seat
abattant^M

filler pipe
tube^M de remplissage^M du réservoir^M

cistern ball
clapet^M

valve seat
siège^M

toilet bowl
cuvette^F

conical washer
rondelle^F conique

cold-water supply
conduite^F principale

shutoff valve
robinet^M d'arrêt^M

trap
siphon^M

waste pipe
tuyau^M de chute^F

wax seal
anneau^M d'étanchéité^F en cire^F

examples of branching

exemples^M de branchement^M

sink with waste disposal unit
évier^M-broyeur^M

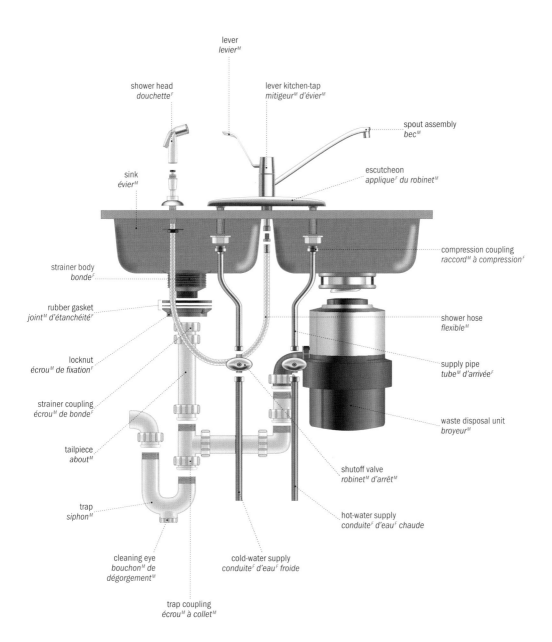

lever
levier^M

shower head
douchette^F

lever kitchen-tap
mitigeur^M d'évier^M

spout assembly
bec^M

sink
évier^M

escutcheon
applique^F du robinet^M

compression coupling
raccord^M à compression^F

strainer body
bonde^F

rubber gasket
joint^M d'étanchéité^F

shower hose
flexible^M

locknut
écrou^M de fixation^F

supply pipe
tube^M d'arrivée^F

strainer coupling
écrou^M de bonde^F

waste disposal unit
broyeur^M

tailpiece
about^M

shutoff valve
robinet^M d'arrêt^M

trap
siphon^M

hot-water supply
conduite^F d'eau^F chaude

cleaning eye
bouchon^M de
dégorgement^M

cold-water supply
conduite^F d'eau^F froide

trap coupling
écrou^M à collet^M

network connection

branchement^M au réseau^M

HOUSE

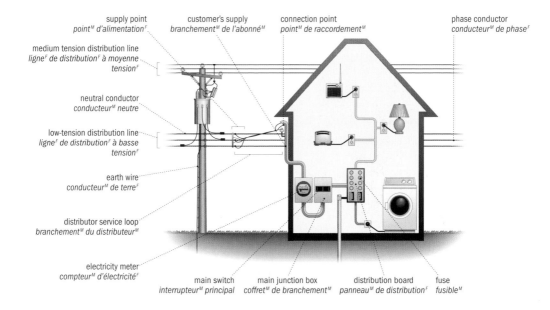

supply point
point^M d'alimentation^F

customer's supply
branchement^M de l'abonné^M

connection point
point^M de raccordement^M

phase conductor
conducteur^M de phase^F

medium tension distribution line
ligne^F de distribution^F à moyenne
tension^F

neutral conductor
conducteur^M neutre

low-tension distribution line
ligne^F de distribution^F à basse
tension^F

earth wire
conducteur^M de terre^F

distributor service loop
branchement^M du distributeur^M

electricity meter
compteur^M d'électricité^F

main switch
interrupteur^M principal

main junction box
coffret^M de branchement^M

distribution board
panneau^M de distribution^F

fuse
fusible^M

contact devices

dispositifs^M de contact^M

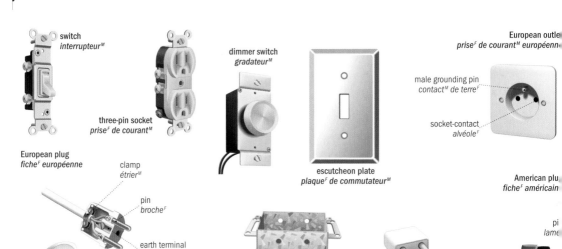

switch
interrupteur^M

three-pin socket
prise^F de courant^M

dimmer switch
gradateur^M

European outle
prise^F de courant^M européenn

male grounding pin
contact^M de terre^F

socket-contact
alvéole^F

European plug
fiche^F européenne

clamp
étrier^M

pin
broche^F

earth terminal
contact^M de terre^F

terminal
borne^F

cover
couvercle^M

escutcheon plate
plaque^F de commutateur^M

electrical box
boîte^F d'encastrement^M

plug adapter
adaptateur^M de fiche^F

American plu
fiche^F américain

pi
lame

earthing pi
contact^M de terre

lighting

éclairage^M

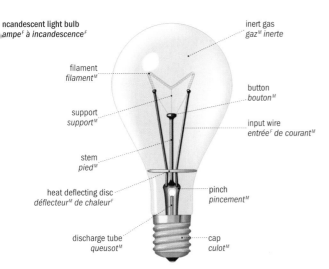

incandescent light bulb
lampe^F à incandescence^F

inert gas
gaz^M inerte

filament
filament^M

button
bouton^M

support
support^M

input wire
entrée^F de courant^M

stem
pied^M

heat deflecting disc
déflecteur^M de chaleur^F

pinch
pincement^M

discharge tube
queusot^M

cap
culot^M

tube
ampoule^F

lampholder
douille^F de lampe^F

screw cap
culot^M à vis^F

energy saving bulb
lampe^F à économie^F d'énergie^F

fluorescent tube
tube^M fluorescent

bulb
ampoule^F

tube retention clip
attache^F du tube^M

mounting plate
plaque^F de montage^M

electronic ballast
ballast^M électronique

housing
boîtier^M

cap
culot^M

bayonet cap
culot^M à baïonnette^F

tungsten-halogen bulb
lampe^F à halogène^M

fluorescent tube
tube^M fluorescent

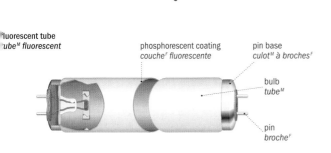

phosphorescent coating
couche^F fluorescente

pin base
culot^M à broches^F

bulb
tube^M

pin
broche^F

pin
broche^F

armchair

fauteuil^M

HOUSE

parts
parties^F

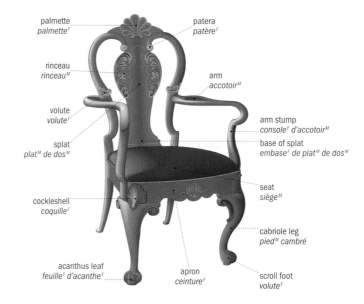

palmette
palmette^F

patera
patère^F

rinceau
rinceau^M

arm
accotoir^M

volute
volute^F

arm stump
console^F *d'accotoir*^M

splat
plat^M *de dos*^M

base of splat
embase^F *de plat*^M *de dos*^M

cockleshell
coquille^F

seat
siège^M

cabriole leg
pied^M *cambré*

acanthus leaf
feuille^F *d'acanthe*^F

apron
ceinture^F

scroll foot
volute^F

examples of armchairs
exemples^M *de fauteuils*^M

Wassily chair
fauteuil^M *Wassily*

director's chair
fauteuil^M *metteur*^M *en scène*^F

rocking chair
fauteuil^M *à bascule*^F

cabriole chair
cabriolet^M

méridienne
méridienne^F

chaise longue
récamier^M

club chair
fauteuil^M *club*^M

bergère
bergère^F

sofa
canapé^M

two-seater settee
causeuse^F

chesterfield
canapé^M *capitonné*

side chair

chaise^F

parts
parties^F

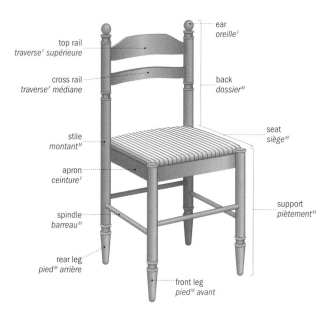

ear
oreille^F

top rail
traverse^F *supérieure*

cross rail
traverse^F *médiane*

back
dossier^M

stile
montant^M

seat
siège^M

apron
ceinture^F

support
piètement^M

spindle
barreau^M

rear leg
pied^M *arrière*

front leg
pied^M *avant*

examples of chairs
exemples^M *de chaises*^F

rocking chair
chaise^F à bascule^F

stacking chairs
chaises^F empilables

folding chair
chaise^F pliante

recliner
chaise^F longue

seats

sièges^M

ottoman
pouf^M

bench
banc^M

banquette
banquette^F

footstool
tabouret^M

bean bag chair
fauteuil^M-sac^M

step chair
chaise^F-escabeau^M

bar stool
tabouret^M de bar^M

table

table^F

gate-leg table
table^F à abattants^M

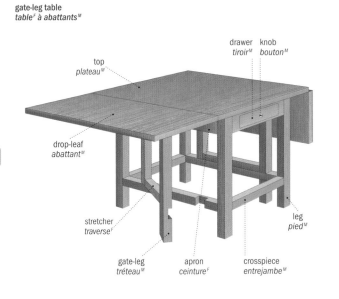

drawer
tiroir^M

knob
bouton^M

top
plateau^M

drop-leaf
abattant^M

stretcher
traverse^F

gate-leg
tréteau^M

apron
ceinture^F

crosspiece
entrejambe^M

leg
pied^M

examples of tables
exemples^M de tables^F

extending table
table^F à rallonges^F

top
plateau^M

extension
rallonge^F

nest of tables
tables^F gigognes

serving trolley
desserte^F

storage furniture

meubles^M de rangement^M

armoire
armoire^F

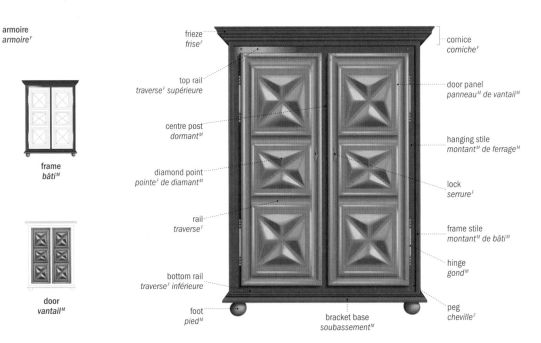

frame
bâti^M

door
vantail^M

frieze
frise^F

top rail
traverse^F supérieure

centre post
dormant^M

diamond point
pointe^F de diamant^M

rail
traverse^F

bottom rail
traverse^F inférieure

foot
pied^M

bracket base
soubassement^M

cornice
corniche^F

door panel
panneau^M de vantail^M

hanging stile
montant^M de ferrage^M

lock
serrure^F

frame stile
montant^M de bâti^M

hinge
gond^M

peg
cheville^F

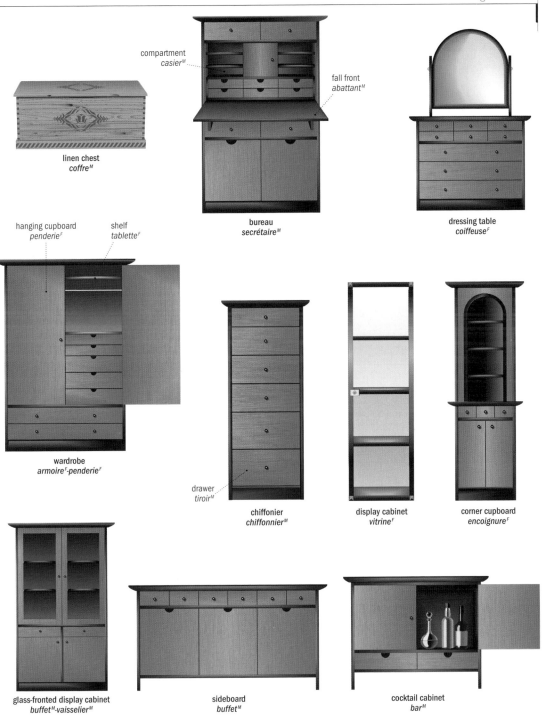

linen chest
coffre^M

compartment
casier^M

fall front
abattant^M

bureau
secrétaire^M

dressing table
coiffeuse^F

hanging cupboard
penderie^F

shelf
tablette^F

wardrobe
armoire^F-penderie^F

drawer
tiroir^M

chiffonier
chiffonnier^M

display cabinet
vitrine^F

corner cupboard
encoignure^F

glass-fronted display cabinet
buffet^M-vaisselier^M

sideboard
buffet^M

cocktail cabinet
bar^M

bed

lit^M

sofa bed
canapé^M convertible

futon
futon^M

frame
cadre^M

parts
parties^F

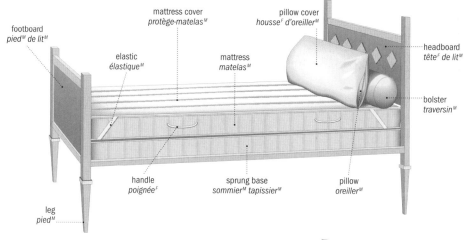

footboard
pied^M de lit^M

mattress cover
protège-matelas^M

pillow cover
housse^F d'oreiller^M

headboard
tête^F de lit^M

elastic
élastique^M

mattress
matelas^M

bolster
traversin^M

handle
poignée^F

sprung base
sommier^M tapissier^M

pillow
oreiller^M

leg
pied^M

bed linen
literie^F

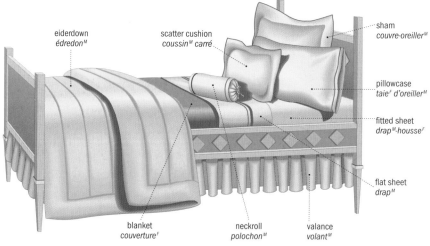

eiderdown
édredon^M

scatter cushion
coussin^M carré

sham
couvre-oreiller^M

pillowcase
taie^F d'oreiller^M

fitted sheet
drap^M-housse^F

flat sheet
drap^M

blanket
couverture^F

neckroll
polochon^M

valance
volant^M

children's furniture
meubles^M d'enfants^M

nursery
lit^M pliant

changing table
plan^M à langer

top rail
bordure^F

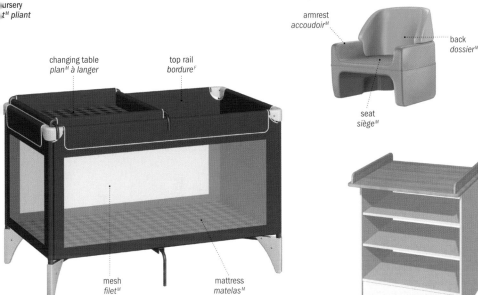

mesh
filet^M

mattress
matelas^M

booster seat
rehausseur^M

armrest
accoudoir^M

back
dossier^M

seat
siège^M

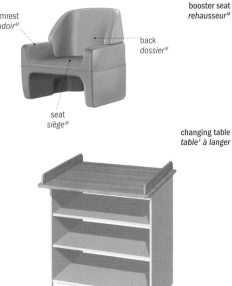

changing table
table^F à langer

HOUSE

high chair
chaise^F haute

back
dossier^M

tray
plateau^M

waist belt
ceinture^F ventrale

footrest
repose-pieds^M

leg
pied^M

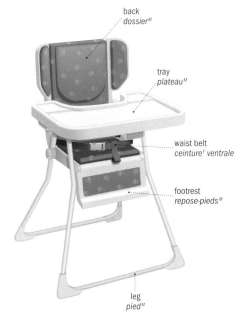

cot
lit^M à barreaux^M

headboard
tête^F de lit^M

barrier
barrière^F

slat
barreau^M

caster
roulette^F

drawer
tiroir^M

mattress
matelas^M

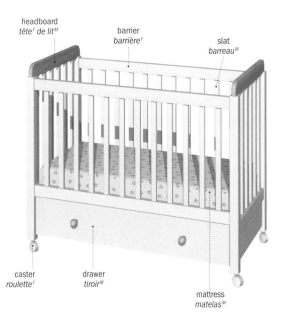

lights

luminaires^M

ceiling fitting
plafonnier^M

clamp spotlight
spot^M à pince^F

hanging pendant
suspension^F

halogen desk lamp
lampe^F de bureau^M
halogène

arm
bras^M

adjustable lamp
lampe^F d'architecte

base
socle^M

on-off switch
interrupteur^M

arm
bras^M

shade
abat-jour^M

shade
abat-jour^M

bed lamp
lampe^F liseuse

spring
ressort^M

adjustable clamp
support^M de fixation^F

shade
abat-jour^M

base
socle^M

stand
pied^M

standard lamp
lampadaire^M

table lamp
lampe^F de table^F

desk lamp
lampe^F de bureau^M

chandelier
lustre^M

sconce
coupelle^F

crystal drop
pendeloque^F

crystal button
pampille^F

column
fût^M

track lighting
rail^M *d'éclairage*^M

track frame
gouttière^F

contact lever
manette^F *de contact*^M

transformer
transformateur^M

spot
spot^M

wall lantern
lanterne^F *murale*

swivel wall lamp
applique^F *orientable*

wall light
applique^F

multiple light fitting
rampe^F *d'éclairage*^M

post lantern
lanterne^F *de pied*^M

domestic appliances

appareils^M électroménagers

steam iron
fer^M à vapeur^F

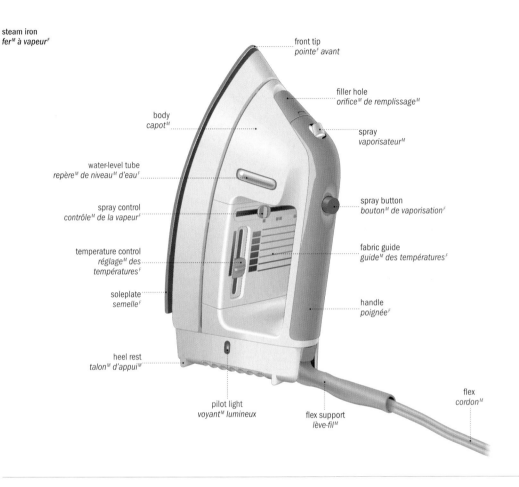

front tip
pointe^F avant

filler hole
orifice^M de remplissage^M

body
capot^M

spray
vaporisateur^M

water-level tube
repère^M de niveau^M d'eau^F

spray control
contrôle^M de la vapeur^F

spray button
bouton^M de vaporisation^F

temperature control
réglage^M des températures^F

fabric guide
guide^M des températures^F

soleplate
semelle^F

handle
poignée^F

heel rest
talon^M d'appui^M

flex
cordon^M

pilot light
voyant^M lumineux

flex support
lève-fil^M

hand vacuum cleaner
aspirateur^M à main^F

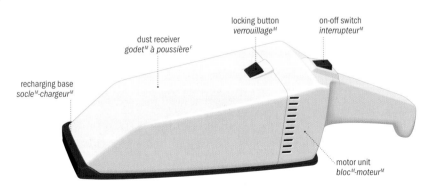

locking button
verrouillage^M

on-off switch
interrupteur^M

dust receiver
godet^M à poussière^F

recharging base
socle^M-chargeur^M

motor unit
bloc^M-moteur^M

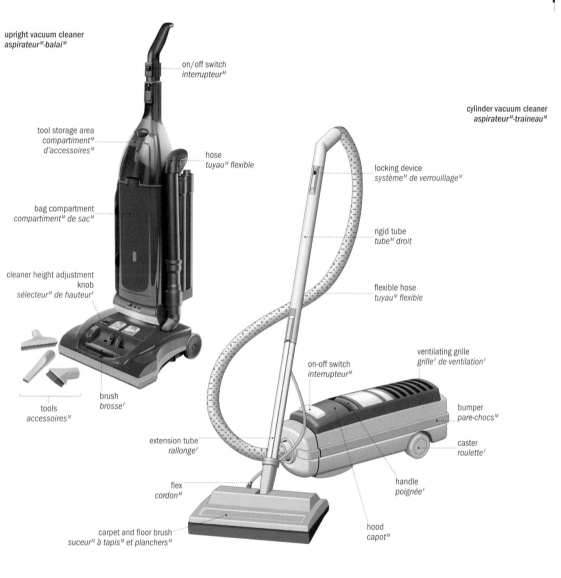

upright vacuum cleaner
*aspirateur*M*-balai*M

on/off switch
*interrupteur*M

tool storage area
*compartiment*M
*d'accessoires*M

hose
*tuyau*M *flexible*

bag compartment
*compartiment*M *de sac*M

cleaner height adjustment
knob
*sélecteur*M *de hauteur*F

tools
*accessoires*M

brush
*brosse*F

cylinder vacuum cleaner
*aspirateur*M*-traineau*M

locking device
*système*M *de verrouillage*M

rigid tube
*tube*M *droit*

flexible hose
*tuyau*M *flexible*

ventilating grille
*grille*F *de ventilation*F

on-off switch
*interrupteur*M

bumper
*pare-chocs*M

caster
*roulette*F

extension tube
*rallonge*F

handle
*poignée*F

flex
*cordon*M

carpet and floor brush
*suceur*M *à tapis*M *et planchers*M

hood
*capot*M

HOUSE

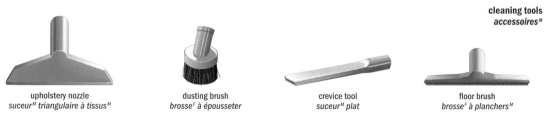

cleaning tools
*accessoires*M

upholstery nozzle
*suceur*M *triangulaire à tissus*M

dusting brush
*brosse*F *à épousseter*

crevice tool
*suceur*M *plat*

floor brush
*brosse*F *à planchers*M

domestic appliances

HOUSE

extractor hood
hotte^F

gas cooke
cuisinière^F à gaz

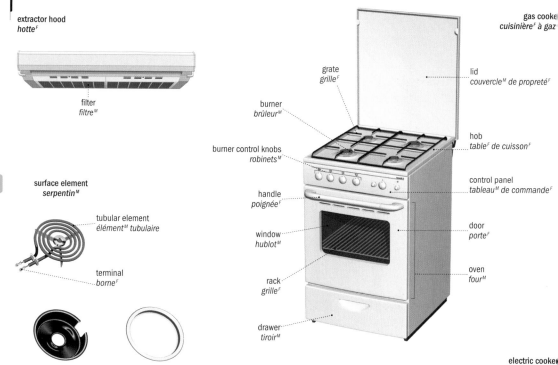

filter
filtre^M

grate
grille^F

lid
couvercle^M de propreté^F

surface element
serpentin^M

burner
brûleur^M

hob
table^F de cuisson^F

burner control knobs
robinets^M

tubular element
élément^M tubulaire

control panel
tableau^M de commande^F

handle
poignée^F

terminal
borne^F

window
hublot^M

door
porte^F

rack
grille^F

oven
four^M

drip bowl
cuvette^F

trim ring
anneau^M

drawer
tiroir^M

electric cooke
cuisinière^F électrique

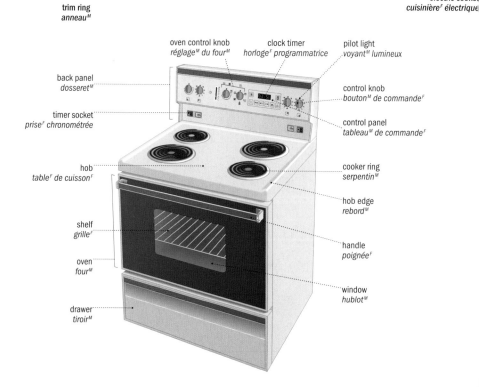

oven control knob
réglage^M du four^M

clock timer
horloge^F programmatrice

pilot light
voyant^M lumineux

back panel
dosseret^M

control knob
bouton^M de commande^F

timer socket
prise^F chronométrée

control panel
tableau^M de commande^F

hob
table^F de cuisson^F

cooker ring
serpentin^M

hob edge
rebord^M

shelf
grille^F

handle
poignée^F

oven
four^M

window
hublot^M

drawer
tiroir^M

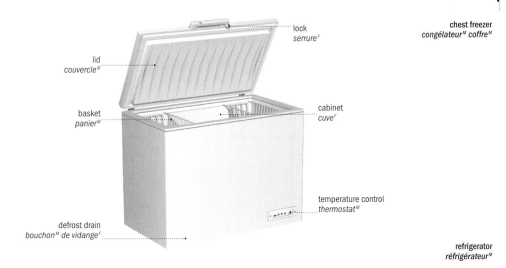

chest freezer
congélateur^M *coffre*^{M}

lock
serrure^F

lid
couvercle^M

basket
panier^M

cabinet
cuve^F

temperature control
thermostat^M

defrost drain
bouchon^M *de vidange*^{F}

refrigerator
réfrigérateur^M

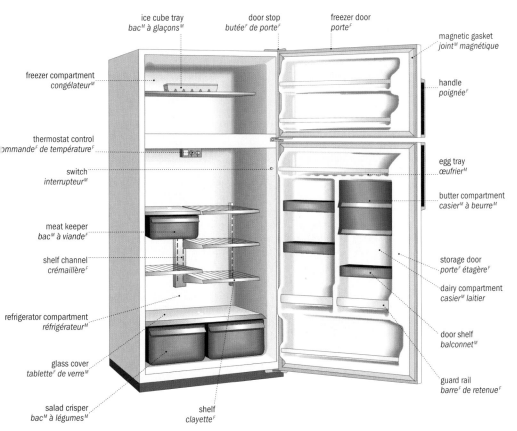

ice cube tray
bac^M *à glaçons*^{M}

door stop
butée^F *de porte*^{F}

freezer door
porte^F

magnetic gasket
joint^M *magnétique*

freezer compartment
congélateur^M

handle
poignée^F

thermostat control
commande^F *de température*^{F}

egg tray
œufrier^M

switch
interrupteur^M

butter compartment
casier^M *à beurre*^{M}

meat keeper
bac^M *à viande*^{F}

shelf channel
crémaillère^F

storage door
porte^F *étagère*^{F}

dairy compartment
casier^M *laitier*

refrigerator compartment
réfrigérateur^M

door shelf
balconnet^M

glass cover
tablette^F *de verre*^{M}

salad crisper
bac^M *à légumes*^{M}

shelf
clayette^F

guard rail
barre^F *de retenue*^{F}

HOUSE

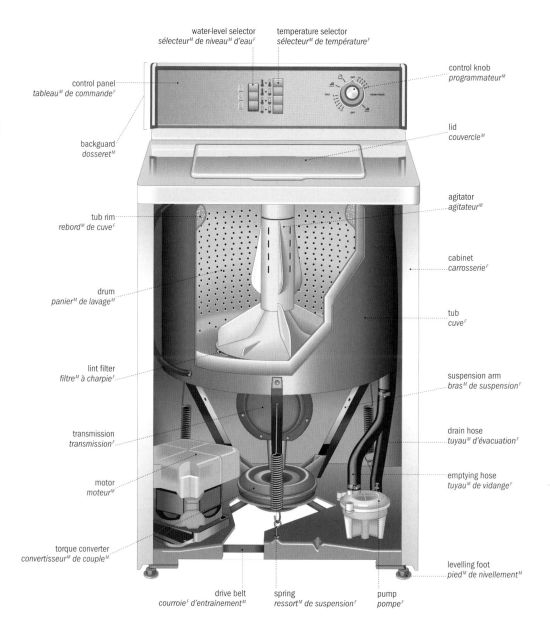

domestic appliances

HOUSE

washing machine
lave-linge^M

water-level selector
sélecteur^M *de niveau*^M *d'eau*^F

temperature selector
sélecteur^M *de température*^F

control knob
programmateur^M

control panel
tableau^M *de commande*^F

lid
couvercle^M

backguard
dosseret^M

agitator
agitateur^M

tub rim
rebord^M *de cuve*^F

cabinet
carrosserie^F

drum
panier^M *de lavage*^M

tub
cuve^F

lint filter
filtre^M *à charpie*^F

suspension arm
bras^M *de suspension*^F

transmission
transmission^F

drain hose
tuyau^M *d'évacuation*^F

motor
moteur^M

emptying hose
tuyau^M *de vidange*^F

torque converter
convertisseur^M *de couple*^M

levelling foot
pied^M *de nivellement*^M

drive belt
courroie^F *d'entraînement*^M

spring
ressort^M *de suspension*^F

pump
pompe^F

domestic appliances

electric tumble dryer
*sèche-linge*M *électrique*

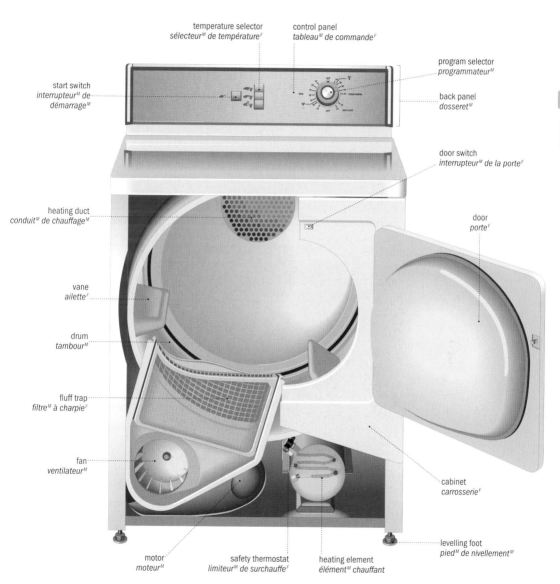

temperature selector
*sélecteur*M *de température*F

control panel
*tableau*M *de commande*F

program selector
*programmateur*M

start switch
*interrupteur*M *de*
*démarrage*M

back panel
*dosseret*M

door switch
*interrupteur*M *de la porte*F

door
*porte*F

heating duct
*conduit*M *de chauffage*M

vane
*ailette*F

drum
*tambour*M

fluff trap
*filtre*M *à charpie*F

fan
*ventilateur*M

cabinet
*carrosserie*F

levelling foot
*pied*M *de nivellement*M

motor
*moteur*M

safety thermostat
*limiteur*M *de surchauffe*F

heating element
*élément*M *chauffant*

HOUSE

domestic appliances

HOUSE

control panel
tableau^M de commande^F

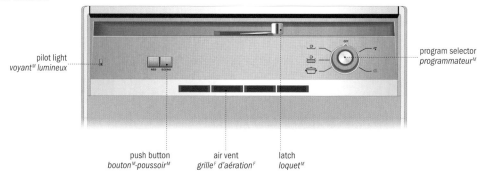

pilot light
voyant^M lumineux

program selector
programmateur^M

push button
bouton^M-poussoir^M

air vent
grille^F d'aération^F

latch
loquet^M

dishwasher
lave-vaisselle^M

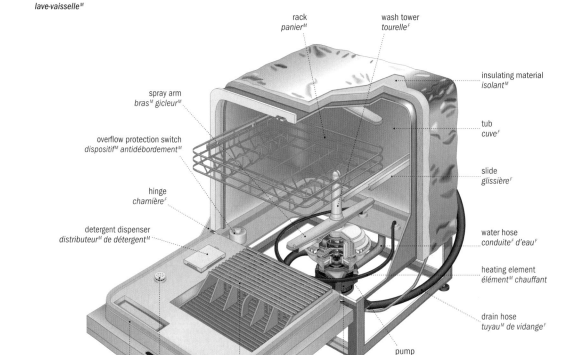

rack
panier^M

wash tower
tourelle^F

insulating material
isolant^M

spray arm
bras^M gicleur^M

tub
cuve^F

overflow protection switch
dispositif^M antidébordement^M

slide
glissière^F

hinge
charnière^F

detergent dispenser
distributeur^M de détergent^M

water hose
conduite^F d'eau^F

heating element
élément^M chauffant

drain hose
tuyau^M de vidange^F

pump
pompe^F

gasket
joint^M

levelling foot
pied^M de nivellement^M

rinse-aid dispenser
*distributeur^M de produit^M de
rinçage^M*

cutlery basket
panier^M à couverts^M

motor
moteur^M

household equipment
articles^M ménagers

kitchen towel
torchon^M

scouring pad
éponge^F à récurer

dustpan
pelle^F à poussière^F

broom
balai^M

mop
balai^M à franges^F

handle
manche^M

brush
brosse^F

block
monture^F

fibres
fibres^F

refuse container
poubelle^F

lid
couvercle^M

handle
poignée^F

fibres
fibres^F

bucket
seau^M

pouring spout
bec^M verseur

handle
anse^F

HOUSE

plumbing tools

plomberie^F : outils^M

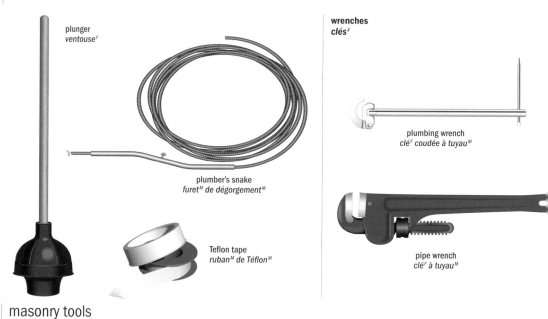

plunger
ventouse^F

plumber's snake
furet^M de dégorgement^M

Teflon tape
ruban^M de Téflon^M

wrenches
clés^F

plumbing wrench
clé^F coudée à tuyau^M

pipe wrench
clé^F à tuyau^M

masonry tools

maçonnerie^F : outils^M

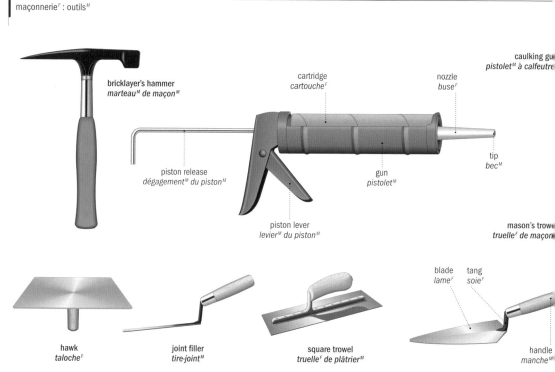

bricklayer's hammer
marteau^M de maçon^M

cartridge
cartouche^F

caulking gun
pistolet^M à calfeutre

nozzle
buse^F

piston release
dégagement^M du piston^M

gun
pistolet^M

tip
bec^M

piston lever
levier^M du piston^M

mason's trowe
truelle^F de maçon

blade
lame^F

tang
soie^F

handle
manche^M

hawk
taloche^F

joint filler
tire-joint^M

square trowel
truelle^F de plâtrier^M

electricity tools
*électricité*F *: outils*M

inspection light
*baladeuse*F

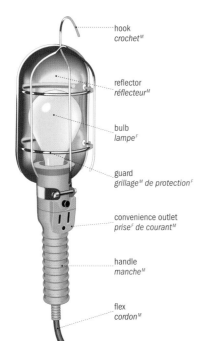

hook
*crochet*M

reflector
*réflecteur*M

bulb
*lampe*F

guard
*grillage*M *de protection*F

convenience outlet
*prise*F *de courant*M

handle
*manche*M

flex
*cordon*M

test-lamp
*vérificateur*M *de circuit*M

wire nut
*capuchon*M *de connexion*F

tester screwdriver
*vérificateur*M *de tension*F

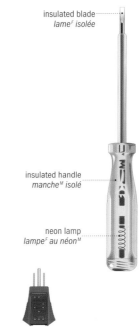

insulated blade
*lame*F *isolée*

insulated handle
*manche*M *isolé*

neon lamp
*lampe*F *au néon*M

socket tester
*vérificateur*M *de prise*F *de courant*M

multipurpose tool
*pince*F *universelle*

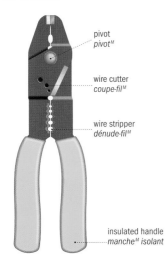

pivot
*pivot*M

wire cutter
*coupe-fil*M

wire stripper
*dénude-fil*M

insulated handle
*manche*M *isolant*

needle-nose pliers
*pince*F *à long bec*M

combination pliers
*pince*F *d'électricien*M

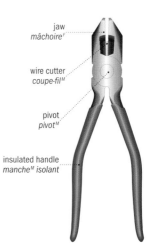

jaw
*mâchoire*F

wire cutter
*coupe-fil*M

pivot
*pivot*M

insulated handle
*manche*M *isolant*

soldering and welding tools

soudage^M : outils^M

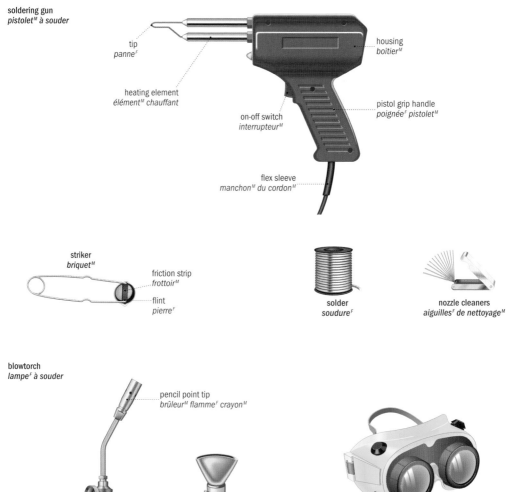

soldering gun
pistolet^M à souder

tip
panne^F

housing
boîtier^M

heating element
élément^M chauffant

pistol grip handle
poignée^F pistolet^M

on-off switch
interrupteur^M

flex sleeve
manchon^M du cordon^M

striker
briquet^M

friction strip
frottoir^M

flint
pierre^F

solder
soudure^F

nozzle cleaners
aiguilles^F de nettoyage^M

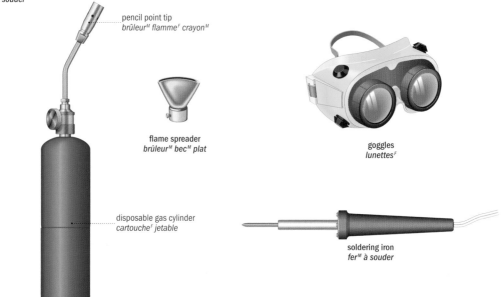

blowtorch
lampe^F à souder

pencil point tip
brûleur^M flamme^F crayon^M

flame spreader
brûleur^M bec^M plat

goggles
lunettes^F

disposable gas cylinder
cartouche^F jetable

soldering iron
fer^M à souder

painting upkeep

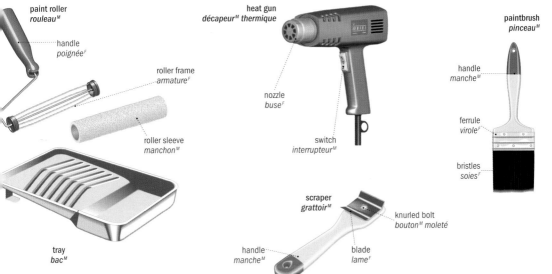

paint roller
rouleau^M

handle
poignée^F

roller frame
armature^F

roller sleeve
manchon^M

tray
bac^M

heat gun
décapeur^M thermique

nozzle
buse^F

switch
interrupteur^M

scraper
grattoir^M

knurled bolt
bouton^M moleté

handle
manche^M

blade
lame^F

paintbrush
pinceau^M

handle
manche^M

ferrule
virole^F

bristles
soies^F

ladders and stepladders

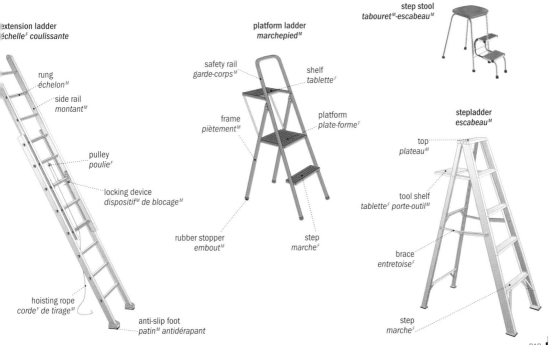

extension ladder
échelle^F coulissante

rung
échelon^M

side rail
montant^M

pulley
poulie^F

locking device
dispositif^M de blocage^M

hoisting rope
corde^F de tirage^M

anti-slip foot
patin^M antidérapant

platform ladder
marchepied^M

safety rail
garde-corps^M

frame
piètement^M

rubber stopper
embout^M

shelf
tablette^F

platform
plate-forme^F

step
marche^F

step stool
tabouret^M-escabeau^M

stepladder
escabeau^M

top
plateau^M

tool shelf
tablette^F porte-outil^M

brace
entretoise^F

step
marche^F

carpentry: nailing tools

menuserie^F : outils^M pour clouer

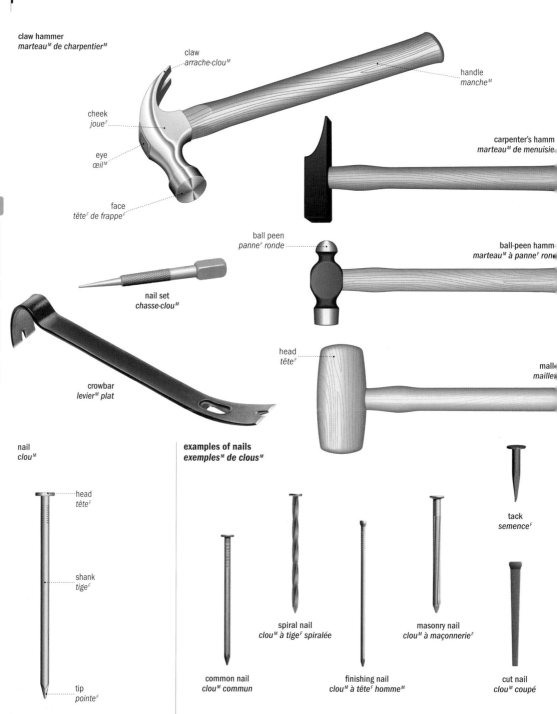

claw hammer
marteau^M de charpentier^M

claw
arrache-clou^M

handle
manche^M

cheek
joue^F

carpenter's hamm
marteau^M de menuisie

eye
œil^M

face
tête^F de frappe^F

ball peen
panne^F ronde

ball-peen hamm
marteau^M à panne^F ron

nail set
chasse-clou^M

head
tête^F

mall
maille

crowbar
levier^M plat

nail
clou^M

examples of nails
exemples^M de clous^M

head
tête^F

tack
semence^F

shank
tige^F

spiral nail
clou^M à tige^F spiralée

masonry nail
clou^M à maçonnerie^F

tip
pointe^F

common nail
clou^M commun

finishing nail
clou^M à tête^F homme^M

cut nail
clou^M coupé

DO-IT-YOURSELF AND GARDENING

carpentry: screwing tools

menuiserie^F : outils^M pour visser

screwdriver
tournevis^M

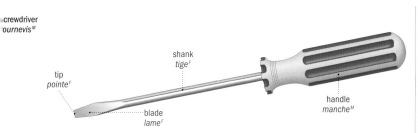

shank
tige^F

tip
pointe^F

handle
manche^M

blade
lame^F

spiral screwdriver
tournevis^M à spirale^F

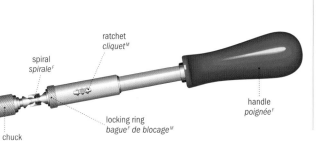

ratchet
cliquet^M

spiral
spirale^F

blade
lame^F

handle
poignée^F

locking ring
bague^F de blocage^M

jaw
mors^M

chuck
mandrin^M

cordless screwdriver
tournevis^M sans fil^M

bit
embout^M

handle
poignée^F

tip
pointe^F

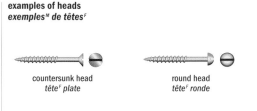

reversing switch
inverseur^M de marche^F

battery
batterie^F

screw
vis^F

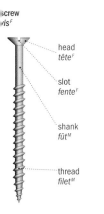

head
tête^F

slot
fente^F

shank
fût^M

thread
filet^M

examples of tips
exemples^M de pointes^F

square-headed tip
pointe^F carrée

cross-headed tip
pointe^F cruciforme

flat tip
pointe^F plate

spring toggle
ailette^F à ressort^M

toggle bolt
boulon^M à ailettes^F

expansion bolt
boulon^M à gaine^F d'expansion^F

examples of heads
exemples^M de têtes^F

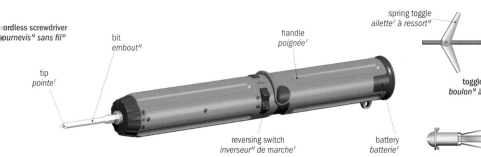

countersunk head
tête^F plate

round head
tête^F ronde

one way head
tête^F à sens^M unique

cross head
tête^F cruciforme

socket head
tête^F creuse

raised head
tête^F bombée

carpentry: gripping and tightening tools

menuiserie^F : outils^M pour serrer

DO-IT-YOURSELF AND GARDENING

pliers
pinces^F

water pump pliers
pince^F multiprise

straight jaw
mâchoire^F droite

slip joint pliers
pince^F à joint^M coulissant

curved jaw
mâchoire^F incurvée

bolt
boulon^M

adjustable channel
cran^M de réglage^M

handle
branche^F

slip joint
joint^M à coulisse^F

nut
écrou^M

handle
branche^F

mole wrench
pince^F-étau^M

spring
ressort^M

lever
levier^M

adjusting screw
vis^F de réglage^M

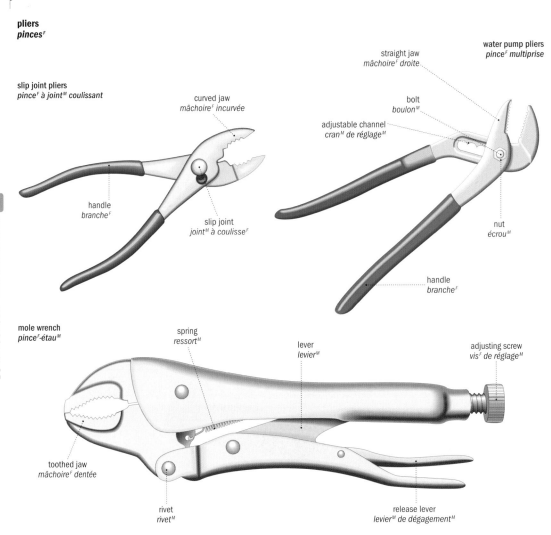

toothed jaw
mâchoire^F dentée

rivet
rivet^M

release lever
levier^M de dégagement^M

washers
rondelles^F

flat washer
rondelle^F plate

spring washer
rondelle^F à ressort^M

external tooth lock washer
rondelle^F à denture^F extérieure

internal tooth lock washer
rondelle^F à denture^F intérieure

carpentry: gripping and tightening tools

wrenches
clés^F

fixed jaw
mâchoire^F *fixe*

adjustable spanner
clé^F *à molette*^{F}

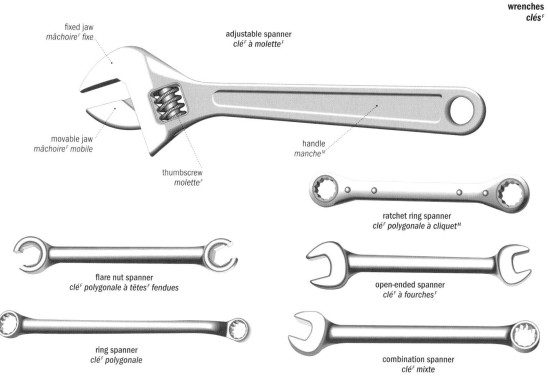

movable jaw
mâchoire^F *mobile*

handle
manche^M

thumbscrew
molette^F

ratchet ring spanner
clé^F *polygonale à cliquet*^{M}

flare nut spanner
clé^F *polygonale à têtes*^{F} *fendues*

open-ended spanner
clé^F *à fourches*^{F}

ring spanner
clé^F *polygonale*

combination spanner
clé^F *mixte*

ratchet socket wrench
clé^F *à douille*^{F} *à cliquet*^{M}

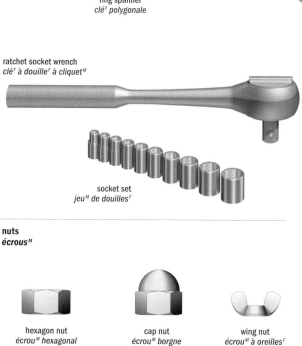

socket set
jeu^M *de douilles*^{F}

bolts
boulons^M

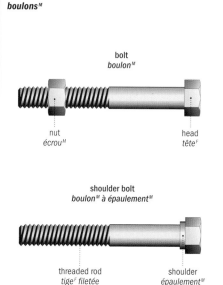

bolt
boulon^M

nut
écrou^M

head
tête^F

shoulder bolt
boulon^M *à épaulement*^{M}

threaded rod
tige^F *filetée*

shoulder
épaulement^M

nuts
écrous^M

hexagon nut
écrou^M *hexagonal*

cap nut
écrou^M *borgne*

wing nut
écrou^M *à oreilles*^{F}

carpentry: gripping and tightening tools

G-clamp
serre-joint M

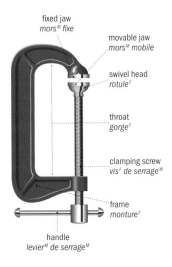

fixed jaw
mors M *fixe*

movable jaw
mors M *mobile*

swivel head
rotule F

throat
gorge F

clamping screw
vis F *de serrage* M

frame
monture F

handle
levier M *de serrage* M

vice
étau M

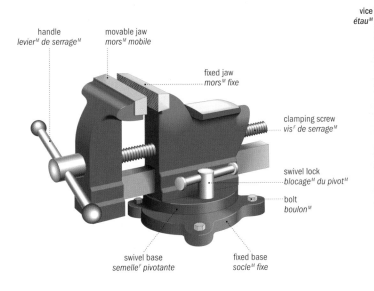

handle
levier M *de serrage* M

movable jaw
mors M *mobile*

fixed jaw
mors M *fixe*

clamping screw
vis F *de serrage* M

swivel lock
blocage M *du pivot* M

bolt
boulon M

swivel base
semelle F *pivotante*

fixed base
socle M *fixe*

pipe clamp
serre-joint M *à tuyau* M

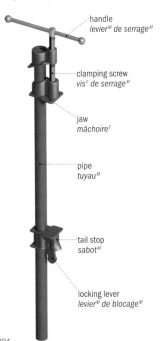

handle
levier M *de serrage* M

clamping screw
vis F *de serrage* M

jaw
mâchoire F

pipe
tuyau M

tail stop
sabot M

locking lever
levier M *de blocage* M

work bench and vice
établi M *étau* M

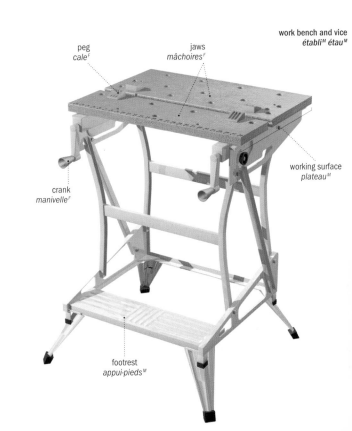

peg
cale F

jaws
mâchoires F

crank
manivelle F

working surface
plateau M

footrest
appui-pieds M

carpentry: measuring and marking tools

menuiserie*F* : instruments*M* de traçage*M* et de mesure*F*

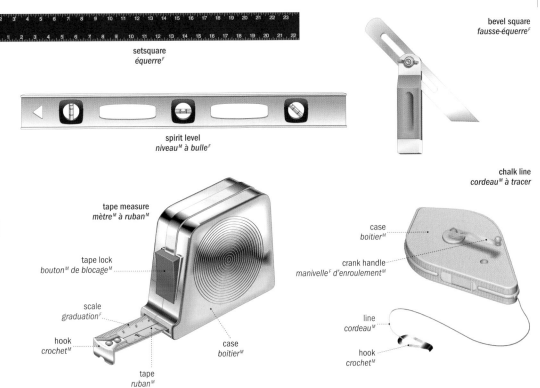

setsquare
*équerre*F*

bevel square
*fausse-équerre*F*

spirit level
*niveau*M* à bulle*F*

chalk line
*cordeau*M* à tracer

tape measure
*mètre*M* à ruban*M*

tape lock
*bouton*M* de blocage*M*

scale
*graduation*F*

hook
*crochet*M*

case
*boitier*M*

tape
*ruban*M*

case
*boitier*M*

crank handle
*manivelle*F* d'enroulement*M*

line
*cordeau*M*

hook
*crochet*M*

carpentry: miscellaneous material

menuiserie*F* : matériel*M* divers

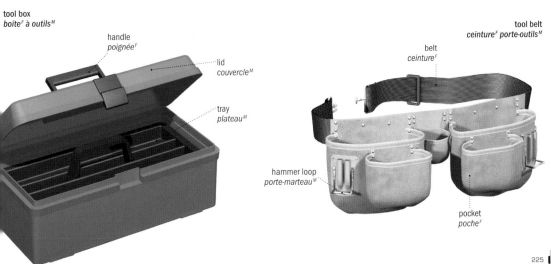

tool box
*boîte*F* à outils*M*

handle
*poignée*F*

lid
*couvercle*M*

tray
*plateau*M*

tool belt
*ceinture*F* porte-outils*M*

belt
*ceinture*F*

hammer loop
*porte-marteau*M*

pocket
*poche*F*

carpentry: sawing tools

menuiserie^F : outils^M pour scier

coping saw
scie^F à chantourner

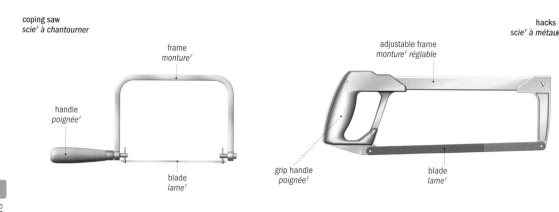

frame
monture^F

handle
poignée^F

blade
lame^F

hacks
scie^F à métau

adjustable frame
monture^F réglable

grip handle
poignée^F

blade
lame^F

compass saw
scie^F à guichet^M

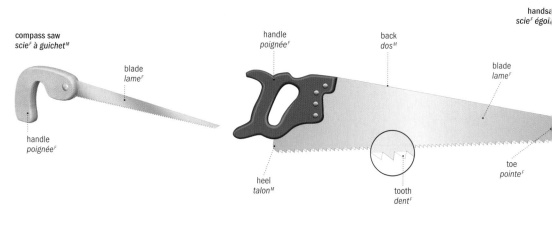

blade
lame^F

handle
poignée^F

handle
poignée^F

back
dos^M

handsa
scie^F égoï

blade
lame^F

heel
talon^M

tooth
dent^F

toe
pointe^F

hand mitre saw
scie^F à onglet^M manuelle

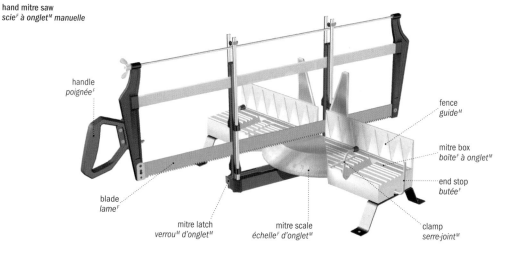

handle
poignée^F

fence
guide^M

mitre box
boîte^F à onglet^M

end stop
butée^F

blade
lame^F

mitre latch
verrou^M d'onglet^M

mitre scale
échelle^F d'onglet^M

clamp
serre-joint^M

jigsaw
scie^F sauteuse

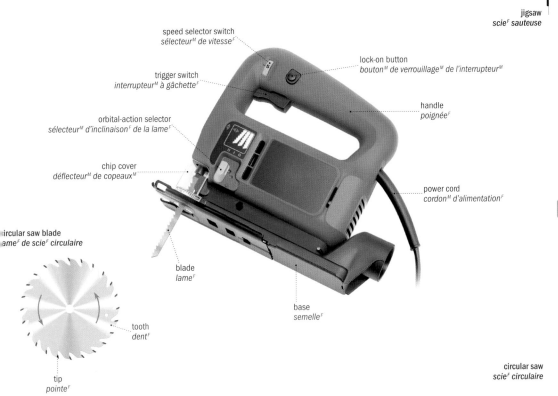

speed selector switch
sélecteur^M de vitesse^F

lock-on button
bouton^M de verrouillage^M de l'interrupteur^M

trigger switch
interrupteur^M à gâchette^F

handle
poignée^F

orbital-action selector
sélecteur^M d'inclinaison^F de la lame^F

chip cover
déflecteur^M de copeaux^M

power cord
cordon^M d'alimentation^F

circular saw blade
lame^F de scie^F circulaire

blade
lame^F

base
semelle^F

tooth
dent^F

tip
pointe^F

circular saw
scie^F circulaire

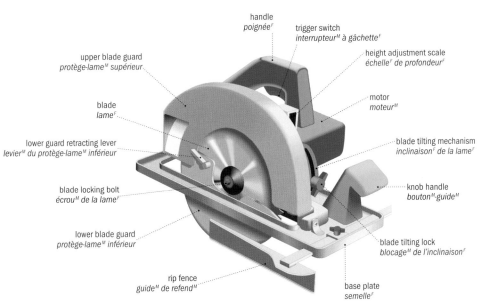

handle
poignée^F

trigger switch
interrupteur^M à gâchette^F

height adjustment scale
échelle^F de profondeur^F

upper blade guard
protège-lame^M supérieur

motor
moteur^M

blade
lame^F

blade tilting mechanism
inclinaison^F de la lame^F

lower guard retracting lever
levier^M du protège-lame^M inférieur

blade locking bolt
écrou^M de la lame^F

knob handle
bouton^M-guide^M

lower blade guard
protège-lame^M inférieur

blade tilting lock
blocage^M de l'inclinaison^F

rip fence
guide^M de refend^M

base plate
semelle^F

carpentry: drilling tools

menuserie^F : outils^M pour percer

cordless drill-driver
perceuse^F-visseuse^F sans fil^M

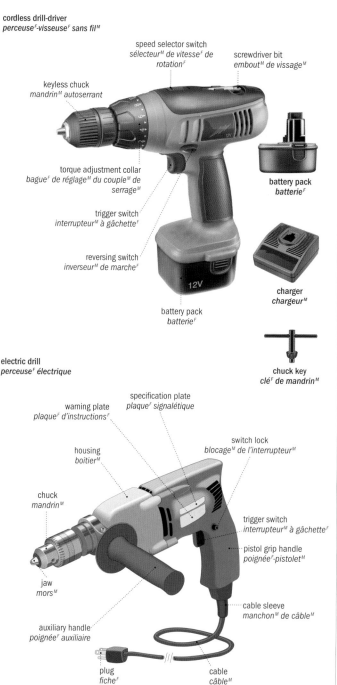

speed selector switch
sélecteur^M de vitesse^F de rotation^F

screwdriver bit
embout^M de vissage^M

keyless chuck
mandrin^M autoserrant

torque adjustment collar
bague^F de réglage^M du couple^M de serrage^M

battery pack
batterie^F

trigger switch
interrupteur^M à gâchette^F

reversing switch
inverseur^M de marche^F

battery pack
batterie^F

charger
chargeur^M

chuck key
clé^F de mandrin^M

electric drill
perceuse^F électrique

specification plate
plaque^F signalétique

warning plate
plaque^F d'instructions^F

switch lock
blocage^M de l'interrupteur^M

housing
boîtier^M

chuck
mandrin^M

trigger switch
interrupteur^M à gâchette^F

pistol grip handle
poignée^F-pistolet^M

jaw
mors^M

cable sleeve
manchon^M de câble^M

auxiliary handle
poignée^F auxiliaire

plug
fiche^F

cable
câble^M

examples of bits and drills
exemples^M de mèches^F et de forets^M

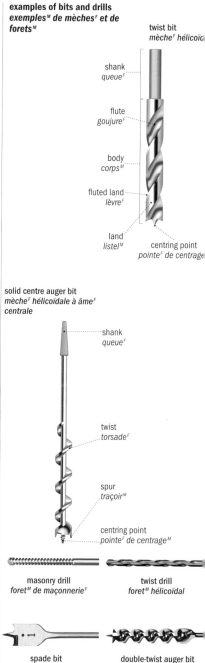

twist bit
mèche^F hélicoïc

shank
queue^F

flute
goujure^F

body
corps^M

fluted land
lèvre^F

land
listel^M

centring point
pointe^F de centrage

solid centre auger bit
mèche^F hélicoïdale à âme^F centrale

shank
queue^F

twist
torsade^F

spur
traçoir^M

centring point
pointe^F de centrage^M

masonry drill
foret^M de maçonnerie^F

twist drill
foret^M hélicoïdal

spade bit
mèche^F à centre^M plat

double-twist auger bit
mèche^F hélicoïdale à doubl' torsade^F

carpentry: shaping tools

menuiserie^F : outils^M pour façonner

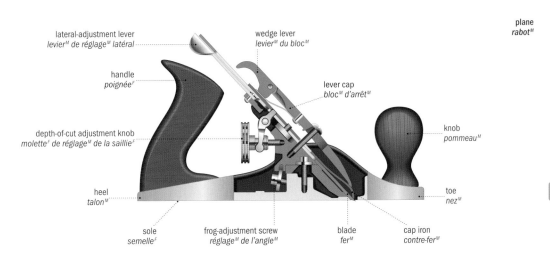

plane
rabot^M

lateral-adjustment lever
levier^M de réglage^M latéral

wedge lever
levier^M du bloc^M

handle
poignée^F

lever cap
bloc^M d'arrêt^M

depth-of-cut adjustment knob
molette^F de réglage^M de la saillie^F

knob
pommeau^M

heel
talon^M

toe
nez^M

sole
semelle^F

frog-adjustment screw
réglage^M de l'angle^M

blade
fer^M

cap iron
contre-fer^M

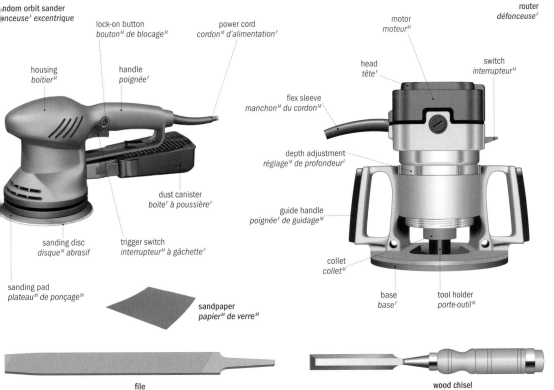

random orbit sander
ponceuse^F excentrique

lock-on button
bouton^M de blocage^M

power cord
cordon^M d'alimentation^F

router
défonceuse^F

motor
moteur^M

head
tête^F

switch
interrupteur^M

housing
boîtier^M

handle
poignée^F

flex sleeve
manchon^M du cordon^M

depth adjustment
réglage^M de profondeur^F

dust canister
boîte^F à poussière^F

guide handle
poignée^F de guidage^M

sanding disc
disque^M abrasif

trigger switch
interrupteur^M à gâchette^F

collet
collet^M

sanding pad
plateau^M de ponçage^M

base
base^F

tool holder
porte-outil^M

sandpaper
papier^M de verre^M

file
lime^F

wood chisel
ciseau^M à bois^M

pleasure garden

jardin^M d'agrément^M

DO-IT-YOURSELF AND GARDENING

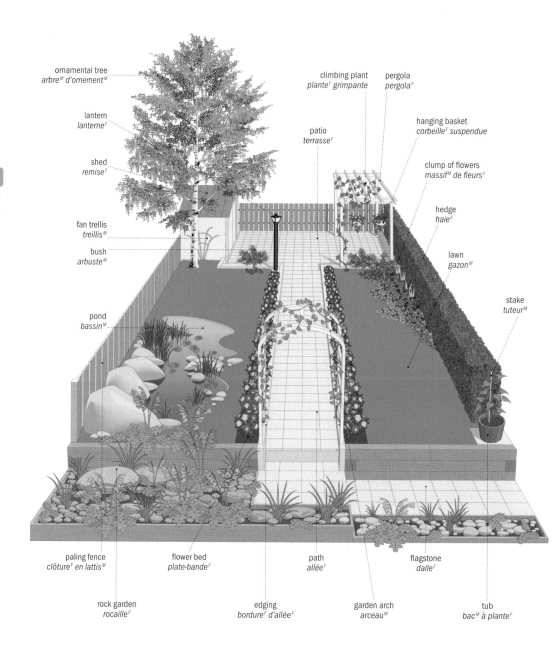

ornamental tree
arbre^M d'ornement^M

lantern
lanterne^F

shed
remise^F

fan trellis
treillis^M

bush
arbuste^M

pond
bassin^M

climbing plant
plante^F grimpante

pergola
pergola^F

patio
terrasse^F

hanging basket
corbeille^F suspendue

clump of flowers
massif^M de fleurs^F

hedge
haie^F

lawn
gazon^M

stake
tuteur^M

paling fence
clôture^F en lattis^M

flower bed
plate-bande^F

path
allée^F

flagstone
dalle^F

rock garden
rocaille^F

edging
bordure^F d'allée^F

garden arch
arceau^M

tub
bac^M à plante^F

miscellaneous equipment
équipement^M divers

compost bin
bac^M à compost^M

container
caisse^F

wheelbarrow
brouette^F

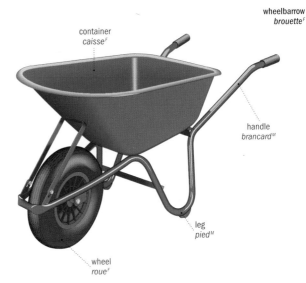

handle
brancard^M

leg
pied^M

wheel
roue^F

seeding and planting tools
outils^M pour semer et planter

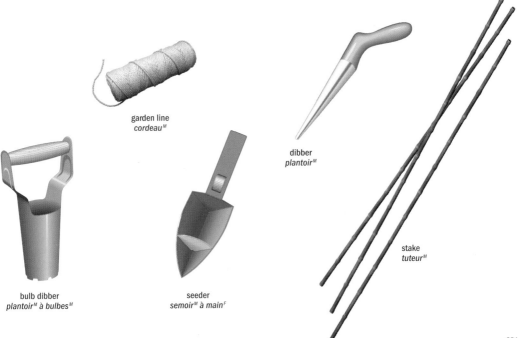

garden line
cordeau^M

dibber
plantoir^M

bulb dibber
plantoir^M à bulbes^M

seeder
semoir^M à main^F

stake
tuteur^M

DO-IT-YOURSELF AND GARDENING

hand tools
jeu^M de petits outils^M

small hand cultivator
griffe^F à fleurs^F

trowel
transplantoir^M

weeder
tire-racine^M

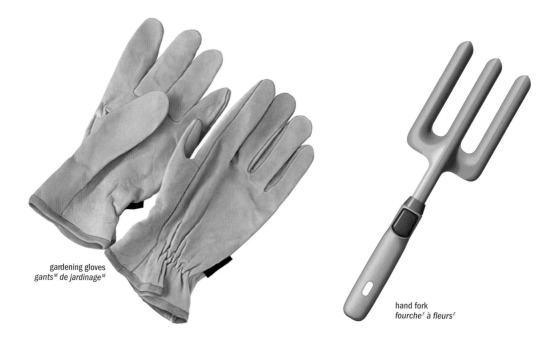

gardening gloves
gants^M de jardinage^M

hand fork
fourche^F à fleurs^F

tools for loosening the earth

outils^M pour remuer la terre^F

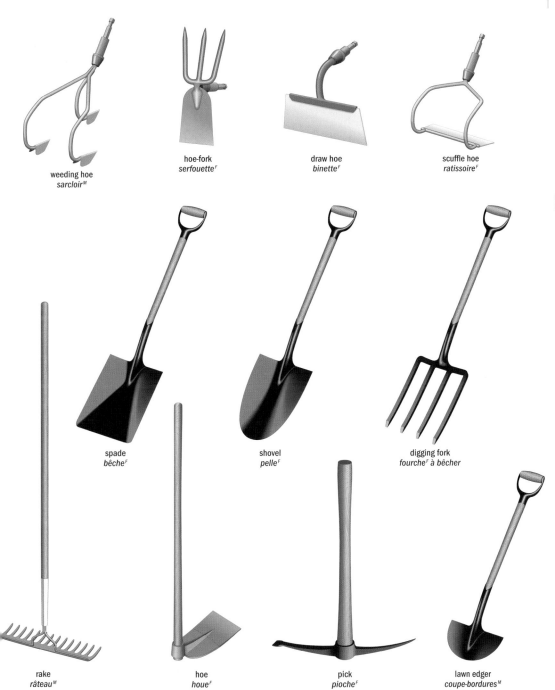

weeding hoe
sarcloir^M

hoe-fork
serfouette^F

draw hoe
binette^F

scuffle hoe
ratissoire^F

spade
bêche^F

shovel
pelle^F

digging fork
fourche^F *à bêcher*

rake
râteau^M

hoe
houe^F

pick
pioche^F

lawn edger
coupe-bordures^M

DO-IT-YOURSELF AND GARDENING

pruning and cutting tools

outils^M pour couper

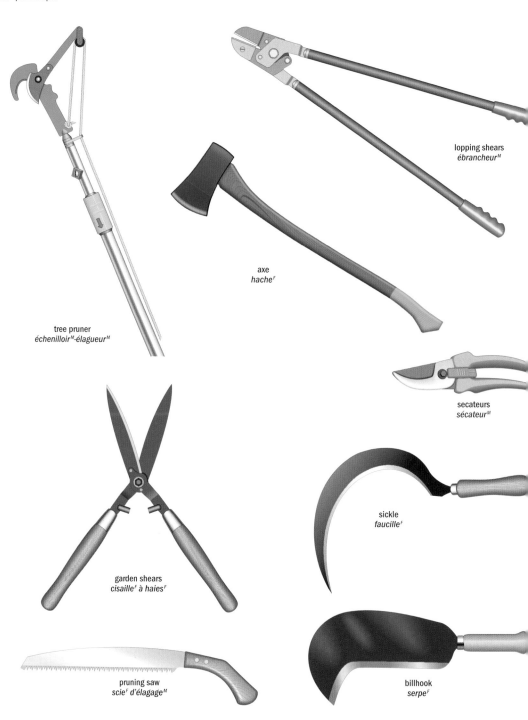

lopping shears
ébrancheur^M

axe
hache^F

tree pruner
échenilloir^M-*élagueur*^M

secateurs
sécateur^M

sickle
faucille^F

garden shears
cisaille^F *à haies*^F

pruning saw
scie^F *d'élagage*^M

billhook
serpe^F

hedge trimmer
taille-haies M

flex
cordon M

hand protector
bouclier M

trigger
gâchette F

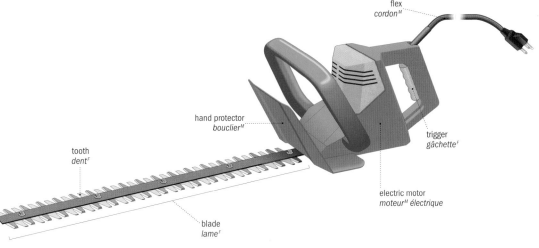

tooth
dent F

electric motor
moteur M *électrique*

blade
lame F

chainsaw
tronçonneuse F

air filter
filtre M *à air* M

anti-vibration handle
poignée F *antivibrations* F

chain brake
frein M *de chaîne* F

stop button
bouton M *d'arrêt* M

security trigger
gâchette F *de sécurité* F

bar nose
nez M *du guide* M

guide bar
guide-chaîne M

handle
poignée F

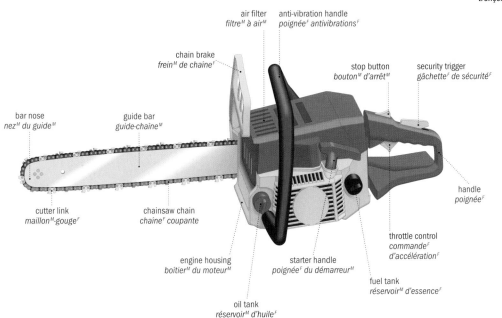

cutter link
maillon M*-gouge* F

chainsaw chain
chaîne F *coupante*

throttle control
commande F
d'accélération F

engine housing
boîtier M *du moteur* M

starter handle
poignée F *du démarreur* M

fuel tank
réservoir M *d'essence* F

oil tank
réservoir M *d'huile* F

watering tools

outils^M pour arroser

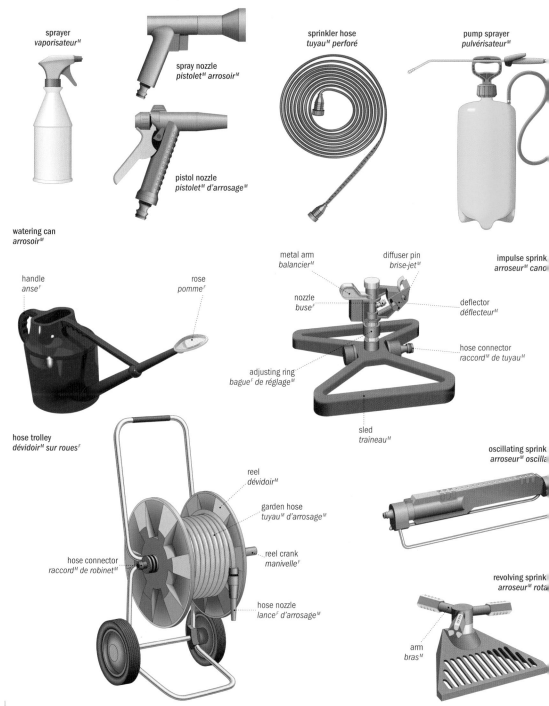

sprayer
vaporisateur^M

spray nozzle
pistolet^M arrosoir^M

pistol nozzle
pistolet^M d'arrosage^M

sprinkler hose
tuyau^M perforé

pump sprayer
pulvérisateur^M

watering can
arrosoir^M

handle
anse^F

rose
pomme^F

metal arm
balancier^M

diffuser pin
brise-jet^M

impulse sprink
arroseur^M cano

nozzle
buse^F

deflector
déflecteur^M

hose connector
raccord^M de tuyau^M

adjusting ring
bague^F de réglage^M

sled
traineau^M

hose trolley
dévidoir^M sur roues^F

reel
dévidoir^M

garden hose
tuyau^M d'arrosage^M

hose connector
raccord^M de robinet^M

reel crank
manivelle^F

hose nozzle
lance^F d'arrosage^M

oscillating sprink
arroseur^M oscilla

revolving sprink
arroseur^M rota

arm
bras^M

lawn care

soins^M de la pelouse^F

trimmer
taille-bordures^M

flex
cordon^M

lawn rake
balai^M à feuilles^F

electric motor
moteur^M électrique

protective casing
carter^M de sécurité^F

nylon line
fil^M de nylon^M

lawn aerator
aérateur^M à gazon^M

handle
guidon^M

throttle
sélecteur^M de régime^M

safety handle
poignée^F de sécurité^F

ignition key
clé^F de contact^M

power mower
tondeuse^F à moteur^M

grassbox
bac^M de ramassage^M

starter
démarreur^M manuel

motor
moteur^M

filler cap
bouchon^M de remplissage^M

throttle cable
câble^M d'accélération^F

deflector
déflecteur^M

sparking plug
bougie^F

casing
carter^M

headgear

coiffure^F

men's headgear
coiffures^F d'homme^M

trilby
chapeau^M de feutre^M

hatband
bourdalou^M

crown
calotte^F

binding
galon^M

brim
bord^M

bow
nœud^M plat

boater
canotier^M

skullcap
calotte^F

bowler
melon^M

astrakhan cap
calot^M

top hat
haut-de-forme^M

shapka
chapka^M

hunting cap
casquette^F norvégienne

ear flap
cache-oreilles^M abattant

cap
casquette^F

panama
panama^M

peak
visière^F

women's headgear
*coiffures*F *de femme*F

pillbox hat
*tambourin*M

cartwheel hat
*capeline*F

cloche
*cloche*F

toque
*toque*F

rain hat
*bob*M

crown
*calotte*F

turban
*turban*M

sou'wester
*suroît*M

brim
*bord*M

unisex headgear
*coiffures*F *unisexes*

balaclava
*cagoule*F

beret
*béret*M

bobble hat
*bonnet*M *à pompon*M

peak
*visière*F

trilby
*feutre*M

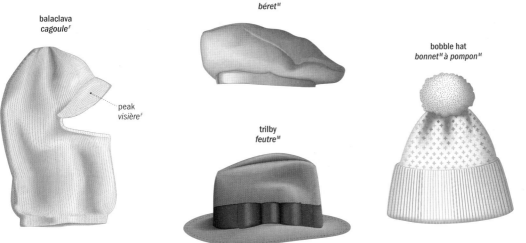

shoes

chaussures^F

men's shoes
chaussures^F d'homme^M

parts of a shoe
parties^F d'une chaussure^F

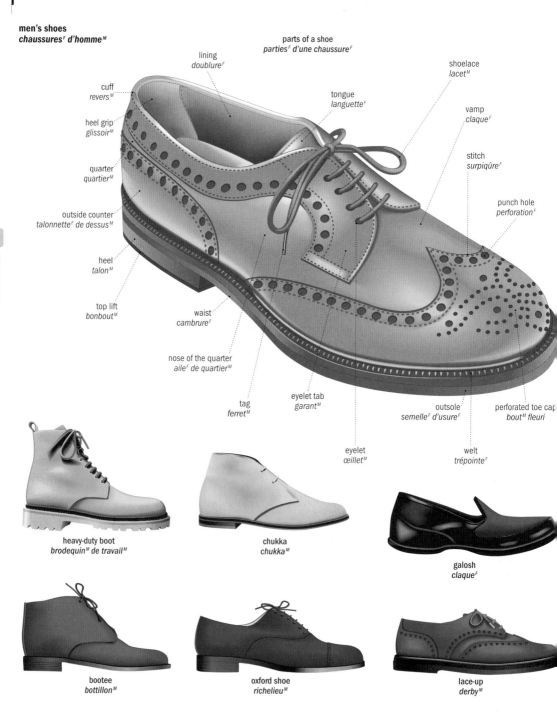

lining
doublure^F

cuff
revers^M

heel grip
glissoir^M

quarter
quartier^M

outside counter
talonnette^F de dessus^M

heel
talon^M

top lift
bonbout^M

nose of the quarter
aile^F de quartier^M

tag
ferret^M

waist
cambrure^F

eyelet tab
garant^M

eyelet
œillet^M

tongue
languette^F

shoelace
lacet^M

vamp
claque^F

stitch
surpiqûre^F

punch hole
perforation^F

outsole
semelle^F d'usure^F

perforated toe cap
bout^M fleuri

welt
trépointe^F

heavy-duty boot
brodequin^M de travail^M

chukka
chukka^M

galosh
claque^F

bootee
bottillon^M

oxford shoe
richelieu^M

lace-up
derby^M

women's shoes
chaussures^F de femme^F

ankle-strap
sandale^F

pump
ballerine^F

slingback shoe
escarpin^M-sandale^F

court
escarpin^M

one-bar shoe
Charles IX^M

T-strap shoe
salomé^M

casual shoe
trotteur^M

thigh-boot
cuissarde^F

boot
botte^F

ankle boot
bottine^F

CLOTHING

unisex shoes
*chaussures*F *unisexes*

mule
*mule*F

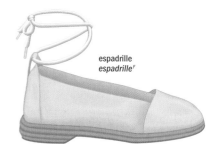

espadrille
*espadrille*F

plimsoll
*tennis*M

slip-on
*mocassin*M

toe-strap
*nu-pied*M

moccasin
*mocassin*M

flip-flop
*tong*M

clog
*socque*M

sandal
*sandalette*F

hiking boot
*brodequin*M *de randonnée*F

men's gloves
gants^M *d'homme*^{M}

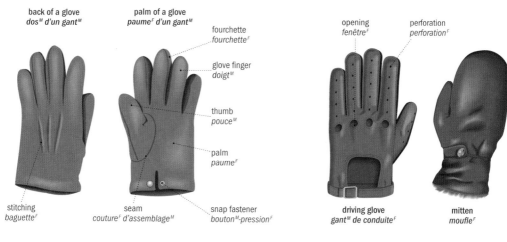

back of a glove
dos^M *d'un gant*^{M}

palm of a glove
paume^F *d'un gant*^{M}

fourchette
fourchette^F

glove finger
doigt^M

thumb
pouce^M

palm
paume^F

stitching
baguette^F

seam
couture^F *d'assemblage*^{M}

snap fastener
bouton^M-*pression*^{F}

opening
fenêtre^F

perforation
perforation^F

driving glove
gant^M *de conduite*^{F}

mitten
moufle^F

CLOTHING

women's gloves
gants^M *de femme*^{F}

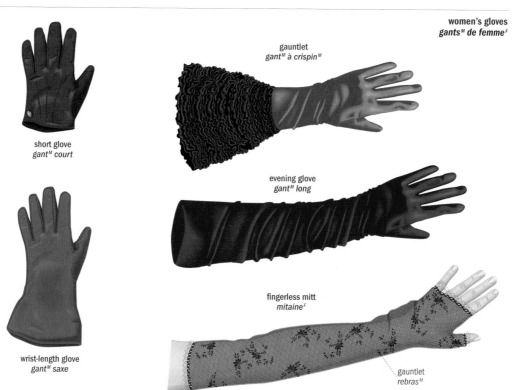

short glove
gant^M *court*

gauntlet
gant^M *à crispin*^{M}

evening glove
gant^M *long*

fingerless mitt
mitaine^F

wrist-length glove
gant^M *saxe*

gauntlet
rebras^M

CLOTHING

jackets
*veston*ᴹ *et veste*ᶠ

double-breasted jacket
*veston*ᴹ *croisé*

collar
*col*ᴹ

peaked lapel
*revers*ᴹ *à cran*ᴹ *aigu*

lining
*doublure*ᶠ

breast welt pocket
*pochette*ᶠ

sleeve
*manche*ᶠ

flap
*rabat*ᴹ

outside ticket pocket
*poche*ᶠ-*ticket*ᴹ

patch pocket
*poche*ᶠ *plaquée*

side back vent
*fente*ᶠ *latérale*

waistcoat
*gilet*ᴹ

V-neck
*encolure*ᶠ *en V*

lining
*doublure*ᶠ

welt
*patte*ᶠ

front
*devant*ᴹ

seaming
*découpe*ᶠ

welt pocket
*poche*ᶠ *gilet*ᴹ

adjustable waist tab
*tirant*ᴹ *de réglage*ᴹ

single-breasted jacket
*veste*ᶠ *droite*

lapel
*revers*ᴹ

notch
*cran*ᴹ

front
*devant*ᴹ

lining
*doublure*ᶠ

pocket handkerchief
*pochette*ᶠ

back
*dos*ᴹ

sleeve
*manche*ᶠ

flap pocket
*poche*ᶠ *tiroir*ᴹ

centre back vent
*fente*ᶠ *médiane*

shirt
chemise^F

collar
col^M

yoke
empiècement^M

set-in sleeve
manche^F *montée*

collar point
pointe^F *de col*^M

breast pocket
poche^F *poitrine*^F

button facing
patte^F *de boutonnage*^M

front
devant^M

pointed tab end
patte^F *capucin*^M

button
bouton^M

cuff
poignet^M

shirttail
pan^M

buttondown collar
col^M *pointes*^F *boutonnées*

cravat
lavallière^F

collar stiffener
baleine^F *de col*^M

bow tie
nœud^M *papillon*^M

spread collar
col^M *italien*

necktie
cravate^F

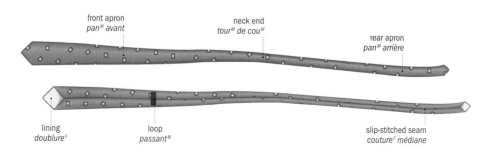

front apron
pan^M *avant*

neck end
tour^M *de cou*^M

rear apron
pan^M *arrière*

lining
doublure^F

loop
passant^M

slip-stitched seam
couture^F *médiane*

CLOTHING

trousers
pantalon^M

belt loop
passant^M

waistband
ceinture^F *montée*

front top pocket
poche^F *cavalière*

knife pleat
pli^M *plat*

waistband extension
patte^F *boutonnée*

fly
braguette^F

crease
pli^M

turn-up
revers^M

back pocket
poche^F*-revolver*^M

brace clip
pince^F

braces
bretelles^F

elastic webbing
bande^F *élastique*

adjustment slide
coulisse^F

leather end
patte^F

button loop
boutonnière^F

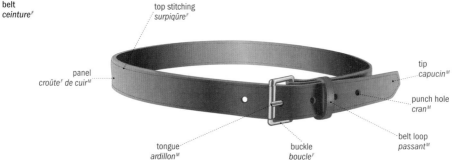

belt
ceinture^F

top stitching
surpiqûre^F

panel
croûte^F *de cuir*^M

tip
capucin^M

punch hole
cran^M

tongue
ardillon^M

buckle
boucle^F

belt loop
passant^M

CLOTHING

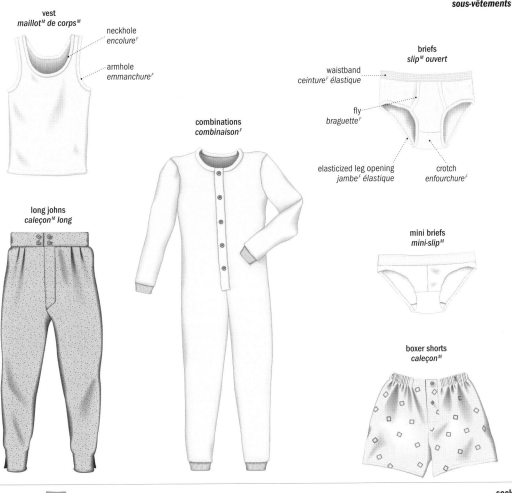

vest
maillot^M *de corps*^M

neckhole
encolure^F

armhole
emmanchure^F

combinations
combinaison^F

briefs
slip^M *ouvert*

waistband
ceinture^F *élastique*

fly
braguette^F

elasticized leg opening
jambe^F *élastique*

crotch
enfourchure^F

long johns
caleçon^M *long*

mini briefs
mini-slip^M

boxer shorts
caleçon^M

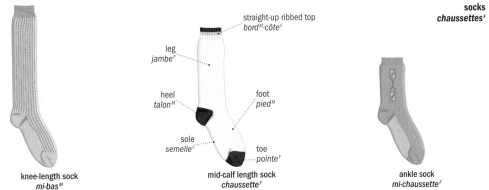

straight-up ribbed top
bord^M-*côte*^F

leg
jambe^F

heel
talon^M

foot
pied^M

sole
semelle^F

toe
pointe^F

knee-length sock
mi-bas^M

mid-calf length sock
chaussette^F

ankle sock
mi-chaussette^F

coats
manteaux^M et blousons^M

CLOTHING

raincoat
imperméable^M

collar
col^M

raglan sleeve
manche^F raglan

notched lapel
revers^M cranté

tab
patte^F

broad welt side pocket
poche^F raglan

buttonhole
boutonnière^F

side panel
pan^M

overcoat
pardessus^M

notched lapel
revers^M cranté

breast pocket
poche^F poitrine^F

breast dart
pince^F de taille^F

flap pocket
poche^F à rabat^M

trench coat
trench^M

two-way collar
col^M transformable

epaulet
patte^F d'épaule^F

gun flap
bavolet^M

raglan sleeve
manche^F raglan

sleeve strap loop
passant^M

double-breasted buttoning
double boutonnage^M

belt
ceinture^F

belt loop
passant^M

buckle
boucle^F de ceinture^F

sleeve strap
patte^F de serrage^M

broad welt side pocket
poche^F raglan

three-quarter coat
paletot^M

CLOTHING

parka
parka^F

snap-fastening tab
patte^F *à boutons*^M-*pression*^F

zip fastener
fermeture^F *à glissière*^F

sheepskin jacket
canadienne^F

duffle coat
duffle-coat^M

hood
capuchon^M

yoke
empiècement^M

frog
brandebourg^M

patch pocket
poche^F *plaquée*

toggle
büchette^F

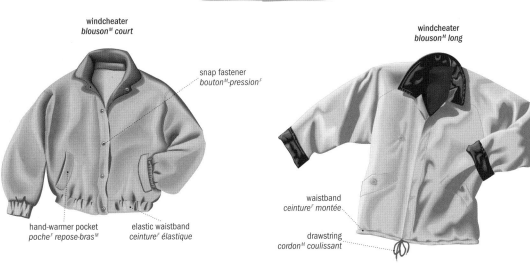

windcheater
blouson^M *court*

snap fastener
bouton^M-*pression*^F

windcheater
blouson^M *long*

waistband
ceinture^F *montée*

hand-warmer pocket
poche^F *repose-bras*^M

elastic waistband
ceinture^F *élastique*

drawstring
cordon^M *coulissant*

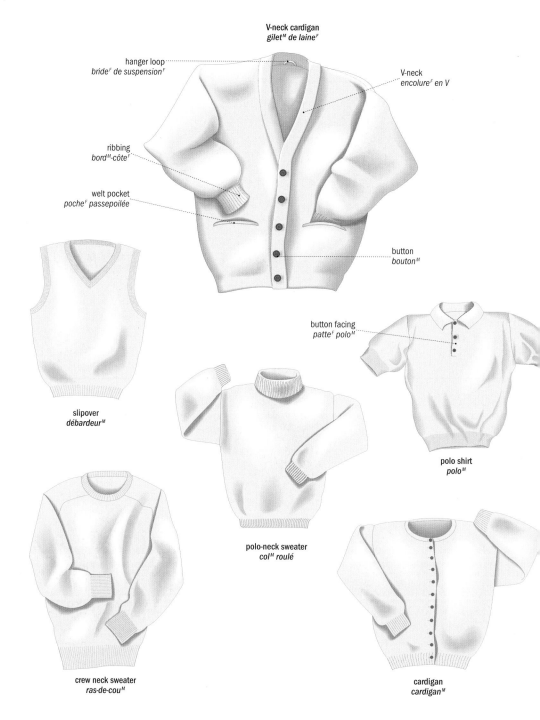

V-neck cardigan
gilet^M de laine^F

hanger loop
bride^F de suspension^F

V-neck
encolure^F en V

ribbing
bord^M-côte^F

welt pocket
poche^F passepoilée

button
bouton^M

button facing
patte^F polo^M

slipover
débardeur^M

polo shirt
polo^M

polo-neck sweater
col^M roulé

crew neck sweater
ras-de-cou^M

cardigan
cardigan^M

CLOTHING

suit
tailleur^M

jacket
veste^F

skirt
jupe^F

raglan
raglan^M

raglan sleeve
manche^F raglan

fly front closing
boutonnage^M sous patte^F

broad welt side pocket
poche^F raglan

coats
manteaux^M

riding coat
redingote^F

pelerine
pèlerine^F

pelerine
pèlerine^F

seam pocket
*poche^F prise dans une
couture^F*

cape
cape^F

arm slit
passe-bras^M

pea jacket
caban^M

tailored collar
col^M tailleur^M

hand warmer pocket
poche^F repose-bras^M

mock pocket
fausse poche^F

overcoat
manteau^M

car coat
paletot^M

jacket
veste^F

poncho
poncho^M

CLOTHING

CLOTHING

examples of dresses
exemples^M *de robes*^F

sheath dress
robe^F *fourreau*^M

princess dress
robe^F *princesse*^F

coat dress
robe^F*-manteau*^M

polo dress
robe^F*-polo*^M

house dress
robe^F *de maison*^F

shirtwaist dress
robe^F *chemisier*^M

drop waist dress
robe^F *taille*^F *basse*

A-line dress
robe^F *trapèze*^M

sundress
robe^F *bain*^M*-de-soleil*^M

wrapover dress
robe^F *enveloppe*^F

tunic dress
robe^F *tunique*^F

pinafore
chasuble^F

examples of skirts
exemples^M de jupes^F

gored skirt
jupe^F à lés^M

kilt
kilt^M

sarong
paréo^M

wrapover skirt
jupe^F portefeuille^M

sheath skirt
jupe^F fourreau^M

ruffled skirt
jupe^F à volants^M étagés

straight skirt
jupe^F droite

yoke skirt
jupe^F à empiècement^M

gather skirt
jupe^F froncée

culottes
jupe^F-culotte^F

examples of pleats
exemples^M de plis^M

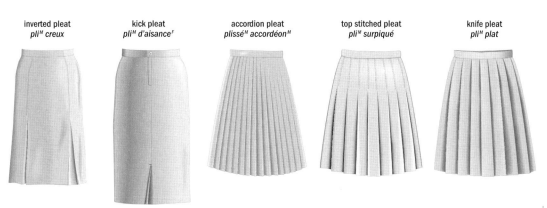

inverted pleat
pli^M creux

kick pleat
pli^M d'aisance^F

accordion pleat
plissé^M accordéon^M

top stitched pleat
pli^M surpiqué

knife pleat
pli^M plat

CLOTHING

examples of trousers
exemples^M de pantalons^M

shorts
short^M

Bermuda shorts
bermuda^M

knickerbockers
knicker^M

pedal pushers
corsaire^M

jeans
jean^M

ski pants
fuseau^M

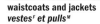

footstrap
sous-pied^M

jumpsuit
combinaison^F-pantalon^M

dungarees
salopette^F

bell bottoms
pantalon^M pattes^F d'éléphant^M

waistcoats and jackets
vestes^F et pulls^M

bolero
boléro^M

spencer
spencer^M

blazer
blazer^M

safari jacket
saharienne^F

waistcoat
gilet^M

twin-set
tandem^M

crew neck sweater
ras-de-cou^M

cardigan
cardigan^M

gusset pocket
poche^F *soufflet*^M

examples of blouses
***exemples*^M *de chemisiers*^M**

CLOTHING

body
body^M

sailor tunic
marinière^F

crotch piece
patte^F *d'entrejambe*^M

yoke
empiècement^M

gather
fronce^F

shirttail
pan^M

classic blouse
chemisier^M *classique*

button-through smock
tablier^M*-blouse*^F

overshirt
liquette^F

smock
tunique^F

wrapover top
cache-cœur^M

polo shirt
polo^M

tunic
casaque^F

nightwear
vêtements^M *de nuit*^F

nightgown
chemise^F *de nuit*^F

baby doll
nuisette^F

kimono
kimono^M

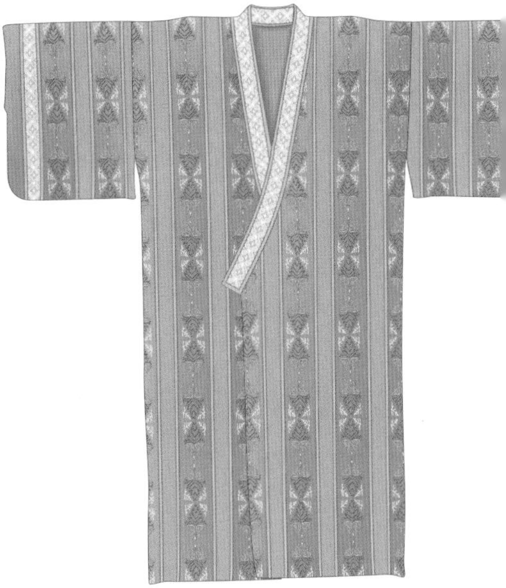

pyjamas
pyjama^M

negligee
déshabillé^M

bathrobe
peignoir^M

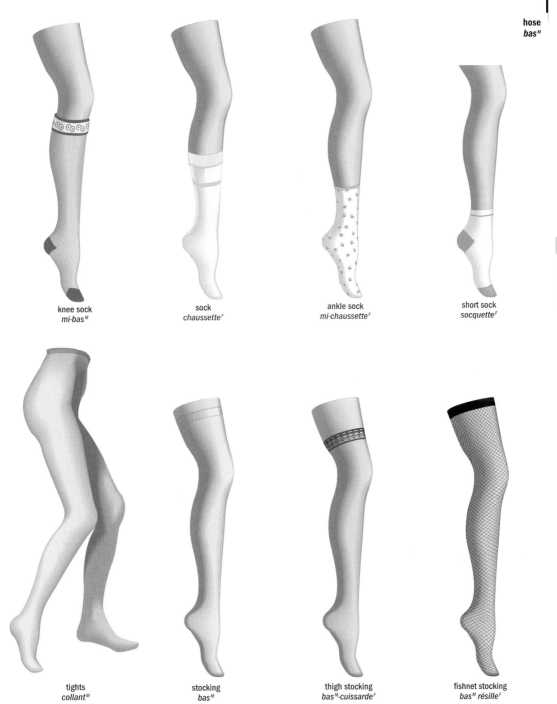

CLOTHING

knee sock
mi-bas^M

sock
chaussette^F

ankle sock
mi-chaussette^F

short sock
socquette^F

tights
collant^M

stocking
bas^M

thigh stocking
bas^M-*cuissarde*^F

fishnet stocking
bas^M *résille*^F

underwear
sous-vêtements^M

corselette
combiné^M

camisole
caraco^M

teddy
teddy^M

body
body^M

panty corselette
combiné^M-*culotte*^F

half-slip
jupon^M

princess seaming
découpe^F *princesse*^F

foundation slip
fond^M *de robe*^F

slip
combinaison^F-*jupon*^M

CLOTHING

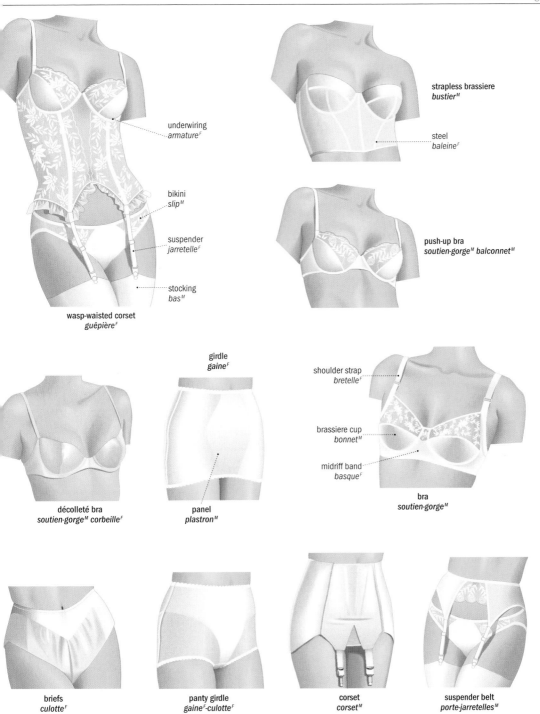

underwiring
armature^F

strapless brassiere
bustier^M

steel
baleine^F

bikini
slip^M

suspender
jarretelle^F

push-up bra
soutien-gorge^M *balconnet*^M

stocking
bas^M

wasp-waisted corset
guêpière^F

girdle
gaine^F

shoulder strap
bretelle^F

brassiere cup
bonnet^M

midriff band
basque^F

décolleté bra
soutien-gorge^M *corbeille*^F

panel
plastron^M

bra
soutien-gorge^M

briefs
culotte^F

panty girdle
gaine^F-*culotte*^F

corset
corset^M

suspender belt
porte-jarretelles^M

CLOTHING

newborn children's clothing

vêtements^M de nouveau-né^M

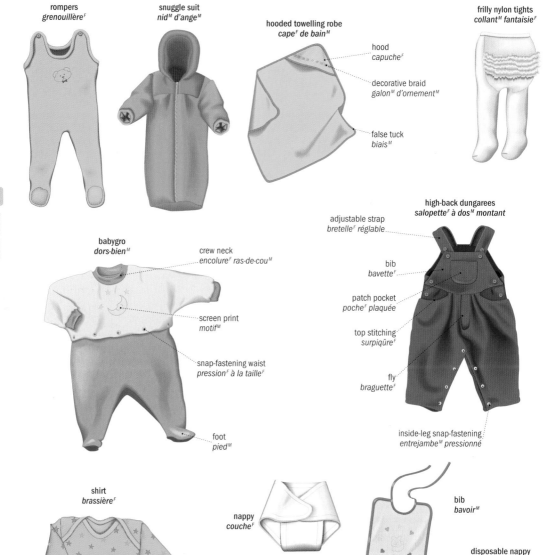

rompers
grenouillère^F

snuggle suit
nid^M d'ange^M

hooded towelling robe
cape^F de bain^M

hood
capuche^F

decorative braid
galon^M d'ornement^M

false tuck
biais^M

frilly nylon tights
collant^M fantaisie^F

high-back dungarees
salopette^F à dos^M montant

adjustable strap
bretelle^F réglable

bib
bavette^F

patch pocket
poche^F plaquée

top stitching
surpiqûre^F

fly
braguette^F

inside-leg snap-fastening
entrejambe^M pressionné

babygro
dors-bien^M

crew neck
encolure^F ras-de-cou^M

screen print
motif^M

snap-fastening waist
pression^F à la taille^F

foot
pied^M

shirt
brassière^F

nappy
couche^F

bib
bavoir^M

frilly pants
culotte^F à ruchés^M

ruching
ruché^M

disposable nappy
couche^F-culotte^F

Velcro® closure
fermeture^F Velcro®

waterproof pants
poche^F intérieure isolante

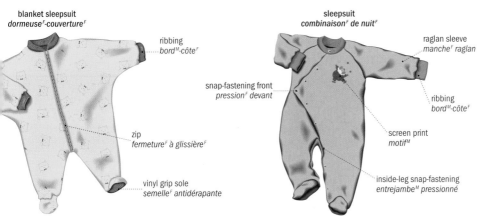

blanket sleepsuit
dormeuse^F-couverture^F

ribbing
bord^M-côte^F

snap-fastening front
pression^F devant

zip
fermeture^F à glissière^F

vinyl grip sole
semelle^F antidérapante

sleepsuit
combinaison^F de nuit^F

raglan sleeve
manche^F raglan

ribbing
bord^M-côte^F

screen print
motif^M

inside-leg snap-fastening
entrejambe^M pressionné

children's clothing

vêtements^M d'enfant^M

CLOTHING

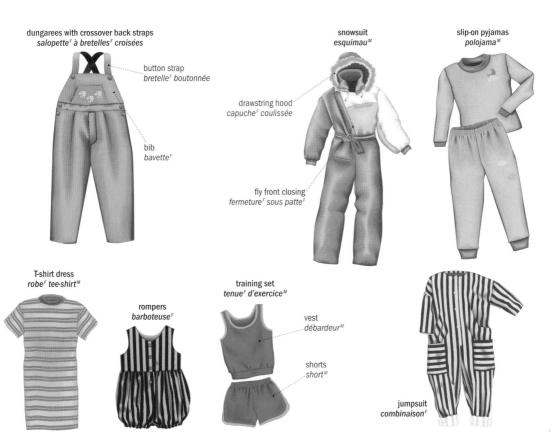

dungarees with crossover back straps
salopette^F à bretelles^F croisées

button strap
bretelle^F boutonnée

bib
bavette^F

snowsuit
esquimau^M

drawstring hood
capuche^F coulissée

fly front closing
fermeture^F sous patte^F

slip-on pyjamas
polojama^M

T-shirt dress
robe^F tee-shirt^M

rompers
barboteuse^F

training set
tenue^F d'exercice^M

vest
débardeur^M

shorts
short^M

jumpsuit
combinaison^F

sportswear

tenue^F d'exercice^M

running shoe
chaussure^F de sport^M

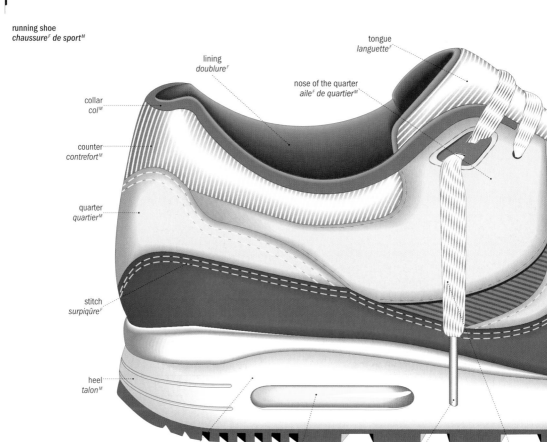

tongue
languette^F

lining
doublure^F

nose of the quarter
aile^F de quartier^M

collar
col^M

counter
contrefort^M

quarter
quartier^M

stitch
surpiqûre^F

heel
talon^M

middle sole
semelle^F intercalaire

air cushion
coussin^M d'air^M

tag
ferret^M

shoelace
lacet^M

training suit
survêtement^M

jogging pants
pantalon^M molleton^M

hooded sweat shirt
sweat-shirt^M à capuche^F

sweat shirt
sweat-shirt^M

swimming trunks
slip^M *de bain*^M

swimsuit
maillot^M *de bain*^M

exercise wear
vêtement^M *d'exercice*^M

eyelet
œillet^M

vamp
claque^F

punch hole
perforation^F

leotard
justaucorps^M

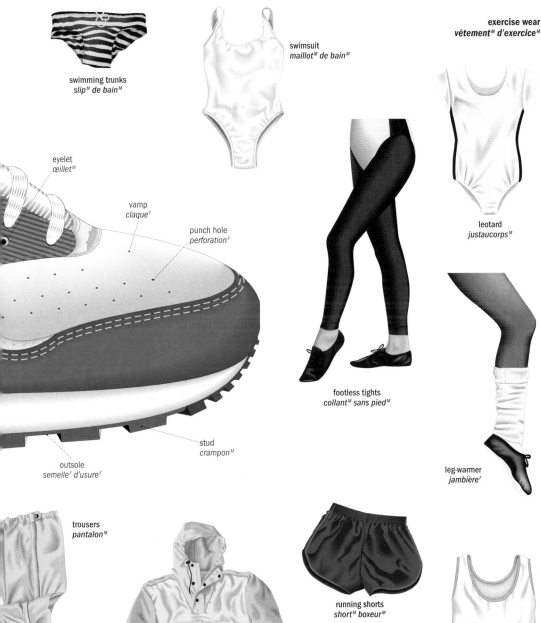

footless tights
collant^M *sans pied*^M

stud
crampon^M

outsole
semelle^F *d'usure*^F

leg-warmer
jambière^F

trousers
pantalon^M

running shorts
short^M *boxeur*^M

anorak
anorak^M

vest
débardeur^M

jewellery
bijouterie^F

PERSONAL ADORNMENT AND ARTICLES

earrings
boucles^F d'oreille^F

clip earrings	screw earrings	ear studs	drop earrings	hoop earrings
boucles^F d'oreille^F à pince^F	*boucles^F d'oreille^F à vis^F*	*boucles^F d'oreille^F à tige^F*	*pendants^M d'oreille^F*	*anneaux^M*

necklaces
colliers^M

matinee-length necklace
collier^M de perles^F, longueur^F matinée^F

velvet-band choker
collier^M-de-chien^M

pendant
pendentif^M

rope	opera-length necklace	bib necklace	choker	locket
sautoir^M	*sautoir^M, longueur^F opéra^M*	*collier^M de soirée^F*	*ras-de-cou^M*	*médaillon^M*

bracelets
bracelets^M

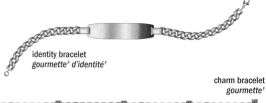

identity bracelet
gourmette^F d'identité^F

charm bracelet
gourmette^F

bangle
bracelet^M tubulaire

rings
bagues^F

band ring	signet ring	solitaire ring	engagement ring	wedding ring
jonc^M	*chevalière^F*	*solitaire^M*	*bague^F de fiançailles^F*	*alliance^F*

manicure
manucure[F]

manicure set
trousse[F] *de manucure*[F]

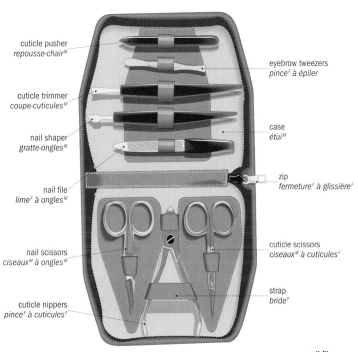

cuticle pusher
repousse-chair[M]

cuticle trimmer
coupe-cuticules[M]

nail shaper
gratte-ongles[M]

nail file
lime[F] *à ongles*[M]

nail scissors
ciseaux[M] *à ongles*[M]

cuticle nippers
pince[F] *à cuticules*[F]

eyebrow tweezers
pince[F] *à épiler*

case
étui[M]

zip
fermeture[F] *à glissière*[F]

cuticle scissors
ciseaux[M] *à cuticules*[F]

strap
bride[F]

nail varnish
vernis[M] *à ongles*[M]

safety scissors
ciseaux[M] *de sûreté*[F]

nail file
polissoir[M] *d'ongles*[M]

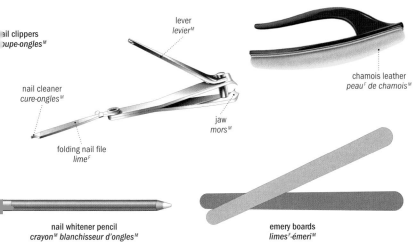

lever
levier[M]

ail clippers
oupe-ongles[M]

nail cleaner
cure-ongles[M]

folding nail file
lime[F]

chamois leather
peau[F] *de chamois*[M]

jaw
mors[M]

nail whitener pencil
crayon[M] *blanchisseur d'ongles*[M]

emery boards
limes[F]*-émeri*[M]

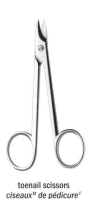

toenail scissors
ciseaux[M] *de pédicure*[F]

PERSONAL ADORNMENT AND ARTICLES

265

make-up

maquillage^M

make-up
maquillage^M

compact
poudrier^M

blusher brush
pinceau^M pour fard^M à joues^F

powder puff
houpette^F

powder blusher
fard^M à joues^F en poudre^F

pressed powder
poudre^F pressée

synthetic sponge
éponge^F synthétique

loose powder
poudre^F libre

loose powder brush
*pinceau^M pour poudre^F
libre*

liquid foundation
fond^M de teint^M liquide

fan brush
pinceau^M éventail^M

eye make-up
maquillage^M des yeux^M

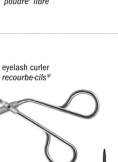

eyelash curler
recourbe-cils^M

brow brush and lash comb
brosse^F-peigne^M pour cils^M et sourcils^M

eyebrow pencil
crayon^M à sourcils^M

mascara brush
brosse^F à mascara^M

liquid eyeliner
eye-liner^M liquide

sponge-tipped applicator
applicateur^M-mousse^F

cake mascara
mascara^M en pain^M

eyeshadow
ombre^F à paupières^F

liquid mascara
mascara^M liquide

lip make-up
maquillage^M des lèvres^F

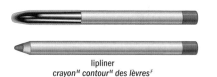

lipbrush
pinceau^M à lèvres^F

lipliner
crayon^M contour^M des lèvres^F

lipstick
rouge^M à lèvres^F

body care
soins^M du corps^M

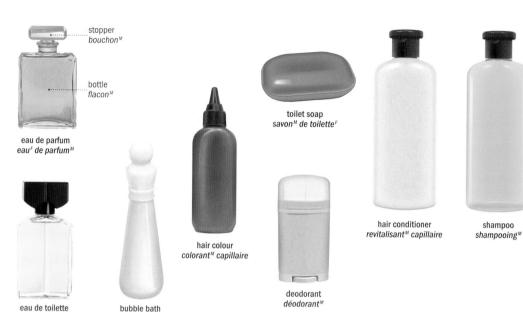

stopper
bouchon^M

bottle
flacon^M

eau de parfum
eau^F de parfum^M

toilet soap
savon^M de toilette^F

hair conditioner
revitalisant^M capillaire

shampoo
shampooing^M

eau de toilette
eau^F de toilette^F

bubble bath
bain^M moussant

hair colour
colorant^M capillaire

deodorant
déodorant^M

face flannel
gant^M de toilette^F

face flannel
débarbouillette^F

massage glove
gant^M de crin^M

vegetable sponge
éponge^F végétale

natural sponge
éponge^F de mer^F

back brush
brosse^F pour le dos^M

bath sheet
drap^M de bain^M

bath towel
serviette^F de toilette^F

bath brush
brosse^F pour le bain^M

hairdressing

coiffure^F

hairbrushes
brosses^F à cheveux^M

flat-back brush
brosse^F pneumatique

round brush
brosse^F ronde

quill brush
brosse^F anglaise

vent brush
brosse^F-araignée^F

combs
peignes^M

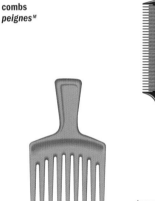

teaser comb
peigne^M à crêper

barber comb
peigne^M de coiffeur^M

rake comb
démêloir^M

Afro pick
peigne^M afro

tail comb
peigne^M à tige^F

pitchfork comb
combiné^M 2 dans 1

hair roller
bigoudi^M

roller
rouleau^M

hairpin
épingle^F à cheveux^M

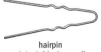

hair grip
pince^F à cheveux^M

hair roller pin
épingle^F à bigoudi^M

wave clip
pince^F à boucles^F de cheveux^M

hair clip
pince^F de mise^F en plis^M

hair slide
barrette^F

hairdressing

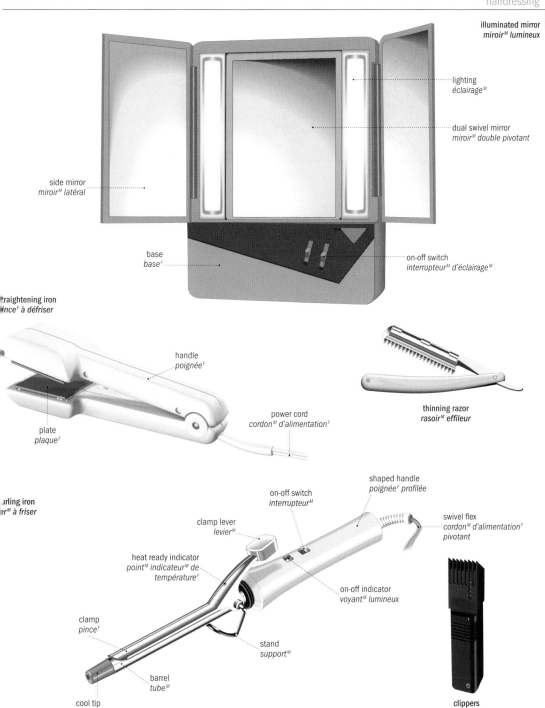

illuminated mirror
miroir^M *lumineux*

lighting
éclairage^M

dual swivel mirror
miroir^M *double pivotant*

side mirror
miroir^M *latéral*

base
base^F

on-off switch
interrupteur^M *d'éclairage*^M

straightening iron
pince^F *à défriser*

handle
poignée^F

plate
plaque^F

power cord
cordon^M *d'alimentation*^F

thinning razor
rasoir^M *effileur*

curling iron
fer^M *à friser*

shaped handle
poignée^F *profilée*

on-off switch
interrupteur^M

swivel flex
cordon^M *d'alimentation*^F
pivotant

clamp lever
levier^M

heat ready indicator
point^M *indicateur*^M *de*
température^F

on-off indicator
voyant^M *lumineux*

clamp
pince^F

stand
support^M

barrel
tube^M

cool tip
embout^M *isolant*

clippers
tondeuse^F

PERSONAL ADORNMENT AND ARTICLES

hairdressing

PERSONAL ADORNMENT AND ARTICLES

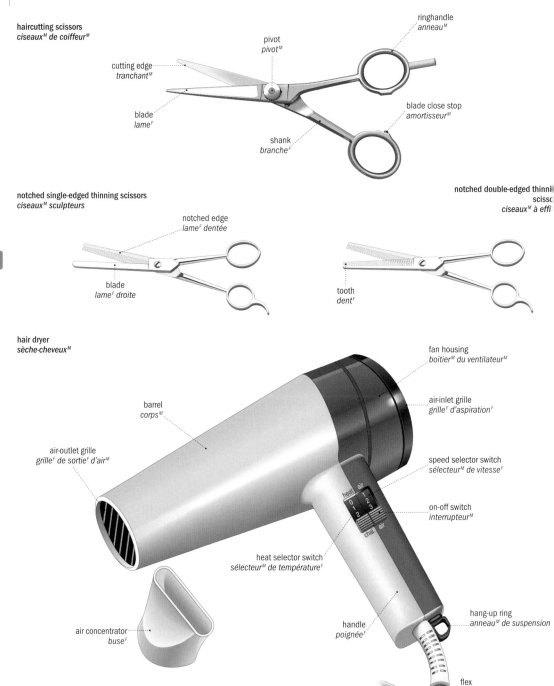

haircutting scissors
ciseaux^M *de coiffeur*^M

pivot
pivot^M

ringhandle
anneau^M

cutting edge
tranchant^M

blade
lame^F

shank
branche^F

blade close stop
amortisseur^M

notched single-edged thinning scissors
ciseaux^M *sculpteurs*

notched edge
lame^F *dentée*

blade
lame^F *droite*

notched double-edged thinning scissors
ciseaux^M *à effiler*

tooth
dent^F

hair dryer
sèche-cheveux^M

fan housing
boîtier^M *du ventilateur*^M

barrel
corps^M

air-inlet grille
grille^F *d'aspiration*^F

air-outlet grille
grille^F *de sortie*^F *d'air*^M

speed selector switch
sélecteur^M *de vitesse*^F

on-off switch
interrupteur^M

heat selector switch
sélecteur^M *de température*^F

hang-up ring
anneau^M *de suspension*^F

air concentrator
buse^F

handle
poignée^F

flex
cordon^M *d'alimentation*^F

shaving
rasage^M

electric razor
rasoir^M électrique

floating head
tête^F flottante

trimmer
tondeuse^F

screen
grille^F

closeness setting
sélecteur^M de coupe^F

cleaning brush
brosse^F de nettoyage^M

housing
boitier^M

charge indicator
indicateur^M de charge^F

charging light
voyant^M de charge^F

shaving foam
mousse^F à raser

flex
cordon^M d'alimentation^F

on-off switch
interrupteur^M

charging socket
prise^F de charge^F

shaving brush
blaireau^M

plug adapter
adaptateur^M de fiche^F

cut-throat razor
rasoir^M à manche^M

blade
lame^F

bristle
soie^F

aftershave
après-rasage^M

handle
manche^M

pivot
pivot^M

double-edged razor
rasoir^M à double
tranchant^M

disposable razor
rasoir^M jetable

blade dispenser
distributeur^M de lames^F

head
tête^F

collar
anneau^M

shaving mug
bol^M à raser

double-edged razor blade
lame^F à double tranchant^M

handle
manche^M

PERSONAL ADORNMENT AND ARTICLES

dental care

hygiène^F dentaire

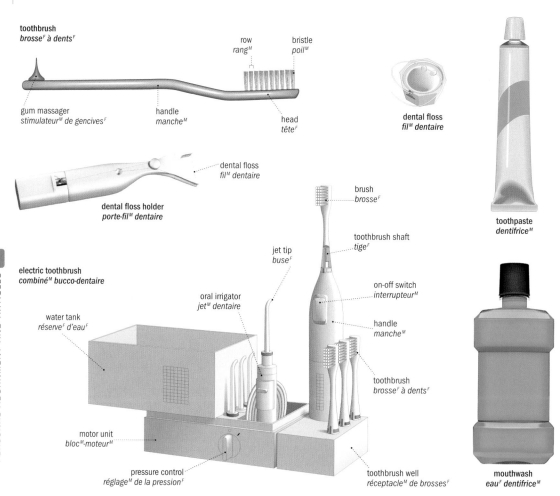

toothbrush
brosse^F à dents^F

row
rang^M

bristle
poil^M

gum massager
stimulateur^M de gencives^F

handle
manche^M

head
tête^F

dental floss
fil^M dentaire

dental floss
fil^M dentaire

dental floss holder
porte-fil^M dentaire

brush
brosse^F

toothbrush shaft
tige^F

jet tip
buse^F

toothpaste
dentifrice^M

electric toothbrush
combiné^M bucco-dentaire

oral irrigator
jet^M dentaire

on-off switch
interrupteur^M

water tank
réserve^F d'eau^F

handle
manche^M

toothbrush
brosse^F à dents^F

motor unit
bloc^M-moteur^M

pressure control
réglage^M de la pression^F

toothbrush well
réceptacle^M de brosses^F

mouthwash
eau^F dentifrice^M

contact lenses

lentilles^F de contact^M

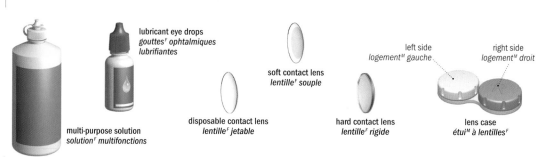

lubricant eye drops
gouttes^F ophtalmiques
lubrifiantes

left side
logement^M gauche

right side
logement^M droit

soft contact lens
lentille^F souple

multi-purpose solution
solution^F multifonctions

disposable contact lens
lentille^F jetable

hard contact lens
lentille^F rigide

lens case
étui^M à lentilles^F

spectacles

lunettes^F

parts of spectacles
parties^F des lunettes^F

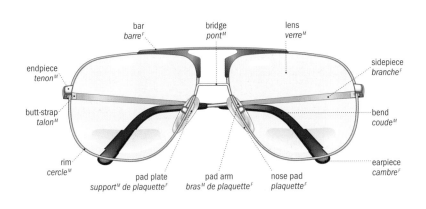

bar
barre^F

bridge
pont^M

lens
verre^M

endpiece
tenon^M

sidepiece
branche^F

butt-strap
talon^M

bend
coude^M

rim
cercle^M

earpiece
cambre^F

pad plate
support^M de plaquette^F

pad arm
bras^M de plaquette^F

nose pad
plaquette^F

examples of spectacles
exemples^M de lunettes^F

opera glasses
lorgnette^F

sunglasses
lunettes^F de soleil^M

half-glasses
demi-lune^F

umbrella and stick

parapluie^M et canne^F

umbrella
parapluie^M

umbrella stand
porte-parapluies^M

walking stick
canne^F

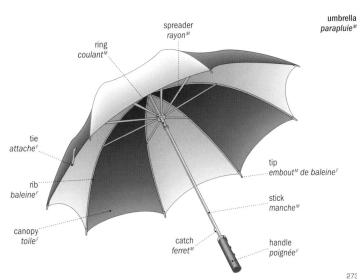

spreader
rayon^M

ring
coulant^M

tie
attache^F

rib
baleine^F

canopy
toile^F

tip
embout^M de baleine^F

stick
manche^M

catch
ferret^M

handle
poignée^F

PERSONAL ADORNMENT AND ARTICLES

leather goods

articles^M de maroquinerie^F

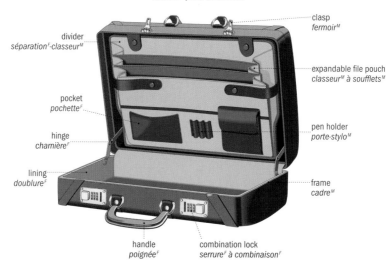

attaché case
mallette^F porte-documents^M

clasp
fermoir^M

divider
séparation^F-classeur^M

expandable file pouch
classeur^M à soufflets^M

pocket
pochette^F

hinge
charnière^F

pen holder
porte-stylo^M

lining
doublure^F

frame
cadre^M

handle
poignée^F

combination lock
serrure^F à combinaison^F

bottom-fold document case
porte-documents^M à soufflet^M

briefcas
serviette

retractable handle
poignée^F rentrante

exterior pocket
poche^F extérieure

tab
patte^F

key lock
serrure^F à clé^F

gusset
soufflet^M

calculator/cheque book holder
porte-chéquier^M

credit card walle
porte-cartes

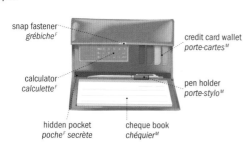

snap fastener
grébiche^F

credit card wallet
porte-cartes^M

calculator
calculette^F

pen holder
porte-stylo^M

hidden pocket
poche^F secrète

cheque book
chéquier^M

wallet section
poche^F américaine

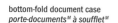

transparent pockets
feuillets^M

tab
patte^F

slot
fente^F

window
volet^M transparent

wallet
portefeuille^M

coin purse
porte-monnaie^M

key case
porte-clés^M

purse
bourse^F *à monnaie*^M

passport case
porte-passeport^M

wallet
porte-coupures^M

writing case
écritoire^F

cheque book cover
porte-chéquier^M

spectacles case
étui^M *à lunettes*^F

underarm briefcase
porte-documents^M *plat*

handbags

sacs^M *à main*^F

drawstring bag
sac^M *seau*^M

satchel bag
sac^M *cartable*^M

eyelet
œillet^M

drawstring
lacet^M *de serrage*^M

front pocket
poche^F *frontale*

handle
poignée^F

flap
rabat^M

clasp
fermoir^M

lock
serrure^F

handbags

box bag
sac^M boîte^F

small drawstring bag
balluchon^M

shoulder bag
sac^M à bandoulière^F

buckle
boucle^F

shoulder strap
bandoulière^F

muff
manchon^M

shoulder bag with zip
sac^M besace^F

accordion bag
sac^M accordéon^M

gusset
soufflet^M

tote bag
sac^M fourre-tout^M

men's bag
pochette^F d'homme^M

duffle bag
sac^M marin^M

holdall
sac^M polochon^M

shopping bag
sac^M à provisions^F

shopping bag
cabas^M

luggage

bagages^M

toilet bag
trousse^F de toilette^F

travel bag
sac^M de vol^M

handle
poignée^F

exterior pocket
poche^F extérieure

shoulder strap
bandoulière^F

flight bag
sac^M fourre-tout^M

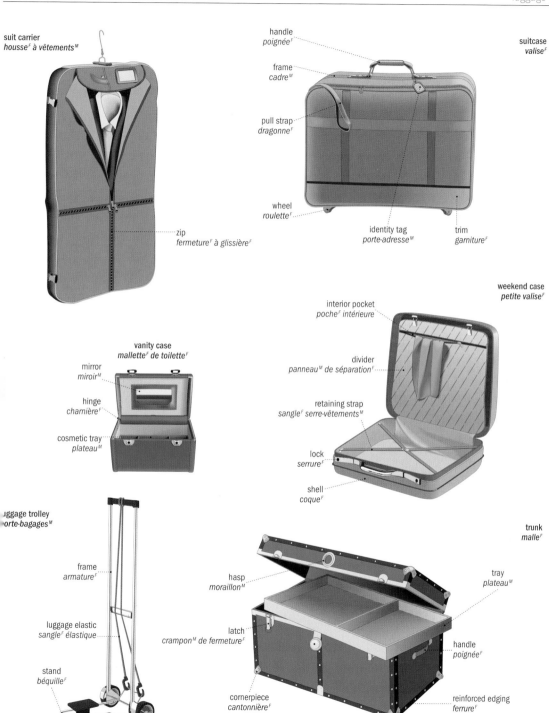

suit carrier
*housse*F *à vêtements*M

handle
*poignée*F

suitcase
*valise*F

frame
*cadre*M

pull strap
*dragonne*F

wheel
*roulette*F

identity tag
*porte-adresse*M

trim
*garniture*F

zip
*fermeture*F *à glissière*F

weekend case
*petite valise*F

interior pocket
*poche*F *intérieure*

divider
*panneau*M *de séparation*F

vanity case
*mallette*F *de toilette*F

mirror
*miroir*M

hinge
*charnière*F

cosmetic tray
*plateau*M

retaining strap
*sangle*F *serre-vêtements*M

lock
*serrure*F

shell
*coque*F

luggage trolley
*porte-bagages*M

trunk
*malle*F

frame
*armature*F

hasp
*moraillon*M

tray
*plateau*M

luggage elastic
*sangle*F *élastique*

latch
*crampon*M *de fermeture*F

handle
*poignée*F

stand
*béquille*F

cornerpiece
*cantonnière*F

reinforced edging
*ferrure*F

pyramid

pyramide^F

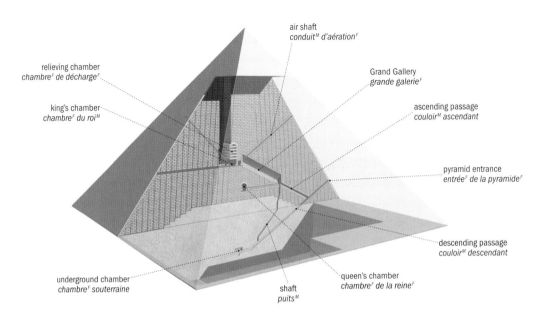

air shaft
conduit^M d'aération^F

relieving chamber
chambre^F de décharge^F

Grand Gallery
grande galerie^F

king's chamber
chambre^F du roi^M

ascending passage
couloir^M ascendant

pyramid entrance
entrée^F de la pyramide^F

descending passage
couloir^M descendant

underground chamber
chambre^F souterraine

shaft
puits^M

queen's chamber
chambre^F de la reine^F

Greek theatre

théâtre^M grec

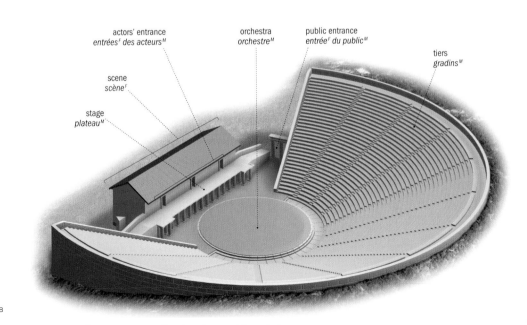

actors' entrance
entrées^F des acteurs^M

orchestra
orchestre^M

public entrance
entrée^F du public^M

tiers
gradins^M

scene
scène^F

stage
plateau^M

Greek temple

temple^M grec

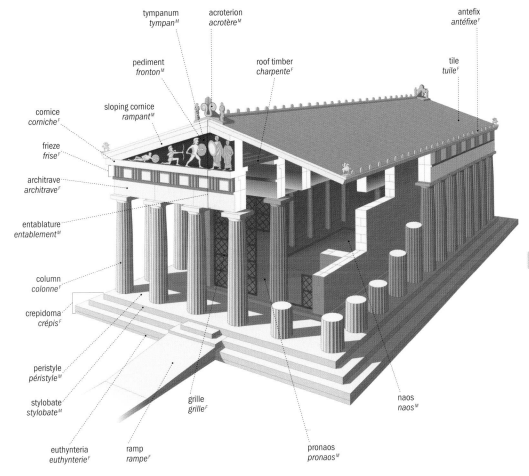

tympanum
tympan^M

acroterion
acrotère^M

antefix
antéfixe^F

pediment
fronton^M

roof timber
charpente^F

tile
tuile^F

cornice
corniche^F

sloping cornice
rampant^M

frieze
frise^F

architrave
architrave^F

entablature
entablement^M

column
colonne^F

crepidoma
crépis^F

peristyle
péristyle^M

stylobate
stylobate^M

euthynteria
euthynterie^F

ramp
rampe^F

grille
grille^F

pronaos
pronaos^M

naos
naos^M

plan
plan^M

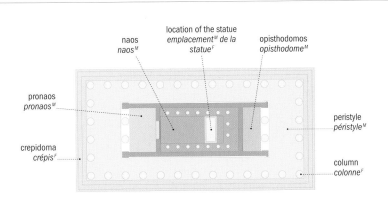

naos
naos^M

location of the statue
emplacement^M de la
statue^F

opisthodomos
opisthodome^M

pronaos
pronaos^M

peristyle
péristyle^M

crepidoma
crépis^F

column
colonne^F

ARTS AND ARCHITECTURE

Roman house

maison^F romaine

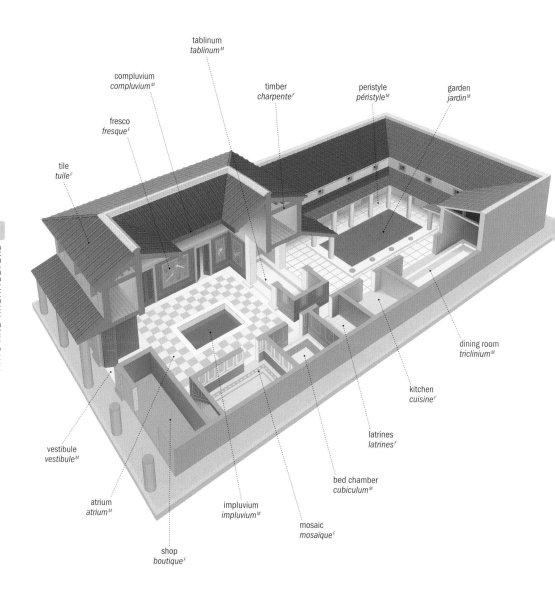

tablinum
tablinum^M

compluvium
compluvium^M

timber
charpente^F

peristyle
péristyle^M

garden
jardin^M

fresco
fresque^F

tile
tuile^F

dining room
triclinium^M

kitchen
cuisine^F

latrines
latrines^F

vestibule
vestibule^M

bed chamber
cubiculum^M

atrium
atrium^M

impluvium
impluvium^M

mosaic
mosaïque^F

shop
boutique^F

Roman amphitheatre

amphithéâtre^M romain

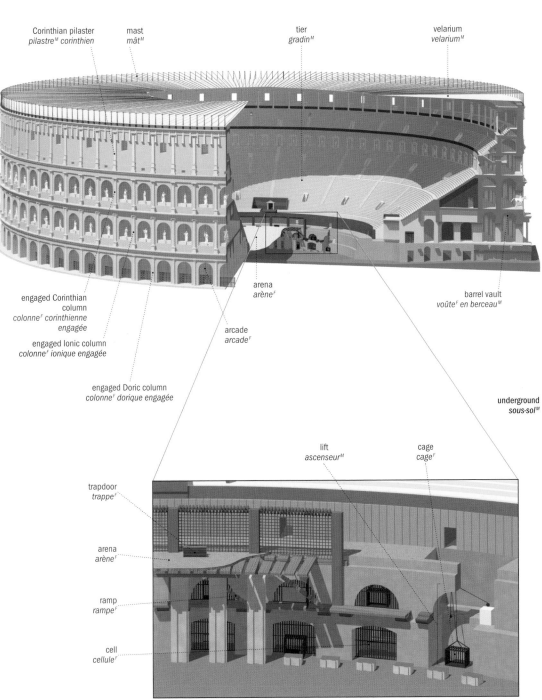

Corinthian pilaster
pilastre^M corinthien

mast
mât^M

tier
gradin^M

velarium
velarium^M

engaged Corinthian
column
*colonne^F corinthienne
engagée*

engaged Ionic column
colonne^F ionique engagée

engaged Doric column
colonne^F dorique engagée

arena
arène^F

arcade
arcade^F

barrel vault
voûte^F en berceau^M

underground
sous-sol^M

lift
ascenseur^M

cage
cage^F

trapdoor
trappe^F

arena
arène^F

ramp
rampe^F

cell
cellule^F

ARTS AND ARCHITECTURE

castle

château^M fort

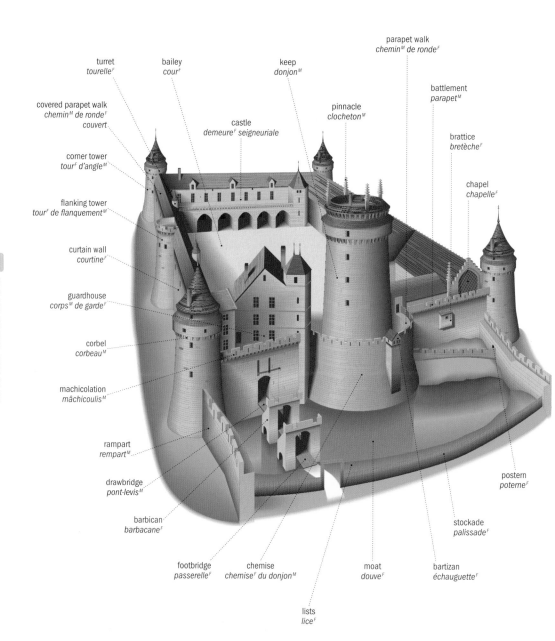

parapet walk
chemin^M de ronde^F

turret
tourelle^F

bailey
cour^F

keep
donjon^M

battlement
parapet^M

covered parapet walk
chemin^M de ronde^F
couvert

pinnacle
clocheton^M

brattice
bretèche^F

castle
demeure^F seigneuriale

corner tower
tour^F d'angle^M

chapel
chapelle^F

flanking tower
tour^F de flanquement^M

curtain wall
courtine^F

guardhouse
corps^M de garde^F

corbel
corbeau^M

machicolation
mâchicoulis^M

rampart
rempart^M

postern
poterne^F

drawbridge
pont-levis^M

barbican
barbacane^F

stockade
palissade^F

footbridge
passerelle^F

chemise
chemise^F du donjon^M

moat
douve^F

bartizan
échauguette^F

lists
lice^F

ARTS AND ARCHITECTURE

pagoda
pagode[F]

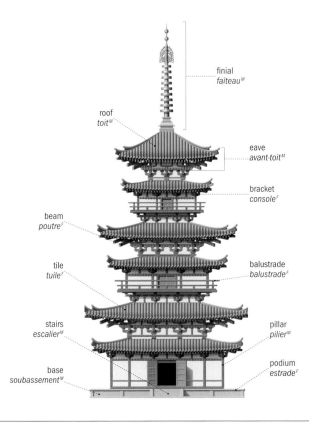

finial
faiteau[M]

roof
toit[M]

eave
avant-toit[M]

bracket
console[F]

beam
poutre[F]

balustrade
balustrade[F]

tile
tuile[F]

stairs
escalier[M]

pillar
pilier[M]

base
soubassement[M]

podium
estrade[F]

Aztec temple
temple[M] aztèque

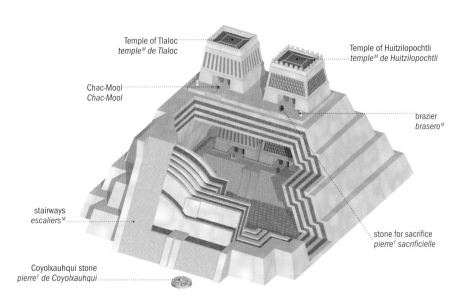

Temple of Tlaloc
temple[M] de Tlaloc

Temple of Huitzilopochtli
temple[M] de Huitzilopochtli

Chac-Mool
Chac-Mool

brazier
brasero[M]

stairways
escaliers[M]

stone for sacrifice
pierre[F] sacrificielle

Coyolxauhqui stone
pierre[F] de Coyolxauhqui

cathedral

cathédrale^F

Gothic cathedral
cathédrale^F gothique

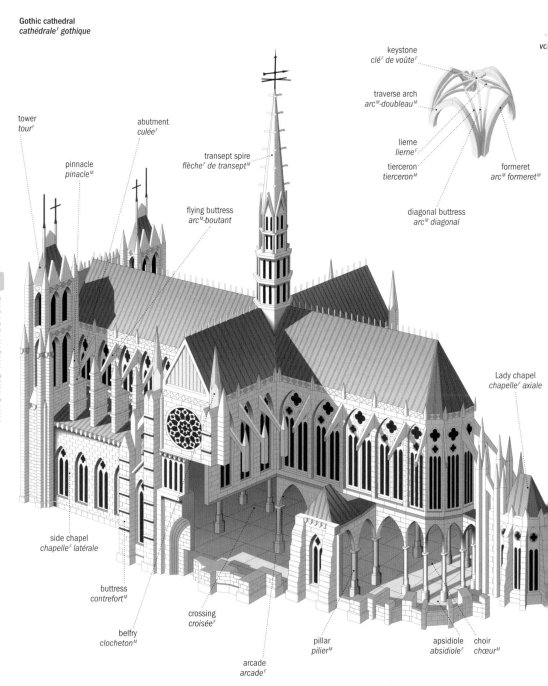

keystone
clé^F de voûte^F

VO

traverse arch
arc^M-doubleau^M

tower
tour^F

abutment
culée^F

lierne
lierne^F

pinnacle
pinacle^M

transept spire
flèche^F de transept^M

tierceron
tierceron^M

formeret
arc^M formeret^M

flying buttress
arc^M-boutant

diagonal buttress
arc^M diagonal

Lady chapel
chapelle^F axiale

side chapel
chapelle^F latérale

buttress
contrefort^M

crossing
croisée^F

belfry
clocheton^M

arcade
arcade^F

pillar
pilier^M

apsidiole
absidiole^F

choir
chœur^M

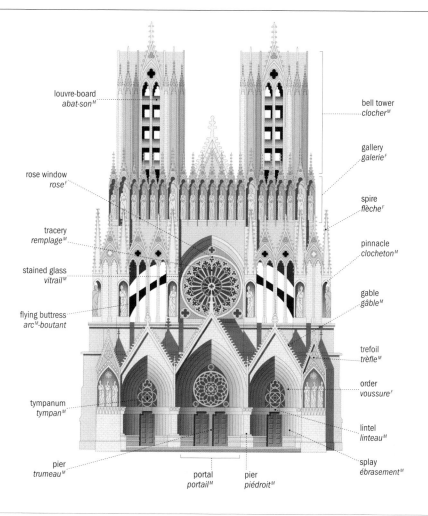

façade
façade^F

louvre-board
abat-son^M

bell tower
clocher^M

gallery
galerie^F

rose window
rose^F

spire
flèche^F

tracery
remplage^M

pinnacle
clocheton^M

stained glass
vitrail^M

gable
gâble^M

flying buttress
arc^M*-boutant*

trefoil
trèfle^M

order
voussure^F

tympanum
tympan^M

lintel
linteau^M

pier
trumeau^M

portal
portail^M

pier
piédroit^M

splay
ébrasement^M

plan
plan^M

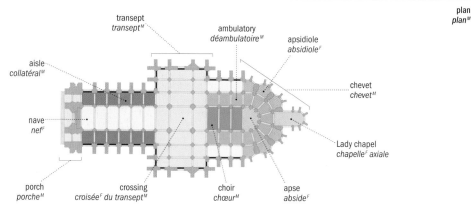

transept
transept^M

ambulatory
déambulatoire^M

apsidiole
absidiole^F

aisle
collatéral^M

chevet
chevet^M

nave
nef^F

Lady chapel
chapelle^F *axiale*

porch
porche^M

crossing
croisée^F *du transept*^M

choir
chœur^M

apse
abside^F

ARTS AND ARCHITECTURE

285

elements of architecture

éléments^M d'architecture^F

examples of doors
exemples^M de portes^F

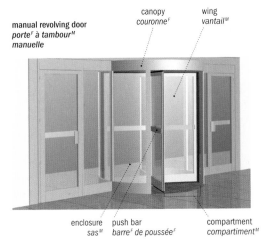

manual revolving door
porte^F à tambour^M
manuelle

canopy
couronne^F

wing
vantail^M

enclosure
sas^M

push bar
barre^F de poussée^F

compartment
compartiment^M

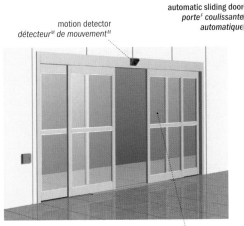

automatic sliding door
porte^F coulissante
automatique

motion detector
détecteur^M de mouvement^M

wing
vantail^M

conventional door
porte^F classique

folding door
porte^F pliante

strip
lanière^F

strip door
porte^F à lanières^F

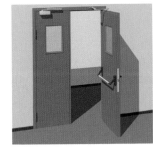

fire door
porte^F coupe-feu

concertina-type folding
door
porte^F accordéon^M

sliding door
porte^F coulissante

sectional garage door
porte^F de garage^M
sectionnelle

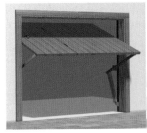

up-and-over garage door
porte^F de garage^M
basculante

ARTS AND ARCHITECTURE

elements of architecture

examples of windows
exemples^M de fenêtres^F

sliding folding window
fenêtre^F en accordéon^M

casement window opening inwards
fenêtre^F à la française^F

casement window
fenêtre^F à l'anglaise^F

louvred window
fenêtre^F à jalousies^F

sliding window
fenêtre^F coulissante

sash window
fenêtre^F à guillotine^F

horizontal pivoting window
fenêtre^F basculante

vertical pivoting window
fenêtre^F pivotante

lift

ascenseur^M

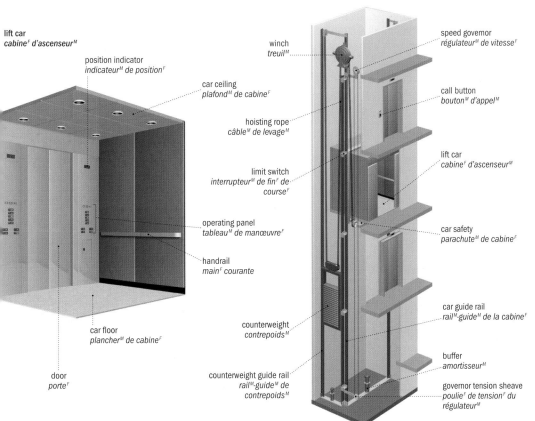

lift car
cabine^F d'ascenseur^M

position indicator
indicateur^M de position^F

car ceiling
plafond^M de cabine^F

winch
treuil^M

speed governor
régulateur^M de vitesse^F

hoisting rope
câble^M de levage^M

call button
bouton^M d'appel^M

limit switch
interrupteur^M de fin^F de course^F

lift car
cabine^F d'ascenseur^M

operating panel
tableau^M de manœuvre^F

car safety
parachute^M de cabine^F

handrail
main^F courante

car floor
plancher^M de cabine^F

counterweight
contrepoids^M

car guide rail
rail^M-guide^M de la cabine^F

door
porte^F

counterweight guide rail
rail^M-guide^M de contrepoids^M

buffer
amortisseur^M

governor tension sheave
poulie^F de tension^F du régulateur^M

ARTS AND ARCHITECTURE

traditional dwellings

maisons^F traditionnelles

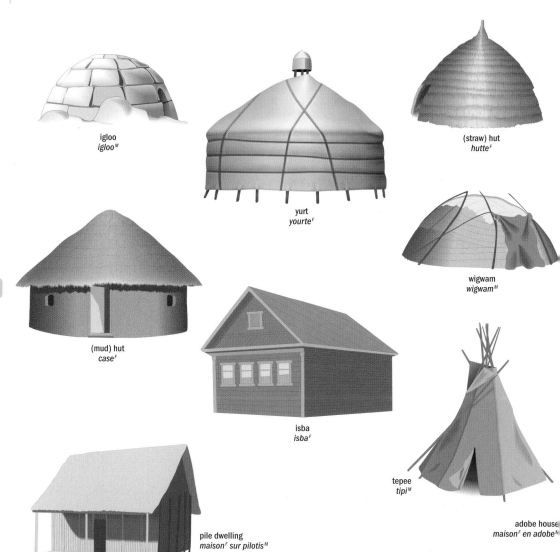

igloo
igloo^M

yurt
yourte^F

(straw) hut
hutte^F

wigwam
wigwam^M

(mud) hut
case^F

isba
isba^F

tepee
tipi^M

pile dwelling
maison^F *sur pilotis*^M

adobe house
maison^F *en adobe*^M

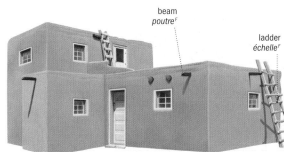

beam
poutre^F

ladder
échelle^F

town houses
maisons^F de ville^F

two-storey house
maison^F à deux étages^M

one-storey-house
maison^F de plain-pied^M

semi-detached houses
maison^F jumelée

terraced houses
maisons^F en rangée^F

freehold flats
appartements^M en copropriété^F

high-rise block
tour^F d'habitation^F

ARTS AND ARCHITECTURE

shooting stage

plateau^M de tournage^M

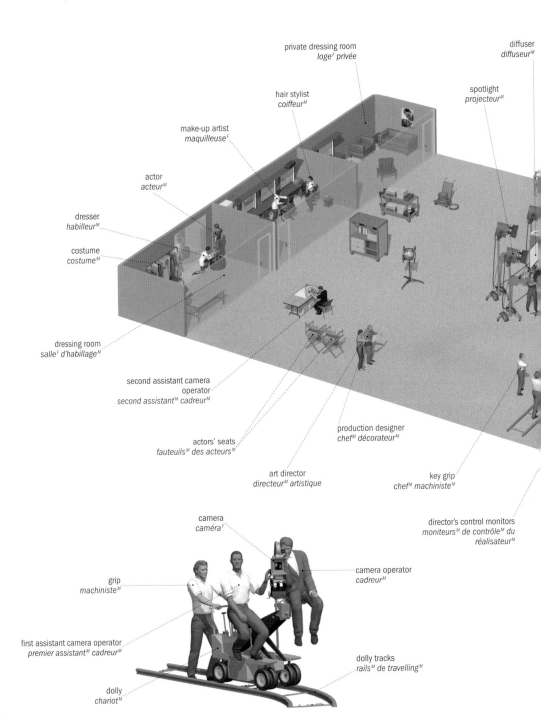

private dressing room
loge^F privée

diffuser
diffuseur^M

hair stylist
coiffeur^M

spotlight
projecteur^M

make-up artist
maquilleuse^F

actor
acteur^M

dresser
habilleur^M

costume
costume^M

dressing room
salle^F d'habillage^M

second assistant camera
operator
second assistant^M cadreur^M

production designer
chef^M décorateur^M

actors' seats
fauteuils^M des acteurs^M

art director
directeur^M artistique

key grip
chef^M machiniste^M

director's control monitors
moniteurs^M de contrôle^M du réalisateur^M

camera
caméra^F

camera operator
cadreur^M

grip
machiniste^M

first assistant camera operator
premier assistant^M cadreur^M

dolly tracks
rails^M de travelling^M

dolly
chariot^M

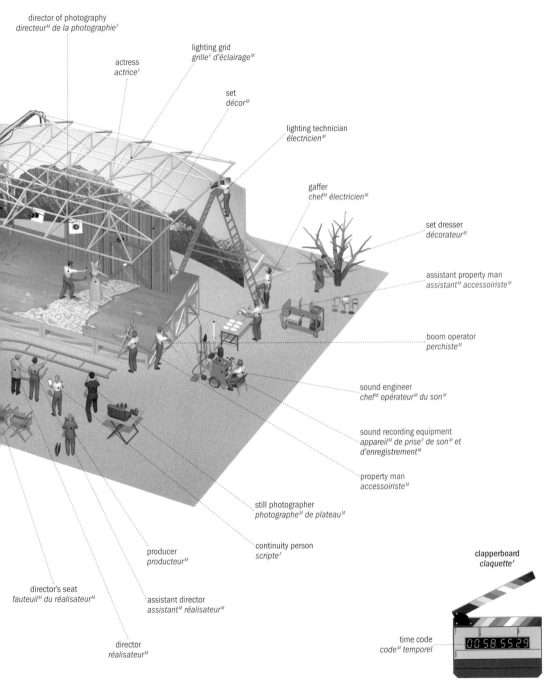

director of photography
*directeur*M *de la photographie*F

lighting grid
*grille*F *d'éclairage*M

actress
*actrice*F

set
*décor*M

lighting technician
*électricien*M

gaffer
*chef*M *électricien*M

set dresser
*décorateur*M

assistant property man
*assistant*M *accessoiriste*M

boom operator
*perchiste*M

sound engineer
*chef*M *opérateur*M *du son*M

sound recording equipment
*appareil*M *de prise*F *de son*M *et*
*d'enregistrement*M

property man
*accessoiriste*M

still photographer
*photographe*M *de plateau*M

continuity person
*scripte*F

producer
*producteur*M

director's seat
*fauteuil*M *du réalisateur*M

assistant director
*assistant*M *réalisateur*M

director
*réalisateur*M

clapperboard
*claquette*F

time code
*code*M *temporel*

theatre

salle^F de spectacle^M

ARTS AND ARCHITECTURE

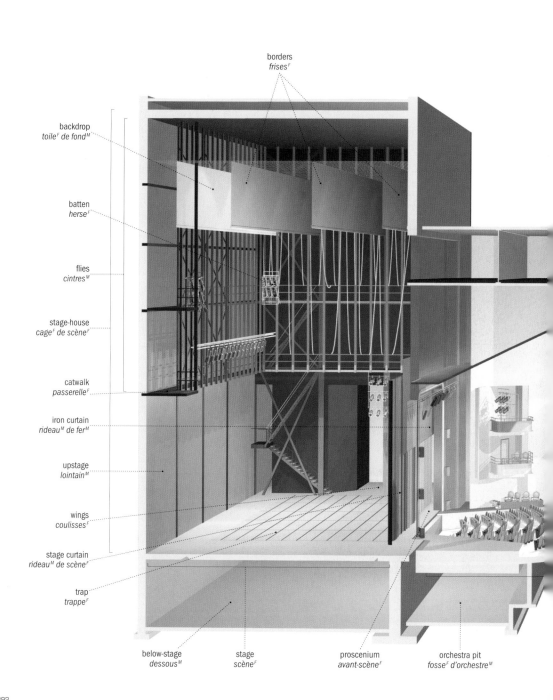

borders
frises^F

backdrop
toile^F de fond^M

batten
herse^F

flies
cintres^M

stage-house
cage^F de scène^F

catwalk
passerelle^F

iron curtain
rideau^M de fer^M

upstage
lointain^M

wings
coulisses^F

stage curtain
rideau^M de scène^F

trap
trappe^F

below-stage
dessous^M

stage
scène^F

proscenium
avant-scène^F

orchestra pit
fosse^F d'orchestre^M

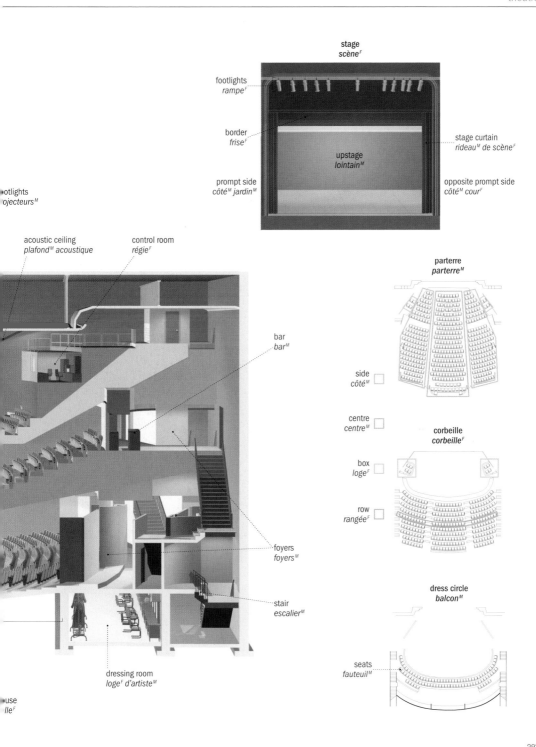

stage
scène^F

footlights
rampe^F

border
frise^F

upstage
lointain^M

stage curtain
rideau^M *de scène*^F

prompt side
côté^M *jardin*^M

opposite prompt side
côté^M *cour*^F

otlights
ojecteurs^M

acoustic ceiling
plafond^M *acoustique*

control room
régie^F

parterre
parterre^M

bar
bar^M

side
côté^M

centre
centre^M

corbeille
corbeille^F

box
loge^F

row
rangée^F

foyers
foyers^M

stair
escalier^M

dress circle
balcon^M

seats
fauteuil^M

dressing room
loge^F *d'artiste*^M

use
lle^F

cinema

cinéma^M

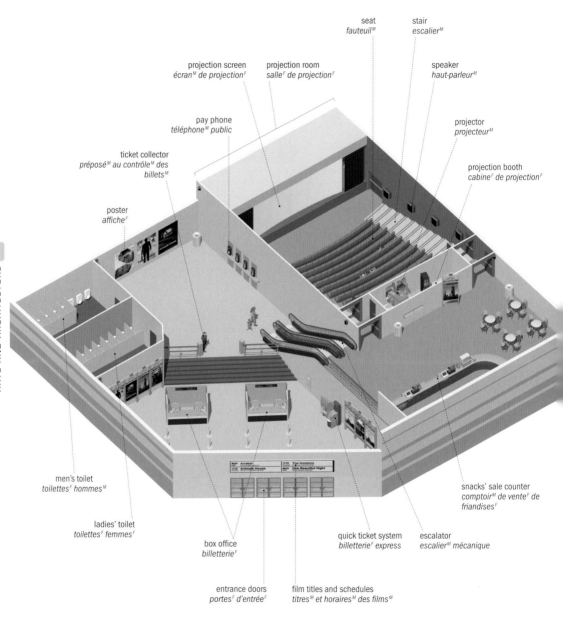

seat
fauteuil^M

stair
escalier^M

projection screen
écran^M de projection^F

projection room
salle^F de projection^F

speaker
haut-parleur^M

pay phone
téléphone^M public

projector
projecteur^M

ticket collector
préposé^M au contrôle^M des
billets^M

projection booth
cabine^F de projection^F

poster
affiche^F

men's toilet
toilettes^F hommes^M

snacks' sale counter
comptoir^M de vente^F de
friandises^F

ladies' toilet
toilettes^F femmes^F

box office
billetterie^F

quick ticket system
billetterie^F express

escalator
escalier^M mécanique

entrance doors
portes^F d'entrée^F

film titles and schedules
titres^M et horaires^M des films^M

symphony orchestra

orchestre^M symphonique

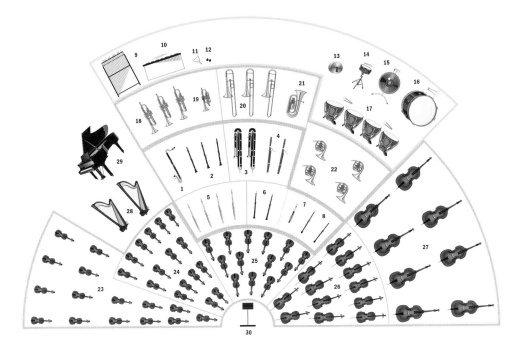

odwind family	**12** castanets
ille^F des bois^M	castagnettes^F

ss clarinet	**7**	piccolo	**13**	cymbals		
rinette^F basse		piccolo^M		cymbales^F		

brass family
famille^F des cuivres^M

violin family
famille^F du violon^M

rinets	**8**	cors anglais	**14**	snare drum	**18**	trumpets	**23**	first violins	
rinettes^F		cors^M anglais		caisse^F claire		trompettes^F		premiers violons^M	

ntrabassoons		**percussion instruments**	**15**	gong	**19**	cornet	**24**	second violins	
ntrebassons^M		*instruments^M à percussion^F*		gong^M		cornet^M à pistons^M		seconds violons^M	

ssoons					**20**	trombones	**25**	violas	
ssons^M	**9**	tubular bells	**16**	bass drum		trombones^M		altos^M	
		carillon^M tubulaire		grosse caisse^F					

es	**10**	xylophone	**17**	timpani	**21**	tuba	**26**	cellos	
tes^F		xylophone^M		timbales^F		tuba^M		violoncelles^M	

oes	**11**	triangle	**28**	harps	**22**	French horns	**27**	double basses	
utbois^M		triangle^M		harpes^F		cors^M d'harmonie^F		contrebasses^F	

29 piano	**30** conductor's podium		
piano^M	pupitre^M du chef^M d'orchestre^M		

traditional musical instruments

instruments^M traditionnels

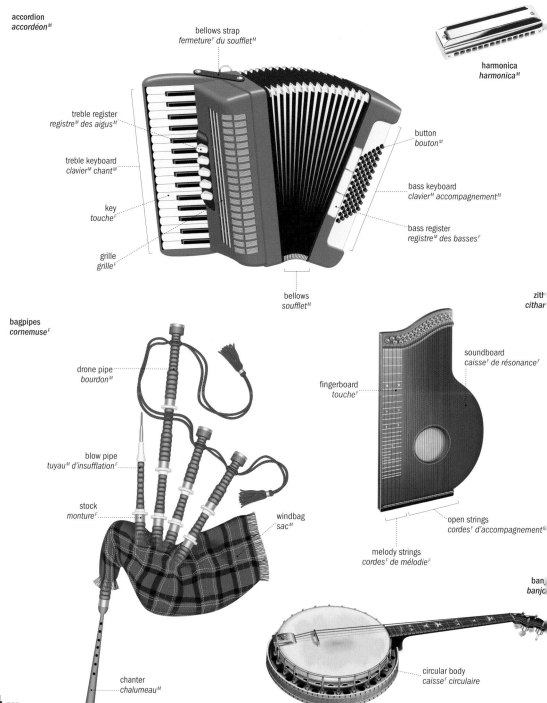

accordion
accordéon^M

bellows strap
fermeture^F du soufflet^M

harmonica
harmonica^M

treble register
registre^M des aigus^M

button
bouton^M

treble keyboard
clavier^M chant^M

bass keyboard
clavier^M accompagnement^M

key
touche^F

bass register
registre^M des basses^F

grille
grille^F

bellows
soufflet^M

zith...
cithar...

bagpipes
cornemuse^F

soundboard
caisse^F de résonance^F

drone pipe
bourdon^M

fingerboard
touche^F

blow pipe
tuyau^M d'insufflation^F

stock
monture^F

windbag
sac^M

open strings
cordes^F d'accompagnement$^{(...)}$

melody strings
cordes^F de mélodie^F

ban...
banj...

chanter
chalumeau^M

circular body
caisse^F circulaire

kora
kora^F

neck
manche^M

strings
cordes^F

tuning ring
attache^F *d'accordage*^M

balalaika
balalaïka^F

mandolin
mandoline^F

hand post
support^F *de main*^F

snare head
peau^F *de timbre*^M

triangular body
caisse^F *triangulaire*

sound box
caisse^F *de résonance*^F

bridge
chevalet^M

pear-shaped body
caisse^F *bombée*

tailpiece
cordier^M

lyre
lyre^F

tongue
lame^F

crossbar
traverse^F

frame
cadre^M

drumstick
mailloche^F

arm
montant^M

Jew's harp
guimbarde^F

plectrum
médiator^M

djembe
djembé^M

soundboard
caisse^F *de résonance*^F

talking drum
tambour^M *d'aisselle*^F

batter skin
peau^F *de batterie*^F

panpipe
flûte^F *de Pan*

sound box
caisse^F *de résonance*^F

tension rope
corde^F *de tension*^F

ARTS AND ARCHITECTURE

297

musical notation

notation^F musicale

staff
portée^F

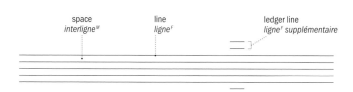

space
interligne^M

line
ligne^F

ledger line
ligne^F supplémentaire

clefs
clés^F

treble clef
clé^F de sol^M

bass clef
clé^F de fa^M

alto clef
clé^F d'ut^M

time signatures
mesures^F

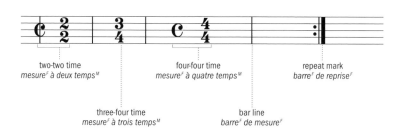

two-two time
mesure^F à deux temps^M

four-four time
mesure^F à quatre temps^M

repeat mark
barre^F de reprise^F

three-four time
mesure^F à trois temps^M

bar line
barre^F de mesure^F

intervals
intervalles^M

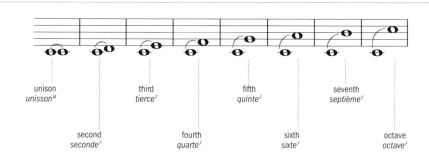

unison
unisson^M

third
tierce^F

fifth
quinte^F

seventh
septième^F

second
seconde^F

fourth
quarte^F

sixth
sixte^F

octave
octave^F

scale
gamme^F

c	d	e	f	g	a	b	c
do^M	*ré^M*	*mi^M*	*fa^M*	*sol^M*	*la^M*	*si^M*	*do^M*

rest values
valeur^F des silences^M

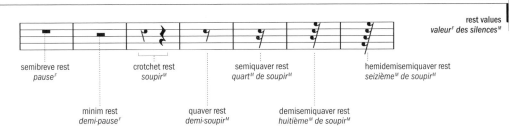

semibreve rest
pause^F

crotchet rest
soupir^M

semiquaver rest
quart^M de soupir^M

hemidemisemiquaver rest
seizième^M de soupir^M

minim rest
demi-pause^F

quaver rest
demi-soupir^M

demisemiquaver rest
huitième^M de soupir^M

ornaments
ornements^M

appoggiatura
appoggiature^F

trill
trille^M

turn
gruppetto^M

mordent
mordant^M

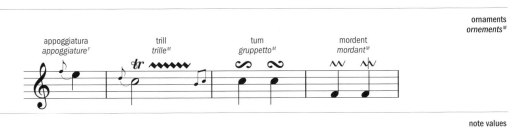

note values
valeur^F des notes^F

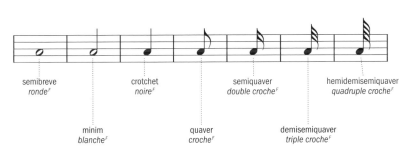

semibreve
ronde^F

crotchet
noire^F

semiquaver
double croche^F

hemidemisemiquaver
quadruple croche^F

minim
blanche^F

quaver
croche^F

demisemiquaver
triple croche^F

accidentals
altérations^F

flat
bémol^M

double sharp
double dièse^M

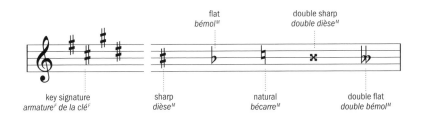

key signature
armature^F de la clé^F

sharp
dièse^M

natural
bécarre^M

double flat
double bémol^M

other signs
autres signes^M

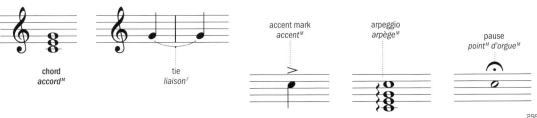

chord
accord^M

tie
liaison^F

accent mark
accent^M

arpeggio
arpège^M

pause
point^M d'orgue^M

ARTS AND ARCHITECTURE

299

examples of instrumental groups

exemples^M de groupes^M instrumentaux

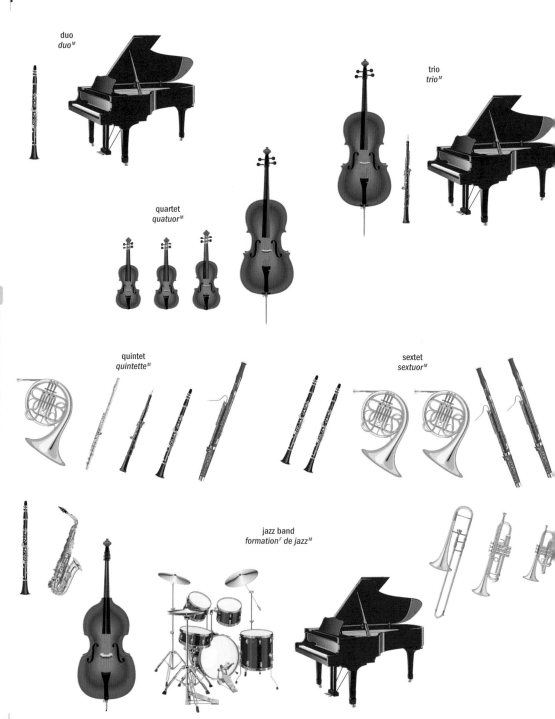

duo
duo^M

trio
trio^M

quartet
quatuor^M

quintet
quintette^M

sextet
sextuor^M

jazz band
formation^F *de jazz*^M

stringed instruments
instruments^M à cordes^F

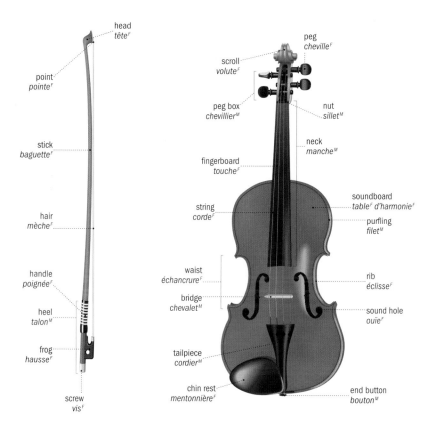

w
chet^M

head
tête^F

point
pointe^F

stick
baguette^F

hair
mèche^F

handle
poignée^F

heel
talon^M

frog
hausse^F

screw
vis^F

violin
violon^M

peg
cheville^F

scroll
volute^F

peg box
chevillier^M

nut
sillet^M

neck
manche^M

fingerboard
touche^F

string
corde^F

soundboard
table^F d'harmonie^F

purfling
filet^M

waist
échancrure^F

rib
éclisse^F

bridge
chevalet^M

sound hole
ouïe^F

tailpiece
cordier^M

chin rest
mentonnière^F

end button
bouton^M

violin family
famille^F du violon^M

double bass
contrebasse^F

cello
violoncelle^M

viola
alto^M

violin
violon^M

ARTS AND ARCHITECTURE

stringed instruments

harp
harpe[F]

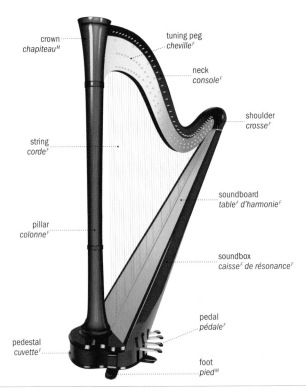

crown ········
chapiteau[M]

tuning peg
cheville[F]

neck
console[F]

shoulder
crosse[F]

string
corde[F]

soundboard
table[F] *d'harmonie*[F]

pillar
colonne[F]

soundbox
caisse[F] *de résonance*[F]

pedal
pédale[F]

pedestal
cuvette[F] ········

foot
········ *pied*[M]

acoustic guitar
guitare[F] *acoustique*

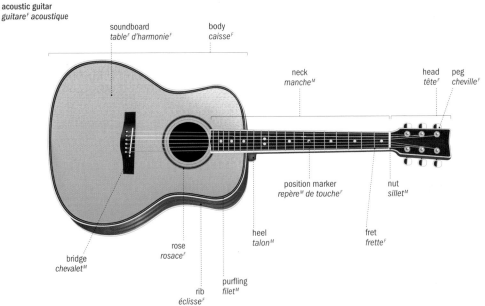

soundboard
table[F] *d'harmonie*[F]

body
caisse[F]

neck
manche[M]

head
tête[F]

peg
cheville[F]

position marker
repère[M] *de touche*[F]

nut
sillet[M]

heel
talon[M]

fret
frette[F]

bridge
chevalet[M]

rose
rosace[F]

purfling
filet[M]

rib
éclisse[F]

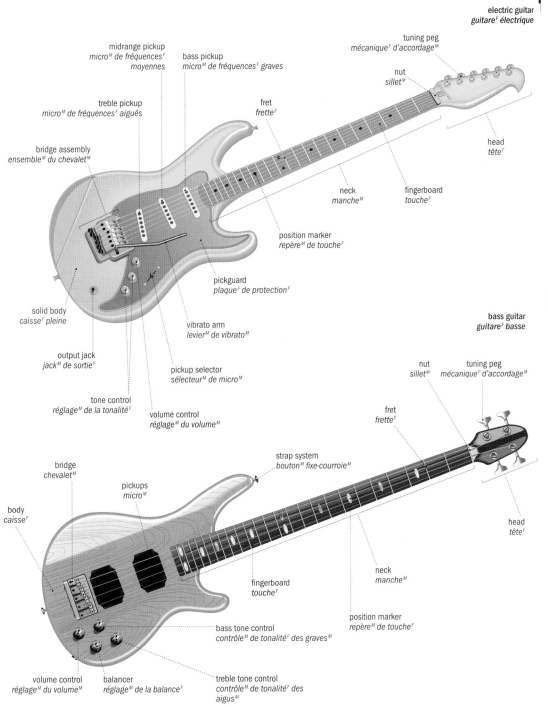

electric guitar
guitare[F] *électrique*

tuning peg
mécanique[F] *d'accordage*[M]

midrange pickup
micro[M] *de fréquences*[F]
moyennes

bass pickup
micro[M] *de fréquences*[F] *graves*

nut
sillet[M]

treble pickup
micro[M] *de fréquences*[F] *aiguës*

fret
frette[F]

bridge assembly
ensemble[M] *du chevalet*[M]

head
tête[F]

neck
manche[M]

fingerboard
touche[F]

position marker
repère[M] *de touche*[F]

pickguard
plaque[F] *de protection*[F]

solid body
caisse[F] *pleine*

bass guitar
guitare[F] *basse*

vibrato arm
levier[M] *de vibrato*[M]

output jack
jack[M] *de sortie*[F]

nut
sillet[M]

tuning peg
mécanique[F] *d'accordage*[M]

pickup selector
sélecteur[M] *de micro*[M]

tone control
réglage[M] *de la tonalité*[F]

volume control
réglage[M] *du volume*[M]

fret
frette[F]

strap system
bouton[M] *fixe-courroie*[M]

bridge
chevalet[M]

pickups
micro[M]

body
caisse[F]

head
tête[F]

neck
manche[M]

fingerboard
touche[F]

position marker
repère[M] *de touche*[F]

bass tone control
contrôle[M] *de tonalité*[F] *des graves*[M]

volume control
réglage[M] *du volume*[M]

balancer
réglage[M] *de la balance*[F]

treble tone control
contrôle[M] *de tonalité*[F] *des
aigus*[M]

keyboard instruments

instruments^M à clavier^M

ARTS AND ARCHITECTURE

upright piano
piano^M droit

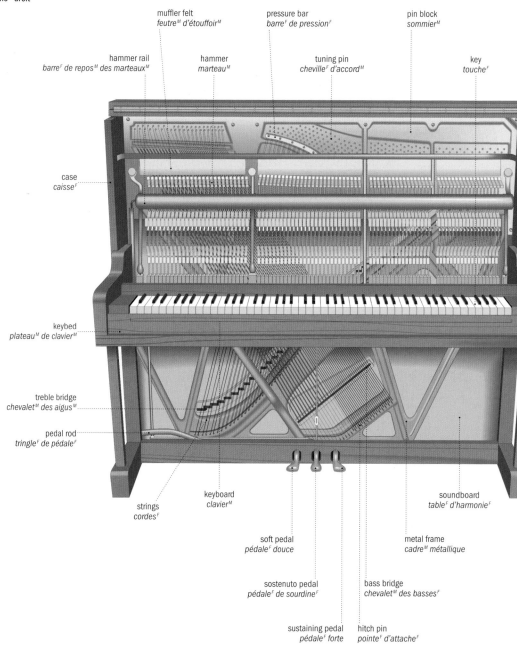

muffler felt
feutre^M d'étouffoir^M

pressure bar
barre^F de pression^F

pin block
sommier^M

hammer rail
barre^F de repos^M des marteaux^M

hammer
marteau^M

tuning pin
cheville^F d'accord^M

key
touche^F

case
caisse^F

keybed
plateau^M de clavier^M

treble bridge
chevalet^M des aigus^M

pedal rod
tringle^F de pédale^F

strings
cordes^F

keyboard
clavier^M

soundboard
table^F d'harmonie^F

soft pedal
pédale^F douce

metal frame
cadre^M métallique

sostenuto pedal
pédale^F de sourdine^F

bass bridge
chevalet^M des basses^F

sustaining pedal
pédale^F forte

hitch pin
pointe^F d'attache^F

organ
orgue^M

organ console
console^F *d'orgue*^M

stop knob
bouton^M *de registre*^M

music rest
pupitre^M

swell organ manual
clavier^M *de récit*^M

coupler-tilt tablet
domino^M *d'accouplement*^M

choir organ manual
clavier^M *de positif*^M

great organ manual
clavier^M *de grand orgue*^M

manuals
claviers^M *manuels*

thumb piston
bouton^M *de combinaisons*^F

crescendo pedal
pédale^F *crescendo*^M

toe piston
pédale^F *de combinaisons*^F

pedal key
touche^F *de pédalier*^M

swell pedals
pédales^F *d'expression*^F

pedal keyboard
clavier^M *à pédales*^F

reed pipe
tuyau^M *à anche*^F

flue pipe
tuyau^M *à bouche*^F

resonator
pavillon^M

tuning wire
rasette^F

body
corps^M

block
noyau^M

wedge
coin^M

upper lip
lèvre^F *supérieure*

mouth
bouche^F

shallot
anche^F

tongue
languette^F

languid
biseau^M

flue
lumière^F

lower lip
lèvre^F *inférieure*

boot
pied^M

foot
pied^M

foot hole
orifice^M *du pied*^M

foot hole
orifice^M *du pied*^M

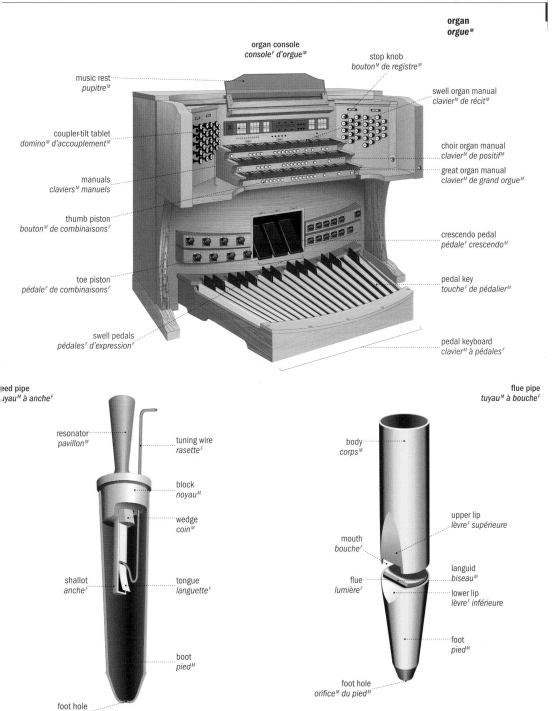

ARTS AND ARCHITECTURE

wind instruments

instruments^M à vent^M

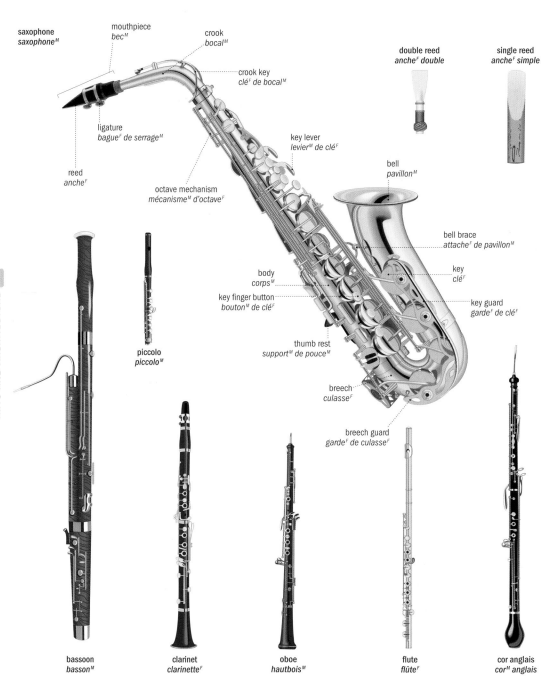

saxophone
saxophone^M

mouthpiece
bec^M

crook
bocal^M

crook key
clé^F de bocal^M

ligature
bague^F de serrage^M

key lever
levier^M de clé^F

reed
anche^F

octave mechanism
mécanisme^M d'octave^F

double reed
anche^F double

single reed
anche^F simple

bell
pavillon^M

bell brace
attache^F de pavillon^M

key
clé^F

body
corps^M

key finger button
bouton^M de clé^F

key guard
garde^F de clé^F

piccolo
piccolo^M

thumb rest
support^M de pouce^M

breech
culasse^F

breech guard
garde^F de culasse^F

bassoon
basson^M

clarinet
clarinette^F

oboe
hautbois^M

flute
flûte^F

cor anglais
cor^M anglais

trumpet
trompette^F

finger button
bouton^M *de piston*^M

little finger hook
crochet^M *de petit doigt*^M

bell
pavillon^M

mouthpipe
branche^F *d'embouchure*^F

ring
bague^F

mouthpiece receiver
boisseau^M *d'embouchure*^F

mouthpiece
embouchure^F

tuning slide
coulisse^F *d'accord*^M

first valve slide
coulisse^F *du premier piston*^M

third valve slide
coulisse^F *du troisième piston*^M

water key
soupape^F *d'évacuation*^F

thumb hook
crochet^M *de pouce*^M

valve
piston^M

mute
sourdine^F

valve casing
corps^M *de piston*^M

second valve slide
coulisse^F *du deuxième piston*^M

French horn
cor^M *d'harmonie*^F

cornet
cornet^M *à pistons*^M

bugle
clairon^M

saxhorn
saxhorn^M

tuba
tuba^M

trombone
trombone^M

percussion instruments

instruments^M à percussion^F

drums
batterie^F

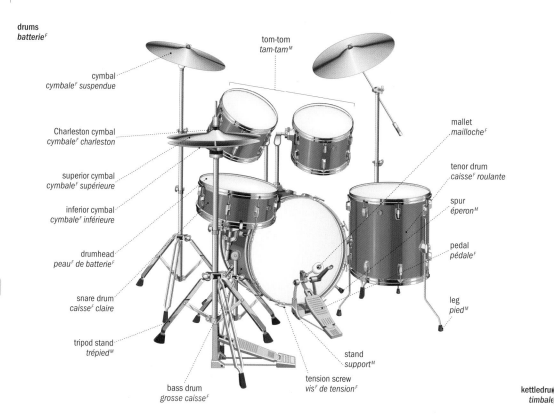

tom-tom
tam-tam^M

cymbal
cymbale^F suspendue

Charleston cymbal
cymbale^F charleston

superior cymbal
cymbale^F supérieure

inferior cymbal
cymbale^F inférieure

drumhead
peau^F de batterie^F

snare drum
caisse^F claire

tripod stand
trépied^M

bass drum
grosse caisse^F

tension screw
vis^F de tension^F

stand
support^M

mallet
mailloche^F

tenor drum
caisse^F roulante

spur
éperon^M

pedal
pédale^F

leg
pied^M

kettledru
timbale

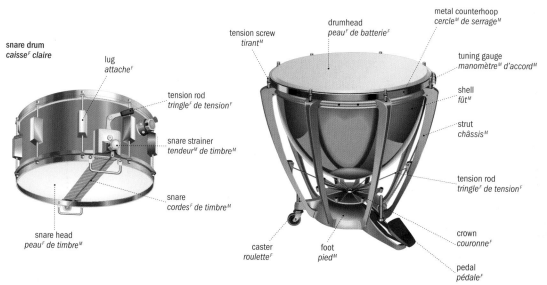

snare drum
caisse^F claire

lug
attache^F

tension rod
tringle^F de tension^F

snare strainer
tendeur^M de timbre^M

snare
cordes^F de timbre^M

snare head
peau^F de timbre^M

tension screw
tirant^M

drumhead
peau^F de batterie^F

metal counterhoop
cercle^M de serrage^M

tuning gauge
manomètre^M d'accord^M

shell
fût^M

strut
châssis^M

tension rod
tringle^F de tension^F

crown
couronne^F

pedal
pédale^F

caster
roulette^F

foot
pied^M

sleigh bells
grelots^M

set of bells
clochettes^F

sistrum
sistre^M

castanets
castagnettes^F

cymbals
cymbales^F

bongos
bongo^M

tambourine
tambour^M de basque^M

triangle
triangle^M

head
peau^F

jingle
cymbalette^F

metal rod
battant^M

wire brush
balai^M métallique

gong
gong^M

sticks
baguettes^F

xylophone
xylophone^M

resonator
tube^M de résonance^F

frame
châssis^M

tubular bells
carillon^M tubulaire

bar
lame^F

mallets
mailloches^F

electronic instruments

instruments^M électroniques

sequencer
séquenceur^M

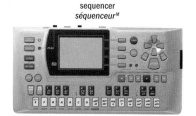

samp▶
échantillonneu

headphone jack
prise^F casque^M

function display
affichage^M des fonctions^F

disc drive
lecteur^M de disquette^F

expander
expandeur^M

synthesizer
synthétiseur^M

volume control
contrôle^M du volume^M

fine data entry control
modification^F fine des variables^F

disc drive
lecteur^M de disquette^F

system buttons
fonctions^F système^M

function display
affichage^M des fonctions^F

sequencer control
contrôle^M du séquenceur^M

fast data entry control
modification^F rapide des variables^F

program selector
sélecteur^M de programme^M

keyboard
clavier^M

modulation wheel
modulation^F du timbre^M du son^M

voice edit buttons
programmation^F des voix^F

pitch wheel
modulation^F de la hauteur^F du son^M

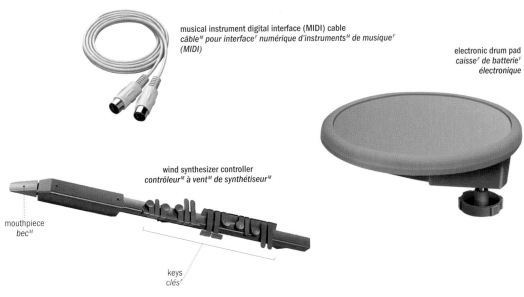

musical instrument digital interface (MIDI) cable
câble^M pour interface^F numérique d'instruments^M de musique^F (MIDI)

electronic drum pad
caisse^F de batterie^F électronique

wind synthesizer controller
contrôleur^M à vent^M de synthétiseur^M

mouthpiece
bec^M

keys
clés^F

electronic piano
piano^M électronique

rhythm selector
sélecteur^M de rythme^M

music rest
pupitre^M

tempo control
réglage^M de tempo^M

volume control
réglage^M du volume^M

power switch
interrupteur^M d'alimentation^F

headphone jack
prise^F casque^M

voice selector
sélecteur^M de voix^F

soft pedal
pédale^F douce

sustaining pedal
pédale^F forte

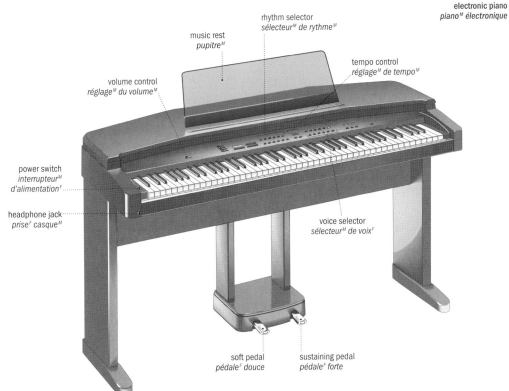

writing instruments

instruments^M d'écriture^F

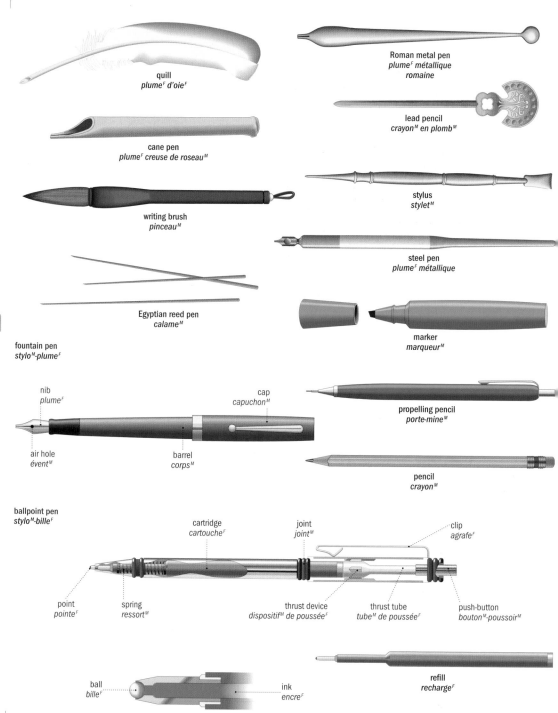

quill
plume^F d'oie^F

cane pen
plume^F creuse de roseau^M

writing brush
pinceau^M

Egyptian reed pen
calame^M

Roman metal pen
plume^F métallique
romaine

lead pencil
crayon^M en plomb^M

stylus
stylet^M

steel pen
plume^F métallique

marker
marqueur^M

fountain pen
stylo^M-plume^F

nib
plume^F

cap
capuchon^M

air hole
évent^M

barrel
corps^M

propelling pencil
porte-mine^M

pencil
crayon^M

ballpoint pen
stylo^M-bille^F

cartridge
cartouche^F

joint
joint^M

clip
agrafe^F

point
pointe^F

spring
ressort^M

thrust device
dispositif^M de poussée^F

thrust tube
tube^M de poussée^F

push-button
bouton^M-poussoir^M

ball
bille^F

ink
encre^F

refill
recharge^F

newspaper

journal[M]

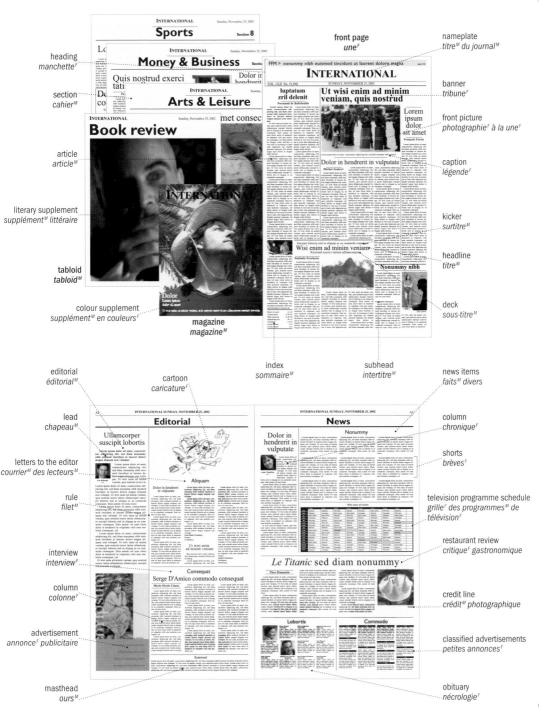

heading
manchette[F]

section
cahier[M]

article
article[M]

literary supplement
supplément[M] littéraire

tabloid
tabloïd[M]

colour supplement
supplément[M] en couleurs[F]

front page
une[F]

nameplate
titre[M] du journal[M]

banner
tribune[F]

front picture
photographie[F] à la une[F]

caption
légende[F]

kicker
surtitre[M]

headline
titre[M]

deck
sous-titre[M]

magazine
magazine[M]

editorial
éditorial[M]

cartoon
caricature[F]

index
sommaire[M]

subhead
intertitre[M]

news items
faits[M] divers

lead
chapeau[M]

letters to the editor
courrier[M] des lecteurs[M]

rule
filet[M]

interview
interview[F]

column
colonne[F]

advertisement
annonce[F] publicitaire

masthead
ours[M]

column
chronique[F]

shorts
brèves[F]

television programme schedule
grille[F] des programmes[M] de
télévision[F]

restaurant review
critique[F] gastronomique

credit line
crédit[M] photographique

classified advertisements
petites annonces[F]

obituary
nécrologie[F]

photography

photographie^F

single-lens reflex (SLR) camera : front view
*appareil^M à visée^F reflex mono-objectif^M :
vue^F avant*

film rewind knob
rebobinage^M

accessory shoe
griffe^F porte-accessoires^M

exposure adjustment knob
correction^F d'exposition^F

hot-shoe contact
contact^M électrique

film advance mode
mode^M d'entraînement^M du film^M

data panel
écran^M de contrôle^M

exposure mode
mode^M d'exposition^F

program selector
sélecteur^M de fonctions^F

multiple exposure mode
surimpression^F

on/off switch
commutateur^M marche^F/arrêt^M

film speed
sensibilité^F du film^M

shutter release button
déclencheur^M

self-timer indicator
témoin^M du retardateur^M

remote control terminal
prise^F de télécommande^F

camera body
boîtier^M

focus mode selector
mode^M de mise^F au point^M

lens release button
déverrouillage^M de l'objectif^M

depth-of-field preview button
vérification^F de la profondeur^F de champ^M

lens
objectif^M

lenses
objectifs^M

telephoto lens
téléobjectif^M

zoom lens
objectif^M zoom^M

wide-angle lens
objectif^M grand-angulaire

macro lens
objectif^M macro

lens accessori
accessoires^M de l'objecti

lens cap
capuchon^M d'objectif^M

lens hood
parasoleil^M

polarizing filter
filtre^M de polarisation^F

photography

menu button
*touche^F de sélection^F des
menus^M*

power switch
*commutateur^M
d'alimentation^F*

digital reflex camera : camera back
*appareil^M à visée^F reflex numérique :
dos^M*

settings display button
*touche^F d'affichage^M des
réglages^M*

viewfinder
viseur^M

strap eyelet
œillet^M d'attache^F

cover
couvercle^M

multi-image jump button
*touche^F de saut^M
d'images^F*

video and digital terminals
prises^F vidéo et numérique

index/enlarge button
*touche^F
d'index^M/agrandissement^M*

remote control terminal
prise^F de télécommande^F

compact memory card
carte^F de mémoire^F

image review button
*touche^F de visualisation^F des
images^F*

liquid crystal display
*écran^M à cristaux^M
liquides*

erase button
touche^F d'effacement^M

four-way selector
*sélecteur^M
quadridirectionnel*

eject button
bouton^M d'éjection^F

still cameras
***appareils^M
photographiques***

rangefinder camera
appareil^M à télémètre^M couplé

Polaroid® Land camera
Polaroid$^{®M}$

medium format SLR (6 x 6)
appareil^M reflex 6 X 6 mono-objectif^M

digital camera
appareil^M numérique

disposable camera
appareil^M jetable

view camera
chambre^F photographique

satellite broadcasting

télédiffusion[F] par satellite[M]

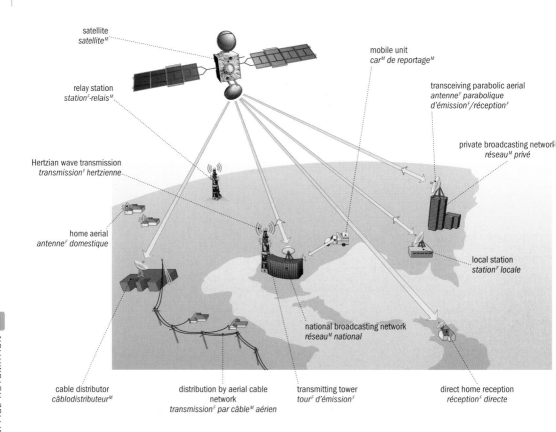

satellite
satellite[M]

mobile unit
car[M] de reportage[M]

transceiving parabolic aerial
antenne[F] parabolique
d'émission[F]/réception[F]

relay station
station[F]-relais[M]

private broadcasting network
réseau[M] privé

Hertzian wave transmission
transmission[F] hertzienne

home aerial
antenne[F] domestique

local station
station[F] locale

national broadcasting network
réseau[M] national

cable distributor
câblodistributeur[M]

distribution by aerial cable
network
transmission[F] par câble[M] aérien

transmitting tower
tour[F] d'émission[F]

direct home reception
réception[F] directe

telecommunication satellites

satellites[M] de télécommunications[F]

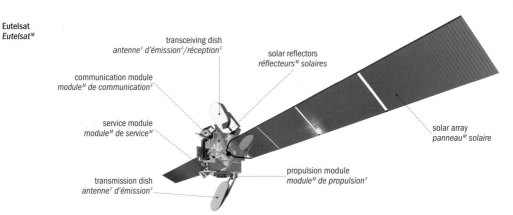

Eutelsat
Eutelsat[M]

transceiving dish
antenne[F] d'émission[F]/réception[F]

solar reflectors
réflecteurs[M] solaires

communication module
module[M] de communication[F]

service module
module[M] de service[M]

solar array
panneau[M] solaire

transmission dish
antenne[F] d'émission[F]

propulsion module
module[M] de propulsion[F]

telecommunications by satellite

télécommunications[F] par satellite[M]

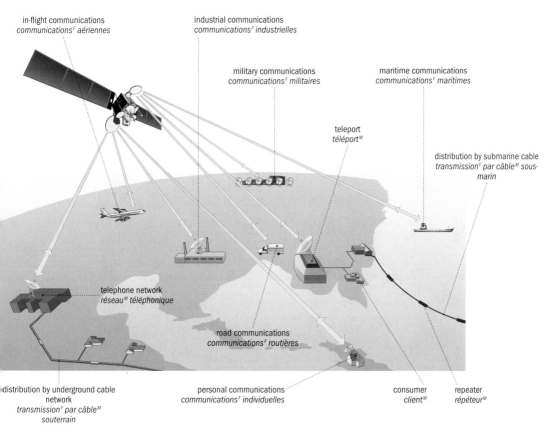

in-flight communications
communications[F] aériennes

industrial communications
communications[F] industrielles

military communications
communications[F] militaires

maritime communications
communications[F] maritimes

teleport
téléport[M]

distribution by submarine cable
transmission[F] par câble[M] sous-marin

telephone network
réseau[M] téléphonique

road communications
communications[F] routières

distribution by underground cable network
transmission[F] par câble[M] souterrain

personal communications
communications[F] individuelles

consumer
client[M]

repeater
répéteur[M]

telecommunication satellites

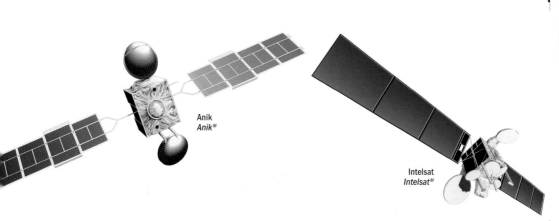

Anik
Anik[M]

Intelsat
Intelsat[M]

COMMUNICATIONS AND OFFICE AUTOMATION

television

télévision[F]

television set
téléviseur[M]

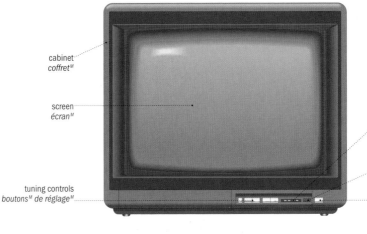

cabinet
coffret[M]

screen
écran[M]

indicators
lampes[F] *témoins*[M]

remote control sensor
capteur[M] *de télécommande*[F]

tuning controls
boutons[M] *de réglage*[M]

power button
interrupteur[M]
d'alimentation[F]

picture tube
tube[M]*-image*[F]

funnel
cône[M]

colour selection filter
masque[M] *de sélection*[F] *des*
couleurs[F]

electron gun
canon[M] *à électrons*[M]

base
culot[M]

neck
col[M]

protective window
vitre[F] *protectrice*

screen
écran[M]

electron beam
faisceau[M] *d'électrons*[M]

electron gun
canon[M] *à électrons*[M]

grid
grille[F]

red beam
faisceau[M] *rouge*

green beam
faisceau[M] *vert*

magnetic field
champ[M] *magnétique*

blue beam
faisceau[M] *bleu*

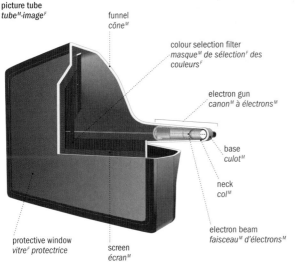

DVD player
lecteur[M] *de DVD*[M] *vidéo*

power button
interrupteur[M]
d'alimentation[F]

disc tray
plateau[M] *de chargement*[M]

display
afficheur[M]

digital versatile disc (DVD)
disque[M] *numérique*
polyvalent (DVD)

COMMUNICATIONS AND OFFICE AUTOMATION

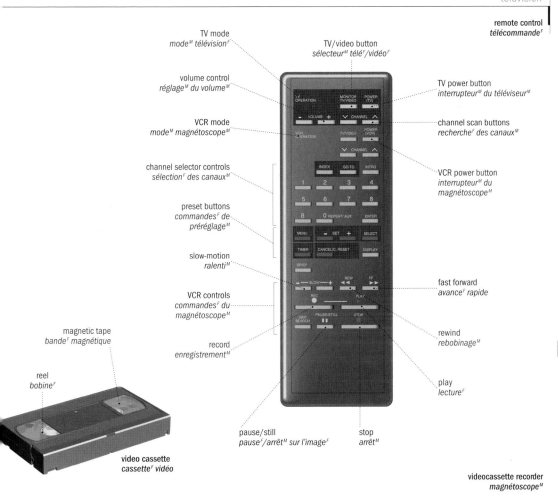

remote control
télécommande^F

TV mode
mode^M *télévision*^F

TV/video button
sélecteur^M *télé*^F/*vidéo*^F

volume control
réglage^M *du volume*^M

TV power button
interrupteur^M *du téléviseur*^M

VCR mode
mode^M *magnétoscope*^M

channel scan buttons
recherche^F *des canaux*^M

channel selector controls
sélection^F *des canaux*^M

VCR power button
interrupteur^M *du*
magnétoscope^M

preset buttons
commandes^F *de*
préréglage^M

slow-motion
ralenti^M

VCR controls
commandes^F *du*
magnétoscope^M

fast forward
avance^F *rapide*

magnetic tape
bande^F *magnétique*

record
enregistrement^M

reel
bobine^F

rewind
rebobinage^M

play
lecture^F

pause/still
pause^F/*arrêt*^M *sur l'image*^F

stop
arrêt^M

video cassette
cassette^F *vidéo*

videocassette recorder
magnétoscope^M

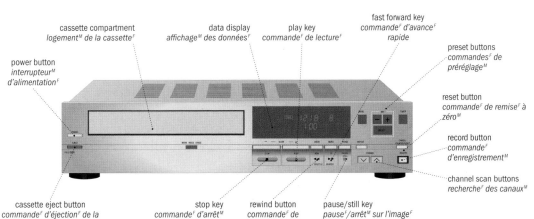

cassette compartment
logement^M *de la cassette*^F

data display
affichage^M *des données*^F

play key
commande^F *de lecture*^F

fast forward key
commande^F *d'avance*^F
rapide

preset buttons
commandes^F *de*
préréglage^M

power button
interrupteur^M
d'alimentation^F

reset button
commande^F *de remise*^F *à*
zéro^M

record button
commande^F
d'enregistrement^M

channel scan buttons
recherche^F *des canaux*^M

cassette eject button
commande^F *d'éjection*^F *de la*
cassette^F

stop key
commande^F *d'arrêt*^M

rewind button
commande^F *de*
rebobinage^M

pause/still key
pause^F/*arrêt*^M *sur l'image*^F

COMMUNICATIONS AND OFFICE AUTOMATION

television

analogue camcorder : front view
caméscope^M analogique : vue^F
avant

edit search button
touche^F de raccord^M
d'enregistrement^M

electronic viewfinder
viseur^M électronique

eyecup
œilleton^M

videotape operation controls
commandes^F de la bande^F
vidéo

display panel
panneau^M de l'écran^M

zoom lens
objectif^M zoom^M

nightshot switch
commutateur^M de prise^F de vues^F
nocturne

power/functions switch
commutateur^M
alimentation^F/fonctions^F

cassette compartment
logement^M de la cassette^F

microphone
microphone^M

focus selector
sélecteur^M de mise^F au
point^M

near/far dial
molette^F de réglage^M
près/loin

compact video cassette adapter
adaptateur^M de cassette^F vidéo
compacte

analogue camcorder : back view
caméscope^M analogique : vue^F
arrière

eyepiece
oculaire^M

power zoom button
commande^F électrique du zoom^M

recording start/stop button
touche^F d'enregistrement^M

speaker
haut-parleur^M

rechargeable battery pack
batterie^F rechargeable

image adjustment buttons
touches^F de réglage^M de
l'image^F

liquid crystal display
écran^M à cristaux^M
liquides

indicators display button
touche^F d'affichage^M des
indicateurs^M

date display/recording button
touche^F de la date^F

end search button
touche^F de raccord^M
d'enregistrement^M

time display/recording button
touche^F de l'heure^F

special effects buttons
touches^F d'effets^M
spéciaux

title display button
touche^F d'affichage^M de titre^M

special effects selection dial
molette^F de sélection^F des effets^M
spéciaux

television

dish aerial
antenne^F parabolique

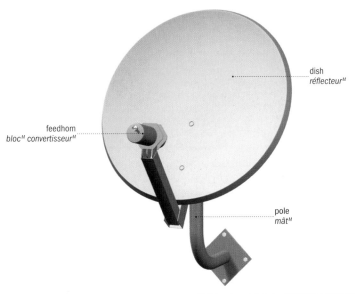

dish
réflecteur^M

feedhorn
bloc^M convertisseur^M

pole
mât^M

receiver
terminal^M numérique

card reader
lecteur^M de carte^F

remote control
télécommande^F

home theatre
home cinéma^M

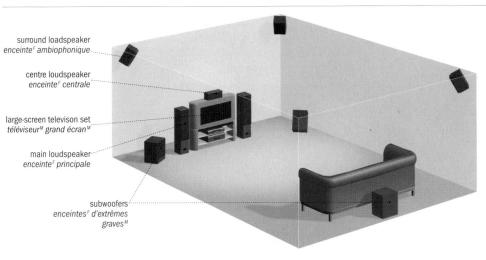

surround loadspeaker
enceinte^F ambiophonique

centre loudspeaker
enceinte^F centrale

large-screen televison set
téléviseur^M grand écran^M

main loudspeaker
enceinte^F principale

subwoofers
enceintes^F d'extrêmes graves^M

COMMUNICATIONS AND OFFICE AUTOMATION

stereo sound system

chaîne^F stéréo

ampli-tuner : front view
ampli^M-syntoniseur^M : vue^F
avant

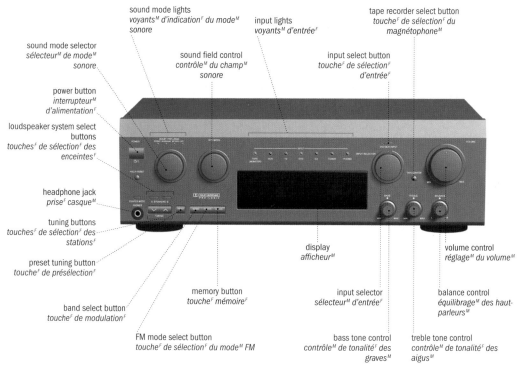

sound mode lights
voyants^M d'indication^F du mode^M
sonore

input lights
voyants^M d'entrée^F

tape recorder select button
touche^F de sélection^F du
magnétophone^M

sound mode selector
sélecteur^M de mode^M
sonore

sound field control
contrôle^M du champ^M
sonore

input select button
touche^F de sélection^F
d'entrée^F

power button
interrupteur^M
d'alimentation^F

loudspeaker system select
buttons
touches^F de sélection^F des
enceintes^F

headphone jack
prise^F casque^M

tuning buttons
touches^F de sélection^F des
stations^F

preset tuning button
touche^F de présélection^F

band select button
touche^F de modulation^F

FM mode select button
touche^F de sélection^F du mode^M FM

memory button
touche^F mémoire^F

display
afficheur^M

input selector
sélecteur^M d'entrée^F

bass tone control
contrôle^M de tonalité^F des
graves^M

volume control
réglage^M du volume^M

balance control
équilibrage^M des haut-
parleurs^M

treble tone control
contrôle^M de tonalité^F des
aigus^M

ampli-tuner : back view
ampli^M-syntoniseur^M : vue^F
arrière

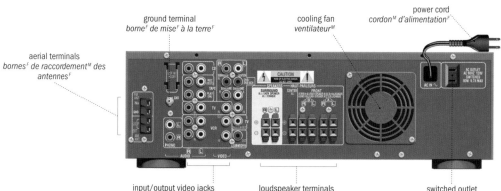

ground terminal
borne^F de mise^F à la terre^F

cooling fan
ventilateur^M

power cord
cordon^M d'alimentation^F

aerial terminals
bornes^F de raccordement^M des
antennes^F

input/output video jacks
prises^F d'entrée^F/de sortie^F audio/vidéo

loudspeaker terminals
bornes^F de raccordement^M des
enceintes^F

switched outlet
prise^F de courant^M
commutée

stereo sound system

cassette tape deck
platine^F cassette^F

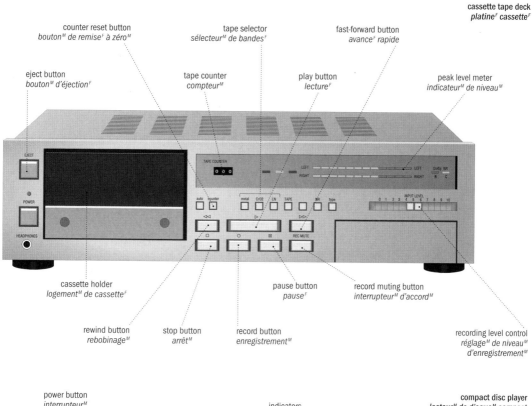

counter reset button
bouton^M de remise^F à zéro^M

tape selector
sélecteur^M de bandes^F

fast-forward button
avance^F rapide

eject button
bouton^M d'éjection^F

tape counter
compteur^M

play button
lecture^F

peak level meter
indicateur^M de niveau^M

cassette holder
logement^M de cassette^F

pause button
pause^F

record muting button
interrupteur^M d'accord^M

rewind button
rebobinage^M

stop button
arrêt^M

record button
enregistrement^M

recording level control
*réglage^M de niveau^M
d'enregistrement^M*

power button
*interrupteur^M
d'alimentation^F*

indicators
voyants^M de contrôle^M

compact disc player
lecteur^M de disque^M compact

disc compartment
logement^M du plateau^M

track number
numéro^M de la piste^F

memory key
touche^F mémoire^F

repeat keys
touches^F de répétition^F

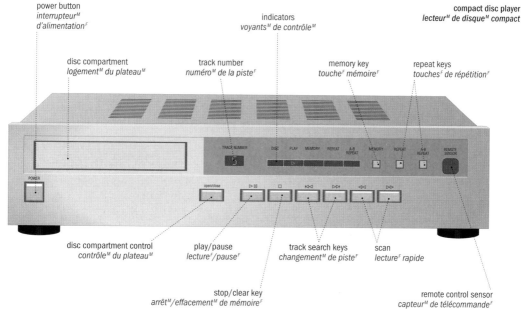

disc compartment control
contrôle^M du plateau^M

play/pause
lecture^F/pause^F

track search keys
changement^M de piste^F

scan
lecture^F rapide

stop/clear key
arrêt^M/effacement^M de mémoire^F

remote control sensor
capteur^M de télécommande^F

COMMUNICATIONS AND OFFICE AUTOMATION

stereo sound system

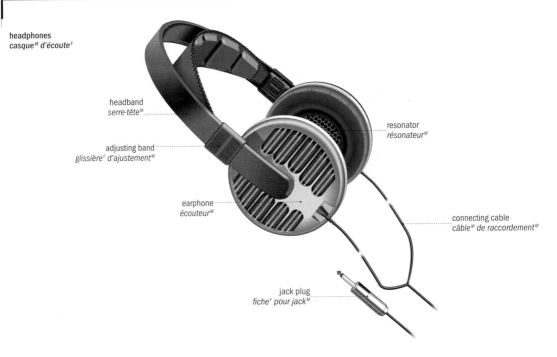

headphones
casque^M d'écoute^F

headband
serre-tête^M

adjusting band
glissière^F d'ajustement^M

earphone
écouteur^M

resonator
résonateur^M

connecting cable
câble^M de raccordement^M

jack plug
fiche^F pour jack^M

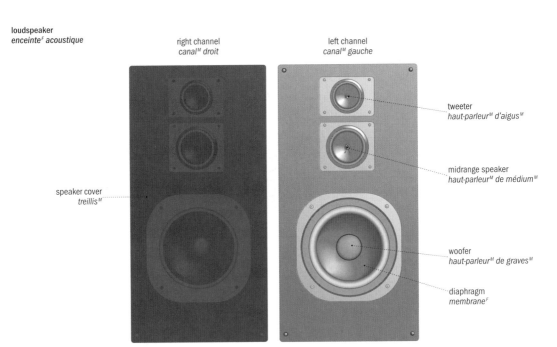

loudspeaker
enceinte^F acoustique

right channel
canal^M droit

left channel
canal^M gauche

tweeter
haut-parleur^M d'aigus^M

midrange speaker
haut-parleur^M de médium^M

speaker cover
treillis^M

woofer
haut-parleur^M de graves^M

diaphragm
membrane^F

mini stereo sound system

minichaine^F stéréo

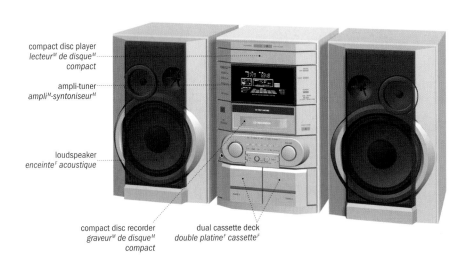

compact disc player
*lecteur^M de disque^M
compact*

ampli-tuner
ampli^M-syntoniseur^M

loudspeaker
enceinte^F acoustique

compact disc recorder
*graveur^M de disque^M
compact*

dual cassette deck
double platine^F cassette^F

portable sound systems

appareils^M de son^M portatifs

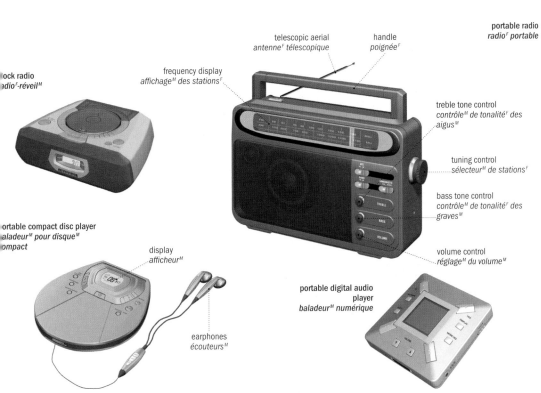

portable radio
radio^F portable

telescopic aerial
antenne^F télescopique

handle
poignée^F

frequency display
affichage^M des stations^F

clock radio
radio^F-réveil^M

treble tone control
*contrôle^M de tonalité^F des
aigus^M*

tuning control
sélecteur^M de stations^F

bass tone control
*contrôle^M de tonalité^F des
graves^M*

portable compact disc player
*baladeur^M pour disque^M
compact*

display
afficheur^M

volume control
réglage^M du volume^M

portable digital audio
player
baladeur^M numérique

earphones
écouteurs^M

COMMUNICATIONS AND OFFICE AUTOMATION

portable sound systems

personal radio cassette player
baladeur^M

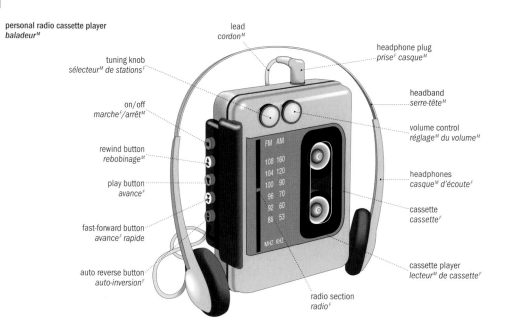

lead
cordon^M

headphone plug
prise^F *casque*^M

tuning knob
sélecteur^M *de stations*^F

headband
serre-tête^M

on/off
marche^F/*arrêt*^M

volume control
réglage^M *du volume*^M

rewind button
rebobinage^M

headphones
casque^M *d'écoute*^F

play button
avance^F

cassette
cassette^F

fast-forward button
avance^F *rapide*

cassette player
lecteur^M *de cassette*^F

auto reverse button
auto-inversion^F

radio section
radio^F

portable CD radio cassette recorder
radiocassette^F *laser*^M

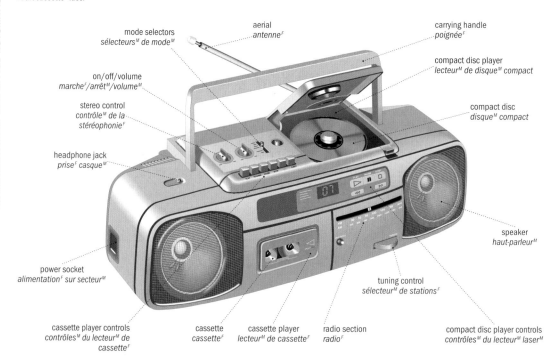

mode selectors
sélecteurs^M *de mode*^M

aerial
antenne^F

carrying handle
poignée^F

compact disc player
lecteur^M *de disque*^M *compact*

on/off/volume
marche^F/*arrêt*^M/*volume*^M

compact disc
disque^M *compact*

stereo control
contrôle^M *de la*
stéréophonie^F

headphone jack
prise^F *casque*^M

speaker
haut-parleur^M

power socket
alimentation^F *sur secteur*^M

tuning control
sélecteur^M *de stations*^F

cassette player controls
contrôles^M *du lecteur*^M *de*
cassette^F

cassette
cassette^F

cassette player
lecteur^M *de cassette*^F

radio section
radio^F

compact disc player controls
contrôles^M *du lecteur*^M *laser*^M

communication by telephone

communication^F par téléphone^M

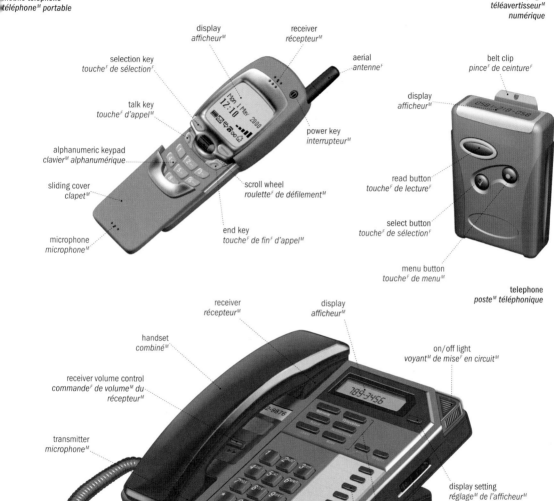

mobile telephone
téléphone^M portable

display
afficheur^M

receiver
récepteur^M

selection key
touche^F de sélection^F

aerial
antenne^F

talk key
touche^F d'appel^M

power key
interrupteur^M

alphanumeric keypad
clavier^M alphanumérique

sliding cover
clapet^M

scroll wheel
roulette^F de défilement^M

microphone
microphone^M

end key
touche^F de fin^F d'appel^M

numeric pager
téléavertisseur^M numérique

belt clip
pince^F de ceinture^F

display
afficheur^M

read button
touche^F de lecture^F

select button
touche^F de sélection^F

menu button
touche^F de menu^M

telephone
poste^M téléphonique

receiver
récepteur^M

display
afficheur^M

handset
combiné^M

on/off light
voyant^M de mise^F en circuit^M

receiver volume control
commande^F de volume^M du récepteur^M

transmitter
microphone^M

display setting
réglage^M de l'afficheur^M

ringing volume control
commande^F de volume^M de la sonnerie^F

handset flex
cordon^M de combiné^M

memory button
commande^F mémoire^F

function selectors
sélecteurs^M de fonctions^F

push buttons
clavier^M

telephone list
répertoire^M téléphonique

automatic dialling index
index^M de composition^F automatique

COMMUNICATIONS AND OFFICE AUTOMATION

communication by telephone

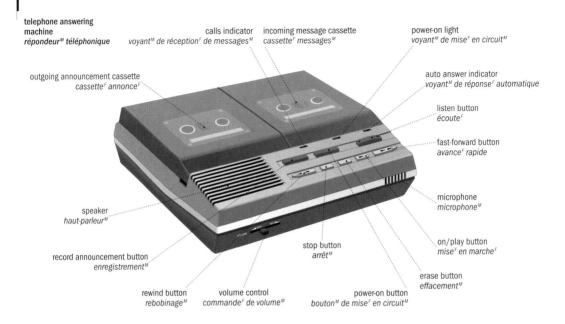

telephone answering
machine
répondeur^M *téléphonique*

calls indicator
voyant^M *de réception*^F *de messages*^M

incoming message cassette
cassette^F *messages*^M

power-on light
voyant^M *de mise*^F *en circuit*^M

outgoing announcement cassette
cassette^F *annonce*^F

auto answer indicator
voyant^M *de réponse*^F *automatique*

listen button
écoute^F

fast-forward button
avance^F *rapide*

microphone
microphone^M

speaker
haut-parleur^M

on/play button
mise^F *en marche*^F

record announcement button
enregistrement^M

stop button
arrêt^M

erase button
effacement^M

rewind button
rebobinage^M

volume control
commande^F *de volume*^M

power-on button
bouton^M *de mise*^F *en circuit*^M

fax machine
télécopieur^M

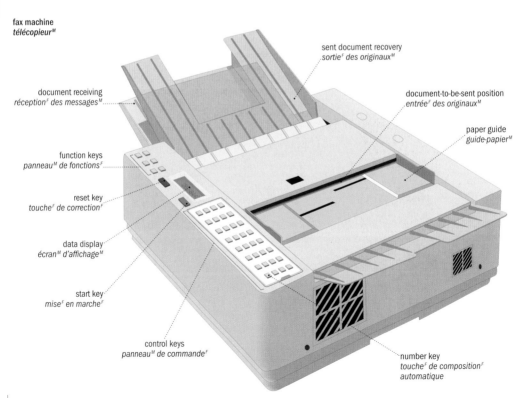

sent document recovery
sortie^F *des originaux*^M

document receiving
réception^F *des messages*^M

document-to-be-sent position
entrée^F *des originaux*^M

paper guide
guide-papier^M

function keys
panneau^M *de fonctions*^F

reset key
touche^F *de correction*^F

data display
écran^M *d'affichage*^M

start key
mise^F *en marche*^F

control keys
panneau^M *de commande*^F

number key
touche^F *de composition*^F
automatique

personal computer

micro-ordinateur^M

video monitor
écran^M

vertical control
réglage^M *vertical*

horizontal control
réglage^M *horizontal*

centring control
réglage^M *de centrage*^M

contrast control
réglage^M *du contraste*^M

power indicator
témoin^M *d'alimentation*^F

power switch
interrupteur^M

brightness control
réglage^M *de la luminosité*^F

tower case : back view
boîtier^M *tour*^F : *vue*^F
arrière

tower case : front view
boîtier^M *tour*^F : *vue*^F *avant*

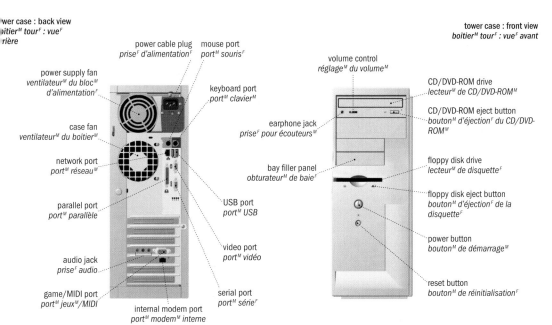

power cable plug
prise^F *d'alimentation*^F

mouse port
port^M *souris*^F

power supply fan
ventilateur^M *du bloc*^M
d'alimentation^F

keyboard port
port^M *clavier*^M

case fan
ventilateur^M *du boîtier*^M

earphone jack
prise^F *pour écouteurs*^M

network port
port^M *réseau*^M

bay filler panel
obturateur^M *de baie*^F

parallel port
port^M *parallèle*

USB port
port^M *USB*

audio jack
prise^F *audio*

video port
port^M *vidéo*

game/MIDI port
port^M *jeux*^M/*MIDI*

serial port
port^M *série*^F

internal modem port
port^M *modem*^M *interne*

volume control
réglage^M *du volume*^M

CD/DVD-ROM drive
lecteur^M *de CD/DVD-ROM*^M

CD/DVD-ROM eject button
bouton^M *d'éjection*^F *du CD/DVD-
ROM*^M

floppy disk drive
lecteur^M *de disquette*^F

floppy disk eject button
bouton^M *d'éjection*^F *de la
disquette*^F

power button
bouton^M *de démarrage*^M

reset button
bouton^M *de réinitialisation*^F

input devices

périphériques^M d'entrée^F

keyboard and pictograms
clavier^M et pictogrammes^M

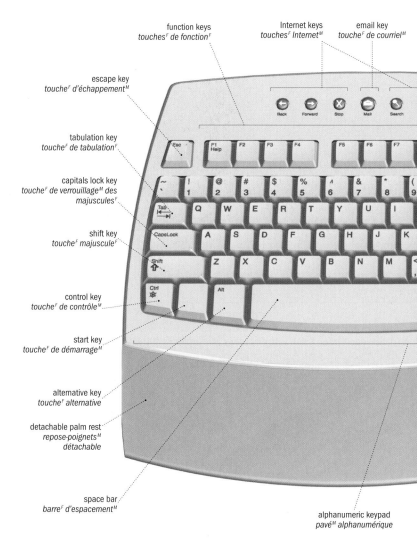

function keys
touches^F de fonction^F

Internet keys
touches^F Internet^M

email key
touche^F de courriel^M

escape key
touche^F d'échappement^M

tabulation key
touche^F de tabulation^F

capitals lock key
touche^F de verrouillage^M des majuscules^F

shift key
touche^F majuscule^F

control key
touche^F de contrôle^M

start key
touche^F de démarrage^M

alternative key
touche^F alternative

detachable palm rest
repose-poignets^M détachable

space bar
barre^F d'espacement^M

alphanumeric keypad
pavé^M alphanumérique

escape
échappement^M

tabulation left
tabulation^F à gauche

tabulation right
tabulation^F à droite

capitals lock
verrouillage^M des majuscules^F

alternate : level 3 select
alternative : sélection^F du niveau^M 3

shift : level 2 select
majuscule^F : sélection^F du niveau^M 2

control : group select
contrôle^M : sélection^F de groupe^M

control
contrôle^M

alternate
alternative

space
espace^F

non-breaking space
espace^F insécable

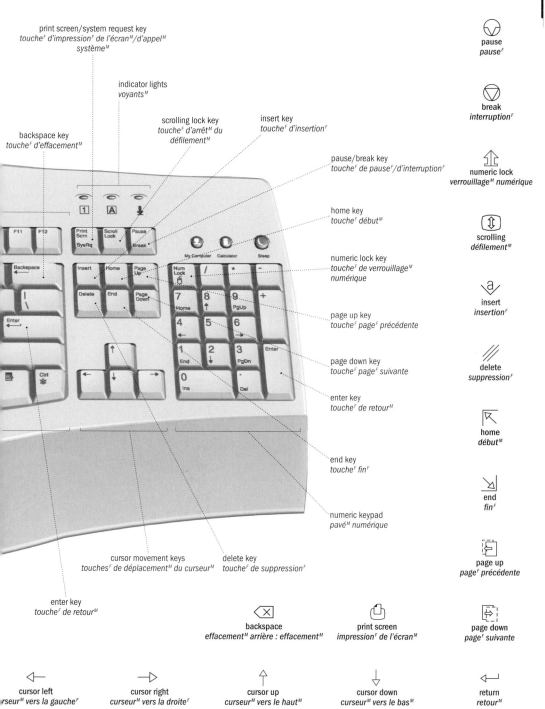

print screen/system request key
*touche^F d'impression^F de l'écran^M/d'appel^M
système^M*

indicator lights
voyants^M

scrolling lock key
*touche^F d'arrêt^M du
défilement^M*

insert key
touche^F d'insertion^F

backspace key
touche^F d'effacement^M

pause/break key
touche^F de pause^F/d'interruption^F

home key
touche^F début^M

numeric lock key
*touche^F de verrouillage^M
numérique*

page up key
touche^F page^F précédente

page down key
touche^F page^F suivante

enter key
touche^F de retour^M

end key
touche^F fin^F

numeric keypad
pavé^M numérique

cursor movement keys
touches^F de déplacement^M du curseur^M

delete key
touche^F de suppression^F

enter key
touche^F de retour^M

pause
pause^F

break
interruption^F

numeric lock
verrouillage^M numérique

scrolling
défilement^M

insert
insertion^F

delete
suppression^F

home
début^M

end
fin^F

page up
page^F précédente

backspace
effacement^M arrière : effacement^M

print screen
impression^F de l'écran^M

page down
page^F suivante

cursor left
~rseur^M vers la gauche^F

cursor right
curseur^M vers la droite^F

cursor up
curseur^M vers le haut^M

cursor down
curseur^M vers le bas^M

return
retour^M

COMMUNICATIONS AND OFFICE AUTOMATION

input devices

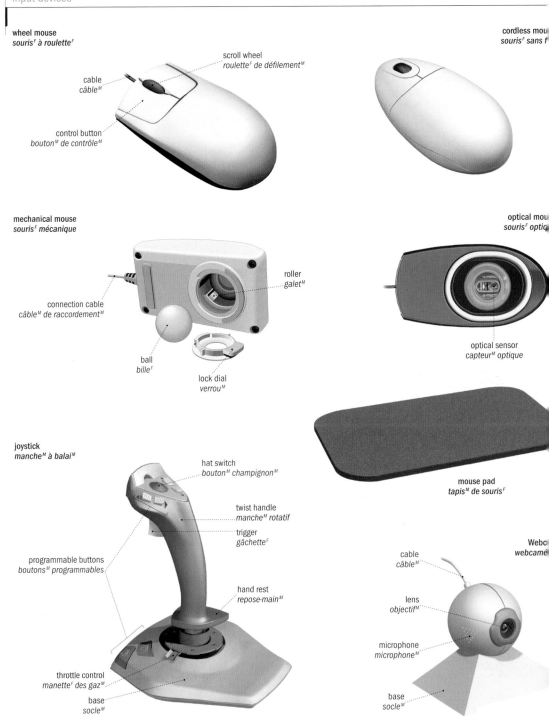

wheel mouse
souris^F à roulette^F

scroll wheel
roulette^F de défilement^M

cable
câble^M

control button
bouton^M de contrôle^M

cordless mou
souris^F sans f

mechanical mouse
souris^F mécanique

connection cable
câble^M de raccordement^M

roller
galet^M

ball
bille^F

lock dial
verrou^M

optical mou
souris^F optiq

optical sensor
capteur^M optique

mouse pad
tapis^M de souris^F

joystick
manche^M à balai^M

hat switch
bouton^M champignon^M

twist handle
manche^M rotatif

trigger
gâchette^F

programmable buttons
boutons^M programmables

hand rest
repose-main^M

throttle control
manette^F des gaz^M

base
socle^M

Webc
webcamé

cable
câble^M

lens
objectif^M

microphone
microphone^M

base
socle^M

output devices
périphériques de sortie*

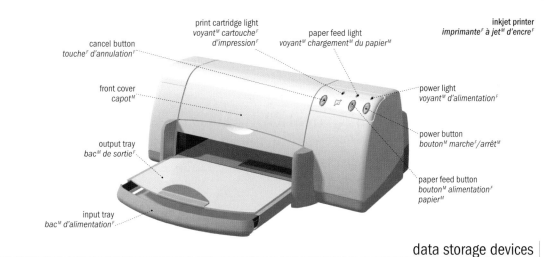

inkjet printer
imprimante à jet* d'encre*

print cartridge light
voyant cartouche*
d'impression*

cancel button
touche d'annulation*

paper feed light
voyant chargement* du papier*

front cover
capot

power light
voyant d'alimentation*

output tray
bac de sortie*

power button
bouton marche*/arrêt*

paper feed button
bouton alimentation*
papier*

input tray
bac d'alimentation*

data storage devices
périphériques de stockage*

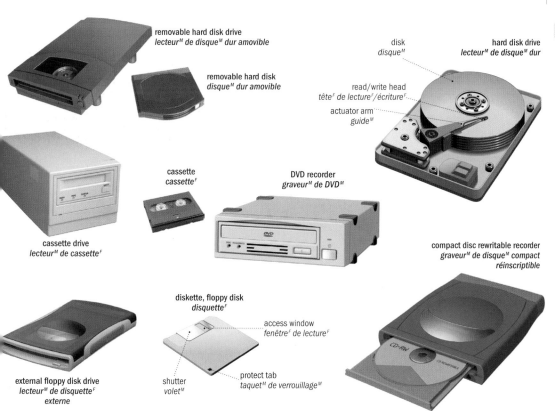

removable hard disk drive
lecteur de disque* dur amovible*

disk
disque

hard disk drive
lecteur de disque* dur*

removable hard disk
disque dur amovible*

read/write head
tête de lecture*/écriture*

actuator arm
guide

cassette
cassette

DVD recorder
graveur de DVD*

cassette drive
lecteur de cassette*

compact disc rewritable recorder
graveur de disque* compact*
réinscriptible

diskette, floppy disk
disquette

access window
fenêtre de lecture*

external floppy disk drive
lecteur de disquette*
externe

shutter
volet

protect tab
taquet de verrouillage*

Internet

Internet[M]

URL (uniform resource locator)
*adresse[F] URL[F] (localisateur[M] universel de
ressources[F])*

communication protocol
protocole[M] de communication[F]

domain name
nom[M] de domaine[M]

file format
format[M] du fichier[M]

http://www.un.org/aboutun/index.htm

double slash
double barre[F] oblique

second-level domain
*domaine[M] de second
niveau[M]*

file
fichier[M]

server
serveur[M]

top-level domain
domaine[M] de premier niveau[M]

directory
répertoire[M]

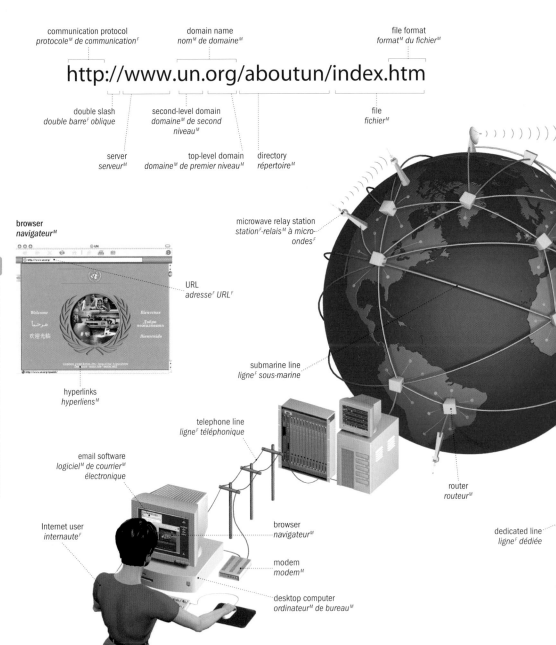

browser
navigateur[M]

URL
adresse[F] URL[F]

hyperlinks
hyperliens[M]

microwave relay station
*station[F]-relais[M] à micro-
ondes[F]*

submarine line
ligne[F] sous-marine

telephone line
ligne[F] téléphonique

email software
*logiciel[M] de courrier[M]
électronique*

router
routeur[M]

Internet user
internaute[F]

browser
navigateur[M]

dedicated line
ligne[F] dédiée

modem
modem[M]

desktop computer
ordinateur[M] de bureau[M]

Internet uses

utilisations[F] d'Internet[M]

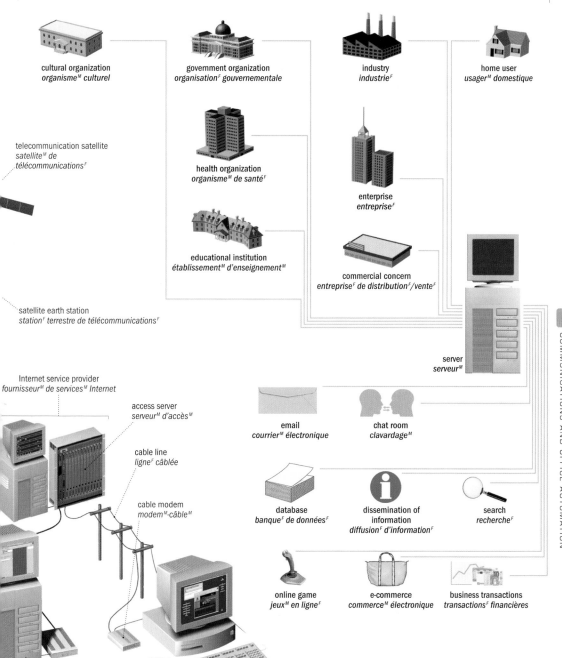

cultural organization
organisme[M] culturel

government organization
organisation[F] gouvernementale

industry
industrie[F]

home user
usager[M] domestique

telecommunication satellite
*satellite[M] de
télécommunications[F]*

health organization
organisme[M] de santé[F]

enterprise
entreprise[F]

educational institution
établissement[M] d'enseignement[M]

commercial concern
entreprise[F] de distribution[F]/vente[F]

satellite earth station
station[F] terrestre de télécommunications[F]

server
serveur[M]

Internet service provider
fournisseur[M] de services[M] Internet

access server
serveur[M] d'accès[M]

cable line
ligne[F] câblée

email
courrier[M] électronique

chat room
clavardage[M]

cable modem
modem[M]-câble[M]

database
banque[F] de données[F]

dissemination of
information
diffusion[F] d'information[F]

search
recherche[F]

online game
jeux[M] en ligne[F]

e-commerce
commerce[M] électronique

business transactions
transactions[F] financières

server
serveur[M]

COMMUNICATIONS AND OFFICE AUTOMATION

laptop computer

ordinateur^M portable

laptop computer : front view
ordinateur^M portable : vue^F avant

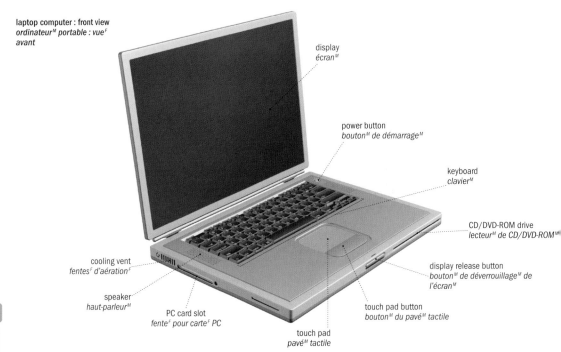

display
écran^M

power button
bouton^M de démarrage^M

keyboard
clavier^M

CD/DVD-ROM drive
lecteur^M de CD/DVD-ROM^M

cooling vent
fentes^F d'aération^F

display release button
bouton^M de déverrouillage^M de l'écran^M

speaker
haut-parleur^M

PC card slot
fente^F pour carte^F PC

touch pad button
bouton^M du pavé^M tactile

touch pad
pavé^M tactile

laptop computer : rear view
ordinateur^M portable : vue^F arrière

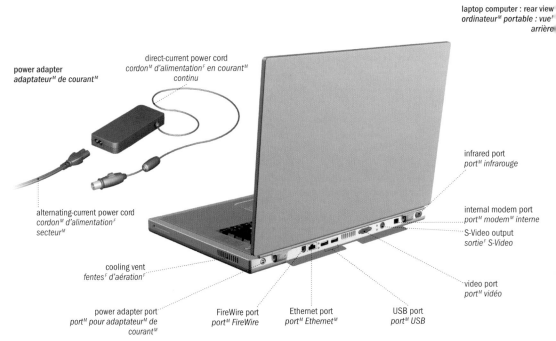

power adapter
adaptateur^M de courant^M

direct-current power cord
cordon^M d'alimentation^F en courant^M continu

infrared port
port^M infrarouge

alternating-current power cord
cordon^M d'alimentation^F secteur^M

internal modem port
port^M modem^M interne

S-Video output
sortie^F S-Video

cooling vent
fentes^F d'aération^F

video port
port^M vidéo

power adapter port
port^M pour adaptateur^M de courant^M

FireWire port
port^M FireWire

Ethernet port
port^M Ethernet^M

USB port
port^M USB

pocket computer

ordinateur^M de poche^F

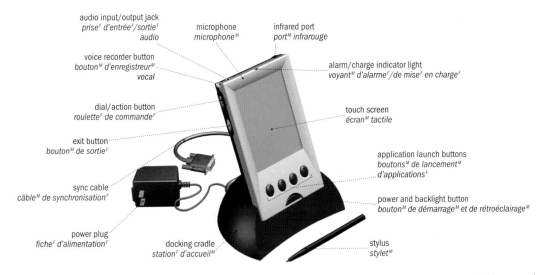

audio input/output jack
prise^F d'entrée^F/sortie^F
audio

microphone
microphone^M

infrared port
port^M infrarouge

voice recorder button
bouton^M d'enregistreur^M
vocal

alarm/charge indicator light
voyant^M d'alarme^F/de mise^F en charge^F

dial/action button
roulette^F de commande^F

touch screen
écran^M tactile

exit button
bouton^M de sortie^F

application launch buttons
boutons^M de lancement^M
d'applications^F

sync cable
câble^M de synchronisation^F

power and backlight button
bouton^M de démarrage^M et de rétroéclairage^M

power plug
fiche^F d'alimentation^F

docking cradle
station^F d'accueil^M

stylus
stylet^M

stationery

articles^M de bureau^M

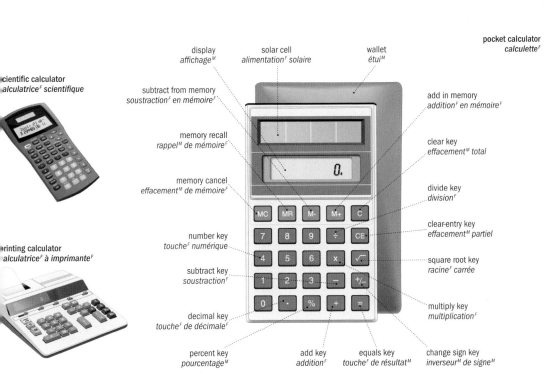

pocket calculator
calculette^F

display
affichage^M

solar cell
alimentation^F solaire

wallet
étui^M

scientific calculator
calculatrice^F scientifique

subtract from memory
soustraction^F en mémoire^F

add in memory
addition^F en mémoire^F

memory recall
rappel^M de mémoire^F

clear key
effacement^M total

memory cancel
effacement^M de mémoire^F

divide key
division^F

clear-entry key
effacement^M partiel

number key
touche^F numérique

printing calculator
calculatrice^F à imprimante^F

subtract key
soustraction^F

square root key
racine^F carrée

multiply key
multiplication^F

decimal key
touche^F de décimale^F

percent key
pourcentage^M

add key
addition^F

equals key
touche^F de résultat^M

change sign key
inverseur^M de signe^M

COMMUNICATIONS AND OFFICE AUTOMATION

stationery

for time use
pour l'emploi^M du temps^M

calendar pad
bloc^M-éphéméride^F

tear-off calendar
calendrier^M-mémorandum^M

organize
organiseur^M

display
écran^M

alphabetical keypad
pavé^M alphabétique

numeric keypad
pavé^M numérique

appointment book
agenda^M

memo pad
bloc^M-notes^F

for correspondence
pour la
correspondance^F

rubber stamp
timbre^M caoutchouc^M

numbering stamp
numéroteur^M

date stamp
timbre^M dateur

stamp pad
tampon^M encreur

desk tray
boîte^F à courrier^M

telephone index
répertoire^M téléphonique

rotary file
fichier^M rotatif

stationery

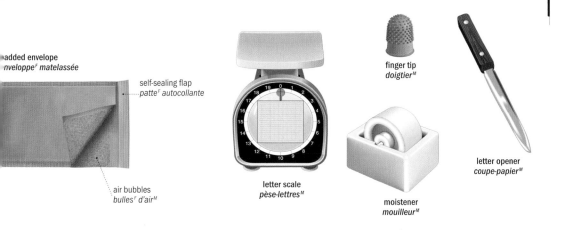

added envelope
nveloppe^F *matelassée*

self-sealing flap
patte^F *autocollante*

air bubbles
bulles^F *d'air*^M

letter scale
pèse-lettres^M

finger tip
doigtier^M

moistener
mouilleur^M

letter opener
coupe-papier^M

for filing
pour le classement^M

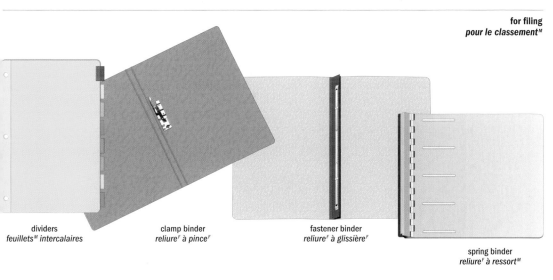

dividers
feuillets^M *intercalaires*

clamp binder
reliure^F *à pince*^F

fastener binder
reliure^F *à glissière*^F

spring binder
reliure^F *à ressort*^M

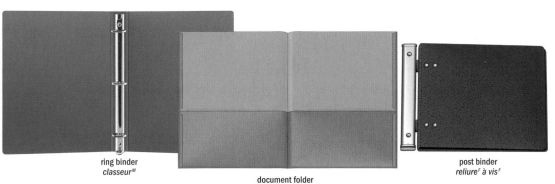

ring binder
classeur^M

document folder
pochette^F *d'information*^F

post binder
reliure^F *à vis*^F

COMMUNICATIONS AND OFFICE AUTOMATION

stationery

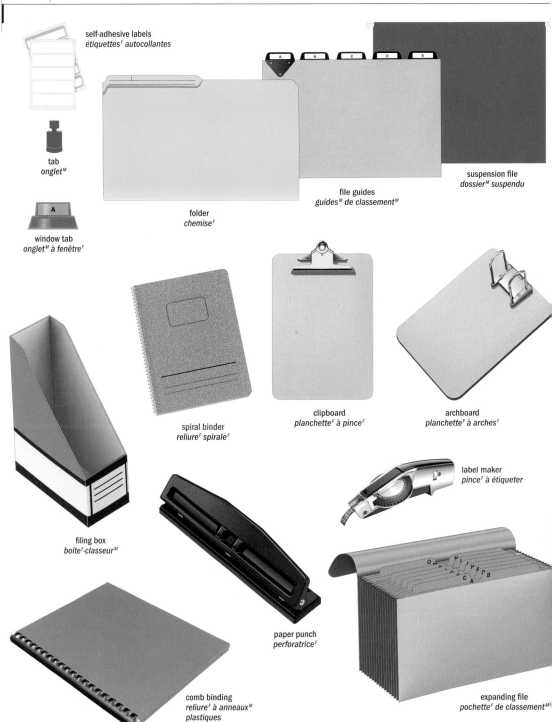

self-adhesive labels
étiquettes^F *autocollantes*

tab
onglet^M

window tab
onglet^M *à fenêtre*^F

folder
chemise^F

file guides
guides^M *de classement*^M

suspension file
dossier^M *suspendu*

spiral binder
reliure^F *spirale*^F

clipboard
planchette^F *à pince*^F

archboard
planchette^F *à arches*^F

filing box
boîte^F-*classeur*^M

label maker
pince^F *à étiqueter*

paper punch
perforatrice^F

comb binding
reliure^F *à anneaux*^M
plastiques

expanding file
pochette^F *de classement*^M

miscellaneous articles
articles^M divers

paper clips
trombones^M

drawing pins
punaises^F

paper fasteners
attaches^F parisiennes

box sealing tape
dispenser
dévidoir^M pistolet^M

hub
moyeu^M

pencil sharpener
taille-crayon^M

tape guide
guide-bande^M

tension adjustment screw
*vis^F de réglage^M de
tension^F*

cutting blade
lame^F

eraser
gomme^F

spike file
pique-notes^M

staple remover
dégrafeuse^F

tape dispenser
dévidoir^M de ruban^M adhésif

handle
poignée^F

stapler
agrafeuse^F

glue stick
bâtonnet^M de colle^F

staples
agrafes^F

book ends
serre-livres^M

paper-clip holder
*distributeur^M de
trombones^M*

pencil sharpener
taille-crayon^M

magnet
aimant^M

bulletin board
tableau^M d'affichage^M

cutting head
tête^F de coupe^F

waste basket
corbeille^F à papier^M

waste basket
corbeille^F à papier^M

posting surface
surface^F d'affichage^M

paper shredder
destructeur^M de documents^M

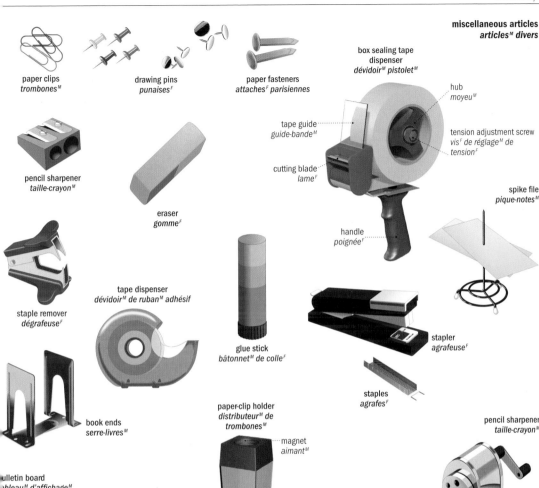

road system

système^M routier

cross section of a road
coupe^F d'une route^F

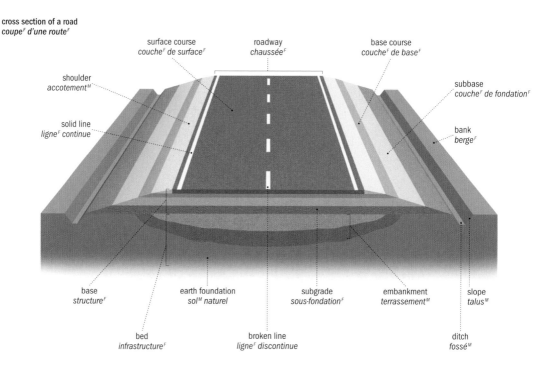

surface course
couche^F de surface^F

roadway
chaussée^F

base course
couche^F de base^F

shoulder
accotement^M

subbase
couche^F de fondation^F

solid line
ligne^F continue

bank
berge^F

base
structure^F

earth foundation
sol^M naturel

subgrade
sous-fondation^F

embankment
terrassement^M

slope
talus^M

bed
infrastructure^F

broken line
ligne^F discontinue

ditch
fossé^M

examples of interchanges
exemples^M d'échangeurs^M

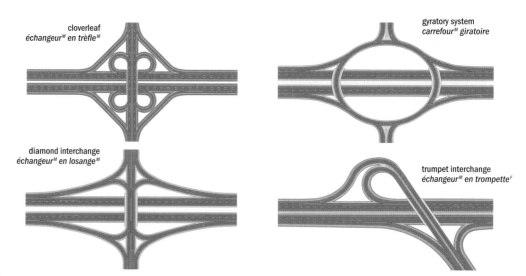

cloverleaf
échangeur^M en trèfle^M

gyratory system
carrefour^M giratoire

diamond interchange
échangeur^M en losange^M

trumpet interchange
échangeur^M en trompette^F

cloverleaf
échangeur^M en trèfle^M

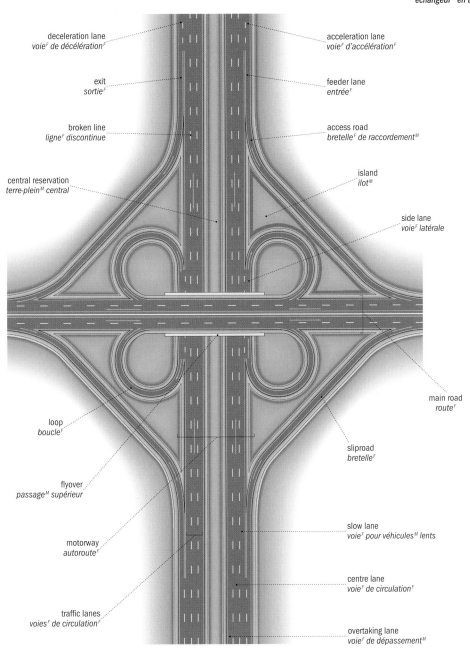

deceleration lane
voie^F de décélération^F

acceleration lane
voie^F d'accélération^F

exit
sortie^F

feeder lane
entrée^F

broken line
ligne^F discontinue

access road
bretelle^F de raccordement^M

central reservation
terre-plein^M central

island
ilot^M

side lane
voie^F latérale

main road
route^F

loop
boucle^F

sliproad
bretelle^F

flyover
passage^M supérieur

slow lane
voie^F pour véhicules^M lents

motorway
autoroute^F

centre lane
voie^F de circulation^F

traffic lanes
voies^F de circulation^F

overtaking lane
voie^F de dépassement^M

TRANSPORT AND MACHINERY

343

fixed bridges

ponts^M fixes

beam bridge
pont^M à poutre^F

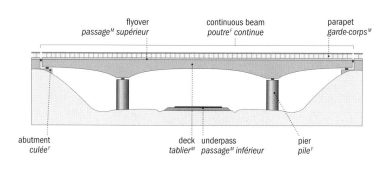

flyover
passage^M supérieur

continuous beam
poutre^F continue

parapet
garde-corps^M

abutment
culée^F

deck
tablier^M

underpass
passage^M inférieur

pier
pile^F

suspension bridge
pont^M suspendu à câble^M porteur

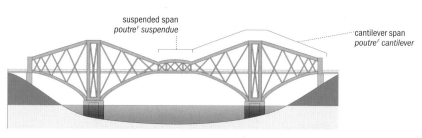

deck
tablier^M

suspension cable
câble^M porteur

suspender
suspente^F

tower
pylône^M

approach ramp
rampe^F d'accès^M

abutment
culée^F

anchorage block
massif^M d'ancrage^M des câbles^M

foundation of tower
fondation^F de pylône^M

centre span
travée^F centrale

side span
travée^F latérale

cantilever bridge
pont^M cantilever

suspended span
poutre^F suspendue

cantilever span
poutre^F cantilever

movable bridges

ponts^M mobiles

swing bridge
pont^M tournant

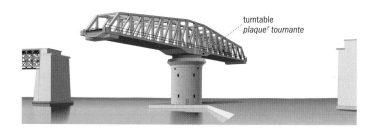

turntable
plaque^F tournante

TRANSPORT AND MACHINERY

movable bridges

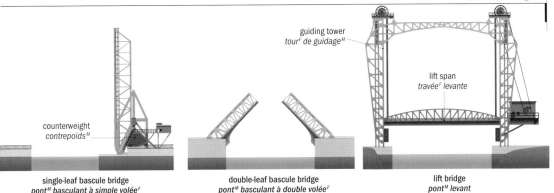

counterweight
contrepoids^M

guiding tower
tour^F de guidage^M

lift span
travée^F levante

single-leaf bascule bridge
pont^M basculant à simple volée^F

double-leaf bascule bridge
pont^M basculant à double volée^F

lift bridge
pont^M levant

road tunnel
tunnel^M routier

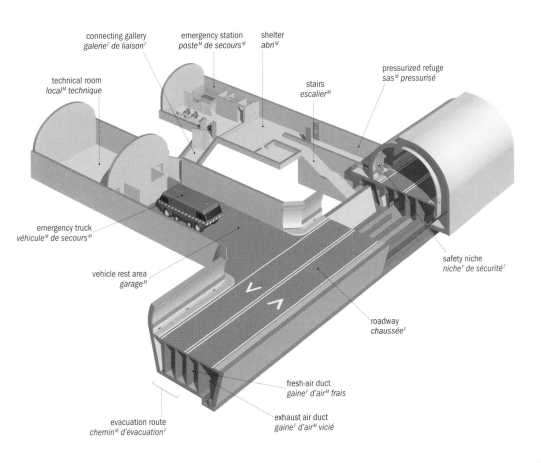

connecting gallery
galerie^F de liaison^F

emergency station
poste^M de secours^M

shelter
abri^M

pressurized refuge
sas^M pressurisé

technical room
local^M technique

stairs
escalier^M

emergency truck
véhicule^M de secours^M

safety niche
niche^F de sécurité^F

vehicle rest area
garage^M

roadway
chaussée^F

fresh-air duct
gaine^F d'air^M frais

evacuation route
chemin^M d'évacuation^F

exhaust air duct
gaine^F d'air^M vicié

TRANSPORT AND MACHINERY

service station

station^F-service^M

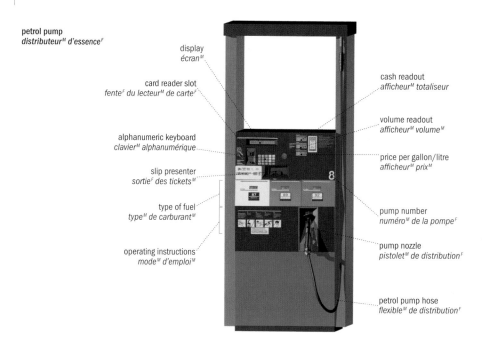

petrol pump
distributeur^M d'essence^F

display
écran^M

card reader slot
fente^F du lecteur^M de carte^F

cash readout
afficheur^M totaliseur

volume readout
afficheur^M volume^M

alphanumeric keyboard
clavier^M alphanumérique

price per gallon/litre
afficheur^M prix^M

slip presenter
sortie^F des tickets^M

type of fuel
type^M de carburant^M

pump number
numéro^M de la pompe^F

operating instructions
mode^M d'emploi^M

pump nozzle
pistolet^M de distribution^F

petrol pump hose
flexible^M de distribution^F

service station
station^F-service^M

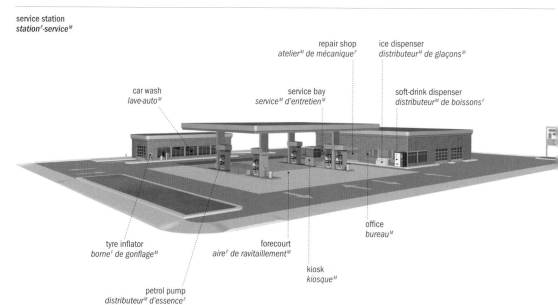

repair shop
atelier^M de mécanique^F

ice dispenser
distributeur^M de glaçons^M

car wash
lave-auto^M

service bay
service^M d'entretien^M

soft-drink dispenser
distributeur^M de boissons^F

tyre inflator
borne^F de gonflage^M

forecourt
aire^F de ravitaillement^M

office
bureau^M

kiosk
kiosque^M

petrol pump
distributeur^M d'essence^F

TRANSPORT AND MACHINERY

car

automobile^F

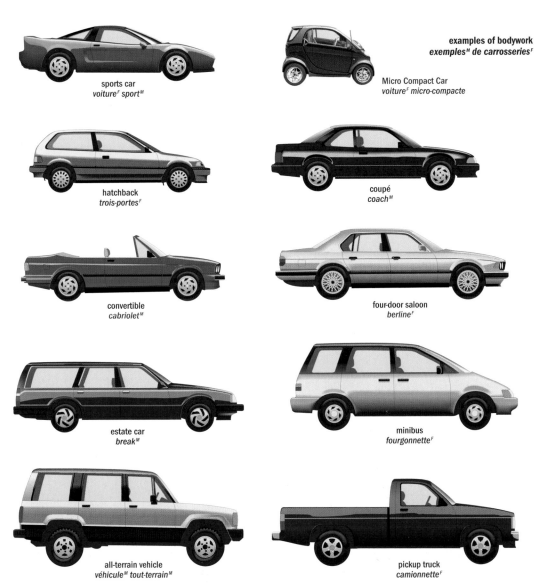

examples of bodywork
exemples^M de carrosseries^F

sports car
voiture^F sport^M

Micro Compact Car
voiture^F micro-compacte

hatchback
trois-portes^F

coupé
coach^M

convertible
cabriolet^M

four-door saloon
berline^F

estate car
break^M

minibus
fourgonnette^F

all-terrain vehicle
véhicule^M tout-terrain^M

pickup truck
camionnette^F

stretch-limousine
limousine^F

TRANSPORT AND MACHINERY

body
carrosserie^F

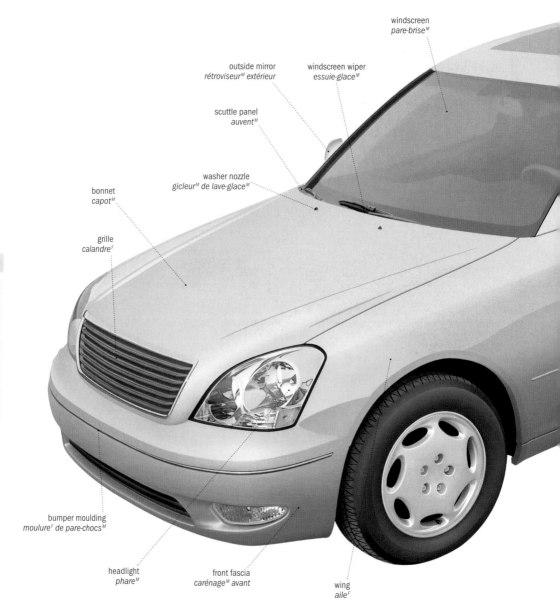

windscreen
pare-brise^M

outside mirror
rétroviseur^M *extérieur*

windscreen wiper
essuie-glace^M

scuttle panel
auvent^M

washer nozzle
gicleur^M *de lave-glace*^M

bonnet
capot^M

grille
calandre^F

bumper moulding
moulure^F *de pare-chocs*^M

headlight
phare^M

front fascia
carénage^M *avant*

wing
aile^F

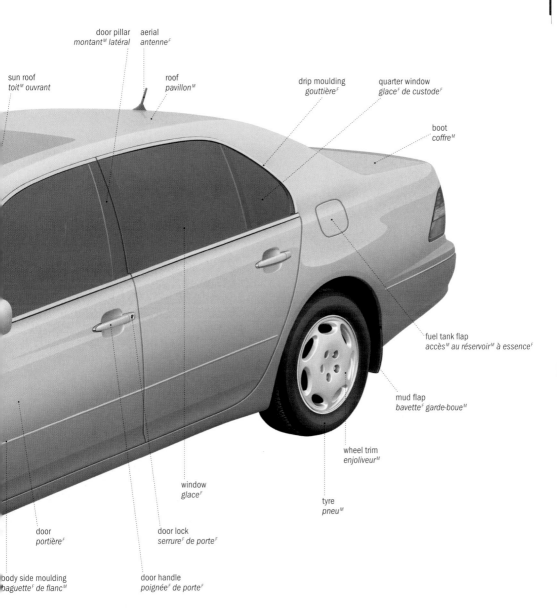

door pillar
montant^M latéral

aerial
antenne^F

sun roof
toit^M ouvrant

roof
pavillon^M

drip moulding
gouttière^F

quarter window
glace^F de custode^F

boot
coffre^M

fuel tank flap
accès^M au réservoir^M à essence^F

mud flap
bavette^F garde-boue^M

wheel trim
enjoliveur^M

window
glace^F

tyre
pneu^M

door
portière^F

door lock
serrure^F de porte^F

body side moulding
baguette^F de flanc^M

door handle
poignée^F de porte^F

TRANSPORT AND MACHINERY

car

car systems : main parts
principaux organes^M *des systèmes*^M
automobiles

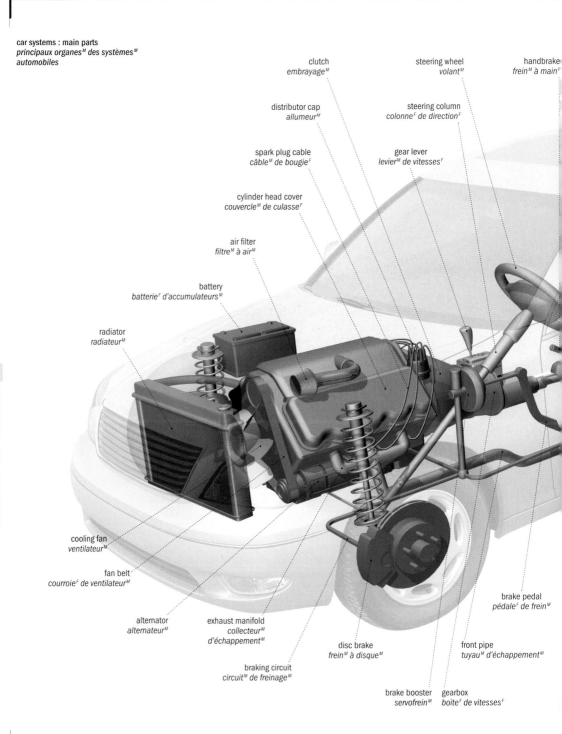

clutch
embrayage^M

steering wheel
volant^M

handbrake
frein^M *à main*^F

distributor cap
allumeur^M

steering column
colonne^F *de direction*^F

spark plug cable
câble^M *de bougie*^F

gear lever
levier^M *de vitesses*^F

cylinder head cover
couvercle^M *de culasse*^F

air filter
filtre^M *à air*^M

battery
batterie^F *d'accumulateurs*^M

radiator
radiateur^M

cooling fan
ventilateur^M

fan belt
courroie^F *de ventilateur*^M

alternator
alternateur^M

exhaust manifold
collecteur^M
d'échappement^M

disc brake
frein^M *à disque*^M

front pipe
tuyau^M *d'échappement*^M

braking circuit
circuit^M *de freinage*^M

brake booster
servofrein^M

gearbox
boîte^F *de vitesses*^F

brake pedal
pédale^F *de frein*^M

TRANSPORT AND MACHINERY

350

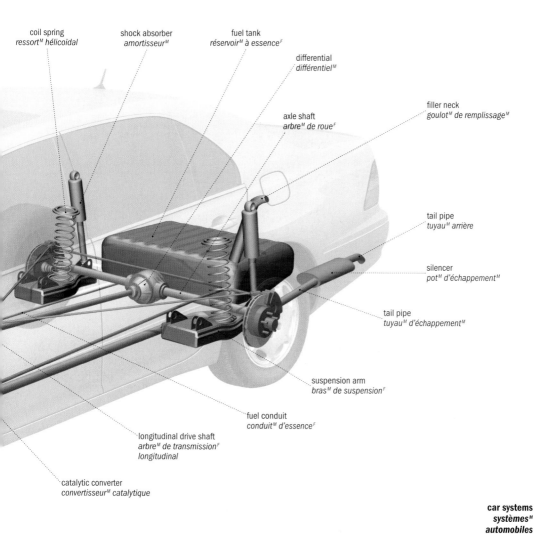

coil spring
ressort^M *hélicoïdal*

shock absorber
amortisseur^M

fuel tank
réservoir^F *à essence*^F

differential
différentiel^M

filler neck
goulot^M *de remplissage*^M

axle shaft
arbre^M *de roue*^F

tail pipe
tuyau^M *arrière*

silencer
pot^M *d'échappement*^M

tail pipe
tuyau^M *d'échappement*^M

suspension arm
bras^M *de suspension*^F

fuel conduit
conduit^M *d'essence*^F

longitudinal drive shaft
arbre^M *de transmission*^F
longitudinal

catalytic converter
convertisseur^M *catalytique*

car systems
***systèmes*^M**
automobiles

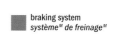
suspension system
système^M *de suspension*^F

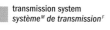
transmission system
système^M *de transmission*^F

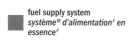
fuel supply system
système^M *d'alimentation*^F *en*
essence^F

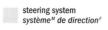
steering system
système^M *de direction*^F

braking system
système^M *de freinage*^M

electrical system
système^M *électrique*

exhaust system
système^M *d'échappement*^M

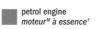
petrol engine
moteur^M *à essence*^F

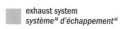
cooling system
système^M *de*
refroidissement^M

TRANSPORT AND MACHINERY

car

front lights
feux^M avant

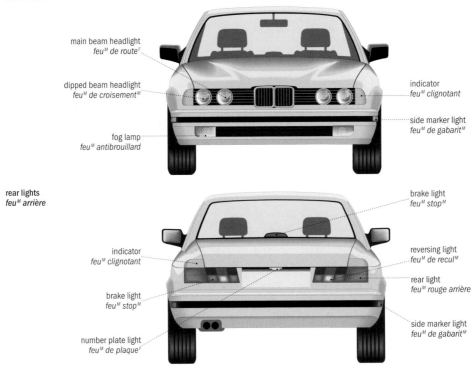

main beam headlight
feu^M de route^F

dipped beam headlight
feu^M de croisement^M

fog lamp
feu^M antibrouillard

indicator
feu^M clignotant

side marker light
feu^M de gabarit^M

rear lights
feu^M arrière

brake light
feu^M stop^M

indicator
feu^M clignotant

reversing light
feu^M de recul^M

rear light
feu^M rouge arrière

brake light
feu^M stop^M

side marker light
feu^M de gabarit^M

number plate light
feu^M de plaque^F

door
portière^F

interior door handle
poignée^F intérieure

window
glace^F

door grip
poignée^F de maintien^M

interior door lock button
bouton^M de verrouillage^M

outside mirror control
commande^F du rétroviseur^M

armrest
appui^M-bras^M

lock
serrure^F

window winder handle
manivelle^F de lève-glace^M

trim panel
panneau^M de garnissage^M

hinge
charnière^F

inner door shell
caisson^M de porte^F

door pocket
vide-poches^M

car

bucket seat : front view
siège^M-baquet^M : vue^F de face^F

bucket seat : side view
siège^M-baquet^M : vue^F de profil^M

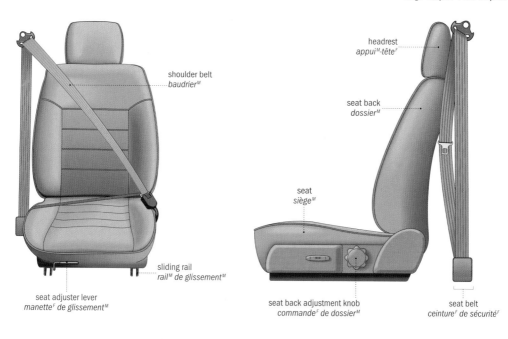

shoulder belt
baudrier^M

headrest
appui^M-tête^F

seat back
dossier^M

seat
siège^M

sliding rail
rail^M de glissement^M

seat adjuster lever
manette^F de glissement^M

seat back adjustment knob
commande^F de dossier^M

seat belt
ceinture^F de sécurité^F

rear seat
banquette^F arrière

armrest
appui^M-bras^M

lap belt
sangle^F

buckle
boucle^F

bench seat
banquette^F

TRANSPORT AND MACHINERY

car

dashboard
tableau^M de bord^M

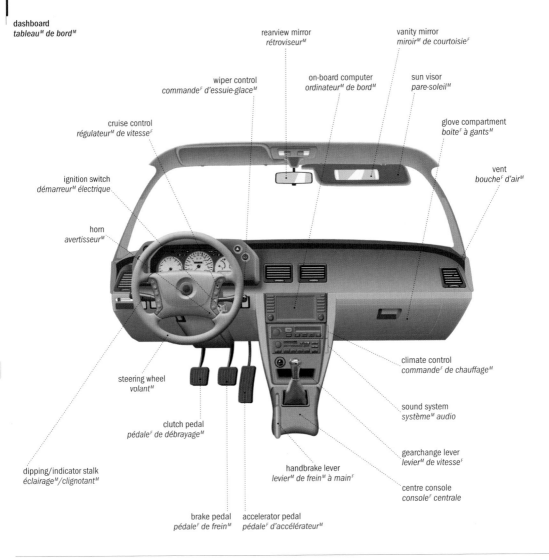

rearview mirror
rétroviseur^M

vanity mirror
miroir^M de courtoisie^F

wiper control
commande^F d'essuie-glace^M

on-board computer
ordinateur^M de bord^M

sun visor
pare-soleil^M

cruise control
régulateur^M de vitesse^F

glove compartment
boîte^F à gants^M

ignition switch
démarreur^M électrique

vent
bouche^F d'air^M

horn
avertisseur^M

climate control
commande^F de chauffage^M

steering wheel
volant^M

sound system
système^M audio

clutch pedal
pédale^F de débrayage^M

gearchange lever
levier^M de vitesse^F

dipping/indicator stalk
éclairage^M/clignotant^M

handbrake lever
levier^M de frein^M à main^F

centre console
console^F centrale

brake pedal
pédale^F de frein^M

accelerator pedal
pédale^F d'accélérateur^M

air bag restraint system
système^M de retenue^F à sacs^M
gonflables

air bag
sac^M gonflable

safing sensor
détecteur^M de sécurité^F

primary crash sensor
détecteur^M d'impact^M primaire

electrical cable
câble^M électrique

TRANSPORT AND MACHINERY

instrument panel
instruments^M de bord^M

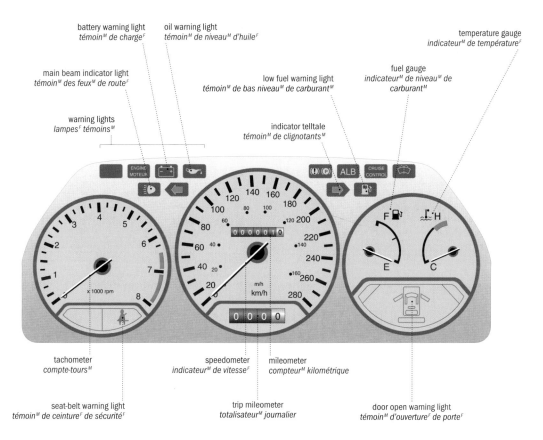

battery warning light
témoin^M de charge^F

oil warning light
témoin^M de niveau^M d'huile^F

temperature gauge
indicateur^M de température^F

main beam indicator light
témoin^M des feux^M de route^F

low fuel warning light
témoin^M de bas niveau^M de carburant^M

fuel gauge
indicateur^M de niveau^M de carburant^M

warning lights
lampes^F témoins^M

indicator telltale
témoin^M de clignotants^M

tachometer
compte-tours^M

speedometer
indicateur^M de vitesse^F

mileometer
compteur^M kilométrique

seat-belt warning light
témoin^M de ceinture^F de sécurité^F

trip mileometer
totalisateur^M journalier

door open warning light
témoin^M d'ouverture^F de porte^F

windscreen wiper
essuie-glace^M

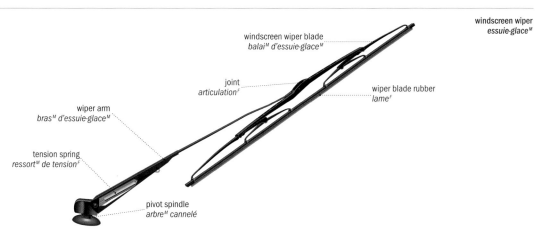

windscreen wiper blade
balai^M d'essuie-glace^M

joint
articulation^F

wiper blade rubber
lame^F

wiper arm
bras^M d'essuie-glace^M

tension spring
ressort^M de tension^F

pivot spindle
arbre^M cannelé

TRANSPORT AND MACHINERY

355

car

accessories
*accessoires*ᴹ

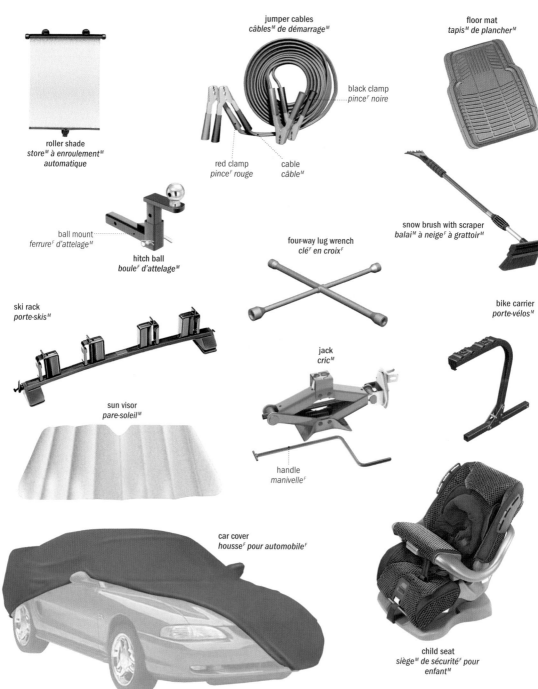

jumper cables
*câbles*ᴹ *de démarrage*ᴹ

floor mat
*tapis*ᴹ *de plancher*ᴹ

black clamp
*pince*ᶠ *noire*

roller shade
*store*ᴹ *à enroulement*ᴹ
automatique

red clamp
*pince*ᶠ *rouge*

cable
*câble*ᴹ

ball mount
*ferrure*ᶠ *d'attelage*ᴹ

hitch ball
*boule*ᶠ *d'attelage*ᴹ

four-way lug wrench
*clé*ᶠ *en croix*ᶠ

snow brush with scraper
*balai*ᴹ *à neige*ᶠ *à grattoir*ᴹ

ski rack
*porte-skis*ᴹ

bike carrier
*porte-vélos*ᴹ

jack
*cric*ᴹ

sun visor
*pare-soleil*ᴹ

handle
*manivelle*ᶠ

car cover
*housse*ᶠ *pour automobile*ᶠ

child seat
*siège*ᴹ *de sécurité*ᶠ *pour*
*enfant*ᴹ

brakes
freins^M

disc brake
frein^M à disque^M

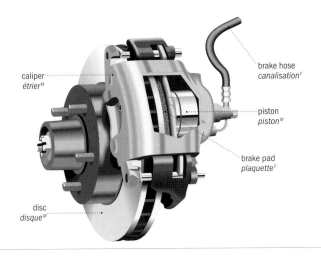

caliper
étrier^M

brake hose
canalisation^F

piston
piston^M

brake pad
plaquette^F

disc
disque^M

drum brake
frein^M à tambour^M

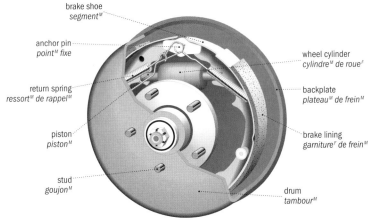

brake shoe
segment^M

anchor pin
point^M fixe

return spring
ressort^M de rappel^M

piston
piston^M

stud
goujon^M

wheel cylinder
cylindre^M de roue^F

backplate
plateau^M de frein^M

brake lining
garniture^F de frein^M

drum
tambour^M

antilock braking system (ABS)
*système^M de freinage^M
antiblocage*

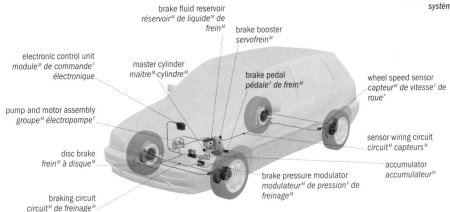

brake fluid reservoir
*réservoir^M de liquide^M de
frein^M*

brake booster
servofrein^M

electronic control unit
*module^M de commande^F
électronique*

master cylinder
maître^M-cylindre^M

brake pedal
pédale^F de frein^M

wheel speed sensor
*capteur^M de vitesse^F de
roue^F*

pump and motor assembly
groupe^M électropompe^F

disc brake
frein^M à disque^M

sensor wiring circuit
circuit^M capteurs^M

accumulator
accumulateur^M

brake pressure modulator
*modulateur^M de pression^F de
freinage^M*

braking circuit
circuit^M de freinage^M

TRANSPORT AND MACHINERY

tyre
pneu^M

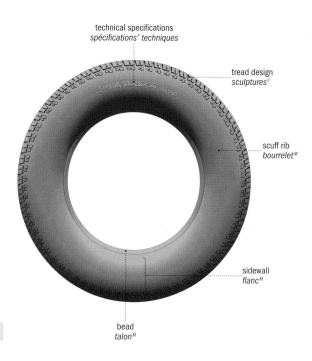

technical specifications
spécifications^F techniques

tread design
sculptures^F

scuff rib
bourrelet^M

sidewall
flanc^M

bead
talon^M

examples of tyres
exemples^M de pneus^M

performance tyre
pneu^M de performance^F

all-season tyre
pneu^M toutes saisons^F

studded tyre
pneu^M à crampons^M

winter tyre
pneu^M d'hiver^M

touring tyre
pneu^M autoroutier

radiator
radiateur^M

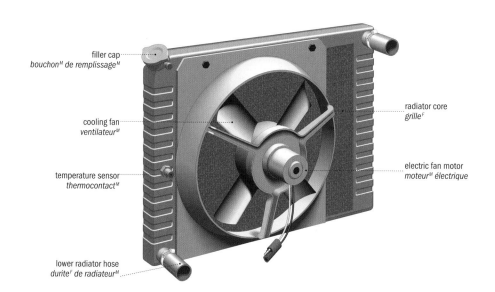

filler cap
bouchon^M de remplissage^M

cooling fan
ventilateur^M

temperature sensor
thermocontact^M

lower radiator hose
durite^F de radiateur^M

radiator core
grille^F

electric fan motor
moteur^M électrique

TRANSPORT AND MACHINERY

spark plug

bougie^F d'allumage^M

groove
cannelure^F

spark plug
borne^F

centre electrode
électrode^F centrale

insulator
isolateur^M

hex nut
écrou^M hexagonal

spark plug seat
joint^M de bougie^F

spark plug body
culot^M

side electrode
électrode^F de masse^F

spark plug gap
écartement^M des électrodes^F

battery

batterie^F d'accumulateurs^M

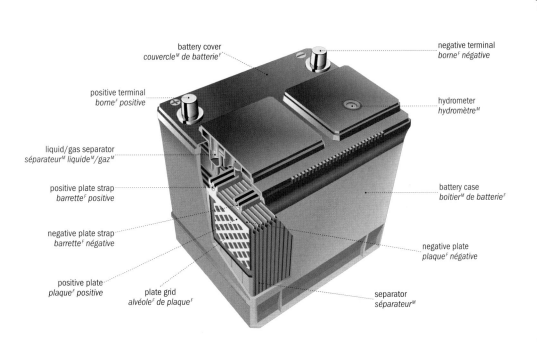

battery cover
couvercle^M de batterie^F

negative terminal
borne^F négative

positive terminal
borne^F positive

hydrometer
hydromètre^M

liquid/gas separator
séparateur^M liquide^M/gaz^M

positive plate strap
barrette^F positive

battery case
boitier^M de batterie^F

negative plate strap
barrette^F négative

negative plate
plaque^F négative

positive plate
plaque^F positive

plate grid
alvéole^F de plaque^F

separator
séparateur^M

TRANSPORT AND MACHINERY

petrol engine

moteur^M à essence^F

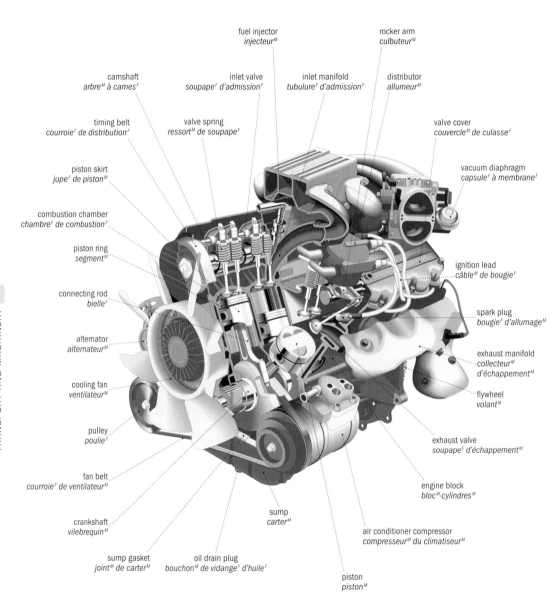

fuel injector
injecteur^M

rocker arm
culbuteur^M

camshaft
arbre^M à cames^F

inlet valve
soupape^F d'admission^F

inlet manifold
tubulure^F d'admission^F

distributor
allumeur^M

timing belt
courroie^F de distribution^F

valve spring
ressort^M de soupape^F

valve cover
couvercle^M de culasse^F

piston skirt
jupe^F de piston^M

vacuum diaphragm
capsule^F à membrane^F

combustion chamber
chambre^F de combustion^F

piston ring
segment^M

ignition lead
câble^M de bougie^F

connecting rod
bielle^F

spark plug
bougie^F d'allumage^M

alternator
alternateur^M

exhaust manifold
collecteur^M
d'échappement^M

cooling fan
ventilateur^M

flywheel
volant^M

pulley
poulie^F

exhaust valve
soupape^F d'échappement^M

fan belt
courroie^F de ventilateur^M

engine block
bloc^M-cylindres^M

crankshaft
vilebrequin^M

sump
carter^M

air conditioner compressor
compresseur^M du climatiseur^M

sump gasket
joint^M de carter^M

oil drain plug
bouchon^M de vidange^F d'huile^F

piston
piston^M

caravan

caravane^F

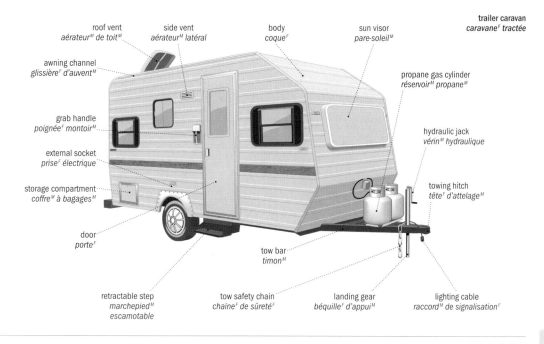

trailer caravan
caravane^F tractée

roof vent
aérateur^M de toit^M

side vent
aérateur^M latéral

body
coque^F

sun visor
pare-soleil^M

awning channel
glissière^F d'auvent^M

propane gas cylinder
réservoir^M propane^M

grab handle
poignée^F montoir^M

hydraulic jack
vérin^M hydraulique

external socket
prise^F électrique

towing hitch
tête^F d'attelage^M

storage compartment
coffre^M à bagages^M

door
porte^F

tow bar
timon^M

retractable step
marchepied^M
escamotable

tow safety chain
chaîne^F de sûreté^F

landing gear
béquille^F d'appui^M

lighting cable
raccord^M de signalisation^F

trailer tent
caravane^F pliante

roof
toit^M

canopy
auvent^M

window
fenêtre^F

bunk
lit^M

spare tyre
roue^F de secours^M

body
coque^F

stabilizer jack
béquille^F d'appoint^M

screen door
porte^F moustiquaire^F

camper
auto^F-caravane^F

air conditioner
climatiseur^M

luggage rack
porte-bagages^M

ladder
échelle^F

bus

autobus^M

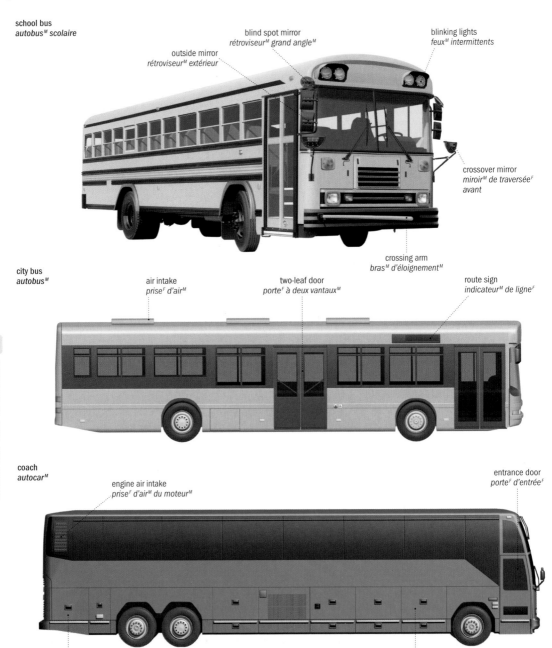

school bus
autobus^M scolaire

outside mirror
rétroviseur^M extérieur

blind spot mirror
rétroviseur^M grand angle^M

blinking lights
feux^M intermittents

crossover mirror
*miroir^M de traversée^F
avant*

crossing arm
bras^M d'éloignement^M

city bus
autobus^M

air intake
prise^F d'air^M

two-leaf door
porte^F à deux vantaux^M

route sign
indicateur^M de ligne^F

coach
autocar^M

engine air intake
prise^F d'air^M du moteur^M

entrance door
porte^F d'entrée^F

engine compartment
compartiment^M moteur^M

baggage compartment
soute^F à bagages^M

double-decker bus
autobus^M *à impériale*^F

route sign
indicateur^M *de ligne*^F

upper deck
impériale^F

minibus
minibus^M

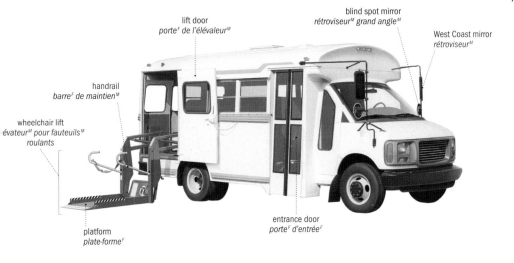

lift door
porte^F *de l'élévateur*^M

blind spot mirror
rétroviseur^M *grand angle*^M

West Coast mirror
rétroviseur^M

handrail
barre^F *de maintien*^M

wheelchair lift
évateur^M *pour fauteuils*^M
roulants

platform
plate-forme^F

entrance door
porte^F *d'entrée*^F

articulated bus
autobus^M *articulé*

articulated joint
section^F *articulée*

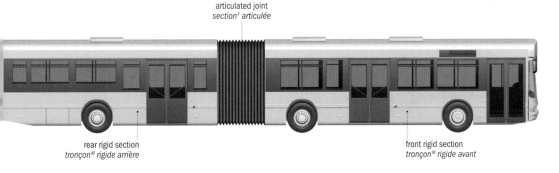

rear rigid section
tronçon^M *rigide arrière*

front rigid section
tronçon^M *rigide avant*

TRANSPORT AND MACHINERY

trucking

camionnage^M

tractor unit
tracteur^M routier

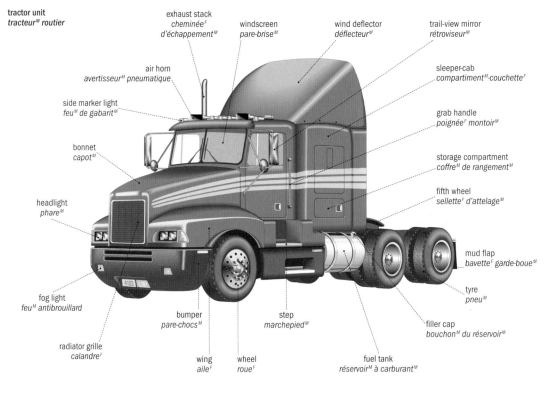

exhaust stack
*cheminée^F
d'échappement^M*

windscreen
pare-brise^M

wind deflector
déflecteur^M

trail-view mirror
rétroviseur^M

air horn
avertisseur^M pneumatique

sleeper-cab
compartiment^M-couchette^F

side marker light
feu^M de gabarit^M

grab handle
poignée^F montoir^M

bonnet
capot^M

storage compartment
coffre^M de rangement^M

headlight
phare^M

fifth wheel
sellette^F d'attelage^M

mud flap
bavette^F garde-boue^M

tyre
pneu^M

fog light
feu^M antibrouillard

bumper
pare-chocs^M

step
marchepied^M

filler cap
bouchon^M du réservoir^M

radiator grille
calandre^F

wing
aile^F

wheel
roue^F

fuel tank
réservoir^M à carburant^M

examples of trucks
exemples^M de camions^M

tanker body
citerne^F

tanker
camion^M-citerne^F

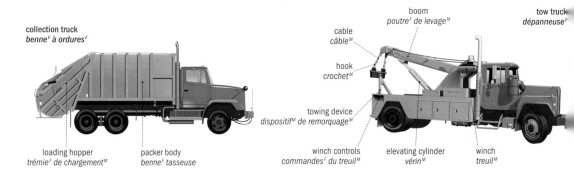

collection truck
benne^F à ordures^F

boom
poutre^F de levage^M

tow truck
dépanneuse^F

cable
câble^M

hook
crochet^M

towing device
dispositif^M de remorquage^M

loading hopper
trémie^F de chargement^M

packer body
benne^F tasseuse

winch controls
commandes^F du treuil^M

elevating cylinder
vérin^M

winch
treuil^M

TRANSPORT AND MACHINERY

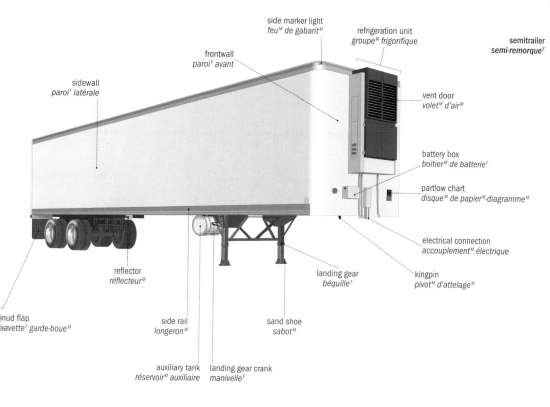

semitrailer
semi-remorque^F

side marker light
feu^M de gabarit^M

refrigeration unit
groupe^M frigorifique

frontwall
paroi^F avant

sidewall
paroi^F latérale

vent door
volet^M d'air^M

battery box
boitier^M de batterie^F

partlow chart
disque^M de papier^M-diagramme^M

electrical connection
accouplement^M électrique

kingpin
pivot^M d'attelage^M

landing gear
béquille^F

reflector
réflecteur^M

mud flap
bavette^F garde-boue^M

side rail
longeron^M

sand shoe
sabot^M

auxiliary tank
réservoir^M auxiliaire

landing gear crank
manivelle^F

van
camion^M porteur^M fourgon^M

concrete mixer truck
camion^M-toupie^F

street sweeper
balayeuse^F

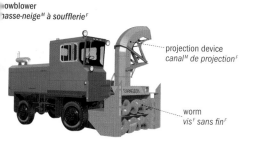

snowblower
chasse-neige^M à soufflerie^F

projection device
canal^M de projection^F

worm
vis^F sans fin^F

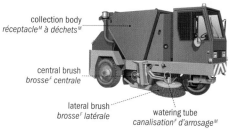

collection body
réceptacle^M à déchets^M

central brush
brosse^F centrale

lateral brush
brosse^F latérale

watering tube
canalisation^F d'arrosage^M

TRANSPORT AND MACHINERY

motorcycle

moto^F

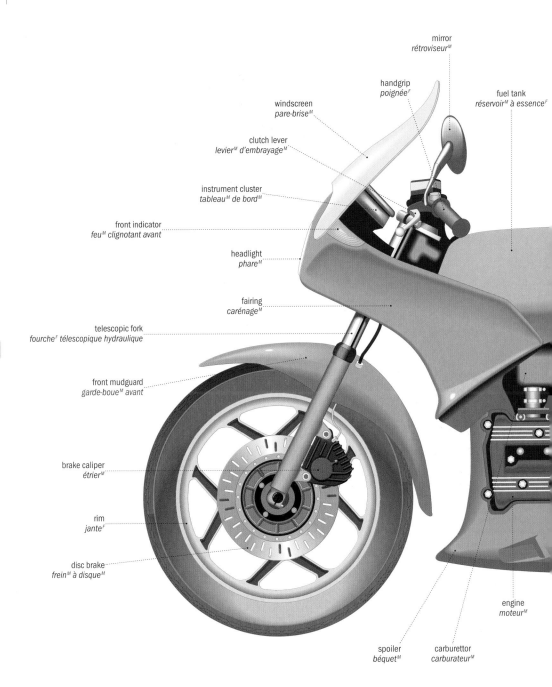

mirror
rétroviseur^M

handgrip
poignée^F

fuel tank
réservoir^M *à essence*^F

windscreen
pare-brise^M

clutch lever
levier^M *d'embrayage*^M

instrument cluster
tableau^M *de bord*^M

front indicator
feu^M *clignotant avant*

headlight
phare^M

fairing
carénage^M

telescopic fork
fourche^F *télescopique hydraulique*

front mudguard
garde-boue^M *avant*

brake caliper
étrier^M

rim
jante^F

disc brake
frein^M *à disque*^M

spoiler
béquet^M

carburettor
carburateur^M

engine
moteur^M

bubble
coque^F

crash helmet
***casque*^M *de protection*^F**

visor
visière^F

visor hinge
charnière^F *de la visière*^F

air inlet
grille^F *d'entrée*^F *d'air*^M

chin protector
mentonnière^F

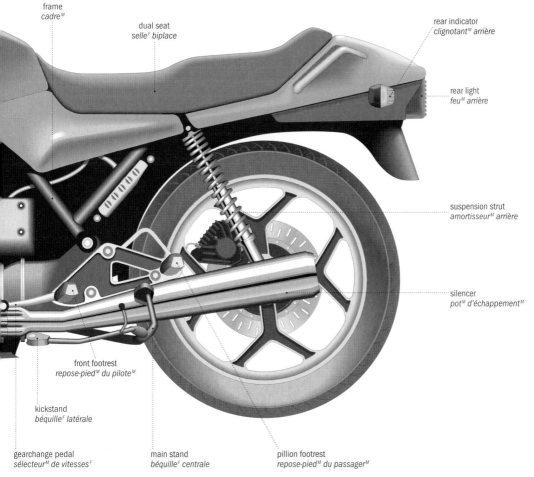

frame
cadre^M

dual seat
selle^F *biplace*

rear indicator
clignotant^M *arrière*

rear light
feu^M *arrière*

suspension strut
amortisseur^M *arrière*

silencer
pot^M *d'échappement*^M

front footrest
repose-pied^M *du pilote*^M

kickstand
béquille^F *latérale*

gearchange pedal
sélecteur^M *de vitesses*^F

main stand
béquille^F *centrale*

pillion footrest
repose-pied^M *du passager*^M

TRANSPORT AND MACHINERY

motorcycle

instrument cluster
tableau^M de bord^M

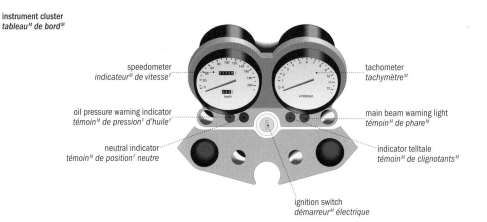

speedometer
indicateur^M de vitesse^F

tachometer
tachymètre^M

oil pressure warning indicator
témoin^M de pression^F d'huile^F

main beam warning light
témoin^M de phare^M

neutral indicator
témoin^M de position^F neutre

indicator telltale
témoin^M de clignotants^M

ignition switch
démarreur^M électrique

motorcycle : view from above
moto^F : vue^F en plongée^F

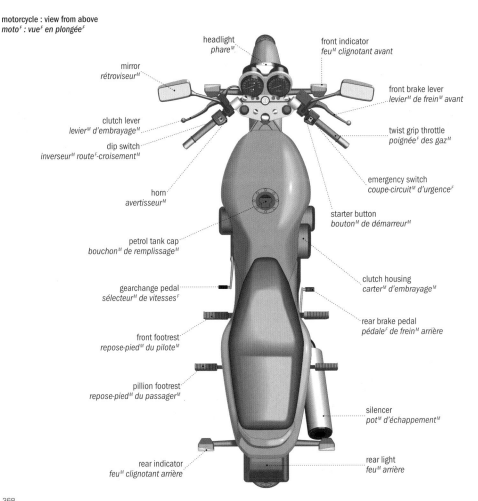

headlight
phare^M

front indicator
feu^M clignotant avant

mirror
rétroviseur^M

front brake lever
levier^M de frein^M avant

clutch lever
levier^M d'embrayage^M

twist grip throttle
poignée^F des gaz^M

dip switch
inverseur^M route^F-croisement^M

emergency switch
coupe-circuit^M d'urgence^F

horn
avertisseur^M

starter button
bouton^M de démarreur^M

petrol tank cap
bouchon^M de remplissage^M

clutch housing
carter^M d'embrayage^M

gearchange pedal
sélecteur^M de vitesses^F

rear brake pedal
pédale^F de frein^M arrière

front footrest
repose-pied^M du pilote^M

pillion footrest
repose-pied^M du passager^M

silencer
pot^M d'échappement^M

rear indicator
feu^M clignotant arrière

rear light
feu^M arrière

motorcycle

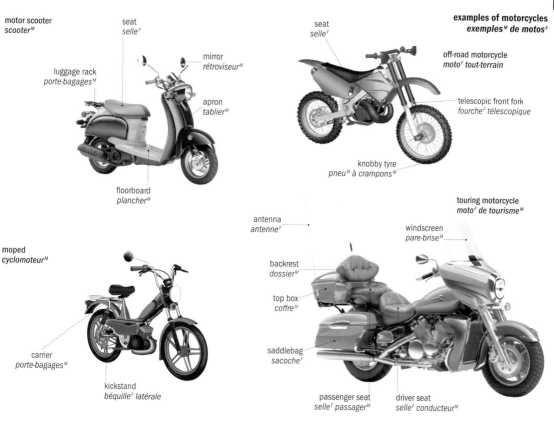

motor scooter
scooter^M

seat
selle^F

mirror
rétroviseur^M

luggage rack
porte-bagages^M

apron
tablier^M

floorboard
plancher^M

moped
cyclomoteur^M

carrier
porte-bagages^M

kickstand
béquille^F *latérale*

seat
selle^F

examples of motorcycles
exemples^M *de motos*^F

off-road motorcycle
moto^F *tout-terrain*

telescopic front fork
fourche^F *télescopique*

knobby tyre
pneu^M *à crampons*^M

touring motorcycle
moto^F *de tourisme*^M

antenna
antenne^F

windscreen
pare-brise^M

backrest
dossier^M

top box
coffre^M

saddlebag
sacoche^F

passenger seat
selle^F *passager*^M

driver seat
selle^F *conducteur*^M

quad bike

quad^M

rear cargo rack
porte-bagages^M *arrière*

rear bumper
garde-boue^M *arrière*

silencer
pot^M *d'échappement*^M

seat
selle^F

fuel tank
réservoir^M *à essence*^F

handgrip
poignée^F

bumper
pare-chocs^M

front shock absorber
amortisseur^M *avant*

gear lever
sélecteur^M *de vitesses*^F

TRANSPORT AND MACHINERY

bicycle

bicyclette^F

parts of a bicycle
parties^F d'une bicyclette^F

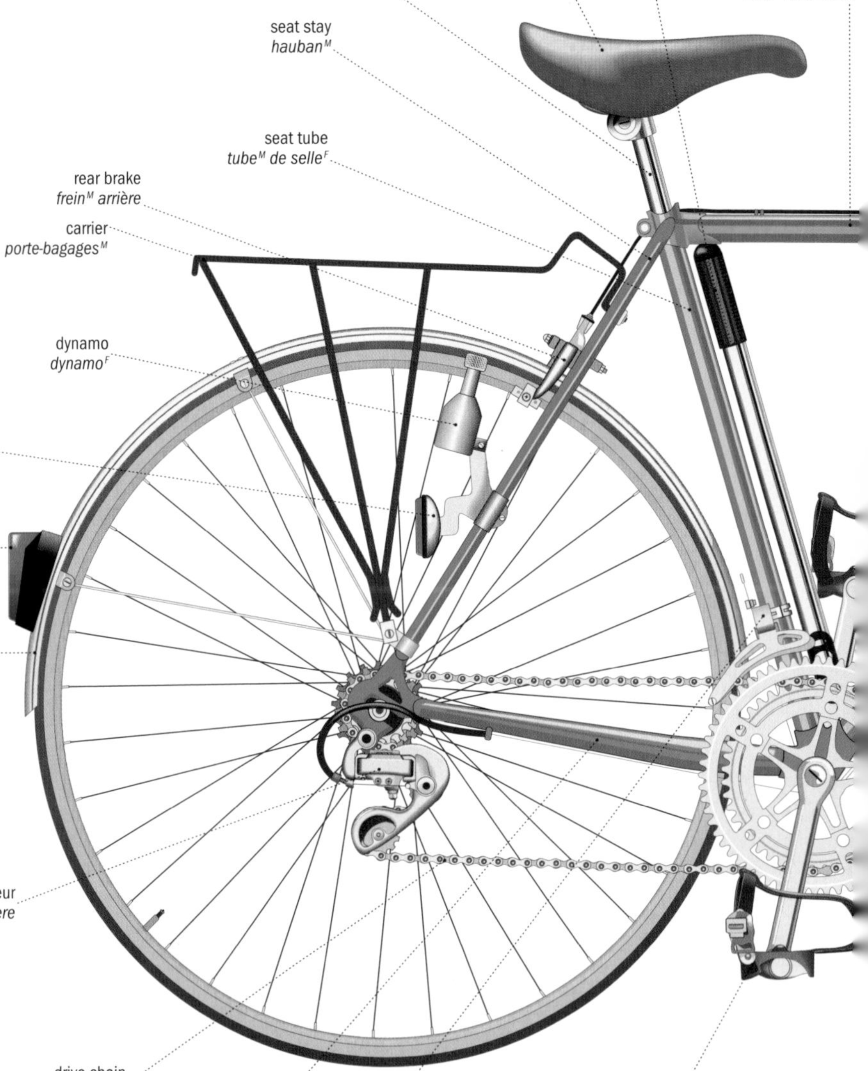

saddle
selle^F

tyre pump
pompe^F

saddle pillar
tige^F de selle^F

crossbar
tube^M horizontal

seat stay
hauban^M

seat tube
tube^M de selle^F

rear brake
frein^M arrière

carrier
porte-bagages^M

dynamo
dynamo^F

reflector
catadioptre^M

rear light
feu^M arrière

mudguard
garde-boue^M

rear derailleur
dérailleur^M arrière

drive chain
chaîne^F

chain stay
base^F

front derailleur
dérailleur^M avant

pedal
pédale^F

toe clip
cale-pied^M

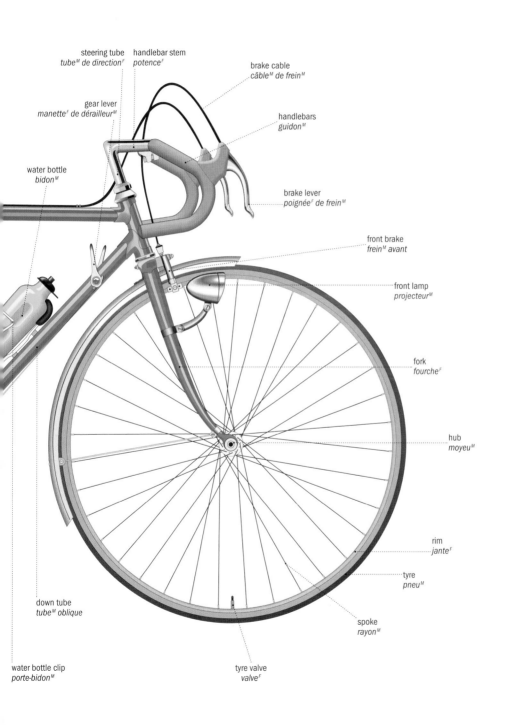

steering tube
tube^M de direction^F

handlebar stem
potence^F

brake cable
câble^M de frein^M

gear lever
manette^F de dérailleur^M

handlebars
guidon^M

water bottle
bidon^M

brake lever
poignée^F de frein^M

front brake
frein^M avant

front lamp
projecteur^M

fork
fourche^F

hub
moyeu^M

rim
jante^F

tyre
pneu^M

down tube
tube^M oblique

spoke
rayon^M

water bottle clip
porte-bidon^M

tyre valve
valve^F

bicycle

power train
*mécanisme^M de
propulsion^F*

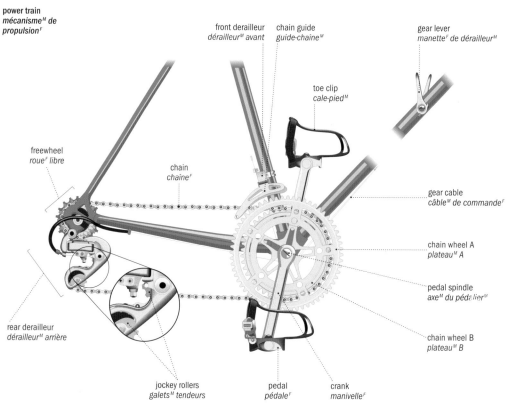

front derailleur
dérailleur^M avant

chain guide
guide-chaîne^M

gear lever
manette^F de dérailleur^M

toe clip
cale-pied^M

freewheel
roue^F libre

chain
chaîne^F

gear cable
câble^M de commande^F

chain wheel A
plateau^M A

pedal spindle
axe^M du pédalier^M

rear derailleur
dérailleur^M arrière

chain wheel B
plateau^M B

jockey rollers
galets^M tendeurs

pedal
pédale^F

crank
manivelle^F

accessories
accessoires^M

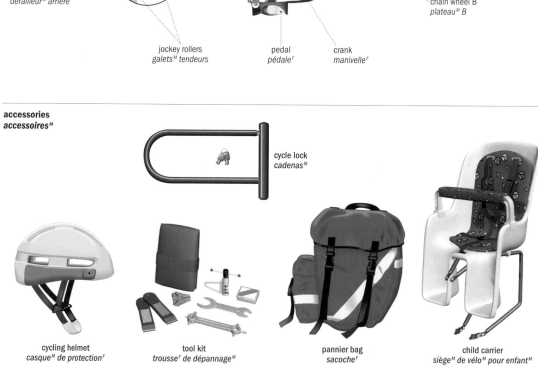

cycle lock
cadenas^M

cycling helmet
casque^M de protection^F

tool kit
trousse^F de dépannage^M

pannier bag
sacoche^F

child carrier
siège^M de vélo^M pour enfant^M

TRANSPORT AND MACHINERY

child's tricycle
*tricycle*M *d'enfant*M

examples of bicycles
exemplesM **de bicyclettes**F

BMX bike
*vélo*M *cross*M

Dutch bicycle
*bicyclette*F *hollandaise*

all-terrain bicycle
*VTT*M

city bicycle
*bicyclette*F *de ville*F

road bicycle
*bicyclette*F *de course*F

touring bicycle
*bicyclette*F *de tourisme*M

tandem
*tandem*M

TRANSPORT AND MACHINERY

passenger station

gare^F de voyageurs^M

office
locaux^M administratifs

timetable
panneau^M indicateur

luggage trolley
chariot^M à bagages^M

luggage lockers
consigne^F automatique

glass roof
verrière^F

metal structure
structure^F métallique

platform number
numéro^M de quai^M

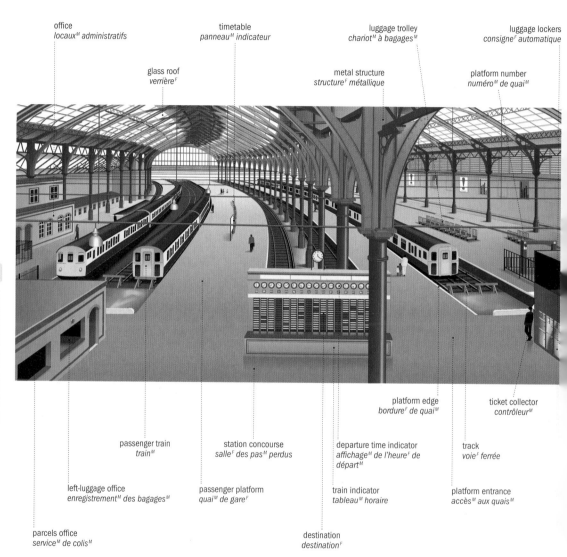

platform edge
bordure^F de quai^M

ticket collector
contrôleur^M

passenger train
train^M

station concourse
salle^F des pas^M perdus

departure time indicator
affichage^M de l'heure^F de départ^M

track
voie^F ferrée

left-luggage office
enregistrement^M des bagages^M

passenger platform
quai^M de gare^F

train indicator
tableau^M horaire

platform entrance
accès^M aux quais^M

parcels office
service^M de colis^M

destination
destination^F

railway station

gare^F

passenger station
gare^F de voyageurs^M

station platform
quai^M

commuter train
train^M de banlieue^F

main line
grandes lignes^F

suburban commuter railway
voie^F de banlieue^F

siding
voie^F de service^M

buffers
butoir^M

level crossing
passage^M à niveau^M

car park
parking^M

platform shelter
abri^M

footbridge
passerelle^F

semaphore signal
sémaphore^M

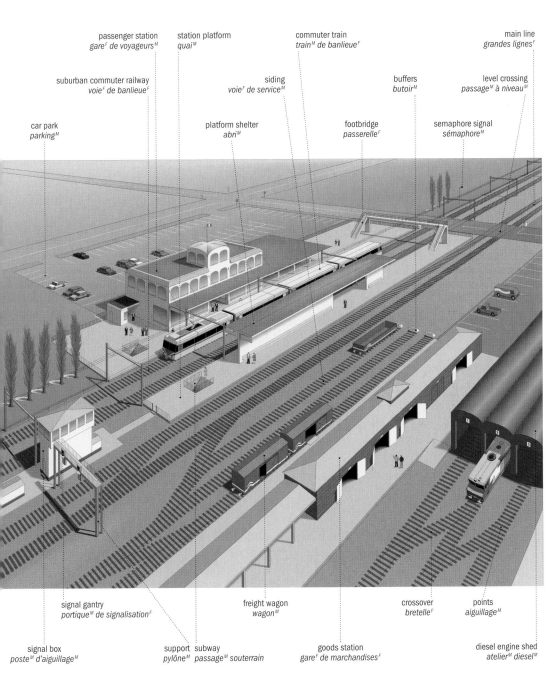

signal gantry
portique^M de signalisation^F

freight wagon
wagon^M

crossover
bretelle^F

points
aiguillage^M

signal box
poste^M d'aiguillage^M

support
pylône^M

subway
passage^M souterrain

goods station
gare^F de marchandises^F

diesel engine shed
atelier^M diesel^M

high-speed train

train^M à grande vitesse^F (T.G.V.)

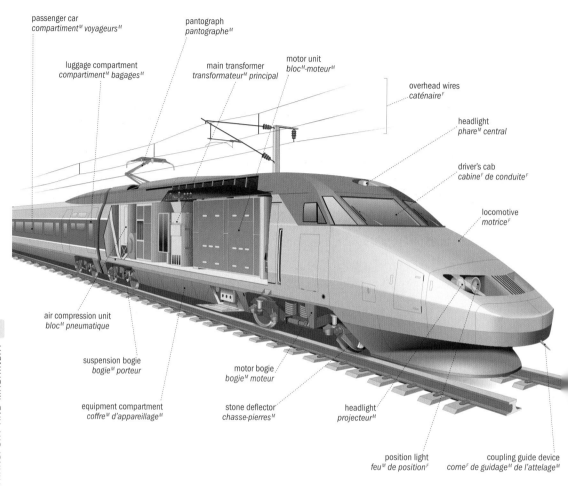

passenger car
compartiment^M voyageurs^M

pantograph
pantographe^M

luggage compartment
compartiment^M bagages^M

main transformer
transformateur^M principal

motor unit
bloc^M-moteur^M

overhead wires
caténaire^F

headlight
phare^M central

driver's cab
cabine^F de conduite^F

locomotive
motrice^F

air compression unit
bloc^M pneumatique

suspension bogie
bogie^M porteur

motor bogie
bogie^M moteur

equipment compartment
coffre^M d'appareillage^M

stone deflector
chasse-pierres^M

headlight
projecteur^M

position light
feu^M de position^F

coupling guide device
corne^F de guidage^M de l'attelage^M

types of passenger coach

types^M de voitures^F

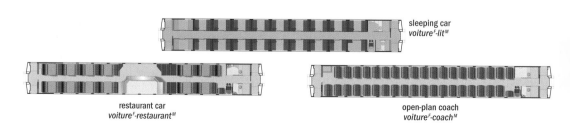

sleeping car
voiture^F-lit^M

restaurant car
voiture^F-restaurant^M

open-plan coach
voiture^F-coach^M

diesel-electric locomotive

locomotive[F] diesel-électrique

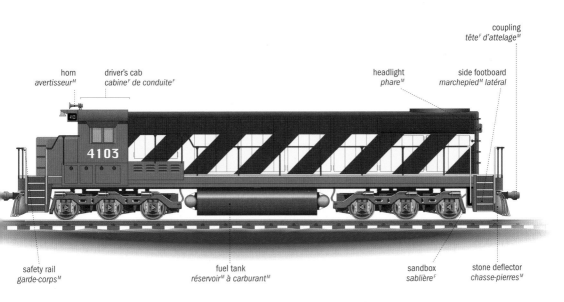

coupling
tête[F] d'attelage[M]

horn
avertisseur[M]

driver's cab
cabine[F] de conduite[F]

headlight
phare[M]

side footboard
marchepied[M] latéral

4103

safety rail
garde-corps[M]

fuel tank
réservoir[M] à carburant[M]

sandbox
sablière[F]

stone deflector
chasse-pierres[M]

examples of freight wagons

exemples[M] de wagons[M]

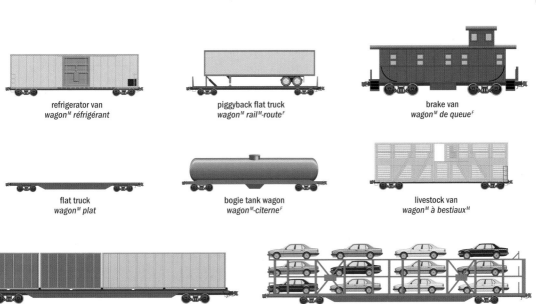

refrigerator van
wagon[M] réfrigérant

piggyback flat truck
wagon[M] rail[M]-route[F]

brake van
wagon[M] de queue[F]

flat truck
wagon[M] plat

bogie tank wagon
wagon[M]-citerne[F]

livestock van
wagon[M] à bestiaux[M]

container truck
wagon[M] porte-conteneurs[M]

three-tier car carrier
wagon[M] porte-automobiles[M]

underground railway

chemin^M de fer^M métropolitain

underground station
station^F de métro^M

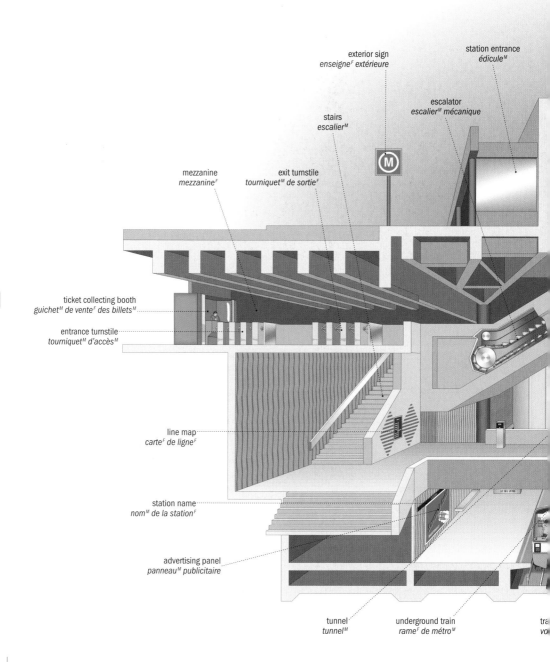

exterior sign
enseigne^F extérieure

station entrance
édicule^M

escalator
escalier^M mécanique

stairs
escalier^M

mezzanine
mezzanine^F

exit turnstile
tourniquet^M de sortie^F

ticket collecting booth
guichet^M de vente^F des billets^M

entrance turnstile
tourniquet^M d'accès^M

line map
carte^F de ligne^F

station name
nom^M de la station^F

advertising panel
panneau^M publicitaire

tunnel
tunnel^M

underground train
rame^F de métro^M

tra
vo

TRANSPORT AND MACHINERY

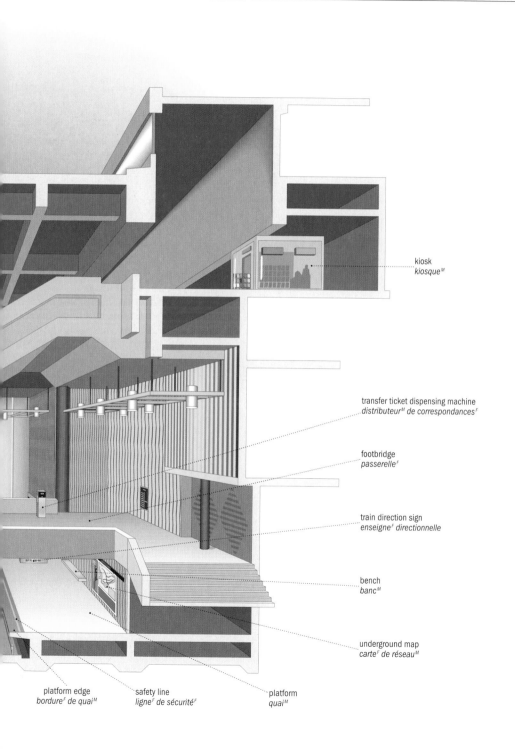

kiosk
kiosque^M

transfer ticket dispensing machine
distributeur^M *de correspondances*^F

footbridge
passerelle^F

train direction sign
enseigne^F *directionnelle*

bench
banc^M

underground map
carte^F *de réseau*^M

platform edge
bordure^F *de quai*^M

safety line
ligne^F *de sécurité*^F

platform
quai^M

TRANSPORT AND MACHINERY

underground railway

passenger car
voiture^F

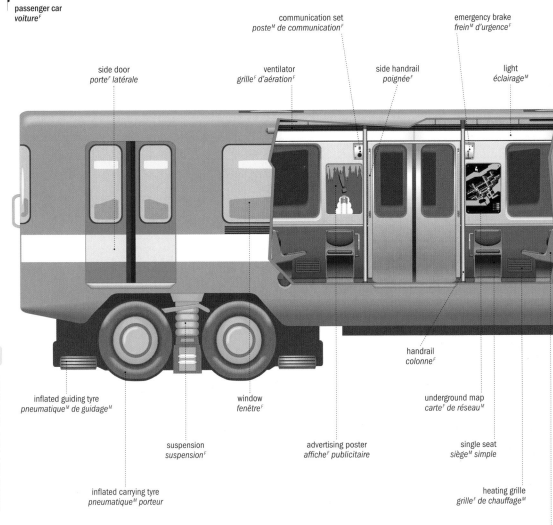

communication set
poste^M *de communication*^F

emergency brake
frein^M *d'urgence*^F

side door
porte^F *latérale*

ventilator
grille^F *d'aération*^F

side handrail
poignée^F

light
éclairage^M

handrail
colonne^F

inflated guiding tyre
pneumatique^M *de guidage*^M

window
fenêtre^F

underground map
carte^F *de réseau*^M

suspension
suspension^F

advertising poster
affiche^F *publicitaire*

single seat
siège^M *simple*

inflated carrying tyre
pneumatique^M *porteur*

heating grille
grille^F *de chauffage*^M

double seat
siège^M *double*

underground train
rame^F *de métro*^M

motor car
motrice^F

trailer car
remorque^F

motor car
motrice^F

TRANSPORT AND MACHINERY

harbour
port[M] maritime

canal lock
écluse[F]

container-loading bridge
portique[M] de chargement[M] de
conteneurs[M]

oil terminal
terminal[M] pétrolier

dry dock
bassin[M] de radoub[M]

transit shed
hangar[M] de transit[M]

tanker
pétrolier[M]

quayside crane
grue[F] à flèche[F]

bulk terminal
terminal[M] de vrac[M]

cold store
entrepôt[M] frigorifique

ferryboat
transbordeur[M]

gate
porte[F]

quay
quai[M]

lighthouse
phare[M]

passenger terminal
gare[F] maritime

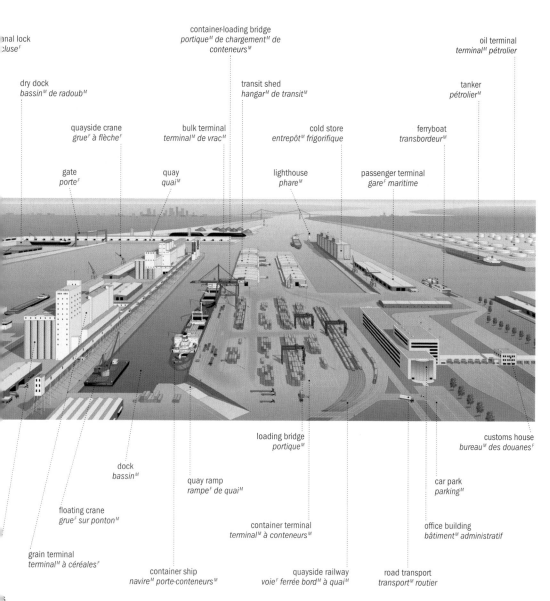

loading bridge
portique[M]

customs house
bureau[M] des douanes[F]

dock
bassin[M]

quay ramp
rampe[F] de quai[M]

car park
parking[M]

floating crane
grue[F] sur ponton[M]

container terminal
terminal[M] à conteneurs[M]

office building
bâtiment[M] administratif

grain terminal
terminal[M] à céréales[F]

container ship
navire[M] porte-conteneurs[M]

quayside railway
voie[F] ferrée bord[M] à quai[M]

road transport
transport[M] routier

examples of boats and ships

exemples^M de bateaux^M et d'embarcations^F

drill ship
navire^M de forage^M

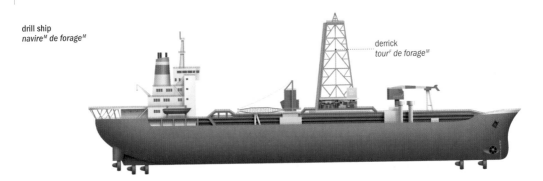

derrick
tour^F de forage^M

bulk carrier
vraquier^M

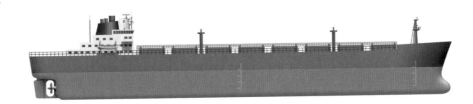

container ship
navire^M porte-conteneurs^M

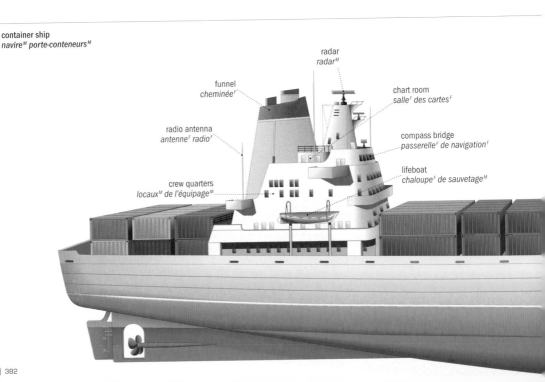

radar
radar^M

funnel
cheminée^F

chart room
salle^F des cartes^F

radio antenna
antenne^F radio^F

compass bridge
passerelle^F de navigation^F

lifeboat
chaloupe^F de sauvetage^M

crew quarters
locaux^M de l'équipage^M

hovercraft
aéroglisseur^M

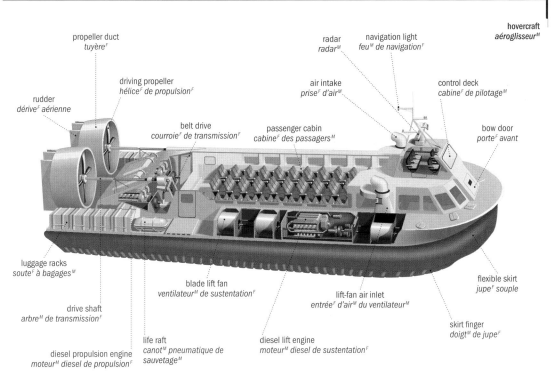

propeller duct
tuyère^F

driving propeller
hélice^F *de propulsion*^F

rudder
dérive^F *aérienne*

belt drive
courroie^F *de transmission*^F

passenger cabin
cabine^F *des passagers*^M

radar
radar^M

navigation light
feu^M *de navigation*^F

air intake
prise^F *d'air*^M

control deck
cabine^F *de pilotage*^M

bow door
porte^F *avant*

luggage racks
soute^F *à bagages*^M

blade lift fan
ventilateur^M *de sustentation*^F

lift-fan air inlet
entrée^F *d'air*^M *du ventilateur*^M

flexible skirt
jupe^F *souple*

drive shaft
arbre^M *de transmission*^F

life raft
canot^M *pneumatique de
sauvetage*^M

diesel lift engine
moteur^M *diesel de sustentation*^F

skirt finger
doigt^M *de jupe*^F

diesel propulsion engine
moteur^M *diesel de propulsion*^F

masthead light
feu^M *de tête*^F *de mât*^M

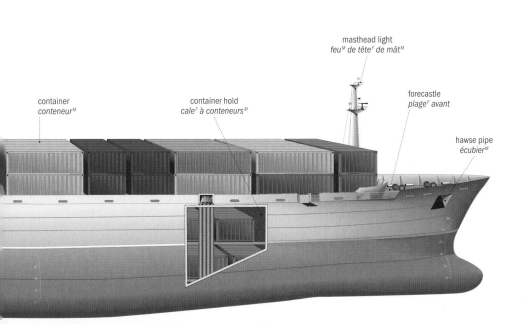

container
conteneur^M

container hold
cale^F *à conteneurs*^M

forecastle
plage^F *avant*

hawse pipe
écubier^M

examples of boats and ships

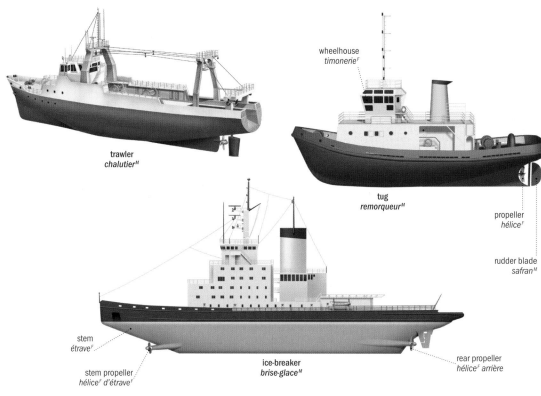

trawler
*chalutier*M

wheelhouse
*timonerie*F

tug
*remorqueur*M

propeller
*hélice*F

rudder blade
*safran*M

stem
*étrave*F

stem propeller
*hélice*F *d'étrave*F

ice-breaker
*brise-glace*M

rear propeller
*hélice*F *arrière*

tanker
*pétrolier*M

radar mast
*mât*M *radar*M

radio antenna
*antenne*F *radio*F

separator
*séparateur*M

davit
*bossoir*M

gangway
*coupée*F

engine room
*salle*F *de contrôle*M *des
machines*F

rudder
*gouvernail*M

propeller
*hélice*F

pump room
*chambre*F *des pompes*F

transverse bulkhead
*cloison*F *transversale*

lengthways bulkhead
*cloison*F *longitudinale*

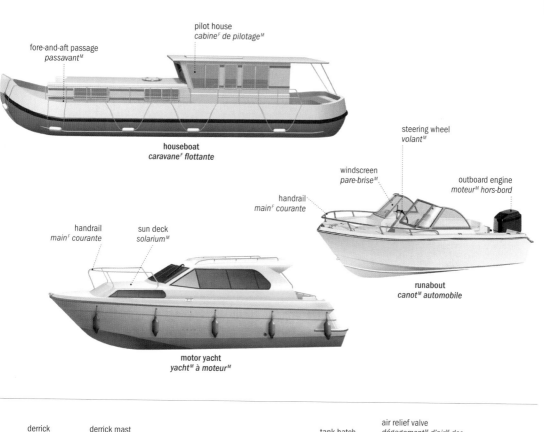

fore-and-aft passage
passavant^M

pilot house
cabine^F *de pilotage*^M

houseboat
caravane^F *flottante*

steering wheel
volant^M

windscreen
pare-brise^M

outboard engine
moteur^M *hors-bord*

handrail
main^F *courante*

runabout
canot^M *automobile*

handrail
main^F *courante*

sun deck
solarium^M

motor yacht
yacht^M *à moteur*^M

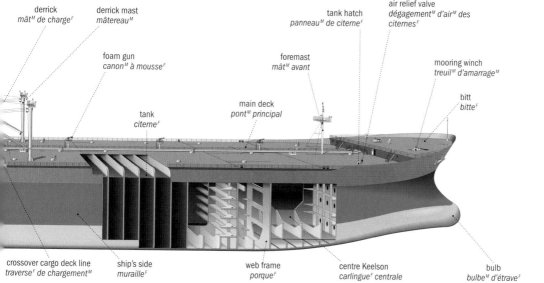

derrick
mât^M *de charge*^F

derrick mast
mâtereau^M

tank hatch
panneau^M *de citerne*^F

air relief valve
dégagement^M *d'air*^M *des
citernes*^F

foam gun
canon^M *à mousse*^F

foremast
mât^M *avant*

mooring winch
treuil^M *d'amarrage*^M

tank
citerne^F

main deck
pont^M *principal*

bitt
bitte^F

crossover cargo deck line
traverse^F *de chargement*^M

ship's side
muraille^F

web frame
porque^F

centre Keelson
carlingue^F *centrale*

bulb
bulbe^M *d'étrave*^F

examples of boats and ships

ferry
*transbordeur*ᴹ

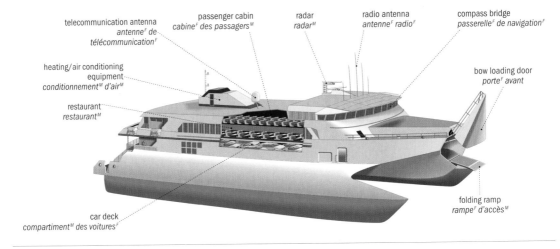

telecommunication antenna
*antenne*ᶠ *de
télécommunication*ᶠ

passenger cabin
*cabine*ᶠ *des passagers*ᴹ

radar
*radar*ᴹ

radio antenna
*antenne*ᶠ *radio*ᶠ

compass bridge
*passerelle*ᶠ *de navigation*ᶠ

heating/air conditioning
equipment
*conditionnement*ᴹ *d'air*ᴹ

bow loading door
*porte*ᶠ *avant*

restaurant
*restaurant*ᴹ

folding ramp
*rampe*ᶠ *d'accès*ᴹ

car deck
*compartiment*ᴹ *des voitures*ᶠ

cruiseliner
*paquebot*ᴹ

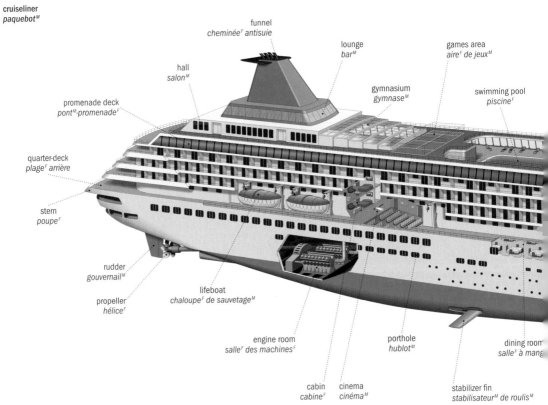

funnel
*cheminée*ᶠ *antisuie*

lounge
*bar*ᴹ

games area
*aire*ᶠ *de jeux*ᴹ

hall
*salon*ᴹ

gymnasium
*gymnase*ᴹ

swimming pool
*piscine*ᶠ

promenade deck
*pont*ᴹ-*promenade*ᶠ

quarter-deck
*plage*ᶠ *arrière*

stern
*poupe*ᶠ

rudder
*gouvernail*ᴹ

lifeboat
*chaloupe*ᶠ *de sauvetage*ᴹ

propeller
*hélice*ᶠ

engine room
*salle*ᶠ *des machines*ᶠ

porthole
*hublot*ᴹ

dining room
*salle*ᶠ *à mang...*

cabin
*cabine*ᶠ

cinema
*cinéma*ᴹ

stabilizer fin
*stabilisateur*ᴹ *de roulis*ᶠ

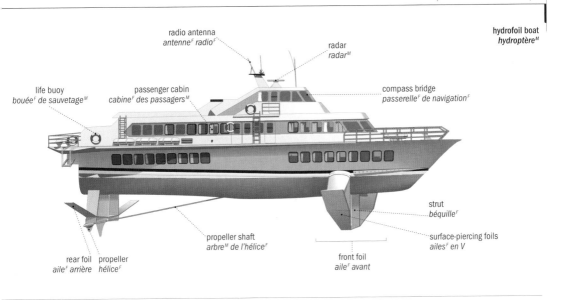

hydrofoil boat
hydroptère^M

radio antenna
antenne^F *radio*^F

radar
radar^M

life buoy
bouée^F *de sauvetage*^M

passenger cabin
cabine^F *des passagers*^M

compass bridge
passerelle^F *de navigation*^F

strut
béquille^F

propeller shaft
arbre^M *de l'hélice*^F

surface-piercing foils
ailes^F *en V*

rear foil
aile^F *arrière*

propeller
hélice^F

front foil
aile^F *avant*

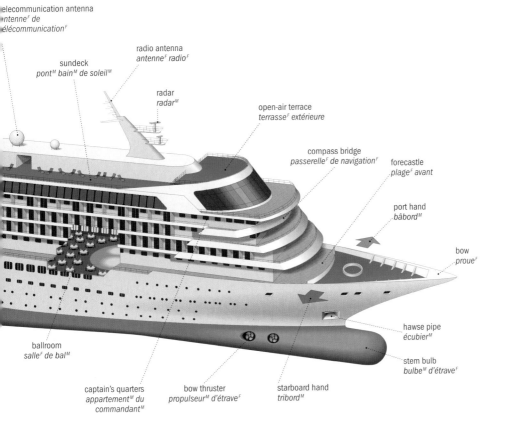

elecommunication antenna
ntenne^F de
élécommunication^F

sundeck
pont^M *bain*^M *de soleil*^M

radio antenna
antenne^F *radio*^F

radar
radar^M

open-air terrace
terrasse^F *extérieure*

compass bridge
passerelle^F *de navigation*^F

forecastle
plage^F *avant*

port hand
bâbord^M

bow
proue^F

hawse pipe
écubier^M

stem bulb
bulbe^M *d'étrave*^F

ballroom
salle^F *de bal*^M

captain's quarters
appartement^M *du*
commandant^M

bow thruster
propulseur^M *d'étrave*^F

starboard hand
tribord^M

TRANSPORT AND MACHINERY

airport

aéroport^M

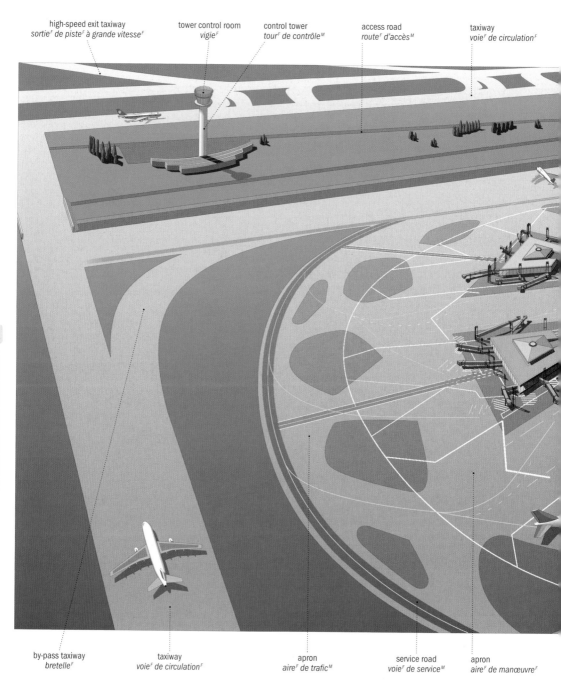

high-speed exit taxiway
sortie^F de piste^F à grande vitesse^F

tower control room
vigie^F

control tower
tour^F de contrôle^M

access road
route^F d'accès^M

taxiway
voie^F de circulation^F

by-pass taxiway
bretelle^F

taxiway
voie^F de circulation^F

apron
aire^F de trafic^M

service road
voie^F de service^M

apron
aire^F de manœuvre^F

passenger terminal
aérogare[F] *de passagers*[M]

maintenance hangar
hangar[M]

parking area
aire[F] *de stationnement*[M]

telescopic corridor
passerelle[F] *télescopique*

service area
aire[F] *de service*[M]

boarding walkway
quai[M] *d'embarquement*[M]

taxiway line
marques[F] *de circulation*[F]

satellite terminal
aérogare[F] *satellite*[M]

airport

passenger terminal
aérogare[F]

information counter
comptoir[M] *de renseignements*[M]

baggage claim area
zone[F] *de retrait*[M] *des bagages*[M]

hotel reservation desk
bureau[M] *de réservation*[F] *de chambres*[F]
d'hôtel[M]

ticket counter
comptoir[M] *de vente*[F] *des billets*[M]

lobby
hall[M] *public*

automatically-controlled
door
porte[F] *automatique*

baggage check-in counter
comptoir[M] *d'enregistrement*[M]

car park
parc[M] *à voitures*[F]

platform
débarcadère[M]

conveyor belt
tapis[M] *roulant*

rail shuttle service
navette[F] *ferroviaire*

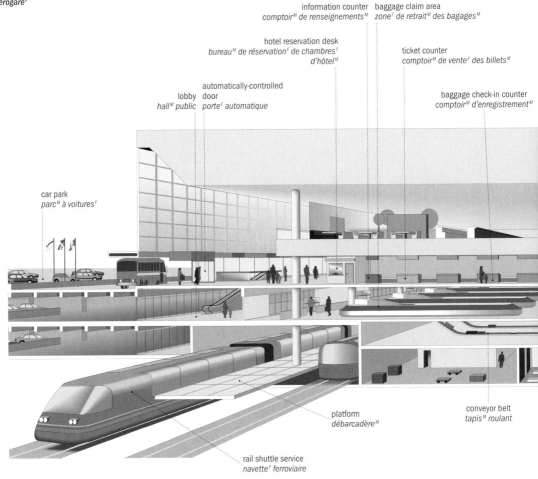

runway
piste[F]

holding area marking
marque[F] *de point*[M] *d'attente*[F]

runway designation marking
marques[F] *d'identification*[F]

runway centre line markings
marque[F] *d'axe*[M] *de piste*[F]

runway side stripe markings
marques[F] *latérales de piste*[F]

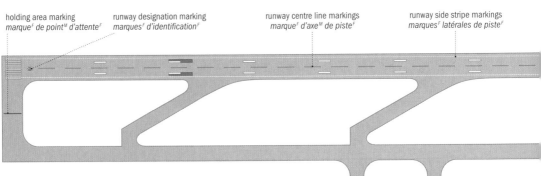

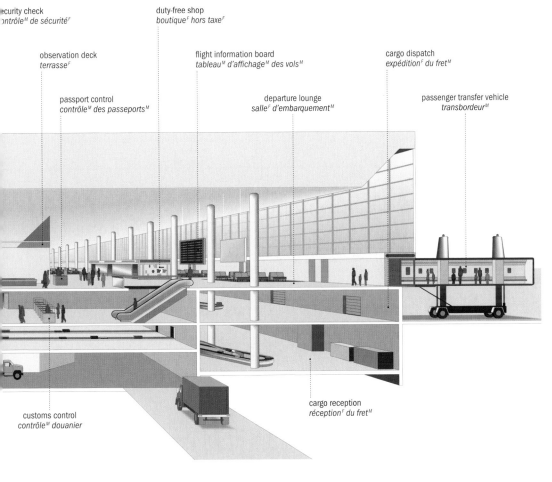

security check
contrôle^M de sécurité^F

duty-free shop
boutique^F hors taxe^F

observation deck
terrasse^F

flight information board
tableau^M d'affichage^M des vols^M

cargo dispatch
expédition^F du fret^M

passport control
contrôle^M des passeports^M

departure lounge
salle^F d'embarquement^M

passenger transfer vehicle
transbordeur^M

cargo reception
réception^F du fret^M

customs control
contrôle^M douanier

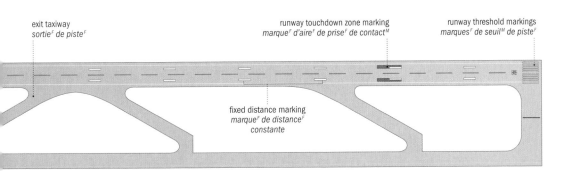

exit taxiway
sortie^F de piste^F

runway touchdown zone marking
marque^F d'aire^F de prise^F de contact^M

runway threshold markings
marques^F de seuil^M de piste^F

fixed distance marking
marque^F de distance^F
constante

long-range jet airliner

avion^M long-courrier^M

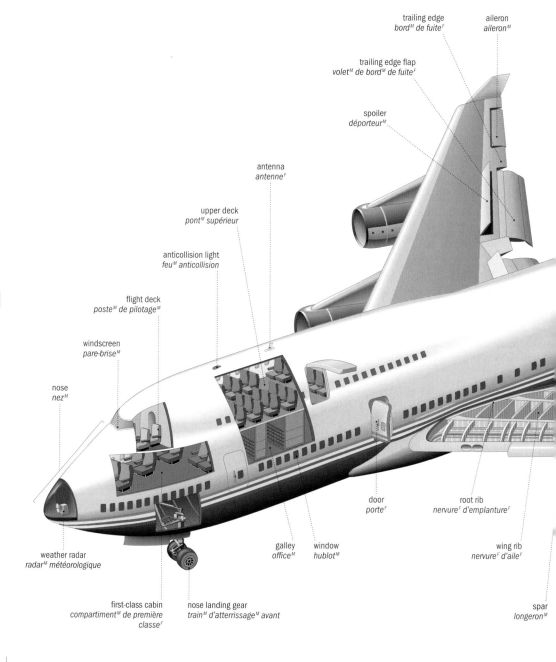

trailing edge
bord^M de fuite^F

aileron
aileron^M

trailing edge flap
volet^M de bord^M de fuite^F

spoiler
déporteur^M

antenna
antenne^F

upper deck
pont^M supérieur

anticollision light
feu^M anticollision

flight deck
poste^M de pilotage^M

windscreen
pare-brise^M

nose
nez^M

door
porte^F

root rib
nervure^F d'emplanture^F

weather radar
radar^M météorologique

galley
office^M

window
hublot^M

wing rib
nervure^F d'aile^F

first-class cabin
*compartiment^M de première
classe^F*

nose landing gear
train^M d'atterrissage^M avant

spar
longeron^M

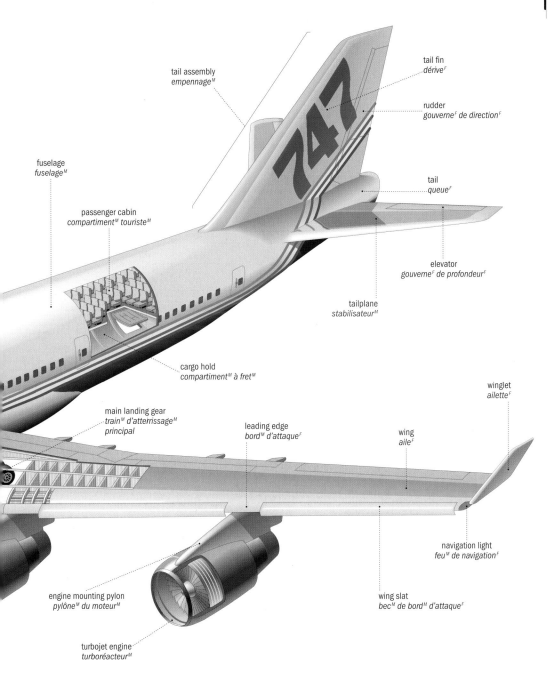

tail assembly
empennage^M

tail fin
dérive^F

rudder
gouverne^F *de direction*^F

fuselage
fuselage^M

tail
queue^F

passenger cabin
compartiment^M *touriste*^M

elevator
gouverne^F *de profondeur*^F

tailplane
stabilisateur^M

cargo hold
compartiment^M *à fret*^M

winglet
ailette^F

main landing gear
train^M *d'atterrissage*^M
principal

leading edge
bord^M *d'attaque*^F

wing
aile^F

navigation light
feu^M *de navigation*^F

engine mounting pylon
pylône^M *du moteur*^M

wing slat
bec^M *de bord*^M *d'attaque*^F

turbojet engine
turboréacteur^M

TRANSPORT AND MACHINERY

examples of aircraft

exemples^M d'avions^M

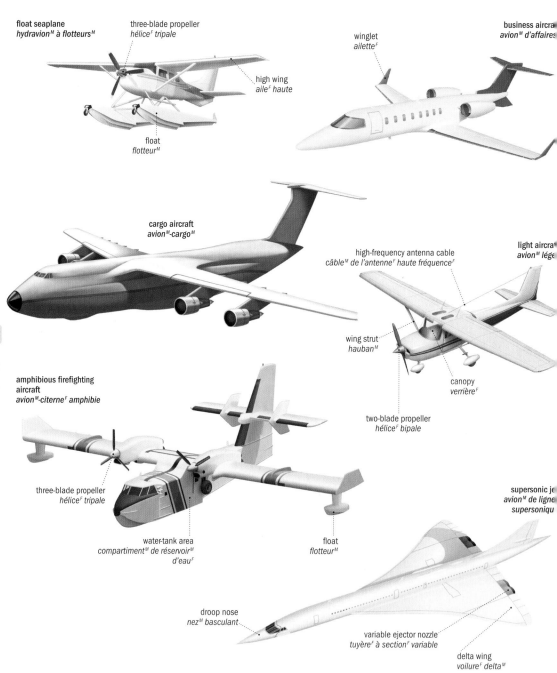

float seaplane
hydravion^M à flotteurs^M

three-blade propeller
hélice^F tripale

high wing
aile^F haute

float
flotteur^M

winglet
ailette^F

business aircra
avion^M d'affaires

cargo aircraft
avion^M-cargo^M

high-frequency antenna cable
câble^M de l'antenne^F haute fréquence^F

light aircra
avion^M lége

wing strut
hauban^M

canopy
verrière^F

amphibious firefighting
aircraft
avion^M-citerne^F amphibie

two-blade propeller
hélice^F bipale

three-blade propeller
hélice^F tripale

supersonic je
avion^M de ligne
supersoniqu

water-tank area
compartiment^M de réservoir^M
d'eau^F

float
flotteur^M

droop nose
nez^M basculant

variable ejector nozzle
tuyère^F à section^F variable

delta wing
voilure^F delta^M

TRANSPORT AND MACHINERY

movements of an aircraft

mouvements^M de l'avion^M

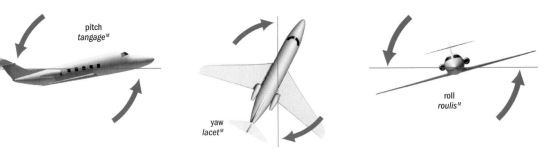

pitch
tangage^M

yaw
lacet^M

roll
roulis^M

helicopter

hélicoptère^M

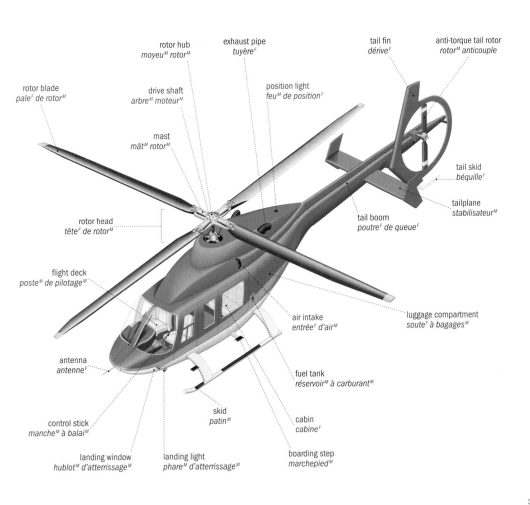

rotor hub
moyeu^M rotor^M

exhaust pipe
tuyère^F

tail fin
dérive^F

anti-torque tail rotor
rotor^M anticouple

rotor blade
pale^F de rotor^M

drive shaft
arbre^M moteur^M

position light
feu^M de position^F

mast
mât^M rotor^M

tail skid
béquille^F

rotor head
tête^F de rotor^M

tailplane
stabilisateur^M

tail boom
poutre^F de queue^F

flight deck
poste^M de pilotage^M

luggage compartment
soute^F à bagages^M

air intake
entrée^F d'air^M

antenna
antenne^F

fuel tank
réservoir^M à carburant^M

control stick
manche^M à balai^M

skid
patin^M

cabin
cabine^F

landing window
hublot^M d'atterrissage^M

landing light
phare^M d'atterrissage^M

boarding step
marchepied^M

TRANSPORT AND MACHINERY

material handling

manutention[F]

forklift truck
chariot[M] élévateur

mast
mât[M]

crosshead
tête[F] du vérin[M] de levage[M]

lifting chain
chaîne[F] de levage[M]

hydraulic system
système[M] hydraulique

carriage
tablier[M]

fork
bras[M] de fourche[F]

forks
fourches[F]

overhead guard
toit[M] de protection[F]

mast operating lever
levier[M] de manœuvre[F] du m...

engine compartment
moteur[M]

frame
châssis[M]

barrow
diable[M]

pallet truck
transpalette[F] manuelle

wing pallet
palette[F] à ailes[F]

top deckboard
plancher[M] supérieur

entry
entrée[F]

stringer
entretoise[F]

bottom deckboard
plancher[M] inférieur

TRANSPORT AND MACHINERY

cranes
grues^F et portique^M

tower crane
grue^F à tour^F

jib tie
tirant^M

travelling crab
chariot^M

jib
flèche^F

counterjib ballast
contrepoids^M

counterjib
contre-flèche^F

crab pulley
poulie^F de chariot^M

operator's cab
cabine^F de commande^F

crane runway
chemin^M de roulement^M

hoisting rope
câble^M de levage^M

hook
crochet^M

hoisting block
treuil^M de levage^M

tower mast
tour^F

counterweight
lest^M

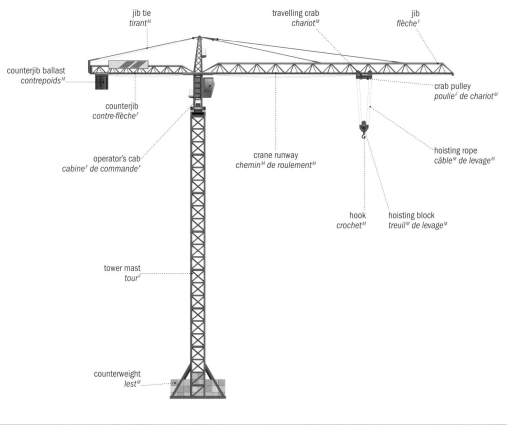

truck crane
grue^F sur porteur^M

telescopic boom
flèche^F télescopique

elevating cylinder
vérin^M de dressage^M

operator's cab
cabine^F de commande^F

jack
stabilisateur^M

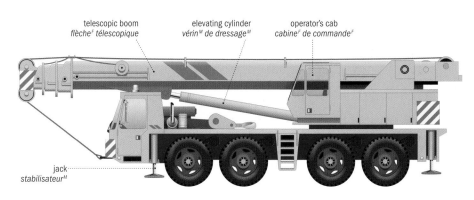

TRANSPORT AND MACHINERY

bulldozer

bouteur^M

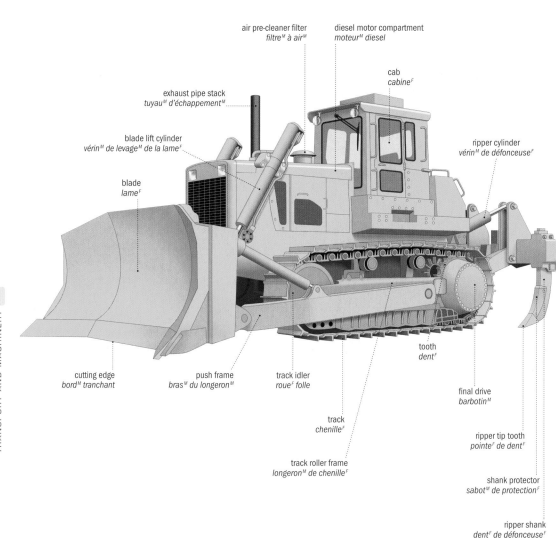

air pre-cleaner filter
filtre^M à air^M

diesel motor compartment
moteur^M diesel

cab
cabine^F

exhaust pipe stack
tuyau^M d'échappement^M

ripper cylinder
vérin^M de défonceuse^F

blade lift cylinder
vérin^M de levage^M de la lame^F

blade
lame^F

cutting edge
bord^M tranchant

push frame
bras^M du longeron^M

track idler
roue^F folle

tooth
dent^F

final drive
barbotin^M

track
chenille^F

ripper tip tooth
pointe^F de dent^F

track roller frame
longeron^M de chenille^F

shank protector
sabot^M de protection^F

ripper shank
dent^F de défonceuse^F

TRANSPORT AND MACHINERY

tracklaying tractor
tracteur^M à chenilles^F

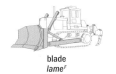

blade
lame^F

ripper
défonceuse^F

backhoe loader

chargeuse^F-pelleteuse^F

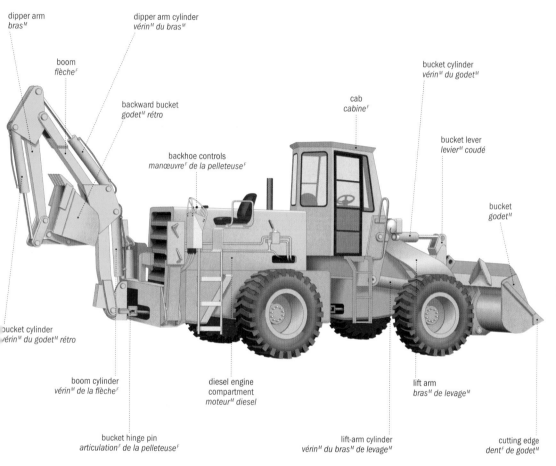

dipper arm
bras^M

dipper arm cylinder
vérin^M du bras^M

boom
flèche^F

bucket cylinder
vérin^M du godet^M

backward bucket
godet^M rétro

cab
cabine^F

backhoe controls
manœuvre^F de la pelleteuse^F

bucket lever
levier^M coudé

bucket
godet^M

bucket cylinder
vérin^M du godet^M rétro

boom cylinder
vérin^M de la flèche^F

diesel engine
compartment
moteur^M diesel

lift arm
bras^M de levage^M

bucket hinge pin
articulation^F de la pelleteuse^F

lift-arm cylinder
vérin^M du bras^M de levage^M

cutting edge
dent^F de godet^M

front-end loader
chargeuse^F frontale

wheel tractor
tracteur^M

backhoe
pelleteuse^F

TRANSPORT AND MACHINERY

scraper

décapeuse^F

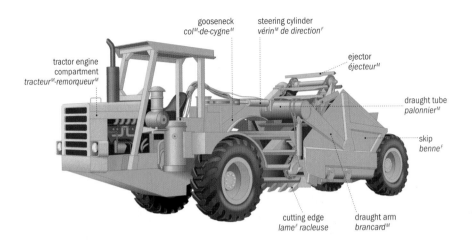

gooseneck
col^M-de-cygne^M

steering cylinder
vérin^M de direction^F

ejector
éjecteur^M

tractor engine
compartment
tracteur^M-remorqueur^M

draught tube
palonnier^M

skip
benne^F

cutting edge
lame^F racleuse

draught arm
brancard^M

hydraulic shovel

pelle^F hydraulique

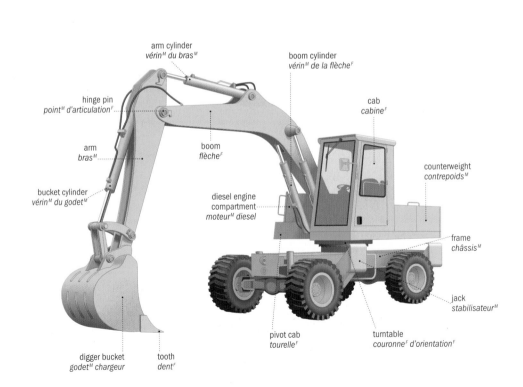

arm cylinder
vérin^M du bras^M

boom cylinder
vérin^M de la flèche^F

hinge pin
point^M d'articulation^F

cab
cabine^F

arm
bras^M

boom
flèche^F

counterweight
contrepoids^M

bucket cylinder
vérin^M du godet^M

diesel engine
compartment
moteur^M diesel

frame
châssis^M

jack
stabilisateur^M

digger bucket
godet^M chargeur

tooth
dent^F

pivot cab
tourelle^F

turntable
couronne^F d'orientation^F

grader
niveleuse^F

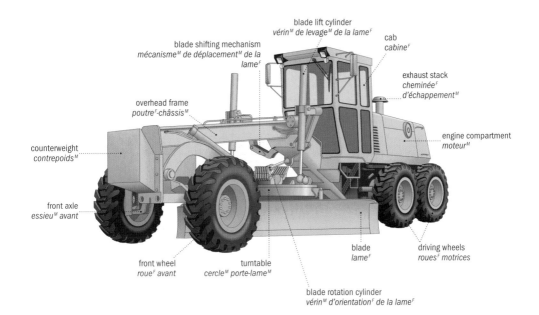

blade lift cylinder
vérin^M de levage^M de la lame^F

cab
cabine^F

blade shifting mechanism
mécanisme^M de déplacement^M de la lame^F

exhaust stack
cheminée^F d'échappement^M

overhead frame
poutre^F-châssis^M

engine compartment
moteur^M

counterweight
contrepoids^M

front axle
essieu^M avant

front wheel
roue^F avant

turntable
cercle^M porte-lame^M

blade
lame^F

driving wheels
roues^F motrices

blade rotation cylinder
vérin^M d'orientation^F de la lame^F

tipper truck
camion^M-benne^F

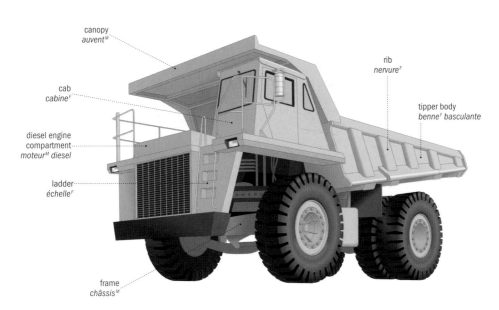

canopy
auvent^M

rib
nervure^F

cab
cabine^F

tipper body
benne^F basculante

diesel engine compartment
moteur^M diesel

ladder
échelle^F

frame
châssis^M

production of electricity from geothermal energy

production^F d'électricité^F par énergie^F géothermique

turbine generator
turbine^F alternateur^M

condenser
condenseur^M

steam
vapeur^F

high-tension electricity transmission
transport^M de l'électricité^F à haute
tension^F

separator
séparateur^M

voltage increase
élévation^F de la tension^F

water-steam mix
mélange^M eau^F-vapeur^F

cooling tower
tour^F de refroidissement^M

upper confining bed
toit^M imperméable

water
eau^F

geothermal field
champ^M géothermique

lower confining bed
substratum^M imperméable

production well
puits^M de production^F

confined aquifer
aquifère^M captif

injection well
puits^M d'injection^F

magma chamber
réservoir^M magmatique

thermal energy

énergie^F thermique

**production of electricity from thermal
energy**
production^F d'électricité^F par énergie^F
thermique

crusher
broyeur^M

stack
cheminée^F

cooling tower
tour^F de refroidissement^M

coal storage yard
parc^M à charbon^M

high-tension electricity transmission
transport^M de l'électricité^F à haute
tension^F

voltage decrease
abaissement^M de la
tension^F

conveyor
convoyeur^M

belt loader
sauterelle^F

pulverizer
pulvérisateur^M

steam generator
générateur^M de vapeur^F

transmission to consumer
transport^M vers les usagers

coal-fired thermal power
station
centrale^F thermique au
charbon^M

condenser
condenseur^M

turbo-alternator unit
groupe^M turbo-alternateur^M

voltage increase
élévation^F de la tension^F

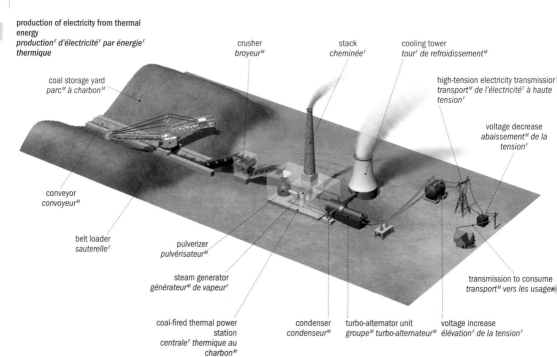

oil
pétrole[M]

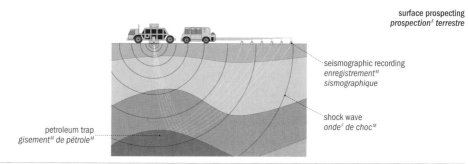

surface prospecting
prospection[F] *terrestre*

seismographic recording
enregistrement[M]
sismographique

shock wave
onde[F] *de choc*[M]

petroleum trap
gisement[M] *de pétrole*[M]

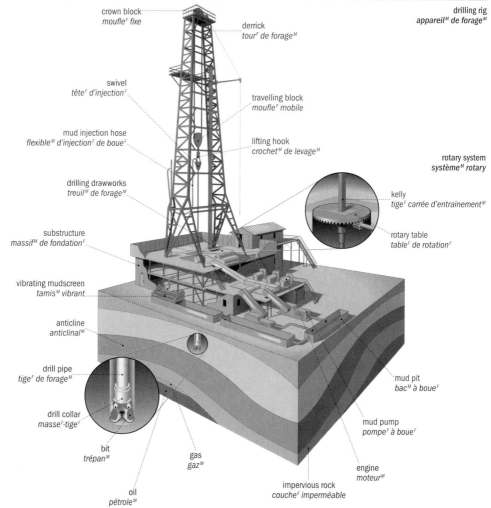

drilling rig
appareil[M] *de forage*[M]

crown block
moufle[F] *fixe*

derrick
tour[F] *de forage*[M]

swivel
tête[F] *d'injection*[F]

travelling block
moufle[F] *mobile*

mud injection hose
flexible[M] *d'injection*[F] *de boue*[F]

lifting hook
crochet[M] *de levage*[M]

rotary system
système[M] *rotary*

drilling drawworks
treuil[M] *de forage*[M]

kelly
tige[F] *carrée d'entraînement*[M]

substructure
massif[M] *de fondation*[F]

rotary table
table[F] *de rotation*[F]

vibrating mudscreen
tamis[M] *vibrant*

anticline
anticlinal[M]

drill pipe
tige[F] *de forage*[M]

mud pit
bac[M] *à boue*[F]

drill collar
masse[F]*-tige*[F]

mud pump
pompe[F] *à boue*[F]

bit
trépan[M]

gas
gaz[M]

engine
moteur[M]

oil
pétrole[M]

impervious rock
couche[F] *imperméable*

floating-roof tank
*réservoir*M *à toit*M *flottant*

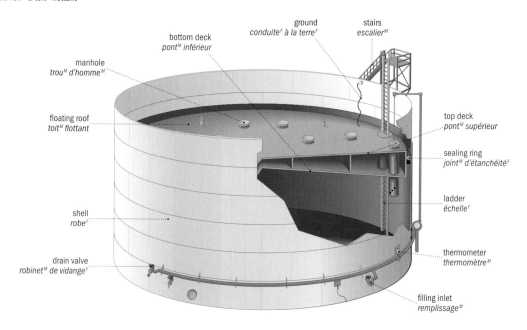

ground
*conduite*F *à la terre*F

stairs
*escalier*M

bottom deck
*pont*M *inférieur*

manhole
*trou*M *d'homme*M

floating roof
*toit*M *flottant*

top deck
*pont*M *supérieur*

sealing ring
*joint*M *d'étanchéité*F

ladder
*échelle*F

shell
*robe*F

thermometer
*thermomètre*M

drain valve
*robinet*M *de vidange*F

filling inlet
*remplissage*M

crude-oil pipeline
*réseau*M *d'oléoducs*M

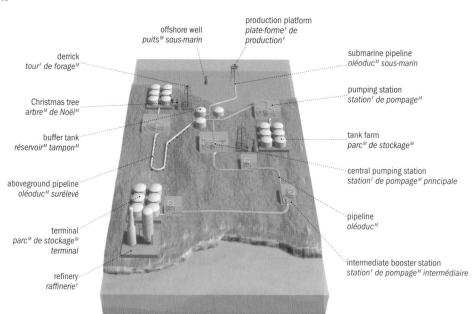

offshore well
*puits*M *sous-marin*

production platform
*plate-forme*F *de
production*F

derrick
*tour*F *de forage*M

submarine pipeline
*oléoduc*M *sous-marin*

Christmas tree
*arbre*M *de Noël*M

pumping station
*station*F *de pompage*M

buffer tank
*réservoir*M *tampon*M

tank farm
*parc*M *de stockage*M

aboveground pipeline
*oléoduc*M *surélevé*

central pumping station
*station*F *de pompage*M *principale*

terminal
*parc*M *de stockage*M
terminal

pipeline
*oléoduc*M

refinery
*raffinerie*F

intermediate booster station
*station*F *de pompage*M *intermédiaire*

ENERGY

oil

refinery products
produits^M de la raffinerie^F

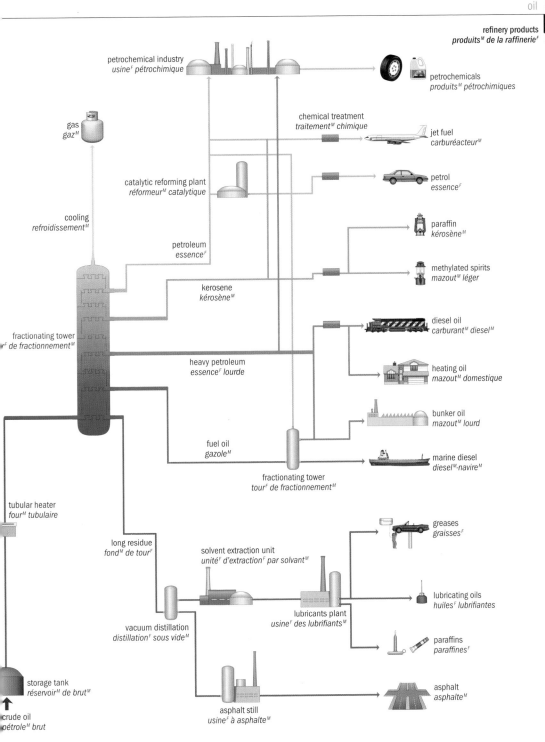

petrochemical industry
usine^F pétrochimique

petrochemicals
produits^M pétrochimiques

chemical treatment
traitement^M chimique

jet fuel
carburéacteur^M

gas
gaz^M

catalytic reforming plant
réformeur^M catalytique

petrol
essence^F

cooling
refroidissement^M

paraffin
kérosène^M

petroleum
essence^F

methylated spirits
mazout^M léger

kerosene
kérosène^M

diesel oil
carburant^M diesel^M

fractionating tower
^F de fractionnement^M

heavy petroleum
essence^F lourde

heating oil
mazout^M domestique

bunker oil
mazout^M lourd

fuel oil
gazole^M

marine diesel
diesel^M-navire^M

fractionating tower
tour^F de fractionnement^M

tubular heater
four^M tubulaire

greases
graisses^F

long residue
fond^M de tour^F

solvent extraction unit
unité^F d'extraction^F par solvant^M

lubricating oils
huiles^F lubrifiantes

lubricants plant
usine^F des lubrifiants^M

vacuum distillation
distillation^F sous vide^M

paraffins
paraffines^F

storage tank
réservoir^M de brut^M

asphalt
asphalte^M

crude oil
pétrole^M brut

asphalt still
usine^F à asphalte^M

ENERGY

405

hydroelectric complex

complexe^M hydroélectrique

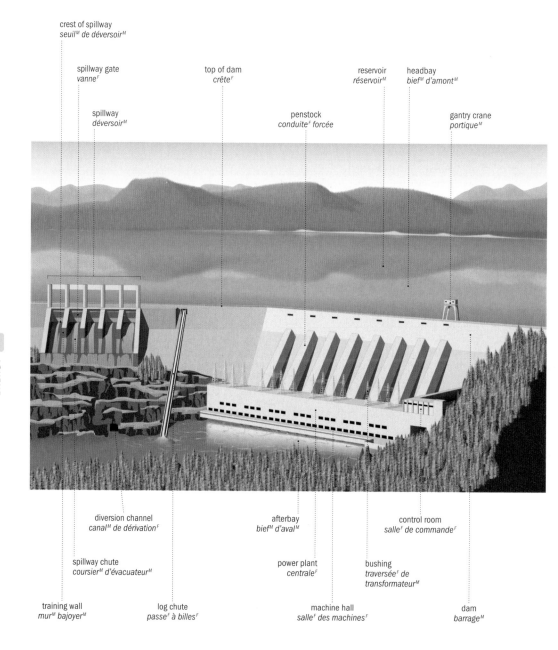

crest of spillway
seuil^M de déversoir^M

spillway gate
vanne^F

top of dam
crête^F

reservoir
réservoir^M

headbay
bief^M d'amont^M

spillway
déversoir^M

penstock
conduite^F forcée

gantry crane
portique^M

diversion channel
canal^M de dérivation^F

afterbay
bief^M d'aval^M

control room
salle^F de commande^F

spillway chute
coursier^M d'évacuateur^M

power plant
centrale^F

bushing
traversée^F de
transformateur^M

training wall
mur^M bajoyer^M

log chute
passe^F à billes^F

machine hall
salle^F des machines^F

dam
barrage^M

cross section of a hydroelectric power plant
coupe^F d'une centrale^F hydroélectrique

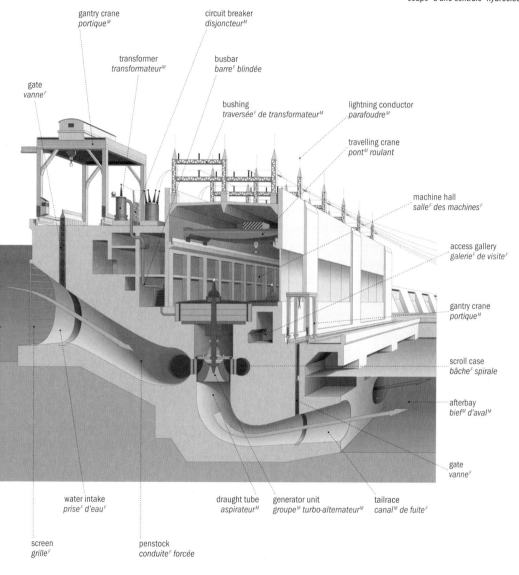

gantry crane
portique^M

circuit breaker
disjoncteur^M

transformer
transformateur^M

busbar
barre^F blindée

gate
vanne^F

bushing
traversée^F de transformateur^M

lightning conductor
parafoudre^M

travelling crane
pont^M roulant

machine hall
salle^F des machines^F

access gallery
galerie^F de visite^F

gantry crane
portique^M

scroll case
bâche^F spirale

afterbay
bief^M d'aval^M

gate
vanne^F

water intake
prise^F d'eau^F

draught tube
aspirateur^M

generator unit
groupe^M turbo-alternateur^M

tailrace
canal^M de fuite^F

screen
grille^F

penstock
conduite^F forcée

reservoir
réservoir^M

ENERGY

production of electricity from nuclear energy

production^F d'électricité^F par énergie^F nucléaire

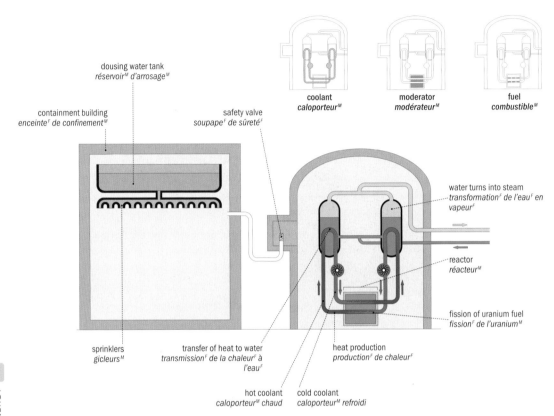

coolant
caloporteur^M

moderator
modérateur^M

fuel
combustible^M

dousing water tank
réservoir^M d'arrosage^M

containment building
enceinte^F de confinement^M

safety valve
soupape^F de sûreté^F

water turns into steam
transformation^F de l'eau^F en
vapeur^F

reactor
réacteur^M

fission of uranium fuel
fission^F de l'uranium^M

sprinklers
gicleurs^M

transfer of heat to water
transmission^F de la chaleur^F à
l'eau^F

heat production
production^F de chaleur^F

hot coolant
caloporteur^M chaud

cold coolant
caloporteur^M refroidi

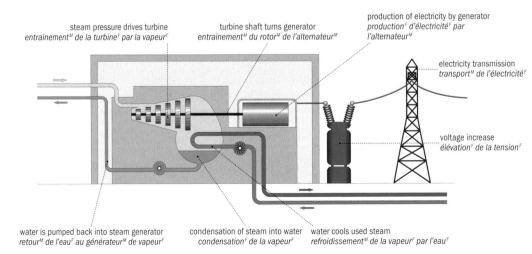

steam pressure drives turbine
entrainement^M de la turbine^F par la vapeur^F

turbine shaft turns generator
entrainement^M du rotor^M de l'alternateur^M

production of electricity by generator
production^F d'électricité^F par
l'alternateur^M

electricity transmission
transport^M de l'électricité^F

voltage increase
élévation^F de la tension^F

water is pumped back into steam generator
retour^M de l'eau^F au générateur^M de vapeur^F

condensation of steam into water
condensation^F de la vapeur^F

water cools used steam
refroidissement^M de la vapeur^F par l'eau^F

ENERGY

fuel bundle

grappe^F de combustible^M

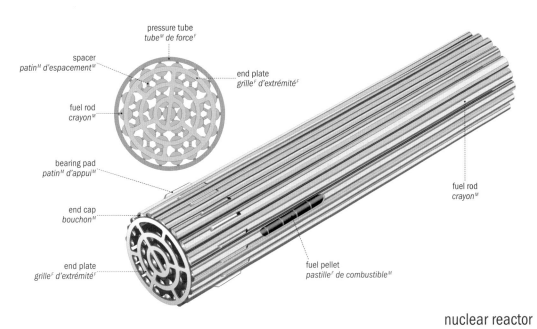

pressure tube
tube^M de force^F

spacer
patin^M d'espacement^M

end plate
grille^F d'extrémité^F

fuel rod
crayon^M

bearing pad
patin^M d'appui^M

end cap
bouchon^M

end plate
grille^F d'extrémité^F

fuel rod
crayon^M

fuel pellet
pastille^F de combustible^M

nuclear reactor

réacteur^M nucléaire

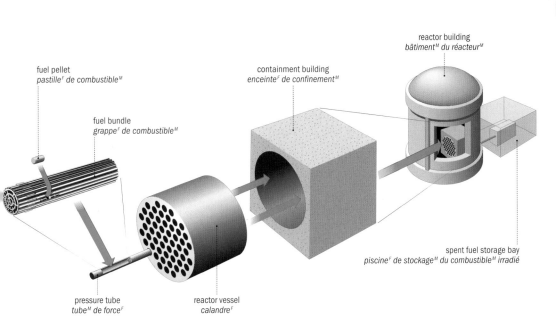

fuel pellet
pastille^F de combustible^M

fuel bundle
grappe^F de combustible^M

containment building
enceinte^F de confinement^M

reactor building
bâtiment^M du réacteur^M

spent fuel storage bay
piscine^F de stockage^M du combustible^M irradié

pressure tube
tube^M de force^F

reactor vessel
calandre^F

ENERGY

solar cell

photopile^F

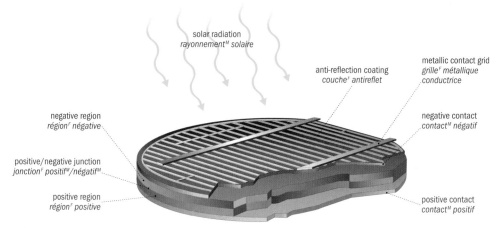

solar radiation
rayonnement^M solaire

anti-reflection coating
couche^F antireflet

metallic contact grid
grille^F métallique
conductrice

negative contact
contact^M négatif

negative region
région^F négative

positive/negative junction
jonction^F positif^M/négatif^M

positive region
région^F positive

positive contact
contact^M positif

flat-plate solar collector

capteur^M solaire plan

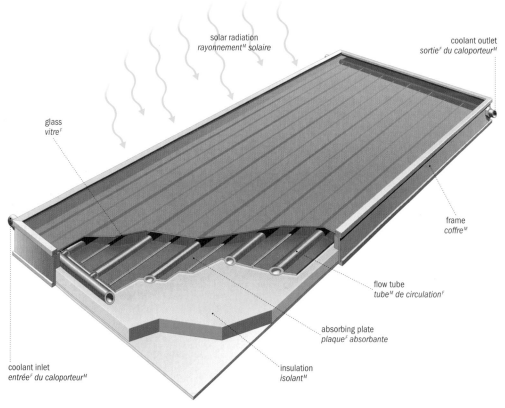

solar radiation
rayonnement^M solaire

coolant outlet
sortie^F du caloporteur^M

glass
vitre^F

frame
coffre^M

flow tube
tube^M de circulation^F

absorbing plate
plaque^F absorbante

coolant inlet
entrée^F du caloporteur^M

insulation
isolant^M

ENERGY

solar-cell system

circuit^M de photopiles^F

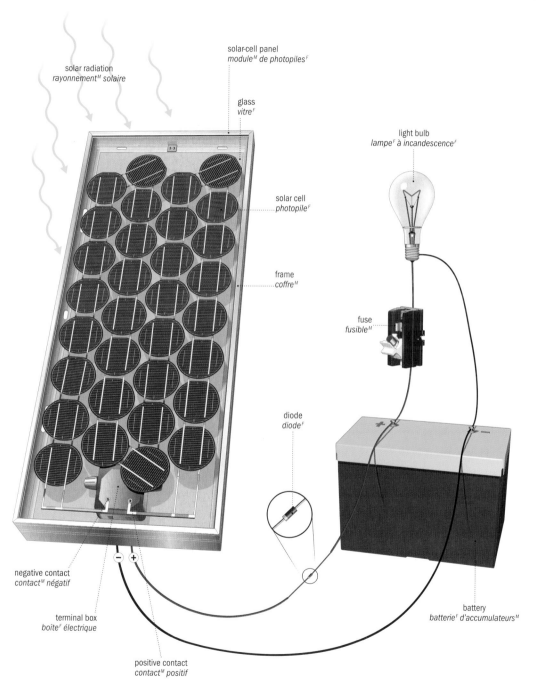

solar radiation
rayonnement^M solaire

solar-cell panel
module^M de photopiles^F

glass
vitre^F

light bulb
lampe^F à incandescence^F

solar cell
photopile^F

frame
coffre^M

fuse
fusible^M

diode
diode^F

negative contact
contact^M négatif

terminal box
boîte^F électrique

positive contact
contact^M positif

battery
batterie^F d'accumulateurs^M

ENERGY

windmill
moulin^M à vent^M

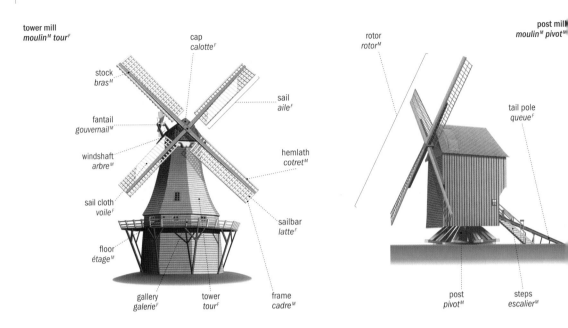

tower mill
moulin^M tour^F

post mill
moulin^M pivot^M

stock
bras^M

cap
calotte^F

rotor
rotor^M

sail
aile^F

tail pole
queue^F

fantail
gouvernail^M

windshaft
arbre^M

hemlath
cotret^M

sail cloth
voile^F

sailbar
latte^F

floor
étage^M

gallery
galerie^F

tower
tour^F

frame
cadre^M

post
pivot^M

steps
escalier^M

wind turbines and electricity production
éoliennes^F et production^F d'électricité^F

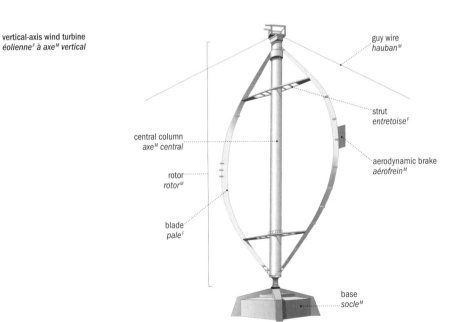

vertical-axis wind turbine
éolienne^F à axe^M vertical

guy wire
hauban^M

strut
entretoise^F

central column
axe^M central

aerodynamic brake
aérofrein^M

rotor
rotor^M

blade
pale^F

base
socle^M

horizontal-axis wind turbine
éolienne^F à axe^M horizontal

nacelle cross-section
coupe^F de la nacelle^F

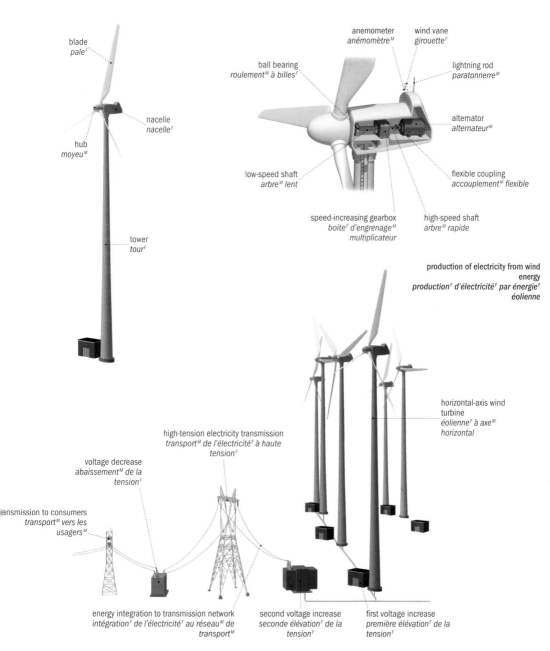

blade
pale^F

nacelle
nacelle^F

hub
moyeu^M

tower
tour^F

anemometer
anémomètre^M

wind vane
girouette^F

ball bearing
roulement^M à billes^F

lightning rod
paratonnerre^M

alternator
alternateur^M

low-speed shaft
arbre^M lent

flexible coupling
accouplement^M flexible

speed-increasing gearbox
*boîte^F d'engrenage^M
multiplicateur*

high-speed shaft
arbre^M rapide

production of electricity from wind
energy
*production^F d'électricité^F par énergie^F
éolienne*

horizontal-axis wind
turbine
*éolienne^F à axe^M
horizontal*

high-tension electricity transmission
*transport^M de l'électricité^F à haute
tension^F*

voltage decrease
*abaissement^M de la
tension^F*

transmission to consumers
*transport^M vers les
usagers^M*

energy integration to transmission network
*intégration^F de l'électricité^F au réseau^M de
transport^M*

second voltage increase
*seconde élévation^F de la
tension^F*

first voltage increase
*première élévation^F de la
tension^F*

ENERGY

413

matter

matière^F

atom
atome^M

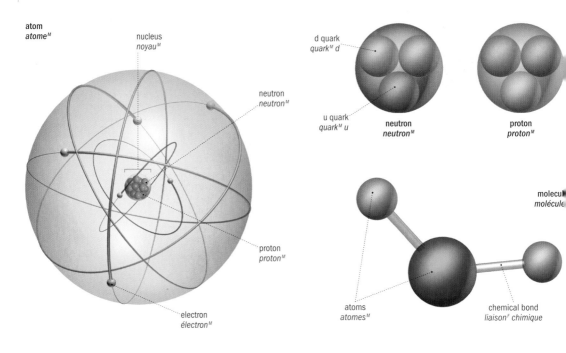

nucleus
noyau^M

d quark
quark^M *d*

u quark
quark^M *u*

neutron
neutron^M

proton
proton^M

neutron
neutron^M

proton
proton^M

electron
électron^M

molecul
molécule

atoms
atomes^M

chemical bond
liaison^F *chimique*

states of matter
états^M *de la matière*^F

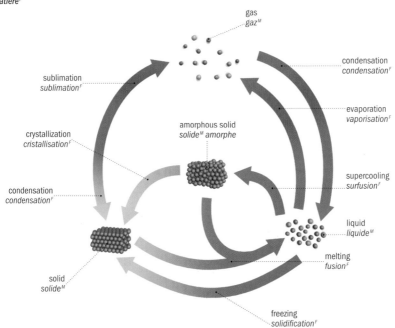

gas
gaz^M

sublimation
sublimation^F

condensation
condensation^F

evaporation
vaporisation^F

crystallization
cristallisation^F

amorphous solid
solide^M *amorphe*

supercooling
surfusion^F

condensation
condensation^F

liquid
liquide^M

melting
fusion^F

solid
solide^M

freezing
solidification^F

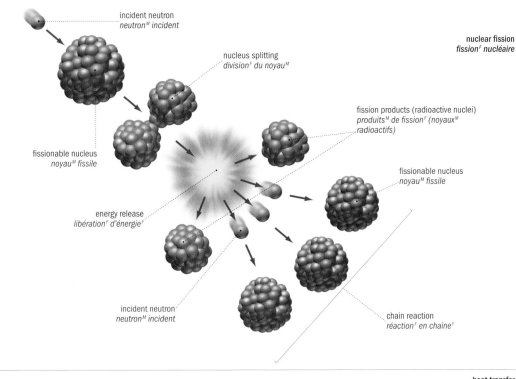

incident neutron
neutron^M incident

nucleus splitting
division^F du noyau^M

fission products (radioactive nuclei)
produits^M de fission^F (noyaux^M radioactifs)

fissionable nucleus
noyau^M fissile

fissionable nucleus
noyau^M fissile

energy release
libération^F d'énergie^F

incident neutron
neutron^M incident

chain reaction
réaction^F en chaîne^F

heat transfer
transfert^M de la chaleur^F

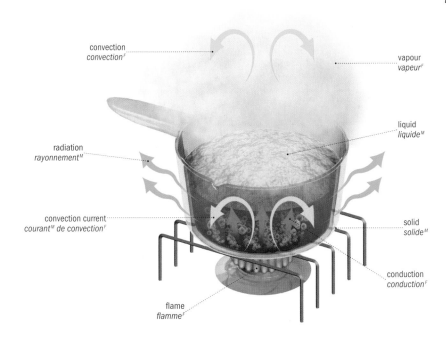

convection
convection^F

vapour
vapeur^F

liquid
liquide^M

radiation
rayonnement^M

convection current
courant^M de convection^F

solid
solide^M

conduction
conduction^F

flame
flamme^F

SCIENCE

magnetism

magnétisme^M

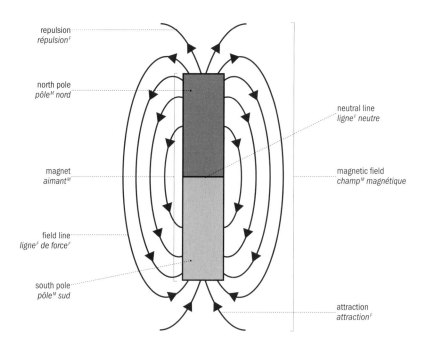

repulsion
répulsion^F

north pole
pôle^M nord

magnet
aimant^M

field line
ligne^F de force^F

south pole
pôle^M sud

neutral line
ligne^F neutre

magnetic field
champ^M magnétique

attraction
attraction^F

parallel electrical circuit

circuit^M électrique en parallèle^F

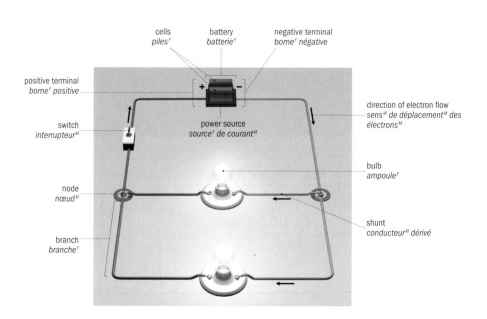

cells
piles^F

battery
batterie^F

negative terminal
borne^F négative

positive terminal
borne^F positive

switch
interrupteur^M

node
nœud^M

branch
branche^F

power source
source^F de courant^M

direction of electron flow
sens^M de déplacement^M des
électrons^M

bulb
ampoule^F

shunt
conducteur^M dérivé

dry cells

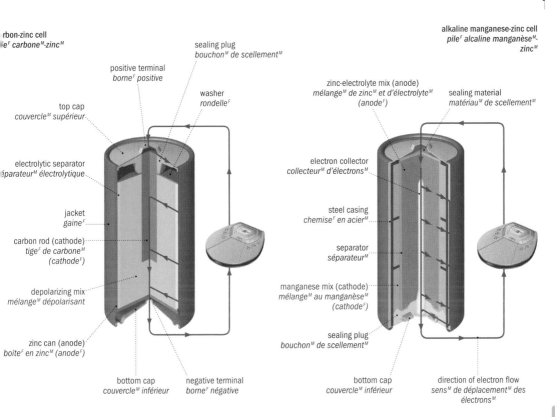

rbon-zinc cell
e^F carbone^M-zinc^M

alkaline manganese-zinc cell
pile^F alcaline manganèse^M-zinc^M

sealing plug
bouchon^M de scellement^M

positive terminal
borne^F positive

zinc-electrolyte mix (anode)
mélange^M de zinc^M et d'électrolyte^M (anode^F)

sealing material
matériau^M de scellement^M

washer
rondelle^F

top cap
couvercle^M supérieur

electron collector
collecteur^M d'électrons^M

electrolytic separator
séparateur^M électrolytique

steel casing
chemise^F en acier^M

jacket
gaine^F

carbon rod (cathode)
tige^F de carbone^M (cathode^F)

separator
séparateur^M

depolarizing mix
mélange^M dépolarisant

manganese mix (cathode)
mélange^M au manganèse^M (cathode^F)

zinc can (anode)
boîte^F en zinc^M (anode^F)

sealing plug
bouchon^M de scellement^M

bottom cap
couvercle^M inférieur

negative terminal
borne^F négative

bottom cap
couvercle^M inférieur

direction of electron flow
sens^M de déplacement^M des électrons^M

electronics

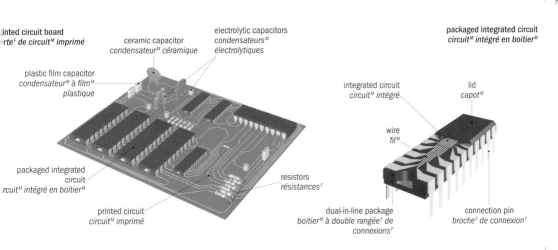

inted circuit board
rte^F de circuit^M imprimé

ceramic capacitor
condensateur^M céramique

electrolytic capacitors
condensateurs^M électrolytiques

packaged integrated circuit
circuit^M intégré en boîtier^M

plastic film capacitor
condensateur^M à film^M plastique

integrated circuit
circuit^M intégré

lid
capot^M

wire
fil^M

packaged integrated circuit
rcuit^M intégré en boîtier^M

resistors
résistances^F

printed circuit
circuit^M imprimé

dual-in-line package
boîtier^M à double rangée^F de connexions^F

connection pin
broche^F de connexion^F

electromagnetic spectrum

spectre^M électromagnétique

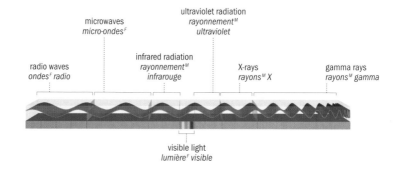

microwaves
micro-ondes^F

ultraviolet radiation
rayonnement^M
ultraviolet

radio waves
ondes^F radio

infrared radiation
rayonnement^M
infrarouge

X-rays
rayons^M X

gamma rays
rayons^M gamma

visible light
lumière^F visible

wave

onde^F

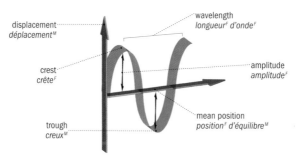

displacement
déplacement^M

wavelength
longueur^F d'onde^F

crest
crête^F

amplitude
amplitude^F

mean position
position^F d'équilibre^M

trough
creux^M

colour synthesis

synthèse^F des couleurs^F

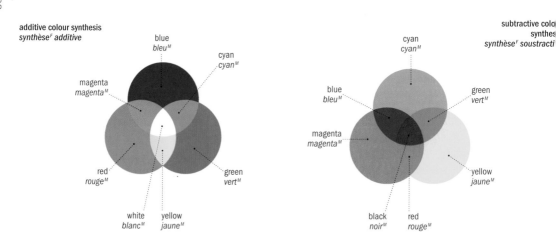

additive colour synthesis
synthèse^F additive

blue
bleu^M

cyan
cyan^M

magenta
magenta^M

red
rouge^M

green
vert^M

white
blanc^M

yellow
jaune^M

**subtractive colo|
synthes|
synthèse^F soustracti|

cyan
cyan^M

blue
bleu^M

green
vert^M

magenta
magenta^M

yellow
jaune^M

black
noir^M

red
rouge^M

vision
vision^F

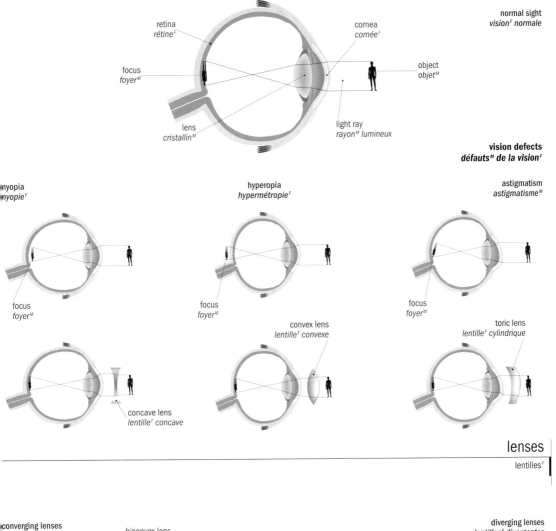

normal sight
vision^F normale

retina
rétine^F

cornea
cornée^F

focus
foyer^M

object
objet^M

lens
cristallin^M

light ray
rayon^M lumineux

vision defects
défauts^M de la vision^F

myopia
myopie^F

hyperopia
hypermétropie^F

astigmatism
astigmatisme^M

focus
foyer^M

focus
foyer^M

focus
foyer^M

convex lens
lentille^F convexe

toric lens
lentille^F cylindrique

concave lens
lentille^F concave

lenses
lentilles^F

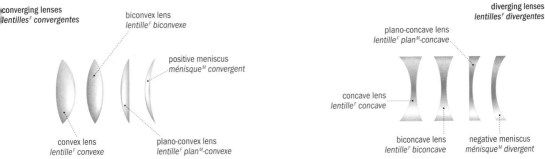

converging lenses
lentilles^F convergentes

biconvex lens
lentille^F biconvexe

positive meniscus
ménisque^M convergent

convex lens
lentille^F convexe

plano-convex lens
lentille^F plan^M-convexe

diverging lenses
lentilles^F divergentes

plano-concave lens
lentille^F plan^M-concave

concave lens
lentille^F concave

biconcave lens
lentille^F biconcave

negative meniscus
ménisque^M divergent

SCIENCE

pulsed ruby laser

laser^M à rubis^M pulsé

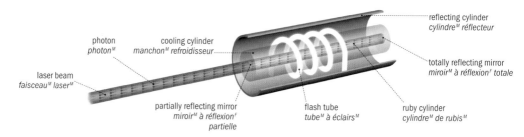

photon
photon^M

cooling cylinder
manchon^M refroidisseur

reflecting cylinder
cylindre^M réflecteur

totally reflecting mirror
miroir^M à réflexion^F totale

laser beam
faisceau^M laser^M

partially reflecting mirror
miroir^M à réflexion^F
partielle

flash tube
tube^M à éclairs^M

ruby cylinder
cylindre^M de rubis^M

prism binoculars

jumelles^F à prismes^M

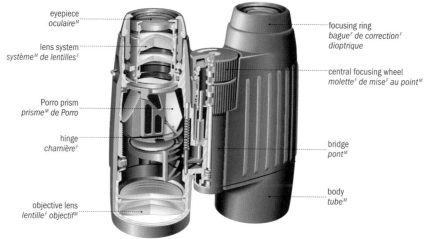

eyepiece
oculaire^M

lens system
système^M de lentilles^F

Porro prism
prisme^M de Porro

hinge
charnière^F

objective lens
lentille^F objectif^M

focusing ring
bague^F de correction^F
dioptrique

central focusing wheel
molette^F de mise^F au point^M

bridge
pont^M

body
tube^M

telescopic sight

lunette^F de visée^F

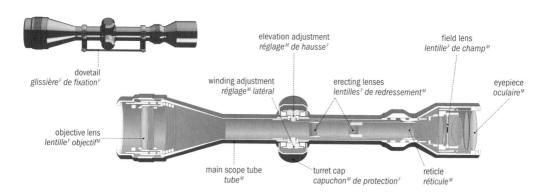

dovetail
glissière^F de fixation^F

elevation adjustment
réglage^M de hausse^F

field lens
lentille^F de champ^M

winding adjustment
réglage^M latéral

erecting lenses
lentilles^F de redressement^M

eyepiece
oculaire^M

objective lens
lentille^F objectif^M

main scope tube
tube^M

turret cap
capuchon^M de protection^F

reticle
réticule^M

SCIENCE

magnifying glass and microscopes

loupe*F* et microscopes*M*

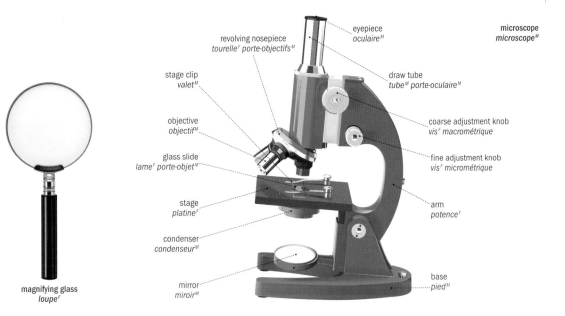

microscope
*microscope*M

eyepiece
*oculaire*M

revolving nosepiece
*tourelle*F *porte-objectifs*M

draw tube
*tube*M *porte-oculaire*M

stage clip
*valet*M

coarse adjustment knob
*vis*F *macrométrique*

objective
*objectif*M

fine adjustment knob
*vis*F *micrométrique*

glass slide
*lame*F *porte-objet*M

stage
*platine*F

arm
*potence*F

condenser
*condenseur*M

mirror
*miroir*M

base
*pied*M

magnifying glass
*loupe*F

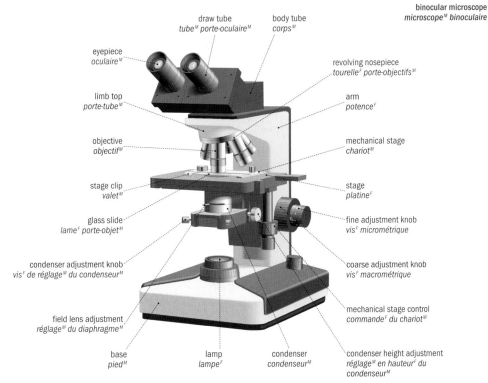

binocular microscope
*microscope*M *binoculaire*

draw tube
*tube*M *porte-oculaire*M

body tube
*corps*M

eyepiece
*oculaire*M

revolving nosepiece
*tourelle*F *porte-objectifs*M

limb top
*porte-tube*M

arm
*potence*F

objective
*objectif*M

mechanical stage
*chariot*M

stage clip
*valet*M

stage
*platine*F

glass slide
*lame*F *porte-objet*M

fine adjustment knob
*vis*F *micrométrique*

condenser adjustment knob
*vis*F *de réglage*M *du condenseur*M

coarse adjustment knob
*vis*F *macrométrique*

field lens adjustment
*réglage*M *du diaphragme*M

mechanical stage control
*commande*F *du chariot*M

base
*pied*M

lamp
*lampe*F

condenser
*condenseur*M

condenser height adjustment
*réglage*M *en hauteur*F *du condenseur*M

measurement of weight

mesure^F de la masse^F

beam balance
balance^F à fléau^M

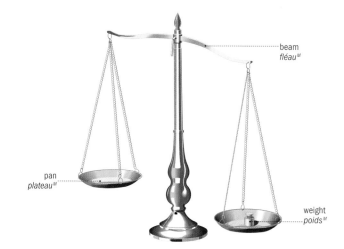

beam
fléau^M

pan
plateau^M

weight
poids^M

steelyard
balance^F romaine

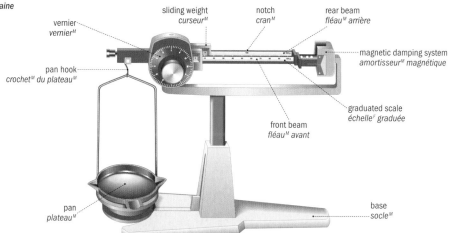

vernier
vernier^M

sliding weight
curseur^M

notch
cran^M

rear beam
fléau^M arrière

pan hook
crochet^M du plateau^M

magnetic damping system
amortisseur^M magnétique

front beam
fléau^M avant

graduated scale
échelle^F graduée

pan
plateau^M

base
socle^M

Roberval's balance
balance^F de Roberval

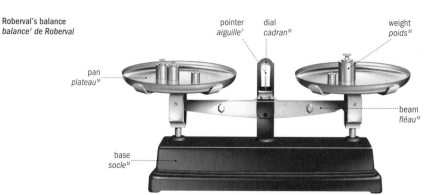

pointer
aiguille^F

dial
cadran^M

weight
poids^M

pan
plateau^M

beam
fléau^M

base
socle^M

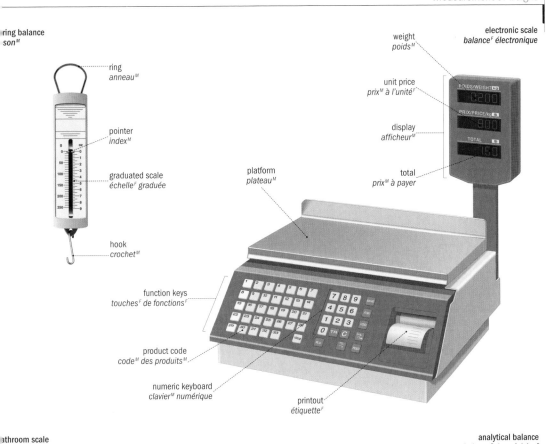

ring balance
son[M]

ring
anneau[M]

pointer
index[M]

graduated scale
échelle[F] *graduée*

hook
crochet[M]

platform
plateau[M]

weight
poids[M]

electronic scale
balance[F] *électronique*

unit price
prix[M] *à l'unité*[F]

display
afficheur[M]

total
prix[M] *à payer*

POIDS/WEIGHT

PRIX/PRICE/kg

TOTAL

function keys
touches[F] *de fonctions*[F]

product code
code[M] *des produits*[M]

numeric keyboard
clavier[M] *numérique*

printout
étiquette[F]

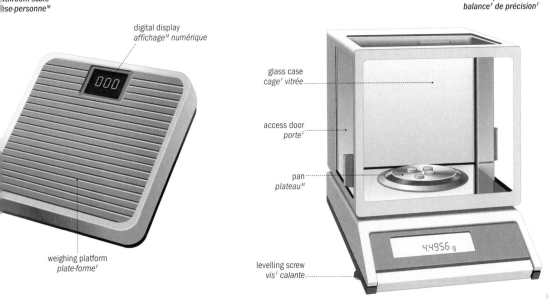

athroom scale
se-personne[M]

digital display
affichage[M] *numérique*

weighing platform
plate-forme[F]

analytical balance
balance[F] *de précision*[F]

glass case
cage[F] *vitrée*

access door
porte[F]

pan
plateau[M]

levelling screw
vis[F] *calante*

4.4956 g

SCIENCE

measurement of temperature

mesure^F de la température^F

thermometer
thermomètre^M

Fahrenheit scale
échelle^F Fahrenheit

Celsius scale
échelle^F Celsius

degrees Fahrenheit
°F

degrees Celsius
°C

alcohol column
colonne^F d'alcool^M

alcohol bulb
réservoir^M d'alcool^M

clinical thermometer
thermomètre^M médical

capillary tube
tube^M capillaire

expansion chamber
chambre^F d'expansion^F

scale
graduation^F

stem
tige^F

column of mercury
colonne^F de mercure^M

mercury bulb
réservoir^M de mercure^M

constriction
étranglement^M

measurement of time

mesure^F du temps^M

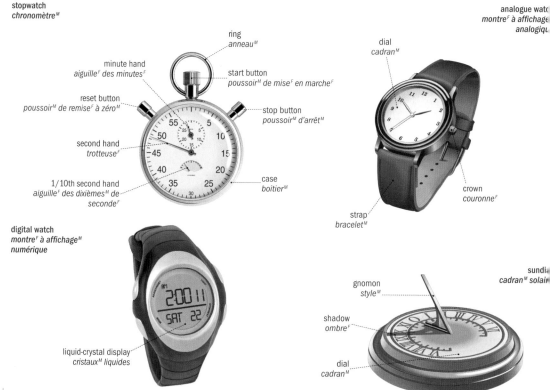

stopwatch
chronomètre^M

ring
anneau^M

minute hand
aiguille^F des minutes^F

start button
poussoir^M de mise^F en marche^F

reset button
poussoir^M de remise^F à zéro^M

stop button
poussoir^M d'arrêt^M

second hand
trotteuse^F

1/10th second hand
aiguille^F des dixièmes^M de seconde^F

case
boitier^M

analogue watch
montre^F à affichage analogique

dial
cadran^M

crown
couronne^F

strap
bracelet^M

digital watch
montre^F à affichage^M numérique

liquid-crystal display
cristaux^M liquides

sundial
cadran^M solaire

gnomon
style^M

shadow
ombre^F

dial
cadran^M

measurement of length
mesure^F *de la longueur*^F

ruler
règle^F *graduée*

scale
graduation^F

measurement of thickness
mesure^F *de l'épaisseur*^F

vernier caliper
pied^M *à coulisse*^F *à vernier*^M

clamping screws
vis^F *de blocage*^M

clamping block
bloc^M *de pression*^F

main scale
graduation^F *de la règle*^F

vernier
vernier^M

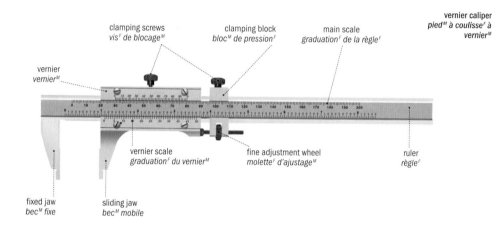

vernier scale
graduation^F *du vernier*^M

fine adjustment wheel
molette^F *d'ajustage*^M

ruler
règle^F

fixed jaw
bec^M *fixe*

sliding jaw
bec^M *mobile*

SCIENCE

micrometer caliper
micromètre^M *palmer*^M

anvil
touche^F *fixe*

spindle
touche^F *mobile*

finely threaded screw
vis^F *micrométrique*

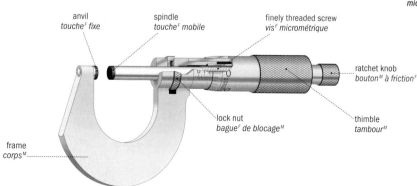

ratchet knob
bouton^M *à friction*^F

lock nut
bague^F *de blocage*^M

thimble
tambour^M

frame
corps^M

international system of units

système^M international d'unités^F

measurement of electric current
mesure^F du courant^M électrique

A

ampere
ampère^M

measurement of electric potential difference
mesure^F de la différence^F de potentiel^M électrique

volt
volt^M

measurement of electric resistance
mesure^F de la résistance^F électrique

Ω

ohm
ohm^M

measurement of electric charge
mesure^F de la charge^F électrique

C

coulomb
coulomb^M

measurement of power
mesure^F de la puissance^F

W

watt
watt^M

measurement of frequency
mesure^F de la fréquence^F

Hz

hertz
hertz^M

measurement of luminous intensity
mesure^F de l'intensité^F lumineuse

cd

candela
candela^F

measurement of energy
mesure^F de l'énergie^F

J

joule
joule^M

measurement of length
mesure^F de la longueur^F

m

metre
mètre^M

measurement of mass
mesure^F de la masse^F

kg

kilogram
kilogramme^M

measurement of pressure
mesure^F de la pression^F

Pa

pascal
pascal^M

measurement of force
mesure^F de la force^F

N

newton
newton^M

measurement of time
mesure^F du temps^M

s

second
seconde^F

measurement of amount of substance
mesure^F de la quantité^F de matière^F

mol

mole
mole^F

measurement of radioactivity
mesure^F de la radioactivité^F

Bq

becquerel
becquerel^M

measurement of Celsius temperature
mesure^F de la température^F Celsius

°C

degree Celsius
degré^M Celsius

measurement of thermodynamic temperature
mesure^F de la température^F thermodynamique

K

kelvin
kelvin^M

biology

biologie^F

female
femelle^F

Rh-

blood factor negative
facteur^M Rhésus négatif

born
naissance^F

male
mâle^M

Rh+

blood factor positive
facteur^M Rhésus positif

†

died
mort^F

mathematics
mathématiques[F]

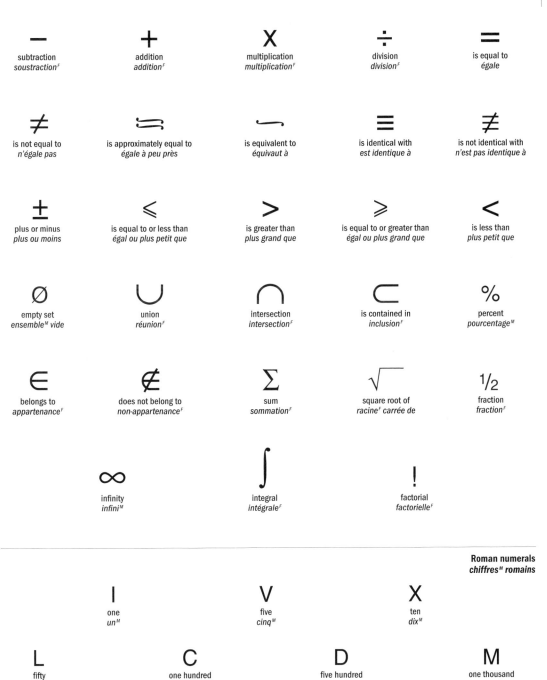

—	+	X	÷	=
subtraction	addition	multiplication	division	is equal to
soustraction[F]	*addition*[F]	*multiplication*[F]	*division*[F]	*égale*

≠	⇆	⌣	≡	≢
is not equal to	is approximately equal to	is equivalent to	is identical with	is not identical with
n'égale pas	*égale à peu près*	*équivaut à*	*est identique à*	*n'est pas identique à*

±	≤	>	⩾	<
plus or minus	is equal to or less than	is greater than	is equal to or greater than	is less than
plus ou moins	*égal ou plus petit que*	*plus grand que*	*égal ou plus grand que*	*plus petit que*

Ø	∪	∩	⊂	%
empty set	union	intersection	is contained in	percent
ensemble[M] *vide*	*réunion*[F]	*intersection*[F]	*inclusion*[F]	*pourcentage*[M]

∈	∉	Σ	√	½
belongs to	does not belong to	sum	square root of	fraction
appartenance[F]	*non-appartenance*[F]	*sommation*[F]	*racine*[F] *carrée de*	*fraction*[F]

∞	∫	!
infinity	integral	factorial
infini[M]	*intégrale*[F]	*factorielle*[F]

Roman numerals
chiffres*[M] *romains

I	V	X
one	five	ten
un[M]	*cinq*[M]	*dix*[M]

L	C	D	M
fifty	one hundred	five hundred	one thousand
cinquante[M]	*cent*[M]	*cinq cents*[M]	*mille*[M]

geometry

géométrie[F]

○	′	″	π	⊥
degree	minute	second	pi	perpendicular
degré[M]	minute[F]	seconde[F]	pi[M]	perpendiculaire[F]

‖	⊬	∟	⟍	∠
is parallel to	is not parallel to	right angle	obtuse angle	acute angle
parallèle	non-parallèle	angle[M] droit	angle[M] obtus	angle[M] aigu

geometrical shapes

formes[F] géométriques

examples of angles
exemples[M] d'angles[M]

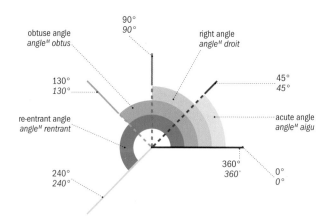

obtuse angle
angle[M] obtus

90°
90°

right angle
angle[M] droit

130°
130°

45°
45°

re-entrant angle
angle[M] rentrant

acute angle
angle[M] aigu

240°
240°

360°
360°

0°
0°

plane surfaces
surfaces[F]

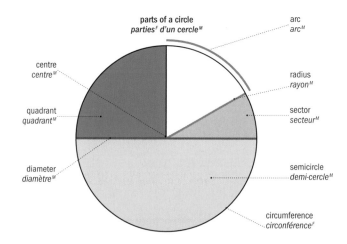

parts of a circle
parties[F] d'un cercle[M]

arc
arc[M]

centre
centre[M]

radius
rayon[M]

quadrant
quadrant[M]

sector
secteur[M]

diameter
diamètre[M]

semicircle
demi-cercle[M]

circumference
circonférence[F]

SCIENCE

polygons
polygones[M]

triangle
triangle[M]

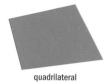

square
carré[M]

rectangle
rectangle[M]

rhombus
losange[M]

trapezoid
trapèze[M]

parallelogram
parallélogramme[M]

quadrilateral
quadrilatère[M]

regular pentagon
pentagone[M] *régulier*

regular hexagon
hexagone[M] *régulier*

regular heptagon
heptagone[M] *régulier*

regular octagon
octogone[M] *régulier*

quadrilateral
regular nonagon
ennéagone[M] *régulier*

regular decagon
décagone[M] *régulier*

regular hendecagon
hendécagone[M] *régulier*

regular dodecagon
dodécagone[M] *régulier*

solids
volumes[M]

helix
hélice[F]

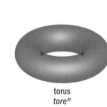

torus
tore[M]

hemisphere
hémisphère[M]

sphere
sphère[F]

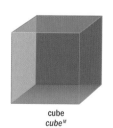

cube
cube[M]

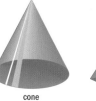

cone
cône[M]

pyramid
pyramide[F]

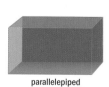

cylinder
cylindre[M]

parallelepiped
parallélépipède[M]

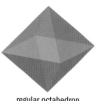

regular octahedron
octaèdre[M] *régulier*

SCIENCE

conurbation

agglomération*F*

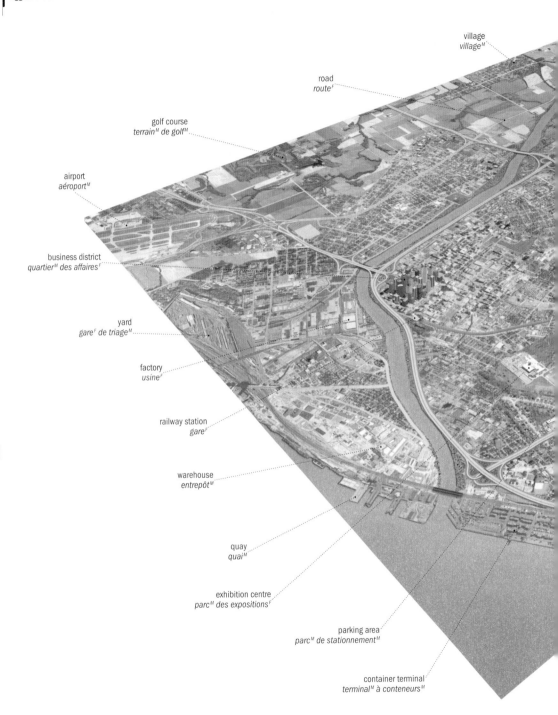

village
*village*M

road
*route*F

golf course
*terrain*M *de golf*M

airport
*aéroport*M

business district
*quartier*M *des affaires*F

yard
*gare*F *de triage*M

factory
*usine*F

railway station
*gare*F

warehouse
*entrepôt*M

quay
*quai*M

exhibition centre
*parc*M *des expositions*F

parking area
*parc*M *de stationnement*M

container terminal
*terminal*M *à conteneurs*M

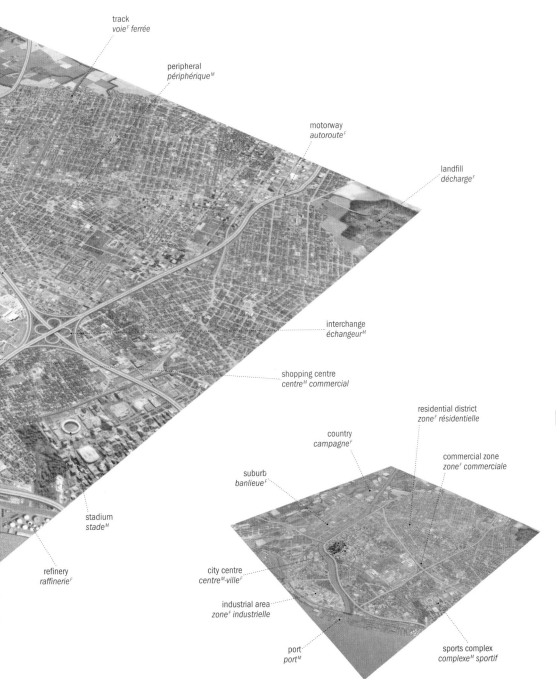

track
voie^F *ferrée*

peripheral
périphérique^M

motorway
autoroute^F

landfill
décharge^F

interchange
échangeur^M

shopping centre
centre^M *commercial*

residential district
zone^F *résidentielle*

country
campagne^F

commercial zone
zone^F *commerciale*

suburb
banlieue^F

stadium
stade^M

refinery
raffinerie^F

city centre
centre^M-*ville*^F

industrial area
zone^F *industrielle*

port
port^M

sports complex
complexe^M *sportif*

city centre

centre^M-ville^F

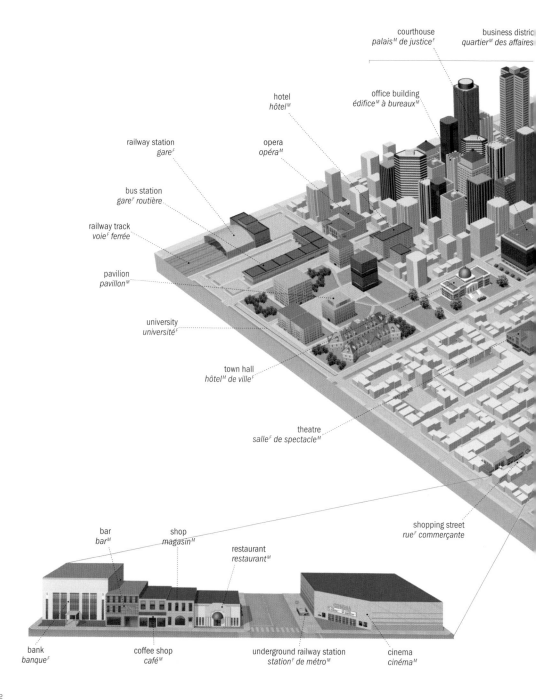

courthouse
palais^M de justice^F

business distric
quartier^M des affaires

hotel
hôtel^M

office building
édifice^M à bureaux^M

railway station
gare^F

opera
opéra^M

bus station
gare^F routière

railway track
voie^F ferrée

pavilion
pavillon^M

university
université^F

town hall
hôtel^M de ville^F

theatre
salle^F de spectacle^M

shopping street
rue^F commerçante

bar
bar^M

shop
magasin^M

restaurant
restaurant^M

bank
banque^F

coffee shop
café^M

underground railway station
station^F de métro^M

cinema
cinéma^M

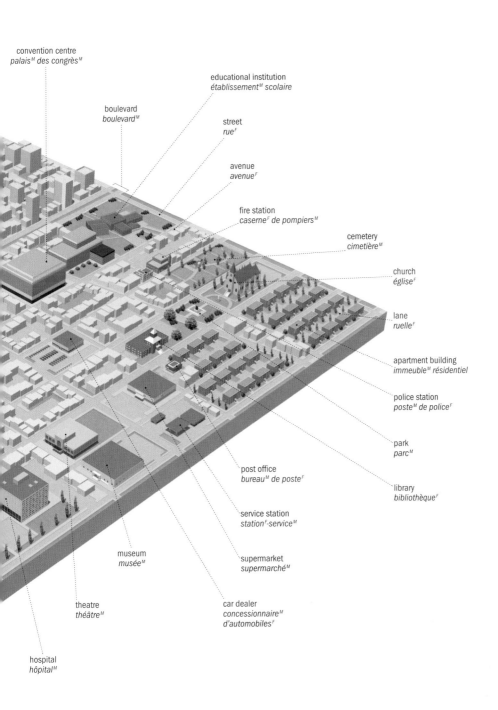

convention centre
palais^M *des congrès*^M

educational institution
établissement^M *scolaire*

boulevard
boulevard^M

street
rue^F

avenue
avenue^F

fire station
caserne^F *de pompiers*^M

cemetery
cimetière^M

church
église^F

lane
ruelle^F

apartment building
immeuble^M *résidentiel*

police station
poste^M *de police*^F

park
parc^M

post office
bureau^M *de poste*^F

library
bibliothèque^F

service station
station^F*-service*^M

museum
musée^M

supermarket
supermarché^M

theatre
théâtre^M

car dealer
concessionnaire^M
d'automobiles^F

hospital
hôpital^M

SOCIETY

cross section of a street

coupe^F d'une rue^F

pavement
trottoir^M

street light
réverbère^M

central reservation
terre-plein^M

roadway
chaussée^F

traffic lights
feux^M de circulation^F

fire hydrant
borne^F d'incendie^M

kerb
bordure^F de trottoir^M

manhole
regard^M de visite^F

pedestrian crossing
passage^M pour piétons^M

surface water drain
branchement^M pluvial

bus stop
arrêt^M d'autobus^M

barrier
barrière^F

bus shelter
abribus^M

sewer
égout^M

water main
conduite^F d'eau^F potable

electricity cable
câble^M électrique

traffic lights
feux^M de circulation^F

red light
feu^M rouge

main sewer
égout^M collecteur

telephone cable
câble^M téléphonique

amber light
feu^M jaune

gas main
conduite^F de gaz^M

green light
feu^M vert

water main
conduite^F d'eau^F potable

pedestrian lights
feux^M pour piétons^M

pedestrian call button
bouton^M d'appel^M pour piétons^M

office building
édifice^M à bureaux^M

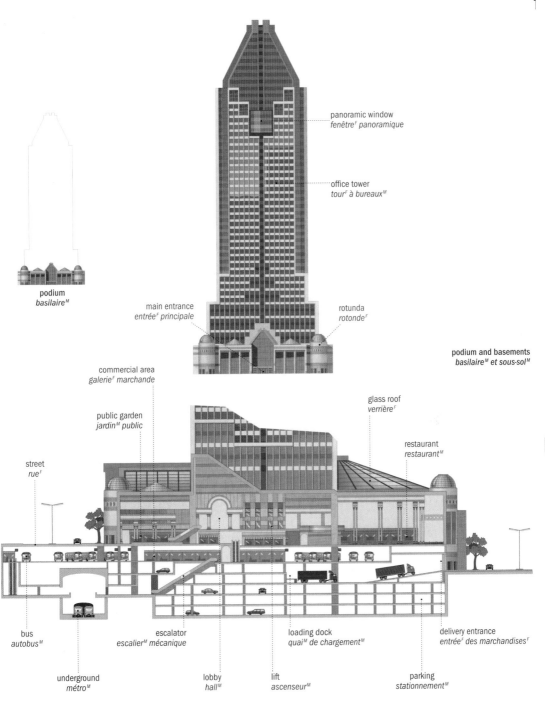

panoramic window
fenêtre^F panoramique

office tower
tour^F à bureaux^M

main entrance
entrée^F principale

rotunda
rotonde^F

podium
basilaire^M

podium and basements
basilaire^M et sous-sol^M

commercial area
galerie^F marchande

glass roof
verrière^F

public garden
jardin^M public

restaurant
restaurant^M

street
rue^F

bus
autobus^M

escalator
escalier^M mécanique

loading dock
quai^M de chargement^M

delivery entrance
entrée^F des marchandises^F

underground
métro^M

lobby
hall^M

lift
ascenseur^M

parking
stationnement^M

SOCIETY

shopping centre

centre^M commercial

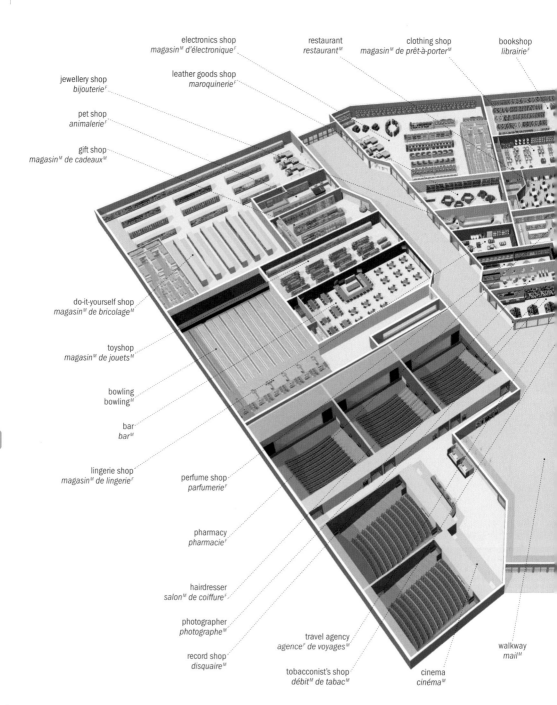

electronics shop
magasin^M d'électronique^F

restaurant
restaurant^M

clothing shop
magasin^M de prêt-à-porter^M

bookshop
librairie^F

jewellery shop
bijouterie^F

leather goods shop
maroquinerie^F

pet shop
animalerie^F

gift shop
magasin^M de cadeaux^M

do-it-yourself shop
magasin^M de bricolage^M

toyshop
magasin^M de jouets^M

bowling
bowling^M

bar
bar^M

lingerie shop
magasin^M de lingerie^F

perfume shop
parfumerie^F

pharmacy
pharmacie^F

hairdresser
salon^M de coiffure^F

photographer
photographe^M

record shop
disquaire^M

travel agency
agence^F de voyages^M

tobacconist's shop
débit^M de tabac^M

cinema
cinéma^M

walkway
mail^M

SOCIETY

shopping centre

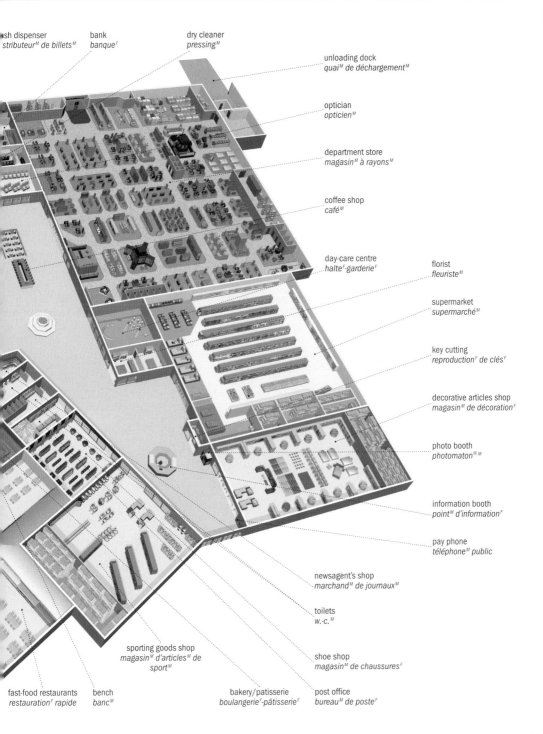

cash dispenser
distributeur^M de billets^M

bank
banque^F

dry cleaner
pressing^M

unloading dock
quai^M de déchargement^M

optician
opticien^M

department store
magasin^M à rayons^M

coffee shop
café^M

day-care centre
halte^F-garderie^F

florist
fleuriste^M

supermarket
supermarché^M

key cutting
reproduction^F de clés^F

decorative articles shop
magasin^M de décoration^F

photo booth
photomaton^{® M}

information booth
point^M d'information^F

pay phone
téléphone^M public

newsagent's shop
marchand^M de journaux^M

toilets
w.-c. ^M

sporting goods shop
magasin^M d'articles^M de sport^M

shoe shop
magasin^M de chaussures^F

fast-food restaurants
restauration^F rapide

bench
banc^M

bakery/patisserie
boulangerie^F-pâtisserie^F

post office
bureau^M de poste^F

SOCIETY

437

restaurant

restaurant^M

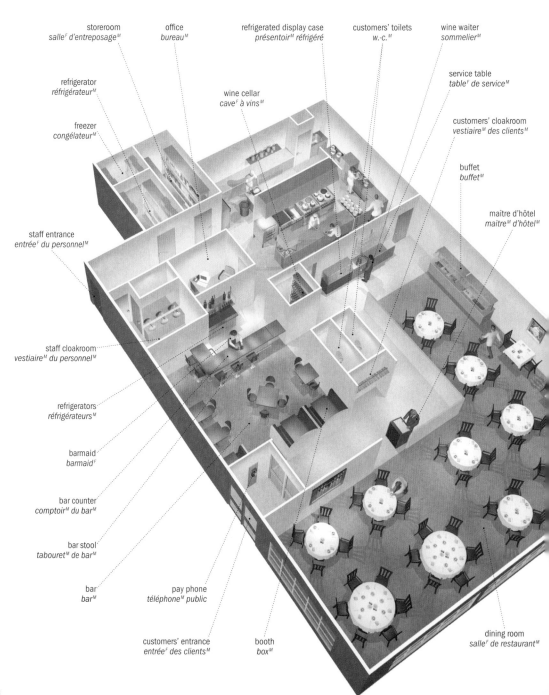

storeroom
salle^F d'entreposage^M

office
bureau^M

refrigerated display case
présentoir^M réfrigéré

customers' toilets
w.-c.^M

wine waiter
sommelier^M

service table
table^F de service^M

refrigerator
réfrigérateur^M

wine cellar
cave^F à vins^M

customers' cloakroom
vestiaire^M des clients^M

freezer
congélateur^M

buffet
buffet^M

staff entrance
entrée^F du personnel^M

maître d'hôtel
maître^M d'hôtel^M

staff cloakroom
vestiaire^M du personnel^M

refrigerators
réfrigérateurs^M

barmaid
barmaid^F

bar counter
comptoir^M du bar^M

bar stool
tabouret^M de bar^M

bar
bar^M

pay phone
téléphone^M public

customers' entrance
entrée^F des clients^M

booth
box^M

dining room
salle^F de restaurant^M

hotel
hôtel[M]

reception level
niveau[M] *de la*
réception[F]

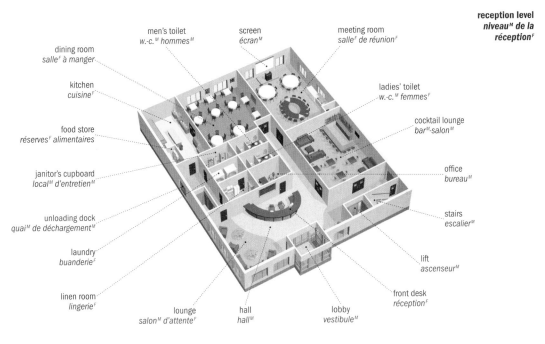

men's toilet
w.-c.[M] *hommes*[M]

screen
écran[M]

meeting room
salle[F] *de réunion*[F]

dining room
salle[F] *à manger*

kitchen
cuisine[F]

ladies' toilet
w.-c.[M] *femmes*[F]

cocktail lounge
bar[M]-*salon*[M]

food store
réserves[F] *alimentaires*

office
bureau[M]

janitor's cupboard
local[M] *d'entretien*[M]

unloading dock
quai[M] *de déchargement*[M]

stairs
escalier[M]

laundry
buanderie[F]

lift
ascenseur[M]

linen room
lingerie[F]

front desk
réception[F]

lounge
salon[M] *d'attente*[F]

hall
hall[M]

lobby
vestibule[M]

hotel room
chambres[F] *d'hôtel*[M]

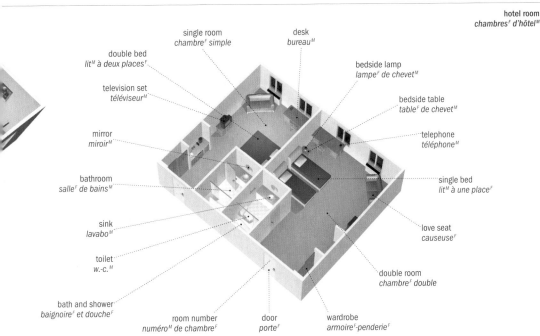

single room
chambre[F] *simple*

desk
bureau[M]

double bed
lit[M] *à deux places*[F]

bedside lamp
lampe[F] *de chevet*[M]

television set
téléviseur[M]

bedside table
table[F] *de chevet*[M]

mirror
miroir[M]

telephone
téléphone[M]

bathroom
salle[F] *de bains*[M]

single bed
lit[M] *à une place*[F]

sink
lavabo[M]

love seat
causeuse[F]

toilet
w.-c.[M]

double room
chambre[F] *double*

bath and shower
baignoire[F] *et douche*[F]

room number
numéro[M] *de chambre*[F]

door
porte[F]

wardrobe
armoire[F]-*penderie*[F]

SOCIETY

court

tribunal^M

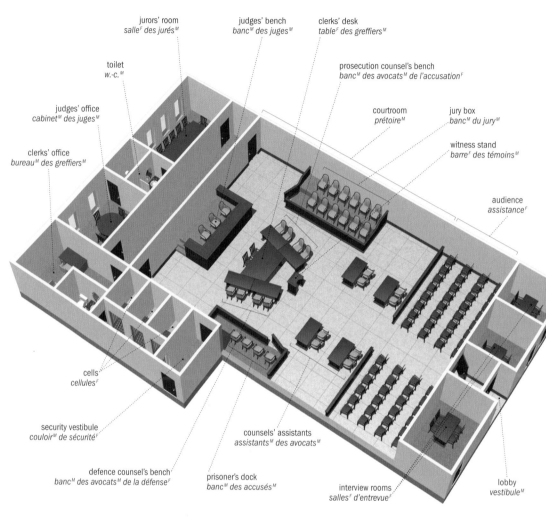

jurors' room
salle^F des jurés^M

judges' bench
banc^M des juges^M

clerks' desk
table^F des greffiers^M

toilet
w.-c.^M

prosecution counsel's bench
banc^M des avocats^M de l'accusation^F

judges' office
cabinet^M des juges^M

courtroom
prétoire^M

jury box
banc^M du jury^M

clerks' office
bureau^M des greffiers^M

witness stand
barre^F des témoins^M

audience
assistance^F

cells
cellules^F

security vestibule
couloir^M de sécurité^F

counsels' assistants
assistants^M des avocats^M

defence counsel's bench
banc^M des avocats^M de la défense^F

prisoner's dock
banc^M des accusés^M

interview rooms
salles^F d'entrevue^F

lobby
vestibule^M

examples of currency abbreviations

exemples^M d'unités^F monétaires

dollar
dollar^M

cent
cent^M

¢

rupee
roupie^F

euro
euro^M

€

new shekel
nouveau shekel^M

peso
peso^M

¥

yen
yen^M

pound
livre^F

SOCIETY

money and modes of payment
monnaie^F et modes^M de paiement^M

coin: obverse
pièce^F : avers^M

date
millésime^M

initials of issuing bank
initiales^F de la banque^F
émettrice

security thread
fil^M de sécurité^F

banknote: front
billet^M de banque^F : recto^M

hologram foil strip
bande^F métallisée
holographique

official signature
signature^F officielle

watermark
filigrane^M

colour shifting ink
encre^F à couleur^F
changeante

edge
tranche^F

portrait
effigie^F

serial number
numéro^M de série^F

coin: reverse
pièce^F : revers^M

European Union flag
drapeau^M de l'Union^F
Européenne

banknote: back
billet^M de banque^F : verso^M

serial number
numéro^M de série^F

outer ring
couronne^F

denomination
valeur^F

motto
devise^F

denomination
valeur^F

currency name
nom^M de la monnaie^F

magnetic strip
bande^F magnétique

cheques
chèques^M

holder's signature
signature^F du titulaire^M

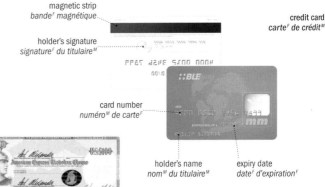

credit card
carte^F de crédit^M

card number
numéro^M de carte^F

traveller's cheque
chèque^M de voyage^M

holder's name
nom^M du titulaire^M

expiry date
date^F d'expiration^F

bank

banque^F

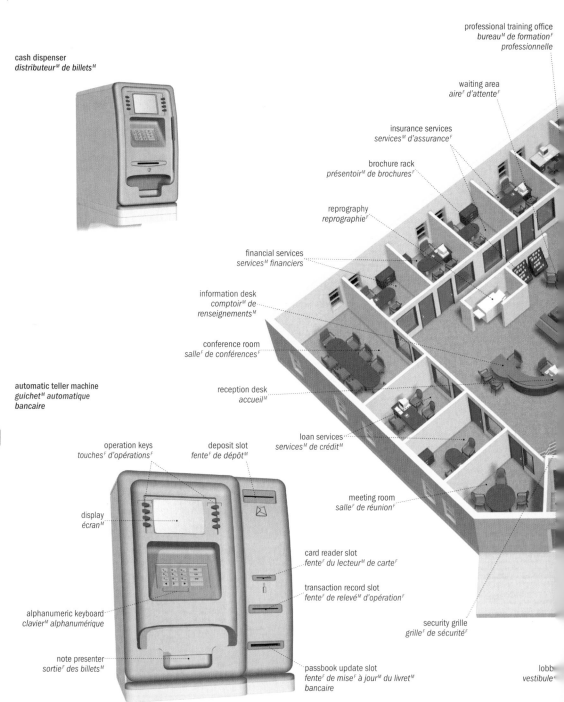

cash dispenser
distributeur^M de billets^M

automatic teller machine
*guichet^M automatique
bancaire*

professional training office
*bureau^M de formation^F
professionnelle*

waiting area
aire^F d'attente^F

insurance services
services^M d'assurance^F

brochure rack
présentoir^M de brochures^F

reprography
reprographie^F

financial services
services^M financiers

information desk
*comptoir^M de
renseignements^M*

conference room
salle^F de conférences^F

reception desk
accueil^M

loan services
services^M de crédit^M

meeting room
salle^F de réunion^F

security grille
grille^F de sécurité^F

lobb
vestibule

operation keys
touches^F d'opérations^F

deposit slot
fente^F de dépôt^M

display
écran^M

card reader slot
fente^F du lecteur^M de carte^F

transaction record slot
fente^F de relevé^M d'opération^F

alphanumeric keyboard
clavier^M alphanumérique

note presenter
sortie^F des billets^M

passbook update slot
*fente^F de mise^F à jour^M du livret^M
bancaire*

SOCIETY

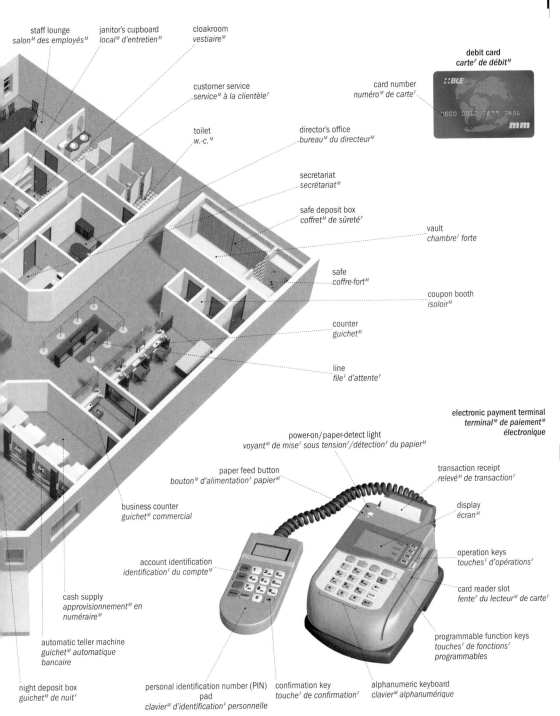

staff lounge
salon^M des employés^M

janitor's cupboard
local^M d'entretien^M

cloakroom
vestiaire^M

debit card
carte^F de débit^M

customer service
service^M à la clientèle^F

card number
numéro^M de carte^F

::BLE

'000 0012 7899 3456

mm

toilet
w.-c. ^M

director's office
bureau^M du directeur^M

secretariat
secrétariat^M

safe deposit box
coffret^M de sûreté^F

vault
chambre^F forte

safe
coffre-fort^M

coupon booth
isoloir^M

counter
guichet^M

line
file^F d'attente^F

electronic payment terminal
terminal^M de paiement^M
électronique

power-on/paper-detect light
voyant^M de mise^F sous tension^F/détection^F du papier^M

transaction receipt
relevé^M de transaction^F

paper feed button
bouton^M d'alimentation^F papier^M

display
écran^M

business counter
guichet^M commercial

account identification
identification^F du compte^M

operation keys
touches^F d'opérations^F

cash supply
approvisionnement^M en
numéraire^M

card reader slot
fente^F du lecteur^M de carte^F

automatic teller machine
guichet^M automatique
bancaire

programmable function keys
touches^F de fonctions^F
programmables

night deposit box
guichet^M de nuit^F

personal identification number (PIN)
pad
clavier^M d'identification^F personnelle

confirmation key
touche^F de confirmation^F

alphanumeric keyboard
clavier^M alphanumérique

SOCIETY

school
école[F]

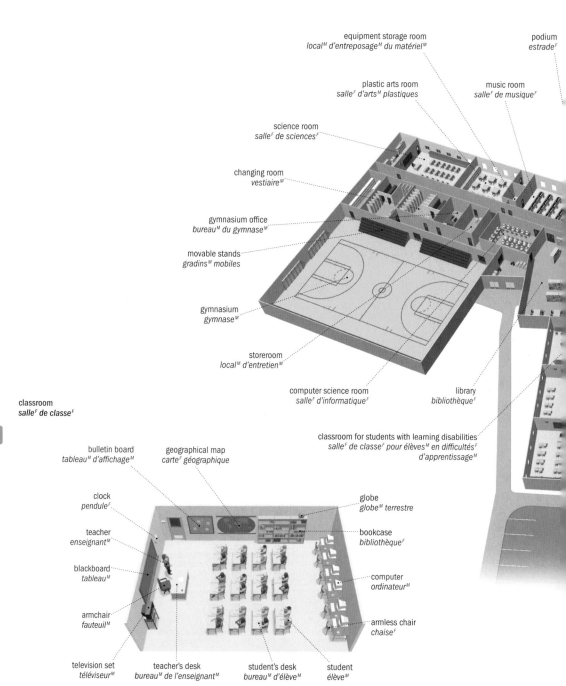

equipment storage room
local[M] *d'entreposage*[M] *du matériel*[M]

podium
estrade[F]

plastic arts room
salle[F] *d'arts*[M] *plastiques*

music room
salle[F] *de musique*[F]

science room
salle[F] *de sciences*[F]

changing room
vestiaire[M]

gymnasium office
bureau[M] *du gymnase*[M]

movable stands
gradins[M] *mobiles*

gymnasium
gymnase[M]

storeroom
local[M] *d'entretien*[M]

computer science room
salle[F] *d'informatique*[F]

library
bibliothèque[F]

classroom
salle[F] *de classe*[F]

classroom for students with learning disabilities
salle[F] *de classe*[F] *pour élèves*[M] *en difficultés*[F]
d'apprentissage[M]

bulletin board
tableau[M] *d'affichage*[M]

geographical map
carte[F] *géographique*

clock
pendule[F]

globe
globe[M] *terrestre*

teacher
enseignant[M]

bookcase
bibliothèque[F]

blackboard
tableau[M]

computer
ordinateur[M]

armchair
fauteuil[M]

armless chair
chaise[F]

television set
téléviseur[M]

teacher's desk
bureau[M] *de l'enseignant*[M]

student's desk
bureau[M] *d'élève*[M]

student
élève[M]

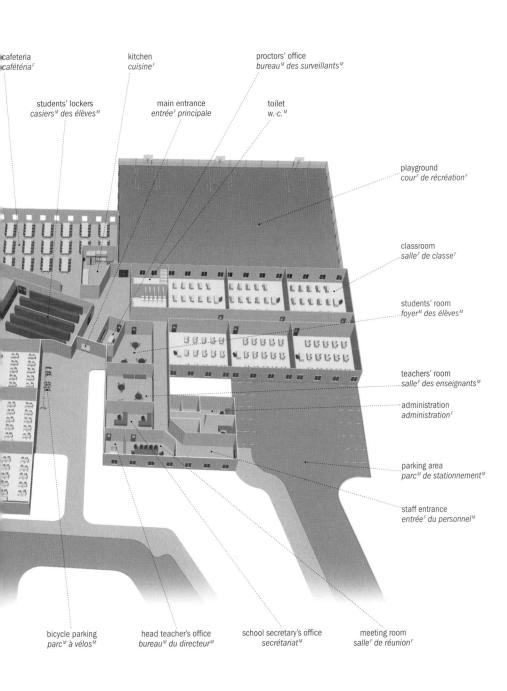

cafeteria
cafétéria^F

kitchen
cuisine^F

proctors' office
bureau^M des surveillants^M

students' lockers
casiers^M des élèves^M

main entrance
entrée^F principale

toilet
w.-c.^M

playground
cour^F de récréation^F

classroom
salle^F de classe^F

students' room
foyer^M des élèves^M

teachers' room
salle^F des enseignants^M

administration
administration^F

parking area
parc^M de stationnement^M

staff entrance
entrée^F du personnel^M

bicycle parking
parc^M à vélos^M

head teacher's office
bureau^M du directeur^M

school secretary's office
secrétariat^M

meeting room
salle^F de réunion^F

SOCIETY

445

church

église^F

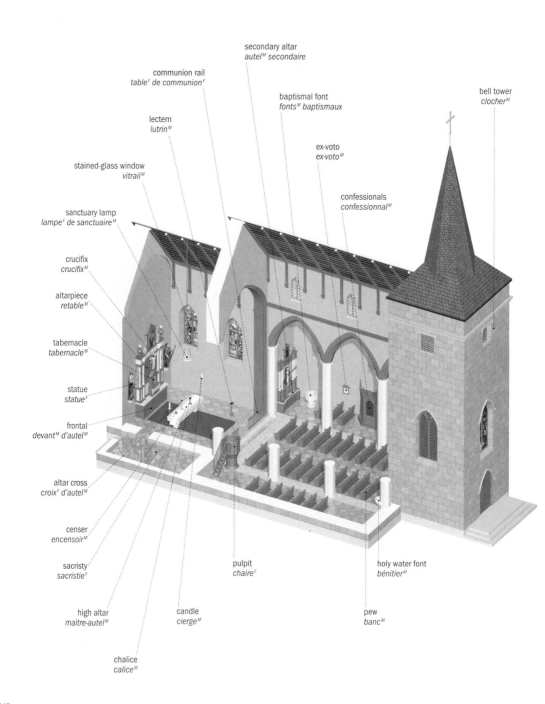

secondary altar
autel^M secondaire

communion rail
table^F de communion^F

baptismal font
fonts^M baptismaux

bell tower
clocher^M

lectern
lutrin^M

ex-voto
ex-voto^M

stained-glass window
vitrail^M

confessionals
confessionnal^M

sanctuary lamp
lampe^F de sanctuaire^M

crucifix
crucifix^M

altarpiece
retable^M

tabernacle
tabernacle^M

statue
statue^F

frontal
devant^M d'autel^M

altar cross
croix^F d'autel^M

censer
encensoir^M

sacristy
sacristie^F

pulpit
chaire^F

holy water font
bénitier^M

high altar
maître-autel^M

candle
cierge^M

pew
banc^M

chalice
calice^M

SOCIETY

synagogue

synagogue^F

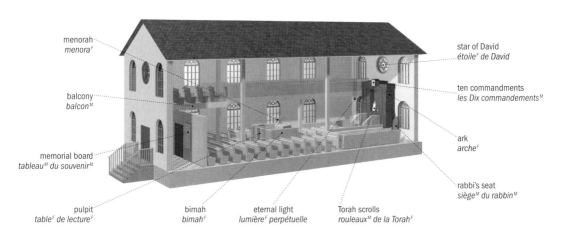

menorah
menora^F

star of David
étoile^F de David

ten commandments
les Dix commandements^M

balcony
balcon^M

ark
arche^F

memorial board
tableau^M du souvenir^M

rabbi's seat
siège^M du rabbin^M

pulpit
table^F de lecture^F

bimah
bimah^F

eternal light
lumière^F perpétuelle

Torah scrolls
rouleaux^M de la Torah^F

mosque

mosquée^F

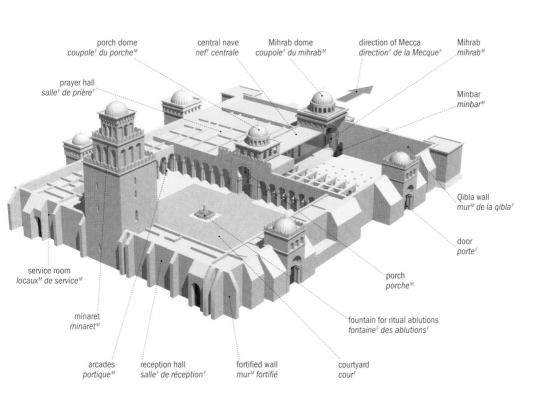

porch dome
coupole^F du porche^M

central nave
nef^F centrale

Mihrab dome
coupole^F du mihrab^M

direction of Mecca
direction^F de la Mecque^F

Mihrab
mihrab^M

prayer hall
salle^F de prière^F

Minbar
minbar^M

Qibla wall
mur^M de la qibla^F

door
porte^F

service room
locaux^M de service^M

porch
porche^M

minaret
minaret^M

fountain for ritual ablutions
fontaine^F des ablutions^F

arcades
portique^M

reception hall
salle^F de réception^F

fortified wall
mur^M fortifié

courtyard
cour^F

flags

drapeaux^M

Americas
Amériques^F

1 Canada
Canada^M

2 United States of America
États-Unis^M d'Amérique^F

3 Mexico
Mexique^M

4 Honduras
Honduras^M

5 Guatemala
Guatemala^M

6 Belize
Belize^M

7 El Salvador
El Salvador^M

8 Nicaragua
Nicaragua^M

9 Costa Rica
Costa Rica^M

10 Panama
Panama^M

11 Colombia
Colombie^F

12 Venezuela
Venezuela^M

13 Guyana
Guyana^F

14 Suriname
Suriname^M

15 Ecuador
Équateur^M

16 Peru
Pérou^M

17 Brazil
Brésil^M

18 Bolivia
Bolivie^F

19 Paraguay
Paraguay^M

20 Chile
Chili^M

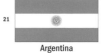

21 Argentina
Argentine^F

22 Uruguay
Uruguay^M

Caribbean Islands
Antilles^F

23 Bahamas
Bahamas^F

24 Cuba
Cuba^F

25 Jamaica
Jamaïque^F

26 Haiti
Haïti^M

SOCIETY

27 Saint Kitts and Nevis
Saint-Kitts-et-Nevis[M]

28 Antigua and Barbuda
Antigua-et-Barbuda[F]

29 Dominica
Dominique[F]

30 Saint Lucia
Sainte-Lucie[F]

31 Saint Vincent and the
Grenadines
Saint-Vincent[M]-et-les
Grenadines[F]

32 Dominican Republic
République[F] dominicaine

33 Barbados
Barbade[F]

34 Grenada
Grenade[F]

35 Trinidad and Tobago
Trinité-et-Tobago[F]

36 Andorra
Andorre[F]

37 Portugal
Portugal[M]

38 Spain
Espagne[F]

Europe
Europe[F]

39 United Kingdom of Great Britain and Northern
Ireland
Royaume-Uni[M] de Grande-Bretagne[F] et d'Irlande[F]
du Nord[M]

40 France
France[F]

41 Ireland
Irlande[F]

42 Belgium
Belgique[F]

43 Luxembourg
Luxembourg[M]

44 Netherlands
Pays-Bas[M]

SOCIETY

flags

45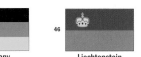
Germany
Allemagne[F]

46
Liechtenstein
Liechtenstein[M]

47
Switzerland
Suisse[F]

48
Austria
Autriche[F]

49
Italy
Italie[F]

50
San Marino
Saint-Marin[M]

51
Vatican City State
État[M] *de la cité*[F] *du Vatican*[M]

52
Monaco
Monaco[M]

53
Malta
Malte[F]

54
Cyprus
Chypre[F]

55
Greece
Grèce[F]

56
Albania
Albanie[F]

57
Macedonia
Ex-République[F] *yougoslave de Macédoine*[F]

58
Bulgaria
Bulgarie[F]

59
Yugoslavia
Yougoslavie[F]

60
Bosnia-Herzegovina
Bosnie-Herzégovine[F]

61
Croatia
Croatie[F]

62
Slovenia
Slovénie[F]

63
Hungary
Hongrie[F]

64
Romania
Roumanie[F]

65
Slovakia
Slovaquie[F]

66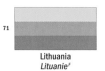
Czech Republic
République[F] *tchèque*

67
Poland
Pologne[F]

68
Denmark
Danemark[M]

69
Iceland
Islande[F]

70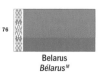
Norway
Norvège[F]

71
Lithuania
Lituanie[F]

72
Sweden
Suède[F]

73
Finland
Finlande[F]

74 **Estonia**
Estonie[F]

75 **Latvia**
Lettonie[F]

76 **Belarus**
Bélarus[M]

77 **Ukraine**
Ukraine[F]

78 **Moldova**
République[F] *de Moldova*[F]

79 **Russian Federation**
Fédération[F] *de Russie*[F]

Africa
Afrique[F]

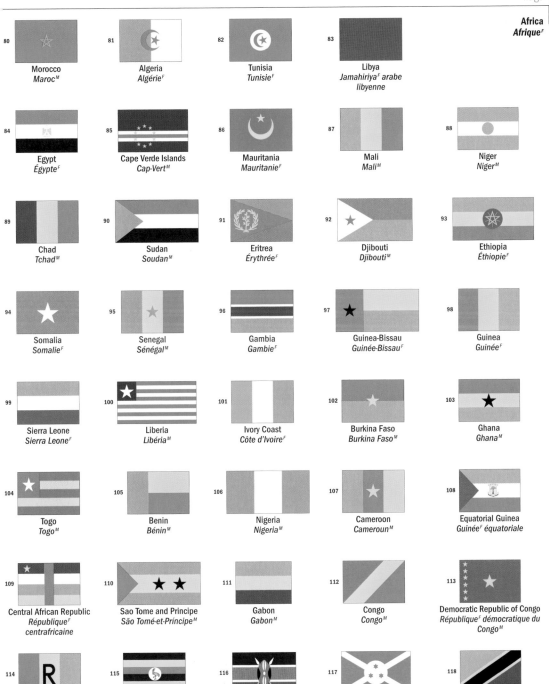

80 Morocco
Maroc[M]

81 Algeria
Algérie[F]

82 Tunisia
Tunisie[F]

83 Libya
Jamahiriya[F] *arabe libyenne*

84 Egypt
Égypte[F]

85 Cape Verde Islands
Cap-Vert[M]

86 Mauritania
Mauritanie[F]

87 Mali
Mali[M]

88 Niger
Niger[M]

89 Chad
Tchad[M]

90 Sudan
Soudan[M]

91 Eritrea
Érythrée[F]

92 Djibouti
Djibouti[M]

93 Ethiopia
Éthiopie[F]

94 Somalia
Somalie[F]

95 Senegal
Sénégal[M]

96 Gambia
Gambie[F]

97 Guinea-Bissau
Guinée-Bissau[F]

98 Guinea
Guinée[F]

99 Sierra Leone
Sierra Leone[F]

100 Liberia
Libéria[M]

101 Ivory Coast
Côte d'Ivoire[F]

102 Burkina Faso
Burkina Faso[M]

103 Ghana
Ghana[M]

104 Togo
Togo[M]

105 Benin
Bénin[M]

106 Nigeria
Nigeria[M]

107 Cameroon
Cameroun[M]

108 Equatorial Guinea
Guinée[F] *équatoriale*

109 Central African Republic
République[F] *centrafricaine*

110 Sao Tome and Principe
São Tomé-et-Príncipe[M]

111 Gabon
Gabon[M]

112 Congo
Congo[M]

113 Democratic Republic of Congo
République[F] *démocratique du Congo*[M]

114 Rwanda
Rwanda[M]

115 Uganda
Ouganda[M]

116 Kenya
Kenya[M]

117 Burundi
Burundi[M]

118 Tanzania
République[F]-*Unie de Tanzanie*[F]

SOCIETY

flags

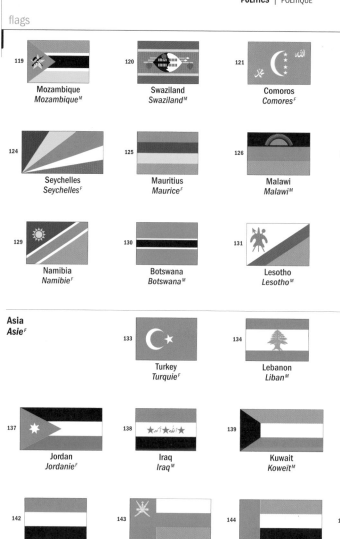
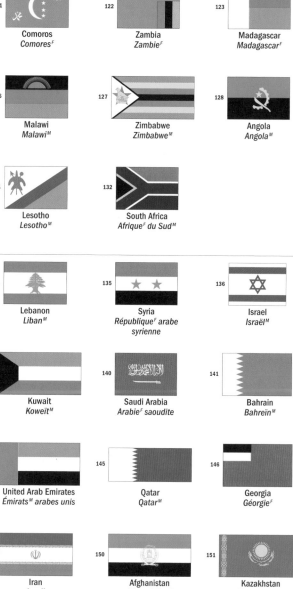
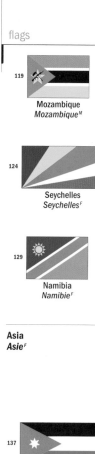
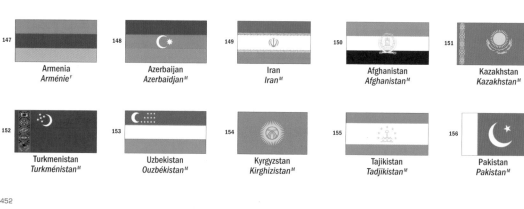

119 Mozambique
Mozambique^M

120 Swaziland
Swaziland^M

121 Comoros
Comores^F

122 Zambia
Zambie^F

123 Madagascar
Madagascar^F

124 Seychelles
Seychelles^F

125 Mauritius
Maurice^F

126 Malawi
Malawi^M

127 Zimbabwe
Zimbabwe^M

128 Angola
Angola^M

129 Namibia
Namibie^F

130 Botswana
Botswana^M

131 Lesotho
Lesotho^M

132 South Africa
Afrique^F *du Sud*^M

Asia
Asie^F

133 Turkey
Turquie^F

134 Lebanon
Liban^M

135 Syria
République^F *arabe syrienne*

136 Israel
Israël^M

137 Jordan
Jordanie^F

138 Iraq
Iraq^M

139 Kuwait
Koweït^M

140 Saudi Arabia
Arabie^F *saoudite*

141 Bahrain
Bahreïn^M

142 Yemen
Yémen^M

143 Oman
Oman^M

144 United Arab Emirates
Émirats^M *arabes unis*

145 Qatar
Qatar^M

146 Georgia
Géorgie^F

147 Armenia
Arménie^F

148 Azerbaijan
Azerbaïdjan^M

149 Iran
Iran^M

150 Afghanistan
Afghanistan^M

151 Kazakhstan
Kazakhstan^M

152 Turkmenistan
Turkménistan^M

153 Uzbekistan
Ouzbékistan^M

154 Kyrgyzstan
Kirghizistan^M

155 Tajikistan
Tadjikistan^M

156 Pakistan
Pakistan^M

SOCIETY

157 Maldives
Maldives^F

158 India
Inde^F

159 Sri Lanka
Sri Lanka^M

160 Nepal
Népal^M

161 China
Chine^F

2 Mongolia
Mongolie^F

163 Bhutan
Bhoutan^M

164 Bangladesh
Bangladesh^M

165 Myanmar
Myanmar^M

166 Laos
République^F démocratique populaire lao

167 Thailand
Thaïlande^F

168 Vietnam
Viet Nam^M

169 Cambodia
Cambodge^M

170 Brunei Darussalam
Brunéi Darussalam^M

171 Malaysia
Malaisie^F

172 Singapore
Singapour^F

173 Indonesia
Indonésie^F

174 Japan
Japon^M

175 Democratic People's Republic of Korea
République^F populaire démocratique de Corée^F

176 Republic of Korea
République^F de Corée^F

77 Philippines
Philippines^F

178 Palau
Palaos^M

179 Micronesia
États^M fédérés de Micronésie^F

Oceania and Polynesia
Océanie^F et Polynésie^F

180 Marshall Islands
Îles^F Marshall

181 Nauru
Nauru^F

182 Kiribati
Kiribati^F

183 Tuvalu
Tuvalu^M

184 Samoa
Samoa^F

185 Tonga
Tonga^F

186 Vanuatu
Vanuatu^M

187 Fiji
Fidji^F

188 Solomon Islands
Îles^F Salomon

189 Papua New Guinea
Papouasie-Nouvelle-Guinée^F

190 Australia
Australie^F

191 New Zealand
Nouvelle-Zélande^F

SOCIETY

fire prevention

prévention^F des incendies^M

fire-fighting material
matériel^M de lutte^F contre les
incendies^M

firefight▪
sapeur^M-pompie▪

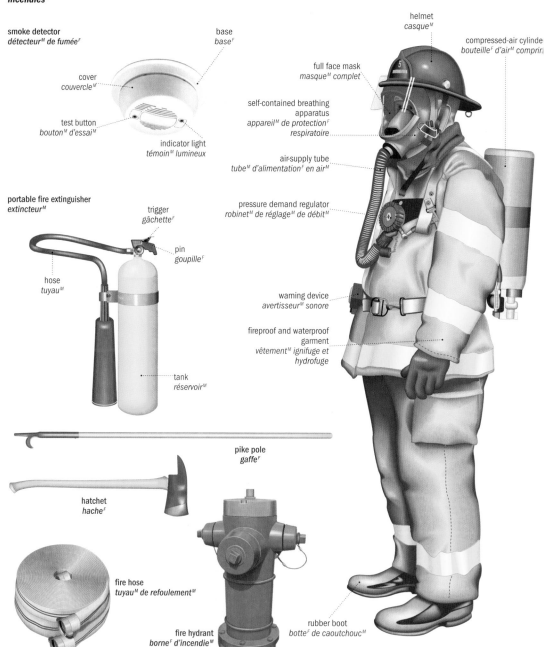

smoke detector
détecteur^M de fumée^F

base
base^F

cover
couvercle^M

test button
bouton^M d'essai^M

indicator light
témoin^M lumineux

helmet
casque^M

compressed-air cylinde▪
bouteille^F d'air^M comprim▪

full face mask
masque^M complet

self-contained breathing
apparatus
appareil^M de protection^F
respiratoire

air-supply tube
tube^M d'alimentation^F en air^M

portable fire extinguisher
extincteur^M

trigger
gâchette^F

pin
goupille^F

hose
tuyau^M

tank
réservoir^M

pressure demand regulator
robinet^M de réglage^M de débit^M

warning device
avertisseur^M sonore

fireproof and waterproof
garment
vêtement^M ignifuge et
hydrofuge

pike pole
gaffe^F

hatchet
hache^F

fire hose
tuyau^M de refoulement^M

fire hydrant
borne^F d'incendie^M

rubber boot
botte^F de caoutchouc^M

SOCIETY

fire engines
véhicules^M d'incendie^M

pumper
fourgon^M-pompe^F

control wheel
volant^M de manœuvre^F

control panel
panneau^M de commande^F

spotlight
projecteur^M orientable

water cannon
lance^F-canon^M

suction hose
tuyau^M d'aspiration^F

fitting
pièce^F de jonction^F

light bar
rampe^F de signalisation^F

siren
corne^F de feu^M

loudspeaker
haut-parleur^M

hydrant intake
orifice^M d'alimentation^F

rear step
marchepied^M arrière

storage compartment
coffre^M de rangement^M

hydrant intake
orifice^M d'alimentation^F

water pressure gauge
manomètre^M

grab handle
poignée^F montoir^M

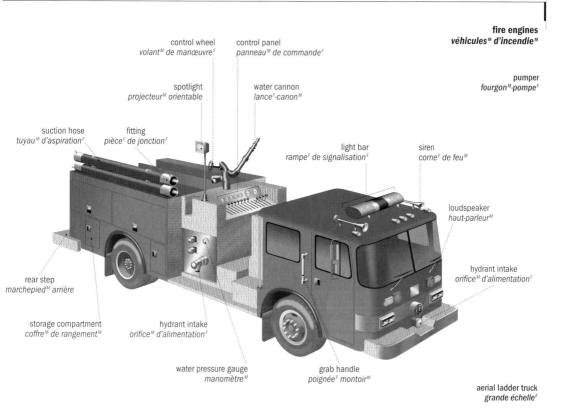

aerial ladder truck
grande échelle^F

telescopic boom
flèche^F télescopique

rotating light
gyrophare^M

ladder pipe nozzle
lance^F à eau^F

elevating cylinder
vérin^M de dressage^M

turntable mounting
tourelle^F

tower ladder
parc^M à échelles^F

top ladder
échelle^F de tête^F

spotlight
projecteur^M orientable

SOCIETY

storage compartment
coffre^M de rangement^M

jack
stabilisateur^M

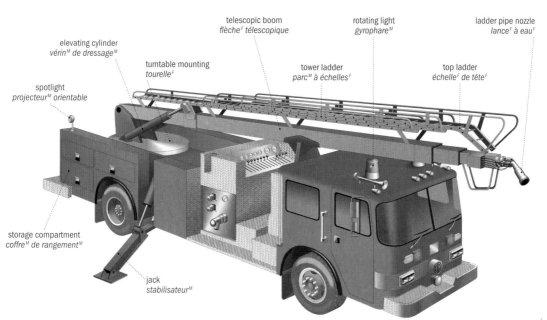

crime prevention

prévention^F de la criminalité^F

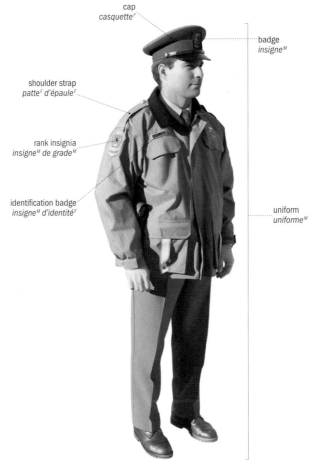

police officer
agent^M de police^F

cap
casquette^F

badge
insigne^M

shoulder strap
patte^F d'épaule^F

rank insignia
insigne^M de grade^M

identification badge
insigne^M d'identité^F

uniform
uniforme^M

duty belt
ceinturon^M de service^M

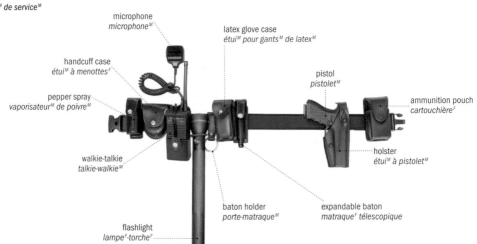

microphone
microphone^M

latex glove case
étui^M pour gants^M de latex^M

handcuff case
étui^M à menottes^F

pistol
pistolet^M

pepper spray
vaporisateur^M de poivre^M

ammunition pouch
cartouchière^F

walkie-talkie
talkie-walkie^M

holster
étui^M à pistolet^M

baton holder
porte-matraque^M

expandable baton
matraque^F télescopique

flashlight
lampe^F-torche^F

dashboard equipment
équipement^M *du tableau*^M *de bord*^M

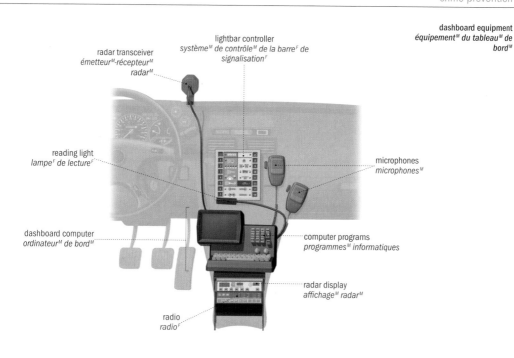

lightbar controller
système^M *de contrôle*^M *de la barre*^F *de signalisation*^F

radar transceiver
émetteur^M-*récepteur*^M *radar*^M

reading light
lampe^F *de lecture*^F

microphones
microphones^M

dashboard computer
ordinateur^M *de bord*^M

computer programs
programmes^M *informatiques*

radar display
affichage^M *radar*^M

radio
radio^F

police car
voiture^F *de police*^F

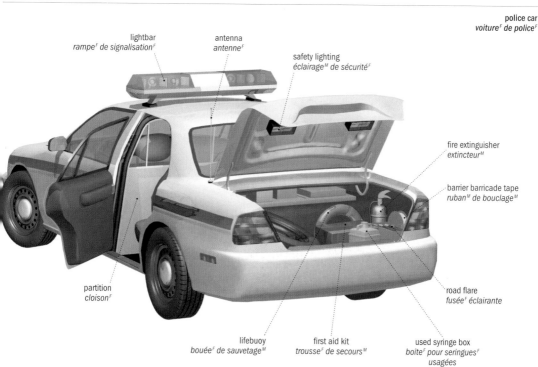

lightbar
rampe^F *de signalisation*^F

antenna
antenne^F

safety lighting
éclairage^M *de sécurité*^F

fire extinguisher
extincteur^M

barrier barricade tape
ruban^M *de bouclage*^M

partition
cloison^F

road flare
fusée^F *éclairante*

lifebuoy
bouée^F *de sauvetage*^M

first aid kit
trousse^F *de secours*^M

used syringe box
boîte^F *pour seringues*^F *usagées*

SOCIETY

ear protection

protection^F de l'ouïe^F

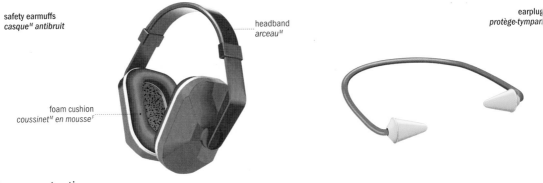

safety earmuffs
casque^M antibruit

headband
arceau^M

foam cushion
coussinet^M en mousse^F

earplug
protège-tympan

eye protection

protection^F des yeux^M

safety glasses
lunettes^F de sécurité^F

safety goggl
lunettes^F de protectio

head protection

protection^F de la tête^F

hard hat
casque^M de sécurité^F

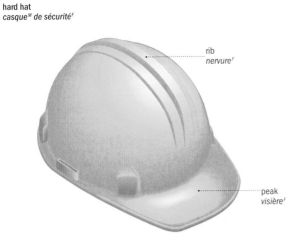

rib
nervure^F

peak
visière^F

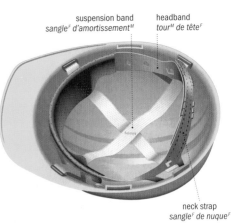

suspension band
sangle^F d'amortissement^M

headband
tour^M de tête^F

neck strap
sangle^F de nuque^F

respiratory system protection

protection^F des voies^F respiratoires

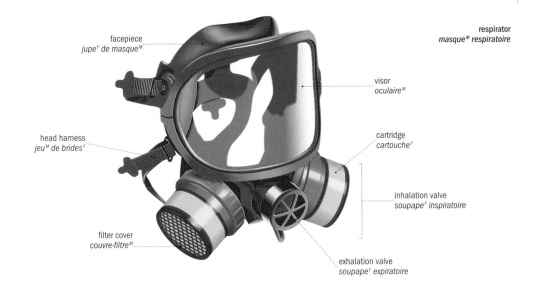

respirator
masque^M respiratoire

facepiece
jupe^F de masque^M

visor
oculaire^M

head harness
jeu^M de brides^F

cartridge
cartouche^F

inhalation valve
soupape^F inspiratoire

filter cover
couvre-filtre^M

exhalation valve
soupape^F expiratoire

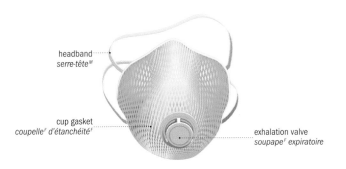

half-mask respirator
masque^M bucco-nasal

headband
serre-tête^M

cup gasket
coupelle^F d'étanchéité^F

exhalation valve
soupape^F expiratoire

foot protection

protection^F des pieds^M

SOCIETY

safety boot
brodequin^M de sécurité^F

toe guard
protège-orteils^M

reinforced toe
embout^M de protection^F

ambulance

ambulance^F

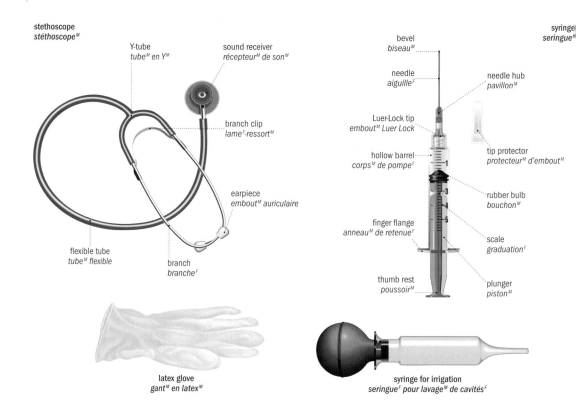

stethoscope
stéthoscope^M

Y-tube
tube^M *en Y*^M

sound receiver
récepteur^M *de son*^M

branch clip
lame^F*-ressort*^M

earpiece
embout^M *auriculaire*

flexible tube
tube^M *flexible*

branch
branche^F

syringe
seringue^F

bevel
biseau^M

needle
aiguille^F

needle hub
pavillon^M

Luer-Lock tip
embout^M *Luer Lock*

tip protector
protecteur^M *d'embout*^M

hollow barrel
corps^M *de pompe*^F

rubber bulb
bouchon^M

finger flange
anneau^M *de retenue*^F

scale
graduation^F

thumb rest
poussoir^M

plunger
piston^M

latex glove
gant^M *en latex*^M

syringe for irrigation
seringue^F *pour lavage*^M *de cavités*^F

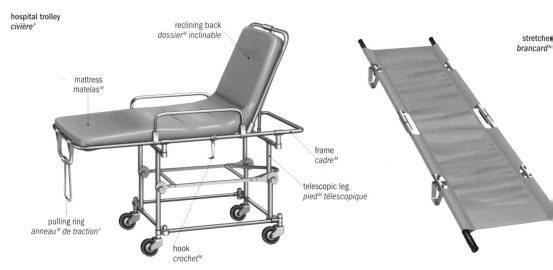

hospital trolley
civière^F

reclining back
dossier^M *inclinable*

mattress
matelas^M

frame
cadre^M

telescopic leg
pied^M *télescopique*

pulling ring
anneau^M *de traction*^F

hook
crochet^M

stretcher
brancard^M

first aid kit

trousse^F de secours^M

trousse*F* de secours*M*

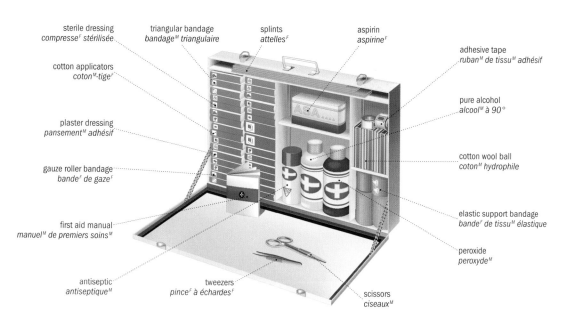

sterile dressing
compresse*F* stérilisée

cotton applicators
coton*M*-tige*F*

plaster dressing
pansement*M* adhésif

gauze roller bandage
bande*F* de gaze*F*

first aid manual
manuel*M* de premiers soins*M*

antiseptic
antiseptique*M*

triangular bandage
bandage*M* triangulaire

splints
attelles*F*

tweezers
pince*F* à échardes*F*

aspirin
aspirine*F*

scissors
ciseaux*M*

adhesive tape
ruban*M* de tissu*M* adhésif

pure alcohol
alcool*M* à 90°

cotton wool ball
coton*M* hydrophile

elastic support bandage
bande*F* de tissu*M* élastique

peroxide
peroxyde*M*

clinical thermometers

thermomètres*M* médicaux

digital thermometer
thermomètre*M* numérique

mercury thermometer
thermomètre*M* à mercure*M*

blood pressure monitor

tensiomètre*M*

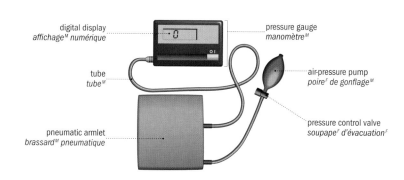

digital display
affichage*M* numérique

tube
tube*M*

pneumatic armlet
brassard*M* pneumatique

pressure gauge
manomètre*M*

air-pressure pump
poire*F* de gonflage*M*

pressure control valve
soupape*F* d'évacuation*F*

SOCIETY

hospital

hôpital^M

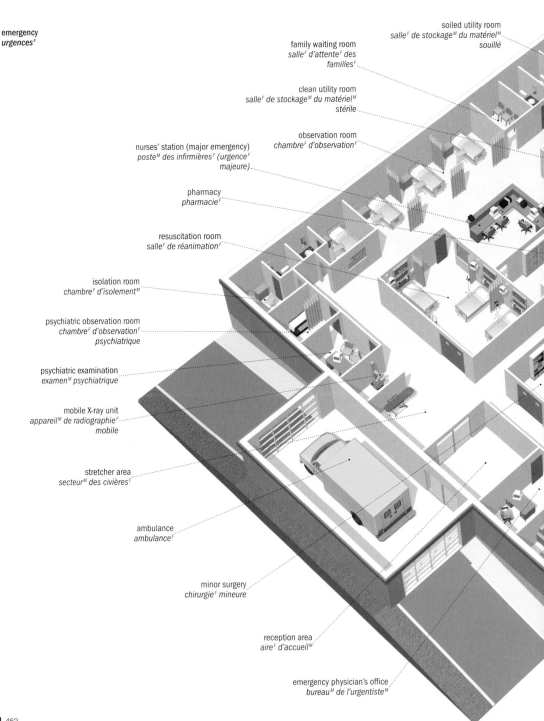

emergency
urgences^F

soiled utility room
salle^F de stockage^M du matériel^M
souillé

family waiting room
salle^F d'attente^F des
familles^F

clean utility room
salle^F de stockage^M du matériel^M
stérile

observation room
chambre^F d'observation^F

nurses' station (major emergency)
poste^M des infirmières^F (urgence^F
majeure)

pharmacy
pharmacie^F

resuscitation room
salle^F de réanimation^F

isolation room
chambre^F d'isolement^M

psychiatric observation room
chambre^F d'observation^F
psychiatrique

psychiatric examination
examen^M psychiatrique

mobile X-ray unit
appareil^M de radiographie^F
mobile

stretcher area
secteur^M des civières^F

ambulance
ambulance^F

minor surgery
chirurgie^F mineure

reception area
aire^F d'accueil^M

emergency physician's office
bureau^M de l'urgentiste^M

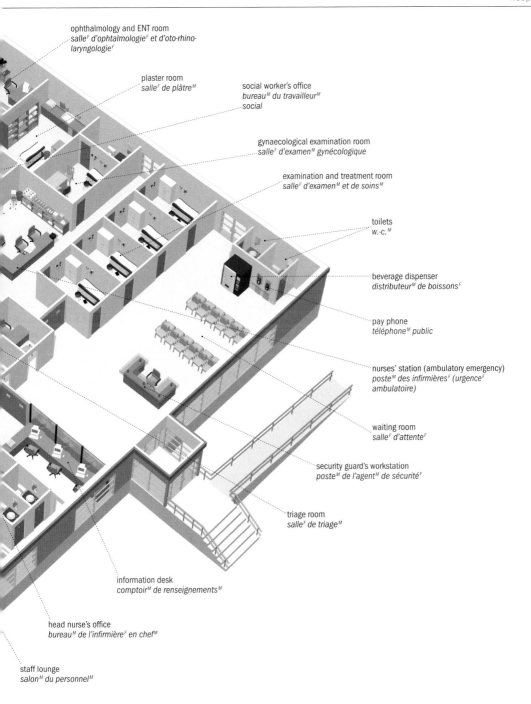

ophthalmology and ENT room
salle^F d'ophtalmologie^F et d'oto-rhino-
laryngologie^F

plaster room
salle^F de plâtre^M

social worker's office
bureau^M du travailleur^M
social

gynaecological examination room
salle^F d'examen^M gynécologique

examination and treatment room
salle^F d'examen^M et de soins^M

toilets
w.-c. ^M

beverage dispenser
distributeur^M de boissons^F

pay phone
téléphone^M public

nurses' station (ambulatory emergency)
poste^M des infirmières^F (urgence^F
ambulatoire)

waiting room
salle^F d'attente^F

security guard's workstation
poste^M de l'agent^M de sécurité^F

triage room
salle^F de triage^M

information desk
comptoir^M de renseignements^M

head nurse's office
bureau^M de l'infirmière^F en chef^M

staff lounge
salon^M du personnel^M

hospital

patient room
chambre^F d'hôpital^M

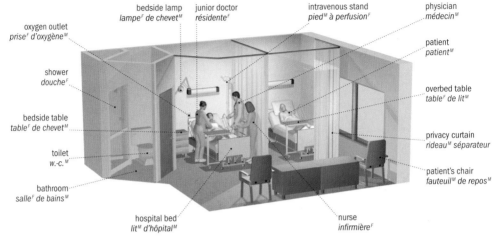

oxygen outlet
prise^F d'oxygène^M

bedside lamp
lampe^F de chevet^M

junior doctor
résidente^F

intravenous stand
pied^M à perfusion^F

physician
médecin^M

shower
douche^F

patient
patient^M

bedside table
table^F de chevet^M

overbed table
table^F de lit^M

toilet
w.-c.^M

privacy curtain
rideau^M séparateur

bathroom
salle^F de bains^M

patient's chair
fauteuil^M de repos^M

hospital bed
lit^M d'hôpital^M

nurse
infirmière^F

operating suite
bloc^M opératoire

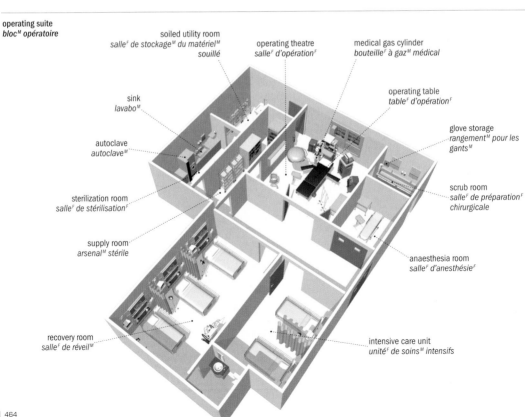

soiled utility room
salle^F de stockage^M du matériel^M souillé

operating theatre
salle^F d'opération^F

medical gas cylinder
bouteille^F à gaz^M médical

sink
lavabo^M

operating table
table^F d'opération^F

autoclave
autoclave^M

glove storage
rangement^M pour les gants^M

sterilization room
salle^F de stérilisation^F

scrub room
salle^F de préparation^F chirurgicale

supply room
arsenal^M stérile

anaesthesia room
salle^F d'anesthésie^F

recovery room
salle^F de réveil^M

intensive care unit
unité^F de soins^M intensifs

SOCIETY

ambulatory care unit
unité^F de soins^M
ambulatoires

specimen collection centre waiting room
salle^F d'attente^F du centre^M de prélèvements^M

surgeon's sink
lavabo^M du chirurgien^M

pathology laboratory
laboratoire^M de pathologie^F

sterilization room
salle^F de stérilisation^F

operating theatre
salle^F d'opération^F

undressing booth
cabine^F de déshabillage^M

secondary waiting room
salle^F d'attente^F
secondaire

observation room
chambre^F d'observation^F

toilets
w.-c.^{M}

social services
services^M sociaux

staff cloakroom
vestiaire^M du personnel^M

nurses' lounge
salle^F de repos^M des
infirmières^F

specimen collection room
salle^F de prélèvements^M

treatment room
salle^F de soins^M

main entrance
entrée^F principale

medical equipment storage room
salle^F de rangement^M du matériel^M
médical

reception area
aire^F d'accueil^M

audiometric examination room
salle^F d'examen^M audiométrique

medical records
archives^F médicales

main waiting room
salle^F d'attente^F principale

examination room
salle^F d'examen^M

pharmacy
pharmacie^F

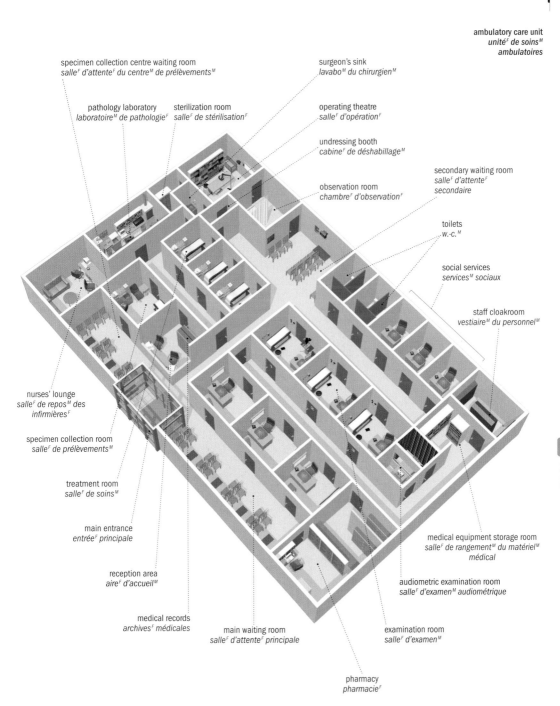

SOCIETY

walking aids

aides^F à la marche^F

forearm crutch
béquille^F d'avant-bras^M

underarm crutch
béquille^F commune

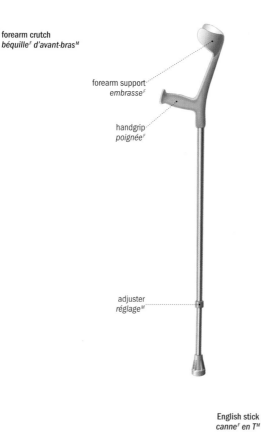

forearm support·
embrasse^F

underarm rest
crosse^F

handgrip·
poignée^F

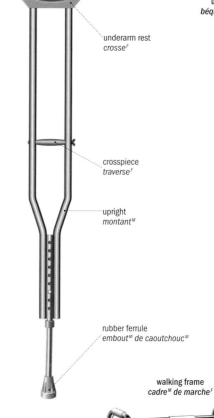

crosspiece
traverse^F

upright
montant^M

adjuster
réglage^M

rubber ferrule
embout^M de caoutchouc^M

English stick
canne^F en T^M

walking frame
cadre^M de marche^F

quadruped stick
canne^F avec quadripode^M

ortho-stick
canne^F avec poignée^F
orthopédique

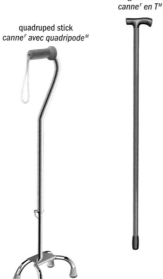

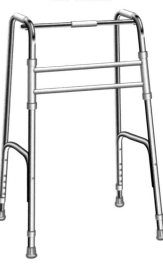

walking stick
canne^F en C^M

wheelchair

fauteuil^M roulant

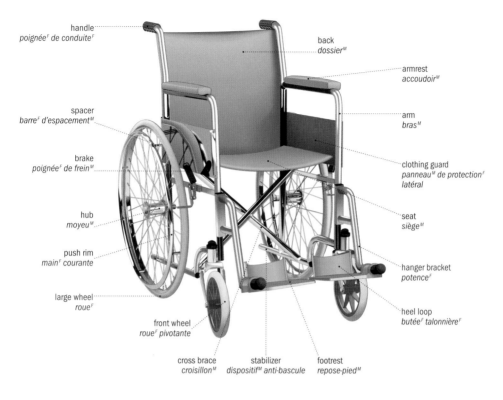

handle
poignée^F de conduite^F

back
dossier^M

armrest
accoudoir^M

spacer
barre^F d'espacement^M

arm
bras^M

brake
poignée^F de frein^M

clothing guard
panneau^M de protection^F
latéral

seat
siège^M

hub
moyeu^M

push rim
main^F courante

hanger bracket
potence^F

large wheel
roue^F

heel loop
butée^F talonnière^F

front wheel
roue^F pivotante

cross brace
croisillon^M

stabilizer
dispositif^M anti-bascule

footrest
repose-pied^M

pharmaceutical forms of medication

formes^F pharmaceutiques des médicaments^M

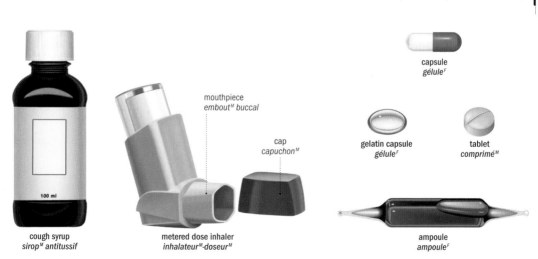

capsule
gélule^F

mouthpiece
embout^M buccal

cap
capuchon^M

gelatin capsule
gélule^F

tablet
comprimé^M

100 ml

cough syrup
sirop^M antitussif

metered dose inhaler
inhalateur^M-doseur^M

ampoule
ampoule^F

SOCIETY

dice and dominoes

dés^M et dominos^M

ordinary die
dé^M régulier

poker die
dé^M à poker^M

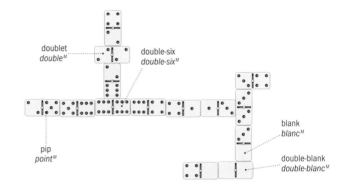

doublet
double^M

double-six
double-six^M

pip
point^M

blank
blanc^M

double-blank
double-blanc^M

card games

cartes^F

symbols
symboles^M

heart
cœur^M

diamond
carreau^M

club
trèfle^M

spade
pique^M

Joker
Joker^M

Ace
As^M

King
Roi^M

Queen
Dame^F

Jack
Valet^M

standard poker hands
combinaisons^F au poker^M

high card
carte^F isolée

one pair
paire^F

two pairs
double paire^F

three-of-a-kind
brelan^M

straight
séquence^F

flush
couleur^F

full house
main^F pleine

four-of-a-kind
carré^M

straight flush
quinte^F

royal flush
quinte^F royale

SPORTS AND GAMES

468

board game
jeux^M de plateau^M

backgammon
jacquet^M

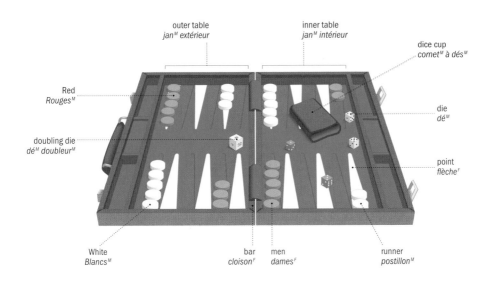

outer table
jan^M extérieur

inner table
jan^M intérieur

dice cup
cornet^M à dés^M

Red
Rouges^M

die
dé^M

doubling die
dé^M doubleur^M

point
flèche^F

White
Blancs^M

bar
cloison^F

men
dames^F

runner
postillon^M

Monopoly®
Monopoly®^M

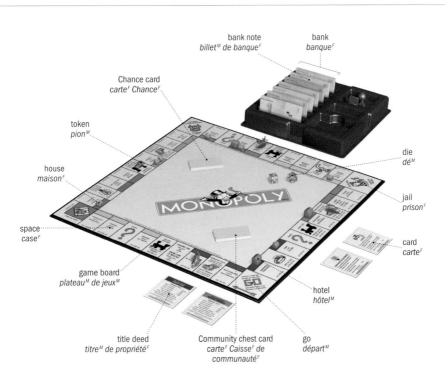

bank note
billet^M de banque^F

bank
banque^F

Chance card
carte^F Chance^F

token
pion^M

die
dé^M

house
maison^F

jail
prison^F

space
case^F

card
carte^F

game board
plateau^M de jeux^M

hotel
hôtel^M

title deed
titre^M de propriété^F

Community chest card
carte^F Caisse^F de
communauté^F

go
départ^M

SPORTS AND GAMES

469

board game

chess
*échecs*M

chessboard
*échiquier*M

Queen's side
*aile*F *Dame*F

King's side
*aile*F *Roi*M

me
pièce

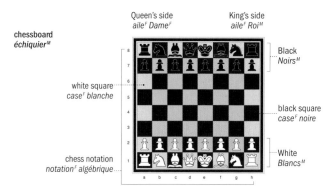

Black
*Noirs*M

white square
*case*F *blanche*

black square
*case*F *noire*

chess notation
*notation*F *algébrique*

White
*Blancs*M

Pawn
*Pion*M

Castle
*Tour*F

Bishop
*Fou*M

Knight
*Cavalier*M

types of move
*types*M *de déplacements*M

diagonal move
*déplacement*M *diagonal*

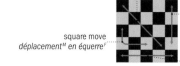

vertical move
*déplacement*M *vertical*

square move
*déplacement*M *en équerre*F

horizontal move
*déplacement*M *horizontal*

King
*Roi*M

Queen
*Dame*F

go
*go*M

major motion
principaux mouvements

board
*terrain*M

handicap spot
*point*M *de handicap*M

centre
*centre*M

black stone
*pierre*F *noire*

white stone
*pierre*F *blanche*

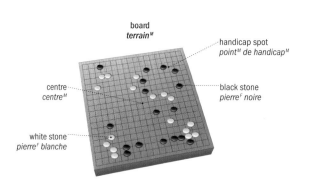

connection
*connexion*F

contact
*contact*M

capture
*capture*F

draughts
*jeu*M *de dames*F

draught
*Dame*F

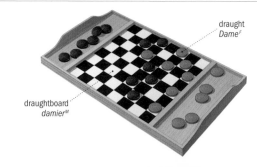

draughtboard
*damier*M

video entertainment system
système^M de jeux^M vidéo

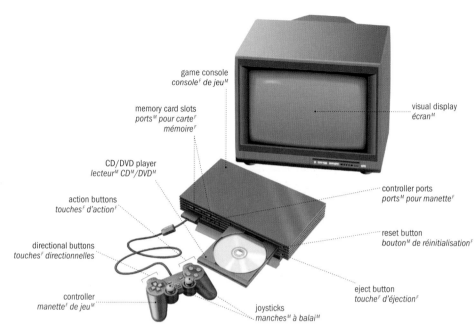

game console
console^F de jeu^M

memory card slots
ports^M pour carte^F
mémoire^F

visual display
écran^M

CD/DVD player
lecteur^M CD^M/DVD^M

action buttons
touches^F d'action^F

controller ports
ports^M pour manette^F

directional buttons
touches^F directionnelles

reset button
bouton^M de réinitialisation^F

controller
manette^F de jeu^M

joysticks
manches^M à balai^M

eject button
touche^F d'éjection^F

game of darts
jeu^M de fléchettes^F

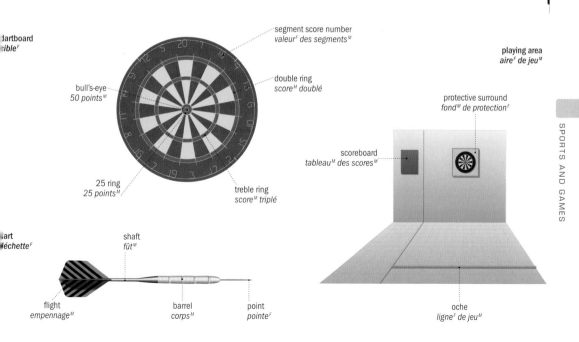

dartboard
cible^F

segment score number
valeur^F des segments^M

playing area
aire^F de jeu^M

bull's-eye
50 points^M

double ring
score^M doublé

protective surround
fond^M de protection^F

scoreboard
tableau^M des scores^M

25 ring
25 points^M

treble ring
score^M triplé

dart
fléchette^F

shaft
fût^M

flight
empennage^M

barrel
corps^M

point
pointe^F

oche
ligne^F de jeu^M

SPORTS AND GAMES

arena

stade^M

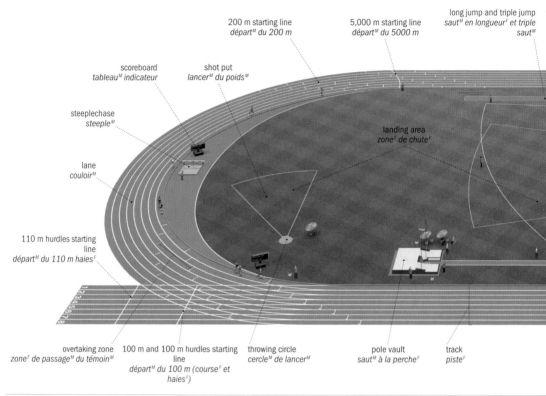

200 m starting line
départ^M du 200 m

5,000 m starting line
départ^M du 5000 m

long jump and triple jump
saut^M en longueur^F et triple
saut^M

scoreboard
tableau^M indicateur

shot put
lancer^M du poids^M

steeplechase
steeple^M

landing area
zone^F de chute^F

lane
couloir^M

110 m hurdles starting
line
départ^M du 110 m haies^F

overtaking zone
zone^F de passage^M du témoin^M

100 m and 100 m hurdles starting
line
départ^M du 100 m (course^F et
haies^F)

throwing circle
cercle^M de lancer^M

pole vault
saut^M à la perche^F

track
piste^F

equipment
équipement^M

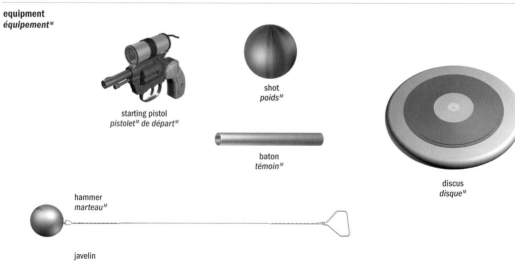

starting pistol
pistolet^M de départ^M

shot
poids^M

baton
témoin^M

discus
disque^M

hammer
marteau^M

javelin
javelot^M

SPORTS AND GAMES

472

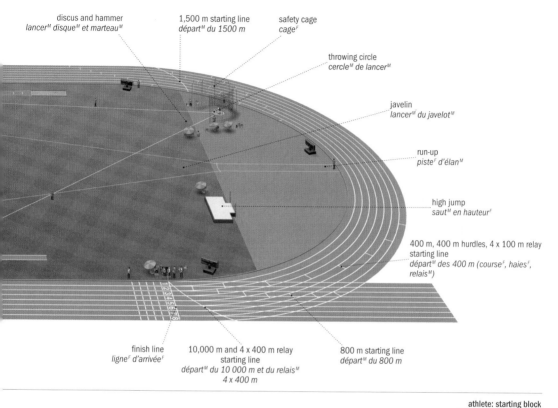

discus and hammer
lancer^M disque^M et marteau^M

1,500 m starting line
départ^M du 1500 m

safety cage
cage^F

throwing circle
cercle^M de lancer^M

javelin
lancer^M du javelot^M

run-up
piste^F d'élan^M

high jump
saut^M en hauteur^F

400 m, 400 m hurdles, 4 x 100 m relay
starting line
*départ^M des 400 m (course^F, haies^F,
relais^M)*

finish line
ligne^F d'arrivée^F

10,000 m and 4 x 400 m relay
starting line
*départ^M du 10 000 m et du relais^M
4 x 400 m*

800 m starting line
départ^M du 800 m

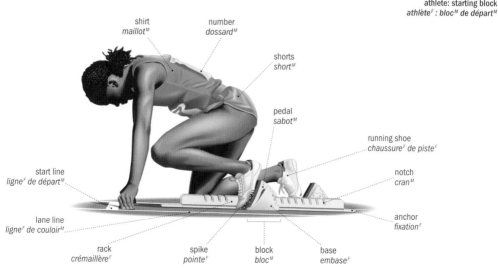

athlete: starting block
athlète^F : bloc^M de départ^M

shirt
maillot^M

number
dossard^M

shorts
short^M

pedal
sabot^M

running shoe
chaussure^F de piste^F

notch
cran^M

start line
ligne^F de départ^M

anchor
fixation^F

lane line
ligne^F de couloir^M

rack
crémaillère^F

spike
pointe^F

block
bloc^M

base
embase^F

baseball

baseball^M

player positions
position^F des joueurs^M

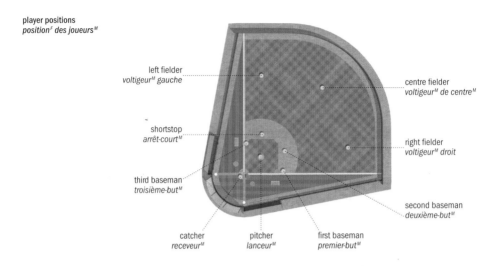

left fielder
voltigeur^M gauche

centre fielder
voltigeur^M de centre^M

shortstop
arrêt-court^M

right fielder
voltigeur^M droit

third baseman
troisième-but^M

second baseman
deuxième-but^M

catcher
receveur^M

pitcher
lanceur^M

first baseman
premier-but^M

field
terrain^M

third base
troisième but^M

coach's box
*rectangle^M des
instructeurs^M*

foul line
ligne^F de jeu^M

dugout
abri^M des joueurs^M

backstop
écran^M de protection^F

on-deck circle
cercle^M d'attente^F

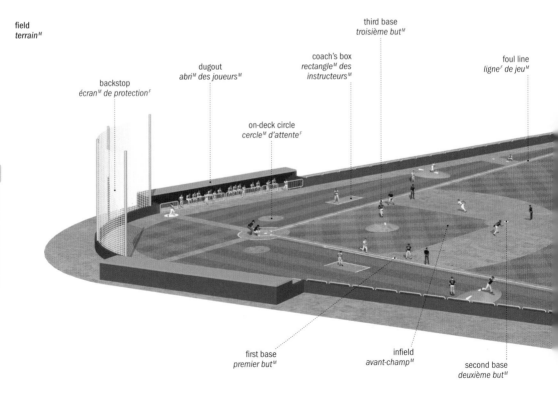

first base
premier but^M

infield
avant-champ^M

second base
deuxième but^M

pitch
lancer^M

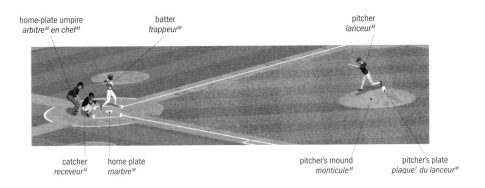

home-plate umpire
arbitre^M *en chef*^M

batter
frappeur^M

pitcher
lanceur^M

catcher
receveur^M

home plate
marbre^M

pitcher's mound
monticule^M

pitcher's plate
plaque^F *du lanceur*^M

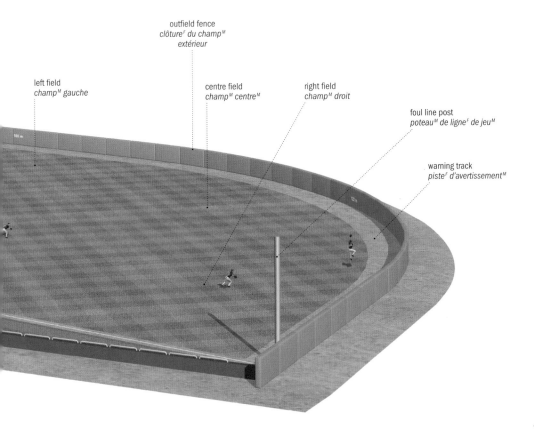

outfield fence
clôture^F *du champ*^M
extérieur

left field
champ^M *gauche*

centre field
champ^M *centre*^M

right field
champ^M *droit*

foul line post
poteau^M *de ligne*^F *de jeu*^M

warning track
piste^F *d'avertissement*^M

baseball

baseball
balle^F de baseball^M

bat
bâton^M

batter's helmet
casque^M de frappeur^M

batter
frappeur^M

catcher
receveur^M

throat protector
protège-gorge^M

mask
masque^M

frame
grille^F

chest protector
plastron^M

catcher's glove
gant^M de receveur^M

team shirt
maillot^M d'équipe^F

undershirt
maillot^M de corps^M

batting glove
gant^M de frappeur^M

trousers
pantalon^M

stirrup sock
chaussette^F-étrier^M

spiked shoe
chaussure^F à crampons^M

toe guard
protège-orteils^M

leg guard
jambière^F

knee pad
genouillère^F

ankle guard
protège-cheville^M

baseball

knob
pommeau^M

handle
manche^M

crest
écusson^M

hitting area
surface^F de frappe^F

bat
bâton^M

fielder's glove
gant^M

web
panier^M

ross section of a baseball
oupe^F de la balle^F

cork ball
balle^F de liège^M

yarn ball
balle^F de fil^M

strap
patte^F

thumb
pouce^M

finger
doigt^M

palm
paume^F

heel
talon^M

lace
lacet^M

cover
enveloppe^F

stitches
couture^F

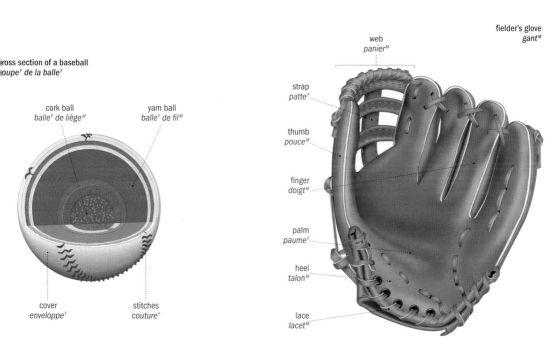

softball

softball^M

softball glove
gant^M de softball^M

softball
balle^F de softball^M

softball bat
bâton^M de softball^M

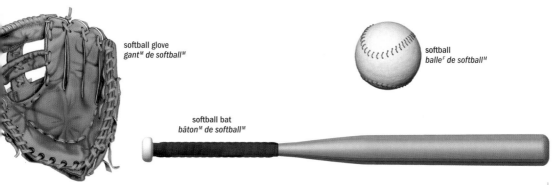

SPORTS AND GAMES

477

cricket

cricket^M

cricket player: batsman
joueur^M de cricket^M : batteur^M

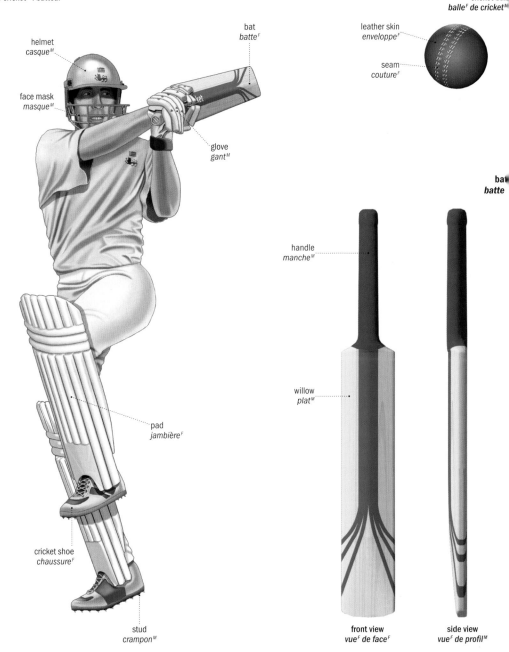

cricket ball
balle^F de cricket^M

bat
batte^F

helmet
casque^M

face mask
masque^M

glove
gant^M

leather skin
enveloppe^F

seam
couture^F

bat
batte

handle
manche^M

willow
plat^M

pad
jambière^F

cricket shoe
chaussure^F

stud
crampon^M

front view
vue^F de face^F

side view
vue^F de profil^M

field
*terrain*M

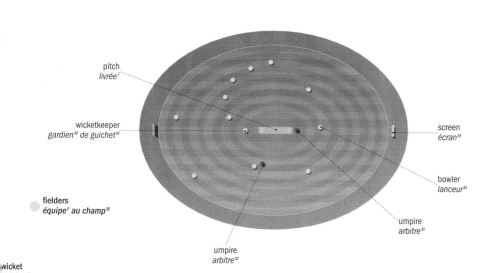

pitch
*livrée*F

wicketkeeper
*gardien*M *de guichet*M

screen
*écran*M

bowler
*lanceur*M

fielders
*équipe*F *au champ*M

umpire
*arbitre*M

umpire
*arbitre*M

wicket
*guichet*M

bail
*barreau*M

pitch
*livrée*F

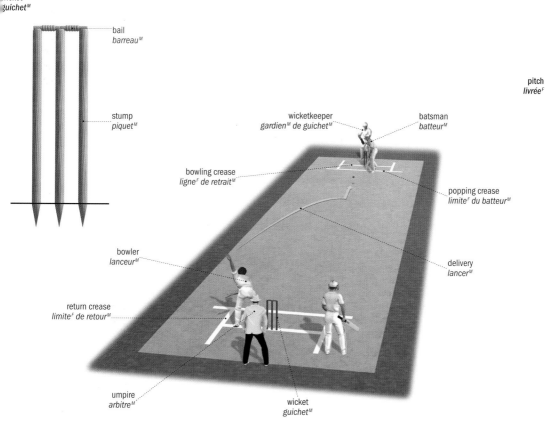

stump
*piquet*M

wicketkeeper
*gardien*M *de guichet*M

batsman
*batteur*M

bowling crease
*ligne*F *de retrait*M

popping crease
*limite*F *du batteur*M

bowler
*lanceur*M

delivery
*lancer*M

return crease
*limite*F *de retour*M

umpire
*arbitre*M

wicket
*guichet*M

SPORTS AND GAMES

association football

football^M

footballer
footballeur^M

team shirt
maillot^M d'équipe^F

goalkeeper's gloves
gants^M de gardien^M de but^M

shorts
short^M

screw-in studs
*crampons^M
interchangeables*

football boot
chaussure^F de football^M

shin guard
protège-tibia^M

sock
chaussette^F

football
ballon^M de football^M

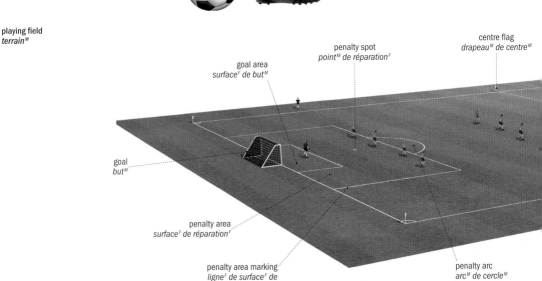

playing field
terrain^M

penalty spot
point^M de réparation^F

centre flag
drapeau^M de centre^M

goal area
surface^F de but^M

goal
but^M

penalty area
surface^F de réparation^F

penalty area marking
*ligne^F de surface^F de
réparation^F*

penalty arc
arc^M de cercle^M

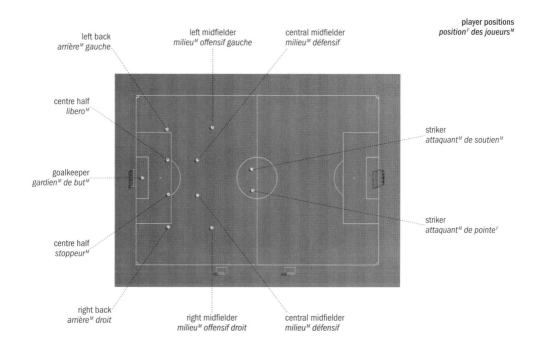

player positions
position^F des joueurs^M

left back
arrière^M gauche

left midfielder
milieu^M offensif gauche

central midfielder
milieu^M défensif

centre half
libero^M

striker
attaquant^M de soutien^M

goalkeeper
gardien^M de but^M

striker
attaquant^M de pointe^F

centre half
stoppeur^M

right back
arrière^M droit

right midfielder
milieu^M offensif droit

central midfielder
milieu^M défensif

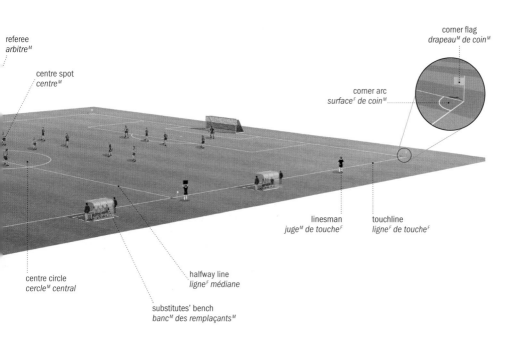

referee
arbitre^M

corner flag
drapeau^M de coin^M

centre spot
centre^M

corner arc
surface^F de coin^M

linesman
juge^M de touche^F

touchline
ligne^F de touche^F

centre circle
cercle^M central

halfway line
ligne^F médiane

substitutes' bench
banc^M des remplaçants^M

SPORTS AND GAMES

rugby

rugby[M]

player positions
position[F] des joueurs[M]

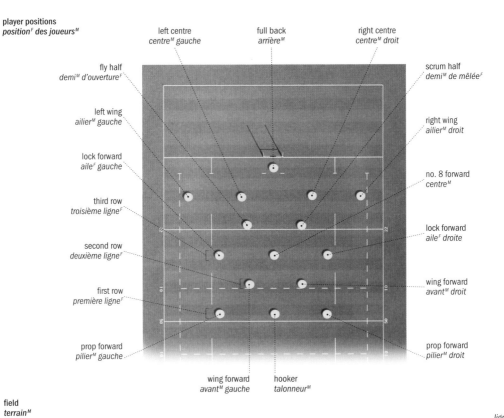

left centre
centre[M] gauche

full back
arrière[M]

right centre
centre[M] droit

fly half
demi[M] d'ouverture[F]

scrum half
demi[M] de mêlée[F]

left wing
ailier[M] gauche

right wing
ailier[M] droit

lock forward
aile[F] gauche

no. 8 forward
centre[M]

third row
troisième ligne[F]

lock forward
aile[F] droite

second row
deuxième ligne[F]

wing forward
avant[M] droit

first row
première ligne[F]

prop forward
pilier[M] gauche

prop forward
pilier[M] droit

wing forward
avant[M] gauche

hooker
talonneur[M]

field
terrain[M]

10 m line
ligne[F] des 10 m

flag
drapeau[M]

goal line
ligne[F] de but[M]

goal
but[M]

22 m line
ligne[F] des 22 m

dead ball line
ligne[F] de ballon[M] mort

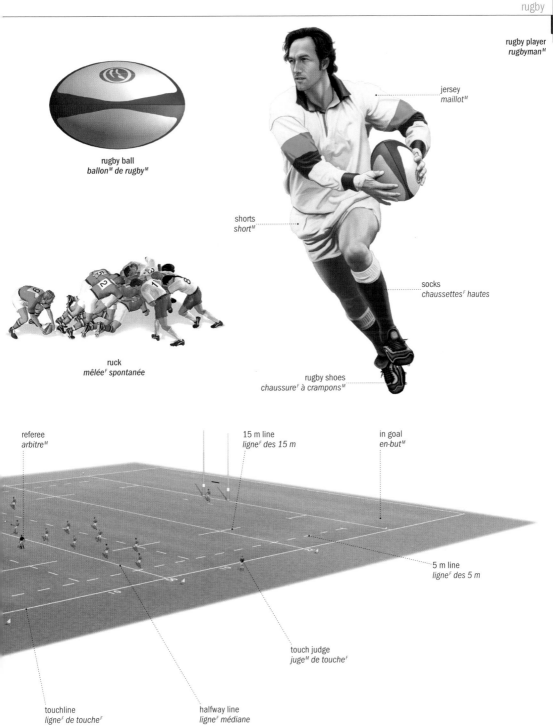

rugby player
rugbyman^M

jersey
maillot^M

rugby ball
ballon^M de rugby^M

shorts
short^M

socks
chaussettes^F hautes

ruck
mêlée^F spontanée

rugby shoes
chaussure^F à crampons^M

referee
arbitre^M

15 m line
ligne^F des 15 m

in goal
en-but^M

5 m line
ligne^F des 5 m

touch judge
juge^M de touche^F

touchline
ligne^F de touche^F

halfway line
ligne^F médiane

SPORTS AND GAMES

483

American football

football^M américain

scrimmage: defence
mêlée^F : défense^F

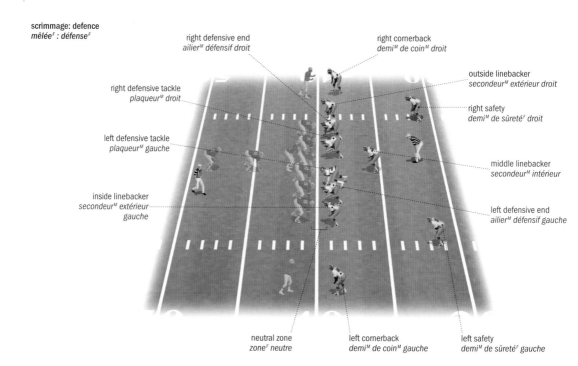

right defensive end
ailier^M défensif droit

right cornerback
demi^M de coin^M droit

outside linebacker
secondeur^M extérieur droit

right defensive tackle
plaqueur^M droit

right safety
demi^M de sûreté^F droit

left defensive tackle
plaqueur^M gauche

middle linebacker
secondeur^M intérieur

inside linebacker
*secondeur^M extérieur
gauche*

left defensive end
ailier^M défensif gauche

neutral zone
zone^F neutre

left cornerback
demi^M de coin^M gauche

left safety
demi^M de sûreté^F gauche

playing field for American football
terrain^M de football^M américain

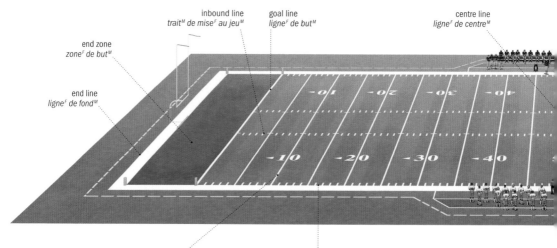

inbound line
trait^M de mise^F au jeu^M

goal line
ligne^F de but^M

centre line
ligne^F de centre^M

end zone
zone^F de but^M

end line
ligne^F de fond^M

yard line
ligne^F des verges^F

sideline
ligne^F de touche^F

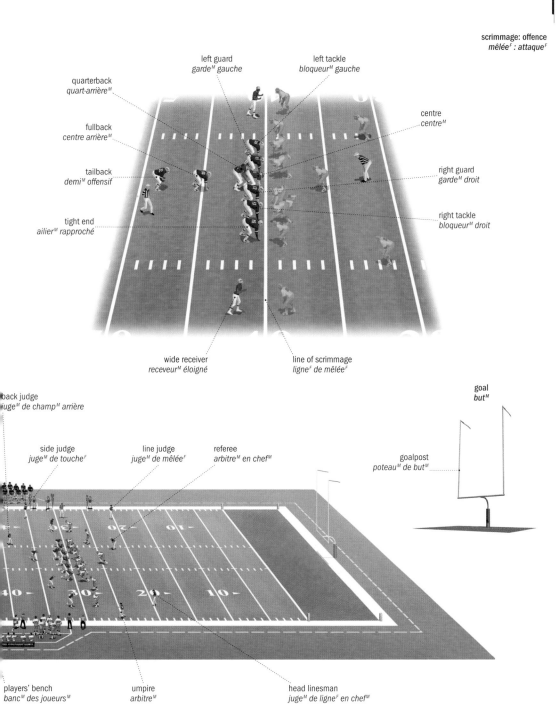

scrimmage: offence
mêlée^F : attaque^F

quarterback
quart-arrière^M

left guard
garde^M gauche

left tackle
bloqueur^M gauche

centre
centre^M

fullback
centre arrière^M

right guard
garde^M droit

tailback
demi^M offensif

tight end
ailier^M rapproché

right tackle
bloqueur^M droit

wide receiver
receveur^M éloigné

line of scrimmage
ligne^F de mêlée^F

back judge
juge^M de champ^M arrière

goal
but^M

side judge
juge^M de touche^F

line judge
juge^M de mêlée^F

referee
arbitre^M en chef^M

goalpost
poteau^M de but^M

players' bench
banc^M des joueurs^M

umpire
arbitre^M

head linesman
juge^M de ligne^F en chef^M

American football

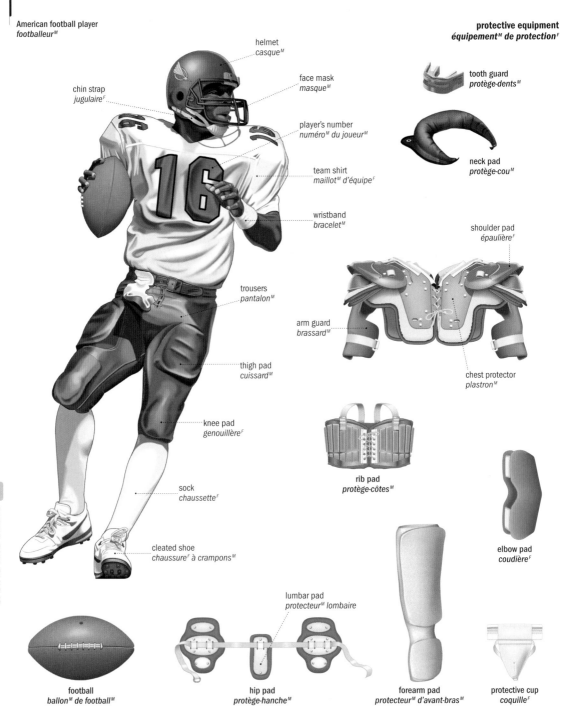

American football player
*footballeur*M

protective equipment
*équipement*M *de protection*F

helmet
*casque*M

face mask
*masque*M

chin strap
*jugulaire*F

player's number
*numéro*M *du joueur*M

team shirt
*maillot*M *d'équipe*F

wristband
*bracelet*M

tooth guard
*protège-dents*M

neck pad
*protège-cou*M

shoulder pad
*épaulière*F

trousers
*pantalon*M

arm guard
*brassard*M

chest protector
*plastron*M

thigh pad
*cuissard*M

knee pad
*genouillère*F

rib pad
*protège-côtes*M

sock
*chaussette*F

cleated shoe
*chaussure*F *à crampons*M

elbow pad
*coudière*F

lumbar pad
*protecteur*M *lombaire*

football
*ballon*M *de football*M

hip pad
*protège-hanche*M

forearm pad
*protecteur*M *d'avant-bras*M

protective cup
*coquille*F

volleyball
volleyball^M

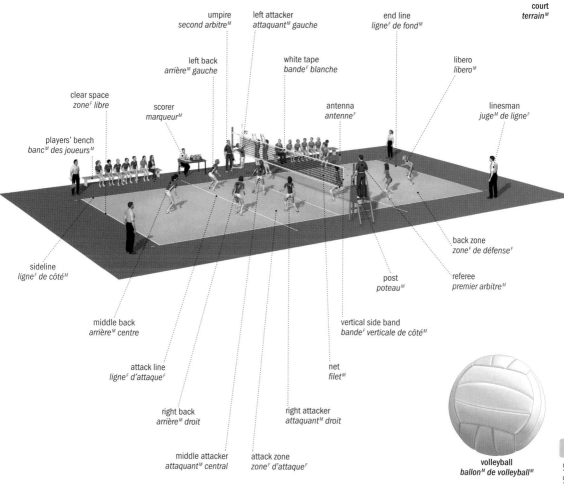

court
terrain^M

umpire
second arbitre^M

left attacker
attaquant^M gauche

end line
ligne^F de fond^M

libero
libero^M

left back
arrière^M gauche

white tape
bande^F blanche

antenna
antenne^F

linesman
juge^M de ligne^F

clear space
zone^F libre

scorer
marqueur^M

players' bench
banc^M des joueurs^M

sideline
ligne^F de côté^M

back zone
zone^F de défense^F

post
poteau^M

referee
premier arbitre^M

middle back
arrière^M centre

vertical side band
bande^F verticale de côté^M

attack line
ligne^F d'attaque^F

net
filet^M

right back
arrière^M droit

right attacker
attaquant^M droit

middle attacker
attaquant^M central

attack zone
zone^F d'attaque^F

volleyball
ballon^M de volleyball^M

techniques
techniques^F

tip
touche^F

bump
manchette^F

serve
service^M

basketball

basketball^M

basketball player
joueur^M de basketball^M

shirt
maillot^M

basketball
ballon^M de basket^M

player's number
numéro^M du joueur^M

shorts
short^M

shoe
chaussure^F

scorer
marqueur^M

court
terrain^M

clock operator
chronométreur^M des trente secondes^F

timekeeper
chronométreur^M

referee
aide^M-arbitre^M

referee
arbitre^M

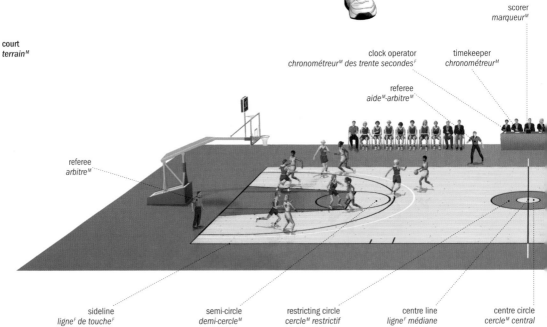

sideline
ligne^F de touche^F

semi-circle
demi-cercle^M

restricting circle
cercle^M restrictif

centre line
ligne^F médiane

centre circle
cercle^M central

SPORTS AND GAMES

player positions
position^F des joueurs^M

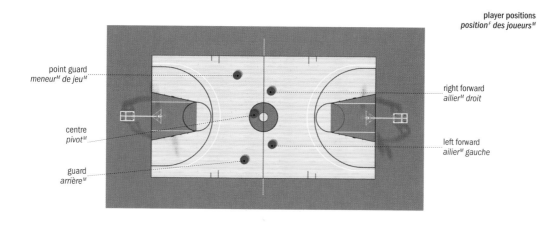

point guard
meneur^M de jeu^M

right forward
ailier^M droit

centre
pivot^M

left forward
ailier^M gauche

guard
arrière^M

backstop
but^M

backboard
panneau^M

rim
anneau^M

net
filet^M

coach
ntraineur^M

backboard support
support^M de panneau^M

basket
panier^M

ssistant coach
ntraineur^M adjoint

trainer
soigneur^M

padded upright
montant^M rembourré

padded base
socle^M rembourré

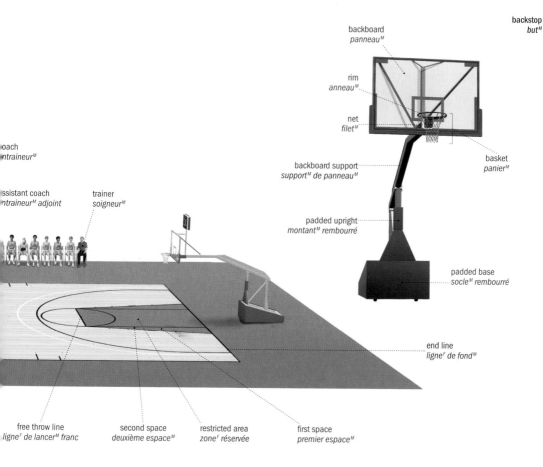

end line
ligne^F de fond^M

free throw line
ligne^F de lancer^M franc

second space
deuxième espace^M

restricted area
zone^F réservée

first space
premier espace^M

SPORTS AND GAMES

tennis
tennis^M

court
court^M

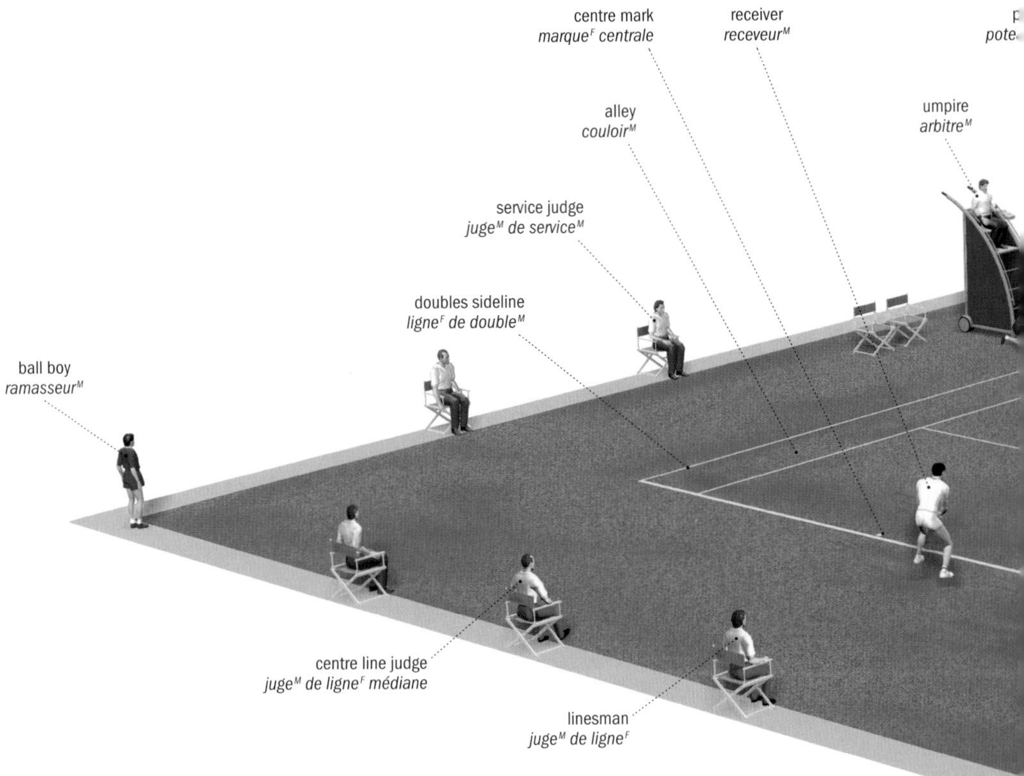

centre mark
marque^F centrale

receiver
receveur^M

p
pote

alley
couloir^M

umpire
arbitre^M

service judge
juge^M de service^M

doubles sideline
ligne^F de double^M

ball boy
ramasseur^M

centre line judge
juge^M de ligne^F médiane

linesman
juge^M de ligne^F

strokes
coups^M

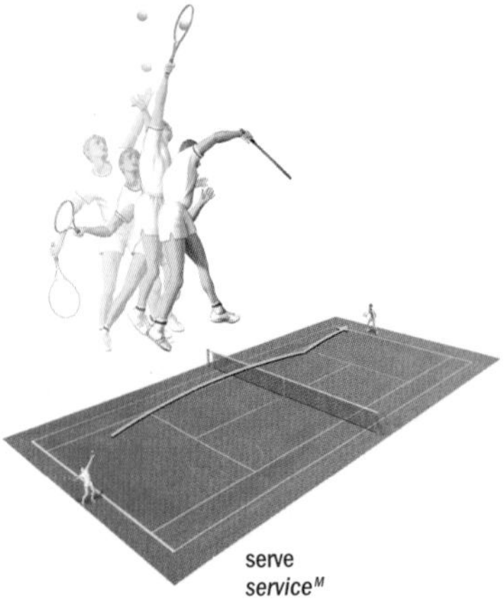

serve
service^M

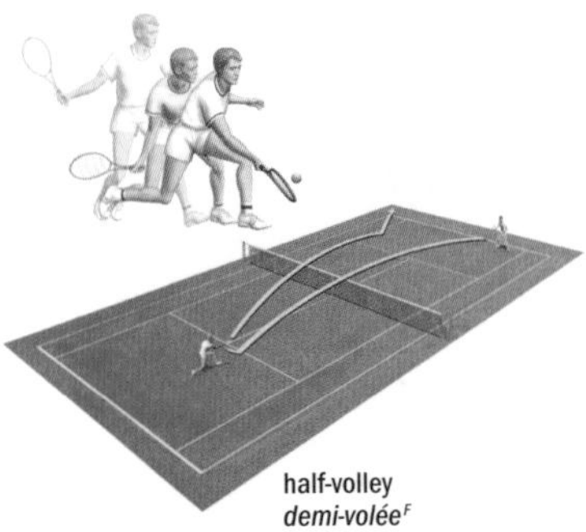

half-volley
demi-volée^F

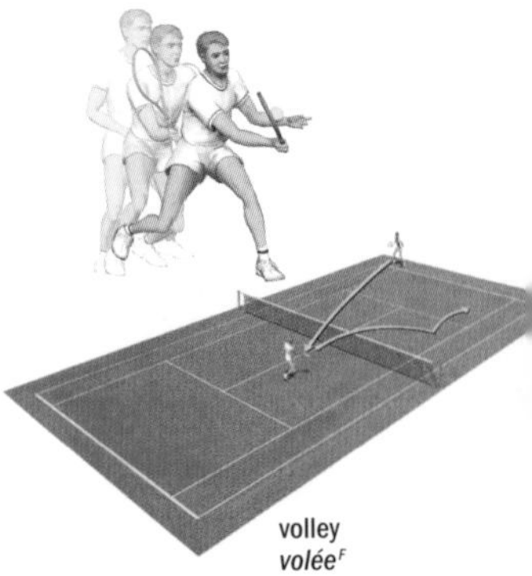

volley
volée^F

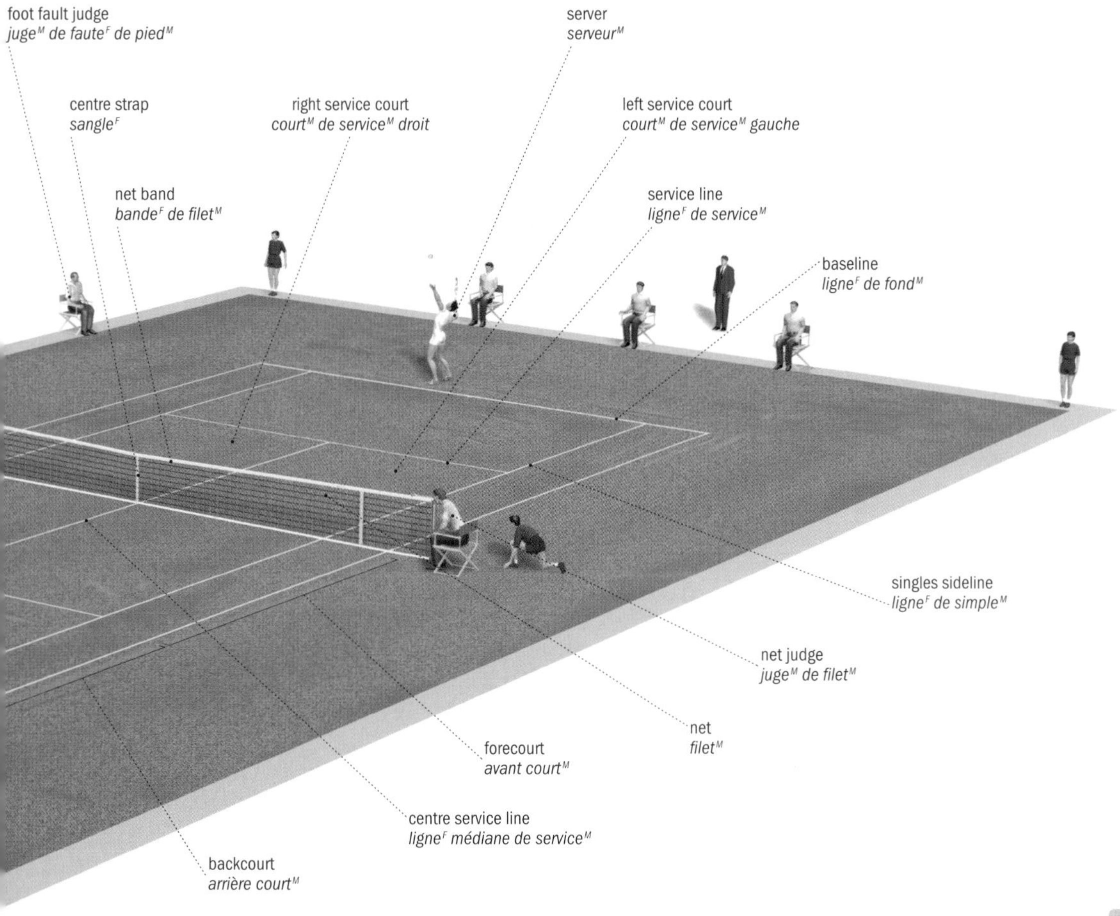

foot fault judge
juge^M de faute^F de pied^M

server
serveur^M

centre strap
sangle^F

right service court
court^M de service^M droit

left service court
court^M de service^M gauche

net band
bande^F de filet^M

service line
ligne^F de service^M

baseline
ligne^F de fond^M

singles sideline
ligne^F de simple^M

net judge
juge^M de filet^M

net
filet^M

forecourt
avant court^M

centre service line
ligne^F médiane de service^M

backcourt
arrière court^M

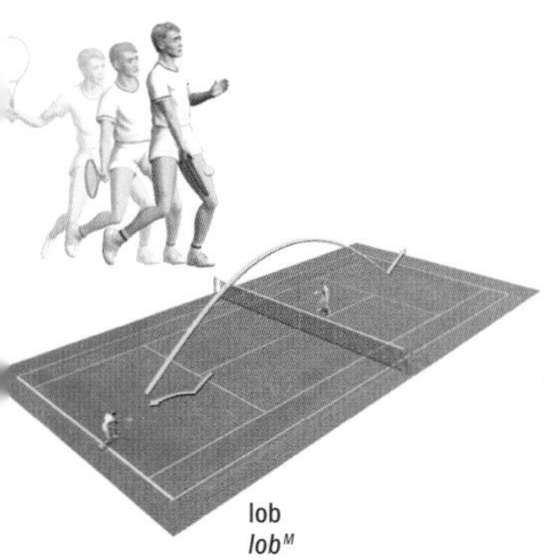

lob
lob^M

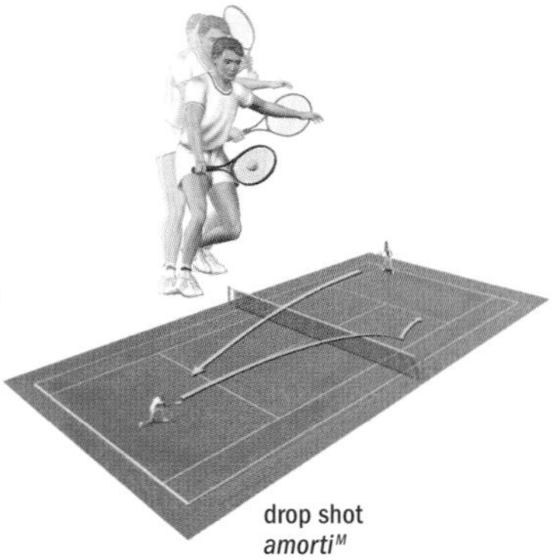

drop shot
amorti^M

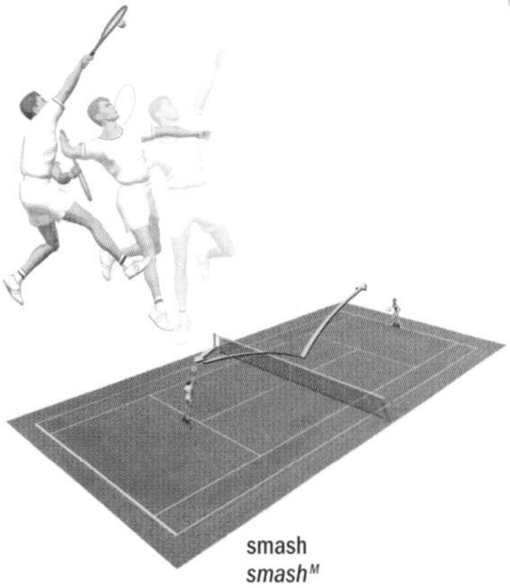

smash
smash^M

tennis

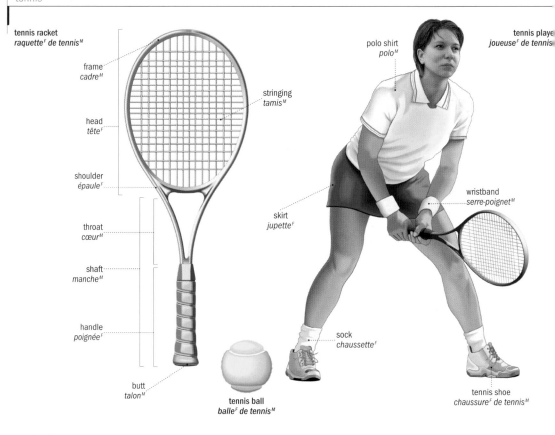

tennis racket
raquette^F de tennis^M

frame
cadre^M

head
tête^F

shoulder
épaule^F

throat
cœur^M

shaft
manche^M

handle
poignée^F

butt
talon^M

stringing
tamis^M

skirt
jupette^F

sock
chaussette^F

tennis ball
balle^F de tennis^M

polo shirt
polo^M

tennis player
joueuse^F de tennis

wristband
serre-poignet^M

tennis shoe
chaussure^F de tennis^M

scoreboard
tableau^M d'affichage^M

previous sets
manches^F précédentes

players
joueurs^M

set
manche^F

points
points^M

game
jeu^M

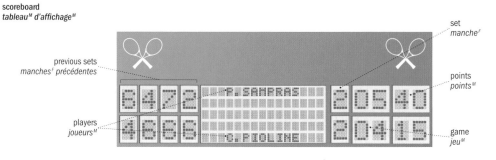

playing surfaces
surfaces^F de jeu^M

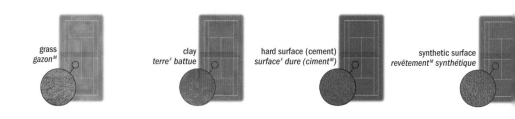

grass
gazon^M

clay
terre^F battue

hard surface (cement)
surface^F dure (ciment^M)

synthetic surface
revêtement^M synthétique

table tennis
tennis^M de table^F

table
table^F

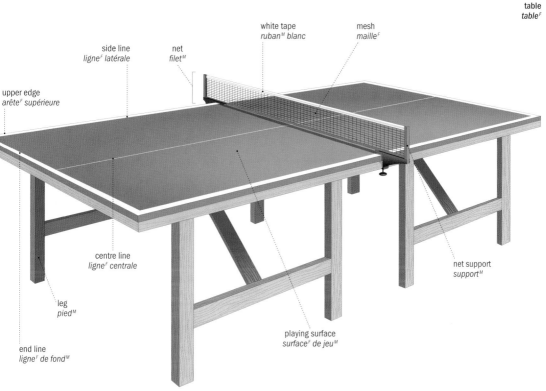

white tape
ruban^M blanc

mesh
maille^F

side line
ligne^F latérale

net
filet^M

upper edge
arête^F supérieure

centre line
ligne^F centrale

net support
support^M

leg
pied^M

end line
ligne^F de fond^M

playing surface
surface^F de jeu^M

table tennis bat
raquette^F de tennis^M de table^F

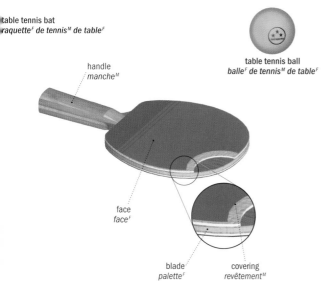

table tennis ball
balle^F de tennis^M de table^F

types of grip
types^M de prises^F

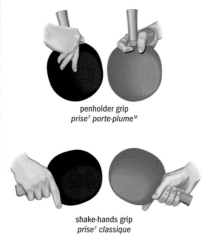

penholder grip
prise^F porte-plume^M

handle
manche^M

face
face^F

blade
palette^F

covering
revêtement^M

shake-hands grip
prise^F classique

badminton

badminton^M

court
terrain^M

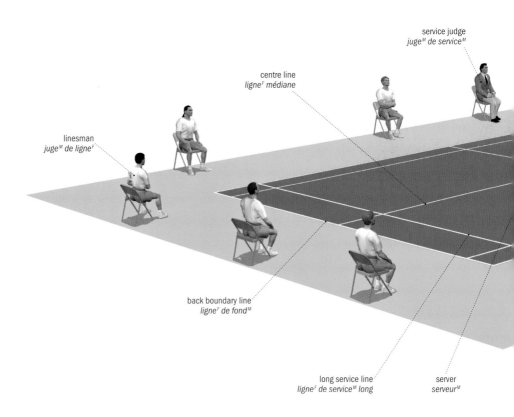

service judge
juge^M de service^M

centre line
ligne^F médiane

linesman
juge^M de ligne^F

back boundary line
ligne^F de fond^M

long service line
ligne^F de service^M long

server
serveur^M

badminton racket
raquette^F de badminton^M

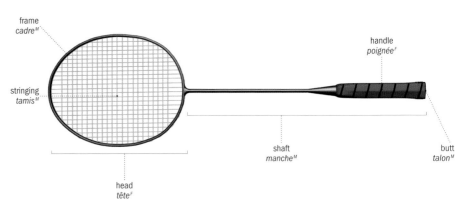

frame
cadre^M

handle
poignée^F

stringing
tamis^M

shaft
manche^M

butt
talon^M

head
tête^F

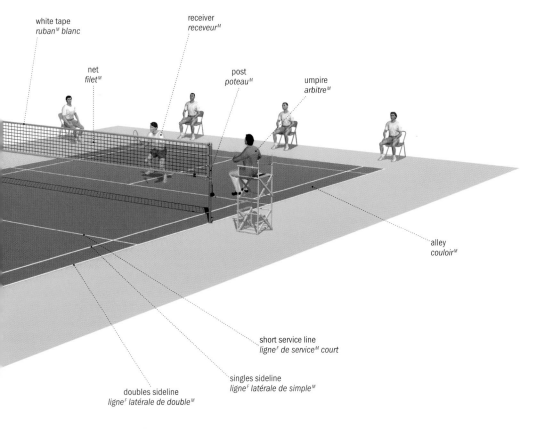

white tape
ruban^M blanc

receiver
receveur^M

net
filet^M

post
poteau^M

umpire
arbitre^M

alley
couloir^M

short service line
ligne^F de service^M court

singles sideline
ligne^F latérale de simple^M

doubles sideline
ligne^F latérale de double^M

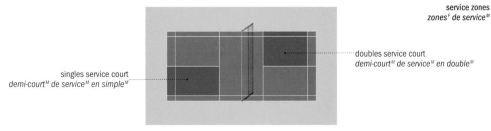

service zones
zones^F de service^M

doubles service court
demi-court^M de service^M en double^M

singles service court
demi-court^M de service^M en simple^M

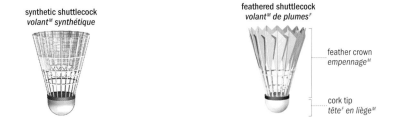

synthetic shuttlecock
volant^M synthétique

feathered shuttlecock
volant^M de plumes^F

feather crown
empennage^M

cork tip
tête^F en liège^M

gymnastics

gymnastique^F

event platform
podium^M des épreuves^F

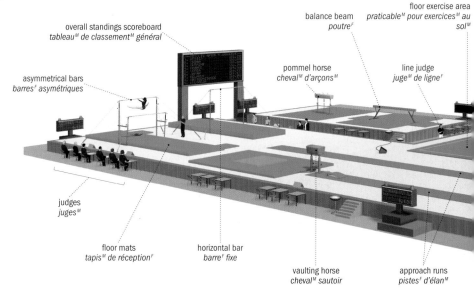

overall standings scoreboard
tableau^M de classement^M général

balance beam
poutre^F

floor exercise area
praticable^M pour exercices^M au sol^M

asymmetrical bars
barres^F asymétriques

pommel horse
cheval^M d'arçons^M

line judge
juge^M de ligne^F

judges
juges^M

floor mats
tapis^M de réception^F

horizontal bar
barre^F fixe

vaulting horse
cheval^M sautoir

approach runs
pistes^F d'élan^M

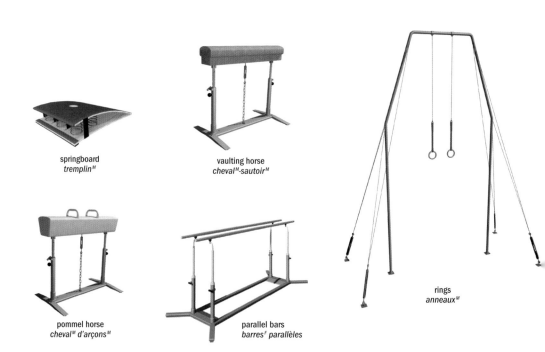

springboard
tremplin^M

vaulting horse
cheval^M-sautoir^M

pommel horse
cheval^M d'arçons^M

parallel bars
barres^F parallèles

rings
anneaux^M

scoreboard
tableau^M *de pointage*^M

gymnast's name
nom^M *du gymnaste*^M

nationality
nationalité^F

current event scoreboard
pointage^M *de l'épreuve*^F *en cours*^M

score
note^F

judges
juges^M

vaulting horse
cheval^M *sautoir*

rings
anneaux^M

parallel bars
barres^F *parallèles*

magnesium powder
magnésie^F

judges
juges^M

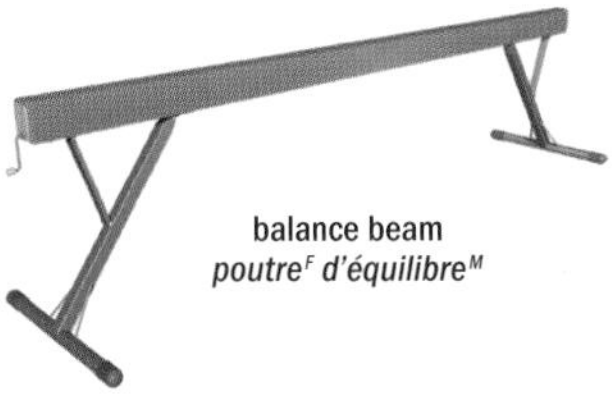

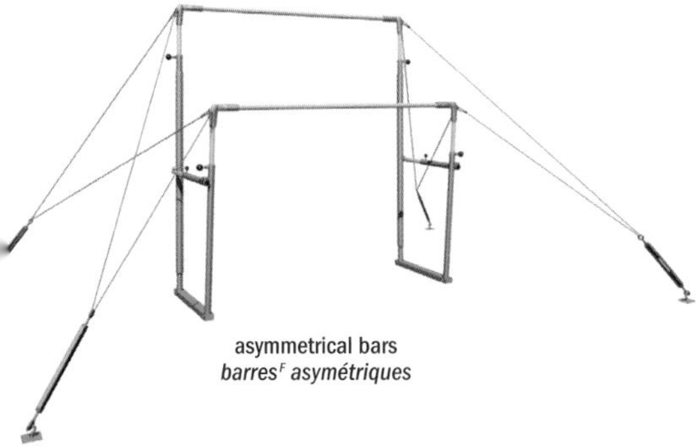

asymmetrical bars
barres^F *asymétriques*

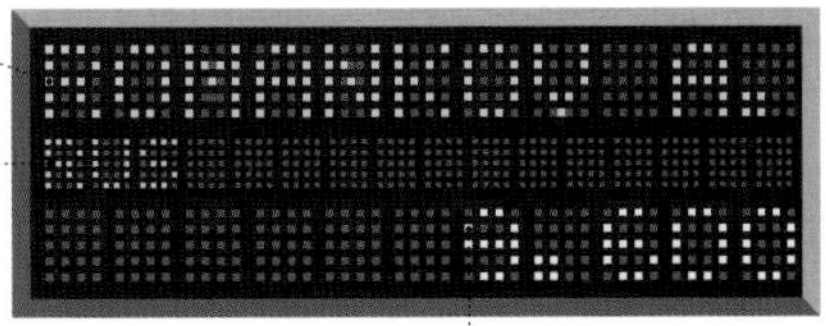

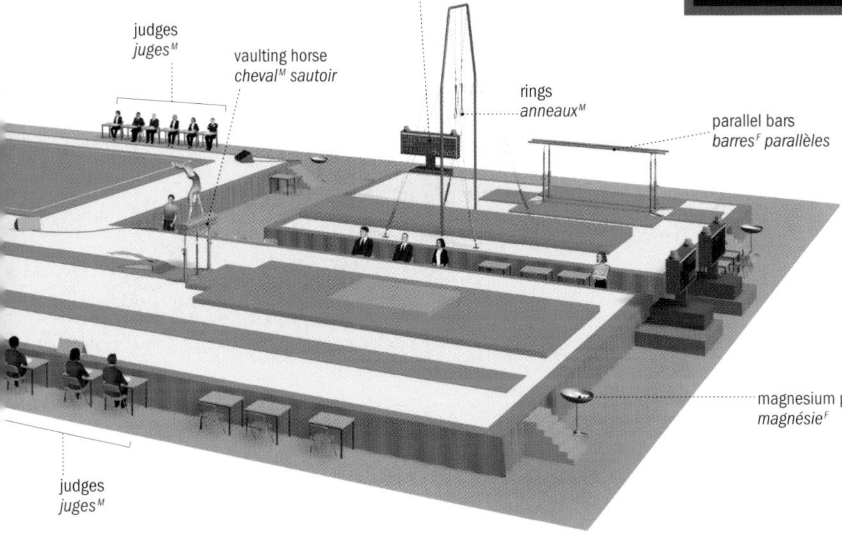

balance beam
poutre^F *d'équilibre*^M

horizontal bar
barre^F *fixe*

SPORTS AND GAMES

boxing

boxe^F

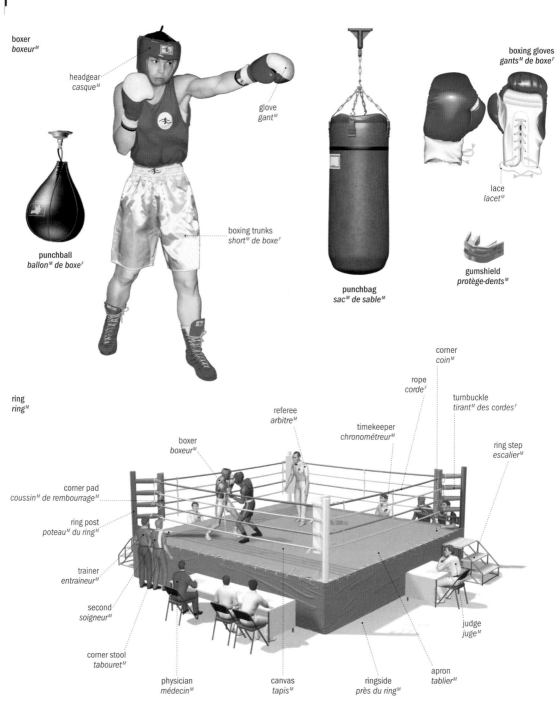

boxer
boxeur^M

headgear
casque^M

glove
gant^M

boxing gloves
gants^M *de boxe*^F

lace
lacet^M

boxing trunks
short^M *de boxe*^F

punchball
ballon^M *de boxe*^F

punchbag
sac^M *de sable*^M

gumshield
protège-dents^M

corner
coin^M

rope
corde^F

turnbuckle
tirant^M *des cordes*^F

ring
ring^M

referee
arbitre^M

timekeeper
chronométreur^M

ring step
escalier^M

boxer
boxeur^M

corner pad
coussin^M *de rembourrage*^M

ring post
poteau^M *du ring*^M

trainer
entraîneur^M

second
soigneur^M

judge
juge^M

corner stool
tabouret^M

physician
médecin^M

canvas
tapis^M

ringside
près du ring^M

apron
tablier^M

judo
judo[M]

scorers and timekeepers
marqueurs[M] et
chronométreurs[M]

mat
tapis[M]

medical team
équipe[F] médicale

contestant
combattant[M]

safety area
surface[F] de sécurité[F]

danger area
zone[F] de danger[M]

scoreboard
tableau[M] d'affichage[M]

contest area
surface[F] de combat[M]

referee
arbitre[M]

judge
juge[M]

examples of holds
exemples[M] de prises[F]

judogi
judogi[M]

jacket
veste[F]

holding
immobilisation[F]

stomach throw
projection[F] en cercle[M]

sweeping hip throw
hanche[F] ailée

major outer reaping throw
grand fauchage[M] extérieur

major inner reaping throw
grand fauchage[M] intérieur

naked strangle
étranglement[M]

trousers
pantalon[M]

belt
ceinture[F]

arm lock
clé[F] de bras[M]

one-arm shoulder throw
projection[F] d'épaule[F] par un côté[M]

SPORTS AND GAMES

499

weightlifting

haltérophilie[F]

barbell
haltère[M] long

wrist band
poignet[M] de force[F]

weightlifting belt
ceinture[F] d'haltérophilie[F]

singlet
maillot[M] de corps[M]

shorts
culotte[F]

knee wrap
genouillère[F]

strap
lanière[F]

weightlifting shoe
chaussure[F] d'haltérophilie[F]

clean and jerk
épaulé[M]-jeté[M]

snatch
arraché[M]

fitness equipment

appareils[M] de conditionnement[M] physique

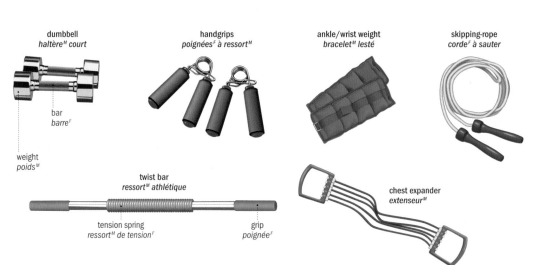

dumbbell
haltère[M] court

handgrips
poignées[F] à ressort[M]

ankle/wrist weight
bracelet[M] lesté

skipping-rope
corde[F] à sauter

bar
barre[F]

weight
poids[M]

twist bar
ressort[M] athlétique

tension spring
ressort[M] de tension[F]

grip
poignée[F]

chest expander
extenseur[M]

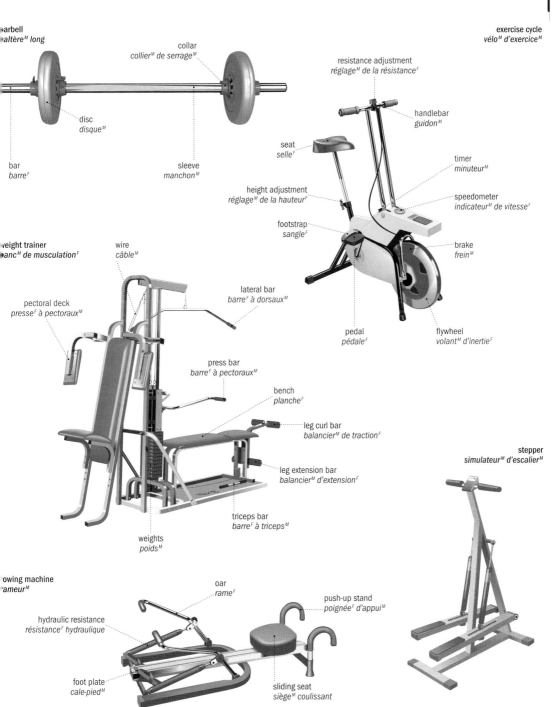

barbell
altère^M long

collar
collier^M de serrage^M

disc
disque^M

bar
barre^F

sleeve
manchon^M

exercise cycle
vélo^M d'exercice^M

resistance adjustment
réglage^M de la résistance^F

handlebar
guidon^M

seat
selle^F

timer
minuteur^M

height adjustment
réglage^M de la hauteur^F

speedometer
indicateur^M de vitesse^F

footstrap
sangle^F

brake
frein^M

weight trainer
banc^M de musculation^F

wire
câble^M

lateral bar
barre^F à dorsaux^M

pectoral deck
presse^F à pectoraux^M

press bar
barre^F à pectoraux^M

bench
planche^F

leg curl bar
balancier^M de traction^F

pedal
pédale^F

flywheel
volant^M d'inertie^F

stepper
simulateur^M d'escalier^M

leg extension bar
balancier^M d'extension^F

triceps bar
barre^F à triceps^M

weights
poids^M

rowing machine
rameur^M

oar
rame^F

push-up stand
poignée^F d'appui^M

hydraulic resistance
résistance^F hydraulique

foot plate
cale-pied^M

sliding seat
siège^M coulissant

billiards

billard^M

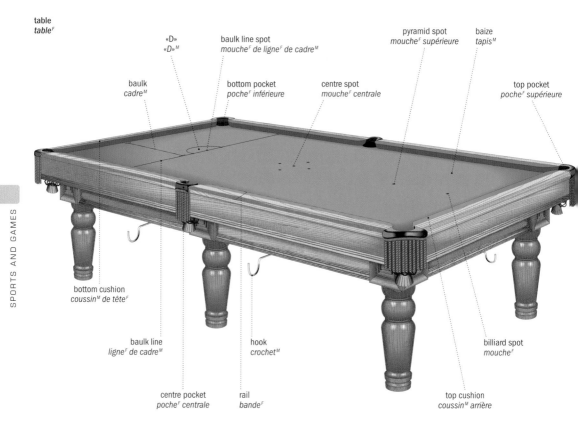

carom billiards
billard^M français

cue ball
bille^F de choc^M

red ball
bille^F rouge

white spot ball
bille^F de visée^F blanche

poo
billard^M poo

object balls
billes^F numérotées

pocket
poche^F

cue ball
bille^F de choc^M

table
table^F

«D»
«D»^M

baulk line spot
mouche^F de ligne^F de cadre^M

pyramid spot
mouche^F supérieure

baize
tapis^M

baulk
cadre^M

bottom pocket
poche^F inférieure

centre spot
mouche^F centrale

top pocket
poche^F supérieure

bottom cushion
coussin^M de tête^F

baulk line
ligne^F de cadre^M

hook
crochet^M

billiard spot
mouche^F

centre pocket
poche^F centrale

rail
bande^F

top cushion
coussin^M arrière

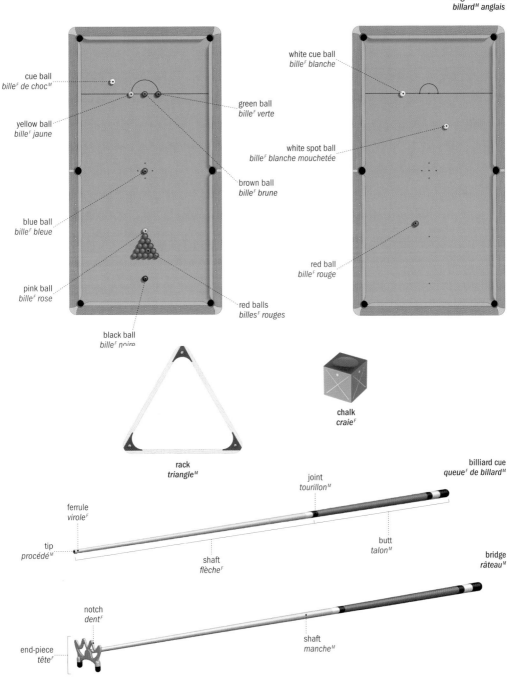

snooker
snooker^M

English billiards
billard^M anglais

cue ball
bille^F de choc^M

white cue ball
bille^F blanche

green ball
bille^F verte

yellow ball
bille^F jaune

white spot ball
bille^F blanche mouchetée

brown ball
bille^F brune

blue ball
bille^F bleue

red ball
bille^F rouge

pink ball
bille^F rose

red balls
billes^F rouges

black ball
bille^F noire

chalk
craie^F

rack
triangle^M

joint
tourillon^M

billiard cue
queue^F de billard^M

ferrule
virole^F

butt
talon^M

bridge
râteau^M

tip
procédé^M

shaft
flèche^F

notch
dent^F

shaft
manche^M

end-piece
tête^F

golf

golf^M

course
parcours^M

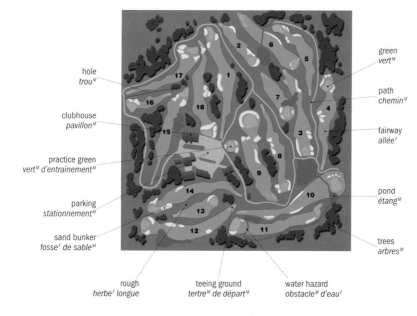

hole
trou^M

clubhouse
pavillon^M

practice green
vert^M *d'entraînement*^M

parking
stationnement^M

sand bunker
fosse^F *de sable*^M

green
vert^M

path
chemin^M

fairway
allée^F

pond
étang^M

trees
arbres^M

rough
herbe^F *longue*

teeing ground
tertre^M *de départ*^M

water hazard
obstacle^M *d'eau*^F

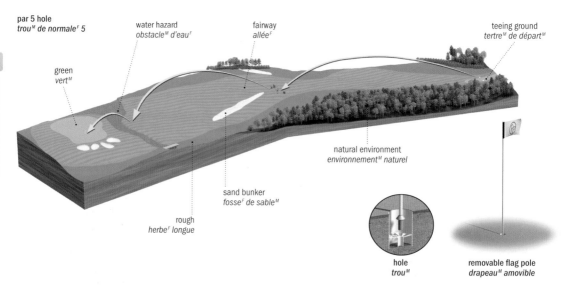

par 5 hole
trou^M *de normale*^F 5

water hazard
obstacle^M *d'eau*^F

fairway
allée^F

teeing ground
tertre^M *de départ*^M

green
vert^M

natural environment
environnement^M *naturel*

sand bunker
fosse^F *de sable*^M

rough
herbe^F *longue*

hole
trou^M

removable flag pole
drapeau^M *amovible*

types of golf club
types^M de bâtons^M de golf^M

golf ball
balle^F de golf^M

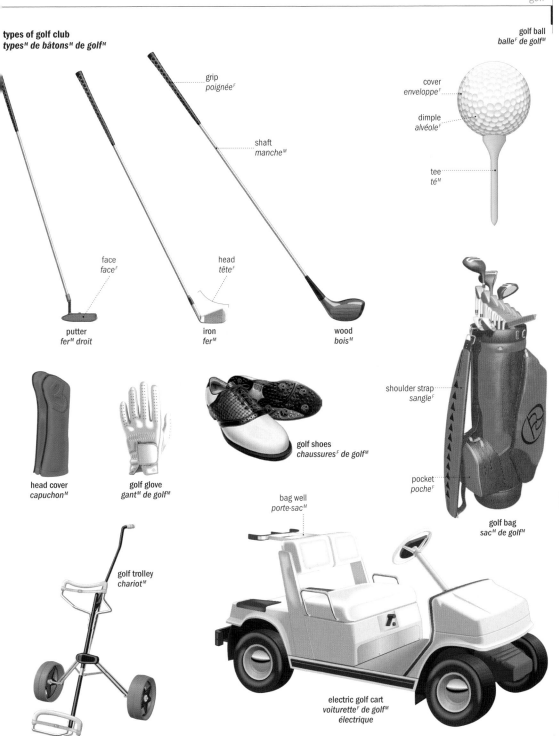

grip
poignée^F

cover
enveloppe^F

shaft
manche^M

dimple
alvéole^F

tee
té^M

face
face^F

head
tête^F

putter
fer^M droit

iron
fer^M

wood
bois^M

shoulder strap
sangle^F

head cover
capuchon^M

golf glove
gant^M de golf^M

golf shoes
chaussures^F de golf^M

pocket
poche^F

bag well
porte-sac^M

golf bag
sac^M de golf^M

golf trolley
chariot^M

electric golf cart
voiturette^F de golf^M
électrique

SPORTS AND GAMES

ice hockey

hockey^M sur glace^F

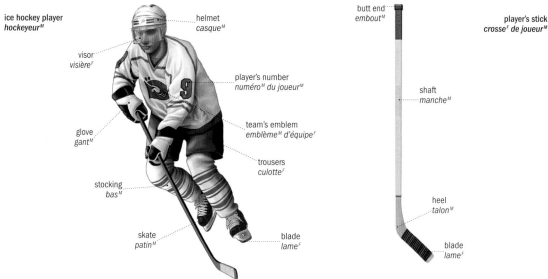

ice hockey player
hockeyeur^M

visor
visière^F

helmet
casque^M

player's number
numéro^M du joueur^M

team's emblem
emblème^M d'équipe^F

glove
gant^M

trousers
culotte^F

stocking
bas^M

skate
patin^M

blade
lame^F

butt end
embout^M

player's stick
crosse^F de joueur^M

shaft
manche^M

heel
talon^M

blade
lame^F

rink
patinoire^F

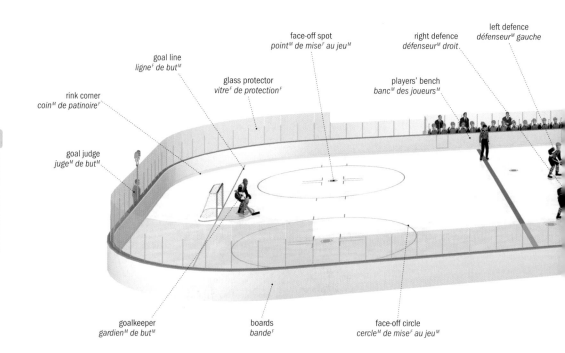

goal line
ligne^F de but^M

face-off spot
point^M de mise^F au jeu^M

right defence
défenseur^M droit

left defence
défenseur^M gauche

glass protector
vitre^F de protection^F

players' bench
banc^M des joueurs^M

rink corner
coin^M de patinoire^F

goal judge
juge^M de but^M

goalkeeper
gardien^M de but^M

boards
bande^F

face-off circle
cercle^F de mise^F au jeu^M

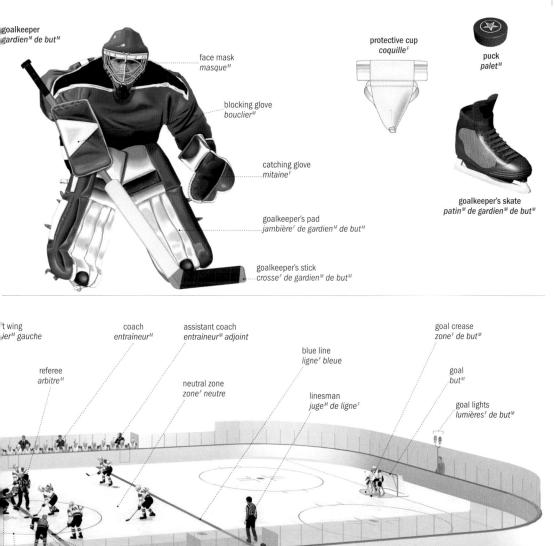

goalkeeper
gardien^M de but^M

face mask
masque^M

blocking glove
bouclier^M

catching glove
mitaine^F

goalkeeper's pad
jambière^F de gardien^M de but^M

goalkeeper's stick
crosse^F de gardien^M de but^M

protective cup
coquille^F

puck
palet^M

goalkeeper's skate
patin^M de gardien^M de but^M

t wing
ier^M gauche

coach
entraîneur^M

assistant coach
entraîneur^M adjoint

blue line
ligne^F bleue

goal crease
zone^F de but^M

referee
arbitre^M

neutral zone
zone^F neutre

linesman
juge^M de ligne^F

goal
but^M

goal lights
lumières^F de but^M

penalty bench official
préposé^M au banc^M des pénalités^F

penalty bench
banc^M des pénalités^F

centre line
ligne^F centrale

centre face-off circle
cercle^M central

centre
centre^M

right wing
ailier^M droit

officials' bench
banc^M des officiels^M

speed skating

patinage^M de vitesse^F

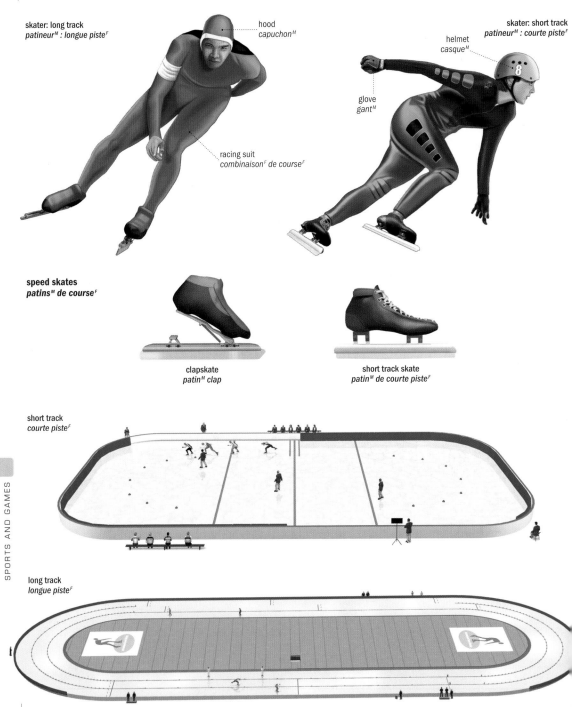

skater: long track
patineur^M : longue piste^F

hood
capuchon^M

skater: short track
patineur^M : courte piste^F

helmet
casque^M

glove
gant^M

racing suit
combinaison^F de course^F

speed skates
patins^M de course^F

clapskate
patin^M clap

short track skate
patin^M de courte piste^F

short track
courte piste^F

long track
longue piste^F

figure skating
patinage^M artistique

figure skate
patin^M de figure^F

lining
doublure^F

tongue
languette^F

hook
crochet^M

backstay
tige^F

lace
lacet^M

boot
chaussure^F

eyelet
œillet^M

dance blade
lame^F de danse^F sur glace^F

heel
talon^M

sole
semelle^F

free-skating blade
lame^F pour programme^M
libre

stanchion
montant^M

toe pick
dent^F

edge
carre^F

blade
lame^F

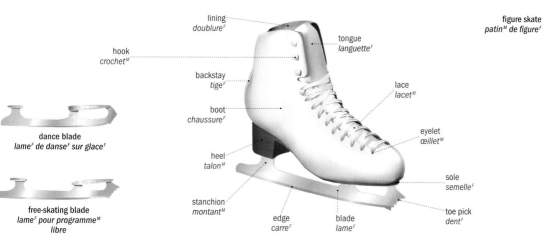

examples of jumps
exemples^M de sauts^M

Salchow
salchow^M

Axel
axel^M

toe loop
boucle^F piquée

flip
flip^M

Lutz
lutz^M

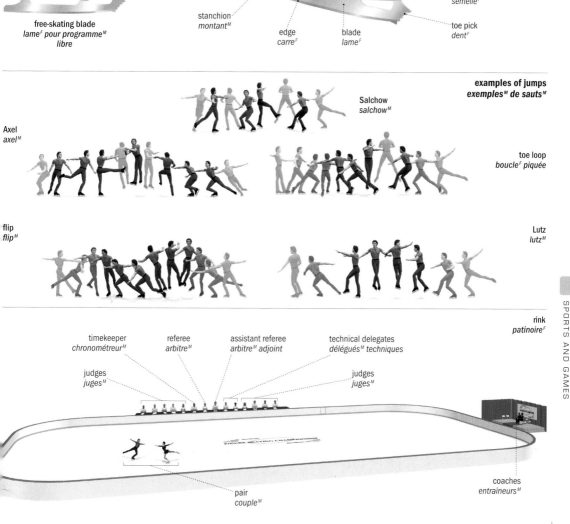

rink
patinoire^F

timekeeper
chronométreur^M

referee
arbitre^M

assistant referee
arbitre^M adjoint

technical delegates
délégués^M techniques

judges
juges^M

judges
juges^M

coaches
entraineurs^M

pair
couple^M

SPORTS AND GAMES

alpine skiing

ski^M alpin

alpine skier
skieur^M alpin

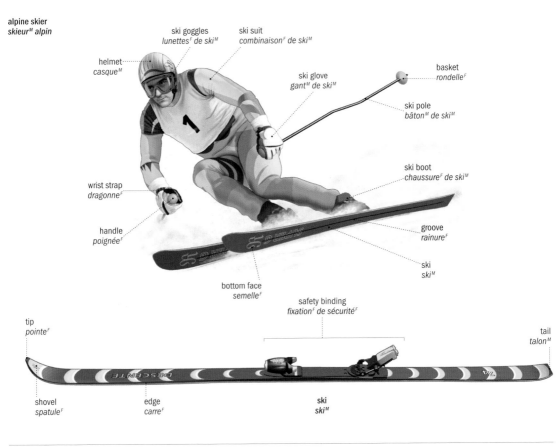

ski goggles
lunettes^F de ski^M

ski suit
combinaison^F de ski^M

helmet
casque^M

ski glove
gant^M de ski^M

basket
rondelle^F

ski pole
bâton^M de ski^M

ski boot
chaussure^F de ski^M

wrist strap
dragonne^F

handle
poignée^F

groove
rainure^F

ski
ski^M

bottom face
semelle^F

safety binding
fixation^F de sécurité^F

tip
pointe^F

tail
talon^M

shovel
spatule^F

edge
carre^F

ski
ski^M

examples of skis
exemples^M de skis^M

slalom ski
ski^M de slalom^M

slalom G ski
ski^M de grand slalom^M

downhill/Super G ski
ski^M de descente^F/super-G^M

technical events
épreuves[F]

downhill
descente[F]

super giant slalom
super-géant[M]

giant slalom
slalom[M] *géant*

special slalom
slalom[M] *spécial*

ski boot
chaussure[F] *de ski*[M]

inner boot
chausson[M] *intérieur*

upper cuff
collier[M]

tongue
languette[F]

upper
tige[F]

upper strap
courroie[F] *de tige*[F]

upper shell
coque[F] *supérieure*

buckle
boucle[F]

adjustable catch
cran[M] *de réglage*[M]

hinge
charnière[F]

sole
semelle[F]

lower shell
coque[F] *inférieure*

safety binding
fixation[F] *de sécurité*[F]

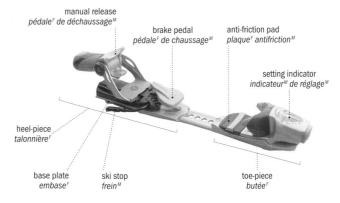

manual release
pédale[F] *de déchaussage*[M]

brake pedal
pédale[F] *de chaussage*[M]

anti-friction pad
plaque[F] *antifriction*[M]

setting indicator
indicateur[M] *de réglage*[M]

heel-piece
talonnière[F]

base plate
embase[F]

ski stop
frein[M]

toe-piece
butée[F]

SPORTS AND GAMES

ski resort

station^F de ski^M

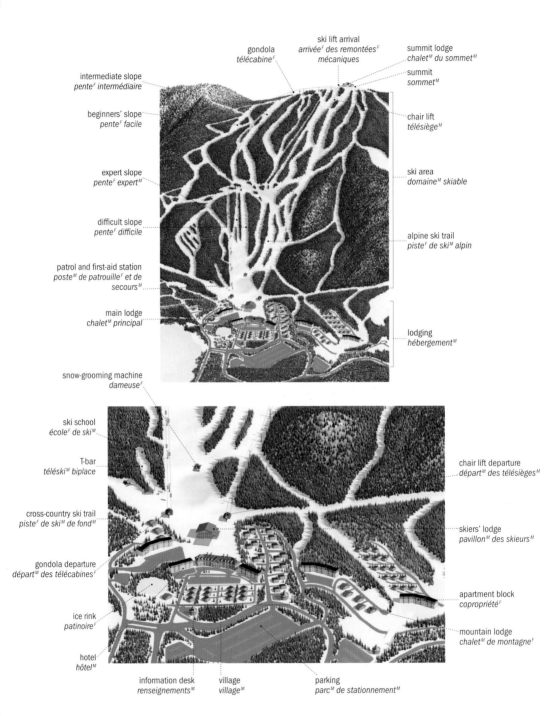

intermediate slope
pente^F intermédiaire

gondola
télécabine^F

ski lift arrival
arrivée^F des remontées^F
mécaniques

summit lodge
chalet^M du sommet^M

summit
sommet^M

beginners' slope
pente^F facile

chair lift
télésiège^M

expert slope
pente^F expert^M

ski area
domaine^M skiable

difficult slope
pente^F difficile

alpine ski trail
piste^F de ski^M alpin

patrol and first-aid station
poste^M de patrouille^F et de
secours^M

main lodge
chalet^M principal

lodging
hébergement^M

snow-grooming machine
dameuse^F

ski school
école^F de ski^M

chair lift departure
départ^M des télésièges^M

T-bar
téléski^M biplace

cross-country ski trail
piste^F de ski^M de fond^M

skiers' lodge
pavillon^M des skieurs^M

gondola departure
départ^M des télécabines^F

apartment block
copropriété^F

ice rink
patinoire^F

mountain lodge
chalet^M de montagne^F

hotel
hôtel^M

information desk
renseignements^M

village
village^M

parking
parc^M de stationnement^M

snowboarding
surf^M des neiges^F

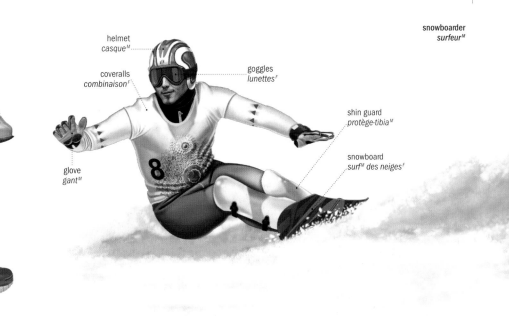

snowboarder
surfeur^M

helmet
casque^M

coveralls
combinaison^F

goggles
lunettes^F

shin guard
protège-tibia^M

snowboard
surf^M des neiges^F

glove
gant^M

hard boot
botte^F rigide

flexible boot
botte^F souple

freestyle snowboard
surf^M acrobatique

alpine snowboard
surf^M alpin

ski jumping
saut^M à ski^M

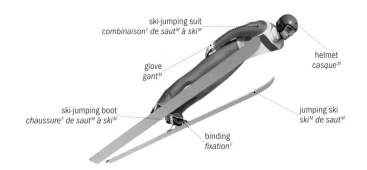

ski jumper
sauteur^M

ski-jumping suit
combinaison^F de saut^M à ski^M

helmet
casque^M

glove
gant^M

ski-jumping boot
chaussure^F de saut^M à ski^M

jumping ski
ski^M de saut^M

binding
fixation^F

cross-country skiing

ski^M de fond^M

cross-country skier
skieur^M de fond^M

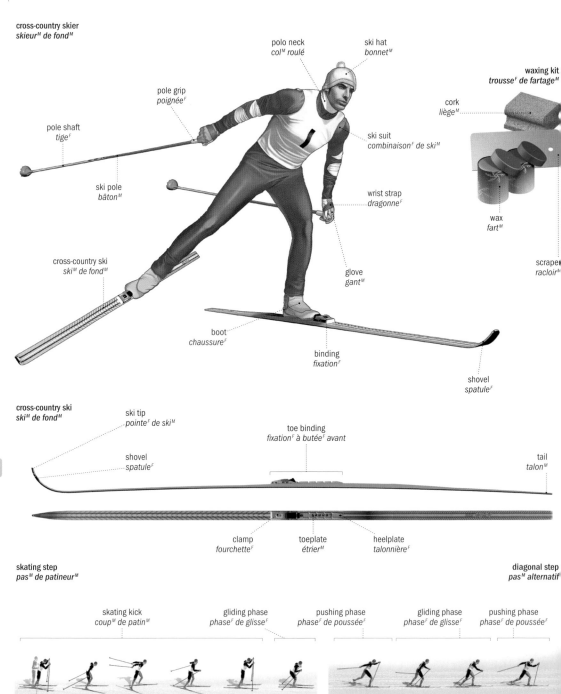

polo neck
col^M roulé

ski hat
bonnet^M

waxing kit
trousse^F de fartage^M

pole grip
poignée^F

cork
liège^M

pole shaft
tige^F

ski suit
combinaison^F de ski^M

ski pole
bâton^M

wrist strap
dragonne^F

wax
fart^M

cross-country ski
ski^M de fond^M

scraper
racloir^M

glove
gant^M

boot
chaussure^F

binding
fixation^F

shovel
spatule^F

cross-country ski
ski^M de fond^M

ski tip
pointe^F de ski^M

toe binding
fixation^F à butée^F avant

tail
talon^M

shovel
spatule^F

clamp
fourchette^F

toeplate
étrier^M

heelplate
talonnière^F

skating step
pas^M de patineur^M

diagonal step
pas^M alternatif

skating kick
coup^M de patin^M

gliding phase
phase^F de glisse^F

pushing phase
phase^F de poussée^F

gliding phase
phase^F de glisse^F

pushing phase
phase^F de poussée^F

curling
curling^M

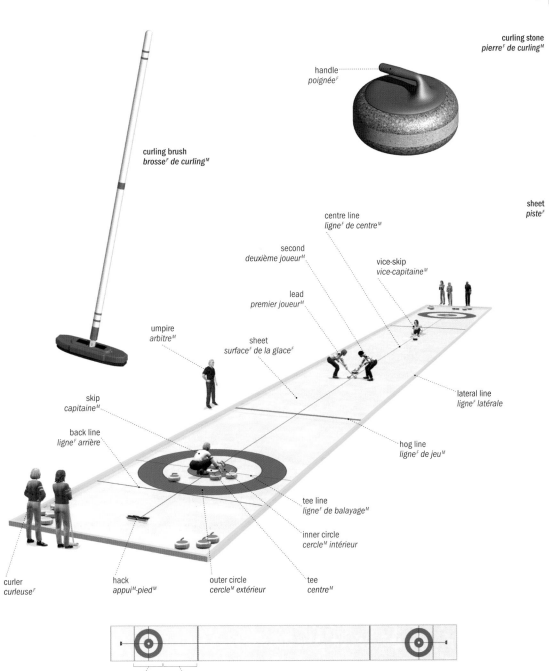

curling stone
pierre^F de curling^M

handle
poignée^F

curling brush
brosse^F de curling^M

sheet
piste^F

centre line
ligne^F de centre^M

second
deuxième joueur^M

vice-skip
vice-capitaine^M

lead
premier joueur^M

umpire
arbitre^M

sheet
surface^F de la glace^F

lateral line
ligne^F latérale

skip
capitaine^M

hog line
ligne^F de jeu^M

back line
ligne^F arrière

tee line
ligne^F de balayage^M

inner circle
cercle^M intérieur

curler
curleuse^F

hack
appui^M-pied^M

outer circle
cercle^M extérieur

tee
centre^M

house
maison^F

free guard zone
zone^F de garde^F protégée

swimming

natation^F

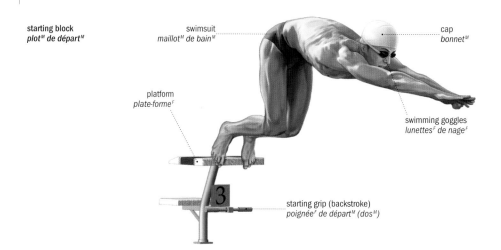

starting block
plot^M de départ^M

swimsuit
maillot^M de bain^M

cap
bonnet^M

platform
plate-forme^F

swimming goggles
lunettes^F de nage^F

starting grip (backstroke)
poignée^F de départ^M (dos^M)

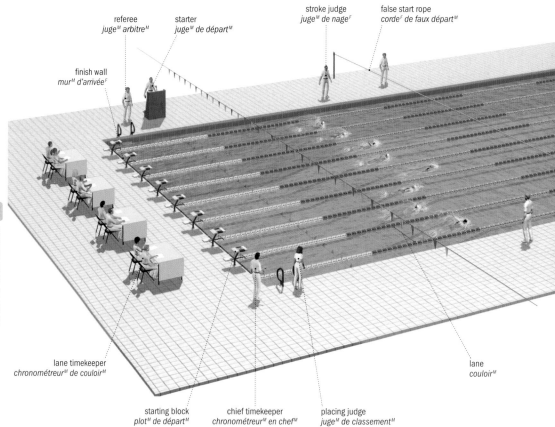

referee
juge^M arbitre^M

starter
juge^M de départ^M

stroke judge
juge^M de nage^F

false start rope
corde^F de faux départ^M

finish wall
mur^M d'arrivée^F

lane timekeeper
chronométreur^M de couloir^M

lane
couloir^M

starting block
plot^M de départ^M

chief timekeeper
chronométreur^M en chef^M

placing judge
juge^M de classement^M

types of stroke
types^M de nages^F

crawl stroke
crawl^M

butterfly stroke
papillon^M

breaststroke
brasse^F

backstroke
nage^F sur le dos^M

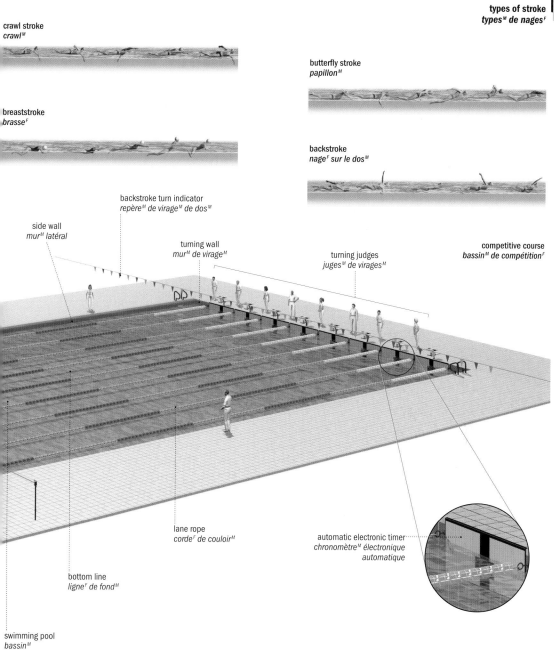

backstroke turn indicator
repère^M de virage^M de dos^M

side wall
mur^M latéral

turning wall
mur^M de virage^M

turning judges
juges^M de virages^M

competitive course
bassin^M de compétition^F

lane rope
corde^F de couloir^M

automatic electronic timer
*chronomètre^M électronique
automatique*

bottom line
ligne^F de fond^M

swimming pool
bassin^M

diving

plongeon[M]

starting positions
positions[F] de départ[M]

flights
vols[M]

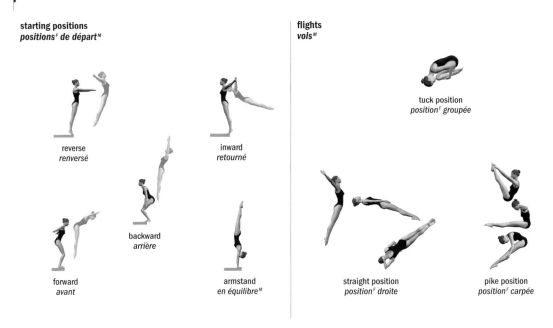

tuck position
position[F] groupée

reverse
renversé

inward
retourné

backward
arrière

forward
avant

armstand
en équilibre[M]

straight position
position[F] droite

pike position
position[F] carpée

diving apparatus
plongeoir[M]

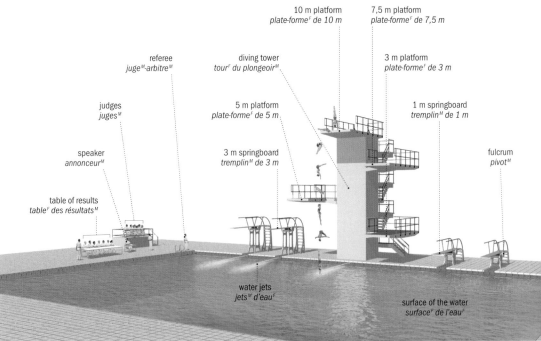

10 m platform
plate-forme[F] de 10 m

7,5 m platform
plate-forme[F] de 7,5 m

referee
juge[M]-arbitre[M]

diving tower
tour[F] du plongeoir[M]

3 m platform
plate-forme[F] de 3 m

judges
juges[M]

5 m platform
plate-forme[F] de 5 m

1 m springboard
tremplin[M] de 1 m

speaker
annonceur[M]

3 m springboard
tremplin[M] de 3 m

fulcrum
pivot[M]

table of results
table[F] des résultats[M]

water jets
jets[M] d'eau[F]

surface of the water
surface[F] de l'eau[F]

sailboard
planche^F à voile^F

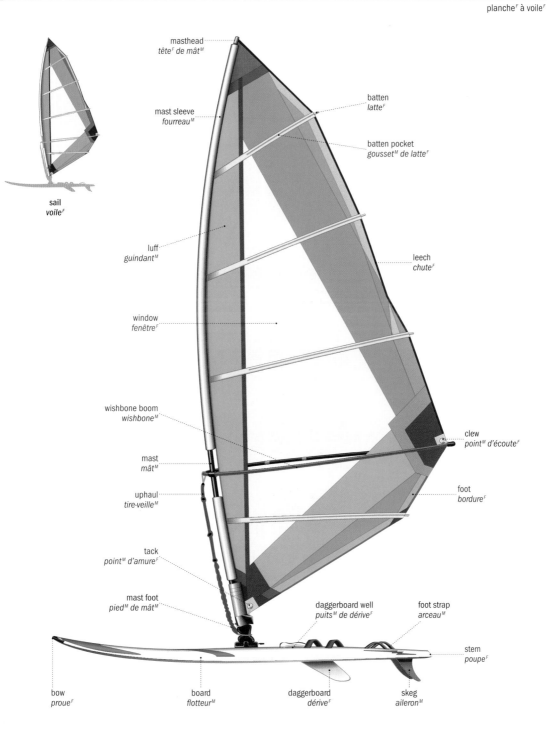

sail
voile^F

masthead
tête^F de mât^M

mast sleeve
fourreau^M

batten
latte^F

batten pocket
gousset^M de latte^F

luff
guindant^M

leech
chute^F

window
fenêtre^F

wishbone boom
wishbone^M

clew
point^M d'écoute^F

mast
mât^M

foot
bordure^F

uphaul
tire-veille^M

tack
point^M d'amure^F

mast foot
pied^M de mât^M

daggerboard well
puits^M de dérive^F

foot strap
arceau^M

stern
poupe^F

bow
proue^F

board
flotteur^M

daggerboard
dérive^F

skeg
aileron^M

SPORTS AND GAMES

sailing

voile[F]

sailing boat
dériveur[M]

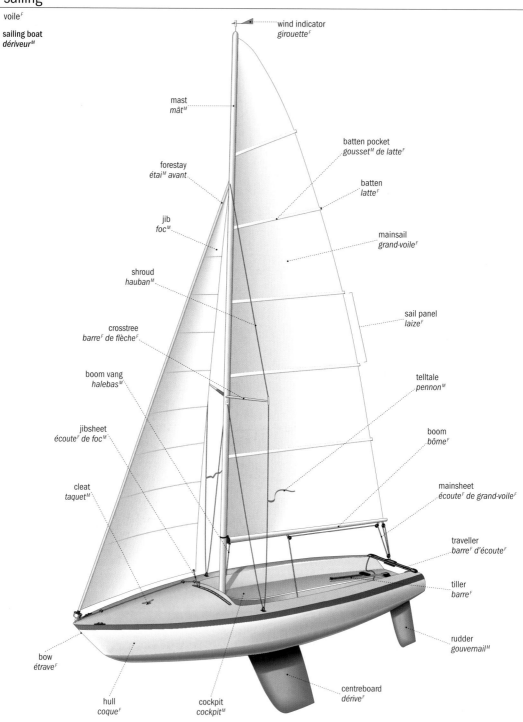

wind indicator
girouette[F]

mast
mât[M]

batten pocket
gousset[M] *de latte*[F]

forestay
étai[M] *avant*

batten
latte[F]

jib
foc[M]

mainsail
grand-voile[F]

shroud
hauban[M]

sail panel
laize[F]

crosstree
barre[F] *de flèche*[F]

boom vang
halebas[M]

telltale
pennon[M]

jibsheet
écoute[F] *de foc*[M]

boom
bôme[F]

cleat
taquet[M]

mainsheet
écoute[F] *de grand-voile*[F]

traveller
barre[F] *d'écoute*[F]

tiller
barre[F]

rudder
gouvernail[M]

bow
étrave[F]

centreboard
dérive[F]

hull
coque[F]

cockpit
cockpit[M]

sailing

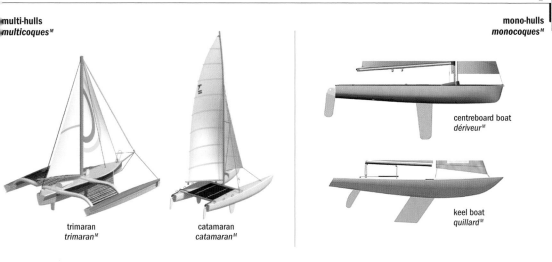

multi-hulls
multicoques^M

mono-hulls
monocoques^M

centreboard boat
dériveur^M

keel boat
quillard^M

trimaran
trimaran^M

catamaran
catamaran^M

upperworks
accastillage^M

snap shackle
mousqueton^M *à ressort*^M

hank
mousqueton^M

shackle
manille^F

fairlead
chaumard^M

cleat
taquet^M

winch
winch^M

turnbuckle
ridoir^M

clam cleat
taquet^M *coinceur*

sheet lead
filoir^M *d'écoute*^F

traveller
barre^F *d'écoute*^F

sliding rail
rail^M *de glissement*^M

car
chariot^M

clam cleat
taquet^M *coinceur*

end stop
butée^F

SPORTS AND GAMES

road racing

cyclisme^M sur route^F

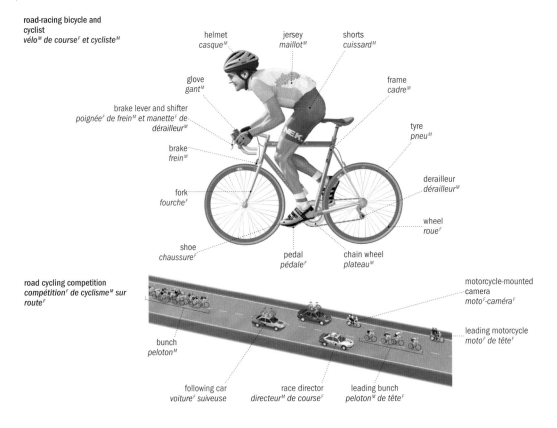

road-racing bicycle and cyclist
vélo^M de course^F et cycliste^M

helmet
casque^M

jersey
maillot^M

shorts
cuissard^M

glove
gant^M

frame
cadre^M

brake lever and shifter
poignée^F de frein^M et manette^F de dérailleur^M

tyre
pneu^M

brake
frein^M

derailleur
dérailleur^M

fork
fourche^F

wheel
roue^F

shoe
chaussure^F

pedal
pédale^F

chain wheel
plateau^M

road cycling competition
compétition^F de cyclisme^M sur route^F

motorcycle-mounted camera
moto^F-caméra^F

leading motorcycle
moto^F de tête^F

bunch
peloton^M

following car
voiture^F suiveuse

race director
directeur^M de course^F

leading bunch
peloton^M de tête^F

mountain biking

vélo^M de montagne^F

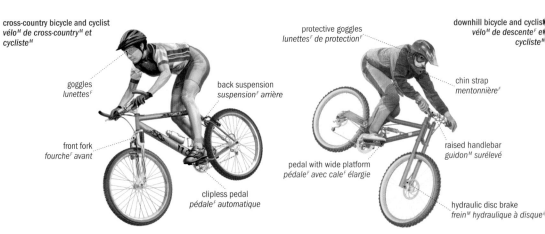

cross-country bicycle and cyclist
vélo^M de cross-country^M et cycliste^M

protective goggles
lunettes^F de protection^F

downhill bicycle and cyclist
vélo^M de descente^F et cycliste^M

goggles
lunettes^F

back suspension
suspension^F arrière

chin strap
mentonnière^F

front fork
fourche^F avant

pedal with wide platform
pédale^F avec cale^F élargie

raised handlebar
guidon^M surélevé

clipless pedal
pédale^F automatique

hydraulic disc brake
frein^M hydraulique à disque

SPORTS AND GAMES

personal watercraft
scooter^M de mer^F

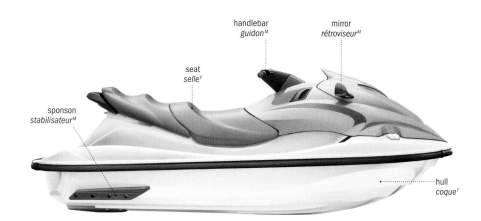

handlebar
guidon^M

mirror
rétroviseur^M

seat
selle^F

sponson
stabilisateur^M

hull
coque^F

snowmobile
motoneige^F

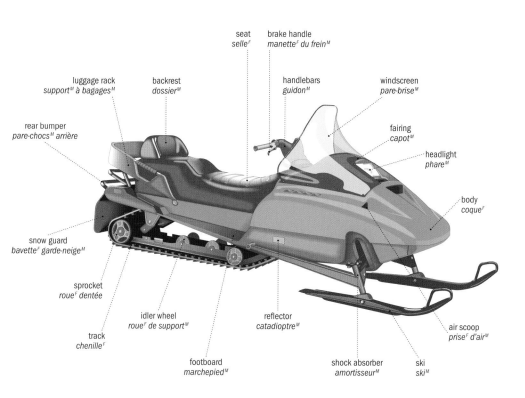

seat
selle^F

brake handle
manette^F du frein^M

luggage rack
support^M à bagages^M

backrest
dossier^M

handlebars
guidon^M

windscreen
pare-brise^M

rear bumper
pare-chocs^M arrière

fairing
capot^M

headlight
phare^M

body
coque^F

snow guard
bavette^F garde-neige^M

sprocket
roue^F dentée

idler wheel
roue^F de support^M

reflector
catadioptre^M

air scoop
prise^F d'air^M

track
chenille^F

footboard
marchepied^M

shock absorber
amortisseur^M

ski
ski^M

SPORTS AND GAMES

motor racing

course^F automobile

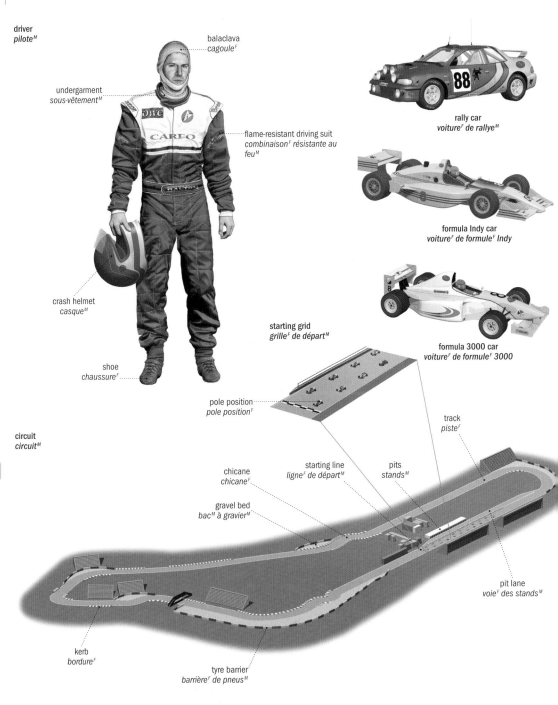

driver
pilote^M

balaclava
cagoule^F

undergarment
sous-vêtement^M

flame-resistant driving suit
combinaison^F résistante au feu^M

crash helmet
casque^M

shoe
chaussure^F

rally car
voiture^F de rallye^M

formula Indy car
voiture^F de formule^F Indy

formula 3000 car
voiture^F de formule^F 3000

starting grid
grille^F de départ^M

pole position
pole position^F

track
piste^F

circuit
circuit^M

chicane
chicane^F

starting line
ligne^F de départ^M

pits
stands^M

gravel bed
bac^M à gravier^M

pit lane
voie^F des stands^M

kerb
bordure^F

tyre barrier
barrière^F de pneus^M

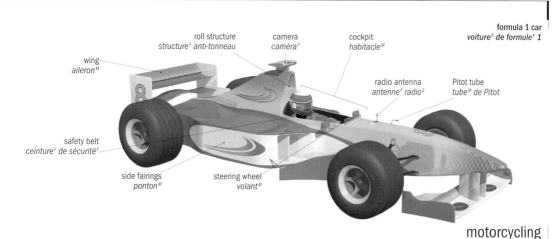

formula 1 car
*voiture*F *de formule*F *1*

roll structure
*structure*F *anti-tonneau*

camera
*caméra*F

cockpit
*habitacle*M

wing
*aileron*M

radio antenna
*antenne*F *radio*F

Pitot tube
*tube*M *de Pitot*

safety belt
*ceinture*F *de sécurité*F

side fairings
*ponton*M

steering wheel
*volant*M

motorcycling
*motocyclisme*M

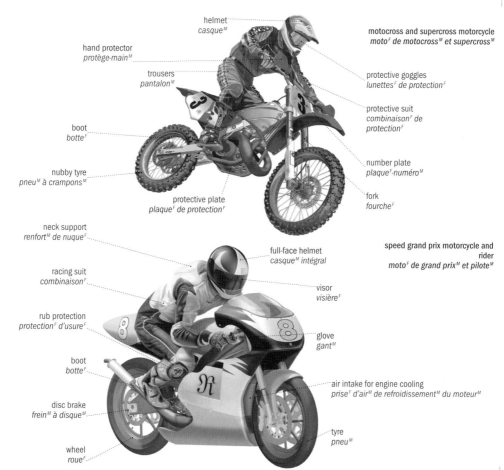

helmet
*casque*M

motocross and supercross motorcycle
*moto*F *de motocross*M *et supercross*M

hand protector
*protège-main*M

protective goggles
*lunettes*F *de protection*F

trousers
*pantalon*M

protective suit
*combinaison*F *de
protection*F

boot
*botte*F

number plate
*plaque*F-*numéro*M

nubby tyre
*pneu*M *à crampons*M

fork
*fourche*F

protective plate
*plaque*F *de protection*F

neck support
*renfort*M *de nuque*F

**speed grand prix motorcycle and
rider**
*moto*F *de grand prix*M *et pilote*M

full-face helmet
*casque*M *intégral*

racing suit
*combinaison*F

visor
*visière*F

rub protection
*protection*F *d'usure*F

glove
*gant*M

boot
*botte*F

air intake for engine cooling
*prise*F *d'air*M *de refroidissement*M *du moteur*M

disc brake
*frein*M *à disque*M

tyre
*pneu*M

wheel
*roue*F

skateboarding

planche^F à roulettes^F

skateboard
planche^F à roulettes^F

skateboarder
planchiste^M

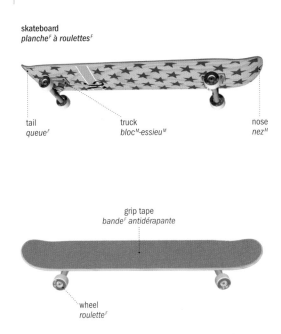

tail
queue^F

truck
bloc^M-essieu^M

nose
nez^M

grip tape
bande^F antidérapante

wheel
roulette^F

knee pad
genouillère^F

elbow pad
protège-coude^M

helmet
casque^M

coping
arête^F

ramp
rampe^F

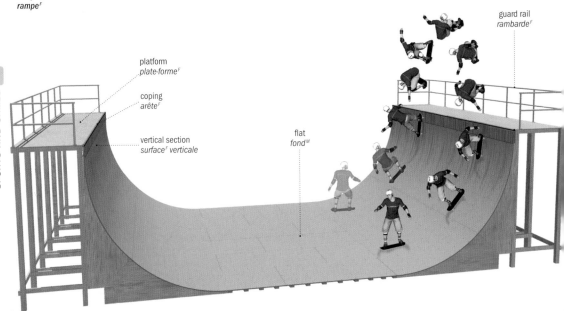

platform
plate-forme^F

coping
arête^F

vertical section
surface^F verticale

flat
fond^M

guard rail
rambarde^F

inline skating
patin^M à roues^F alignées

acrobatic skate
patin^M acrobatique

inner boot
chausson^M intérieur

upper shell
coque^F supérieure

skater
patineuse^F

helmet
casque^M

elbow pad
coudière^F

knee pad
genouillère^F

frame
platine^F

wheel
roue^F

wrist guard
protège-poignet^M

roller speed skate
patin^M de vitesse^F

roller skate
patin^M à roues^F alignées

upper shell
coque^F supérieure

inner boot
chausson^M intérieur

adjustable buckle
boucle^F de réglage^M

roller hockey skate
patin^M de hockey^M

boot
chaussure^F

axle
essieu^M

heel stop
frein^M de talon^M

wheel
roue^F

truck
bloc^M-essieu^M

SPORTS AND GAMES

camping

camping^M

examples of tents
exemples^M de tentes^F

two-person tent
tente^F deux places^F

flysheet
double toit^M

door
porte^F

canopy
auvent^M

guy line
hauban^M

peg
piquet^M

tension adjuster
tendeur^M

elastic loop
Sandow^®M

zip
fermeture^F à glissière^F

inner tent
tente^F intérieure

family tent
tente^F familiale

window awning
auvent^M de fenêtre^F

living room
séjour^M

guy line
hauban^M

elastic loop
Sandow^®M

bedroom
chambre^F

sewn-in groundsheet
tapis^M de sol^M cousu

wall
mur^M

peg loop
boucle^F de piquet^M

canvas divider
cloison^F

frame
armature^F

screen window
fenêtre^F moustiquaire^F

wagon tent
tente^F grange^F

wall tent
tente^F rectangulaire

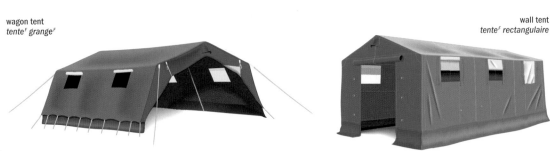

ridge tent
tente^F canadienne

flysheet
double toit^M

roof pole
mât^M de toit^M

elastic strainer
Sandow^®M

inner tent
tente^F intérieure

door
porte^F

peg loop
boucle^F de piquet^M

sewn-in groundsheet
tapis^M de sol^M cousu

peg
piquet^M

one-person tent
tente^F individuelle

dome tent
tente^F dôme^M

igloo tent
tente^F igloo^M

propane or butane appliances
accessoires^M au propane^M ou au butane^M

lantern
lanterne^F

globe
globe^M

burner frame
bâti^M du brûleur^M

pressure regulator
régulateur^M de pression^F

pump
pompe^F

leakproof cap
bouchon^M antifuite

gas container
réservoir^M

heater
chaufferette^F

two-burner camp stove
réchaud^M à deux feux^M

burner
brûleur^M

gas container
réservoir^M

wire frame
grille^F stabilisatrice

single-burner camp stove
réchaud^M à un feu^M

control valve
robinet^M relais^M

camping

examples of sleeping bags
exemples^M de sacs^M de couchage^M

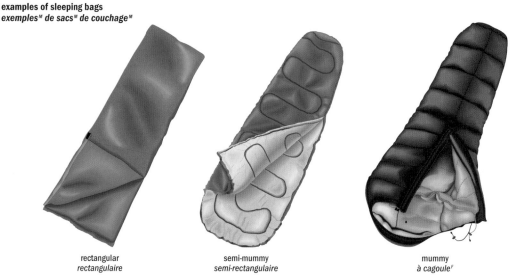

rectangular
rectangulaire

semi-mummy
semi-rectangulaire

mummy
à cagoule^F

bed and mattress
lit^M et matelas^M

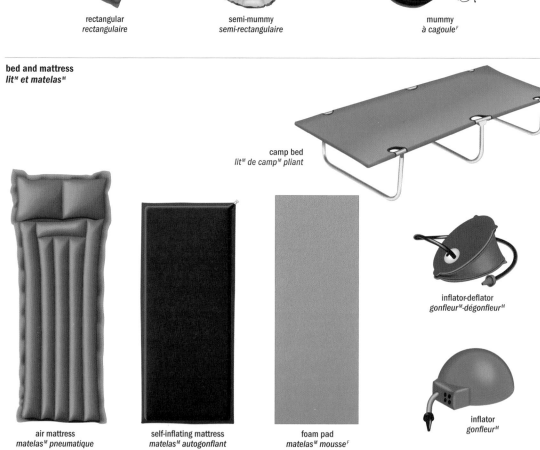

camp bed
lit^M de camp^M pliant

inflator-deflator
gonfleur^M-dégonfleur^M

inflator
gonfleur^M

air mattress
matelas^M pneumatique

self-inflating mattress
matelas^M autogonflant

foam pad
matelas^M mousse^F

cutlery set
ustensiles^M de campeur^M

cooking set
popote^F

spoon
cuiller^F

belt loop
ganse^F

plate
assiette^F plate

fork
fourchette^F

pouch
étui^M

saucepan
faitout^M

knife
couteau^M

handle
queue^F

frying pan
poêle^F

coffee pot
cafetière^F

cup
tasse^F

camping equipment
matériel^M de camping^M

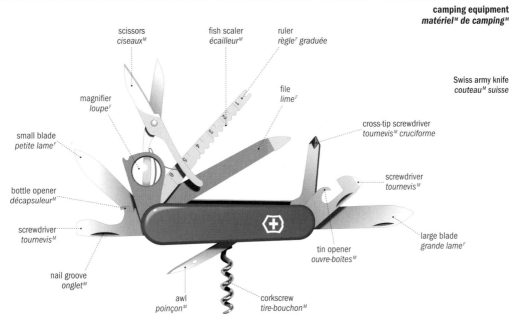

scissors
ciseaux^M

fish scaler
écailleur^M

ruler
règle^F graduée

Swiss army knife
couteau^M suisse

magnifier
loupe^F

file
lime^F

cross-tip screwdriver
tournevis^M cruciforme

small blade
petite lame^F

screwdriver
tournevis^M

bottle opener
décapsuleur^M

screwdriver
tournevis^M

large blade
grande lame^F

nail groove
onglet^M

tin opener
ouvre-boîtes^M

awl
poinçon^M

corkscrew
tire-bouchon^M

camping

backpack
sac^M *à dos*^M

top flap
rabat^M

shoulder strap
bretelle^F

tightening buckle
boucle^F *de réglage*^M

side compression strap
sangle^F *de compression*^F

front compression strap
sangle^F *de fermeture*^F

strap loop
passe-sangle^M

waist belt
ceinture^F

folding shovel
pelle^F*-pioche*^F *pliante*

vacuum flask
bouteille^F *isolante*

bottle
bouteille^F

stopper
bouchon^M

cup
tasse^F

hurricane lamp
lampe^F*-tempête*^F

canteen
gourde^F

cooler
glacière^F

water carrier
bidon^M *à eau*^F

SPORTS AND GAMES

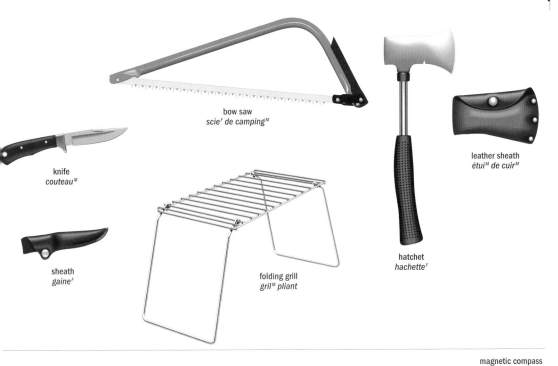

bow saw
scie^F de camping^M

knife
couteau^M

sheath
gaine^F

folding grill
gril^M pliant

leather sheath
étui^M de cuir^M

hatchet
hachette^F

magnetic compass
boussole^F magnétique

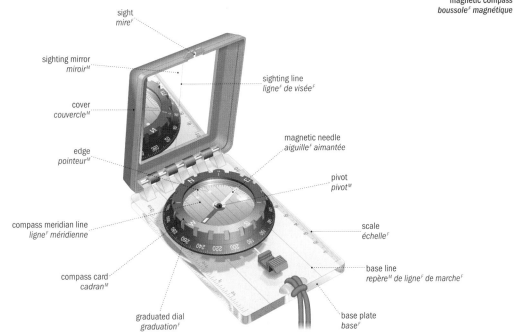

sight
mire^F

sighting mirror
miroir^M

cover
couvercle^M

edge
pointeur^M

compass meridian line
ligne^F méridienne

compass card
cadran^M

graduated dial
graduation^F

sighting line
ligne^F de visée^F

magnetic needle
aiguille^F aimantée

pivot
pivot^M

scale
échelle^F

base line
repère^M de ligne^F de marche^F

base plate
base^F

hunting

chasse^F

rifle (rifled bore)
carabine^F (canon^M rayé)

breechblock
bloc^M de culasse^F

muzzle
*bouche^*

pistol grip
poignée^F

hammer
chien^M

telescopic sight
lunette^F de visée^F

rear sight
hausse^F

front sight
guidon^M

butt plate
plaque^F de couche^F

trigger guard
pontet^M

barrel
canon^M

stock
crosse^F

lever
levier^M

trigger
détente^F

muzzle
bouche^F

shotgun (smooth-bore)
fusil^M (canon^M lisse)

pistol grip
poignée^F

hammer
chien^M

ventilated rib
bande^F ventilée

front sight
guidon^M

butt plate
plaque^F de couche^F

breechblock
bloc^M de culasse^F

forearm
fût^M

barrel
canon^M

trigger guard
pontet^M

trigger
détente^F

stock
crosse^F

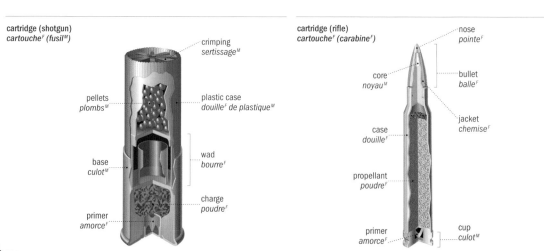

cartridge (shotgun)
cartouche^F (fusil^M)

crimping
sertissage^M

pellets
plombs^M

plastic case
douille^F de plastique^M

base
culot^M

wad
bourre^F

primer
amorce^F

charge
poudre^F

cartridge (rifle)
cartouche^F (carabine^F)

nose
pointe^F

core
noyau^M

bullet
balle^F

case
douille^F

jacket
chemise^F

propellant
poudre^F

primer
amorce^F

cup
culot^M

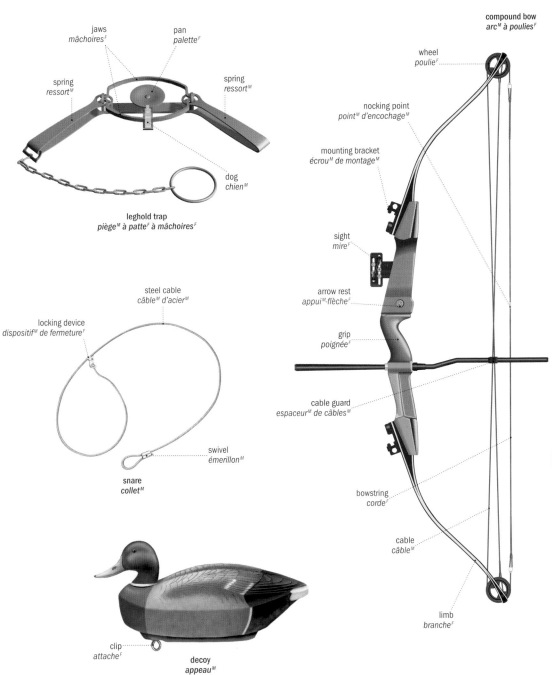

jaws
mâchoires^F

pan
palette^F

spring
ressort^M

spring
ressort^M

dog
chien^M

leghold trap
piège^M *à patte*^F *à mâchoires*^F

compound bow
arc^M *à poulies*^F

wheel
poulie^F

nocking point
point^M *d'encochage*^M

mounting bracket
écrou^M *de montage*^M

sight
mire^F

arrow rest
appui^M*-flèche*^F

grip
poignée^F

cable guard
espaceur^M *de câbles*^M

bowstring
corde^F

cable
câble^M

limb
branche^F

steel cable
câble^M *d'acier*^M

locking device
dispositif^M *de fermeture*^F

swivel
émerillon^M

snare
collet^M

clip
attache^F

decoy
appeau^M

SPORTS AND GAMES

535

fishing
pêche^F

flyfishing
pêche^F à la mouche^F

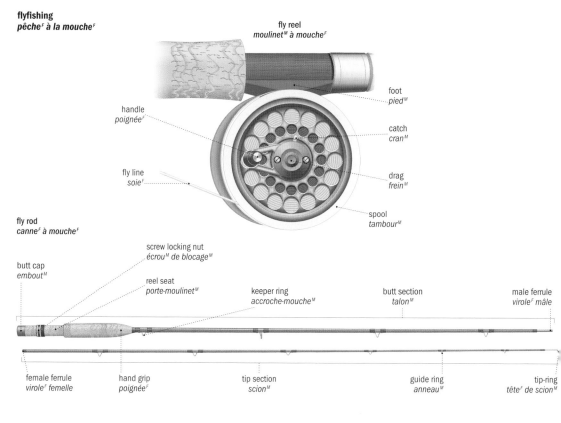

fly reel
moulinet^M à mouche^F

foot
pied^M

handle
poignée^F

catch
cran^M

fly line
soie^F

drag
frein^M

spool
tambour^M

fly rod
canne^F à mouche^F

screw locking nut
écrou^M de blocage^M

butt cap
embout^M

reel seat
porte-moulinet^M

keeper ring
accroche-mouche^M

butt section
talon^M

male ferrule
virole^F mâle

female ferrule
virole^F femelle

hand grip
poignée^F

tip section
scion^M

guide ring
anneau^M

tip-ring
tête^F de scion^M

artificial fly
mouche^F artificielle

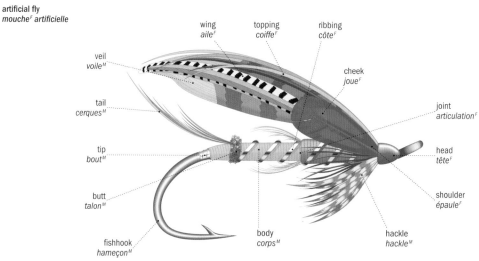

wing
aile^F

topping
coiffe^F

ribbing
côte^F

veil
voile^M

cheek
joue^F

tail
cerques^M

joint
articulation^F

tip
bout^M

head
tête^F

butt
talon^M

shoulder
épaule^F

fishhook
hameçon^M

body
corps^M

hackle
hackle^M

casting
pêcheᶠ au lancerᴹ

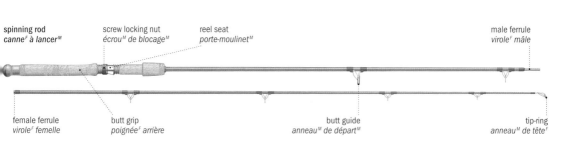

spinning rod
canneᶠ à lancerᴹ

screw locking nut
écrouᴹ de blocageᴹ

reel seat
porte-moulinetᴹ

male ferrule
viroleᶠ mâle

female ferrule
viroleᶠ femelle

butt grip
poignéeᶠ arrière

butt guide
anneauᴹ de départᴹ

tip-ring
anneauᴹ de têteᶠ

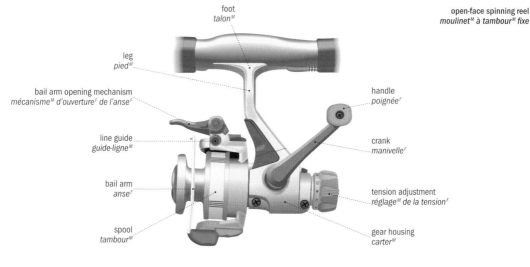

foot
talonᴹ

open-face spinning reel
moulinetᴹ à tambourᴹ fixe

leg
piedᴹ

bail arm opening mechanism
mécanismeᴹ d'ouvertureᶠ de l'anseᶠ

handle
poignéeᶠ

line guide
guide-ligneᴹ

crank
manivelleᶠ

bail arm
anseᶠ

tension adjustment
réglageᴹ de la tensionᶠ

spool
tambourᴹ

gear housing
carterᴹ

baitcasting reel
*moulinetᴹ à tambourᴹ
tournant*

spool-release mechanism
*mécanismeᴹ de débrayageᴹ du
tambourᴹ*

spool
tambourᴹ

star drag wheel
étoileᶠ de freinageᴹ

spool axle
axeᴹ de tambourᴹ

crank
manivelleᶠ

stand
piedᴹ

SPORTS AND GAMES

fishing

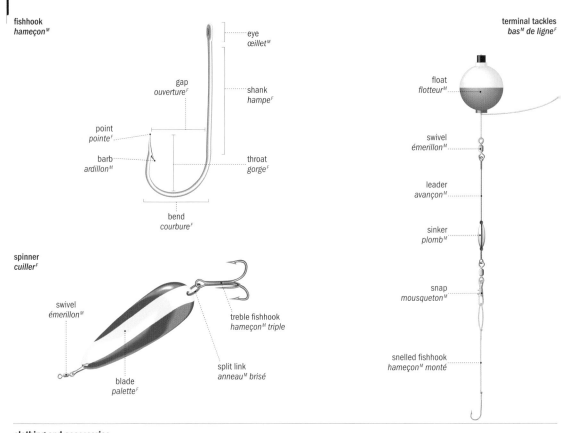

fishhook
hameçon^M

eye
œillet^M

gap
ouverture^F

shank
hampe^F

point
pointe^F

barb
ardillon^M

throat
gorge^F

bend
courbure^F

spinner
cuiller^F

swivel
émerillon^M

treble fishhook
hameçon^M *triple*

split link
anneau^M *brisé*

blade
palette^F

terminal tackles
bas^M *de ligne*^F

float
flotteur^M

swivel
émerillon^M

leader
avançon^M

sinker
plomb^M

snap
mousqueton^M

snelled fishhook
hameçon^M *monté*

clothing and accessories
vêtements^M *et accessoires*^M

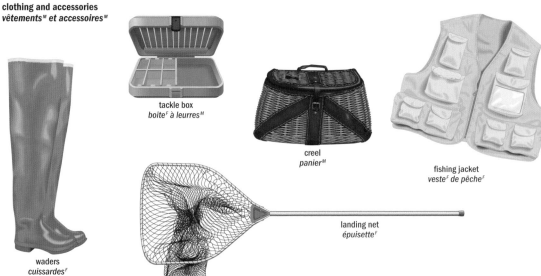

tackle box
boite^F *à leurres*^M

creel
panier^M

fishing jacket
veste^F *de pêche*^F

landing net
épuisette^F

waders
cuissardes^F

English Index

ASTRONOMY > 2-13;   EARTH > 14-49;   PLANT KINGDOM >50-65;   ANIMAL KINGDOM > 66-91;   HUMAN BEING > 92-119;   FOOD AND KITCHEN > 120-181;   HOUSE > 182-215;
DO-IT-YOURSELF AND GARDENING > 216-237;   CLOTHING > 238-263;   PERSONAL ADORNMENT AND ARTICLES > 264-277;   ARTS AND ARCHITECTURE > 278-311;   COMMUNICATIONS AND
OFFICE AUTOMATION > 312-341;   TRANSPORT AND MACHINERY > 342-401;   ENERGY > 402-413;   SCIENCE > 414-429;   SOCIETY > 430-467;   SPORTS AND GAMES > 468-538

539

ENGLISH INDEX

bead 358.
beaker, measuring 171.
beam 283, 288, 422.
beam balance 422.
beam bridge 344.
beam, laser 420.
beam, balance 496.
bean bag chair 201.
bean thread cellophane noodles 147.
bean, adzuki 131.
bean, black 131.
bean, lablab 130.
bean, Lima 131.
bean, mung 131.
bean, pinto 131.
bean, roman 131.
bean, scarlet runner 131.
bean, wax 131.
bean, yard-long 130.
beans 131.
beans, dolichos 130.
beans, green coffee 148.
bear, black 89.
bear, polar 89.
bearing pad 409.
beater 176.
beater ejector 176.
beaters 176.
Beaufort Sea 16.
beaver 82.
becquerel 426.
bed 183, 204, 342.
bed and mattress 530.
bed chamber 280.
bed lamp 206.
bed linen 204.
bed, double 439.
bed, gravel 524.
bed, hospital 464.
bed, single 439.
bed, sofa 204.
bedrock 27, 54.
bedroom 189, 528.
bedside lamp 439, 464.
bedside table 439, 464.
beech 64.
beechnut 133.
beef cubes 152.
beef, cuts of 152.
beef, minced 152.
beehive 122.
beer and wine 120.
beer glass 165.
beetroot 129.
begonia 56.
beginners' slope 512.
Belarus 450.
belfry 284.
Belgium 449.
Belize 448.
bell 306, 307.
bell bottoms 254.
bell brace 306.
bell tower 285, 446.
bellows 296.
bellows strap 296.
belly 83.
belongs to 427.
below-stage 292.
belt 225, 246, 248, 499.
belt drive 383.
belt loader 402.
belt loop 246, 248, 531.
belt, conveyor 49.
belt, duty 456.
belt, fan 350.
belt, Kuiper 2.
belt, safety 525.
belt, tool 225.
belt, waist 205, 532.
beltclip 327.
bench 201, 379, 437, 501.
bench seat 353.
bench, defence counsel's 440.
bench, judges' 440.
bench, prosecution counsel's 440.
bench, substitutes' 481.
bend 273, 538.
Bengal, Bay of 19.
Benin 451.
beret 239.
bergamot 134.
bergère 200.
bergschrund 30.

Bering Sea 14.
Bering Strait 16.
Bermuda shorts 254.
Bernard, Saint 86.
berries 132.
berry, juniper 138.
bevel 460.
bevel square 225.
beverage can 163.
beverage dispenser 463.
Bhutan 453.
bib 260, 261.
bib necklace 264.
biceps of arm 96.
biceps of thigh 97.
biconcave lens 419.
biconvex lens 419.
bicycle 370.
bicycle parking 445.
bicycle, accessories 372.
bicycle, all-terrain 373.
bicycle, city 373.
bicycle, Dutch 373.
bicycle, parts of a 370.
bicycle, road 373.
bicycle, touring 373.
bicycles, examples of 373.
bidet 195.
Bight, Great Australian 15.
bike carrier 356.
bike, BMX 373.
bike, quad 369.
biking, mountain 522.
bikini 259.
bilberry 132.
bill 78.
billhook 234.
billiard cue 503.
billiard spot 502.
billiards 502.
bills, examples of 79.
bimah 447.
bin, compost 231.
bin, recycling 49.
binding 238, 513, 514.
binding, comb 340.
binding, safety 510.
binocular microscope 421.
biology 426.
biosphere, structure of 44.
biparous cyme 57.
birch 64.
bird 78.
bird of prey 79.
bird's eye chilli 139.
bird's nest fern 52.
bird, morphology of 78.
birds 78.
birds, examples of 80.
biscuit cutters 172.
Bishop 470.
bison 84.
bit 221, 403.
bit, screwdriver 228.
bit, spade 228.
bit, twist 228.
bits and drills, examples of 228.
bitt 385.
bitter melon 128.
bivalve shell 73.
bivalve shell, anatomy of 73.
bivalve shell, morphology of 73.
Black 470.
black 418.
black ball 503.
black bean 131.
black bear 89.
black bread 144.
black clamp 356.
black gram 131.
black mustard 138.
black pepper 138.
black pollock 161.
black pudding 156.
black radish 129.
black salsify 129.
Black Sea 14, 18, 19.
black square 470.
black stone 470.
black tea 148.
black-eyed pea 130.
blackberry 132.
blackboard 444.
blackcurrant 132.

blade 52, 55, 167, 169, 177, 180, 216, 219, 221, 226, 227, 229, 235, 270, 271, 398, 401, 412, 413, 493, 506, 509, 538.
blade close stop 270.
blade dispenser 271.
blade lift cylinder 398, 401.
blade lift fan 383.
blade locking bolt 227.
blade rotation cylinder 401.
blade shifting mechanism 401.
blade tilting lock 227.
blade tilting mechanism 227.
blade, cutting 341.
blade, dance 509.
blade, free-skating 509.
blade, rudder 384.
blank 468.
blanket 204.
blanket sleepsuit 261.
blastodisc 79.
blazer 254.
blender 176.
blender, pastry 172.
blending attachment 176.
blind spot mirror 362, 363.
blinking lights 362.
block 215, 305, 473.
block, apartment 512.
block, clamping 425.
blocking glove 507.
blood circulation 102.
blood factor negative 426.
blood factor positive 426.
blood pressure monitor 461.
blood vessel 104, 114.
blood, composition of 104.
blood, deoxygenated 104.
blood, oxygenated 104.
blouses, examples of 255.
blow pipe 296.
blowhole 90.
blowtorch 218.
blue 418.
blue ball 503.
blue beam 318.
blue line 507.
blue mussel 157.
Blue, Danish 151.
blue-veined cheeses 151.
blueberry 132.
bluefish 160.
blusher brush 266.
BMX bike 373.
boa 77.
boar, wild 84.
board 470, 519.
board game 469.
board, bulletin 341, 444.
board, cutting 169.
board, diving 184.
board, game 469.
board, memorial 447.
boarding step 395.
boarding walkway 389.
boards 506.
boat, centreboard 521.
boat, keel 521.
boater 238.
boats and ships, examples of 382.
bobble hat 239.
bodies, celestial 2.
body 118, 180, 208, 228, 255, 258, 302, 303, 305, 306, 348, 361, 420, 523, 536.
body care 267.
body flap 13.
body of fornix 109.
body of nail 114.
body side moulding 349.
body temperature control unit 10.
body tube 421.
body, collection 365.
body, packer 364.
body, tanker 364.
bodywork, examples of 347.
bogie tank wagon 377.
bole 63.
bolero 254.
boletus, edible 123.
Bolivia 448.
bolster 167, 169, 204.
bolt 222, 223, 224.
bolts 223.

bomb, volcanic 28.
bond, chemical 414.
bone, frontal 100.
bone, nasal 100.
bone, occipital 100.
bone, parietal 100.
bone, sphenoid 100.
bone, temporal 100.
bone, zygomatic 100.
bongos 309.
boning knife 169.
bonnet 348, 364.
bony fish 74.
bony fishes 159.
book ends 341.
bookcase 444.
bookshop 436.
boom 364, 399, 400, 520.
boom cylinder 399, 400.
boom operator 291.
boom vang 520.
booster parachute 12.
booster seat 205.
booster, brake 350, 357.
booster, solid rocket 12.
boot 241, 349, 509, 514, 525, 527.
boot, flexible 513.
boot, football 480.
boot, hard 513.
boot, hiking 242.
boot, inner 527.
boot, ski-jumping 513.
bootee 240.
booth 438.
booth, coupon 443.
booth, information 437.
booth, photo 437.
booth, projection 294.
booth, ticket collecting 378.
booth, undressing 465.
borage 142.
bordeaux glass 165.
border 182, 293.
borders 292.
boreal forest 44.
born 426.
Bosnia-Herzegovina 450.
Bothnia, Gulf of 18.
Botswana 452.
bottle 267, 532.
bottle opener 170, 531.
bottle, glass 163.
bottom cap 417.
bottom cushion 502.
bottom deck 404.
bottom deckboard 396.
bottom face 510.
bottom line 517.
bottom pocket 502.
bottom rail 185, 202.
bottom stair 191.
bottom-fold document case 274.
boulevard 25, 433.
bow 238, 301, 387, 519, 520.
bow door 383.
bow loading door 386.
bow saw 533.
bow thruster 387.
bow tie 245.
bow, compound 535.
bow-winged grasshopper 69.
bowl 167, 177, 180.
bowl with serving spout 177.
bowler 238, 479.
bowling 436.
bowling crease 479.
bowstring 535.
box 192, 293.
box bag 276.
box office 294.
box sealing tape dispenser 341.
box, cheese 163.
box, drink 163.
box, jury 440.
box, mitre 226.
box, night deposit 443.
box, safe deposit 443.
box, sound 297.
box, tool 225.
box, top 369.
boxer 498.
boxer shorts 247.
boxing 498.

boxing gloves 498.
boxing trunks 498.
bra 259.
brace 187, 219.
brace clip 246.
bracelets 264.
braces 246.
brachial 96.
brachial artery 102.
brachial plexus 108.
brachioradialis 96, 97.
bracket 283.
bracket base 202.
bracket, mounting 535.
bract 60.
brain 71.
brains 154.
brake 467, 501, 522.
brake booster 350, 357.
brake cable 371.
brake caliper 366.
brake fluid reservoir 357.
brake handle 523.
brake hose 357.
brake lever 371.
brake lever and shifter 522.
brake light 352.
brake lining 357.
brake pad 357.
brake pedal 350, 354, 357, 511.
brake pressure modulator 357.
brake shoe 357.
brake van 377.
brake, disc 350, 357, 525.
brakes 357.
braking circuit 350, 357.
braking system 351.
branch 62, 63, 65, 125, 194, 416, 460.
branch clip 460.
branches 63.
branching, examples of 197.
brandy glass 165.
brass family 295.
brassiere cup 259.
brattice 282.
brazier 283.
Brazil 448.
Brazil nut 133.
bread 144.
bread guide 178.
bread knife 169.
bread maker 179.
bread, multigrain 145.
bread, white 145.
break 331.
breaker 33.
bream, sea 159.
breast 78, 92, 94, 113.
breast dart 248.
breast pocket 245, 248.
breast welt pocket 244.
breaststroke 517.
breech 306.
breech guard 306.
breechblock 534.
breeds, dog 86.
brick carton 163.
brick-bond woodstrip flooring 190.
bricklayer's hammer 216.
bridge 25, 273, 297, 301, 302, 303, 420, 503.
bridge assembly 303.
bridge of nose 117.
bridging 187.
Brie 151.
briefcase 274.
briefs 247, 259.
brightness control 329.
brim 238, 239.
bristle 271, 272.
bristles 219.
broad beans 130.
broad ligament of uterus 113.
broad welt side pocket 248, 251.
broadleaved trees, examples of 64.
broccoli 127.
broccoli raab 127.
brochure rack 442.
broken line 342, 343.
bronchus, lobe 105.
bronchus, main 105.
brook 32.
brook charr 161.

ENGLISH INDEX

ASTRONOMY > 2-13; EARTH > 14-49; PLANT KINGDOM >50-65; ANIMAL KINGDOM > 66-91; HUMAN BEING > 92-119; FOOD AND KITCHEN > 120-181; HOUSE > 182-215;
DO-IT-YOURSELF AND GARDENING > 216-237; CLOTHING > 238-263; PERSONAL ADORNMENT AND ARTICLES > 264-277; ARTS AND ARCHITECTURE > 278-311; COMMUNICATIONS AND
OFFICE AUTOMATION > 312-341; TRANSPORT AND MACHINERY > 342-401; ENERGY > 402-429; SCIENCE > 414-429; SOCIETY > 430-467; SPORTS AND GAMES > 468-538

ENGLISH INDEX

543

ASTRONOMY > 2-13;   EARTH > 14-49;   PLANT KINGDOM >50-65;   ANIMAL KINGDOM > 66-91;   HUMAN BEING > 92-119;   FOOD AND KITCHEN > 120-181;   HOUSE > 182-215;
DO-IT-YOURSELF AND GARDENING > 216-237;   CLOTHING > 238-263;   PERSONAL ADORNMENT AND ARTICLES > 264-277;   ARTS AND ARCHITECTURE > 278-311;   COMMUNICATIONS AND
OFFICE AUTOMATION > 312-341;   TRANSPORT AND MACHINERY > 342-401;   ENERGY > 402-413;   SCIENCE > 414-429;   SOCIETY > 430-467;   SPORTS AND GAMES > 468-538

545

ENGLISH INDEX

ENGLISH INDEX

RONOMY > 2-13;   EARTH > 14-49;   PLANT KINGDOM >50-65;   ANIMAL KINGDOM > 66-91;   HUMAN BEING > 92-119;   FOOD AND KITCHEN > 120-181;   HOUSE > 182-215;
IT-YOURSELF AND GARDENING > 216-237;   CLOTHING > 238-263;   PERSONAL ADORNMENT AND ARTICLES > 264-277;   ARTS AND ARCHITECTURE > 278-311;   COMMUNICATIONS AND
CE AUTOMATION > 312-341;   TRANSPORT AND MACHINERY > 342-401;   ENERGY > 402-413;   SCIENCE > 414-429;   SOCIETY > 430-467;   SPORTS AND GAMES > 468-538

551

ENGLISH INDEX

men's gloves 243.
men's headgear 238.
men's shoes 240.
men's toilet 294, 439.
meninges 109.
menorah 447.
menu button 315, 327.
Mercury 2, 3.
mercury bulb 424.
mercury thermometer 461.
merguez sausage 156.
méridienne 200.
mesa 36.
mesh 205, 493.
mesh bag 162.
mesh strainer 171.
mesocarp 57, 58, 59.
mesopause 37.
mesosphere 37.
metal arm 236.
metal counterhoop 308.
metal frame 304.
metal rod 309.
metal sorting 49.
metal structure 374.
metallic contact grid 410.
metamorphic rocks 26.
meteorological forecast 38.
meteorology 37.
meteorology, station model 39.
metered dose inhaler 467.
methylated spirits 405.
metre 426.
Mexico 448.
Mexico, Gulf of 16.
mezzanine 378.
mezzanine floor 182, 189.
mezzanine stairs 189.
Micro Compact Car 347.
microfilament 66.
micrometer caliper 425.
Micronesia 453.
micronucleus 66.
microphone 320, 327, 328, 332, 337, 456.
microphones 457.
microscope 421.
microscopes, magnifying glass and 421.
microtubule 66.
microwave oven 164, 178.
microwave relay station 334.
microwaves 418.
Mid-Atlantic Ridge 34.
mid-calf length sock 247.
Mid-Indian Ridge 34.
mid-ocean ridge 33.
middle attacker 487.
middle back 487.
middle clouds 42.
middle covert 78.
middle ear 116.
middle finger 115.
middle leg 67, 68.
middle linebacker 484.
middle lobe 105.
middle nasal concha 117.
middle panel 185.
middle phalanx 114.
middle piece 111.
middle primary covert 78.
middle sole 262.
middle toe 78.
midfielder, central 481.
midfielder, left 481.
midfielder, right 481.
midrange pickup 303.
midrange speaker 324.
midrib 51, 55, 60.
midriff band 259.
Mihrab 447.
Mihrab dome 447.
mileometer 355.
military communications 317.
milk 150.
milk chocolate 148.
milk, evaporated 150.
milk, goat's 150.
milk, homogenized 150.
milk, powdered 150.
milk/cream cup 163.
Milky Way 6.
Milky Way (seen from above) 6.
Milky Way (side view) 6.

mill, food 170.
millet 61, 143.
millet: spike 61.
Mimas 3.
minaret 447.
Minbar 447.
minced beef 152.
minced lamb 153.
minced pork 153.
minced veal 152.
mincer 170.
mini briefs 247.
mini stereo sound system 325.
minibus 347, 363.
minim 299.
minim rest 299.
mink 88.
minor sciatic nerve 108.
minor surgery 462.
mint 142.
minute 428.
minute hand 424.
Miranda 3.
mirror 195, 277, 366, 368, 369, 421, 439, 523.
mirror, blind spot 362, 363.
mirror, concave primary 9.
mirror, crossover 362.
mirror, outside 362.
mirror, partially reflecting 420.
mirror, secondary 7, 9.
mirror, totally reflecting 420.
mirror, West Coast 363.
miscellaneous articles 341.
miscellaneous domestic appliances 180.
miscellaneous equipment 231.
miscellaneous utensils 173.
Mississippi River 16.
mist 41.
mitochondrion 50, 66.
mitral valve 104.
mitre box 226.
mitre latch 226.
mitre scale 226.
mitten 243.
mix, depolarizing 417.
mix, water-steam 402.
mixed forest 44.
mixing bowl 176.
mixing bowls 172.
moat 282.
mobile remote servicer 11.
mobile telephone 327.
mobile unit 316.
mobile X-ray unit 462.
moccasin 242.
mock pocket 251.
mode selectors 326.
modem 334.
modem, cable 335.
moderator 408.
modulation wheel 310.
module, centrifuge 11.
module, European experiment 11.
module, Japanese experiment 11.
module, Russian 11.
module, U.S. habitation 11.
Mohorovicic discontinuity 26.
moistener 339.
molar, cross section 101.
molars 101.
molasses 149.
Moldova 450.
mole 426.
mole wrench 222.
molecule 414.
molluscs 72, 157.
Monaco 450.
money and modes of payment 441.
Mongolia 453.
mongoose 88.
monitor lizard 77.
monkfish 160.
mono-hulls 521.
Monopoly® 469.
mons pubis 112.
monument 25.
Moon 2, 4, 5.
Moon's orbit 4, 5.
Moon, phases 5.
moons 2.
mooring winch 385.
mop 215.

moped 369.
moraine, end 30.
moraine, terminal 30.
mordent 299.
morel 123.
Morocco 451.
morphology of a bird 78.
morphology of a bivalve shell 73.
morphology of a butterfly 67.
morphology of a dog 86.
morphology of a dolphin 90.
morphology of a frog 75.
morphology of a gorilla 91.
morphology of a honeybee: worker 68.
morphology of a horse 83.
morphology of a lobster 71.
morphology of a perch 74.
morphology of a rat 82.
morphology of a shark 74.
morphology of a snail 72.
morphology of a spider 70.
morphology of a turtle 76.
morphology of a univalve shell 73.
morphology of a venomous snake: head 76.
morphology of an octopus 72.
mortadella 156.
mortar 170.
mosaic 280.
mosque 447.
mosquito 69.
moss 51.
moss, common hair cap 51.
moss, Irish 123.
moss, structure of 51.
mosses, examples of 51.
moth, atlas 69.
motion detector 286.
motocross and supercross motorcycle 525.
motor 212, 213, 214, 227, 229, 237.
motor bogie 376.
motor car 380.
motor end plate 110.
motor neuron 110.
motor racing 524.
motor root 109, 110.
motor scooter 369.
motor sports 524.
motor unit 176, 177, 180, 208, 272, 376.
motor vehicle pollution 47.
motor yacht 385.
motorcycle 366.
motorcycle : view from above 368.
motorcycle, leading 522.
motorcycle, off-road 369.
motorcycle, touring 369.
motorcycle-mounted camera 522.
motorcycles, examples of 369.
motorcycling 525.
motorway 25, 343, 431.
motorway number 25.
motto 441.
mouflon 84.
mould, charlotte 172.
moulding, bumper 348.
mount, ball 356.
mountain 29.
mountain biking 522.
mountain lodge 512.
mountain range 5, 24, 26.
mountain slope 29.
mountain torrent 29.
Mountains, Appalachian 16.
Mountains, Atlas 20.
Mountains, Carpathian 18.
Mountains, Rocky 16.
Mountains, Transantarctic 15.
Mountains, Ural 18.
mounting bracket 535.
mounting plate 199.
mouse pad 332.
mouse port 329.
mouse, cordless 332.
mouse, field 82.
mouse, mechanical 332.
mouse, optical 332.
mouse, wheel 332.
mouth 71, 72, 73, 75, 90, 94, 116, 305.
mouthparts 68.
mouthpiece 306, 307, 311, 467.
mouthpiece receiver 307.

mouthpipe 307.
mouthwash 272.
movable bridges 344.
movable jaw 223, 224.
movable maxillary 76.
movable stands 444.
movement, horizontal ground 27.
movement, vertical ground 27.
movements of aircraft 395.
Mozambique 452.
Mozambique Channel 20.
mozzarella 150.
Mt Everest 37.
mud flap 349, 364, 365.
mud hut 288.
mud injection hose 403.
mud pit 403.
mud pump 403.
mudflow 31.
mudguard 370.
muff 276.
muffler felt 304.
mule 84, 242.
mullet 160.
multi-hulls 521.
multi-image jump button 315.
multi-purpose solution 272.
multigrain bread 145.
multipack 163.
multiple exposure mode 314.
multiple light fitting 207.
multiplication 427.
multiply key 337.
multipurpose tool 217.
mummy 530.
mung bean 131.
Munster 151.
muscle fibre 110.
muscles 96.
museum 433.
mushroom 52.
mushroom, enoki 123.
mushroom, structure 52.
mushrooms 123.
music 296.
music rest 305, 311.
music room 444.
musical instrument digital interface (MIDI) cable 311.
musical notation 298.
muskmelon 135.
muslin 171.
mustard, American 140.
mustard, black 138.
mustard, Dijon 140.
mustard, English 140.
mustard, German 140.
mustard, powdered 140.
mustard, white 138.
mustard, wholegrain 140.
mute 307.
muzzle 83, 86, 87, 534.
Myanmar 453.
mycelium 52.
myelin sheath 110.
myocardium 104.
myopia 419.

N

nacelle 413.
nacelle cross-section 413.
nail 220.
nail bed 114.
nail cleaner 265.
nail clippers 265.
nail file 265.
nail groove 531.
nail matrix 114.
nail scissors 265.
nail set 220.
nail shaper 265.
nail varnish 265.
nail whitener pencil 265.
nail, common 220.
nail, cut 220.
nail, finishing 220.
nail, masonry 220.
nail, spiral 220.
nails, examples of 220.
naked strangle 499.
name, currency 441.
name, domain 334.
name, gymnast's 497.

name, holder's 441.
nameplate 313.
names, tropical cyclone 43.
Namib Desert 20.
Namibia 452.
naos 279.
nape 78, 93, 95.
nappy 260.
nappy, disposable 260.
naris 117.
nasal bone 100, 117.
nasal cavity 105.
nasal fossae 117.
nasopharynx 117.
national broadcasting network 316.
national park 25.
nationality 497.
natural 299.
natural arch 35.
natural environment 504.
natural greenhouse effect 46.
natural sponge 267.
Nauru 453.
nave 285.
navel 92, 94.
navigation light 383, 393.
Nazca Plate 27.
Neapolitan coffee maker 181.
near/far dial 320.
neck 76, 83, 93, 94, 95, 101, 111, 167, 297, 301, 302, 303, 318.
neck end 245.
neck of femur 99.
neck pad 486.
neck strap 458.
neck support 525.
neck, filler 351.
neckhole 247.
necklaces 264.
neckroll 204.
necktie 245.
nectarine 132.
needle 36, 460.
needle hub 460.
needle, larding 173.
needle, trussing 173.
needle-nose pliers 217.
negative contact 410, 411.
negative meniscus 419.
negative plate 359.
negative plate strap 359.
negative region 410.
negative terminal 359, 416, 417.
negligee 256.
neon lamp 217.
Nepal 453.
Neptune 2, 3.
nerve 114.
nerve fibre 114.
nerve termination 114.
nerve, olfactory 117.
nerve, spinal 109.
nervous system 108.
nest of tables 202.
net 487, 489, 491, 493, 495.
net band 491.
net judge 491.
net support 493.
Netherlands 449.
nettle 127.
network connection 198.
network port 329.
neurons 110.
neutral conductor 198.
neutral indicator 368.
neutral line 416.
neutral zone 484, 507.
neutron 414.
neutron, incident 415.
névé 30.
New Caledonia 15.
new crescent 5.
new moon 5.
new shekel 440.
New Zealand 15, 453.
newborn children's clothing 260.
newel post 191.
Newfoundland Island 16.
news items 313.
newsagent's shop 437.
newspaper 313.
newt 75.
newton 426.
nib 312.

ASTRONOMY > 2-13;   EARTH > 14-49;   PLANT KINGDOM > 50-65;   ANIMAL KINGDOM > 66-91;   HUMAN BEING > 92-119;   FOOD AND KITCHEN > 120-181;   HOUSE > 182-215;
DO-IT-YOURSELF AND GARDENING > 216-237;   CLOTHING > 238-263;   PERSONAL ADORNMENT AND ARTICLES > 264-277;   ARTS AND ARCHITECTURE > 278-311;   COMMUNICATIONS AND
OFFICE AUTOMATION > 312-341;   TRANSPORT AND MACHINERY > 342-401;   ENERGY > 402-413;   SCIENCE > 414-429;   SOCIETY > 430-467;   SPORTS AND GAMES > 468-538.   553

ENGLISH INDEX

ASTRONOMY > 2-13; EARTH > 14-49; PLANT KINGDOM >50-65; ANIMAL KINGDOM > 66-91; HUMAN BEING > 92-119; FOOD AND KITCHEN > 120-181; HOUSE > 182-215;
DO-IT-YOURSELF AND GARDENING > 216-237; CLOTHING > 238-263; PERSONAL ADORNMENT AND ARTICLES > 264-277; ARTS AND ARCHITECTURE > 278-311; COMMUNICATIONS AND
OFFICE AUTOMATION > 312-341; TRANSPORT AND MACHINERY > 342-401; ENERGY > 402-413; SCIENCE > 414-429; SOCIETY > 430-467; SPORTS AND GAMES > 468-538

ENGLISH INDEX

557

ENGLISH INDEX

ENGLISH INDEX

ASTRONOMY > 2-13; EARTH > 14-49; PLANT KINGDOM >50-65; ANIMAL KINGDOM > 66-91; HUMAN BEING > 92-119; FOOD AND KITCHEN > 120-181; HOUSE > 182-215;
DO-IT-YOURSELF AND GARDENING > 216-237; CLOTHING > 238-263; PERSONAL ADORNMENT AND ARTICLES > 264-277; ARTS AND ARCHITECTURE > 278-311; COMMUNICATIONS AND
OFFICE AUTOMATION > 312-341; TRANSPORT AND MACHINERY > 342-401; ENERGY > 402-413; SCIENCE > 414-429; SOCIETY > 430-467; SPORTS AND GAMES > 468-538

561

ENGLISH INDEX

ASTRONOMY > 2-13;   EARTH > 14-49;   PLANT KINGDOM >50-65;   ANIMAL KINGDOM > 66-91;   HUMAN BEING > 92-119;   FOOD AND KITCHEN > 120-181;   HOUSE > 182-215;
DO-IT-YOURSELF AND GARDENING > 216-237;   CLOTHING > 238-263;   PERSONAL ADORNMENT AND ARTICLES > 264-277;   ARTS AND ARCHITECTURE > 278-311;   COMMUNICATIONS AND
OFFICE AUTOMATION > 312-341;   TRANSPORT AND MACHINERY > 342-401;   ENERGY > 402-413;   SCIENCE > 414-429;   SOCIETY > 430-467;   SPORTS AND GAMES > 468-538.

ENGLISH INDEX

French Index

ASTRONOMY > 2-13;   EARTH > 14-49;   PLANT KINGDOM >50-65;   ANIMAL KINGDOM > 66-91;   HUMAN BEING > 92-119;   FOOD AND KITCHEN > 120-181;   HOUSE > 182-215;
DO-IT-YOURSELF AND GARDENING > 216-237;   CLOTHING > 238-263;   PERSONAL ADORNMENT AND ARTICLES > 264-277;   ARTS AND ARCHITECTURE > 278-311;   COMMUNICATIONS AND
OFFICE AUTOMATION > 312-341;   TRANSPORT AND MACHINERY > 342-401;   ENERGY > 402-413;   SCIENCE > 414-429;   SOCIETY > 430-467;   SPORTS AND GAMES > 468-538.

565

568

ASTRONOMY > 2-13;   EARTH > 14-49;   PLANT KINGDOM >50-65;   ANIMAL KINGDOM > 66-91;   HUMAN BEING > 92-119;   FOOD AND KITCHEN > 120-181;   HOUSE > 182-215;
DO-IT-YOURSELF AND GARDENING > 216-237;   CLOTHING > 238-263;   PERSONAL ADORNMENT AND ARTICLES > 264-277;   ARTS AND ARCHITECTURE > 278-311;   COMMUNICATIONS AND
OFFICE AUTOMATION > 312-341;   TRANSPORT AND MACHINERY > 342-401;   ENERGY > 402-413;   SCIENCE > 414-429;   SOCIETY > 430-467;   SPORTS AND GAMES > 468-538.

cercle(m) extérieur 515.
cercle(m) intérieur 515.
cercle(m) polaire antarctique 15, 21, 22.
cercle(m) polaire arctique 21, 22.
cercle(m) porte-lame(m) 401.
cercle(m) restrictif 488.
céréales(f) 61, 143.
cerf(m) de Virginie 84.
cerf(m) du Canada 84.
cerfeuil(m) 142.
cerise(f) 132.
cerne(m) annuel 63.
cerneau(m) 60.
cerques(m) 536.
cerveau(m) 71, 109.
cervelet(m) 109.
cervelle(f) 154.
Chac-Mool 283.
chaîne(f) 370, 372.
chaîne(f) alimentaire 45.
chaîne(f) coupante 235.
chaîne(f) de levage(m) 396.
chaîne(f) de montagnes(f) 5, 24, 26.
chaîne(f) de neurones(m) 110.
chaîne(f) de sûreté(f) 361.
chaîne(f) nerveuse ventrale 71.
chaîne(f) stéréo 322.
chaînette(f) de levage(m) 196.
chaire(f) 446.
chaise(f) 201, 444.
chaise(f) berçante 201.
chaise(f) haute 205.
chaise(f) longue 201.
chaise(f) pliante 201.
chaise(f)-escabeau(m) 201.
chaises(f) empilables 201.
chaises(f), exemples(m) 201.
chalaze(f) 79.
chalet(m) de montagne(f) 512.
chalet(m) du sommet(m) 512.
chalet(m) principal 512.
chaloupe(f) de sauvetage(m) 382, 386.
chalumeau(m) 296.
chalutier(m) 384.
chambranle(m) 185, 186.
chambre(f) 189, 528.
chambre(f) à air(m) 79.
chambre(f) antérieure 119.
chambre(f) d'expansion(f) 424.
chambre(f) d'hôpital(m) 464.
chambre(f) d'isolement(m) 462.
chambre(f) d'observation(f) 462, 465.
chambre(f) d'observation(f) psychiatrique 462.
chambre(f) de combustion(f) 192, 360.
chambre(f) de décharge(f) 278.
chambre(f) de la reine(f) 278.
chambre(f) des pompes(f) 384.
chambre(f) double 439.
chambre(f) du roi(m) 278.
chambre(f) forte 443.
chambre(f) froide 120, 121.
chambre(f) photographique 315.
chambre(f) postérieure 119.
chambre(f) principale, plafond(m) cathédrale(f) 189.
chambre(f) principale, toit(m) cathédrale(f) 189.
chambre(f) pulpaire 101.
chambre(f) simple 439.
chambre(f) souterraine 278.
chambres(f) d'hôtel(m) 439.
chameau(m) 85.
champ(m) centre(m) 475.
champ(m) droit 475.
champ(m) gauche 475.
champ(m) géothermique 402.
champ(m) magnétique 318, 416.
champignon(m) 52.
champignon(m) de couche(f) 123.
champignon(m) mortel 52.
champignon(m) vénéneux 52.
champignon(m), structure(f) 52.
champignons(m) 123.
chanfrein(m) 83.
changement(m) de piste(f) 323.
chanterelle(f) commune 123.
chape(f) 190.
chapeau(m) 52, 313.
chapeau(m) de feutre(m) 238.
chapeau(m) de ventilation(f) 194.
chapelle(f) 282.
chapelle(f) axiale 284.

chapelle(f) latérale 284.
chapiteau(m) 302.
chapka(m) 238.
chapon(m) 155.
charcuterie(f) 156.
charge(f) électrique, mesure(f) 426.
chargeur(m) 228.
chargeuse(f) frontale 399.
chargeuse(f)-pelleteuse(f) 399.
chariot(m) 290, 397, 421, 505, 521.
chariot(m) à bagages(m) 374.
chariot(m) élévateur 396.
chariots(m) 121.
Charles IX(m) 241.
charnière(f) 178, 214, 274, 277, 352, 420, 511.
charnière(f) de la visière(f) 367.
Charon 3.
charpente(f) 187, 279, 280.
chasse(f) 534.
chasse-clou(m) 220.
chasse-neige(m) à soufflerie(f) 365.
chasse-pierres(m) 376, 377.
châssis(m) 308, 309, 396, 400, 401.
chasuble(f) 252.
chat(m) 87.
chat(m) de l'île(f) de Man 87.
chat(m), tête(f) 87.
châtaigne(f) d'eau(f) 124.
château(m) fort 282.
chats(m), races(f) 87.
chauffage(m) 192.
chauffage(m) au bois(m) 192.
chauffe-eau(m) 194.
chaufferette(f) 529.
chaumard(m) 521.
chaussée(f) 342, 345, 434.
chaussette(f) 247, 257, 480, 486, 492.
chaussette(f)-étrier(m) 476.
chaussettes(f) 247.
chaussettes(f) hautes 483.
chausson(m) intérieur 511, 527.
chaussure(f) 478, 488, 509, 514, 522, 524, 527.
chaussure(f) à crampons(m) 476, 483, 486.
chaussure(f) d'haltérophilie(f) 500.
chaussure(f) de football(m) 480.
chaussure(f) de piste(f) 473.
chaussure(f) de ski(m) 510, 511.
chaussure(f) de sport(m) 262.
chaussure(f) de tennis(m) 492.
chaussure(f), parties(f) 240.
chaussures(f) 240.
chaussures(f) d'homme(m) 240.
chaussures(f) de femme(f) 241.
chaussures(f) de golf(m) 505.
chaussures(f) unisexes 242.
chayote(f) 129.
chef(m) décorateur(m) 290.
chef(m) électricien(m) 291.
chef(m) machiniste(m) 290.
chef(m) opérateur(m) du son(m) 291.
chemin(m) 504.
chemin(m) d'évacuation(f) 345.
chemin(m) de fer(m) 25.
chemin(m) de fer(m) métropolitain 378.
chemin(m) de ronde(f) 282.
chemin(m) de ronde(f) couvert 282.
chemin(m) de roulement(m) 397.
cheminée(f) 28, 183, 188, 193, 382, 402.
cheminée(f) à foyer(m) ouvert 192.
cheminée(f) antisuie 386.
cheminée(f) d'échappement(m) 364, 401.
chemise(f) 245, 340, 534.
chemise(f) de nuit(f) 256.
chemise(f) du donjon(m) 282.
chemise(f) en acier(m) 417.
chemisier(m) classique 255.
chemisiers(m), exemples(m) 255.
chêne(m) 64.
chenets(m) 193.
chenille(f) 67, 398, 523.
chèque(m) de voyage(m) 441.
chèques(m) 441.
chéquier(m) 379.
chercheur(m) 8, 9.
chérimole(f) 136.
cheval(m) 83, 85.
cheval(m) d'arçons(m) 496.
cheval(m) d'arçons(m) 496.

cheval(m) sautoir 496, 497.
cheval(m), morphologie(f) 83.
cheval(m)-sautoir(m) 496.
chevalet(m) 297, 301, 302, 303.
chevalet(m) des aigus(m) 304.
chevalet(m) des basses(f) 304.
chevalière(f) 264.
chevelu(m) 63.
chevet(m) 285.
cheveux(m) 93, 95.
cheville(f) 92, 94, 202, 301, 302.
cheville(f) d'accord(m) 304.
chevillier(m) 301.
chèvre(f) 84.
chèvre(m) frais 150.
chevron(m) 187.
chiasma(m) optique 109.
chicane(f) 524.
chicorée(f) de Trévise 126.
chicorée(f) frisée 127.
chien(m) 86, 534, 535.
chien(m), morphologie(f) 86.
chiens(m), races(f) 86.
chiffres(m) romains 427.
Chili(m) 448.
chimie(f) 414.
chimpanzé(m) 91.
Chine(f) 453.
chinois(m) 171.
chipolata(f) 156.
chirurgie(f) mineure 462.
chloroplaste(m) 50.
chocolat(m) 148.
chocolat(m) au lait(m) 148.
chocolat(m) blanc 148.
chocolat(m) noir 148.
chope(f) à bière(f) 165.
chope(f) à café(m) 166.
chorizo(m) 156.
choroïde(f) 119.
chou(m) cavalier(m) 126.
chou(m) de Milan 126.
chou(m) frisé 126.
chou(m) laitue(f) 126.
chou(m) marin 126.
chou(m) pommé blanc 126.
chou(m) pommé rouge 126.
chou(m) pommé vert 126.
chou(m)-fleur(f) 127.
chou(m)-rave(f) 125.
choux(m) de Bruxelles 126.
chœur(m) 284, 285.
chromatine(f) 66.
chromosphère(f) 4.
chronique(f) 313.
chronomètre(f) 424.
chronomètre(m) électronique automatique 517.
chronométreur(m) 488, 498, 509.
chronométreur(m) de couloir(m) 516.
chronométreur(m) des trente secondes(f) 488.
chronométreur(m) en chef(m) 516.
chronométreurs(m) 499.
chrysalide(f) 67.
chukka(m) 240.
chute(f) 31, 519.
chute(f) d'eau(f) 32.
chutney(m) à la mangue(f) 141.
Chypre(f) 450.
cible(f) 471.
ciboule(f) 124.
ciboulette(f) 124.
ciel(m) d'orage(m) 41.
cierge(m) 446.
cigale(f) 69.
cigogne(f) 80.
cil(m) 66, 119.
cilié 55.
cils(m) 87.
cime(f) 63.
cimetière(m) 25, 433.
cimier(m) mobile 7.
cinéma(m) 294, 386, 432, 436.
cinq cents(m) 427.
cinq(m) 427.
cinq-épices(m) chinois 139.
cinquante(m) 427.
cintres(m) 292.
circonférence(f) 428.
circuit(m) capteurs(m) 357.
circuit(m) d'eau(f) chaude 194.
circuit(m) d'eau(f) froide 194.
circuit(m) d'évacuation(f) 194.
circuit(m) de freinage(m) 350, 357.

circuit(m) de photopiles(f) 411.
circuit(m) de plomberie(f) 194.
circuit(m) de ventilation(f) 194.
circuit(m) électrique en parallèle(f) 416.
circuit(m) imprimé 417.
circuit(m) intégré 417.
circuit(m) intégré en boîtier(m) 417.
circuit(m), course(f) automobile 524.
circulation(f) sanguine 102.
circulation(f) sanguine, schéma(m) 103.
cirque(m) 5.
cirque(m) glaciaire 30.
cirro-cumulus(m) 42.
cirro-stratus(m) 42.
cirrus(m) 42.
cisaille(f) à haies(f) 234.
cisaille(f) à volaille(f) 173.
ciseau(m) à bois(m) 229.
ciseaux(m) 461, 531.
ciseaux(m) à cuticules(f) 265.
ciseaux(m) à effiler 270.
ciseaux(m) à ongles(m) 265.
ciseaux(m) de coiffeur(m) 270.
ciseaux(m) de cuisine(f) 173.
ciseaux(m) de pédicure(f) 265.
ciseaux(m) de sûreté(f) 265.
ciseaux(m) sculpteurs 270.
citerne(f) 364, 385.
cithare(f) 296.
citron(m) 134.
citron(m) vert 134.
citrouille(f) 129.
civière(f) 460.
clairon(m) 307.
clapet(m) 196, 327.
claque(f) 240, 263.
claquette(f) 291.
clarinette(f) 306.
clarinette(f) basse 295.
clarinettes(m) 295.
classeur(m) 339.
classeur(m) à soufflets(m) 274.
clavardage(m) 335.
clavicule(f) 98.
clavier(m) 304, 310, 327, 330, 336.
clavier(m) à pédales(f) 305.
clavier(m) accompagnement(m) 296.
clavier(m) alphanumérique 327, 346, 442, 443.
clavier(m) chant(m) 296.
clavier(m) d'identification(f) personnelle 443.
clavier(m) de grand orgue(m) 305.
clavier(m) de positif(m) 305.
clavier(m) de récit(m) 305.
clavier(m) numérique 423.
claviers(m) manuels 305.
clayette(f) 211.
clé(f) 306.
clé(f) à douille(f) à cliquet(m) 223.
clé(f) à fourches(f) 223.
clé(f) à molette(f) 223.
clé(f) à tuyau(m) 216.
clé(f) coudée à tuyau(m) 216.
clé(f) d'ut(m) 298.
clé(f) de bocal(m) 306.
clé(f) de bras(m) 499.
clé(f) de contact(m) 237.
clé(f) de fa(m) 298.
clé(f) de mandrin(m) 228.
clé(f) de sol(m) 298.
clé(f) de voûte(f) 284.
clé(f) en croix(f) 356.
clé(f) mixte 223.
clé(f) polygonale 223.
clé(f) polygonale à cliquet(m) 223.
clé(f) polygonale à têtes(f) fendues 223.
clés(f) 216, 223, 298, 311.
client(m) 317.
clignotant(m) arrière 367.
climatiseur(m) 361.
climats(m) arides 40.
climats(m) de montagne(f) 40.
climats(m) du monde(m) 40.
climats(m) polaires 40.
climats(m) tempérés chauds 40.
climats(m) tempérés froids 40.
climats(m) tropicaux 40.
cliquet(m) 203.
clitoris(m) 112.
cloche(f) 289.
clocher(m) 285, 446.
clocheton(m) 282, 284, 285.

clochettes(f) 309.
cloison(f) 58, 117, 457, 469, 528.
cloison(f) longitudinale 384.
cloison(f) transversale 384.
clôture(f) 122, 182.
clôture(f) du champ(m) extérieur 475.
clôture(f) en lattis(m) 230.
clou(m) 220.
clou(m) à maçonnerie(f) 220.
clou(m) à tête(f) homme(m) 220.
clou(m) à tige(f) spiralée 220.
clou(m) commun 220.
clou(m) coupé 220.
clou(m) de girofle(m) 138.
clous(m), exemples(m) 220.
coach(m) 347.
cobaye(m) 82.
cobra(m) 77.
coccinelle(f) 69.
coccyx(m) 98.
cochlée(f) 116.
cockpit(m) 520.
code(m) des produits(m) 423.
code(m) temporel 291.
coffre(m) 203, 349, 369, 410, 411.
coffre(m) à bagages(m) 361.
coffre(m) d'appareillage(m) 376.
coffre(m) de rangement(m) 364, 455.
coffre-fort(m) 443.
coffret(m) 318.
coffret(m) de branchement(m) 198.
coffret(m) de sûreté(f) 443.
coiffe(f) 53, 536.
coiffeur(m) 290.
coiffeuse(f) 195, 203.
coiffure(f) 238, 268.
coiffures(f) d'homme(m) 238.
coiffures(f) de femme(f) 239.
coiffures(f) unisexes 239.
coin(m) 305, 498.
coin(m) de patinoire(f) 506.
coin(m)-repas(m) 164, 188.
coing(m) 133.
col(m) 29, 244, 245, 248, 262, 318.
col(m) de l'utérus(m) 112.
col(m) du fémur(m) 99.
col(m) italien 245.
col(m) pointes(f) boutonnées 245.
col(m) roulé 250, 514.
col(m) tailleur(m) 251.
col(m) transformable 248.
col(m)-de-cygne(m) 191, 400.
colibri(m) 80.
collant(m) 257.
collant(m) fantaisie(f) 260.
collant(m) sans pied(m) 263.
collatéral(m) 285.
collatérale(f) 110.
colle(f) 190.
collecte(f) sélective 49.
collecteur(m) d'appareil(m) 194.
collecteur(m) d'échappement(m) 350, 360.
collecteur(m) d'électrons(m) 417.
collecteur(m) d'évacuation(f) 194.
collecteur(m) de graisse(f) 179.
collecteur(m) principal 194.
collet(m) 53, 101, 167, 193, 229, 535.
collet(m) de l'axone(m) 110.
colley(m) 86.
collier(m) 174, 511.
collier(m) coupe-feu(m) 193.
collier(m) de perles(f), longueur(f) matinée(f) 264.
collier(m) de serrage(m) 501.
collier(m) de serrage(m) du casque(m) 10.
collier(m) de soirée(f) 264.
collier(m)-de-chien(m) 264.
colliers(m) 264.
colline(f) 29.
colline(f) abyssale 33.
collybie(f) à pied(m) velouté 123.
Colombie(f) 448.
côlon(m) ascendant 106.
côlon(m) descendant 106.
côlon(m) pelvien 106.
côlon(m) transverse 106.
colonne(f) 31, 279, 302, 313, 380.
colonne(f) corinthienne engagée 281.
colonne(f) d'alcool(m) 424.
colonne(f) de collecte du papier(m) 49.
colonne(f) de collecte du verre(m) 49.

ASTRONOMY > 2-13;   EARTH > 14-49;   PLANT KINGDOM > 50-65;   ANIMAL KINGDOM > 66-91;   HUMAN BEING > 92-119;   FOOD AND KITCHEN > 120-181;   HOUSE > 182-215;
DO-IT-YOURSELF AND GARDENING > 216-237;   CLOTHING > 238-263;   PERSONAL ADORNMENT AND ARTICLES > 264-277;   ARTS AND ARCHITECTURE > 278-311;   COMMUNICATIONS AND
OFFICE AUTOMATION > 312-341;   TRANSPORT AND MACHINERY > 342-401;   ENERGY > 402-413;   SCIENCE > 414-429;   SOCIETY > 430-467;   SPORTS AND GAMES > 468-538

569

FRENCH INDEX

couronne(f) 4, 83, 101, 286, 308, 424, 441.
couronne(f) d'orientation(f) 400.
couronnement(m) 191.
courrier(m) des lecteurs(m) 313.
courrier(m) électronique 335.
courroie(f) d'entrainement(m) 212.
courroie(f) de distribution(f) 360.
courroie(f) de tige(f) 511.
courroie(f) de transmission(f) 383.
courroie(f) de ventilateur(m) 350, 360.
cours(m) d'eau(f) 32, 48.
course(f) automobile 524.
coursier(m) d'évacuateur(m) 406.
court péronier(m) latéral 97.
court(m) 490.
court(m) de service(m) droit 491.
court(m) de service(m) gauche 491.
courte piste(f) 508.
courtine(f) 282.
couscous(m) 144.
couscoussier(m) 175.
coussin(m) arrière 502.
coussin(m) carré 204.
coussin(m) d'air(m) 262.
coussin(m) de rembourrage(m) 498.
coussin(m) de tête(f) 502.
coussinet(m) en mousse(f) 458.
couteau(m) 157, 167, 176, 177, 180, 531, 533.
couteau(m) à beurre(m) 168.
couteau(m) à bifteck(m) 168.
couteau(m) à découper 169.
couteau(m) à désosser 169.
couteau(m) à dessert(m) 168.
couteau(m) à filets(m) de sole(f) 169.
couteau(m) à fromage(m) 168.
couteau(m) à huitres(f) 169.
couteau(m) à jambon(m) 169.
couteau(m) à pain(m) 169.
couteau(m) à pamplemousse(m) 169.
couteau(m) à poisson(m) 168.
couteau(m) à zester 169.
couteau(m) d'office(m) 169.
couteau(m) de chef(m) 169.
couteau(m) de cuisine(f) 169.
couteau(m) de table(f) 168.
couteau(m) électrique 177.
couteau(m) suisse 531.
couteaux(m) de cuisine(f), exemples(m) 169.
couteaux(m), exemples(m) 168.
couture(f) 477, 478.
couture(f) d'assemblage(m) 243.
couture(f) médiane 245.
couturier(m) 96.
couvercle(m) 174, 177, 178, 179, 180, 181, 196, 198, 211, 212, 215, 225, 315, 454, 533.
couvercle(m) de batterie(f) 359.
couvercle(m) de culasse(f) 350, 360.
couvercle(m) de propreté(f) 210.
couvercle(m) de réservoir(m) 196.
couvercle(m) inférieur 417.
couvercle(m) supérieur 417.
couverts(m) 167.
couverture(f) 204.
couvre-filtre(m) 459.
couvre-oreiller(m) 204.
Cowper, glande(f) 111.
cœur(m) 58, 71, 73, 104, 105, 154, 192, 468, 492.
crabe(m) 158.
cracker(m) de seigle(m) 145.
cracker(m) scandinave 145.
craie(f) 503.
crampon(m) 263, 478.
crampon(m) de fermeture(f) 277.
crampons(m) interchangeables 480.
cran(m) 244, 246, 422, 473, 536.
cran(m) de réglage(m) 222, 511.
crâne(m) 92.
crâne(m) d'enfant(m) 100.
crâne(m), vue(f) latérale 100.
crapaud(m) commun 75.
cratère(m) 5, 28.
cravate(f) 245.
crawl(m) 517.
crayon(m) 312, 409.
crayon(m) à sourcils(m) 266.
crayon(m) blanchisseur d'ongles(m) 265.
crayon(m) contour(m) des lèvres(f) 266.
crayon(m) en plomb(m) 312.
crédit(m) photographique 313.
crémaillère(f) 178, 191, 211, 473.
crème(f) 150.
crème(f) aigre 150.
crème(f) épaisse 150.
crémier(m) 166.
crénelé 55.
crépis(f) 279.
cresson(m) alénois 127.
cresson(m) de fontaine(f) 127.
crête(f) 29, 33, 406, 418.
creux(m) 33, 167, 418.
creux(m) barométrique 39.
crevasse(f) 30.
crevette(f) 158.
cric(m) 356.
cricket(m) 478.
crinière(f) 83.
criquet(m) mélodieux 69.
cristallin(m) 119, 419.
cristallisation(f) 414.
cristaux(m) liquides 424.
critique(f) gastronomique 313.
Croatie(f) 450.
croche(f) 299.
crochet(m) 70, 73, 186, 217, 225, 364, 397, 423, 460, 502, 509.
crochet(m) à venin(m) 76.
crochet(m) de levage(m) 403.
crochet(m) de petit doigt(m) 307.
crochet(m) de pouce(m) 307.
crochet(m) du plateau(m) 422.
crochet(m) pétrisseur 176.
crocodile(m) 77.
crocus(m) 56.
croisée(f) 284.
croisée(f) du transept(m) 285.
croisillon(m) 467.
croissant(m) 5, 144.
croix(f) d'autel(m) 446.
croix(f) de Saint-André 187.
crosne(m) 124.
crosse(f) 52, 302, 466, 534.
crosse(f) de fougère(f) 125.
crosse(f) de gardien(m) de but(m) 507.
crosse(f) de joueur(m) 506.
crottin(m) de Chavignol 150.
croupe(f) 83.
croupion(m) 78.
croûte(f) basaltique 26.
croûte(f) continentale 26.
croûte(f) de cuir(m) 246.
croûte(f) granitique 26.
croûte(f) océanique 26.
croûte(f) terrestre 26, 27.
croûte(f) terrestre, coupe(f) 26.
crucifix(m) 446.
crustacés(m) 71, 158.
Cuba(f) 448.
cube(m) 429.
cubes(m) d'agneau(m) 153.
cubes(m) de bœuf(m) 152.
cubes(m) de veau(m) 152.
cubiculum(m) 280.
cubital(m) antérieur 96, 97.
cubital(m) postérieur 97.
cubitus(m) 98.
cuiller(f) 167, 531, 538.
cuiller(f) à café(m) 168.
cuiller(f) à dessert(m) 168.
cuiller(f) à égoutter 173.
cuiller(f) à glace(f) 173.
cuiller(f) à goûter 173.
cuiller(f) à soda(m) 168.
cuiller(f) à soupe(f) 168.
cuiller(f) à thé(m) 168.
cuiller(f) de table(f) 168.
cuiller(f) parisienne 173.
cuilleron(m) 167.
cuillers(f) doseuses 171.
cuillers(f), exemples(m) 168.
cuisine(f) 120, 162, 164, 188, 280, 439, 445.
cuisinière(f) à gaz(m) 210.
cuisinière(f) électrique 210.
cuissard(m) 486, 522.
cuissarde(f) 241.
cuissardes(f) 538.
cuisse(f) 83, 86, 93, 95, 111, 112.
cuit-vapeur(m) 175.
cuit-vapeur(m) électrique 179.
cuivres(m), famille(f) 295.
cul-de-sac(m) de Douglas 112.
cul-de-sac(m) dural 109.
cul-de-sac(m) vésico-utérin 112.
culasse(f) 306.
culbuteur(m) 360.
culée(f) 284, 344.
culot(m) 199, 318, 359, 534.
culot(m) à baïonnette(f) 199.
culot(m) à broches(f) 199.
culot(m) à vis(f) 199.
culotte(f) 259, 500, 506.
culotte(f) à ruchés(m) 260.
cumin(m) 138.
cumulo-nimbus(m) 42.
cumulus(m) 42.
cupule(f) 60.
curcuma(m) 138.
cure-ongles(m) 265.
curiosité(f) 25.
curleuse(f) 515.
curling(m) 515.
curry(m) 138.
curseur(m) 422.
curseur(m) vers la droite(f) 331.
curseur(m) vers la gauche(f) 331.
curseur(m) vers le bas(m) 331.
curseur(m) vers le haut(m) 331.
cuve(f) 211, 212, 214.
cuvette(f) 196, 210, 302.
cuvette(f) ramasse-gouttes(m) 181.
cyan(m) 418.
cycle(m) de l'eau(f) 45.
cycle(m) des saisons(f) 38.
cyclisme(m) 522.
cyclisme(m) sur route(f) 522.
cyclomoteur(m) 369.
cyclone(m) 43.
cyclone(m) tropical 43.
cylindre(m) 429.
cylindre(m) de roue(f) 357.
cylindre(m) de rubis(m) 420.
cylindre(m) enregistreur 27.
cylindre(m) réflecteur 420.
cymbale(f) charleston 308.
cymbale(f) inférieure 308.
cymbale(f) supérieure 308.
cymbale(f) suspendue 308.
cymbales(f) 295, 309.
cymbalette(f) 309.
cyme(f) bipare 57.
cyme(f) unipare 57.
cytopharynx(m) 66.
cytoplasme(m) 50, 66, 112.
cytoprocte(m) 66.
cytostome(m) 66.

D

dalle(f) 230.
dalmatien(m) 86.
Dame(f) 468, 470.
dames(f) 469.
dameuse(f) 512.
damier(m) 470.
Danemark(m) 450.
danois(m) 86.
Danube(m) 18.
date(f) d'expiration(f) 441.
datte(f) 132.
dauphin(m) 90.
dauphin(m), morphologie(f) 90.
dé(m) 469.
dé(m) à poker(m) 468.
dé(m) doubleur(m) 469.
dé(m) régulier 468.
déambulatoire(m) 285.
débarbouillette(f) 267.
débarcadère(m) 390.
débardeur(m) 250, 261, 263.
débit(m) de tabac(m) 436.
début(m) 331.
décagone(m) régulier 429.
décapeur(m) thermique 219.
décapeuse(f) 400.
décapsuleur(m) 170, 531.
décharge(f) 431.
déchets(m) industriels 47.
déchets(m) nucléaires 48.
déchiquetage(m) 49.
déclencheur(m) 314.
déclivité(f) du terrain(m) 182.
décomposeurs(m) 45.
décor(m) 291.
décorateur(m) 291.
découpe(f) 244.
découpe(f) princesse(f) 258.
découpes(f) d'agneau(m) 153.
découpes(f) de bœuf(m) 152.
découpes(f) de porc(m) 153.
découpes(f) de veau(m) 152.
défauts(m) de la vision(f) 419.
défense(f) 484.
défenseur(m) droit 506.
défenseur(m) gauche 506.
défilement(m) 331.
déflecteur(m) 236, 237, 364.
déflecteur(m) d'air(m) chaud 192.
déflecteur(m) de chaleur(f) 199.
déflecteur(m) de copeaux(m) 227.
déflecteur(m) de fumée(f) 192.
défonceuse(f) 229, 398.
déforestation(f) 47.
dégagement(m) d'air(m) des citernes(f) 385.
dégagement(m) du piston(m) 216.
dégrafeuse(f) 341.
degré(m) 428.
degré(m) Celsius 426.
Deimos 2.
déjections(f) animales 48.
délégués(m) techniques 509.
delta(m) 32, 35.
deltoïde(m) 96.
démarreur(m) électrique 354, 368.
démarreur(m) manuel 237.
démêloir(m) 268.
demeure(f) seigneuriale 282.
demi(m) d'ouverture(f) 482.
demi(m) de coin(m) droit 484.
demi(m) de coin(m) gauche 484.
demi(m) de mêlée(f) 482.
demi(m) de sûreté(f) droit 484.
demi(m) de sûreté(f) gauche 484.
demi(m) offensif 485.
demi-cercle(m) 428, 488.
demi-court(m) de service(m) en double(m) 495.
demi-court(m) de service(m) en simple(m) 495.
demi-lune(f) 273.
demi-manche(m) 169.
demi-membraneux(m) 97.
demi-pause(f) 299.
demi-soupir(m) 299.
demi-tendineux(m) 97.
demi-volée(f) 490.
dendrite(f) 110.
dénominations(f) des cyclones(m) tropicaux 43.
dénoyauteur(m) 173.
dent(f) 74, 76, 167, 226, 227, 235, 270, 398, 400, 503, 509.
dent(f) de défonceuse(f) 398.
dent(f) de godet(m) 399.
dent(f) de sagesse(f) 101.
denté 55.
dentifrice(m) 272.
dents(f) 101.
denture(f) humaine 101.
dénude-fil(m) 217.
déodorant(m) 267.
dépanneuse(f) 364.
départ(m) 469.
départ(m) des 400 m (course(f), haies(f), relais(m)) 473.
départ(m) des télécabines(f) 512.
départ(m) des télésièges(m) 512.
départ(m) du 10 000 m et du relais(m) 4 x 400 m 473.
départ(m) du 100 m (course(f) et haies(f)) 472.
départ(m) du 110 m haies(f) 472.
départ(m) du 1500 m 473.
départ(m) du 200 m 472.
départ(m) du 5000 m 472.
départ(m) du 800 m 473.
déplacement(m) 418.
déplacement(m) des électrons(m), sens(m) 416, 417.
déplacement(m) diagonal 470.
déplacement(m) en équerre(f) 470.
déplacement(m) horizontal 470.
déplacement(m) vertical 470.
déplacements(m), échecs(m) 470.
déporteur(m) 392.
dépression(f) 39.
dérailleur(m) 522.
dérailleur(m) arrière 370, 372.
dérailleur(m) avant 370, 372.
derby(m) 240.
dérive(f) 393, 395, 519, 520.
dérive(f) aérienne 383.
dériveur(m) 520, 521.
derme(m) 114.
dernier croissant(m) 5.
dernier quartier(m) 5.
dés(m) 468.
descente(f) 511.
descente(f) de gouttière(f) 182.
désert(m) 36, 40, 44.
Désert(m) d'Atacama 17.
Désert(m) de Gobi(m) 19.
désert(m) de pierres(f) 36.
désert(m) de sable(m) 36.
Désert(m) du Kalahari(m) 20.
Désert(m) du Namib(m) 20.
Désert(m) du Sahara(m) 20.
déshabillé(m) 256.
desserte(f) 202.
dessous(m) 292.
destination(f) 374.
destructeur(m) de documents(m) 341.
détecteur(m) d'impact(m) primaire 354.
détecteur(m) de fumée(f) 454.
détecteur(m) de mouvement(m) 286.
détecteur(m) de sécurité(f) 354.
détente(f) 534.
détroit(m) 24.
Détroit(m) de Bass 15.
Détroit(m) de Béring 16.
Détroit(m) de Cook 15.
Détroit(m) de Drake 15, 17.
Détroit(m) de Gibraltar 18.
Détroit(m) de Torres 15.
deuxième but(m) 474.
deuxième espace(m) 489.
deuxième joueur(m) 515.
deuxième ligne(f) 482.
deuxième molaire(f) 101.
deuxième prémolaire(f) 101.
deuxième radial(m) externe 97.
deuxième-but(m) 474.
devant(m) 244, 245.
devant(m) d'autel(m) 446.
déverrouillage(m) de l'objectif(m) 314.
déversement(m) d'hydrocarbures(m) 48.
déversoir(m) 406.
dévidoir(m) 236.
dévidoir(m) de ruban(m) adhésif 341.
dévidoir(m) pistolet(m) 341.
dévidoir(m) sur roues(f) 236.
devise(f) 441.
diable(m) 175, 396.
diamètre(m) 428.
diaphragme(m) 105.
dièse(m) 299.
diesel(m)-navire(m) 405.
différence(f) de potentiel(m) électrique, mesure(f) 426.
différentiel(m) 351.
diffuseur(m) 290.
diffusion(f) d'information(f) 335.
dinde(f) 155.
dindon(m) 81.
diode(f) 411.
Dioné 3.
directeur(m) artistique 290.
directeur(m) de course(f) 522.
directeur(m) de la photographie(f) 291.
direction(f) de la Mecque(f) 447.
direction(f) du vent(m) 39.
direction(f) et force(f) du vent(m) 39.
discontinuité(f) de Gutenberg 26.
discontinuité(f) de Mohorovicic 26.
disjoncteur(m) 407.
dispositif(m) anti-bascule 467.
dispositif(m) antidébordement(m) 214.
dispositif(m) de blocage(m) 219.
dispositif(m) de fermeture(f) 535.
dispositif(m) de poussée(f) 312.
dispositif(m) de remorquage(m) 364.
dispositifs(m) de contact(m) 198.
disposition(f) des informations(f) d'une station(f) 39.
disquaire(m) 436.
disque(m) 6, 333, 357, 472, 501.
disque(m) abrasif 229.
disque(m) compact 326.
disque(m) de papier(m)-diagramme(m) 365.
disque(m) dur amovible 333.
disque(m) numérique polyvalent (DVD) 318.
disques(m) 177.
disquette(f) 333.
distillation(f) sous vide(m) 405.
distributeur(m) d'essence(f) 346.
distributeur(m) de billets(m) 437, 442.

FRENCH INDEX

ASTRONOMY > 2-13; **EARTH** > 14-49; **PLANT KINGDOM** >50-65; **ANIMAL KINGDOM** > 66-91; **HUMAN BEING** > 92-119; **FOOD AND KITCHEN** > 120-181; **HOUSE** > 182-215; **DO-IT-YOURSELF AND GARDENING** > 216-237; **CLOTHING** > 238-263; **PERSONAL ADORNMENT AND ARTICLES** > 264-277; **ARTS AND ARCHITECTURE** > 278-311; **COMMUNICATIONS AND OFFICE AUTOMATION** > 312-341; **TRANSPORT AND MACHINERY** > 342-401; **ENERGY** > 402-413; **SCIENCE** > 414-429; **SOCIETY** > 430-467; **SPORTS AND GAMES** > 468-538

571

ASTRONOMY > 2-13;   EARTH > 14-49;   PLANT KINGDOM >50-65;   ANIMAL KINGDOM > 66-91;   HUMAN BEING > 92-119;   FOOD AND KITCHEN > 120-181;   HOUSE > 182-215;
DO-IT-YOURSELF AND GARDENING > 216-237;   CLOTHING > 238-263;   PERSONAL ADORNMENT AND ARTICLES > 264-277;   ARTS AND ARCHITECTURE > 278-311;   COMMUNICATIONS AND
OFFICE AUTOMATION > 312-341;   TRANSPORT AND MACHINERY > 342-401;   ENERGY > 402-413;   SCIENCE > 414-429;   SOCIETY > 430-467;   SPORTS AND GAMES > 468-538

ASTRONOMY > 2-13;   EARTH > 14-49;   PLANT KINGDOM >50-65;   ANIMAL KINGDOM > 66-91;   HUMAN BEING > 92-119;   FOOD AND KITCHEN > 120-181;   HOUSE > 182-215;
DO-IT-YOURSELF AND GARDENING > 216-237;   CLOTHING > 238-263;   PERSONAL ADORNMENT AND ARTICLES > 264-277;   ARTS AND ARCHITECTURE > 278-311;   COMMUNICATIONS AND
OFFICE AUTOMATION > 312-341;   TRANSPORT AND MACHINERY > 342-401;   ENERGY > 402-413;   SCIENCE > 414-429;   SOCIETY > 430-467;   SPORTS AND GAMES > 468-538.

573

FRENCH INDEX

ASTRONOMY > 2-13; EARTH > 14-49; PLANT KINGDOM > 50-65; ANIMAL KINGDOM > 66-91; HUMAN BEING > 92-119; FOOD AND KITCHEN > 120-181; HOUSE > 182-215;
DO-IT-YOURSELF AND GARDENING > 216-237; CLOTHING > 238-263; PERSONAL ADORNMENT AND ARTICLES > 264-277; ARTS AND ARCHITECTURE > 278-311; COMMUNICATIONS AND
OFFICE AUTOMATION > 312-341; TRANSPORT AND MACHINERY > 342-401; ENERGY > 402-413; SCIENCE > 414-429; SOCIETY > 430-467; SPORTS AND GAMES > 468-538.

575

FRENCH INDEX

FRENCH INDEX

manivelle(f) 170, 224, 236, 356, 365, 372, 537.
manivelle(f) d'enroulement(m) 225.
manivelle(f) de lève-glace(m) 352.
manomètre(m) 455, 461.
manomètre(m) d'accord(m) 308.
manœuvre(f) de la pelleteuse(f) 399.
mante(f) religieuse 69.
manteau(m) 72, 73, 192, 251.
manteau(m) inférieur 26.
manteau(m) supérieur 26.
manteaux(m) 248, 251.
manucure(f) 265.
manuel(m) de premiers soins(m) 461.
manutention(f) 396.
maquereau(m) 159.
maquillage(m) 266.
maquillage(m) des lèvres(f) 266.
maquillage(m) des yeux(m) 266.
maquilleuse(f) 290.
maquis(m) 44.
marbre(m) 475.
marchand(m) de journaux(m) 437.
marche(f) 191, 219.
marche(f) de départ(m) 191.
marche(f)/arrêt(m) 326.
marche(f)/arrêt(m)/volume(m) 326.
marchepied(m) 219, 364, 395, 523.
marchepied(m) arrière 455.
marchepied(m) escamotable 361.
marchepied(m) latéral 377.
margarine(f) 149.
margelle(f) continentale 33.
margose(f) 128.
marinière(f) 255.
marmite(f) 175.
marmotte(f) 82.
Maroc(m) 451.
maroquinerie(f) 436.
marque(f) centrale 490.
marque(f) d'aire(f) de prise(f) de contact(m) 391.
marque(f) d'axe(m) de piste(f) 390.
marque(f) de distance(f) constante 391.
marque(f) de point(m) d'attente(f) 390.
marques(f) d'identification(f) 390.
marques(f) de circulation(f) 389.
marques(f) de seuil(m) de piste(f) 391.
marques(f) latérales de piste(f) 390.
marqueur(m) 312, 487, 488.
marqueurs(m) 499.
marron(m) 133.
Mars 2, 3.
marteau(m) 116, 304, 472.
marteau(m) à panne(f) ronde 220.
marteau(m) de charpentier(m) 220.
marteau(m) de maçon(m) 216.
marteau(m) de menuisier(m) 220.
martin-pêcheur(m) 80.
martinet(m) 80.
martre(f) 88.
mascara(m) en pain(m) 266.
mascara(m) liquide 266.
masque(m) 476, 478, 486, 507.
masque(m) bucco-nasal 459.
masque(m) complet 454.
masque(m) de sélection(f) des couleurs(f) 318.
masque(m) respiratoire 459.
masse(f) 27.
masse(f), mesure(f) 422, 426.
masse(f)-tige(f) 403.
masséter(m) 96.
massif(m) 183.
massif(m) d'ancrage(m) des câbles(m) 344.
massif(m) de fleurs(f) 230.
massif(m) de fondation(f) 403.
massif(m) montagneux 24.
mât(m) 281, 321, 396, 519, 520.
mât(m) avant 385.
mât(m) de charge(f) 385.
mât(m) de toit(m) 529.
mât(m) radar(m) 384.
mât(m) rotor(m) 395.
matelas(m) 204, 205, 460, 530.
matelas(m) autogonflant 530.
matelas(m) mousse(f) 530.
matelas(m) pneumatique 530.
mâtereau(m) 385.
matériau(m) de scellement(m) 417.
matériel(m) de camping(m) 531.
matériel(m) de lutte(f) contre les incendies(m) 454.
mathématiques(f) 427.
matière(f) 414.
matière(f) inorganique 45.
matières(f) grasses 149.
matraque(f) télescopique 456.
matrice(f) de l'ongle(m) 114.
maturation(f), vigne(f) 62.
maturité(f) 62.
Maurice(f) 452.
Mauritanie(f) 451.
maxillaire(m) 74, 117.
maxillaire(m) basculant 76.
maxillaire(m) inférieur 98, 100.
maxillaire(m) supérieur 78, 98, 100.
mazout(m) domestique 405.
mazout(m) léger 405.
mazout(m) lourd 405.
méandre(m) 32.
méat(m) de l'urètre(m) 111.
mécanique(f) d'accordage(m) 303.
mécanique(f) d'accordage(m) 303.
mécanisme(m) d'octave(f) 306.
mécanisme(m) d'ouverture(f) de l'anse(f) 537.
mécanisme(m) de débrayage(m) du tambour(m) 537.
mécanisme(m) de déplacement(m) de la lame(f) 401.
mécanisme(m) de propulsion(f) 372.
mèche(f) 301.
mèche(f) à centre(m) plat 228.
mèche(f) hélicoïdale 228.
mèche(f) hélicoïdale à âme(f) centrale 228.
mèche(f) hélicoïdale à double torsade(f) 228.
médaillon(m) 264.
médecin(m) 464, 498.
médiator(m) 297.
médicaments(m), formes(f) 467.
méditerranéen 40.
Meissner, corpuscule(m) 114.
Mélanésie(f) 15.
mélange(m) au manganèse(m) (cathode(f)) 417.
mélange(m) d'épices(f) cajun 139.
mélange(m) de zinc(m) et d'électrolyte(m) (anode(f)) 417.
mélange(m) dépolarisant 417.
mélange(m) eau(f)-vapeur(f) 402.
mélangeur(m) 176.
mélangeur(m) à main(f) 176.
mélangeur(m) à pâtisserie(f) 172.
mélangeur(m) bain(m)-douche(f) 194.
mélasse(f) 149.
mêlée(f) : attaque(f) 485.
mêlée(f) : défense(f) 484.
mêlée(f) spontanée 483.
mélèze(m) 65.
mélisse(f) 142.
melon(m) 238.
melon(m) à cornes(f) 136.
melon(m) brodé 135.
melon(m) Casaba 135.
melon(m) d'Espagne(f) 135.
melon(m) d'hiver(m) chinois 128.
melon(m) d'Ogen 135.
melon(m) miel(m) 135.
melons(m) 135.
membrane(f) 324.
membrane(f) coquillière 79.
membrane(f) cytoplasmique 50, 66.
membrane(f) du tympan(m) 116.
membrane(f) médiane 60.
membrane(f) nucléaire 50, 66.
membrane(f) pellucide 112.
membrane(f) plasmique 66.
membrane(f) squelettique 50.
membrane(f) vitelline 79.
membre(m) inférieur 103.
membre(m) supérieur 103.
meneur(m) de jeu(m) 489.
méninges(f) 109.
ménisque(m) convergent 419.
ménisque(m) divergent 419.
menora(f) 447.
menthe(f) 142.
menton(m) 78, 94.
mentonnière(f) 301, 367, 522.
menuiserie(f) : instruments(m) de traçage(m) et de mesure(f) 225.
menuiserie(f) : matériel(m) divers 225.
menuiserie(f) : outils(m) pour clouer 220.
menuiserie(f) : outils(m) pour percer 228.
menuiserie(f) : outils(m) pour scier 226.
menuiserie(f) : outils(m) pour serrer 222.
menuiserie(f) : outils(m) pour visser 221.
mer(f) 5, 24, 32.
Mer(f) Adriatique 18.
Mer(f) Baltique(f) 18.
Mer(f) Caspienne 14, 19.
Mer(f) d'Aral 19.
Mer(f) d'Irlande(f) 18.
Mer(f) d'Oman(m) 19.
Mer(f) de Barents 18.
Mer(f) de Beaufort 16.
Mer(f) de Béring 14.
Mer(f) de Chine(f) méridionale 14, 19.
Mer(f) de Chine(f) orientale 19.
Mer(f) de Corail(m) 15.
Mer(f) de Norvège(f) 18.
Mer(f) de Tasman 15.
Mer(f) de Weddell 15.
Mer(f) des Antilles(f) 14, 16.
Mer(f) du Groenland(m) 14.
Mer(f) du Japon(m) 19.
Mer(f) du Nord(m) 14, 18.
Mer(f) Égée 18.
Mer(f) Méditerranée(f) 14, 18, 20.
Mer(f) Noire 14, 18, 19.
Mer(f) Rouge 14, 19, 20.
Mercure 2, 3.
merguez(f) 156.
méridien(m) de Greenwich 22.
méridien(m) est 22.
méridien(m) ouest 22.
méridienne(f) 200.
merlan(m) 161.
mesa(f) 36.
mésocarpe(m) 57, 58, 59.
mésopause(f) 37.
mésosphère(f) 37.
mesure(f) à deux temps(m) 298.
mesure(f) à quatre temps(m) 298.
mesure(f) à trois temps(m) 298.
mesure(f) de l'énergie(f) 426.
mesure(f) de l'épaisseur(f) 425.
mesure(f) de l'intensité(f) lumineuse 426.
mesure(f) de la charge(f) électrique 426.
mesure(f) de la différence(f) de potentiel(m) électrique 426.
mesure(f) de la force(f) 426.
mesure(f) de la fréquence(f) 426.
mesure(f) de la longueur(f) 425, 426.
mesure(f) de la masse(f) 422, 426.
mesure(f) de la pression(f) 426.
mesure(f) de la puissance(f) 426.
mesure(f) de la quantité(f) de matière(f) 426.
mesure(f) de la radioactivité(f) 426.
mesure(f) de la résistance(f) électrique 426.
mesure(f) de la température(f) 424.
mesure(f) de la température(f) Celsius 426.
mesure(f) de la température(f) thermodynamique 426.
mesure(f) du courant(m) électrique 426.
mesure(f) du temps(m) 424, 426.
mesure(f), appareils(m) 424.
mesures(f) 171, 298.
météorologie(f) 37.
mètre(m) 426.
mètre(m) à ruban(m) 225.
métro(m) 435.
meubles(m) d'enfants(m) 205.
meubles(m) de rangement(m) 202.
Mexique(m) 448.
mezzanine(f) 182, 189, 378.
mi(m) 298.
mi-bas(m) 247, 257.
mi-chaussette(f) 247, 257.
micro(m) 303.
micro(m) de fréquences(f) aiguës 303.
micro(m) de fréquences(f) graves 303.
micro(m) de fréquences(f) moyennes 303.
micro-ondes(f) 418.
micro-ordinateur(m) 329.
microfilament(m) 66.
micromètre(m) palmer(m) 425.
micronucleus(m) 66.
microphone(m) 320, 327, 328, 332, 337, 456.
microphones(m) 457.
microscope(m) 421.
microscope(m) binoculaire 421.
microtubule(m) 66.
miel(m) 149.
mihrab(m) 447.
milieu(m) défensif 481.
milieu(m) offensif droit 481.
milieu(m) offensif gauche 481.
mille(m) 427.
millésime(m) 441.
millet(m) 61, 143.
millet(m) : épi(m) 61.
Mimas 3.
minaret(m) 447.
minbar(m) 447.
mini-slip(m) 247.
minibus(m) 363.
minichaîne(f) stéréo 325.
minute(f) 428.
minuterie(f) 178, 179.
minuteur(m) 171, 501.
Miranda 3.
mire(f) 533, 535.
miroir(m) 195, 277, 421, 439, 533.
miroir(m) à réflexion(f) partielle 420.
miroir(m) à réflexion(f) totale 420.
miroir(m) concave 7.
miroir(m) de courtoisie(f) 354.
miroir(m) de lecture(f) 10.
miroir(m) de traversée(f) avant 362.
miroir(m) double pivotant 269.
miroir(m) latéral 269.
miroir(m) lumineux 269.
miroir(m) plan rétractable 7.
miroir(m) primaire 7.
miroir(m) primaire concave 9.
miroir(m) secondaire 7, 9.
mise(f) en balles(f) 49.
mise(f) en marche(f) 328.
Mississippi(m) 16.
mitaine(f) 243, 507.
mitigeur(m) d'évier(m) 197.
mitochondrie(f) 50, 66.
mitre(f) 167, 169, 193.
mitron(m) 183.
mocassin(m) 242.
mode(m) d'emploi(m) 346.
mode(m) d'entraînement(m) du film(m) 314.
mode(m) d'exposition(f) 314.
mode(m) de mise(f) au point(m) 314.
mode(m) magnétoscope(m) 319.
mode(m) télévision(f) 319.
modem(m) 334.
modem(m)-câble(m) 335.
modérateur(m) 408.
modes(m) d'inflorescence(f) 57.
modification(f) fine des variables(f) 310.
modification(f) rapide des variables(f) 310.
modulateur(m) de pression(f) de freinage(m) 357.
modulation(f) de la hauteur(f) du son(m) 310.
modulation(f) du timbre(m) du son(m) 310.
module(m) d'habitation(f) américain 11.
module(m) de commande(f) électronique 357.
module(m) de communication(f) 316.
module(m) de photopiles(f) 411.
module(m) de propulsion(f) 316.
module(m) de service(m) 316.
module(m) russe 11.
moelle(f) 63, 154.
moelle(f) épinière 109, 110.
moelle(f) épinière, structure(f) 109.
Mohorovicic, discontinuité(f) 26.
moineau(m) 80.
molaire(f), coupe(f) 101.
molaires(f) 101.
mole(f) 426.
molécule(f) 414.
molette(f) 223.
molette(f) d'ajustage(m) 425.
molette(f) d'entraînement(m) 180.
molette(f) de mise(f) au point(m) 420.
molette(f) de réglage(m) de la saillie(f) 229.
molette(f) de réglage(m) près/loin 320.
molette(f) de sélection(f) des effets(m) spéciaux 320.
mollet(m) 93, 95.
mollusques(m) 72, 157.
Monaco(m) 450.
Mongolie(f) 453.
moniteurs(m) de contrôle(m) du réalisateur(m) 290.
monnaie(f) et modes(m) de paiement(m) 441.
monocoques(m) 521.
Monopoly®(m) 469.
mont(m) de Vénus 112.
montagne(f) 29.
Montagnes(f) Rocheuses 16.
montant(m) 184, 187, 201, 219, 297, 466, 509.
montant(m) de bâti(m) 202.
montant(m) de ferrage(m) 185, 202.
montant(m) de la serrure(f) 185.
montant(m) de rive(f) 186.
montant(m) embrevé 186.
montant(m) latéral 349.
montant(m) mouton(m) 186.
montant(m) rembourré 489.
monticule(m) 475.
montre(f) à affichage(m) analogique 424.
montre(f) à affichage(m) numérique 424.
Monts(m) Oural(m) 18.
Monts(m) Transantarctiques 15.
monture(f) 215, 224, 226, 296.
monture(f) en fer(m) à cheval(m) 7.
monture(f) réglable 226.
monument(m) 25.
moquette(f) 190.
moraillon(m) 277.
moraine(f) de fond(m) 30.
moraine(f) frontale 30.
moraine(f) latérale 30.
moraine(f) médiane 30.
moraine(f) terminale 30.
mordant(m) 299.
morille(f) 123.
morphologie(f) de l'abeille(f) : ouvrière(f) 68.
morphologie(f) de l'araignée(f) 70.
morphologie(f) de l'escargot(m) 72.
morphologie(f) de l'oiseau(m) 78.
morphologie(f) de la coquille(f) bivalve 73.
morphologie(f) de la coquille(f) univalve 73.
morphologie(f) de la grenouille(f) 75.
morphologie(f) de la perche(f) 74.
morphologie(f) de la pieuvre(f) 72.
morphologie(f) de la tortue(f) 76.
morphologie(f) du cheval(m) 83.
morphologie(f) du chien(m) 86.
morphologie(f) du dauphin(m) 90.
morphologie(f) du gorille(m) 91.
morphologie(f) du homard(m) 71.
morphologie(f) du papillon(m) 67.
morphologie(f) du rat(m) 82.
morphologie(f) du requin(m) 74.
morphologie(f) du serpent(m) venimeux : tête(f) 76.
mors(m) 221, 228, 265.
mors(m) fixe 224.
mors(m) mobile 224.
mort(f) 426.
mortadelle(f) 156.
mortier(m) 170.
morue(f) de l'Atlantique(m) 161.
mosaïque(f) 280.
mosquée(f) 447.
moteur(m) 212, 213, 214, 227, 229, 237, 366, 396, 401, 403.
moteur(m) à essence(f) 351, 360.
moteur(m) de manœuvre(f) 13.
moteur(m) diesel 398, 399, 400, 401.
moteur(m) diesel de propulsion(f) 383.
moteur(m) diesel de sustentation(f) 383.
moteur(m) électrique 235, 237, 358.
moteur(m) hors-bord 385.
moteur(m) principal 13.
motif(m) 260, 261.
moto(f) 366.
moto(f) 368.
moto(f) de grand prix(m) et pilote(m) 525.
moto(f) de motocross(m) et supercross(m) 525.

FRENCH INDEX

ASTRONOMY > 2-13; EARTH > 14-49; PLANT KINGDOM >50-65; ANIMAL KINGDOM > 66-91; HUMAN BEING > 92-119; FOOD AND KITCHEN > 120-181; HOUSE > 182-215; DO-IT-YOURSELF AND GARDENING > 216-237; CLOTHING > 238-263; PERSONAL ADORNMENT AND ARTICLES > 264-277; ARTS AND ARCHITECTURE > 278-311; COMMUNICATIONS AND OFFICE AUTOMATION > 312-341; TRANSPORT AND MACHINERY > 342-401; ENERGY > 402-413; SCIENCE > 414-429; SOCIETY > 430-467; SPORTS AND GAMES > 468-538

577

ASTRONOMY > 2-13;   EARTH > 14-49;   PLANT KINGDOM >50-65;   ANIMAL KINGDOM > 66-91;   HUMAN BEING > 92-119;   FOOD AND KITCHEN > 120-181;   HOUSE > 182-215;
DO-IT-YOURSELF AND GARDENING > 216-237;   CLOTHING > 238-263;   PERSONAL ADORNMENT AND ARTICLES > 264-277;   ARTS AND ARCHITECTURE > 278-311;   COMMUNICATIONS AND
OFFICE AUTOMATION > 312-341;   TRANSPORT AND MACHINERY > 342-401;   ENERGY > 402-413;   SCIENCE > 414-429;   SOCIETY > 430-467;   SPORTS AND GAMES > 468-538;

579

FRENCH INDEX

ASTRONOMY > 2-13;   EARTH > 14-49;   PLANT KINGDOM >50-65;   ANIMAL KINGDOM > 66-91;   HUMAN BEING > 92-119;   FOOD AND KITCHEN > 120-181;   HOUSE > 182-215;
DO-IT-YOURSELF AND GARDENING > 216-237;   CLOTHING > 238-263;   PERSONAL ADORNMENT AND ARTICLES > 264-277;   ARTS AND ARCHITECTURE > 278-311;   COMMUNICATIONS AND
OFFICE AUTOMATION > 312-341;   TRANSPORT AND MACHINERY > 342-401;   ENERGY > 402-413;   SCIENCE > 414-429;   SOCIETY > 430-467;   SPORTS AND GAMES > 468-538

581

FRENCH INDEX

rangée(f) 293.
rangement(m) pour les gants(m) 464.
Ranvier, nœud(m) 110.
râpe(f) 170.
râpe(f) à fromage(m) cylindrique 170.
râpe(f) à muscade(f) 170.
rappel(m) de mémoire(f) 337.
raquette(f) de badminton(m) 494.
raquette(f) de tennis(m) 492.
raquette(f) de tennis(m) de table(f) 493.
ras-de-cou(m) 250, 255, 264.
ras-el-hanout(m) 139.
rasage(m) 271.
rasette(f) 305.
rasoir(m) à double tranchant(m) 271.
rasoir(m) à manche(m) 271.
rasoir(m) effileur 269.
rasoir(m) électrique 271.
rasoir(m) jetable 271.
rat(m) 82.
rat(m), morphologie(f) 82.
rate(f) 103.
râteau(m) 233, 503.
ratissoire(f) 233.
raton(m) laveur 88.
ravier(m) 166.
ravioli(m) 146.
rayon(m) 70, 273, 371, 428.
rayon(m) épineux 74.
rayon(m) lumineux 419.
rayon(m) médullaire 63.
rayon(m) mou 74.
rayonnement(m) 415.
rayonnement(m) infrarouge 46, 418.
rayonnement(m) solaire 45, 46, 410, 411.
rayonnement(m) solaire absorbé 46.
rayonnement(m) solaire réfléchi 46.
rayonnement(m) ultraviolet 46.
rayons(m) gamma 418.
rayons(m) X 418.
ré(m) 298.
réacteur(m) 408.
réacteur(m) nucléaire 409.
réaction(f) en chaîne(f) 415.
réalisateur(m) 291.
rebobinage(m) 314, 319, 323, 326, 328.
rebord(m) 210.
rebord(m) de cuve(f) 212.
rebras(m) 243.
récamier(m) 200.
réceptacle(m) 51, 56, 59.
réceptacle(m) à déchets(m) 365.
réceptacle(m) de brosses(f) 272.
récepteur(m) 327.
récepteur(m) de son(m) 460.
récepteur(m) sensoriel 110.
récepteurs(m) du goût(m) 118.
réception(f) 439.
réception(f) des messages(m) 328.
réception(f) directe 316.
réception(f) du fret(m) 391.
receveur(m) 474, 475, 476, 490, 495.
receveur(m) éloigné 485.
recharge(f) 312.
réchaud(m) 174.
réchaud(m) à deux feux(m) 529.
réchaud(m) à un feu(m) 529.
réchauffement(m) de la planète(f) 46.
recherche(f) 335.
recherche(f) des canaux(m) 319.
Récif(m) de la Grande Barrière(f) 15.
récipient(m) 176.
recourbe-cils(m) 266.
rectangle(m) 429.
rectangle(m) des instructeurs(m) 474.
rectangulaire 530.
rectrice(f) 78.
rectum(m) 106, 111, 112.
recyclage(m) 49.
redingote(f) 251.
réflecteur(m) 217, 321, 365.
réflecteurs(m) solaires 316.
réformeur(m) catalytique 405.
réfrigérateur(m) 164, 211, 438.
réfrigérateurs(m) 438.
refroidissement(m) 405.
refroidissement(m) de la vapeur(f) par l'eau(f) 408.
regard(m) de visite(f) 434.
régie(f) 293.
région(f) auriculaire 78.
région(f) malaire 78.

région(f) négative 410.
région(f) positive 410.
registre(m) des aigus(m) 296.
registre(m) des basses(f) 296.
réglage(m) 466.
réglage(m) de centrage(m) 329.
réglage(m) de hausse(f) 420.
réglage(m) de l'afficheur(m) 327.
réglage(m) de l'angle(m) 229.
réglage(m) de l'écran(m) de l'ordinateur(m) 10.
réglage(m) de la balance(f) 303.
réglage(m) de la hauteur(f) 501.
réglage(m) de la luminosité(f) 329.
réglage(m) de la pression(f) 272.
réglage(m) de la pression(f) d'oxygène(m) 329.
réglage(m) de la résistance(f) 501.
réglage(m) de la tension(f) 537.
réglage(m) de la tonalité(f) 303.
réglage(m) de niveau(m) d'enregistrement(m) 323.
réglage(m) de profondeur(m) 229.
réglage(m) de tempo(m) 311.
réglage(m) des températures(f) 208.
réglage(m) du contraste(m) 329.
réglage(m) du diaphragme(m) 421.
réglage(m) du four(m) 210.
réglage(m) du volume(m) 303, 311, 319, 322, 325, 326, 329.
réglage(m) du volume(m) des communications(f) 10.
réglage(m) en hauteur(f) du condenseur(m) 421.
réglage(m) horizontal 329.
réglage(m) latéral 329.
réglage(m) micrométrique (azimut(m)) 8, 9.
réglage(m) micrométrique (latitude(f)) 8, 9.
réglage(m) vertical 329.
règle(f) 425.
règle(f) graduée 425, 531.
règne(m) végétal 50.
régulateur(m) de pression(f) 174, 529.
régulateur(m) de vitesse(f) 287, 354.
rehausseur(m) 205.
rein(m) 73, 103.
rein(m) droit 107.
rein(m) gauche 107.
reine(f) 68.
reine(f), abeille(f) 68.
reins(m) 83, 93, 95.
rejet(m) 63.
rejet(m) d'oxygène(m) 54.
rejets(m) industriels 47, 48.
relevé(m) de transaction(f) 443.
relief(m) lunaire 5.
reliure(f) à anneaux(m) plastiques 340.
reliure(f) à glissière(f) 339.
reliure(f) à pince(f) 339.
reliure(f) à ressort(m) 339.
reliure(f) à vis(f) 339.
reliure(f) spirale(f) 340.
rémige(f) primaire 78.
rémige(f) secondaire 78.
rémige(f) tertiaire 78.
remise(f) 182, 230.
remorque(f) 380.
remorqueur(m) 384.
rempart(m) 5, 282.
remplage(m) 285.
remplissage(m) 404.
renard(m) 88.
renfort(m) de nuque(f) 525.
réniforme 55.
renne(m) 84.
renseignements(m) 512.
renversé 518.
renvoi(m) 194.
repère(m) de ligne(f) de marche(f) 533.
repère(m) de niveau(m) d'eau(f) 208.
repère(m) de touche(f) 302, 303.
repère(m) de virage(m) de dos(m) 517.
répertoire(m) 334.
répertoire(m) téléphonique 327, 338.
répéteur(m) 317.
répondeur(m) téléphonique 328.
repose-main(m) 332.
repose-pied(m) 467.
repose-pied(m) du passager(m) 367, 368.

repose-pied(m) du pilote(m) 367, 368.
repose-pieds(m) 205.
repose-poignets(m) détachable 330.
repousse-chair(m) 265.
reproduction(f) de clés(f) 437.
reprographie(f) 442.
reptation(f) 31.
reptiles(m) 76.
République(f) arabe syrienne 452.
République(f) centrafricaine 451.
République(f) de Corée(f) 453.
République(f) de Moldova(f) 450.
République(f) démocratique du Congo(m) 451.
République(f) démocratique populaire lao 453.
République(f) dominicaine 449.
République(f) populaire démocratique de Corée(f) 453.
République(f) tchèque 450.
République(f)-Unie de Tanzanie(f) 451.
répulsion(f) 416.
requin(m), morphologie(f) 74.
réseau(m) d'oléoducs(m) 404.
réseau(m) national 316.
réseau(m) nerveux 101.
réseau(m) privé 316.
réseau(m) téléphonique 317.
réserve(f) d'eau(f) 272.
réserves(f) alimentaires 439.
réservoir(m) 13, 181, 406, 407, 454, 529.
réservoir(m) à carburant(m) 364, 377, 395.
réservoir(m) à essence(f) 351, 366, 369.
réservoir(m) à toit(m) flottant 404.
réservoir(m) auxiliaire 365.
réservoir(m) d'alcool(m) 424.
réservoir(m) d'arrosage(m) 408.
réservoir(m) d'eau(f) 181.
réservoir(m) d'essence(f) 235.
réservoir(m) d'huile(f) 235.
réservoir(m) de brut(m) 405.
réservoir(m) de chasse(f) d'eau(f) 195.
réservoir(m) de liquide(m) de frein(m) 357.
réservoir(m) de mercure(m) 424.
réservoir(m) externe 12.
réservoir(m) magmatique 28, 402.
réservoir(m) propane(m) 361.
réservoir(m) tampon(m) 404.
résidente(f) 464.
résidus(m) non recyclables 49.
résistance(f) électrique, mesure(f) 426.
résistance(f) hydraulique 501.
résistances(f) 417.
résonateur(m) 324.
ressort(m) 27, 206, 222, 312, 535.
ressort(m) athlétique 500.
ressort(m) de rappel(m) 357.
ressort(m) de soupape(f) 360.
ressort(m) de suspension(f) 212.
ressort(m) de tension(f) 355, 500.
ressort(m) hélicoïdal 351.
restaurant(m) 386, 432, 435, 436, 438.
restauration(f) rapide 437.
retable(m) 446.
réticule(m) 420.
réticulum(m) endoplasmique 50, 66.
rétine(f) 119, 419.
retour(m) 331.
retour(m) de l'eau(f) au générateur(m) de vapeur(f) 408.
retourné 518.
rétroviseur(m) 354, 363, 364, 366, 368, 369, 523.
rétroviseur(m) extérieur 348, 362.
rétroviseur(m) grand angle(m) 362, 363.
réunion(f) 427.
réverbère(m) 434.
revers(m) 240, 244, 246.
revers(m) à cran(m) aigu 244.
revers(m) cranté 248.
revêtement(m) 187, 493.
revêtement(m) de sécurité(f) 10.
revêtement(m) synthétique 492.
revêtement(m) thermique 12.
revêtements(m) de sol(m) textiles 190.
revitalisant(m) capillaire 267.
rez-de-chaussée(m) 182, 188.

Rhéa 3.
rhino-pharynx(m) 117.
rhinocéros(m) 85.
rhizoïde(m) 51.
rhizome(m) 52.
rhodyménie(m) palmé 123.
rhubarbe(f) 125.
rias(f) 35.
ribosome(m) 50, 66.
richelieu(m) 240.
ricotta(f) 150.
rideau(m) de fer(m) 292.
rideau(m) de scène(f) 292, 293.
rideau(m) séparateur 464.
ridoir(m) 521.
rigatoni(m) 146.
rillettes(f) 156.
rimaye(f) 30.
rinceau(m) 200.
ring(m) 498.
ris(m) 154.
rivet(m) 169, 222.
rivière(f) 24, 32.
rivière(f) souterraine 31.
rizière(f) 47.
riz(m) 61, 143, 147.
riz(m) : épi(m) 61.
riz(m) basmati 147.
riz(m) blanc 147.
riz(m) complet 147.
riz(m) étuvé 147.
riz(m) sauvage 143.
robe(f) 404.
robe(f) bain-de-soleil(m) 252.
robe(f) chemisier(m) 252.
robe(f) de maison(f) 252.
robe(f) enveloppe(f) 252.
robe(f) fourreau(m) 252.
robe(f) princesse(f) 252.
robe(f) taille(f) basse 252.
robe(f) tee-shirt(m) 261.
robe(f) trapèze(m) 252.
robe(f) tunique(f) 252.
robe(f)-manteau(m) 252.
robe(f)-polo(m) 252.
Roberval, balance(f) 422.
robes(f), exemples(m) 252.
robinet(m) 195.
robinet(m) d'arrêt(m) 196, 197.
robinet(m) d'arrêt(m) général 194.
robinet(m) de réglage(m) de débit(m) 454.
robinet(m) de vidange(f) 404.
robinet(m) flotteur à clapet(m) 196.
robinet(m) relais(m) 529.
robinets(m) 210.
robot(m) boulanger(m) 179.
robot(m) de cuisine(f) 177.
roc(m) 27.
rocaille(f) 230.
roche(f) mère(f) 54.
roches(f) d'intrusion(f) 26.
roches(f) ignées 26.
roches(f) métamorphiques 26.
roches(f) sédimentaires 26.
rognons(m) 154.
Roi(m) 468, 470.
romaine(f) 126.
romano(m) 151.
romarin(m) 142.
rond pronateur(m) 96.
rond-point(m) 25.
ronde(f) 299.
rondelle(f) 417, 510.
rondelle(f) à denture(f) extérieure 222.
rondelle(f) à denture(f) intérieure 222.
rondelle(f) à ressort(m) 222.
rondelle(f) conique 196.
rondelle(f) plate 222.
rondelles(f) 222.
rongeur(m) 82.
roquefort(m) 151.
roquette(f) 127.
rorqual(m) 90.
rosace(f) 302.
rose(f) 56, 285.
rose(f) des vents(m) 23.
rosée(f) 41.
rosette(f) 186.
rossignol(m) 80.
rôti(m) 152, 153.
rôti(m) de côtes(m) 152.
rotini(m) 146.
rotonde(f) 435.
rotor(m) 412.
rotor(m) anticouple 395.

rotule(f) 98, 224.
roue(f) 231, 364, 467, 522, 525, 527.
roue(f) avant 401.
roue(f) de secours(m) 361.
roue(f) de support(m) 523.
roue(f) dentée 523.
roue(f) folle 398.
roue(f) libre 372.
roue(f) pivotante 467.
roues(f) motrices 401.
rouge(m) 418.
rouge(m) à lèvres(f) 266.
rouge-gorge(m) 80.
Rouges(m) 469.
rouget(m) barbet(m) 159.
rouleau(m) 219, 268.
rouleau(m) à pâtisserie(f) 172.
rouleau(m) de la Torah(f) 447.
roulement(m) à billes(f) 413.
roulette(f) 205, 209, 277, 308, 526.
roulette(f) de commande(f) 337.
roulette(f) de défilement(m) 327, 332.
roulette(f) de pâtissier(m) 172.
roulis(m) 395.
Roumanie(f) 450.
roupie(f) 440.
route(f) 25, 343, 430.
route(f) d'accès(m) 388.
route(f) secondaire 25.
route(f), coupe(f) 342.
routeur(m) 334.
Royaume-Uni(m) de Grande-Bretagne(f) et d'Irlande(f) du Nord(m) 449.
ruban(m) 225.
ruban(m) blanc 493, 495.
ruban(m) de bouclage(m) 457.
ruban(m) de Téflon(m) 216.
ruban(m) de tissu(m) adhésif 461.
ruche(f) 122.
ruché(m) 260.
rue(f) 25, 433, 435.
rue(f) commerçante 432.
rue(f), coupe(f) 434.
ruelle(f) 433.
Ruffini, corpuscule(m) 114.
rugby(m) 482.
rugbyman(m) 483.
ruisseau(m) 32.
ruissellement(m) 45.
russule(f) verdoyante 123.
rutabaga(m) 129.
Rwanda(m) 451.

sablier(m) 171.
sablière(f) 377.
sablière(f) double 187.
sabot(m) 83, 224, 365, 473.
sabot(m) de protection(f) 398.
sac(m) 296.
sac(m) à bandoulière(f) 276.
sac(m) à dos(m) 532.
sac(m) à provisions(f) 276.
sac(m) accordéon(m) 276.
sac(m) besace(f) 276.
sac(m) boîte(f) 276.
sac(m) cartable(m) 275.
sac(m) de congélation(f) 162.
sac(m) de golf(m) 505.
sac(m) de sable(m) 498.
sac(m) de vol(m) 276.
sac(m) fourre-tout(m) 276.
sac(m) gonflable 354.
sac(m) marin(m) 276.
sac(m) polochon(m) 276.
sac(m) seau(m) 275.
sac(m)-filet(m) 162.
sachet(m) 162.
sacoche(f) 369, 372.
sacristie(f) 446.
sacrum(m) 98, 99.
sacs(m) à main(f) 275.
sacs(m) à provisions(f) 121.
sacs(m) de couchage(m), exemples(m) 530.
safran(m) 138, 384.
saharienne(f) 255.
saindoux(m) 149.
saint-bernard(m) 86.
Saint-Kitts-et-Nevis(m) 449.
Saint-Laurent(m) 16.
Saint-Marin(m) 450.
saint-pierre(m) 161.

582